STATISTICS FOR BUSINESS AND ECONOMICS

BASIC STATISTICS FOR BUSINESS AND ECONOMICS

Earl K. Bowen
Babson College

Martin K. Starr
Columbia University

McGRAW-HILL BOOK COMPANY

Auckland Bogotá Guatemala Hamburg Lisbon
London Madrid Mexico New Delhi Panama Paris
San Juan São Paulo Singapore Sydney Tokyo

LITERATÜR
YAYINCILIK - DAĞITIM - PAZARLAMA
SANAYI VE TİC. LİMİTED ŞİRKETİ

BASIC STATISTICS FOR BUSINESS AND ECONOMICS
INTERNATIONAL EDITION 1982

Exclusive rights by McGraw-Hill Book Co-Singpaore for manufacture and export.
This book cannot be re-exported from the country to which it is consigned bv
McGraw-Hill.

67890KKP94321

This book was set in Electra by Progrcssive Typographers.
The editors were Donald G. Mason, Michael Elia, and James B. Armstrong;
The designer was Jo Jones;
The production supervisor was Dennis J. Conroy.

Library of Congress Cataloging in Publication Data

Bowen, Earl K.
    Basic statistics for business and economics.

    (McGraw-Hill series in quantitative methods for management)
    Includes index.
    1. Commereial statistics 2. Economics - Statistical methods.
3. Statistics. l. Starr, Martin Kenneth, date   II. Title III. Series.
HF1017.B65   519.5   81-17199
ISBN 0-07-006725-2   AACR2

When ordering this title use ISBN 0-07-066188-X
When ordering this title (In Turkey) use ISBN 975-7860-02-6

Literatür Yayıncılık Çukuryurt Sok. 6/3 Mecidiyeköy - İstanbul
Tel: (0212) 272 92 72 - 267 40 56 - 272 96 40 Fax: (0212) 274 22 63
Yayın Koordinatörü: Kenan KOCATÜRK
Matbaa: Motif Matbacılık (0216) 313 15 00
Dizgi   : Ozan GÜNER - Nurgül UÇAR - ARION (0216) 418 61 14-15-16

Printed in Turkey

BASIC STATISTICS FOR BUSINESS AND ECONOMICS

**McGraw-Hill Series in
Quantitative Methods for Management**

**Consulting Editor
Martin K. Starr, Columbia University**

Bowen and Starr: Basic Statistics for Business and Economics
Byrd and Moore: Decision Models for Management
Dannenbring and Starr: Management Science: An Introduction
Fitzsimmons and Sullivan: Service Operations Management
Gohagan: Quantitative Analysis for Public Policy
Heyman and Sobel: Stochastic Models in Operations Research, Volume I:
  Stochastic Processes and Operating Characteristics
McKenna: Quantitative Methods for Public Decision Making
Sobol and Starr: Statistics for Business and Economics:
  An Action Learning Approach
Swanson: Linear Programming: Basic Theory and Applications
Zeleny: Multiple Criteria Decision Making

To
Dorothy Holmes Bowen

CONTENTS

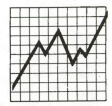

PREFACE

In quantitative courses in general, and in statistics in particular, business students have special need for a text from which they can learn—on their own, if necessary. Students have a right to expect that their text will be written in a language they can understand and that the text will help them to learn. Instructors need a text that provides details they cannot cover in the short time available in class. The purpose of this book is to assume a fair share of the responsibility for both learning and teaching.

The teaching sequence in the text goes like this: new topic is explained. Then completely worked-out examples are given. Next, before moving on, the reader does a "fix-it-in-mind" exercise to make sure that the topic is understood. After a major topic or a few related topics are covered, a set of homework problems is provided. The sequence is tlien repeated. At the end of the chapter there is a "how-to-do-it" summary of methods discussed in the chapter and a set of review problems on the entire chapter.

Answers to the "fix-it-in-mind" exercises are given with the exercises. Answers to *odd-numbered* homework problems are given at the end of the book. Answers to *even-numbered* homework problems and all *review problems*, worked out in detail, are given in the *Instructor's Manual*. (These problems can be userl for examinations or lecture preparation.) The text contains more problems and exercises than any other business statistics book (about 1100 problems and 200 "fix-it-in-mind" exercises).

The text is written for students taking the required first course in business statistics. High school algebra (ability to read formulas—not algebraic manipulation of symbols) is the only prerequisite. The book contains material for two semesters of study, but chapters and parts of chapters have been made independent to permit maximum flexibilitv in the selection of topics for a one-semester or a one-quarter course. The *Instructor's Manual* describes chapter dependencies and lists the sections that are not a prerequisite for later sections.

The book contains all the topics included in beginning courses in business statistics. In addition, Chapter 2 contains a review of basic calculations that students need but often do not know or have forgotten. Also, some topics not usually discussed in other texts have been included because they are particularly relevant to business and economics. Examples include the interpretahon of computer output in regression and analysis of variance (Chapters 13 and 15), the Kendall test ofconcordance (Chapter 16), and productivity indexes (Chapter 17). But on the whole, the content is standard. It is the teaching-learning orientation of this text that makes it different from others with similar content.

A student Study Guide is available which includes chapter review materials as well as additional worked-out problems and examples. It also includes self-testing materials with answers.

The book has benefited from comments and suggestions made by five professors who taught from it during its 3-year trial period at Babson College: Ismael G. Dambolena, David Kopcso, John D. McKenzie, Jr., Arvind A. Shah, and Margaret Weinblatt. During the trial period, approximately 1300 students from the freshman level through the M.B.A. level used the text in courses taught by six full-time and four part-time faculty members.

We express our thanks to the following professors whose insightful reviews led to revisions that improved the trial version of the text: George J. Brabb (Illinois State University), Virginia Krright (Western New England College), Michael Liechenstein (St. John's University), Carl A. Silver (Drexel University), Scot A. Stradley (University of North Dakota), Willbann D. Terpening (University of Notre Dame), Thomas C. Tucker (University ofHouston-Clear Lake City), and Dean W. Wichern (University of Wisconsin).

We express our thanks also to Edward M. Millrnan for his many contributions to the task of explaining statistics to beginners. And to Jo Jones, Michael R. Elia, James B. Armstrong and Dennis J. Conroy go the credit for the design, editing, and production of the book.

We are grateful to the Literary Executor ofthe late Sir Ronald A. Fisher, F.R.S.; to Dr. Frank Yates, F.R.S.; and to Longman Group Ltd., London, for permission to reprint Table IV from their book *Statistical Tables for Biological, Agricultural and Medical Research* (6th edition, 1974).

Earl K. Bowen
Martin K. Starr

1

INTRODUCTION

Business executives and managers are decision makers. Administrators of hospitals, colleges, and other organizations are decision makers. Decisions are based on information, and much of this information is in the form of numbers—numbers which are frequently called *statistics* or *statistical data*. Thus, statistics *are* numbers. On the other hand, statistics is a field of study. Students working toward decision-making careers take one or more courses in statistics. I'll start by discussing what statistics are, then discuss what statistics is, and finally return to decision making.

1.1 STATISTICS ARE

Statistics: *a group of numerical data*

The word *statistics*, which is derived from the word *state*, entered the English vocabulary in the eighteenth century. It was used then, and still is used, to mean one or more sets of numerical data on population, taxes, wealth, exports, imports, crop production, and other items of interest to state officials. Today we use the "set of numerical data" meaning when we refer to baseball statistics, stock market statistics, production statistics, labor statistics, and so on. In the plural, then, statistics, or statistical data, are numbers—not abstract numbers such as those in a table of square roots, but concrete numbers such as inventory counts, measurements, dollar prices and dollar sales, interest rates, and average hourly wage rates.

1.2 STATISTICS IS

Statistic: *a field of study*

Statistics is a field of study. The main parts of this field of study are descriptive statistics, probability, decision analysis, and statistical inference.

Descriptive Statistics

The *median is one* descriptive statistic. *There are others*

The Bureau of the Census has described the ages of people in the United States population as shown in Table 1.1. The table does not show the ages of every person. Instead, it provides an understandable summary description of the ages of many millions of people. Now look at the numbers in the last column—the medians. The top number means that in 1950, 50 percent of the people in the population were under, and 50 percent were over, 30.2 years of age. The 50-50 meaning applies to all the medians. Run your eye down the column and note that the median age first declined, and then rose. The medians in Table 1.1 provide a very condensed summary description of changes in ages.

The Bureau of the Census—a major statistical arm of the United States government—projects a continuing rise in the median age for the remainder of the century. Population and other data compiled by the Bureau are used extensively by decision makers. For example, in deciding how to allocate funds for research and development, drug manufacturers are influenced by the growing numbers of older people. On the other hand, my college—which followed a policy of expansion in the 1960s and early

TABLE 1.1
POPULATION OF THE UNITED STATES BY AGE GROUP, 1950–1977
(In thousands of persons except for median age)

Year	Total all ages	Under 5	5–13	14–17	18–21	22–24	25–34	35–44	45–54	55–64	65 and over	Median age, years
1950	152,271	16,410	22,423	8,444	8,947	7,129	24,036	21,637	17,453	13,396	12,397	30.2
1960	180,671	20,341	32,965	11,219	9,555	6,573	22,919	24,221	20,578	15,625	16,675	29.4
1970	204,878	17,148	36,636	15,910	14,707	9,980	25,294	23,142	23,310	18,664	20,087	27.9
1975	213,540	15,882	33,440	16,934	16,484	11,120	30,918	22,815	23,768	19,774	22,405	28.8
1976	215,142	15,343	32,962	16,393	16,767	11,396	32,049	23,080	23,641	20,065	22,947	29.0
1977	216,817	15,236	32,227	16,783	16,956	11,646	33,149	23,543	23,389	20,395	23,494	29.4

Source: Adapted from the Statistical Abstract of the United States, 1978.

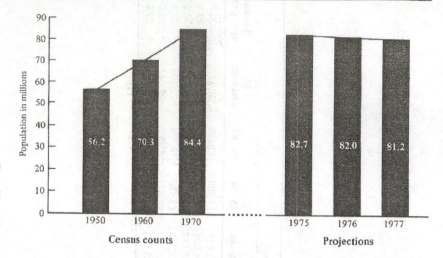

FIGURE 1.1
United States population under 22 years of age—a population change that affected decisions.

Census counts   Projections

1970s—decided to abandon this policy in 1975. You can see why by glancing at Figure 1.1, which shows that the number of current and prospective college age students had stopped growing by the mid-1970s.

The median is also a summary statistic.

The subject area of descriptive statistics includes procedures used to summarize masses of data and present them in an understandable way. It also includes computations of specialized averages, ratios, projections, and other measures which aid in making decisions.

Probability

A probability is a number which measures relative frequency of occurrence over the long run or expresses a degree of belief. We often use the word *chance* rather than *probability*. When we say the probability—or chance—that a tossed coin will land heads up is 50 percent (or 0.5, or 1 out of 2), we are using the relative-frequency meaning of probability. We expect that, if we were to flip a coin many times, heads would occur on about one-half the tosses. Moreover, we expect that the proportion of heads—which is the relative frequency of heads—will get closer to 0.5 as the number of tosses increases.

Relative frequency of heads:

$$\frac{Number\ of\ heads}{Number\ of\ tosses}$$

On the other hand, a businessperson who says there is a 90 percent chance—or 90 percent probability—of selling more than 50,000 units of a product next year is using a degree-of-belief meaning of probability. That belief is influenced by sales in past years and by a judgment of economic and other factors which will be operative next year. To understand why the businessperson's 90 percent probability is not a relative-frequency measure, suppose that the 50,000 units are a 10 percent increase over last year and represent a new high for sales. Then the relative frequency of sales exceeding

50,000 is zero—it has never occurred—not the 90 percent stated by the businessperson.

Probability, as a subject area, develops rules for working with relative frequency or degree-of-belief probabilities. These rules show how to use one or more known probabilities to obtain an unknown but desired probability. As an example, suppose there is a 0.9 probability—a 90 percent chance—that a fire detector will function if there is a fire. Suppose also that the functioning of one detector does not depend on whether another detector functions. If two detectors are installed, you would expect the probability that at least one (that is, one or the other, or both) will function to be greater than 0.9. Probability rules that we shall develop tell us that this is so and that the desired probability is 0.99. Thus, there is a 99 percent chance that at least one of two detectors will function if there is a fire.

As this simple example shows, probability itself (the numbers and the rules) has useful applications. Moreover, probability is the foundation for the more technical subjects in statistics—decision analysis and statistical inference.

Statistical Decision Analysis

Many of us would decide to invest $1000 in a business which, in our opinion, has a 99 percent chance of returning $10,000 to us during the coming year. Few, if any, would make the same decision if the chance of the $10,000 gain is only 1 percent. Similarly, a clothing store owner may decide to order 500 women's dresses for the spring season because she believes there is a high chance (say, 95 percent) of selling all, or most, of the dresses. The owner knows that her profit might be doubled if 1000 dresses were ordered and sold, but dismisses this opportunity for higher profit because the chance of obtaining it is too small (say, 10 percent). Statistical decision analysis is concerned with making a decision when alternative courses of action (e.g., how many dresses to order) exist but the profits and the probabilities associated with the actions vary. Generally, the higher the potential profit, the lower the probability of achieving this profit. Decision analysis will be introduced after your study of probability.

Population, Sample, and Statistical Inference

A statistical inference is a statement made about a *population* but based upon information about a *random sample* selected from the population. The terms *population* and *random sample* have very specific meanings in statistics.

Populations In everyday language, the word *population* means *all* the people in a specific area. We use this meaning when we speak of the population of New York City. In statistics, the word population has a broader meaning. All the accounts in a bank make up a population of bank accounts.

All the houses in a town make up a population of houses. Each individual item in a population—a person, a bank account, or a house—is called an element of the corresponding population. Thus, in the broad statistical sense, population means all the elements of some specified type.

Population *means all the elements*

Information about populations is needed in making decisions. However, in many situations it is too costly or too time-consuming to obtain the desired information about all the elements in a population. In such cases, information is obtained from part of the population. A set of elements consisting of part of a population is called a *sample* of the population. A hint of the variety of areas where samples are used is provided by the following list.

Sample *means some of the elemets*

1. The percent unemployed in the civilian labor force (a population of about 100 million people) is estimated monthly from a sample of about 100 thousand people; that is, a sample of about one worker per 1000 workers.
2. Auditors derive conclusions about the adequacy of accounting methods by examining a sarnple of accounts.
3. A manufacturer monitors the quality of goods produced by examining a sample of the output.

Some sample samples

4. Before placing orders with dress manufacturers, a large mail order firm prepares a special brochure which is sent to a sample of its customers. From orders received, the firm estimates the number of dresses to order, by style and color, for all its customers.
5. Before widespread distribution of a new drug, information on the drug's effects is determined by sampling.
6. Information on employee attitudes is obtained by in-depth interviews with a sample ofemployees.
7. An advertising firm obtains an indicator of the effect of a magazine advertisement by selecting a sample of subscribers and determining what proportion recall the ad and the product advertised.
8. A tire manufacturer wears out test samples of tires to estimate the average mileage to be expected from the tires.
9. An automobile manufacturer questions a sample of consumers to obtain information on their new-car buying expectations.
10. A company-employed economist analyzes a sample of price and sales data to obtain information on the relationship between quantity sold and the prices charged.

Simple Random Samples A simple random salnple is one selected in a manner such that each element of the population has an equal chance of being included in the sample. One way to obtain a simple random sample is this: Write the name ofeach person in the population on a card—one name per card. Then mix the cards thoroughly, and draw out the same number of cards as you wish to have people in the sample. Simple random samples are important in the development of probability and statistical inference. Unless some statement to the contrary appears, you should assume that when I refer to a random sample, I mean a simple sandom sample.

A special type of inference

Statistical Inference We cannot be sure just how closely the characteristics of a random sample reflect those of the population from which the sample was selected. Consequently, any conclusion about a population is called a statistical *inference* if it is based on a random sample from that population. The qualifier *statistical* emphasizes that this is a special type of inference—an inference based on sample evidence. Random samples are important because they make it possible to determine the probability that inferences are correct. For example, suppose a marketing executive learns that in a random sample of the television audience, 40 percent of the viewers watched the series sponsored by her company. She knows it is highly unlikely that the total audience (population) share is exactly 40 percent. It would be helpful if she were told that there is a 0.99 probability that the audience share is between 37 and 43 percent. The population statement (share between 37 and 43 percent) and its accompanying probability (0.99) is a statistical inference. How to make such statements and compute the probabili-ties is part of the study of statistical inference.

1.3 WHY STUDY STATISTICS?

A massive volume of statistical data has been collected in the past, and will be collected at increasing rates in the future. This information explosion would be unmanageable if not for the capacity of modern computer systems to store, process, retrieve, and present information. But who asked for all these data, and who needs them? The answer is almost everyone, in all parts of the economy, public and private, who uses statistical data in making decisions, planning, negotiating, and in other activities. You are studying statistics mainly because you will be involved in making decisions. The following two items illustrate the decision thrust of statistics. They were selected because at least one affects you.

Item: The message from the Surgeon General of the United States illustrated in Figure 1.2 appears on cigarette packages. Why this warning? In large part because data collected on amount of smoking, age, and cause of death showed that the more people smoked, the higher their death rate from lung cancer and some other diseases—in all age categories. It should be noted, however, that the relationship between smoking and lung cancer does not

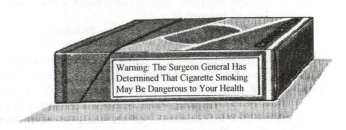

Warning: The Surgeon General Has Determined That Cigarette Smoking May Be Dangerous to Your Health

FIGURE 1.1
The Surgeon General's decision

prove absolutely that smoking causes the disease. Researchers suspect tarry substances in tobacco may be a cause. Nevertheless, the Surgeon General made the decision to require the warning—and tobacco companies decided to market and advertise low-tar cigarettes.

Item: In 1975, Social Security tax deducted from paychecks was at the rate of 5.85 percent on earnings up to a "wage base" of $14,100. In 1977, Congress decided to raise the tax. Statistical data played an important role in this decision. Higher taxes were needed because of increases in the number and the proportion of persons eligible to receive Social Security payments. Moreover, payments to eligible persons rise when prices rise; so price data affected the decision. In 1980, the tax rate was 6.13 percent on earnings up to $25,900. The rate is scheduled to rise through 1990. Furthermore, the "wage base" will increase when the average wage level increases. You can expect to pay higher Social Security taxes as time goes on.

The two items just cited relate mainly to decisions in government. A hint of the range of business decision problems involving statistics is provided by the following list.

Problems in which statistics are, and statistics is, needed

1. Selecting locations for new stores, restaurants, warehouses, fire stations
2. Deciding whether to continue or cancel a new television series
3. Forecasting whether an economic recession is imminent
4. Negotiating a labor contract
5. Determining what to charge (the premium) for fire, casualty, life, health, and other insurances
6. Setting up airline schedules
7. Establishing sales quotas for regional sales territories
8. Deciding how long a replacement warranty to offer on a product
9. Selecting the appropriate media in which to advertise a product
10. Planning production schedules and raw-material purchases for the next 3 months ⌣
11. Deciding which stocks to buy or sell, and when
12. Deciding the quantity of goods to be carried in inventory, and when to reorder
13. Selecting new management trainees
14. Determining the quality of manufactured camera film when the testing destroys the product
15. Deciding whether or not to market a new product
16. Deciding whether to publish a textbook and, if so, how many copies to print
17. Deciding to start a new business
18. Determining what factors promote employee morale and motivation

Advocates use statistics.

Each of the listed items relates to making decisions. Statistical data also are obtained and used by advocates to serve their purposes. By an advocate I mean a person who argues for or defends a cause, proposal, or course of action. In this meaning, Ralph Nader is a consumer advocate. Labor and management representatives become advocates when labor contracts are negotiated. To see advocacy involving statistics at work, let's sit in on a contract negotiation. The negotiators are Fran (for management) and Bob (for the union).

> *Fran: Bob, we follow the consumer price index, just as you do. Prices have been rising, and we go along with you for about a thirty-cent-an-hour increase—maybe a little more—to compensate for increased living costs. But we can't go along with your demand for ten cents for what you call sharing in increased productivity.*
>
> *Bob: Just look at the company's annual reports. Sales are up twenty percent over last year, and the number of employees is just about the same; so sales per worker are up. That's what we mean by increased productivity. Our people do the work, and we demand our fair share of that increase.*
>
> *Fran: Come on, Bob, I just agreed that we would offer you an increase to compensate for increased living costs—and now you turn the coin over. All prices have increased, including the price of our product. The sales increase you quote is due to price increases. It doesn't mean that your people are working harder and making more product per worker.*
>
> *Bob: Even allowing for price increases, productivity still has increased.*
>
> *Fran: That's not true, but I guess we are not going to be able to get together on how to compute productivity statistics. Maybe we could agree on having an impartial consultant prepare some figures we might agree on.*
>
> *Bob: I'll speak to my people and get back to you on that.*
>
> *Fran: What about this matter of increased hazard on the job? Our figures show fewer accidents this year than last.*
>
> *Bob: That's right, but if you figure the number of accidents per 1000 labor-hours worked, it's higher this year than it was last year.*
>
> *Fran: There is nothing unusual about that. The change was small, and that rate always fluctuates a little from year to year.*
>
> *Bob: I know that, Fran, but look at this chart for the last ten years. The rate does fluctuate, but the important fact is that the trend has been definitely upward. It's about time the company either paid more attention to safety or compensated us for increased hazard on the job.*

We have listened to the discussion long enough to observe advocacy involving statistics in action in one business context. But advocacy is widespread. At one time or another most of us become advocates. If you want to be an effective advocate, prepare yourself by obtaining relevant statistical data.

I should mention that statistics—numerical information—may be used to mislead or deceive. Of course, nonnumerical information also may be used for this purpose. However, probably because people feel that numbers should be somehow "correct," misleading by numbers is considered to be a greater sin than misleading by words. A person may feel so strongly about misleading uses of numbers that he or she comes to distrust—and disregard—all statistics. That's burying one's head in the sand. We should be as critical of statistical information as we are of nonnumerical information. We should neither trust all statistics nor distrust all statistics. The point is well stated by W. A. Wallis and H. V. Roberts in their book *Statistics, a New Approach* (The Free Press, Glencoe, Ill., 1956, p. 17). They write that "he who trusts statistics indiscriminately will often be duped unnecessarily. But he who distrusts statistics indiscriminately will often be ignorant unnecessarily."

1.4 LOOKING AHEAD

This book has been written for students—you—rather than for professional stabsticians. I will not ask you to learn mathematical proofs or do complicated algebra. Simple algebra is all you will need to understand and use the symbols and formulas found in the book. You will often be doing arithmetic and taking square roots. A hand calculator will be extremely helpful.

When we start a new topic, I will explain what is involved, then give one or more examples. Frequently, I will then ask you to do an exercise to help you fix the topic in your mind. The answer is given with the exercise so that you will not have to search for it. After a related group oftopics has been discussed, a set of homework problems is provided. The answers to half of the homework problems are given at the end of the book. Additionally, a set of review problems covering a whole chapter appears at the end of each chapter except this one. The review problems will help you prepare for examinations.

This is an applied book. The examples, exercises, and problems are drawn from a wide variety of applications of statistics. Applications help you learn and give you a reason for wanting to learn. Look for applications in your surroundings—the more you find, the more you will learn about statistics.

1.5 PROBLEMS

1. Distinguish between statistics plural and statistics singular.
2. What are the main sections of the field of study called statistics?
3. What is a probability?
4. With what type of decision is statistical decision analysis concerned?
5. In the statistical sense, what is a population?
6. What is a simple random sample?
7. What is a statistical inference?

2

DATA ANALYSIS

2.1 INTRODUCTION

The first six sections of this chapter deal with rounding numbers, significant digits, calculations with approximate numbers, ratios, and percentages. All this material is used in descriptive statistics, and almost all of it is used in probability, statistical decision analysis, and statistical inference.

We use ratios and percentages extensively in comparisons to help us understand the meaning of data. Arranging data in the rows and columns of a table also provides a method for making meaningful comparisons. Comparisons are discussed in Sections 2.8 through 2.10. In the discussion of comparisons, we shall use some basic operations with numbers; so these operations are reviewed in the next six sections.

2.2 ROUNDING NUMBERS

Rounding means dropping one or more of the right-end digits of a decimal number, or replacing with a zero one or more of the right-end digits of a whole number. Then the digit preceding the first dropped digit (or the digit preceding the first digit which is replaced by a zero) may be left unchanged or increased by 1, depending upon the rounding convention adopted. We

Round to the closer number when you can.

shall adopt the "choose the closer" convention. For example, suppose we wish to round 45.68 to three digits by dropping the 8. We may write the rounded number as either 45.6 or 45.7. We choose 45.7 because it is closer to 45.68. However, if 34.54 is to be rounded to three digits, we write 34.5 rather than 34.6 because 34.5 is closer to 34.54.

The "choose the closer" convention does not specify what is to be done in the equally close case. For example, in rounding 76.85 to three digits, both 76.8 and 76.9 are equally close to 76.85. We shall adopt the "choose the

Otherwise, round to an even digit.

even" convention for this case and write 76.8 because it ends with an even digit. On the other hand, 34.15 rounded to three digits will be written as 34.2 rather than 34.1 because 34.2 ends with an even digit. The conventions just illustrated are summarized as follows:

Rules for Rounding Decimal Numbers

1. If the leftmost digit to be dropped is less than 5, do not change the preceding digit. If the leftmost digit to be dropped is greater than 5, or is 5 followed by one or more nonzero digits, increase the preceding digit by 1.
2. If the leftmost digit to be dropped is 5, or 5 followed only by zeros, round to make the preceding digit even.

EXAMPLE Round 125.64735 to five digits.

The digits to be dropped are 735. The leftmost dropped digit is 7, which is greater than 5. We increase the digit preceding 735, which is 4, by 1 and write the rounded number as 125.65.

EXAMPLE   Round 46.5649 to four digits.
In this example, we will retain digits in the first four places. The digits to be dropped are 49. The leftmost dropped digit, 4, is less than 5; so the preceding digit is not changed. The desired rounded number is 46.56.

EXAMPLE   Round 74.6501 to three digits.
In this example, the digits to be dropped, 501, are 5 followed by a nonzero digit (the ending 1); so we increase the preceding digit by 1 and write 74.7.

EXAMPLE   Round 8.6450 to three digits.
This is an example of the equally close case; so we round to the even digit and write 8.64.

I am now going to ask you to do an exercise. This exercise, and others which will appear as you read on, are part of the text. You should do the exercises as they are encountered, because they will help you set ideas firmly in mind. First do the work on scratch paper, and then compare your result with the given answer. You won't get much benefit from the exercises if you look at the answer first and then use trial and error to get that answer. In fact, trial and error may lead you to the answer by the wrong method or for the wrong reason. If you don't see what is involved in an exercise, read the preceding text again. *That's* what the exercises are for—to call your attention to points you should understand before proceeding.

EXERCISE   Round the following numbers to three digits. (a) 2.4749; (b) 136.49; (c) 92.450; (d) 6.3750; (e) 6.36501; (f) 26.962.
ANSWER   (a) 2.47; (b) 136; (c) 92.4; (d) 6.38; (e) 6.37; (f) 27.0.

Rules for Rounding Whole Numbers

The rules for rounding whole numbers by replacing one or more of the right-end digits with a zero correspond to the rules for rounding decimals. The only difference is that instead of referring to the first digit to be dropped, we refer to the first digit to be replaced with a zero. For example, when

$$128,502$$

is rounded to three digits, the digits 502 will be replaced by zeros. In 502, the 5 is followed by a nonzero digit; so we increase the preceding digit, 8, by 1 and write 129,000.

Rounding mixed decimals   A number may contain a whole part and a decimal part. If rounding is to be done in the whole part, we use the rule for rounding whole numbers and drop the decimal part. For example, 4265.72 rounded to three digits becomes 4270. Rounded to four digits, 4265.72 becomes 4266: it would be improper here to write 4266.00 because that implies the number is accurate to two decimal places.

EXERCISE (a) Round 127,632 to three digits. (b) Round 3,163,500 to four digits. (c) Round 316.34 to two digits.
ANSWER (a) 128,000; (b) 3,164,000; (c) 320.

Rounding rules are not laws. Rounding procedures other than those discussed above can be adopted. For example, many people round "5 or more up," so that, to three digits, 136.5 becomes 137, and 137.5 becomes 138. But in retail stores fractional prices are rounded to the next higher cent; "3 for a dollar" becomes 34 cents each. And a life insurance company may round age to the last birthday—so that on the day before a person's 25th birthday the person is taken as being 24 years old. In this text, I shall follow the rounding rules discussed earlier—except on rare occasions which will be noted. If you do the same, our answers should agree—unless one of us made an error.

One reason for rounding is simply that rounded numbers are easier to understand and compare. Another reason, which we will go into next, is that rounding is needed to show how many digits in a number are correct.

2.3 SIGNIFICANT DIGITS AND APPROXIMATE CALCULATIONS

Suppose a car driver keeps miles-traveled and gasoline-used records to the nearest tenth, and finds that 82.6 gallons of gasoline were consumed in traveling a total of 1426.8 miles. The driver then computes on a hand calculator

$$\text{Mileage} = \frac{1426.8}{82.6} = 17.27360775 \text{ miles per gallon}$$

How many digits in the result are accurate? How should the result be rounded? This section provides rules that answer these questions.

Significant Digits

The significant digits in a number are those in the sequence of digits beginning at the left, excluding beginning zeros, which are correct. You should understand that *correct* means not only correctly computed but also correct in the sense that it is possible to know what the correct digit is. For example, in the mileage calculation, 82.6 has three significant digits and 1426.8 has five significant digits. All the digits in the result, 17.27360775 miles per gallon, are arithmetically correct. But if we know the gas consumption to only three significant digits, we can't possibly know the mileage to any more than three significant digits. Additional digits have no meaning. The result, 17.27360775, should be rounded to three digits and stated as 17.3 miles per gallon.

Beginning Zeros Are Not Significant The beginning zero in 0.642 is there simply because the number has a better written appearance than .642.

The zero is not significant. Again, if we write .076, the beginning zero serves only to position the decimal point: It is not counted as a significant digit. In general, then, beginning zeros are not counted as being significant digits. The numbers 0.076 and .076 both have two significant digits.

Ending Zeros May Be Significant If we write 36.0, we mean that the ending zero is significant; otherwise, there would be no reason for writing it. However, some ending zeros may serve only to position the decimal point, and it may not be possible to determine how many of these zeros are significant. Thus, an inventory count stated as about 4500 items may be accurate to the nearest hundred, so that the number has two significant digits. Or, it may be accurate to the nearest ten, so that the number has three significant digits. If we know which of the foregoing is true, we can state the number in a manner which tells how many digits are significant. For example, "to the nearest hundred the inventory is 4500 items."

Rounding Results of Multiplication and Division

22.2
× __3.0__
= 67

After multiplication or division, the result should be rounded to the number of significant digits in the figure having the fewest significant digits.

EXAMPLE Carry out the following operations and write the result, properly rounded.

$$\frac{(0.076)(842.9)}{12.4}$$

I use a calculator to do arithmetic—and I advise strongly that you do the same. In the example at hand, I multiplied 0.076 by 842.9, leaving the product in the calculator. Dividing the product by 12.4, I find the result to be 5.166 and some more digits. The result, properly rounded, is 5.2, because 0.076 has only two (the fewest) significant digits. Note that I rounded the final result, leaving the unrounded result of the previous calculation (the multiplication) in the calculator. You should do the same.

Note: In exercises, to save space, I will use a slash mark (/) to specify division. Using the slash, the last calculation would be expressed as (0.076)(842.9)/12.4.

EXERCISE Carry out the following calculations. Round the result to the proper number of significant digits. (a) (23.958)(2.4); (b) (0.0625)(1284); (c) (12.4)(32.1)/0.0526.
ANSWER (a) 57; (b) 80.2; (c) 7570.

Rounding Results of Addition and Subtraction

2.1
+ __3.48__
= 5.6

In addition and subtraction, the result should be rounded to the rightmost place in which all figures have a significant digit.

Consider the addition

$$\begin{array}{r} 17.2 \\ 8.41 \\ \underline{0.08} \\ 25.69 \end{array}$$

Because the 17.2 does not have a digit in the second decimal place, we cannot know the digit in the second decimal place of the sum. If we retained the second decimal place in the sum, as in 25.69, we would be assuming that the first number was 17.20. But it could have been rounded, say, from 17.21 or from 17.18. Hence we must round the sum to the first decimal place and state it as 25.7. In addition and subtraction, the farthest place to the right where all the component numbers have a significant digit determines how many digits to retain when writing the result.

EXERCISE Carry out the following calculations. Round the result to the proper number of significant digits. (a) 4.23 + 1.2; (b) 23.475 − 10.52; (c) 46.5 + 133.47 − 122.
ANSWER (a) 5.4; (b) 12.96; (c) 58.

Measurements are approximate numbers.

Some numbers are exact. For example, I counted the keys on my calculator: There are exactly 36 of them. Numbers which are not exact are called approximate numbers. As closely as I can judge using a ruler calibrated in millimeters, the width of the lighted display area of my calculator is approximately 158 millimeters. When all numbers used in a calculation are exact, we can retain as many digits as we wish in a result. The rules cited next apply when approximate numbers are used in calculations.

Rules for Calculations Involving Approximate Numbers

1. After multiplication or division of figures, the result should be rounded to the number of significant digits in the figure having the fewest significant digits.
2. After addition and subtraction, the result should be rounded to the rightmost place in which all figures have a significant digit.
3. The square root of a figure should be rounded to the number of significant digits in that figure.

Spurious accuracy means false accuracy. It arises from inattention to the rules for calculations involving approximate numbers or, at times, from deliberate attempts to make a number appear more accurate than it is. In this text we try to avoid spurious accuracy, but it may not always be possible to know, for sure, how many digits in a number are significant. As a guide, when you are in doubt about how many digits to retain in the result of a calculation, retain three or four (but don't count beginning zeros). Do not follow the practice of copying down every digit that is displayed on a hand calculator. This often leads to spurious accuracy or to retaining digits which are meaningless for a particular purpose.

2.4 PROBLEMS

1. Assuming the following numbers are correctly written, how many significant digits does each have? (a) 126.8; (b) 24.0; (c) 4.00; (d) 0.0720.

2. Round the following to two significant digits. (a) 2.563; (b) 8.749; (c) 4.450; (d) 8.750; (e) 0.09755; (f) 0.00403.

3. If neither of the zeros in 2500 is significant, we may specify the number of significant digits by writing 2500 as 25 hundred or 2.5 thousand. Assume none of the zeros in the following is significant, and express the numbers in this way. (a) 1200; (b) 15,000; (c) 12,500; (d) 34,600.

4. (a) A newspaper article quoting a government source states there were 5,500,000 unemployed workers in the United States last month. How many digits in this number do you think are significant? (b) A tabulation by government statisticians states the number unemployed at 5.54 million. Why, do you think, is this number not written as 5,540,000? (See Problem 3.)

5. Do the following calculations on a hand calculator. Round results to the proper number of digits. Use the words hundred, thousand, and so on, where needed (see Problem 3). (a) (3.6)(2.4); (b) (1.37)(2.15); (c) (0.875)(128.4); (d) (56.5)(12,258); (e) (4.3)(526); (f) (0.0207)(0.30); (g) (2.5)(2.5); (h) (5.00)(0.00511); (i) 56.7/27; (j) 810/20; (k) 0.00468/0.02387; (l) 125/0.0050; (m) 12.50/2.10; (n) 746.3/48.1; (o) 62.45 + 31.616; (p) 48 + 2.3 + 247.2; (q) 0.0235 + 0.055; (r) 3.5502 + 2.0; (s) 34.6548 − 12.406; (t) 0.4325 − 0.057; (u) 284.65 − 126.1; (v) 2.42 − 2.4; (w) $\sqrt{247}$; (x) $\sqrt{86}$; (y) $\sqrt{0.000256}$; (z) $\sqrt{(0.875)(0.125)}$.

2.5 RATIOS

Some ratios are so much a part of everyday language that they are understood even when described incompletely. For example, "gas mileage" for a car is understood to mean the ratio "miles per gallon"; that is, number of miles driven divided by number of gallons of gas consumed. However, many ratios are quite specialized and are not part of our everyday language. It is here that care must be exercised in describing the outcome of a ratio calculation.

The Word *per* in Ratios

If a driver divides 1200 miles driven by 60 gallons of gasoline consumed to obtain

$$\frac{1200 \text{ miles}}{60 \text{ gallons}} = 20 \frac{\text{miles}}{\text{gallon}}$$

the result is described as the ratio 20 miles per gallon. That is, the division line translates as *per*, and the unit of the base (the denominator of the ratio) follows the word per.

Miles   *gallon*

EXAMPLE   A company had a net profit of $120,000 on sales totaling $1,600,000. Divide net profit by sales and describe the result.

We compute

$$\frac{\$120,000 \text{ net profit}}{\$1,600,000 \text{ sales}} = 0.075$$

The result is described by saying net profit was $0.075 per dollar of sales, or 7.5 cents per dollar of sales.

EXERCISE   An advertisement costing $2485 led to 875 inquiries by potential customers. Note that 2485/875 = 2.84 and 875/2485 = 0.352. Write a description of (a) the first ratio; (b) the second ratio.

ANSWER   (a) The advertisement cost $2.84 per inquiry received. (b) About 0.352 inquiry was received per dollar spent.

Conventional Bases for Ratios

Observe in the last exercise that 0.352 inquiry per $1 spent can be changed to the equivalent ratio 35.2 inquiries per $100 spent. That is,

$$\frac{0.352}{\$1} = \frac{35.2}{\$100}$$

The conversion to the base 100 was made by multiplying both 0.352 and 1 by 100. The ratio 35.2 inquiries per $100 spent is the easier one to comprehend. It is common practice to convert to bases which are powers of 10 (10, 100, 1000) for ease in comprehension. When possible, the base should be chosen so that the resulting ratio, when rounded, has at least one digit to the left of the decimal point.

EXAMPLE   Eight years ago the numbers of imported and domestic cars sold in the United States were, respectively, 660 thousand and 8380 thousand. Last year corresponding sales were 1420 thousand and 7450 thousand. Compute ratios for the 2 years and write a descriptive comparison of these ratios.

In the example at hand, as in many cases, there are several ways to make the ratio comparison, each of which is correct if it is described properly. One way is to compute

$$8 \text{ years ago:} \frac{660 \text{ thousand imports}}{8380 \text{ thousand domestics}} = 0.0788 \text{ import per domestic}$$

or, multiplying by 1000, 78.8 imports per 1000 domestics.

$$\text{Last year:} \frac{1420 \text{ thousand imports}}{7450 \text{ thousand domestics}} = 0.1906 \text{ import per domestic}$$

or 190.6 imports per 1000 domestics. So we may say that sales of imports per 1000 domestics rose from 78.8 to 190.6 over the 8-year period. For a rougher, but perhaps more easily comprehended, comparison, we may say that sales of imports per 100 domestics rose from about 8 to about 19 over the period.

EXERCISE In June, stock (inventory) of the beer, wine, and distilled alcoholic beverage industry was valued at $2.66 billion, and sales were $2.47 billion. In August, stock was $2.59 billion and sales were $2.63 billion. Compute stock per $100 of sales for June and for August.
ANSWER $108 and $98.5.

Rates

Rates are ratios. Some ratios are referred to or defined as *rates*. Thus, we speak of growth rates, rates of change, interest rates, absentee rates, and so on. This leads us to another way of describing the change in the numbers in the last example. Suppose we define the sales of imported cars divided by the sales of domestic cars as the "import to domestic" rate. This rate was computed as 0.0788 eight years ago, and 0.1906 last year. We now form the ratio

$$\frac{0.1906}{0.0788} = 2.42$$

which we can describe by saying that the import to domestic rate last year was about 2.4 times what it was 8 years ago.

The foregoing examples illustrate that different ratios or rates may be computed from given data. The description of the results depends on the calculation procedure. Remember, though, that the calculation procedure for some ratios is fixed by definition or convention. Thus, in management, the current ratio is always computed as current assets divided by current liabilities. And a productivity ratio is computed as output divided by input—for example, units produced per hour worked.

Compound Units

A compound unit is the product of two unlike units. For example, 20 workers, each working five 8-hour days (40 hours each), work a total

$$(20 \text{ workers})(40 \text{ hours}) = 800 \text{ labor-hours}$$

EXAMPLE To the driver of a passenger car, fuel consumption usually connotes miles per gallon. To a trucking firm, however, a more meaningful ratio takes into account not only miles and gallons but also the amount of freight hauled. Thus, if a loaded trailer truck hauls 22.5 tons of freight a distance of 205 miles and consumes 32.5 gallons of fuel, we compute

$$\frac{(22.5 \text{ tons})(205 \text{ miles})}{32.5 \text{ gallons}} = 142 \text{ ton-miles per gallon}$$

By way of contrast, a passenger car could haul perhaps 1000 pounds (0.5 ton) and at 16 miles per gallon would yield only

$$(0.5 \text{ ton})\left(16 \frac{\text{miles}}{\text{gallon}}\right) = 8 \text{ ton-miles per gallon}$$

EXERCISE A train hauled 1000 tons of goods a distance of 800 miles and had a net revenue of $16,000. Compute revenue per ton-mile.
ANSWER $0.02, or 2 cents per ton-mile.

The Arithmetic Average

Average as a ratio or rate

The arithmetic average (the ordinary average) is computed as the sum of a group of figures divided by the number of figures in the group. It is actually a ratio. To see this, suppose sales by each of four car salespersons were 7, 10, 8, and 13 cars. We can compute the average as

$$\frac{7 + 10 + 8 + 13}{4} = \frac{38}{4} = 9.5$$

which is the ratio of cars sold to salespeople. It is usually stated as an average of 9.5 cars per salesperson.

EXERCISE Sales for Monday through Saturday, in thousands of dollars, were $18.5, $16.2, $20.4, $24.9, $23.0, $14.6. Compute and describe the average of these numbers.
ANSWER Sales averaged $19.6 thousand per day.

2.6 PERCENT

Percent means *per hundred*; so a percent is a ratio expressed with 100 as its base (denominator). When the ratio is calculated, the numerator and denominator should be measured in the same unit. The ratio is calculated as a decimal number and then converted to a percent.

Conversion

Converting decimal to percent

A decimal number is converted to percent by multiplying it by 100 (moving the decimal point two places to the right) and affixing the % symbol. Thus,

0.03 becomes 3%

0.001 becomes 0.1% (one-tenth of 1 percent)

0.625 becomes 62.5%

2.53 becomes 253%

Converting percent to decimal

A percent is converted to its decimal equivalent by dropping the % symbol and dividing by 100 (moving the decimal point two places to the left). An interest rate of 7.54% becomes the decimal 0.0754, and one-half of 1 percent (0.5%) becomes 0.005.

Percent of

If expenses of $300 are incurred in obtaining a sales volume of $1200, we can compute

$$\frac{\$300 \text{ expenses}}{\$1200 \text{ sales}} = 0.25 \text{ or } 25 \text{ percent}$$

Calculating the percent We may say that expenses amounted to 25 percent *of* sales. That is, when a ratio is stated in percent form using the word *of*, the divisor (base) is named after the word *of*. Or, the other way around, if we want to compute what percent *a* is of *b*, then *b* is the base.

We should avoid using the word *of* if the numerator is not in some sense a part of the denominator. For example, current year's sales (say, 96,000 units) are not part of last year's sales (84,000 units). Thus, in the ratio

$$\frac{\text{Current year's sales}}{\text{Last year's sales}} = \frac{96,000}{84,000} = 1.14 \text{ or } 114 \text{ percent}$$

we would say that current year's sales were 114 percent *as great as* last year's sales (*not* 114 percent *of* last year's sales).

EXERCISE For the following sales figures, compute and describe (using the proper terminology) the percent ratios (*a*) current December to current year total; (*b*) current December to December a year ago.

	Current December	Current year total	Last December
Sales ($000)*	$180	$900	$200

* Sales ($000) means sales in thousands of dollars.

ANSWER (*a*) Current December sales were 20 percent of current year's sales. (*b*) Current December sales were 90 percent as great as December sales a year ago.

Calculating a percent of a number To find a percent of a number, we multiply the number by the decimal form of the percent. For example, 17 percent of 250 is

$$0.17(250) = 42.5$$

Similarly, 125 percent of 200 is

$$1.25(200) = 250$$

EXERCISE (*a*) Compute 35 percent of 1600. (*b*) Compute 140 percent of 500.
ANSWER (*a*) 560; (*b*) 700.

Percent Change or Difference

A numerical change is a change *from* one number to another. An increase is a change *from* the smaller of two numbers to the larger number. A decrease is a change *from* the larger of two numbers to the smaller. For consistency, the number "from" which the change occurred is used as the base in computing the percent change. This means that a percent increase is computed by dividing the difference in two numbers by the smaller number. But a percent decrease is computed by dividing the difference by the larger of two numbers. Some alternatives for the words increase and decrease are less than and greater than, above and below.

Consider the following data:

	This month	Last month	Same month last year
Price per unit, cents	65	67	62

Percent decrease Note that price this month is below that of last month; so we have a *decrease* of 2 cents. We use the larger number as the base to compute

$$\frac{2}{67} = 0.02985, \text{ or about } 3.0 \text{ percent}$$

We say this month's price is about 3.0 percent less than, or below, last month's price.

On the other hand, this month's price, 65, is above that of the same month last year, 62; so we have an *increase* of 3 cents. We divide by the ***Percent increase*** *smaller* number to obtain

$$\frac{3}{62} = 0.0484, \text{ or about } 4.8 \text{ percent}$$

Hence, this month's price is about 4.8 percent above, or greater than, that of the same month a year ago.

A percent increase or decrease can be converted to a percent *of*. For example, a 25 percent increase becomes (by adding 100 percent) 125 percent *of*. A 10 percent decrease becomes (by subtracting from 100 percent) 90 percent *of*. A merchant who wants to mark up a cost price of $75 by 25 percent can do so by adding 25 percent of $75 to $75, or by computing 125 percent of $75. Thus,

$$\$75 + 0.25(\$75) = \$75 + \$18.75 = \$93.75$$

or

$$1.25(\$75) = \$93.75$$

EXERCISE (a) A price of $99.95 is to be reduced by 20 percent. Show two ways to compute the new price. (b) Sales this year are $20,900 compared with $22,000 last year. Compute and describe the percent change in sales from last year to this year.

ANSWER (a) $99.95 − 0.20($99.95) = $79.96. Or, 0.80($99.95) = $79.96. (b) Sales this year are 5 percent below sales last year.

Percent Error

The difference between an approximation of a number and the correct number (approximate minus correct) is called the *error*. We shall compute percent error by dividing the error by the correct number and expressing the result as a percent. For example, suppose an approximate inventory record indicates that there are 156 hats in stock, but an actual count shows the correct number is 150. The error is $156 - 150$, or 6. The percent error is

$$\frac{\text{Error}}{\text{Correct number}} = \frac{6}{150} = 0.04 \text{ or } 4 \text{ percent}$$

The approximate inventory record is 4 percent greater than the correct count, or we may say, the record is in error by 4 percent on the high side.

Next, suppose the approximate inventory record had indicated 144 hats. Then the error would have been $144 - 150 = -6$; that is, the record is 6 below the correct count. The percent error would have been

$$\frac{-6}{150} = -0.04 = -4 \text{ percent}$$

or 4 percent on the low side.

If we know the correct number, we use it as the base when computing percent error; this ensures that errors of the same amount above and below the correct number lead to the same percent error, except for sign. Thus, in the foregoing example, $^6/_{150}$ is 4 percent and $-^6/_{150}$ is -4 percent. Observe that if the approximate numbers had been used as bases, $^6/_{156}$ is about 3.85 percent, but $-^6/_{144}$ is about -4.17 percent. I should point out, though, that percent error terminology sometimes is used when the correct number is not known. Suppose, for example, that, in October, a manager says her estimate that November sales will be $220,000 could be in error by 10 percent one way or the other. Here, the correct number is unknown. The manager's statement means she thinks sales will be within $22,000 (10 percent of $220,000) of $220,000; that is, from $198,000 to $242,000.

This may also be written as $220,000 ⊥ $22,000.

EXERCISE Compute percent error if (a) the correct number is 375 and the approximate number is 340; (b) the approximate number is 0.587 and the correct number is 0.545.
ANSWER (a) -9.33 percent; (b) 7.71 percent.

Percentage Relatives

Sometimes a series of numbers is each expressed as a percent of some single number. Usually, this single number (the base) is one of the series or the average of two or more numbers in the series. We shall call such a series of numbers *percentage relatives. The percent symbol is usually omitted when writing or quoting relatives.* The base number, which is the ratio of itself to itself, is 100 percent, or simply 100. Percentage relatives are illustrated in Table 2.1. In the table, the relatives with period 1 as 100 (base) were ob-

TABLE 2.1

	Period				
	1	2	3	4	5
Output (thousand tons)	360.0	400.0	470.0	450.0	490.0
Relative output (period 1 = 100)	100	111.1	130.6	125.0	136.1
Relative output (periods 1–3 = 100)	87.8	97.6	114.6	109.8	119.5

tained by expressing each output as a percent of the period 1 output, 360, and omitting the percent symbol. Average output for periods 1 through 3 was

$$\frac{360.0 + 400.0 + 470.0}{3} = \frac{1230.0}{3} = 410.0$$

and the relatives with period 1–3 = 100 were computed by expressing each output as a percent of 410.0, again omitting the percent symbol.

Such indexes are the subject of Chapter 17. Some important economic indicators are published in the form of percentage relatives. For example, the consumer price index (1967 = 100) serves as a gauge of prices paid by consumers for goods and services. If the current level of the index is 240, the price level (as measured by the index) has risen 140 percent since 1967.

Percentage Points We shall use the term *percentage points* to describe the numerical difference between two percents. For example, in Table 2.1, the output percentage relative (period 1 = 100) rose from 111.1 in period 2 to 136.1 in period 5. This is an increase of

$$136.1 - 111.1 = 25$$

percentage points. Note, however, that the percent increase is

$$\frac{25}{111.1} = 0.225 \quad \text{or} \quad 22.5 \text{ percent}$$

The term percentage points is used to distinguish between the difference of two percent numbers and the percent difference in the numbers.

EXERCISE Unemployment at the end of a year was 7.1 percent of the civilian labor force. At the beginning of the year it had been predicted that the figure would reach 7.4 percent by the year's end. By how much was the prediction in error (*a*) in percentage points? (*b*) in percent?
ANSWER (*a*) 0.3 percentage point too high; (*b*) 4.2 percent on the high side.

Percentage Distributions If each of the numbers in a group is expressed as a percent of the sum of the group, the results are called a *percentage distribution*. For example, in Table 2.2, sales by territory are shown in the top

TABLE 2.2

	Sales territory						
	North East	South East	North Central	South Central	North West	South West	Total
Sales ($000)	$926	$315	$784	$515	$207	$438	$3185
Percent of total	29.1%	9.9%	24.6%	16.2%	6.5%	13.8%	100.1%*

* Percents do not add to 100 because of rounding.

row. Their sum is $3185. The percentage distribution in the next row was computed by expressing the sales figure for each territory as a percent of 3185. The percentage distribution should, of course, have 100 percent as its sum, but as the footnote indicates, rounding can lead to a sum which varies a bit from 100.

EXERCISE Express the following sales data as (a) percentage relatives with average sales per sales territory = 100; (b) a percentage distribution. Round calculations to one decimal place.

	Sales territory		
	East	Central	West
Sales, tons	8500	6000	4100

ANSWER (a) 137.1, 96.8, 66.1; (b) 45.7 percent, 32.3 percent, 22.0 percent.

2.7 PROBLEMS

In Problems 1 to 4, compute a ratio you think might be useful in business. Describe the ratio. Round results to three or four significant digits.

1. A store sold 875 television sets and 1242 radios.
2. A company which has issued 500,000 shares of stock had earnings of $1,210,000.
3. A store stocks canned soups on shelves which occupy 240 cubic feet of space. Soup sales for a period amounted to $2250.
4. During a period when a company had 880 employees there were 66 accidents to employees.
5. Fuel cost for a year was $4250 for an office building containing 25 offices. Compute fuel cost per office per month.
6. Factory sales of refrigerators and freezers, in thousands, 10 years ago were, respectively, 4545 and 1110. Last year the respective figures were 5982 and 3220. (a) Compute the refrigerator-to-freezer ratio for each year and write a descriptive comparison of the ratios. (b) Divide the ratios obtained in (a) and write a description of the outcome.

7. During a year, output valued at $9,113,611 was produced by 246 workers each working fifty 40-hour weeks. Compute dollar output per labor-hour. (A worker-hour is a labor-hour.)

8. A truck carried 22 tons of cargo a distance of 300 miles. Operating expenses (driver, gas, etc.) were $190. Compute operating expenses per ton-mile.

9. Convert the following decimals to percents. (a) 0.475; (b) 0.0875; (c) 0.0025; (d) 1.6414.

10. Convert the following percents to decimals. (a) 34.6 percent; (b) 0.4 percent; (c) 0.0852 percent; (d) 252 percent.

In Problems 11 to 16, compute a percent you think might be useful in business. Describe the percent. Round results to three significant digits.

11. Sales for December were $307,036 and for the year were $2,456,287.

12. Out of a total of 484 toasters made during a day, 4 were found to be defective.

13. Sales this month were $307,036 compared with $331,930 for the same month a year ago.

14. Sales this month were $307,036 compared with $303,245 last month.

15. A standard stereo receiver costs $425, and the super model costs $550.

16. A company has 1024 employees in its California plant and 1462 in its Texas plant.

17. During the current year, output valued at $9,113,611 was produced by 246 workers each working fifty 40-hour weeks. Last year 230 workers each working fifty 40-hour weeks produced output valued at $8,227,353. Compute the percent change in the dollar value of output per labor-hour.

18. During the current month, 9752 radios were produced in 23 working days. Last month, 8316 radios were produced in 21 working days. Compute the percent change in average output per working day.

19. A company budgeted selling expense at 13.7 percent of sales for the next quarter, and the actual figure was found to be 14.3 percent at the end of the quarter. (a) Compute the error in percentage points. (b) Compute the percent error.

20. A physical inventory (actual count) showed the number of tires in stock was 627. Accounting records compiled from data on purchases and sales showed 635. Compute the percent error.

21. Use Table A to compute percentage relatives. Round to the first decimal place. (a) Take period 1 equal to 100. (b) Take the average of periods 1 and 2 = 100.

TABLE A

Period	1	2	3	4
Price, cents per gallon	73.9	77.9	83.9	88.9

22. Sales in territories 1, 2, 3, and 4 in thousands of dollars were, respectively, $42.6, $63.0, $50.2, and $44.2. Make a percentage distribution of sales.
23. The assets of a company for 2 years are shown in Table B. Make a percentage distribution of assets for each year.

TABLE B

Item	This year	Last year
Cash	$ 52,480	$ 59,370
Marketable securities	34,500	28,400
Accounts receivable	374,260	350,580
Inventory	290,570	301,600
Plant and equipment	310,460	280,500

24. An investor in a high tax bracket must pay a 55 percent tax on interest income obtained from corporate bonds. The investor can, however, buy tax-free municipal bonds which provide 5.4 percent interest. What corporate bond interest rate would provide the investor with the equivalent of 5.4 percent tax-free?
25. A credit card company has found that 0.5 percent of cardholders are bad debts (do not pay their bills) and 3.5 percent of the bad debts become bankrupt. What percent of cardholders become bankrupt?

2.8 COMPARISONS: OTHER THINGS EQUAL

The words *other things equal* mean *nothing else changed*. We use the words when we try to explain why a change occurred or to give a reason for an observed difference. For example, we might say that, other things equal, an increase in the dollar volume of sales is due to an increase in advertising expenditures. The real fact of life, however, is that "other things" usually do not stay equal. Thus, a sales increase could be due in part to a price increase, an increase in the sales force, or seasonal or other factors, some of which may not even be identifiable. In business and economics we cannot prevent variations in factors which we would like to hold constant; instead, we make adjustments in an attempt to remove the effect of such factors. Percents and other ratios are often employed for this purpose.

Ratios reduce comparisons to a common base.

The White Sheep Effect

Said Dan to Fran, "Isn't it remarkable that white sheep eat more than black sheep?" Fran replied, "That's not remarkable at all. It simply means there are more white sheep than black sheep."

The white sheep effect—the effect of different totals—is one we often seek to remove by percent or ratio comparisons. Thus, if we compute average food consumption per animal for black sheep and for white sheep, we reduce the number of sheep being compared to one. Then we can compare food consumption in terms of *one* white sheep and *one* black sheep. Adjustments for the white sheep effect are very common.

EXAMPLE Other things equal, a substantial increase in selling expense this year compared with last year usually is a call for taking actions aimed at reducing selling expense. However, the increase may simply reflect a higher sales volume, so that no action is required. The effect of different sales volumes is adjusted for by computing the expense to sales ratio for each year. The results expressed as, say, expenses per $100 of sales, allow us to compare expenses on the same basis for both years.

EXAMPLE Other things equal, the hazards of various jobs are indicated by the numbers of accidents occurring to workers in those jobs. However, we must first adjust for different numbers of workers by computing, say, accidents per 100 workers. If there is reason to believe that variations in this ratio may be due, in part, to varying numbers of hours worked by workers, we go one step further. We can compute accidents per 1000 labor-hours. This gives us ratios which reflect what the number of accidents would be if each job had the same number of workers (1000) and each worked the same length of time (1 hour).

EXERCISE We have data showing different numbers of defective cameras produced by the day shift and the night shift. (a) What white sheep effect may be present? (b) What adjustment can be made to remove this effect?

ANSWER (a) Different total numbers of cameras produced by the day and night shifts. (b) Compute the proportion of defective cameras for each shift—or the number of defective cameras per 100 cameras produced.

The Proportionality Assumption

Adjustments leading to ratio comparisons are based on the *assumption of proportionality*. The assumption is that a ratio computed using one base may be converted to an equal ratio which has a different base. For example, suppose we convert 4 accidents among 250 workers to

$$\frac{4}{250} = \frac{0.016}{1} = \frac{1.6}{100}$$

or 1.6 accidents per 100 workers. We are assuming the ratio of accidents per worker is the same whether we have 100 workers or 250 workers. We cannot know whether or not this is true because we have 250 workers, not 100. The proportionality assumption often is deemed to be reasonable, but there are situations where it may not be. For example, if it costs $4000 to print 1000 books, it is not reasonable to say that it will cost $2000 to print 500 books. To see why, suppose the cost of setting up the press for a run of books is $500, and each book printed after the press has been set up adds $3.50 to cost. Then we compute

$$\text{Cost of 1000-book run} = \$500 + \$3.50(1000) = \$4000$$

$$\text{Cost of 500-book run} = \ \ \$500 + \$3.50(500) = \$2250$$

Note that the cost of 500 books is not half the cost of 1000 books.

The only general advice we can offer on the proportionality assumption is to recognize its existence, and question it when it does not seem to be reasonable.

The Need for Comparisons

Said Fran to Dan, "Drinking and driving do not mix. Statistics show that twenty percent of driving accidents involved drinking drivers." Dan replied, "Your statistics also show that eighty percent of the accidents involved sober drivers."

Fran seems to be saying the 20 percent implies that drinking is a cause of auto accidents. If so, she is supported by studies of the effect of alcohol on reaction time and judgment; they show the chance of accident is higher for drinking drivers than for sober drivers—but that is not my point. My point is that the 20 percent figure, by itself, implies nothing. Dan, of course, is using the same information, and his lone figure, 80 percent, implies nothing. Implications come from comparisons, and it takes at least two numbers to form a comparison. In the fictitious example at hand, we might reason (by proportionality) that if drinking is *not* associated with auto accidents, then the proportion of accidents involving drinking drivers would be about the same as the proportion of drinking drivers in the population. If, however, we find that 10 percent drive after drinking and become involved in 20 percent of the accidents, the numbers imply that accidents are associated with drinking.

We use the words *the data imply* in stating what we think the data mean. Comparisons lead to implications, but do not prove them to be correct. Observed differences may be due to factors that are not taken into account by the comparison. One such factor in the present example could be that drinking drivers tend to be on the road at a time of day when driving is most hazardous, and that accidents are associated with time of day as well as drinking. We need comparisons to suggest implications. The more successful we are at removing the effects of factors other than the one of interest, the more confidence we have in the implication.

EXERCISE A company personnel executive has read a study which reports that 65 percent of successful sales managers are extroverts and wonders whether it might be a good idea to select extroverts when filling sales manager openings. Suggest a comparison which might shed some light on this matter.

ANSWER It would be informative to find out the percent of *unsuccessful* managers who are extroverts, and then compare it with the 65 percent figure.

TABLE 2.3
ABSENTEE DATA BY EDUCATIONAL BACKGROUND

High school graduates			Nongraduates		
Number employed	Number of days absent	Absentee rate, days/employee	Number employed	Number of days absent	Absentee rate, days/employee
595	633	1.06	255	237	0.93

2.9 TABULAR ANALYSIS

Tables serve not only as compact storage places for data but also as an analytical tool. To set the stage for our example of tabular analysis, suppose Dan, a manager, is trying to identify factors which influence employee absenteeism. His first guess is that absenteeism might be related to workers' education level and the distance workers have to travel from home to the job. He has data gathered for a 6-month period and presented as shown in Tables 2.3 and 2.4.

Absentee rates, days absent per employee, adjust for the white sheep effect. The graduate, nongraduate rates in Table 2.3 (1.06 and 0.93) imply (but not strongly) that absenteeism is associated with educational level. Table 2.4 implies absenteeism is associated with distance from the job, and this implication is strengthened by the fact that the rates increase systematically from 0.89 to 1.08 to 1.12. Dan wonders if the higher rate for graduates might be related to distance traveled rather than educational status. That is, reasons Dan, if graduates tend to live farther from the job *and* absenteeism is related to distance from the job, the higher rate for graduates could be related to distance from the job rather than educational status. Consequently, Dan has Table 2.5 prepared, and it appears that his point was well taken. The absentee rates for graduates and nongraduates in the *same* distance category vary little. However, the rates in the *same* educational category increase systematically with distance from the job. The data imply that absenteeism is associated with distance from the job. Dan concludes that absenteeism could be reduced by selecting employees from those who live nearby.

Distance, not education, is the important factor.

The entries (the rates) in Table 2.5 are classified by distance down the

TABLE 2.4
ABSENTEE DATA BY DISTANCE FROM WORK

Distance from employee's home to job								
Less than 1 mile			1–3 miles			More than 3 miles		
Number employed	Days absent	Absentee rate	Number employed	Days absent	Absentee rate	Number employed	Days absent	Absentee rate
319	285	0.89	258	279	1.08	273	306	1.12

TABLE 2.5
ABSENTEE RATE BY DISTANCE FROM JOB
BY EDUCATIONAL STATUS

	Absentee rate	
Miles distant from job	High school graduates	Nongraduates
Less than 1	0.90	0.89
1–3	1.08	1.10
More than 3	1.12	1.12

Analysis by cross classification

side and by educational status across the top. Tables which classify entries in both directions, down and across, are called cross-classified tables. The analytical purpose of a cross-classified table is to hold one or more factors constant when making comparisons—to make some "other things equal." By so doing, we can improve our understanding of what the data imply.

EXERCISE Suppose Dan in the foregoing wishes to consider whether absenteeism is related to sex of employees. Describe how Table 2.5 could be extended to meet his wish. How many entries will the new table have?

ANSWER Make two columns for high school graduates, one headed male and the other female. Do the same for nongraduates. Then obtain and enter the rates. There will be 12 entries.

2.10 VARIABILITY

Suppose you leave an examination feeling that you will obtain a grade of 85. If the paper is returned with a grade of 83, your reaction probably will be no more than a slight shrug of the shoulders. But if the grade is 60, you may get excited enough to ask your instructor to regrade the paper. The point is that, from experience, you expect some variation between your expectations and actual grades obtained but will take action if the variation is large enough. You, of course, have to decide what "large enough" is. A business executive operates in much the same way. For example, suppose that, on the basis of average past performance, selling expense has been budgeted at 8.5 percent of dollar sales. The executive charged with expense control will not take action unless a month's variation above 8.5 percent is large enough—and the executive decides what "large enough" means on the basis of experience. This experience is obtained by observing monthly performance over a period of time, to develop a feel for the usual range of variations and for the amount of variation which would be judged large enough to warrant taking action.

A visual impression of variability can be obtained by charting performance. Thus, Figure 2.1 shows 2 years of monthly selling expense as a percent of sales, with the 24-month average, 8.5 percent, as the central line. By plotting a current month's performance on this chart the executive can visually

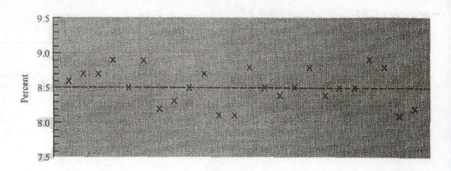

FIGURE 2.1
Selling expense as a
percent of sales
(24-month period).

compare its variation from the average with past variations. The executive
can also resort to the numbers themselves and decide, say, that a figure
exceeding 8.8 percent calls for action, because only 3 of the 24 plotted points
exceed 8.8 percent. We shall have more to say later about the topic of variability. Our purpose here is simply to establish a principle: Comparison of an
observed variation with past variations can be an important aid to a decision
maker.

2.11 PROBLEMS

1. (a) What is meant by the white sheep effect? (b) Cite an example of the
white sheep effect.

In Problems 2 to 5, name at least one "other thing" that may not be "equal,"
and suggest a comparison which adjusts for that factor.

2. Statistics show more auto accidents occur within 15 miles of the
driver's home than on long trips. Other things equal, this implies it is
safer to take long trips than short trips.

3. Exray Company paid its stockholders $2,160,500 in dividends last
year compared with the $1,246,500 paid by Whyray Company. Other
things equal, this shows it was more profitable to own Exray stock than
Whyray stock.

4. Day-shift employees produce more defective units of product than
night-shift employees. Other things equal, this implies poorer quality
control on the day shift.

5. This year a credit card company had 890 cardholders who defaulted
on payment, compared with 780 last year. Other things equal, this implies a worsening of the default problem.

6. Joe is obtaining $16,000 of *spendable* income from his present job
and has an offer of a new job which has a *total* salary 50 percent
greater than his present salary. Consequently, Joe figures the new job
will provide him with 1.5($16,000) = $24,000 of spendable income.
Joe has mistakenly applied the proportionality assumption. Explain
why.

7. Carol owns a small suburban women's fashion shop. To gauge her performance, she compares her operating data (for example, expenses as a percent of sales) with averages obtained from a women's fashion shop trade association to which she belongs. What comparison would be more meaningful to Carol if it were available?

8. An examination of the proportion of total tax revenue collected by a state from its industries shows marked variations among states. Does this mean that a company seeking to gain a tax advantage should locate a new plant in a state where the proportion is low? Explain.

9. A group of workers selected by supervisors as being the best workers was given a manual dexterity test, and 70 percent made better than average grades. Before drawing any conclusion about the relation between the best workers and test results, with what number should the 70 percent be compared?

10. Suppose only 20 percent of the executives in a certain area of business started their careers in the financial department. Before you draw the conclusion that the financial department should be avoided by beginners who hope to become executives, with what number should the 20 percent be compared?

11. The ratio output per labor-hour, as in two chairs per labor-hour, is often referred to as *productivity* (as contrasted to production, which refers to the number of chairs produced). What fault can be found with using the dollar value of output per labor-hour as a measure of productivity?

12. The proportion of women obtaining M.B.A. (Master of Business Administration) degrees has increased substantially in recent years. Suppose a study is to be made to compare average incomes of male and female M.B.A.s to determine whether income inequality exists. Suggest at least one factor which should be adjusted for (held constant) in making income comparisons.

13. Lay out a cross-classified table (showing rulings and headings) which is to contain average hourly wage rates of clerical and production workers in two plants (plant A and plant B) by job classification (I, II, III, IV) and by sex. Include a table title. Put job classifications down the side.

14. A company produces Betatrans in two plants, A and B, periodically. A production lot is either a small lot (100 units) or a large lot (200 units). Plant A has made 20 small lots which contained 60 defective Betatrans and 10 large lots with 140 defectives. Plant B has made 25 small lots containing 170 defective Betatrans and 15 large lots containing 108 defectives. Quality performance is judged by the proportion of defectives to total units made. Make a cross-classified table showing this proportion by lot size (down the side) by plant. What implication is suggested by this table?

15. Assume you are the loan officer of a bank and you are concerned about the matter of delinquent accounts, that is, loans on which borrowers are late in making payments. The bank has 6000 loans outstanding, of

which 130 are delinquent. You are to compute delinquency rates per 100 accounts, compare them, then answer questions. Round rates to three significant digits. (a) You find there are 4200 borrowers (of whom 69 are delinquent) who own their own homes and 1800 borrowers (61 delinquent) who rent. Does delinquency appear to be related to whether a borrower owns or rents? Explain, citing delinquency rates. (b) You find there are 2000 borrowers (52 delinquent) who have held their present job less than 2 years, and 4000 borrowers (78 delinquent) who have 2 or more years on the present job. Does delinquency appear to be related to time on the job? Explain, citing delinquency rates. (c) You find that for less than 2 years on the job, 1400 borrowers (30 delinquent) own and 600 borrowers (22 delinquent) rent, whereas for 2 or more years on the job, 2800 (39 delinquent) own and 1200 (39 delinquent) rent. Compute delinquency rates and tabulate them. Do the relationships in (a) and (b) still hold ? Explain.

16. See Problem 15. (a) You find that 3450 borrowers (78 delinquent) have good credit ratings and 2550 (52 delinquent) have average credit ratings. Does delinquency appear to be associated with credit rating? Explain. (b) You find that among those with good credit ratings and less than 2 years on the job, 750 borrowers (16 delinquent) own their home, 400 (15 delinquent) rent; for good ratings and 2 or more years on the job 1500 (21 delinquent) own, 800 (26 delinquent) rent. Among those with average credit ratings and less than 2 years on the job 650 (14 delinquent) own, 200 (7 delinquent) rent; for average ratings and 2 or more years on the job, 1300 (18 delinquent) own, 400 (13 delinquent) rent. Compute delinquency rates and tabulate them. What do the tabulated rates imply?

17. What is a cross-classified table?

18. (a) A properly adjusted drink-dispensing machine which promises to deliver 8 ounces of coffee after coins are inserted cannot be expected to deliver exactly 8 ounces. Why not? (b) Why, then, do people kick and shake the machine if it delivers only about 4 ounces of coffee?

2.12 SUMMARY

Rounding numbers means dropping one or more of the right-end digits in a decimal number, or replacing one or more of the right-end digits of a whole number with a zero. Rounding rules generally used in statistics are as follows, for decimal numbers:

1. If the leftmost digit to be dropped is less than 5, do not change the preceding digit. If the leftmost digit to be dropped is greater than 5, or is 5 followed by one or more nonzero digits, increase the preceding digit by 1.

2. If the leftmost digit to be dropped is 5, or is 5 followed only by zeros, round to make the preceding digit even.

By changing the words "leftmost digit to be dropped" to the "leftmost digit to be replaced by zero," the rules just stated can be applied for rounding whole numbers.

The *significant digits* in a number are those in the sequence of digits, beginning at the left, which are correct. Beginning zeros are never counted as significant digits. Ending zeros may or may not be significant.

In multiplication and division, the result should be rounded to the number of significant digits in the figure having the fewest significant digits. In addition and subtraction, the result should be rounded to the rightmost place in which all figures have a significant digit. The square root of a figure should be rounded to the number of significant digits in that figure.

In describing a ratio, the division line can be translated as *per*. Thus, 100 miles/5 gallons is 20 miles per (1) gallon. Conventional bases for ratios are powers of 10 (1, 10, 100, and so on).

A *compound* unit is the product of unlike units. Thus, 50 tons times 100 miles is 5000 ton-miles.

Percent means *per hundred*. A decimal number is converted to a percent by multiplying it by 100 and affixing the % symbol. A percent number is converted to a decimal by dividing it by 100 and dropping the % symbol. If we divide a by b and express the result as $c\%$, the result can be described by saying a is $c\%$ of, or *as great as*, b. To find $p\%$ *of* a number x, we convert $p\%$ to a decimal and multiply x by the decimal.

A percent *increase* is computed by dividing the difference between two numbers by the *smaller* number, and converting the result to a percent. The difference is divided by the *larger* of the two numbers in finding a percent decrease.

Percent error is computed by dividing the difference (approximate number − correct number) by the *correct* number, and converting the result to a percent. The difference in two percent numbers is called *percentage points*.

If the numbers in a series are each expressed as a percent of some single number, the resulting percents are called *percentage relatives*. The percent sign usually is omitted in writing percentage relatives.

If each of the numbers in a group is expressed as a percent of the sum of the group, the percents are called a *percentage distribution*.

In comparisons, the term *other things equal* means that nothing else has changed. Percents and other ratios are used extensively to design comparisons in which observed differences are not due simply to the "white sheep" effect, that is, the effect of different totals. By removing the white sheep effect, we can get a better understanding of what the data imply.

Cross-classified tables—tables which classify entries in both directions—also permit us to make comparisons in which one factor (or more than one factor) is held constant (does not change); these tables also help us understand what the data imply.

2.13 REVIEW PROBLEMS

1. Assuming the following approximate numbers are correctly written, how many significant digits does each have? (*a*) 21.80; (*b*) 0.0162; (*c*) 0.085 billion; (*d*) 4.00; (*e*) 1002.3; (*f*) 0.005.
2. Round the following to three significant digits. (*a*) 408.52; (*b*) 0.036972; (*c*) 237,401.62; (*d*) 1.065; (*e*) 1.055; (*f*) 24.449.

3. Selling expense has been computed to be $0.0437 per dollar of sales. (a) Write the rate with 4 to the left of the decimal point and append the proper words. (b) Write the rate with 43 to the left of the decimal point and append the proper words.

4. (a) What is meant by "spurious accuracy"? (b) Why does spurious accuracy occur?

5. If the government reports farm income at $42.0 billion, would the ending zero be considered to be significant? Explain.

6. Carry out the following calculations involving approximate numbers and round the results to the proper number of significant digits. (a) (3.32)(8.4); (b) (0.0365)(12.57); (c) (1.75)(7.00); (d) (0.110)(0.0445); (e) 235.6/12.8; (f) 126.0/3.460; (g) 31.25/12.50; (h) 0.04895/0.11; (i) 32.7 + 3.26 + 0.59; (j) 0.0137 + 0.246 + 0.0028; (k) 286. − 4.5; (l) 0.327 − 0.025; (m) $\sqrt{2164}$; (n) $\sqrt{0.000196}$.

7. If all the numbers in a calculation are exact, how many digits in the outcome of the calculation are significant?

8. Write, correctly rounded, the number that is exactly 65 percent of approximately $2.42 million.

9. The denominator in the following is an exact number. Write the value of the square root, properly rounded.

$$\sqrt{\frac{(0.225)(0.745)}{900}}$$

10. For each of the following, compute a ratio which you think might be meaningful in business. Describe the ratio. (a) A distributor sold 276 crates of oranges and 690 bushels of apples. (b) During a period when a plant had 275 workers, absences totaled 341 labor-days. (c) Out of a total of 2860 loans made by a bank, 10 borrowers defaulted. (d) During a period when a manufacturer carried an inventory of $1,246,000, sales amounted to $3,240,000.

11. In ten 40-hour weeks, 186 workers had 119 accidents. Compute the number of accidents per 1000 labor-hours.

12. Five years ago a dealer sold 72 trucks and 302 passenger cars. Last year, sales were 58 trucks and 435 passenger cars. Compute and write a description of the change in the passenger-car-to-truck ratio.

13. During a month when a scheduled 500-mile flight was taken on 25 days by a plane having 240 available passenger seats, 60 percent of the seats, on the average, were occupied. Passenger operating revenue for the period was $100,818. Compute revenue per passenger-mile.

14. For each of the following, compute a percent figure and round to three significant digits. Describe the result. (a) In a total of 8746 bank balances, 36 were found to be in error. (b) Last month 185 stereos were sold, compared with 208 this month. (c) This month 208 stereos were sold, compared with 225 sold in the same month last year. (d) Total national sales of a company were $2,572,484. Sales in the New England region were $707,768.

15. During 21 working days this month output of a plant was 6867 units. Last month had 24 working days, and output was 6984 units. Compute the percent change in output per working day.

16. A poll predicted political candidate Bronson would obtain 49 percent of the vote. Actual results show Bronson obtained 54 percent. Compute the error (a) in percentage points; (b) in percent.

17. Sales which actually totaled 9100 units for the current month had been predicted earlier at 10,000 units. Compute the percent error.

18. Compute percentage relatives for the board feet prices in Table A. Round to the first decimal place. (*a*) Take period 2 as 100. (*b*) Take the average of periods 1 through 3 as 100.

TABLE A

Period	1	2	3	4	5
Price per 1000 board feet	$130.25	$154.98	$174.35	$150.62	$125.63

19. See Table B. Present a tabular comparison of the percentage distributions of sales by region for the 2 years. Round to the first decimal place.

TABLE B

Sales, thousands of dollars		
Region	This year	Last year
East	$2465	$2415
Central	2084	1814
West	1391	998

20. The sales quota for the Central sales region is 37.5 percent of the national quota, and the Illinois quota is 33 percent of the Central region quota. What is the Illinois quota as a percent of the national quota?

21. An investor earns 10.6 percent on an investment and pays a state tax of 10.75 percent on these earnings. What is the investor's percent return after state tax?

22. Fixed operating expense for a store is $12,000 per week. Net sales revenue is 15 percent of a week's dollar sales volume. What must the store's weekly sales volume be to have a net sales revenue just large enough to cover fixed operating expense?

23. A company learns that it has charged a customer 25 percent too much for an item mistakenly priced at $160. How much should the company refund to the customer?

In Problems 24 to 27 name at least one factor which may not be "equal," and suggest a comparison which adjusts for such a factor.

24. The lung cancer death rate is higher for cigarette smokers than for nonsmokers. Other things equal, this implies that lung cancer is associated with cigarette smoking.

25. The day shift has more employee absences than the night shift. Other things equal, this implies absenteeism is more of a problem among day than among night workers.

26. Selling expense this year was below that of a year ago. Other things equal, this implies improved expense control.

27. A restaurant owner observes an increase in the number of bottles of a certain vintage wine being returned by diners. Other things equal, this implies that the wine is losing quality.

28. An auto manufacturer claims that, because of superior design, gasoline mileage of its midsized car is above that of other midsized cars. Suggest a factor other than design that might account for the difference, and state the comparison needed to account for that factor.

29. An advertisement states that Lowcav toothpaste contains exophyl and 9 out of 10 dentists recommend exophyl. What is the intended implication of the advertisement?

30. A study of executives shows that two-thirds have a certain set of characteristics which the study defines to be executive characteristics. What comparison is missing here?

31. The death rate for soldiers is lower than that for civilians. Does this mean it is safer to be a soldier than a civilian? Explain.

32. Lay out a cross-classified table (showing headings and rulings) which is to contain average interest rates received by owners of corporate bonds and owners of municipal bonds. Bonds vary by quality (safety) and the quality ratings Aaa (safest), Aa, A, Baa are to be considered. Bonds vary also in the number of years before the amount of the bond (not the interest) becomes payable to bond owners. The latter is called time to maturity and the table should have, down the side, the categories less than 5 years, 5 and under 10 years, 10 and under 15 years, and so on through 25 and under 30 years. The title of the table is to be Average Interest Yields for Corporate and Municipal Bonds, by Years to Maturity by Quality Rating.

33. A company operates two production facilities, North Plant and South Plant. A report shows 170 of the 400 employees in North Plant and 91 of the 300 employees in South Plant have negative attitudes toward their supervisors. Further breakdown shows that among North Plant employees, 300 (150 having negative attitudes) are high school graduates and 100 (20 negative) are not graduates. South Plant has 100 (49 negative) graduates and 200 (42 negative) nongraduates. (a) The first data (in the second sentence) imply that perhaps management should do something about supervision in North Plant. Why? (b) Present the remaining data in a cross-classified table, adjusted for the white sheep effect. What do the comparisons imply now?

3

DATA SUMMARIZATION: FREQUENCY DISTRIBUTIONS

3.1 INTRODUCTION

Reducing a mass of data to an easily comprehended summary is a major step in descriptive statistics. In this chapter we shall first construct frequency distribution tables, which provide summary descriptions of sets of data. Then we shall construct charts that give visual representations of patterns which exist in data sets. Finally, we shall discuss some data patterns that are encountered in statistics. I'll start by illustrating what a frequency distribution looks like.

3.2 FREQUENCY DISTRIBUTIONS: AN ILLUSTRATION

Each year, *Fortune* magazine publishes a variety of data on the nation's largest corporations. The data in Tables 3.1 and 3.2 were compiled from that magazine. The numbers in each table are percent returns on investments in the corporations. Thus, for example, an entry of 27 for a corporation means that an investor who bought a share of the corporation's stock at the beginning of the year and sold it at the year's end would have had a total return of 27 percent on the investment. The total return reflects both the amount paid to the shareholder by the corporation (the dividend) and the change in the price of the stock during the year. A negative entry means a loss.

TABLE 3.1
PERCENT RETURN ON INVESTMENT FOR 212 INDUSTRIAL CORPORATIONS
WITH SALES OF $1 BILLION OR MORE

One goal of statistics is to make sense out of such masses of data.

27	46	46	27	50	47	49	28	24	58
45	67	20	31	11	27	8	44	5	39
14	25	-3	79	55	-17	83	49	46	18
29	40	73	28	14	24	32	17	15	19
86	15	60	12	89	97	23	26	60	23
5	-2	41	30	17	15	33	21	11	26
31	19	26	22	42	44	41	52	14	55
27	25	16	33	17	26	17	26	42	12
43	27	-12	50	-1	34	69	31	-12	29
-28	61	27	7	100	68	36	30	18	31
18	18	86	38	37	52	56	2	-1	-13
45	13	9	4	10	60	36	-10	61	22
54	91	93	45	-6	0	9	77	18	3
-17	8	3	78	5	24	47	54	121	12
37	40	-12	29	56	3	54	-30	47	120
9	13	18	33	46	23	47	32	-5	75
98	106	-6	46	50	67	-8	8	98	30
14	49	64	70	37	69	-9	67	49	17
-5	63	48	-15	2	38	33	81	-7	14
67	33	20	-6	48	-14	29	21	58	46
24	108	127	30	21	154	67	-7	34	97
43	4								

Source: Compiled from *Fortune*, May 1977. (Rounded to the nearest whole number.)

TABLE 3.2
PERCENT RETURN ON INVESTMENT FOR 248 INDUSTRIAL CORPORATIONS
WITH SALES FROM $328 MILLION UP TO $1 BILLION

-2	38	17	22	27	68	-8	20	24	31
27	20	65	10	46	51	38	52	28	14
16	49	-13	75	32	76	60	81	54	6
-13	5	55	33	31	59	3	25	25	-10
37	-12	30	-14	6	18	59	1	22	65
76	100	19	72	56	72	31	142	65	3
33	38	44	86	22	74	44	46	58	39
21	94	44	78	84	28	55	52	55	73
72	29	15	-20	57	112	35	71	39	20
26	2	25	-4	23	85	69	22	46	60
50	55	77	35	-7	60	44	56	13	18
51	88	35	38	9	49	16	-32	16	76
14	6	120	62	-12	65	19	41	36	88
6	72	111	44	43	-22	8	66	27	8
39	26	18	3	33	136	4	21	25	20
44	-6	6	95	-8	26	53	28	85	-18
11	46	33	34	45	93	42	167	104	25
33	18	130	35	23	16	22	15	90	92
69	23	80	46	60	68	57	5	40	39
67	58	-9	33	13	28	18	82	-34	-32
16	-7	22	19	46	135	6	119	92	10
53	44	62	24	71	-19	49	54	107	67
95	59	82	4	5	-5	25	44	63	50
38	37	49	44	27	14	44	-39	95	74
128	40	1	83	46	56	73	84		

Source: Compiled from *Fortune*, May 1977. (Rounded to the nearest whole number.)

Are these numbers similar to the numbers in Table 3.1?

Table 3.1 contains percent returns for "billions" corporations, that is, corporations having sales of $1 billion or more. The "hundred-millions" corporations in Table 3.2 had sales from $328 million up to, but not including, $1 billion.

You can get some information from the numbers in Tables 3.1 and 3.2 by "eyeing" them—but not much. For example, the smallest and largest numbers in Table 3.1 are −30 and 154, respectively. But it is difficult to see how the numbers are distributed in the interval from −30 to 154. And it is impossible to compare how the numbers in the two tables are distributed. You might try computing and comparing the average returns on investment. That would be useful—but it would not provide a comparison of the distributions of the numbers.

A frequency distribution summarizes a mass of data.

A numerical frequency distribution is a table which shows how the numbers in a data set (a group of numbers) are distributed in an interval which includes the smallest and largest numbers in the data set. Table 3.3 provides frequency distributions for the two data sets at hand. Percent return classes are shown down the left. A *class* is a description of a group of similar numbers in a data set. The total number of data values in a class is

TABLE 3.3
PERCENT RETURN FREQUENCY DISTRIBUTIONS "BILLIONS" AND
"HUNDRED-MILLIONS" CORPORATIONS

Percent return class	Number of corporations (frequencies)	
	Billions corporations (Table 3.1)	Hundred-millions corporations (Table 3.2)
(50)–(31)*	0	3
(30)–(11)	10	9
(10)–9	31	30
10–29	64	59
30–49	54	56
50–69	29	42
70–89	11	28
90–109	9	11
110–129	3	5
130–149	0	4
150–169	1	1
Sums	212	248

* Numbers in parentheses are negative.

In the 30–49 percent class, the frequency of billions corporations is 54.

called the *class frequency*. For example, Table 3.3 shows a class frequency of 54 for the 30–49 class of "billions" corporations. Thus, 54 of the billions corporations in Table 3.1 have returns of from 30 to 49 percent.

Table 3.3 summarizes the masses of data in Tables 3.1 and 3.2. It also reveals the pattern of the data in each table. Note that the "billions" frequencies increase up to a peak of 64, then decline. The frequency pattern—rising to a peak, then declining—is a fairly common pattern. The "hundred-millions" corporations exhibit the same general pattern.

EXERCISE What proportion of all the "billions" and what proportion of all the "hundred-millions" corporations included in Table 3.3 had returns of at least 30 percent?

ANSWER 0.50 and 0.59, respectively.

3.3 CONSTRUCTING A FREQUENCY DISTRIBUTION

Setting Up the Classes

Class limits

The numbers used to describe classes in a frequency distribution are called *class limits*. For example, in Table 3.3 we see the class limits

$$30-49$$

$$50-69$$

$$70-89$$

The 30–49 class has 30 as its *lower* class limit and 49 as its *upper* class limit.

Between-class width

When the difference between successive lower (and upper) class limits is the same for the classes in a distribution, that difference is called the *between-class* width or, briefly, the *width* for the distribution. I used a width of 20 in making Table 3.3. This may be seen by subtracting successive pairs of lower (or upper) class limits.

The larger the width used in making a frequency distribution, the smaller the number of classes. The smaller the width, the larger the number of classes. We can choose a width that we think is reasonable for the data set at hand—and this choice will determine how many classes there will be. Or we can choose the number of classes to use—and this choice will determine the width. We shall follow the latter procedure—choosing the number of classes.

The analyst must decide arbitrarily how many classes to use to span the difference between the smallest and largest number in a data set. A large number of classes describes the data set in more detail than a small number of classes. The smaller the number of classes, the more condensed is the summarization. However, if the number of classes is "too" large or small, patterns and other significant aspects of the data may be obscured. What you choose for a between-class width will be reflected in the resultant distribution. As a rule of thumb, we shall use from about 5 up to about 20 classes. Generally, smaller numbers of classes are appropriate for small data sets, and larger numbers of classes are appropriate for large data sets.

Suppose a data set has 20 and 180 as its smallest and largest numbers. If we decide to use about 12 classes, we compute the approximate width as follows:

$$\text{Approximate width} = \frac{\text{largest value} - \text{smallest value}}{\text{number of classes}}$$

$$= \frac{180 - 20}{12}$$

$$= \frac{160}{12}$$

$$= 13.3$$

Choose width and class limits for ease of understanding.

We do not have to use the approximate value, 13.3. The final choice is arbitrary. You can make your own choice. I would choose 15 rather than 13.3 or 14 because I find it more natural to count by 15, that is, 0, 15, 30, 45, and so on. Depending upon my assessment of the resulting frequency distribution, I might also make another with a width of 10—and maybe another with a width of 13, or something else—until I obtain what in my judgment is a good representation of the data set at hand.

EXERCISE Suppose the smallest and largest numbers in a data set are $2.95 and $21.45, and that you are going to make a frequency distribution having about 10 classes. What would you choose as the width?
ANSWER I would choose $2.00.

EXAMPLE　Determine the class limits for a frequency distribution for the data of Table 3.4.

Scanning Table 3.4, we find that the smallest and largest values are 4.1 and 9.6. This is a relatively small (60 numbers) data set; so let's use a relatively small number of classes, say, 6. Then

$$\text{Approximate width} = \frac{9.6 - 4.1}{6} = \frac{5.5}{6} = 0.92$$

Let's choose 1 as the between-class width. Next we choose a number for the lower limit of the first class. We can use the smallest data value, 4.1, or a number less than 4.1. Let's choose the whole number 4, which will be written as 4.0 because the data are given to one decimal place. So 4.0 is the lower limit of the first class. Now we add the width, 1, to 4.0 to obtain 5.0 as the lower limit of the second class. Then we have

> First class　　　4.0–
>
> Second class　　5.0–

Because the numbers in Table 3.4 are given to the nearest tenth, the last numbers that would fall in the first and second classes are, respectively, 4.9 and 5.9. Hence, we have the class limits

> First class　　　4.0–4.9
>
> Second class　　5.0–5.9

We continue by adding the width, 1, successively, until we have the following six intervals:

> 4.0–4.9
>
> 5.0–5.9
>
> 6.0–6.9
>
> 7.0–7.9
>
> 8.0–8.9
>
> 9.0–9.9

We check that the last class includes the largest number in Table 3.4.

TABLE 3.4
OUTPUT: UNITS PER LABOR-HOUR FOR 60 WORKING DAYS
(Rounded to the nearest tenth)

5.9	7.7	8.9	5.2	7.3	7.7	6.3	7.3	5.7	5.6
5.6	6.7	6.9	7.0	7.3	6.2	6.5	6.5	9.2	7.1
4.1	4.9	7.5	7.5	9.6	7.9	5.3	5.5	6.1	6.1
8.3	8.1	8.1	4.5	7.3	9.4	5.8	6.7	6.7	6.9
6.9	7.1	6.9	7.7	7.7	8.1	8.7	6.5	6.7	9.1
7.1	6.3	5.1	7.3	8.3	8.9	9.3	5.7	6.0	5.9

The Tally Sheet and Frequency Distribution

After class limits have been set up, a tally sheet can be made with one pass through the data set of Table 3.4. To do this, we enter a tally mark in the appropriate class for each number in the data set. See Table 3.5.

TABLE 3.5
TALLY SHEET FOR DATA OF TABLE 3.4

Class interval	Tally marks
4.0–4.9	///
5.0–5.9	~~////~~ ~~////~~ /
6.0–6.9	~~////~~ ~~////~~ ~~////~~ //
7.0–7.9	~~////~~ ~~////~~ ~~////~~ /
8.0–8.9	~~////~~ ///
9.0–9.9	~~////~~

After counting the tally marks for each class, we make the frequency distribution shown in Table 3.6.

TABLE 3.6
FREQUENCY DISTRIBUTION
FOR TABLE 3.4

Output per labor-hour	Number of days	
4.0–4.9	3	Sums of the tally marks
5.0–5.9	11	
6.0–6.9	17	
7.0–7.9	16	
8.0–8.9	8	
9.0–9.9	5	
	60	

Trying Different Between-Class Widths

An *array* is a data set listed in order of size—from smallest to largest, or vice versa. By constructing an array we see aspects of the data that may go unnoticed when a tally sheet is made directly from a nonordered data set. Moreover, it is easier to make frequency distributions from an array. We can make distributions with different widths, and then choose the one we think best describes the data.

Making a *stem-and-leaf* table is a useful first step when data are to be arrayed. In this table the first part of each number, the stem, is written in one direction (down or across), and the rest of the number, the leaf, in the other

TABLE 3.7
STEM-AND-LEAF TABLE FOR DATA
OF TABLE 3.4

Stem	Leaf
4.	1, 9, 5
5.	9, 2, 7, 6, 6, 3, 5, 8, 1, 7, 9
6.	3, 7, 9, 2, 5, 5, 1, 1, 7, 7, 9, 9, 9, 5, 7, 3, 0
7.	7, 3, 7, 3, 0, 3, 1, 5, 5, 9, 3, 1, 7, 7, 1, 3
8.	9, 3, 1, 1, 1, 7, 3, 9
9.	2, 6, 4, 1, 3

The "4 stem" and
its leaves

direction. For example, the numbers in Table 3.4 have two digits. The smallest number is 4.1 and the largest is 9.6. Table 3.7 shows the first digits, the stems 4., 5., 6., 7., 8., 9., written down the left side. The first number in Table 3.4, 5.9, has a stem of 5. and a leaf of 9. The leaf is recorded by writing 9 in the 5. row of Table 3.7. The second number in Table 3.4, 7.7, is recorded in Table 3.7 with a stem of 7. and a leaf of 7. Proceeding in the manner just illustrated, we obtain the partially ordered set of numbers in Table 3.7. If you turn the book so that the leaves are vertical, you can visualize the data set as a pile of numbers with each leaf number piled over its stem. The stem-and-leaf table itself provides a useful description of the data set.

The leaves of each stem are now placed in order of size to obtain the array shown in Table 3.8. We can use the array to try different between-class widths. Suppose we want to try a frequency distribution with a width of 0.5, using 4.0 as the lower limit of the first class. The classes then will be 4.0–4.4, 4.5–4.9, and so on. Counting from the array in Table 3.8, we find the frequencies for these classes are, respectively, 1 and 2. Table 3.9 shows the frequency counts for all the classes. Incidentally, when going through the array, I saw that 7.3 was the most frequently occurring number. I had not noticed that earlier when I made the tally sheet from the unarrayed data. An array provides information that may go unnoticed if we tally unarrayed data.

TABLE 3.8
ARRAY OF OUTPUTS PER LABOR-HOUR

4.1	4.5	4.9	5.1	5.2	5.3	5.5	5.6	5.6	5.7
5.7	5.8	5.9	5.9	6.0	6.1	6.1	6.2	6.3	6.3
6.5	6.5	6.5	6.7	6.7	6.7	6.7	6.9	6.9	6.9
6.9	7.0	7.1	7.1	7.1	7.3	7.3	7.3	7.3	7.3
7.5	7.5	7.7	7.7	7.7	7.7	7.9	8.1	8.1	8.1
8.3	8.3	8.7	8.9	8.9	9.1	9.2	9.3	9.4	9.6

Source: Table 3.4.

TABLE 3.9
FREQUENCY DISTRIBUTION FOR OUTPUT
PER LABOR-HOUR

Output per labor-hour	Number of days
4.0–4.4	1
4.5–4.9	2
5.0–5.4	3
5.5–5.9	8
6.0–6.4	6
6.5–6.9	11
7.0–7.4	9
7.5–7.9	7
8.0–8.4	5
8.5–8.9	3
9.0–9.4	4
9.5–9.9	1
Frequency total	60

EXERCISE Use Table 3.8 to make a frequency distribution with a width of 1.5, using 4.0 as the lower limit of the first class.

ANSWER The classes are 4.0–5.4; 5.5–6.9; 7.0–8.4; 8.5–9.9. Respective frequencies are 6, 25, 21, 8.

I think the distribution in the exercise does not provide a sufficiently detailed description of the output per labor-hour data set. The distribution in Table 3.9 is perhaps too detailed; so the frequencies lose some meaning. In my judgment, Table 3.6 is a better summary description of the data than Table 3.9 or the table you made for the exercise.

Class Intervals

The limits written to describe classes are called *stated* class limits. However, a frequency distribution may have *real* class limits which differ slightly from the stated limits. The difference is due to rounding.

Suppose milk cartons state that the cartons contain 2 quarts (32 fluid ounces). Suppose next that the contents of a carton are measured to the nearest tenth of an ounce. The convention usually followed in making frequency distributions is to "round 5 or more up." That is, for example, contents of 31.20, 31.21, 31.22, 31.23, and 31.24 ounces, rounded to the nearest tenth, are 31.2. But 31.25 through 31.29 are rounded to 31.3. Consequently, a class with *stated* limits of, for example,

$$31.5–31.7$$

includes the numbers 31.45, 31.46, 31.47, . . . , 31.73, 31.74 and thus has the *real* limits

31.45 up to, but not including, 31.75

Sometimes, the words "up to, but not including" are replaced by "and under." Then the class would be described as "31.45 and under 31.75." Real class limits are arbitrary because they depend upon the rounding procedure followed. You will know what the real limits are if you prepared the data set from which a frequency distribution was made. For frequency distributions prepared by others, we use the "5 in the next place" rule to determine real limits from stated limits. For example, the stated limits

Determine the real class limits from the stated class limits.

31.5–31.7

are given to the first decimal place. Then 5 in the next place is 5 in the second decimal place, or 0.05. Subtracting this 0.05 from the lower stated limit and adding 0.05 to the stated upper limit gives the real limits of 31.45 and 31.75.

EXERCISE The stated class limits for average hourly wage rates are $3.75–$3.99. What are the real limits?
ANSWER $3.745 and $3.995.

When classes describe counts, so that rounding is not involved, real class limits are the same as the stated class limits. For example, suppose the frequency distribution classes describe numbers of defective parts made in a day. Then a class such as 3–5 means exactly 3 or 4 or 5 defective parts. The real limits are 3 and 5, the same as the stated limits.

Class interval   A *class interval* is the difference between the *real* class limits. For example, the stated limits 31.5–31.7 correspond to the real limits 31.45 and 31.75; so the 31.5–31.7 class has a class interval of

$$31.75 - 31.45 = 0.30$$

EXERCISE What is the class interval for the class $3.75–$3.99 of the last exercise?
ANSWER $0.25.

For classes describing counts, the class interval is the difference between the stated limits, because the stated and real limits are the same. Also, when the "and under" method of describing classes is used, the class interval is taken as the difference between the stated limits. For example, the class

$10.00 and under $15.00

means $10.00 and values up to, but not including, $15.00. The class interval is $5.00.

We use the between-class width (the difference between successive lower stated class limits) in setting up the classes of a frequency distribution. The class interval, which may differ from the width, is a term used in describing classes after they have been set up.

Points to Keep in Mind

Judgment and arbitrary decisions are involved when a frequency distribution is made. However, the following points should be kept in mind.

1. The classes must be mutually exclusive; that is, each data number must fall in only one class. Classes such as 4.00–4.50 and 4.50–5.00, where the same number is used for the upper limit of one class and for the lower limit of the next class, are not mutually exclusive. The number 4.50 could be in either class. Use, instead, 4.00–4.49 and 4.50–4.99. Or, if you wish, use 4.00 and under 4.50; 4.50 and under 5.00.
2. The classes must be all-inclusive. That is, the classes must provide a place to record every number in the data set.
3. Try to choose the number of classes and the class limits so that empty classes (classes with 0 frequencies) do not occur.
4. If possible, use the same class interval for all classes. Then, when frequencies in a distribution are compared, observed variations are not related to the sizes of intervals. The variations now tell us something about the data and their pattern.

Unequal Class Intervals

A data set may contain a few numbers which are so far from the majority of numbers that the first or last class must be left open-ended. For example, suppose we are tabulating the incomes of salaried employees in a corporation using a class interval of, say, $5000. The income of a top executive might be $30,000 higher than any other income. Then an attempt to use equal class intervals would result in a table having five classes with zero frequencies. To avoid this, the ending class could be stated in open-ended fashion as, say, "$50,000 and above." The procedure accomplishes the dual purpose of making a compact table and not disclosing top executive salary levels; but, of course, it conceals some data which may be of interest. An example of a lower open-ended class is "below $10,000." Open-ended classes are encountered often in published distributions. And, on occasion, varying class intervals may appear within a distribution.

Open-end classes conceal rather than reveal

Relative Frequency Distributions

A relative frequency distribution is made by dividing each frequency of a distribution by the total frequency and expressing the result (the relative frequency) either as a decimal or as a percent. Relative frequency distributions are particularly useful when comparing distributions having different total frequencies. They provide comparisons in which the total for each distribution is the same, that is, 100 percent if percents are used, or 1.00 if decimals are used. The two rightmost columns of Table 3.10 contain relative (percent) frequencies. Converting to relative frequencies changes frequencies to a common denominator—but it does not change the pattern of a distribution.

TABLE 3.10
PERCENT RETURN FREQUENCY DISTRIBUTIONS "BILLIONS" AND
"HUNDRED-MILLIONS" CORPORATIONS

		Number of corporations (frequencies)		Relative frequencies (percent)	
	Percent return class	Billions corporations	Hundred-millions corporations	Billions corporations	Hundred-millions corporations
Class relative frequency =	(50)–(31)*	0	3	0.0	1.2
	(30)–(11)	10	9	4.7	3.6
	(10)–9	31	30	14.6	12.1
Class frequency	10–29	64	59	30.2	23.8
Sum of frequencies	30–49	54	56	25.5	22.6
	50–69	29	42	13.7	16.9
	70–89	11	28	5.2	11.3
	90–109	9	11	4.2	4.4
	110–129	3	5	1.4	2.0
	130–149	0	4	0.0	1.6
	150–169	1	1	0.5	0.4
	Sums	212	248	100%	99.9%

Source: Tables 3.1 and 3.2
* Numbers in parentheses are negative.

EXERCISE (a) How was the first relative frequency 1.2 percent for the "hundred-millions" corporations in Table 3.10 computed? (b) Which corporation group had the greater frequency in the 30–49 class? (c) Which had the greater relative frequency in the 30–49 class?

ANSWER (a) 3/248 = 0.012097, which rounds to 0.012, or 1.2 percent; (b) the "hundred-millions" group; (c) the "billions" group.

Qualitative Frequency Distributions

The class 10–19 is a numerical, or quantitative, class. Nonquantitative classes are called qualitative classes. For example, manufacturing, mining, and transportation are some of the qualitative classes for type of business

TABLE 3.11
NUMBER OF SALESPERSONS
BY SALES DISTRICT

Sales district	Number of salespersons
North East	52
East Central	192
South East	84
Mid West	176
North West	71
South West	30
Total	605

activity. A list of qualitative classes with a frequency count for each class as in Table 3.11 is called a qualitative frequency distribution.

Class limits and class intervals are concepts which obviously do not apply in qualitative distributions. We work with the number of qualitative classes that exist—for example, the 50 states in the nation. Or we choose the number of classes to serve a particular purpose, for example, the six sales districts in Table 3.11.

3.4 FREQUENCY DISTRIBUTION CHARTS

Visually it is easier to comprehend a data pattern by looking at a chart than by examining numbers in a frequency table.

Histograms

A histogram for a distribution with equal class intervals is a chart made by drawing rectangles whose width is the class interval and whose heights equal the class frequencies. Figure 3.1 is a histogram for the output per labor-hour distribution in Table 3.6.

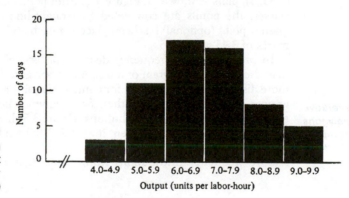

FIGURE 3.1
Histogram showing pattern of output per labor-hour. (*Source:* Table 3.6.)

Frequency Polygons

Use stated class limits to find the class mark. A *class mark* is the average of the stated lower and upper limits of a class. It is chosen to represent all the data values counted in a class. For example, the 4.0–4.9 output per labor-hour class has

$$\text{Class mark} = \frac{\text{lower limit} + \text{upper limit}}{2}$$

$$= \frac{4.0 + 4.9}{2}$$

$$= 4.45$$

TABLE 3.12
A CLASS MARK IS THE AVERAGE OF THE CLASS LIMITS

Output per labor-hour	Class mark	Number of days
4.0–4.9	4.45	3
5.0–5.9	5.45	11
6.0–6.9	6.45	17
7.0–7.9	7.45	16
8.0–8.9	8.45	8
9.0–9.9	9.45	5
		60

as its class mark. Table 3.12 gives the class marks for all the classes in the output per labor-hour distribution. Note that after the class mark for the first class has been computed, successive class marks can be obtained by successive additions of the between-class width, 1.

A frequency polygon is a plot with the class variable on the horizontal scale and frequencies on the vertical scale. Each pair of numbers (class mark, frequency) is then plotted as a point. For example, the first pair in Table 3.12, (4.45, 3), plots as shown on Figure 3.2. After points have been plotted for all classes, the points are connected by straight-line segments. A zero frequency point (optional) has been placed at each end of Figure 3.2—at class marks of 3.45 and 10.45.

In presenting one frequency distribution graphically, the chart maker may use either a histogram or a frequency polygon. However, when two or more distributions are graphed for comparison, it is awkward to try to superimpose one histogram on another. So, frequency polygons are chosen for graphical comparisons of distributions. Figure 3.3 shows frequency polygons comparing returns on investment for the 212 "billions" corporations and the 248 "hundred-millions" corporations discussed earlier in the chapter. The relative frequency distributions from Table 3.10 were used because the

Use relative frequency polygons to compare distributions.

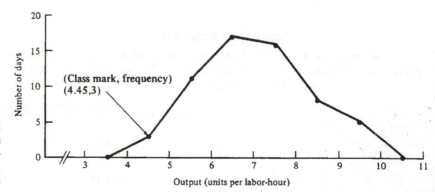

FIGURE 3.2
Frequency polygon showing pattern of output per labor-hour. (*Source:* Table 3.12.)

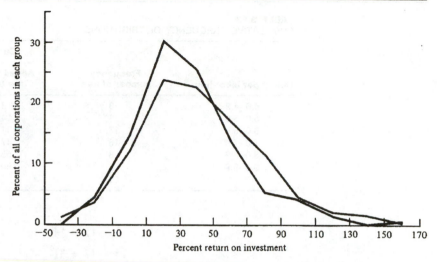

FIGURE 3.3
Comparative relative
frequency polygons of
percent returns. Red
line represents corpo-
rations with sales of $1
billion or more; black
line represents corpora-
tions with sales of
$328 million to
$1 billion. (*Source:*
Table 3.10.)

numbers of corporations in the groups are different. The chart shows clearly
the similar patterns of the data sets. Both polygons rise to a peak over the
same class and then decline. The peaks are somewhat to the left of center of
the charted polygons. But there are differences. For example, note that one
polygon is generally below the other on the left side of the figure but above
the other on the right side.

EXERCISE In terms of the corporation groups and relative frequencies,
state the meaning of the last sentence in the preceding paragraph.
ANSWER "Billions" corporations were relatively more frequent than
"hundred-millions" corporations in the lower half, or so, of returns on investment. But "hundred-millions" corporations were relatively more frequent in the
upper half.

You might also phrase the answer to the exercise by interpreting relative
frequency as probability or chance—as we did in Chapter 1. Then you
would state that a corporation selected at random from all the "hundred-
millions" group had a somewhat better chance of being in the upper half of
the returns on investment than a corporation selected from the "billions"
group.

Cumulative Frequency Distributions

How to construct a
cumulative frequency
distribution

The first two columns of Table 3.13 contain a frequency distribution. The
two rightmost columns are cumulative frequencies determined by adding
frequencies. The "from the top" cumulative frequencies start with first frequency, 3; then the following frequencies are added cumulatively. Thus,

TABLE 3.13
CUMULATIVE FREQUENCY DISTRIBUTIONS

Output per labor-hour	Frequency, number of days	Cumulative frequencies	
		Added from the top	Added from the bottom
4.0–4.9	3	3	60
5.0–5.9	11	14	57
6.0–6.9	17	31	46
7.0–7.9	16	47	29
8.0–8.9	8	55	13
9.0–9.9	5	60	5
	60		

$$3 + 11 = 14$$
$$14 + 17 = 31$$

and so on. The "from the bottom" cumulative frequencies start with the bottom frequency, 5, then add cumulatively upward. Thus,

$$5 + 8 = 13$$
$$13 + 16 = 29$$

Fran and Dan were discussing the meanings of the cumulative frequencies:

Fran: I see how the cumulative frequencies are found by adding. That's simple. But what do they mean?

Dan: The first cumulative from the top is three—the same as the actual frequency in the class. So, on three days, output was from four to four point nine units. But you can also say that on three days output was less than five units. Then the second cumulative means that on fourteen days, output was less than six units.

Fran: I get it. So the last cumulative means that on sixty days—that's all the days—output was less than ten units, even though there is no class for ten units.

Dan: But you can't use the same thinking for the last column—cumulatives from the bottom.

Fran: Right. The bottom number means there were five days in the class—but it also means that on five days output was nine units or more. The next number up means that on thirteen days output was eight units or more.

Dan: I've seen frequency distributions with the largest class limits at the top and the smallest limits at the bottom. If that is the way the table is set up, you would have to turn your thinking around. But that's easy, once you get the idea.

EXERCISE For the 7.0–7.9 class in Table 3.13, what is the meaning of the cumulative frequency (a) 47? (b) 29?

ANSWER (a) On 47 days output per labor-hour was less than 8.0 units. (b) On 29 days, output was 7.0 units or more.

An ogive is a graph of a cumulative frequency distribution.

Ogives An ogive is a line chart of a cumulative frequency distribution. Let's make a "less than" ogive from the data of Table 3.13. We start by making Table 3.14. Then the data points (4, 0), (5, 3), and so on, are plotted

TABLE 3.14
A "LESS THAN" TABLE

Output per labor-hour	Number of days
Less than 4	0
Less than 5	3
Less than 6	14
Less than 7	31
Less than 8	47
Less than 9	55
Less than 10	60

An "or more" ogive

and connected to obtain the ogive in Figure 3.4. Note how this ogive rises to the right. An "or more" ogive, on the other hand, would fall to the right.

Ogives can also be made from cumulative relative frequencies. Ogives for relatives are used when two cumulative distributions with different total frequencies are to be compared.

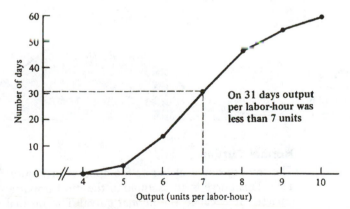

FIGURE 3.4
A cumulative frequency "less than" chart.

3.5 SMOOTH FREQUENCY DISTRIBUTION CURVES

The idea of representing frequencies or relative frequencies by areas under a smooth curve has proved to be exceptionally fruitful. In later chapters we

FIGURE 3.5
Comparative frequen-
cies are either
heights or areas of
rectangles.

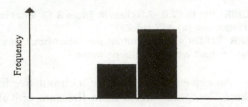

FIGURE 3.5
Comparative frequen-
cies are either
heights or areas of
rectangles.

shall solve probability and statistical inference problems by referring to tables which contain numerical values of areas under such curves. Here, I wish simply to introduce the idea in a nonnumerical fashion and use it in describing some common data patterns. The idea stems from the observation that we can compare frequencies in various classes of a histogram by comparing either the heights of the rectangles or the areas of the rectangles. For example, in Figure 3.5 we can say there are more data values in the right-hand class than in the left-hand class because the right rectangle is higher—or because the area of the right rectangle is greater. The relative heights of the rectangles (which look to be about 2 to 1) are the same as the relative areas of the rectangles, because the base widths of the rectangles are equal.

Now look at Figure 3.6, which shows a histogram with a smooth curve sketched through the midpoints of the tops of the rectangles. The area of each rectangle is approximately the same as the area bounded by the curve, the sides of the rectangle, and the base of the rectangle. Don't be concerned with the word approximately in the last sentence because we are dealing with an idea, not precise arithmetic. The idea is that frequency in an interval can be represented by the area under a curve.

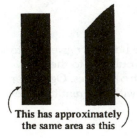

This has approximately
the same area as this

FIGURE 3.6
Smooth-curve repre-
sentation of a
histogram.

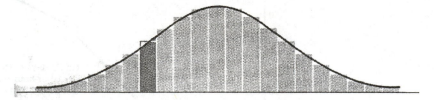

Normal Curves

The smooth curve of Figure 3.6 appears in Figure 3.7 with labels on the axes. This curve is an example of the most important pattern in statistical analysis. It is called the *normal curve*. The normal curve is described as being bell-shaped. It is *symmetrical* about the dashed vertical centerline (which occurs at 75 on Figure 3.7). The word *symmetrical* means that the two halves of the curve are mirror images. If you fold the page on the vertical line of symmetry (the dashed line), the two halves of the curve will coincide. Symmetrical curves "balance" at the center point. The balance

FIGURE 3.7
Normal curve of
employee scores on
aptitude test. Shaded
area represents the
number of employees
in the test-score
interval 75–80.

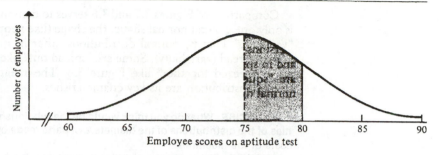

FIGURE 3.7
Normal curve of
employee scores on
aptitude test. Shaded
area represents the
number of employees
in the test-score
interval 75–80.

Number of employees

60   65   70   75   80   85   90

Employee scores on aptitude test

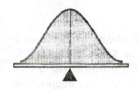

point is called the *mean* or *average* of the distribution represented by the smooth curve. Figure 3.7 shows that test scores pile up around 75 and thin out at either end. *This observation is based upon comparisons of areas under the curve over intervals*, not upon the height of the curve at a particular point. That's because the area under a smooth curve, not the height of the curve, is being used to represent a frequency.

EXERCISE Is an upside-down capital U symmetrical about a vertical line through its center? Does it have the shape of a normal curve? (I leave this for you to answer.)

Real-life data can never be represented exactly by a smooth mathematical frequency curve. However, various types of data exhibit patterns which have an approximately normal shape. Thus, the normal curve is a great aid in describing many data sets. To say that data are approximately normal creates a mental image, making a detailed frequency presentation unnecessary. Thus, scores on aptitude tests and college entrance examinations have approximately normal distributions. Again, parts made by an automatic machine properly adjusted to drill holes of a certain diameter will exhibit variations about the desired diameter; the pattern of variations can be expected to be approximately normal, as illustrated in Figure 3.8.

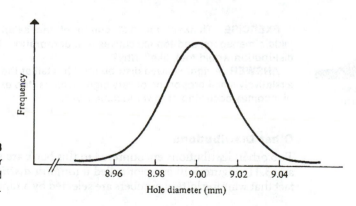

Frequency

8.96   8.98   9.00   9.02   9.04

Hole diameter (mm)

FIGURE 3.8
Normal curve for
diameters of machined
parts.

Comparison of Figures 3.7 and 3.8 serves to demonstrate that while there is only one general normal shape, the shape (like people) comes in different "versions." That is, normal distributions differ in means (balance points) and in spread (variability). Some are "spread out" like Figure 3.7, and some are "squeezed together" like Figure 3.8. The mean and variability of a normal distribution are its key characteristics.

EXERCISE What do you think would be the relationship between the variabilities of the distributions of the diameters of parts made by two machines and the costs of the machines.

ANSWER The lower the machine's variability, the higher is its precision in making parts, and the more costly will be the machine.

Skewed Distributions

Skewness is a term applied to nonsymmetrical distributions which have a longer "tail" in one direction than in the other direction. Look at Figure 3.9. Here we are conveying the idea that individuals owning municipal bonds tend to cluster at older age levels and comparatively few younger people own such bonds. The pattern is said to be *skewed* to the left; the direction of skewness is the direction of the thin "tail."

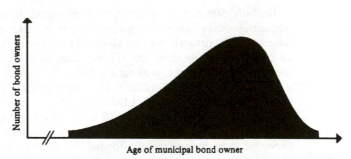

FIGURE 3.9
A left-skewed
distribution.

Age of municipal bond owner

A right-skewed
distribution

EXERCISE Think of the distribution of the salaries of all supervisors, middle managers, and top executives in a corporation. What do you think this distribution would look like? Why?

ANSWER A right-skewed distribution (thin tail at the right), which indicates a relatively small proportion of very high incomes (top executives) with the bulk of incomes occurring at lower income levels.

Other Distributions

Two other distributions encountered in this book are shown in Figures 3.10 and 3.11. Figure 3.10 is a plot called a *uniform distribution*. It reflects the fact that winning lottery numbers are selected by a random procedure which

FIGURE 3.10
A uniform distribution
for winning lottery
numbers.

makes all numbers equally likely to be selected. Hence, we expect a large data set of winning numbers would be approximately evenly (uniformly) distributed over the interval 0000 through 9999.

Figure 3.11 is an example of an *exponential distribution*. It conveys the idea that the time until the arrival of the next customer is more often a short time than a long time. This pattern is encountered in studies made by service facilities, such as banks, which have to schedule personnel (say, the number of bank tellers) and equipment to try to match customer demand.

We are interested in the shaded area, and not in the height of the curve at any point.

In closing this section, I want to remind you that areas under smooth curves over intervals, and not the height of the curve at a point, are the subject of interest. And, while real-life data can never be represented exactly by a smooth mathematical curve, the mental images stimulated by describing a distribution as approximately normal, or right-skewed, or uniform, or exponential are important to communication.

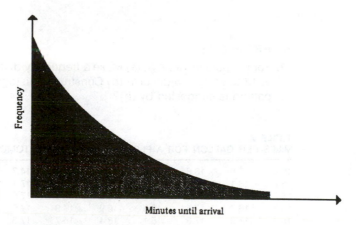

FIGURE 3.11
An exponential distri-
bution for time until
next customer arrives.

3.6 DATA ANALYSIS BY COMPUTER

Computer programmers are people who write instructions which "teach" a computer how to carry out a procedure. A set of instructions for a procedure is called a *program*. A set of programs for carrying out various statistical procedures is called a statistical "package." All the user of a package needs to know is (1) how to enter a set of data into the computer and (2) the command word which will direct the computer to perform a particular procedure and print out the result. A computer can array 1000 data items and start printing out the array in less time than it takes to write this sentence. Given appropriate commands, the computer will make frequency distributions with different classes (as many as you want) and print them out in tabular or histogram form. Computers with plotting capabilities can draw frequency polygons and other line charts. The computer will also calculate percentage distributions, averages, measures of variability, and other numbers which help describe a data set.

If you have not already done so, you should learn how to use a computer package. Check with the computer center at your school or place of work to find what statistical packages are available. The data sets in Sections 3.7 and 3.9 will serve as raw material. Choose a data set and enter it into the computer. Get permission from the computer center to keep your data in the computer's "library" so that you will not have to reenter the data set. Then you can learn more about the package—and get practice in using it—by carrying out new procedures as they are introduced in the book.

Computers are an integral part of all modern organizations. They are of particular importance in statistical work because they can store and handle large masses of data and carry out a great variety of analyses very rapidly. They remove the drudgery—and the errors—of hand calculation. But be sure to enter data accurately. The computer can do only what it is instructed to do, using the data it is given.

3.7 PROBLEMS

1. For the data in Table A: (*a*) Make a frequency distribution table starting at 13.5, using a width of 1. (*b*) Construct a histogram. (*c*) What smooth pattern is suggested by (*b*)?

TABLE A
MILES PER GALLON FOR A FLEET OF 100 AMEX AUTOMOBILES

16.2	17.6	18.6	16.0	17.0	17.0	14.7	16.5	14.9	17.7
15.7	18.1	17.1	17.7	16.9	15.6	17.1	17.7	17.5	15.9
18.2	16.7	14.1	16.1	16.9	17.9	17.0	16.7	17.1	15.9
16.9	16.7	17.5	16.8	16.9	17.9	17.0	14.6	16.8	17.1
15.9	17.8	17.9	15.1	18.4	15.7	17.3	16.9	18.8	17.1
17.9	16.0	17.0	15.2	17.3	16.0	17.8	16.5	15.8	16.4
17.1	18.1	16.8	17.1	18.8	16.0	15.9	17.6	18.4	17.7
16.0	14.9	16.8	17.1	20.2	13.7	17.3	16.8	15.5	17.7
18.1	17.4	17.6	18.6	16.3	17.7	16.1	18.6	16.9	15.6
16.6	17.0	19.1	16.3	19.2	17.3	16.1	15.6	18.2	18.2

2. The dollar amounts of sales to 100 customers at a grocery store are given in Table B. (*a*) Make a frequency tabulation starting at $0, using a width of $10. (*b*) Construct a histogram.

TABLE B
SALES PER CUSTOMER FOR 100 CUSTOMERS, IN DOLLARS

3.89	25.74	13.69	5.22	44.87	3.25	8.30	67.75	2.50	10.11
1.15	4.16	26.35	7.60	18.00	15.65	38.08	3.81	24.65	6.33
60.35	13.00	20.50	6.79	1.36	50.11	10.25	55.17	16.42	49.55
26.04	35.19	0.75	37.06	15.50	5.75	3.72	14.65	5.61	11.20
5.35	3.08	17.88	13.25	11.70	33.00	21.95	28.57	46.73	34.62
7.01	10.65	44.09	4.75	21.40	14.33	57.45	6.77	4.36	6.55
29.30	5.84	14.20	35.72	3.50	10.63	0.98	22.13	38.98	9.62
9.91	42.50	50.37	9.75	28.40	34.14	26.89	12.55	16.27	31.95
51.05	1.94	25.15	63.00	14.21	4.97	13.47	7.84	1.80	8.30
4.91	15.00	13.84	5.05	34.04	76.00	31.75	17.85	54.62	21.40

3. For the data in Table C: (*a*) Make a frequency distribution table. (*b*) Construct a frequency polygon. (*c*) What smooth curve pattern is suggested by (*b*)?

TABLE C
WEEKLY EARNINGS OF 50 MANUFACTURING WORKERS, IN DOLLARS

151	179	163	142	180	195	150	206	194	143
211	193	194	198	187	164	188	175	198	216
182	163	180	155	178	209	172	208	190	185
148	205	158	195	192	184	174	161	199	165
209	206	187	163	131	202	137	179	200	156

4. For the data in Table D (at the top of page 62): (*a*) Make a frequency table. (*b*) Construct a frequency polygon. (*c*) What smooth curve pattern is suggested by (*b*)?
5. Add the percent frequencies in each row of Table 3.10. (*a*) Make a percent frequency table with a width of 10. (*b*) Construct a percent frequency polygon. (*c*) What smooth curve pattern does (*b*) suggest?
6. (*a*) From a recent issue of *Fortune*, make a percent frequency table of return on investment for the 500 largest industrial corporations as in Problem 5(*a*). (*b*) Construct a percent frequency polygon on the same chart as Problem 5(*b*). (*c*) Write a statement describing the relationship of the percent return patterns exhibited by the polygons for Problems 5(*b*) and 6(*b*).
7. The data in Table E (in the middle of page 62) were taken from the 1975 issue of the *Statistical Abstract of the United States*. For these data: (*a*) Make a frequency table. (*b*) Construct a frequency polygon. (*c*) What smooth curve pattern does (*b*) suggest?

TABLE D
SCORES OF 200 JOB APPLICANTS ON A STANDARD APTITUDE TEST

91	100	82	111	94	90	92	87	103	85
102	99	116	106	104	115	93	113	126	113
127	77	105	96	104	105	118	98	101	119
92	98	96	91	108	93	110	110	98	92
96	102	118	106	84	109	82	113	86	118
96	91	92	97	109	96	88	92	117	101
80	107	101	102	93	108	112	116	104	124
88	93	75	87	91	95	98	98	88	97
114	104	106	97	102	103	108	100	79	103
92	81	88	109	83	93	88	108	108	114
101	81	107	84	109	97	112	82	101	92
91	97	93	106	90	102	104	96	97	103
113	97	110	95	107	96	91	96	97	108
98	88	96	106	104	107	100	96	92	93
85	110	83	103	96	71	112	103	107	111
114	95	101	86	101	98	94	106	93	98
97	95	98	112	101	100	106	87	103	122
103	100	91	98	94	86	95	108	87	97
121	112	112	96	100	86	108	105	106	107
99	87	104	100	92	102	89	106	91	97

TABLE E
AVERAGE WEEKLY EARNINGS OF MANUFACTURING WORKERS,
100 METROPOLITAN AREAS, IN DOLLARS

227	190	133	178	177	254	194	163	138	190	191
228	220	172	182	222	211	208	151	130	154	199
220	135	189	195	219	209	252	113	193	199	252
150	164	191	140	133	167	163	205	194	207	129
180	185	193	206	193	158	229	143	179	202	213
137	216	182	149	171	202	180	192	133	164	155
163	177	187	184	174	222	192	190	142	164	163
192	133	211	200	253	200	174	131	187	219	196
161	172	179	209	161	193	198	206	199	206	163
221	193	179	176	163	195	199	187	208	165	235

8. (a) From the latest issue of the *Statistical Abstract of the United States* make a frequency table of average weekly earnings, as in Problem 7(a). (b) Construct a frequency polygon on the same chart as Problem 7(b). (c) Write a statement describing the relationship of the earning patterns exhibited by the polygons for Problems 7(b) and 8(b)

9. Table F is a frequency distribution of monthly rent charges for one-room apartments in an area. (a) What is the class interval of the distribution? (b) Cumulate the frequencies from the *bottom up* and make an "or more" frequency chart.

10. (See Table F.) Make a percent frequency distribution. Then cumulate the percents from the *top down* and make a percent "less than" frequency chart.

TABLE F

Rent, dollars per month	Number of apartments
250–274	8
275–299	23
300–324	52
325–349	86
350–374	68
375–399	56
400–424	37
425–449	26
450–474	11
475–499	7

11. Suppose a frequency chart of the balances in the checking accounts of individuals (not businesses, organizations, etc.) is to be made with dollar balance on the horizontal axis and number of accounts on the vertical axis. In smooth frequency curve terminology, what pattern do you think might emerge? Why?

12. Suppose a frequency chart is to be made with age on the horizontal axis and number of people owning hearing aids on the vertical axis. In smooth curve terminology, what pattern do you think might emerge? Why?

3.8 SUMMARY

A *class* is a group of similar data values described by two numbers called the *class limits*. A *frequency distribution* table shows how many (the frequency) of the values in a data set fall in each of the classes.

When the difference between successive lower (and upper) class limits of a frequency distribution are equal, that difference is called the between-class width or, more briefly, the *width* for the distribution. Frequency distributions generally have from 5 up to 20 classes. The class limits must be chosen so that every data value belongs in one, and only one, class.

After writing the class limits, go through the data set and tally each data value in its class. The classes and the frequencies (tally counts) are the frequency distribution. Distributions having different between-class widths may be constructed before you obtain one which, in your judgment, provides a good representation of the data set at hand. If different widths are to be tried, time can be saved by first arraying the data set in order of size.

Real class limits may be different from the limits stated in a frequency distribution table. For the stated limits

15.5–15.9   16.0–16.4

we use the "5 in the next place" rule to obtain 15.45 and 15.95 as the real limits of the first class. For "and under" classes such as "15 and under 20," and for count data classes such as 0-5 cars sold, the real limits are the same as the stated limits. A *class interval* is the difference between the real class limits. The *class mark* is the average of the stated class limits.

A *relative* frequency distribution is constructed by replacing actual frequencies by the ratios of the actual frequencies to the total frequency: the ratios may be expressed as proportions or percents. Relative frequency distributions should be calculated when two or more distributions that have different total frequencies are to be compared.

Frequency distributions with numerical classes are called *quantitative* distributions: those with nonnumerical classes, such as "male" and "female," are called *qualitative* distributions.

A *histogram* for a distribution with equal class intervals is a chart made by drawing rectangles whose widths are the class interval and whose heights are the class frequencies. A *frequency polygon* is made by plotting a point for each (class mark, class frequency) number pair, then connecting the points by line segments.

Successive addition of frequencies leads to *cumulative* frequencies. Tables containing cumulative frequencies are called *less than* or *or more* distributions, depending upon the direction (from the top or from the bottom) of cumulation. Charts of cumulative frequencies are called *ogives*.

Smooth curves are often used to describe patterns in frequency distributions. Some important distributions are (1) the symmetrical, bell-shaped, *normal* distributions; (2) left-skewed and right-skewed distributions; (3) uniform distributions; and (4) exponential distributions.

Statistical packages available at computer centers can perform a wide variety of statistical analyses—accurately and rapidly. In particular, all the procedures discussed in this chapter can be performed by such a package.

3.9 REVIEW PROBLEMS

1. The data in Table A are account balances in 100 checking accounts. For these data: (*a*) Make a frequency table. (*b*) Construct a histogram.

TABLE A

16.20	46.00	58.22	36.25	101.50	32.72	152.22	161.75	224.75	342.18
169.82	74.19	297.15	419.62	98.98	66.15	77.25	42.57	39.02	31.22
6.94	38.10	25.86	92.14	13.25	335.96	36.75	29.00	189.06	76.87
241.16	384.96	223.25	51.25	128.16	95.27	121.12	144.90	47.94	48.95
43.18	86.19	184.00	39.25	44.06	32.15	62.14	21.44	75.34	486.12
320.16	15.50	11.00	147.50	214.16	116.30	26.42	132.40	103.25	27.50
30.96	110.00	53.00	17.35	2.75	82.37	135.10	95.06	39.30	280.01
54.18	48.76	194.13	362.75	261.15	38.10	88.24	42.00	96.38	49.38
123.75	72.00	21.45	79.00	90.75	65.23	25.09	136.10	34.87	69.01
23.16	33.00	209.00	40.15	60.80	34.16	107.16	41.20	276.85	37.05

2. Make a "less than" ogive from the frequency table constructed for Problem 1.
3. Birthrates, in number of births per 10,000 people, are given in Table B for 147 metropolitan areas in the United States in 1973. The data are from the 1975 *Statistical Abstract of the United States*. For these data: (a) Make a percent frequency distribution table. (b) Construct a percent frequency polygon.

TABLE B

127	139	135	148	162	137	171	150	120	149
140	155	157	156	91	142	120	173	142	149
128	149	120	169	145	156	185	151	184	130
141	158	161	127	145	143	151	151	137	131
151	113	146	166	170	127	139	124	159	159
134	164	151	121	149	166	154	132	154	155
162	167	119	131	161	135	171	164	130	165
141	139	155	128	114	149	163	116	172	168
161	168	134	171	144	158	128	172	184	135
120	119	169	124	137	158	138	139	135	135
152	172	122	175	138	116	176	152	163	139
147	142	133	152	162	170	135	151	163	180
123	174	178	179	135	180	176	186	129	146
181	204	141	123	183	193	202	178	207	230
124	232	238	150	125	144	132			

4. From the latest issue of the *Statistical Abstract of the United States:* (a) Make a percent frequency distribution of birthrates as in Problem 3(a). (b) Make a percent frequency polygon and plot it on the chart drawn for Problem 3(b). (c) Describe any changes shown by comparison of the polygons for Problems 3(b) and 4(b).
5. Construct a percent "or more" ogive from the frequency table obtained for Problem 3(a).
6. In graphical terms, what is meant by saying that a frequency distribution is approximately normal?
7. In graphical terms, what is meant by saying a frequency distribution is approximately uniform?
8. What is the class interval for a frequency distribution which has classes 0.00–24.99, 25.00–49.99, and so on?
9. Each number in Table C (on page 66) was obtained by dividing the dollar value of a corporation's annual earnings by the number of shares of common stock the corporation has issued. Investors who buy a stock are buying the right to share in the issuing corporation's earnings; so investors use earnings per share in their investment decisions. (Other ratios used by investors include price per share; dividends per share; and the *P/E* ratio, which is the ratio price per share divided by earnings per share.) (a) Array the data in order of size. (b) Make a frequency distribution table for the data. (c) Make a histogram for the frequency distribution. (d) In smooth curve terminology, how would you describe the distributions?
10. If a professor gives a difficult test, what would be the shape of the frequency distribution of test grades?

TABLE C
EARNINGS PER SHARE FOR 204 CORPORATIONS

5.90	7.15	1.86	6.52	3.04	5.20	0.95	3.58	3.51	3.90	8.69	3.06
10.08	2.54	2.34	6.14	2.32	2.01	4.90	2.02	3.10	0.76	2.40	4.70
10.45	1.69	4.51	4.26	4.53	0.57	5.19	3.38	2.58	4.05	3.32	3.26
3.20	5.39	7.48	3.53	5.56	3.75	10.79	4.25	4.26	2.90	2.67	4.80
9.08	3.30	10.05	3.64	2.99	2.36	3.42	3.94	4.05	3.30	4.34	4.27
5.18	2.77	5.03 ·	3.10	5.15	3.75	5.33	3.82	2.31	2.80	3.54	1.94
4.19	6.02	3.02	4.19	4.54	7.28	2.28	3.07	3.05	2.64	7.18	5.18
4.12	4.03	7.98	3.93	2.04	4.19	4.82	2.28	1.23	2.44	1.00	4.20
4.00	7.33	1.68	5.10	4.18	5.75	4.62	2.11	2.90	3.39	3.50	1.21
6.09	7.42	4.85	4.47	3.23	5.61	4.21	1.03	4.43	4.10	10.14	3.32
10.11	2.30	3.90	4.04	9.11	3.88	2.14	3.61	2.73	8.30	1.41	7.66
5.03	4.49	1.76	2.21	4.07	4.67	2.44	2.44	3.53	5.76	3.24	4.74
5.04	3.85	3.55	4.76	3.53	2.84	5.04	5.21	3.91	4.97	2.03	2.62
9.30	3.62	2.85	4.74	5.50	4.16	2.42	9.05	1.71	7.75	5.54	3.59
4.38	5.05	5.60	4.05	1.75	6.17	5.23	4.76	6.07	4.11	1.58	3.47
4.86	4.45	2.94	4.14	5.58	4.82	4.71	4.51	4.95	3.31	5.20	4.97
4.33	4.86	1.95	3.55	3.14	4.68	4.37	2.05	2.01	4.71	1.39	2.44

4

DATA SUMMARIZATION: MEASURES OF CENTRAL TENDENCY AND VARIABILITY

4.1 INTRODUCTION

In Chapter 3 you learned how to describe a large data set by reducing it to a frequency distribution having, say, 10 classes. We noted that distributions often exhibit a central tendency, that is, a tendency for higher frequencies near the center of the distribution and lower frequencies at the ends. In this chapter we first discuss four measures of central tendency—the arithmetic mean, the median, the mode, and the geometric mean. Each of these has properties which are not generally shared by the other measures. Consequently, the analyst has to decide which measure to use for a particular data set. Of course, a single measure cannot describe a data set as well as a frequency distribution. However, a single representative measure is easy to comprehend and use.

In the second part of the chapter, two numbers are used to represent a data set. These are (1) the arithmetic mean to measure central tendency and (2) the standard deviation to measure the variability (spread) of the numbers around the arithmetic mean. Let's start by reviewing the summation symbol, which is widely used in statistical formulas.

4.2 SUMMATION NOTATION

Summation is such a common process in statistics and other quantitative fields that a special symbol Σ, the uppercase Greek letter sigma, is used as a shorthand instruction to sum. Thus,

$$\Sigma \text{ prices}$$

means the sum of a group of prices. More specifically, suppose we have five prices which are, in dollars, 3, 6, 4, 7, 8. We may designate the first price as p_1 (p sub one) so that $p_1 = 3$, and similarly for the remaining prices. We have

$$p_1 = 3 \qquad p_2 = 6 \qquad p_3 = 4 \qquad p_4 = 7 \qquad p_5 = 8$$

The sum of all five prices can be expressed by the symbol

$$\sum_{i=1}^{5} p_i \qquad \text{or} \qquad \Sigma_{i=1}^{5} \, p_i$$

Any letter may be used as the index, but i and j are the most common. The letter subscript i is called the *index* of summation. The symbol is read as "the sum of the p_i's with i going from 1 to 5." It means to first let $i = 1$, getting p_1; then let $i = 2$ to get p_2; and so on; and then sum these quantities. That is,

$$\sum_{i=1}^{5} p_i = p_1 + p_2 + p_3 + p_4 + p_5$$

$$= 3 + 6 + 4 + 7 + 8$$

$$= 28$$

Similarly,

$$\sum_{j=1}^{m} y_j \quad \text{or} \quad \Sigma_{j=1}^{m} \, y_j$$

where m is some unspecified whole number, would be expanded by writing

$$\sum_{j=1}^{m} y_j = y_1 + y_2 + y_3 + \cdots + y_m$$

where $\cdots$ is read "and so on."

The index is omitted *when its meaning* *would be obvious.* When *all* possible values are to be summed, it is permissible to omit all or part of the index symbolism. Thus, if p is price, then Σp or Σp_i means the sum of all the prices at hand.

If we think of the contents of the parentheses in

$$\Sigma(\quad)$$

as being the head of a column of numbers, then the symbol means to sum that column, as illustrated next.

EXAMPLE From the following data, compute (*a*) Σx; (*b*) $\Sigma(x - 4)$; (*c*) Σx^2; (*d*) Σxy; (*e*) $(\Sigma x)^2$.

x	y
4	11
2	5
9	8

SOLUTION All the calculations required are shown in Table 4.1.

a. The sum of the x column is $\Sigma x = 15$.
b. $\Sigma(x - 4)$ means to construct a column headed $x - 4$ and find its entries and their sum. Each entry in the column is found by subtracting 4 from the given value of x. $\Sigma(x - 4) = 3$.
c. Σx^2 means to form a column headed x^2 and find its sum. Each entry in the column is the square of the given value of x. $\Sigma x^2 = 101$.
d. Σxy means to form a column headed xy and find its sum. Each entry in the column is the product of the given x and y values. $\Sigma xy = 126$.

TABLE 4.1
SUMMATION CALCULATIONS

x	y	x − 4	x²	xy
4	11	0	16	44
2	5	−2	4	10
9	8	5	81	72
15		3	101	126

Important —
Please reread

e. In $(\Sigma x)^2$, Σx is in parentheses; so $(\Sigma x)^2$ means the square of the sum of the x values. Since $\Sigma x = 15$, we have $(\Sigma x)^2 = (15)^2 = 225$.

In Table 4.1, note that $\Sigma x^2 = 101$ is not equal to $(\Sigma x)^2 = 225$. It is true for some data sets that $\Sigma x^2 = (\Sigma x)^2$, but this is not always (or usually) the case.

EXERCISE From the (x, y) data of Table 4.1, find (a) Σy; (b) Σy^2; (c) $(\Sigma y)^2$; (d) $\Sigma(y - 3)^2$.
ANSWER (a) 24; (b) 210; (c) 576; (d) 93.

4.3 THE ARITHMETIC MEAN (ARITHMETIC AVERAGE)

Questions about large groups of data often are answered by quoting averages, and such averages serve as a part of the information upon which decisions are based. For example, an investor who calls a stockbroker and asks how the stock market is doing may be told that "the Dow was up 2 at noon." This means that the Dow-Jones average of 30 industrial stock prices at noon was 2 points above its opening (10 a.m.) level. This change in the average does not, of course, provide information about the price change of any particular stock; it does, however, indicate the direction and extent of the change in the prices of a selected group of stocks.

Formula for the Arithmetic Mean

In measuring central tendency, we try to find a representative "middle" value for a group of data.

Each of the various measures of central tendency may properly be called an average; so there are various averages. The arithmetic average—also called the arithmetic mean—is the "ordinary" average. It is computed by dividing the sum of N data values by N, where N is the total number of values in a data set. In everyday language—and frequently in statistical language—the word *average* or *mean*, by itself, denotes the arithmetic average. In this book, I shall follow that general convention. Other measures—the median, mode, and geometric mean—will be referred to by their names.

We shall denote the mean of a data set by μ, the Greek letter mu. When we discuss statistical inference, μ will be specialized to be the mean of a population. Sometimes we shall indicate a particular mean with a subscript.

To find μ: Add up the data values; then divide by the number of values.

Thus, μ_x is the mean of a set of x values, and μ_y is the mean of a set of y values.

In sigma notation, the *arithmetic mean* of a set of N values x_1, x_2, x_3, . . . , x_N is

$$\mu_x = \frac{\Sigma_{i=1}^{N} x_i}{N} = \frac{\Sigma x_i}{N} = \frac{\Sigma x}{N}$$

The last statement shows the fully indexed summation symbol and two of its abbreviated forms.

EXERCISE From Table 4.1: (a) What is μ_y? (b) What is the square of the average value of y? (c) What is the average of the squared values of y?
ANSWER (a) 8; (b) 64; (c) 70.

The arithmetic average is one of several numbers which may be chosen to measure central tendency. However, the arithmetic average has some useful *arithmetic* (hence the name) properties not generally possessed by the other measures. These properties will be discussed next.

Total Value Property of μ: $\Sigma x = N\mu$

If we know that over a period of 20 days a company's output averaged 123.5 units per day, the total number of units made must have been $(123.5)(20) = 2470$. That is, if

$$\mu = \frac{\Sigma x}{20} = 123.5$$

then $\Sigma x = 20(123.5) = 2470$

In general, if we multiply both sides of

$$\mu = \frac{\Sigma x}{N}$$

To find Σx: Multiply the mean by the number of data values.

by N we have

$$N\mu = \Sigma x \quad \text{or} \quad \Sigma x = N\mu$$

The last equation is referred to as the *total value property*, because it states that the total value of all the numbers Σx can be obtained if we know how many numbers N there are and their average μ.

EXERCISE Compute the total sales to 400 customers if the average sale per customer was $26.25.
ANSWER $10,500.

The Average and Marginal Addition

Suppose we have produced 4 units at a cost of $220 so the average unit cost for the four is $220/4 = \$55$ per unit. We wish to determine what the additional cost for the next unit, the fifth, should be if the average cost of the five is to be $50 per unit. We reason by the total value property that the total cost of the five units must be

$$5(\$50) = \$250$$

And, because the first 4 cost $220, the additional cost incurred by making the fifth must be

$$\text{Cost of 5} - \text{cost of 4} = \$250 - \$220 = \$30$$

The $30 just computed is called the *marginal* cost of the fifth unit. In general, the marginal cost of a unit is the *additional* cost incurred in the production of that unit.

Marginal and average costs are important in economic analysis. The eco-

A lower marginal cost "pulls" the average down.

nomic idea we have just demonstrated is that average cost goes down if the marginal cost of the next unit is less than the average cost before the next unit is produced. Similarly, the average cost goes up if the marginal cost of the next unit is greater than the average cost before the next unit is produced. Thus, in our example, the average cost went down from $55 because the marginal cost of the next unit, $30, was less than $55. The next exercise will help you to fix the idea in mind.

EXERCISE A student has an average of 61.25 on four tests. One test remains and the course average will be the average of the five test grades. If 60 is the passing grade for the course, what is the lowest fifth test grade which will lead to a passing average?
ANSWER 55.

The Average as a Balance Point

The numbers 1, 14, 19, 31, 50 have an average of $\mu = 23$. Figure 4.1 shows

FIGURE 4.1
The arithmetic mean μ is the balance point.

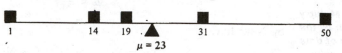

$x_i - \mu$

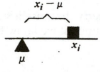

$x_i - \mu$ is a "distance" in Figure 4-1

the numbers as equal small weights placed on a number line at their respective values. If we think of the line as a stick with the weights on it, the stick will balance if it is set on the edge of a fulcrum at μ as shown. The arithmetic counterpart of this balance property is this: If we compute $x_i - \mu$ for each number, the positive and negative values balance so that their sum is zero. That is, for any set of numbers,

$$\Sigma(x_i - \mu) = 0$$

EXERCISE For the numbers 1, 14, 19, 31, 50, which have $\mu = 23$: (a) What are the values of $x_i - \mu$? (b) What is $\Sigma(x_i - \mu)$?
ANSWER (a) $-22, -9, -4, 8, 27$; (b) zero.

Effect of Outliers

A nonswimmer can drown wading across a river whose average depth is 2 feet.

Averages are often used to describe the differences between two groups of data. Averages also are used, at times, as norms or standards as, for example, when the average time needed to assemble an engine is taken as the standard for an assembly line. In these and other applications of the average, we should be aware of the effect of *outliers*, that is, the effect of numbers which differ markedly from most of the numbers in the set being averaged. For example, suppose net profits as a percent of sales for the past five periods have been

5.30   0.10   5.74   5.87   5.49

The average of these numbers is 4.5 percent. The outlier 0.10 percent "pulls down" the average to give a number which is quite unlike all the other observations. If we discard the outlier, we obtain a *modified mean* of 5.6 percent, which probably is a more meaningful number to use in comparisons or for setting a norm.

It is important to examine a data set for outliers. Sometimes an outlier occurs for a reason which can be identified. For example, an unusually severe storm and very cold weather, not expected to recur, could explain the small profit, 0.10 percent. If so, the number should be excluded when the average is computed. Of course, the outlier might be due to an error in calculation which should be corrected before the average is computed.

The Weighted Average

Suppose profits per order for small, medium, and large orders are $1, $3, and $6. The average profit per order is obtained by dividing total profit by the number of orders. It is

$$\mu = \frac{\$1 + \$3 + \$6}{3} = \$3.33$$

Each profit figure has been counted *once* to compute this *simple* or *unweighted* average.

The unweighted average is appropriate when data items are of equal importance. However, when this is not so, we weight each data item according to its importance and compute a *weighted* average. Suppose, in the example at hand, that the numbers of small, medium, and large orders are different, as shown in Table 4.2. Then the simple average of the three profits does not tell us what average profit was actually earned; to find that, each profit is weighted (multiplied) by w, the number of orders having this profit. Thus, we have 120 orders at $1 which contribute $120 to total profit; 60 orders at $3 which contribute $180; and 20 orders at $6 which contribute $120. The total number of orders Σw is 200, and the total profit Σpw is $420. The actual average profit per order is

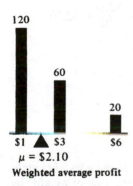

120

60

20

$1 $3 $6
$\mu = \$2.10$

Weighted average profit

TABLE 4.2
WEIGHTED AVERAGE PROFIT PER ORDER

Order size	Profit per order p	Number of orders w	pw
Small	$1	120	$120
Medium	3	60	180
Large	6	20	120
		$\Sigma w = 200$	$\Sigma(pw) = \$420$

Weighted average profit per order $= \dfrac{\Sigma pw}{\Sigma w} = \dfrac{\$420}{200} = \$2.10$

$$\frac{\text{Total profit}}{\text{Number of orders}} = \frac{\Sigma(pw)}{\Sigma w} = \frac{\$420}{200} = \$2.10 \text{ per order}$$

The preponderance of lower-profit orders makes the weighted average lower than the simple average.

In general, if the numbers x_i have respective weights w_i, then

$$Weighted\ average\ of\ the\ x_i\text{'s} = \frac{\Sigma x_i w_i}{\Sigma w_i} = \frac{\Sigma x w}{\Sigma w}$$

That is, to compute the weighted average of a set of numbers, we multiply each number by its weight, add the products, and then divide by the sum of the weights.

EXERCISE Suppose that in a semester you received a grade of 70 in a 3-hour course, 84 in a 4-hour course, and 90 in a 5-hour course. Weight grades by hours and compute your weighted average semester's grade.
ANSWER 83.

Multiplying or dividing a given set of weights by the same number leads to a set of *equal-share* weights. Equal-share weights yield the same weighted average. For example, dividing each of the weights w in Table 4.2 by 2 gives 60, 30, and 10, shown in the w_e column of Table 4.3. Now we compute

$$Weighted\ average\ profit\ per\ order = \frac{\Sigma(pw_e)}{\Sigma w_e} = \frac{\$210}{100} = \$2.10$$

TABLE 4.3
EQUAL-SHARE WEIGHTS

p	w_e	pw_e
$1	60	$60
3	30	90
6	10	60
	100	$210

In general, *a given set of weights and any set of equal-share weights yield the same weighted average*. In particular, we may replace a set of weights by an equal-share set which sums to 1 (100 percent) by dividing each weight by the total of the weights, that is, by expressing the given weights as proportions or percents of the total weight. Then $\Sigma w_e = 1$, and

$$Weighted\ average = \Sigma x w_e \quad (if\ \Sigma w_e = 1)$$

Weights summing to 1 (or 100 percent) are encountered in calculations of average price levels, in probability, and elsewhere.

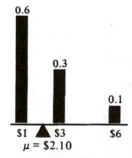

0.6

0.3

0.1

$1　$3　$6
$\mu = \$2.10$

Relative weighted
average profit

EXERCISE (a) Express the weights of Table 4.2 as proportions of the total weight Σw. (b) Using the proportions in (a) as the weights, compute the weighted average profit per order.
ANSWER (a) 0.6, 0.3, 0.1; (b) $2.10/1 = $2.10.

Combining Averages

Suppose a company operates two plants, designated as plants 1 and 2. Plant 1 has $N_1 = 50$ workers having an average hourly wage rate of $\mu_1 = \$3.20$, and plant 2 has $N_2 = 70$ workers having an average hourly wage rate of $\mu_2 = \$3.50$. The average rate paid by the company to all workers is computed as follows:

This is a weighted average of the averages

$$\frac{\Sigma N_i \mu_i}{\Sigma N_i}$$

where the numbers N_i are the weights.

Total paid, plant 1	$N_1 \mu_1$	$= 50(\$3.20)$	$= \$160$
Total paid, plant 2	$N_2 \mu_2$	$= 70(\$3.50)$	$= \$245$
Total paid	$N_1 \mu_1 + N_2 \mu_2$		$= \$405$
Total number of workers	$N_1 + N_2$		$= 120$

$$\text{Average rate per worker} = \frac{N_1 \mu_1 + N_2 \mu_2}{N_1 + N_2} = \frac{\$405}{120} = \$3.38$$

It is worth noting that subscripts are a handy way to designate different values of the same type of quantity. Thus, in the last example, the quantity μ is an average, and μ_1 and μ_2 represent that average for different plants. Similarly, using N_1 and N_2 preserves N to represent number of workers; subscripts designate these numbers for different plants.

Properties of the arithmetic mean

We have seen that the average has the total value property; that is, the total of N numbers can be obtained by multiplying μ by N. The average was also seen to be a balance point; the sum of deviations of the data values from their average $\Sigma(x_i - \mu)$ is zero. Also, we found it reasonable to compute a weighted average when data values differ in importance. And it is possible to combine the averages of two groups of numbers to obtain the overall average. The foregoing statements are true for the arithmetic mean (average). They are not generally true for other measures of central tendency.

EXERCISE Last month an investor acquired 500 shares of a stock at an average price of $42 per share. This month the investor bought 300 shares of the stock at an average price of $36 per share. Find the average price per share paid during the 2 months.
ANSWER $39.75.

Approximating the Average for Grouped Data

Data summarized in a frequency table are called *grouped* data. When data are grouped, their average can be *approximated* by assuming that the average of the numbers in a class is equal to the class mark (the average of the class limits).

Table 4.4 illustrates the calculation of the average of grouped data. The frequency distribution is given in the first two columns. Each class mark x in the third column is taken to represent the average of the numbers in the class. Then the contribution of the numbers in a class to the total value of all

TABLE 4.4
APPROXIMATING THE AVERAGE FOR A
FREQUENCY DISTRIBUTION

Output per labor-hour	Number of days (frequency f)	Class mark x	fx
4.0 and under 5.0	3	4.5	13.5
5.0 and under 6.0	11	5.5	60.5
6.0 and under 7.0	17	6.5	110.5
7.0 and under 8.0	16	7.5	120.0
8.0 and under 9.0	8	8.5	68.0
9.0 and under 10.0	5	9.5	47.5
	60		420.0

the numbers is fx, the product of the class frequency and the class mark. The total value of all the $\Sigma f = 60$ numbers is approximately $\Sigma fx = 420.0$. Hence,

$$\mu \approx \frac{420.0}{60} \approx 7.0$$

The symbol $\approx$ means *equals approximately*. It is used because an accurate average cannot usually be computed from a frequency table: An accurate average can, however, be calculated for the data set from which a frequency distribution is constructed. The data set from which Table 4.4 was constructed had a sum of 418.2; so

$$\mu = \frac{418.2}{60} = 6.97$$

is the accurate average. The approximation $\mu \approx 7.0$ is very close in this case. Generally, for carefully made frequency distributions, the approximate average is adequate for most purposes.

Another type of weighted average: here we weight each class mark by its class frequency.

The formula for calculating *the average of grouped data* is

$$\mu \approx \frac{\Sigma fx}{\Sigma f}$$

The formula instructs us to multiply, or weight, each class mark by the class frequency, add the products, and then divide by the sum of the frequencies.

EXERCISE A frequency distribution has class intervals of 3.00 and under 4.00, 4.00 and under 5.00, 5.00 and under 6.00, with respective frequencies of 4, 10, 6. Estimate μ for the distribution.
ANSWER 4.6.

The average cannot be computed from an open-ended frequency table which gives no information about the sizes of the numbers in the open class. However, if the average of the numbers in the open class is known or can be estimated, this average can be taken as the class mark of the open interval. Then the calculation can proceed in the manner of Table 4.4.

4.4 THE MEDIAN

Determining the Median from an Array

To find the median, first make an array of the data items.

The median of a set of data is a number selected to represent the middle *position* when the data are arrayed in order of size. The middle position in an array of N data items is the position numbered $(N + 1)/2$. If N is odd, there is a data item at the middle position, and we take this item as the median. If N is even, we take the average of the two middle data items as the median. The median is thus the middle value, or the average of the two middle values, in an *arrayed* data set.

Next, find the middle position in the array.

In Table 4.5 there are $N = 5$ data items. The middle *position* in the array is

$$\text{Position } \frac{N + 1}{2} = \frac{5 + 1}{2} = \text{position 3}$$

Then the median is the data item that is (or would be) in the middle position.

so we take the number at that position, 10, as the median. In Table 4.6, $N = 6$ and

$$\text{Position } \frac{N + 1}{2} = \frac{7}{2} = \text{position 3.5}$$

so the middle position is halfway between positions 3 and 4. We take the average of the numbers at these positions $(16 + 20)/2 = 18$ as the median.

TABLE 4.5
DETERMINING THE MEDIAN
FROM AN ARRAY (*N* ODD)

Arrayed x	Position order of x in the array
8	1
9	2
10*	3 ← Middle position
15	4
20	5

* Median is 10.

TABLE 4.6
DETERMINING THE MEDIAN
FROM AN ARRAY (*N* EVEN)

Arrayed y	Position order of y in the array
13	1
14	2
16	3
*	← Middle position
20	4
25	5
30	6

* Median is (16 + 20)/2 = 18.

EXERCISE (*a*) Find the median of 18, 30, 44, 60, 31, 22, 68. (*b*) How would the median of a set of 1000 data items be selected?

ANSWER (*a*) 31. (*b*) Make an ordered array and take the average of the data values at positions 500 and 501 as the median.

In both Tables 4.5 and 4.6 as many data values fall below the median as fall above it. We shall thus find it useful to think of the median as a 50-50 point, with half the data values falling below and half above. The 50-50 description is not always strictly correct, but it is reasonable when we have large data sets in mind.

Effect of Outliers

An outlier can have a marked effect upon the arithmetic average. Note, however, that the data sets

$$1, 2, 2, 3, 4, 4, 5$$

$$1, 2, 2, 3, 4, 4, 5000$$

The value of an outlier does not affect the median.

both have 3 as their median, even though the latter set has the outlier 5000. Consequently, if the effect of outliers is to be avoided, the median is preferred to the average. Remember, though, that the median does not have the total value property and other properties of the arithmetic average that were described in Section 4.3.

Fractiles

A *fractile* is a value below which a specified fraction of the numbers in a data set lie. Thus, the 0.25 fractile or *first quartile* Q_1 is the value below which one-quarter of the data numbers lie. The 0.75 fractile is called the third quartile Q_3. The median is the second quartile Q_2 or the 0.50 fractile. When these fractions are expressed in percentage form, fractiles are called *percentiles*. The 95th percentile is the 0.95 fractile. Q_1, Q_2, and Q_3 are, respectively, the 25th, 50th, and 75th percentiles.

A fractile may be approximate.

It may be necessary to make an arbitrary choice when selecting a fractile. For example, a set of $N = 177$ numbers cannot be divided exactly into fourths; so there is no precise 0.25 fractile. Consequently, a selected fractile may only approximately satisfy its definition. However, such approximations generally are adequate and helpful in describing large data sets.

EXERCISE (a) What is meant by the 0.90 fractile for a data set? (b) What percentile would this be?

ANSWER (a) A value below which nine-tenths of the data items lie; (b) 90th percentile.

Approximating the Median for Grouped Data

To find the approximate median of grouped data, we first find the class that contains the median. Then we approximate the median within that class.

Let N be the total frequency of a distribution. The *median class* of a distribution is the first class where the cumulative frequency equals or exceeds $N/2$. In Table 4.7, the total frequency is $N = 440$. Hence, $N/2 = 220$. The

TABLE 4.7
HOURLY WAGE RATE FREQUENCY DISTRIBUTION

Hourly wage rate, dollars	Number of workers (frequency)	Cumulative frequency
3.00–3.49	68	68
3.50–3.99	142	210
4.00–4.49	100	310
4.50–4.99	60	
5.00–5.49	40	
5.50–5.99	20	
6.00–6.49	10	
	$N = 440$	$\frac{N}{2} = 220$

4.00–4.99 is the median class; 310 exceeds N/2 = 220

cumulative frequency 310 is the first to exceed 220; so the class 4.00–4.49 is the median class.

Now we move into the median class to approximate the median. The cumulative frequency in the previous class is 210; so we need

$$\frac{N}{2} - 210 = 220 - 210 = 10$$

data values from the median class to reach the cumulative frequency of $N/2 = 220$. The median class contains 100 data values. We assume these values are evenly spread over the class interval. We require 10 of these 100 values to get to the 220th value; so we move along from the lower class limit 4.00 a distance which is 10/100 of the class interval. The class interval is 0.50. Hence, we approximate the median Md as

$$Md \approx 4.00 + \frac{10}{100}(0.50) \approx 4.00 + 0.05 = 4.05 \text{ dollars}$$

r is N/2 minus the cumulative frequency for the class before the median class.

In general, let L be the lower limit of the median class, f be the median class frequency, c be the class interval, and r be the number of data items required from the median class to reach a cumulative frequency of $N/2$. The formula for computing *the median of grouped data* is

$$Md \approx L + \frac{r}{f}c$$

EXERCISE Approximate the median from the following frequency table.

Class	Frequency
0.00– 4.99	16
5.00– 9.99	35
10.00–14.99	40
15.00–19.99	39
20.00–24.99	26

ANSWER Approximately 13.4.

If the median class is not open-ended, the median for an open-ended frequency distribution can be determined. This, of course, is not true for the arithmetic mean.

The procedure for approximating the median for a frequency distribution can be applied to approximate other fractiles. For example, to locate Q_1, the first quartile, cumulate frequencies up to $N/4$ to locate the quartile class. Then use the last formula, interpreting L, r, and f with reference to the first quartile class.

4.5 THE MODE

Mode for individual data

Statisticians have adopted the French word *mode*, meaning fashion, to convey the idea of "most frequent." The *mode* of a set of data is the value that occurs most frequently. If a store sells more size 14 women's dresses than any other size, the mode of the dress sizes (the modal dress size) is 14. A data set in which each value occurs only once has no mode.

A data set may be *bimodal* (have two modes) or be *multimodal* (have more than two modes). For example, the following set of belt sizes has two modes, 28 and 36.

26, 28, 28, 28, 28, 28, 30, 30, 32, 34, 36, 36, 36, 36, 36

Sometimes bimodal data sets arise because two different distributions have been mixed. Thus, the belt sizes shown may be for a mixture of belts that men buy for themselves and for their sons.

Mode for grouped data

We can assign a mode to grouped data that have a highest frequency class even though we don't know whether or not any data value occurs more than once. Figure 4.2 is a histogram of the wage rate distribution of Table 4.7. The *modal* (highest frequency) *class* of this distribution is the class 3.50–3.99. We use the frequencies of the modal class and of the two adjacent classes to locate the mode in the modal class. If the adjacent classes have equal frequency, we assume the mode is at the middle of the modal class. If one of the adjacent classes has a higher frequency than the other, we assume the mode is proportionately closer to that class; then we use a formula to locate the mode in the modal class.

The formula for computing *the mode of grouped data* is

The fraction

$$\dfrac{d_1}{d_1 + d_2}$$

locates the mode within the modal class.

$$\text{Mode} = Mo = L + \frac{d_1}{(d_1 + d_2)}\, c$$

where L = lower limit of the modal class

d_1 = modal class frequency minus the frequency in the previous (smaller class limits) class

d_2 = modal class frequency minus the frequency in the next (larger class limits) class

c = class interval

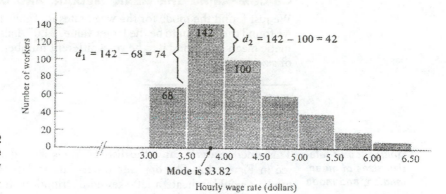

FIGURE 4.2
Determining the mode
from a frequency
distribution.

Mode is $3.82

Hourly wage rate (dollars)

In Figure 4.2, we see that

$$L = 3.50$$

$$d_1 = 142 - 68 = 74$$

$$d_2 = 142 - 100 = 42$$

$$c = 0.50$$

Hence,

$$Mo = L + \frac{d_1}{(d_1 + d_2)} c$$

$$= 3.50 + \frac{74}{(74 + 42)} 0.50$$

$$= 3.50 + \frac{74}{(116)} 0.50$$

$$= 3.50 + 0.32$$

$$= 3.82$$

so $3.82 is the mode for the wage rates in Table 4.7: It is closer to the upper modal class limit because the next class has a higher frequency than the previous class.

EXERCISE Determine the mode for the following frequency distribution.

Class	Frequency
10.0–14.9	94
15.0–19.9	102
20.0–24.9	70

ANSWER 16.0.

4.6 COMPARING THE MEAN, MEDIAN, AND MODE

We just found the mode for the wage rates in Table 4.7 to be $3.82. Earlier we found the median to be the larger value, $4.05. I also calculated the arithmetic mean and found it to be yet a different number, $4.20. Thus, in order of size, we have

Mode	Median	Mean
$3.82	$4.05	$4.20

Significance of relative sizes of mean, median, and mode

This order occurs because the distribution is skewed to the right, as you can see in Figure 4.2. The opposite order—mean less than median less than mode—would indicate a left-skewed distribution. If a distribution is symmetrical and unimodal, the three measures are equal.

Figure 4.3*a–c* illustrates the relationships just described. You should avoid the mistake of calling the peak of a smooth curve the mode. The mode is the value at the point on the horizontal axis directly below the peak—as indicated by the arrows on the figures.

The mode is rarely used in business applications, because a data set may have no mode or it may have two or more modes. But the mode is used often in statistics when frequency distributions are described. The mean is the most commonly used measure of central tendency because (1) a data set always has one, and only one, mean and (2) the mean has the arithmetic properties discussed earlier. For skewed distributions, the median is a better measure of central tendency than the mean, because the mean is pulled away from the central region in the direction of skewness. Moreover, the median has the 50-50 property, which is not generally true for the mean. And, of course, the median (but not the mean) usually can be determined for open-ended frequency distributions.

Definition

4.7 THE GEOMETRIC MEAN

The geometric mean of a set of N numbers is the Nth root of the product of the numbers. The formula for *the geometric mean* is

$$\text{Geometric mean} = GM = \sqrt[N]{\text{product of N numbers}}$$

For example, the $N = 4$ numbers

$$0.5, 1, 4, 8$$

have

$$GM = \sqrt[4]{(0.5)(1)(4)(8)} = \sqrt[4]{16} = 2$$

The arithmetic mean of the numbers is $13.5/4 = 3.375$. The geometric mean is less than the arithmetic mean except in the rare case where all the numbers in the data set are the same; in that rare case, the two means are equal. Consequently, the geometric mean is sometimes used as the average

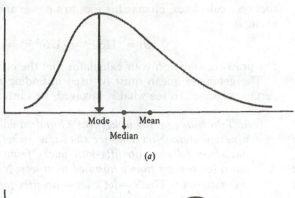

(a)

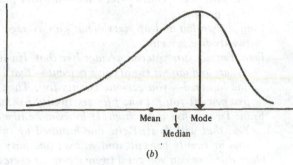

(b)

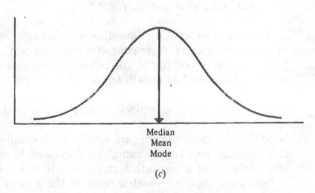

(c)

FIGURE 4.3
(a) Central tendency measures in a right-skewed distribution.
(b) Central tendency measures in a left-skewed distribution.
(c) Central tendency measures coincide in a symmetrical unimodal distribution.

for right-skewed economic data—because it is not affected as much by the skewness as the arithmetic mean.

EXERCISE Compute (a) the geometric mean and (b) the arithmetic mean for the values 1, 3, and 9.
ANSWER (a) 3; (b) 4.33.

You should use your calculator to take roots. That is much simpler and more accurate than the alternative, which is to use logarithms. To take a root on a calculator, change the root to a power and use the power key. For example,

$$\sqrt[8]{126} = (126)^{1/8} = (126)^{0.125} = 1.83$$

For practice, verify on your calculator that the cube root of 125 is 5.

The geometric mean must be used in finding average period-to-period percent change. To see what is involved, let's listen in on Dan and Fran.

100 to 90 to 144

100 to 90,
−10 percent

90 to 144, +60 percent

(−10 + 60)/2 = 25

1.25(100) = 125

1.25(125) = 156.25

1.2(100) = 120
1.2(120) = 144

Dan: Two years ago, my jacket cost a hundred dollars. Last year it sold for ninety dollars. Now I notice the same jacket goes for a hundred and forty-four dollars—up fifty-four bucks from last year! First it went down ten percent from a hundred to ninety. Now it's up from ninety to one forty-four. That's—let's see—up fifty-four on ninety—that's up sixty percent.

Fran: Down ten and up sixty. That's an average yearly percent change of twenty-five percent.

Dan: I'm not sure you can average like that. If you start with one hundred dollars and raise it twenty-five percent—that's one point two five times one hundred—you get one twenty-five. Then raising that by twenty-five percent you get one fifty-six twenty-five, not one forty-four.

Fran: Twenty-five is too high. It looks more like twenty percent per year. Yes, that will do it. Raise one hundred by twenty percent, then raise that by twenty percent, and you get one forty-four.

Dan: But how can you get a twenty percent average from a minus ten percent and a plus sixty percent?

Growth factors

The way to answer Dan's question is to first compute the geometric mean of the growth factors. A *growth factor* is the ratio of a number, say, price or sales, for one period to the corresponding number for a previous period. Dan's jacket price had growth factors of

$$\frac{\$90}{\$100} = 0.90 \quad \text{and} \quad \frac{\$144}{\$90} = 1.60$$

Note that the growth factors are simply the decimal equivalents of the percent changes, plus 1. For example, a decline of 10 percent is −10 percent, and −10 percent is a growth factor of −0.10 + 1 = 0.90.

Now compute the geometric mean of the growth factors. This is

$$GM = \sqrt{(0.90)(1.60)} = (1.44)^{0.5} = 1.20$$

Finally subtract 1 to obtain 1.20 − 1 = 0.20, or 20 percent, as the desired average.

Computing average
period-to-period per-
cent change

The *average period-to-period percent change* is computed by (1) converting the percent changes to growth factors, (2) finding the geometric mean of the growth factors, (3) converting the geometric mean growth factor to a percent change.

✗ **EXAMPLE** Abac Company's year-to-year changes in fuel consumption expenditures were -5, 10, 20, 40, and 60 percent. Using the geometric mean of growth factors, determine the average yearly percent change in expenditures.

SOLUTION Converting the percent changes to growth factors, we obtain

$$0.95 \quad 1.10 \quad 1.20 \quad 1.40 \quad 1.60$$

Then, taking the fifth root (power is 0.2) of the product of the factors, we have

$$GM = [(0.95)(1.10)(1.20)(1.40)(1.60)]^{0.2} = 1.229$$

Subtracting 1 gives $1.229 - 1 = 0.229$, or a 22.9 percent average increase per year.

EXERCISE Month-to-month changes in the prices of a stock were 11, 18, and -15 percent. Using the geometric mean of the growth factors, determine the average monthly percent change in the price of the stock.
ANSWER 3.64 percent.

4.8 PROBLEMS

1. (a) If we have five x values, how would their sum be symbolized using fully indexed sigma notation? (b) If we have P values of y, how would their sum be symbolized using fully indexed sigma notation?
2. (a) Complete (expand) the expression $\sum_{k=1}^{4} z_k$. (b) Complete (expand) the following, using $\cdots$ to mean "and so on."

$$\sum_{j=1}^{L} w_j$$

3. For the x values 6, 7, 13, 14 compute (a) Σx_i; (b) Σx_i^2; (c) $(\Sigma x_i)^2$; (d) μ; (e) $\Sigma(x_i - \mu)$; (f) $\Sigma(x_i - \mu)^2$.
4. For the y values -3, 0, 5, 7, 2, 4 compute (a) Σy_i; (b) Σy_i^2; (c) $(\Sigma y_i)^2$; (d) μ; (e) $\Sigma(y_i - \mu)$; (f) $\Sigma(y_i - \mu)^2$.
5. For the data in Table A, compute (a) Σxy; (b) $(\Sigma x)(\Sigma y)$.

TABLE A

x	y
-3	2
0	5
2	7
3	10

6. For the data in Table B (page 86), compute $\Sigma(x - \mu_x)(y - \mu_y)$.

TABLE B

x	y
1	17
4	6
9	12
11	13
6	15
5	9

7. DMP Company orders watches from suppliers A and B. Delivery times have varied as shown in Table C for the last six orders from each supplier. (a) Find the average delivery time for each supplier. (b) From an inventory scheduling viewpoint, the data imply that DMP should order all watches from A. Explain why.

TABLE C

Supplier	Delivery time, days
A	3 4 3 3 4 4
B	1 5 2 6 3 4

8. (a) Find the average of 4, 3, 5, 2, 6. (b) Find the average of 4, 3, 5, 2, 60. (c) What characteristic of the average is illustrated by comparing the answers to (a) and (b)?

9. In order to have an early estimate of the dollar volume of sales, a mail order company weighs the mail at the beginning of each business day. Past records show that the average dollar volume of sales per pound of mail was $45. (a) Estimate dollar volume of sales on a day when the morning mail weighs 850 pounds. (b) What property of the average was applied in answering (a)?

10. Compute the total weekly amount paid to 86 secretaries who receive an average of $290 per week.

11. A student has grades of 65, 70, 95, and 62 on four quizzes. If the student is to have an average of at least 75 after the next quiz, what is the lowest grade that can be received for the next quiz?

12. Average cost when four units are produced is $10 per unit. What must be the marginal cost of the fifth unit if average cost is to decline to $9 per unit?

13. Sets of values of average cost per unit and marginal cost are both increasing as number of units produced increases. Which set contains the larger values? Why?

14. A smooth uniform distribution has a rectangle as its graph. Suppose the base of the rectangle extends from 20 to 80. What is the mean of the distribution? Why? What are the median and the mode? Why?

15. Suppose a distribution is represented by a right triangle whose hypote-

nuse slants down to the right. If the base of the triangle extends from 0 to 100, will the mean of the distribution be 50? If not, on which side of 50 will the mean lie? Why?

16. What is the numerical value of $\Sigma(x_i - \mu)$ if the sum is taken over all N values of x_i?

17. Average profit was $2.00 per order on 200 small orders and $4.60 per order on 50 large orders. Find average profit per order on all 250 orders.

18. See Problem 17. Holding average profit on large orders constant, what would the average profit per small order have to be if the average profit on the 250 orders is to be $2.80?

19. A company has wage scale classes A, B, and C. In period 1, there were 50 class A workers whose hourly wage rate was $4, 300 class B at $5 per hour, and 150 class C at $6 per hour. In period 2, all hourly rates were increased 10 percent and the numbers of workers in classes A, B, and C were, respectively, 160, 200, and 40. (a) Compute the average hourly wage rate in period 1. (b) Compute the average hourly wage rate in period 2. (c) Are the results of (a) and (b) consistent with the fact that all wage rates were increased by 10 percent in period 2? Explain.

20. During a decline in stock market prices, a stock sold at $50 per share one day, $40 on the next day, and $25 on the third. (a) Find the average daily price per share. (b) An investor bought $1000 worth of the stock on each of the three days. Find the average price paid per share. (c) Explain why the answers for (a) and (b) are different.

21. During period 1, a company sells products A, B, and C at $40, $50, and $60 per ton, respectively. Fifty percent of all tons sold are product A, 30 percent are B, and 20 percent are C. In period 2, the company sells the same proportions of each product but raises the prices of A, B, and C by 10, 3, and 2 percent, respectively. (a) Compute the average price per ton sold in period 1 and in period 2. (b) Compute the percent change from period 1 to period 2 in average price per ton sold. (c) Compute the average of the percent increases in the prices of the products. Why is this different from the answer to part (b)?

22. See Table D. (a) Compute the average selling price per unit for all units sold. (b) Convert each number of units sold to a proportion of the total number sold. (c) Compute the average selling price per unit using the proportions in (b) as weights for the prices.

TABLE D

Item	Number of units sold	Selling price per unit
A	90	$2
B	45	4
C	15	5

23. Approximate the mean salary for Table E (page 88).

TABLE E

Salary class, dollars per week	Number of workers
205.00–214.99	5
215.00–224.99	30
225.00–234.99	40
235.00–244.99	20
245.00–254.99	5

24. Compute the average number of new cars sold per day from Table F.

TABLE F

Number of cars sold	0	1	2	3	4
Number of days	3	19	48	15	5

25. Compute the average size of orders received from Table G.

TABLE G

Size of order, dollars	Relative frequency of orders
0.00– 7.99	0.150
8.00–15.99	0.300
16.00–23.99	0.400
24.00–31.99	0.075
32.00–39.99	0.075

26. (a) Find the median of 4, 3, 5, 2, 6. (b) Find the median of 4, 3, 5, 2, 60 (c) What favorable property of the median is illustrated by comparing the answers to (a) and (b)?

27. The average and median weekly salaries of 86 secretaries in a company are, respectively, $290 and $275. (a) Compute the total weekly amount paid to the secretaries. (b) Why do the data imply that the majority of secretaries earn less than $290 per week? (c) You and a friend do not know what one particular secretary's salary is but can obtain this information. Prior to obtaining the actual figure, each of you names a figure, a bet is made, and the one coming closest wins the bet. Would you choose a figure near $290 or near $275? Why?

28. A regional trade association collected the data in Table H from its 56 member companies. Each number is selling expense as a percent of dollars of sales. For example, the first number, 7.2, means that selling expense for the reporting company was 7.2 percent of sales, or 7.2 cents per dollar of sales. (a) Make an array of the data. (b) Find the median. (c) Find the first and third quartiles.

29. See Table I. (a) Make an array of the data. (b) Find the median miles per gallon. (c) Find the first and third quartiles.

30. For the data of Table E, approximate the median salary.

31. For the data of Table G, approximate the median order size.

TABLE H
SELLING EXPENSE AS PERCENT OF SALES

7.2	8.2	7.4	5.2	6.2	5.8	7.0
7.1	7.8	7.4	7.1	9.3	7.3	6.3
7.5	7.6	7.6	6.5	7.1	5.7	7.3
8.9	8.0	7.7	8.0	8.6	7.9	6.1
5.6	8.2	8.3	7.5	7.7	8.3	8.5
7.1	7.0	6.8	7.6	8.5	7.2	6.6
7.3	7.4	8.7	8.3	6.3	7.2	6.8
8.2	6.7	7.7	7.2	8.8	8.4	7.2

TABLE I
MILES PER GALLON FOR A FLEET OF 100 AMEX AUTOMOBILES

16.2	17.6	18.6	16.0	17.0	17.0	14.7	16.5	14.9	17.7
15.7	18.1	17.1	17.7	16.9	15.6	17.1	17.7	17.5	15.9
18.2	16.7	14.1	16.1	16.9	17.9	17.0	16.7	17.1	15.9
16.9	16.7	17.5	16.8	16.9	17.9	17.0	14.6	16.8	17.1
15.9	17.8	17.9	15.1	18.4	15.7	17.3	16.9	18.8	17.1
17.9	16.0	17.0	15.2	17.3	16.0	17.8	16.5	15.8	16.4
17.1	18.1	16.8	17.1	18.8	16.0	15.9	17.6	18.4	17.7
16.0	14.9	16.8	17.1	20.2	13.7	17.3	16.8	15.5	17.7
18.1	17.4	17.6	18.6	16.3	17.7	16.1	18.6	16.9	15.6
16.6	17.0	19.1	16.3	19.2	17.3	16.1	15.6	18.2	18.2

32. Compute the mode for the salaries in Table E.

33. In the last 5 years the year-to-year sales growth factors for Ahem, Inc., were 0.90, 1.20, 1.25, 1.04, and 1.38. (a) Compute the geometric mean of the growth factors. (b) Using the geometric mean computed in (a), what was Ahem's average percent change in year-to-year sales?

34. Six year-to-year percent changes in the gross national product (GNP) were 11.2, −3.7, 13.6, 17.7, 17.0, and −3.8 percent. (a) Compute the six growth factors. (b) Using the geometric mean of the growth factors, determine the average year-to-year percent change in the GNP.

✻ 4.9 THE STANDARD DEVIATION

When asked how he thought the stock market would perform in the coming year, a famous financier replied that "it will vary." One common characteristic of almost all data sets is that the numbers in the set vary. The arithmetic mean and a variability measure called the *standard deviation* are used extensively in descriptive statistics to summarize a mass of data; they are also used extensively in statistical inference.

The mean and the standard deviation summarize a mass of data.

Standard Deviation Formulas for Ungrouped Data

The difference between a number in a data set and the mean μ of the data set is called a *deviation*. A deviation shows how much a number varies from

TABLE 4.8
COMPUTING THE VARIANCE AND STANDARD DEVIATION OF DELIVERY TIMES
(Squared deviations method)

Delivery time, days, x	Deviation $x - \mu = x - 7$	Squared deviation $(x - \mu)^2$	
			Mean
			$\mu = \dfrac{\Sigma x}{N} = \dfrac{35}{5} = 7$
8	1	1	
9	2	4	**Variance**
6	−1	1	
4	−3	9	$\sigma^2 = \dfrac{\Sigma(x - \mu)^2}{N} = \dfrac{16}{5} = 3.20$
8	1	1	
$\Sigma x = 35$	0	16	
$N = 5$			**Standard deviation**
			$\sigma = \sqrt{\dfrac{\Sigma(x - \mu)^2}{N}} = \sqrt{3.2} = 1.79$ days

the mean. Thus,

$$\text{Deviation} = x - \mu$$

In Table 4.8, the x values are delivery times, in days, for five orders placed by a company with its supplier. The mean delivery time is $\mu = 7$ days, as shown in the table. The second column contains the deviations. We wish to obtain a summary measure of the deviations, but averaging them will not serve the purpose because $\Sigma(x - \mu)$ is always zero (the sum of the positive and the sum of the negative deviations are always equal).

Squaring removes the minus signs and leads to the positive numbers $(x - \mu)^2$ in the third column of the table.

We now average the squared deviations to obtain a variability measure called the *variance*, which is designated by σ^2. The symbol σ is the small Greek letter sigma. Thus,

Variance formula as the average of the squared deviations.

$$\sigma^2 = \frac{\Sigma(x - \mu)^2}{N}$$

Squaring enlarges deviations; so we compensate by taking the square root of the variance to obtain σ, the *standard deviation*.

Standard deviation computed by the squared deviation method

$$\sigma = \sqrt{\frac{\Sigma(x - \mu)^2}{N}}$$

Computations of the variance and standard deviation (the square root of the variance) are shown at the right in Table 4.8. We will demonstrate shortly how σ is used in descriptive statistics. And, as the book progresses, you will learn that σ plays an important role in statistical inference; there σ has the specialized meaning of being the standard deviation of a population. For the moment, we shall concentrate on computations of σ.

EXERCISE Calculate the variance and standard deviation of the data set 6, 4, 8, 10.

ANSWER Variance = $\sigma^2 = 5$; $\sigma = 2.24$.

Standard deviation computed by the average of squares method

The formula which *defines* σ calls for the computation of $(x - \mu)^2$. The simpler "average of squares" method does not require computations of the deviations. The formula is as follows:

$$\sigma = \sqrt{\frac{\Sigma x^2}{N} - \left(\frac{\Sigma x}{N}\right)^2}$$

Observe that the expression within the square root symbol is the *average of the squares of the data items minus the square of their average*. That is,

$$\frac{\Sigma x^2}{N}$$

is the average of the squares, and

$$\left(\frac{\Sigma x}{N}\right)^2 = \mu^2$$

is the square of the average.

Table 4.9 applies the average of squares method to the data of Table 4.8. You can see that the computation in Table 4.9 is simpler than that in Table 4.8. We often use one formula to define a measure (the squared deviation formula defines σ) and a different formula to simplify computations.

TABLE 4.9
STANDARD DEVIATION
(Average of squares method)

Delivery time, days, x	x^2
8	64
9	81
6	36
4	16
8	64
$\Sigma x = 35$	261

$N = 5 \qquad \mu = \dfrac{\Sigma x}{N} = \dfrac{35}{5} = 7$

Average of squares: $\dfrac{\Sigma x^2}{N} = \dfrac{261}{5} = 52.2$

Square of the average: $\left(\dfrac{\Sigma x}{N}\right)^2 = (7)^2 = 49$

$\sigma = \sqrt{\dfrac{\Sigma x^2}{N} - \left(\dfrac{\Sigma x}{N}\right)^2} = \sqrt{52.2 - 49}$

$\quad = \sqrt{3.2}$

$\quad = 1.79$

Approximating the Standard Deviation for Grouped Data

During a 3-month period, some of the machines in a factory had breakdowns causing "down times" during the working day. For example, the top row of Table 4.10 shows that on two occasions there were down times of under 10 minutes. We wish to approximate the standard deviation of down times.

TABLE 4.10
APPROXIMATING σ FOR GROUPED DATA
(Machine down times)

Down time, minutes	Frequency of occurrence f	Class mark x	fx	x^2	fx^2
0 and under 10	2	5	10	25	50
10 and under 20	6	15	90	225	1350
20 and under 30	16	25	400	625	10000
30 and under 40	12	35	420	1225	14700
40 and under 50	7	45	315	2025	14175
50 and under 60	4	55	220	3025	12100
60 and under 70	2	65	130	4225	8450
70 and under 80	1	75	75	5625	5625
	50		1660		66450

$$\frac{\Sigma fx}{\Sigma f} = \frac{1660}{50} = 33.2 \qquad \frac{\Sigma(fx^2)}{\Sigma f} = \frac{66450}{50} = 1329$$

$$\sigma \approx \sqrt{\frac{\Sigma(fx^2)}{\Sigma f} - \left(\frac{\Sigma fx}{\Sigma f}\right)^2} \approx \sqrt{1329 - (33.2)^2} \approx \sqrt{226.76} \approx 15.1 \text{ minutes}$$

We need to find the average of the squares and the square of the average.

To approximate the standard deviation of a set of grouped data, we shall use an average of squares type of calculation because it is simpler than the squared deviations procedure. First, we find the class marks (the averages of the class limits) and call them x, as shown in the third column of the table. You learned earlier in the chapter that μ is approximated for grouped data by the formula

$$\mu \approx \frac{\Sigma fx}{\Sigma f}$$

The formula represents a weighted average of the x values, with the weights being the frequencies. For Table 4.10, fx is shown in the fourth column, and $\mu \approx 33.2$.

Next, we compute the squares of the class marks shown in the x^2 column of Table 4.10. Then we compute a weighted average of these squares, again using the frequencies as weights. The calculation is

$$\frac{\Sigma(fx^2)}{\Sigma f} = \frac{66,450}{50} = 1329$$

Finally, we compute the (weighted) average of the squares minus the square of the (weighted) average, and take the square root. Thus,

$$\sigma \approx \sqrt{1329 - (33.2)^2} \approx \sqrt{226.76} \approx 15.1 \text{ minutes}$$

as shown in the table.

We have, in step-by-step fashion, made use of the formula

Standard deviation formula for grouped data

$$\sigma \approx \sqrt{\frac{\Sigma(fx^2)}{\Sigma f} - \left(\frac{\Sigma fx}{\Sigma f}\right)^2}$$

EXERCISE Approximate the standard deviation for the following frequency distribution.

Class	1 and under 3	3 and under 5	5 and under 7
Frequency	6	3	1

ANSWER $\sigma \approx 1.34$.

4.10 USING THE STANDARD DEVIATION

Normal Distribution Percents

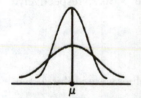

The mean is a measure of central tendency, and the standard deviation is a measure of variability around the mean. The two measures μ and σ are essential in describing normal distributions, and they are very useful for describing large data sets.

All normal distributions have bell-shaped graphs, but different values of μ or σ, or both, lead to different normal distributions. However, about 68 percent of every normal distribution lies in an interval extending from one standard deviation to the left of μ to one standard deviation to the right of μ, that is, in the interval $\mu \pm \sigma$, which is from

$$\mu - \sigma \qquad \text{to} \qquad \mu + \sigma$$

Same mean but different standard deviations

If the interval is extended to two standard deviations on either side of μ—that is, $\mu \pm 2\sigma$—about 95 percent of the distribution is in this interval. Finally, practically all (99.7 percent) of a normal distribution is in the $\mu \pm 3\sigma$ interval. The foregoing intervals and percents are illustrated in Figure 4.4. We shall refer to 68, 95, and 99.7 percent as the *normal percents* for their respective intervals as shown in Table 4.11.

Values of μ and σ together with the normal percents provide useful approximate descriptions for data sets whose distributions are unimodal

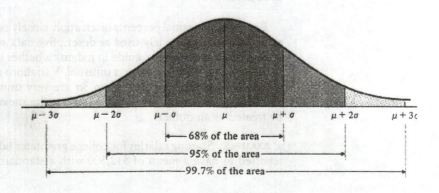

FIGURE 4.4
Normal distribution
percents.

TABLE 4.11
NORMAL PERCENTS

Interval	Normal percent in interval
$\mu \pm \sigma$	68
$\mu \pm 2\sigma$	95
$\mu \pm 3\sigma$	99.7

(have one mode). Of course, the closer the shape of a distribution is to the normal shape, the better the approximation. As an example, I calculated the mean and standard deviation of the percent returns on investment for 212 corporations and found them to be $\mu = 34.4$ and $\sigma = 30.7$, respectively. The interval $\mu \pm \sigma$ therefore is

$$34.4 \pm 30.7$$

or

$$3.7 \text{ to } 65.1$$

Then I counted and found that 151 of the 212 data values were in this $\mu \pm \sigma$ interval. This is

$$\frac{151}{212} = 0.712 \quad \text{or} \quad 71.2 \text{ percent}$$

compared with the normal figure of 68 percent. Similar calculations showed 94 percent were in the $\mu \pm 2\sigma$ interval and 99 percent were in the $\mu \pm 3\sigma$ interval, as compared with the respective normal figures 95 and 99.7 percent.

EXERCISE The down times in Table 4.10 have $\mu \approx 33.2$ minutes and $\sigma \approx$ 15.1 minutes. (a) Calculate the upper and lower values of the $\mu \pm 2\sigma$ interval. (b) Approximately what percent of down times are in the $\mu \pm 2\sigma$ interval?
ANSWER (a) 3 to 63.4. (b) The interval extends from a point in the first class to a point in the next-to-the-last class. We can obtain a low approximation by discarding the frequencies in the first and the last two classes. This leaves $^{45}/_{50}$, or 90 percent.

Because the normal percents often apply closely enough for practical purposes, μ and σ are widely used as descriptive data summaries. The normal percents also are a helpful guide in judging whether the variation of a particular data value from the mean is unusual. Variations of more than 2σ are unusual, and variations of more than 3σ are very unusual. A number that is more than three standard deviations from the mean of its data set should be treated as an outlier.

EXAMPLE Starting salaries for college graduates taking jobs in banking are reported to have a mean of $12,500 with a standard deviation of $700. (a)

Apply the normal percents to describe the salary distribution. (b) Would a salary of $14,000 be unusual?

SOLUTION   (a) We find the $\mu \pm 1\sigma$ limits to be $12,500 \pm \$700$, or from $11,800 to $13,200; these and the $\mu \pm 2\sigma$ and $\mu \pm 3\sigma$ limits are shown in Table 4.12. The intervals and the normal percents describe the distribution. (b) We first calculate $14,000 - \mu$ and find that $14,000 is $1500 above the mean. Dividing this deviation by σ, we have

$$\frac{\text{Deviation}}{\sigma} = \frac{1500}{700} = 2.1$$

This implies that $14,000 would be an unusually high salary because it is more than 2 standard deviations above the mean.

TABLE 4.12
NORMAL PERCENT INTERVALS

Sigma interval	Dollar interval	Normal percent in interval
$\mu \pm \sigma$	$11,800–$13,200	68
$\mu \pm 2\sigma$	11,100– 13,900	95
$\mu \pm 3\sigma$	10,400– 14,600	99.7

This is very important in statistical inference.

Expressing the deviation of an x value from the mean in terms of σ yields what is called a *z value* or a *standardized value of x*. That is, for data value x, the z value is

$$z = \frac{x - \mu}{\sigma}$$

Thus, in the foregoing,

$$z = \frac{14,000 - 12,500}{700} = \frac{1500}{700} = 2.1$$

and $z = 2.1$ means 14,000 is 2.1σ greater than μ.

EXERCISE An automatic machine can produce cylinders whose mean diameter is the machine setting, with a standard deviation of 0.2 mm (millimeters). (a) If the machine setting is 25.4 mm, apply the normal percents to describe the distribution of diameters of cylinders that will be produced. (b) What would be the consequence if the company owning the machine accepts a contract to make cylinders if the contract specifies that the diameter must be between 25.2 and 25.6 mm?

ANSWER

(a) Diameter interval	25.2–25.6	25.0–25.8	24.8–26.0
Percent of cylinders	68	95	99.7

(b) Only about 68 percent of the cylinders made would meet the specifications; so the remaining 32 percent would be defective.

The Chebyshev Inequality

The normal percent approximations do not work well for all data sets. In seeking a rule which does always apply, Chebyshev proved that *at least* three-fourths (75 percent) of the numbers in every data set are within 2 sigma of the mean of the data set. Also, at least eight-ninths of the numbers are always within 3σ of the mean. The rule leading to the three-fourths and eight-ninths is as follows:

The Chebyshev Inequality applies to every data set, no matter what its "shape" is.

Chebyshev inequality Let z be at least 1. Then, in any data set, the proportion of the data values lying in the interval $\mu \pm z\sigma$ is *at least* $1 - 1/z^2$.

Thus, relating $\mu \pm 2\sigma$ to $\mu \pm z\sigma$, we see that z is 2. Hence,

$$1 - \frac{1}{z^2} = 1 - \frac{1}{2^2} = 1 - \frac{1}{4} = \frac{3}{4}$$

so at least three-fourths of the values in any data set lie in the $\mu \pm 2\sigma$ interval.

EXERCISE   What statement can be made about the proportion of numbers in any arbitrary population lying in an interval extending (*a*) three standard deviations on both sides of the mean? (*b*) four standard deviations on both sides of the mean? (*c*) one standard deviation on both sides of the mean?

ANSWER   (*a*) At least $8/9$, or about 89 percent, lie in the interval; (*b*) at least $15/16$, or about 94 percent, lie in the interval; (*c*) at least 0, or 0 percent, lie in the interval. This result, while obviously true, is of no interest.

EXAMPLE   The college graduates hired by an accounting firm are paid a mean salary of \$16,000. The standard deviation of the salaries is \$800. Within what interval centered at the mean do at least 80 percent of the salaries lie?

SOLUTION   The Chebyshev inequality says "at least $1 - 1/z^2$." The example says "at least 80 percent." So the 80 percent, or 0.8, is $1 - 1/z^2$. Hence,

$$0.8 = 1 - \frac{1}{z^2}$$

$$\frac{1}{z^2} = 1 - 0.8 = 0.2$$

$$z^2 = \frac{1}{0.2} = 5$$

$$z = \sqrt{5} = 2.236$$

We find z must be 2.236, which means that $z\sigma$ is

$$2.236(\$800) = \$1789$$

The required interval $\mu \pm z\sigma$ is $\mu \pm 1789$; that is,

$16,000 \pm \$1789$ or $14,211 to \$17,789$

Rounded to three digits, the interval is \$14,200 to \$17,800.

EXERCISE Roadhug tires have a mean tread wear life of 22,000 miles and a standard deviation of 2000 miles. Within what interval centered at the mean do at least 60 percent of the wear lives lie? Round to three digits.
ANSWER 18,800 to 25,200 miles.

The advantage of the Chebyshev inequality is its generality. It holds true for all data sets; so it is worth knowing. The disadvantage of a Chebyshev "at least" statement is that it is not specific—at least 75 percent could be anything from 75 percent up to and including 100 percent.

4.11 EFFECT OF A CONSTANT ON μ AND σ

Consider the set of x values 2, 4, 6, 10, 13. Now add 3 to each x value to get the set of y values 5, 7, 9, 13, 16. Table 4.13 shows the calculation of the mean and the standard deviation of the x values and of the y values. We see that adding 3 to each of a set of numbers whose mean is 7 increases the mean to $7 + 3 = 10$. However, both sets of numbers deviate by the same amounts from their respective means; so the standard deviations of both sets are the same; $\sigma = 4$ in both cases.

TABLE 4.13
ADDING 3 INCREASES μ BY 3 BUT DOES NOT CHANGE σ

x	$x - \mu_x$	$(x - \mu_x)^2$	$y = x + 3$	$y - \mu_y$	$(y - \mu_y)^2$
2	−5	25	5	−5	25
4	−3	9	7	−3	9
6	−1	1	9	−1	1
10	3	9	13	3	9
13	6	36	16	6	36
35		80	50		80

$$\mu_x = \frac{35}{5} = 7 \qquad\qquad \mu_y = \frac{50}{5} = 10$$

$$\sigma_x = \sqrt{\frac{80}{5}} = \sqrt{16} = 4 \qquad\qquad \sigma_y = \sqrt{\frac{80}{5}} = \sqrt{16} = 4$$

EXERCISE Start with the numbers 5, 7, 9, 13, 16 which have $\mu = 10$, $\sigma = 4$. Now obtain a new data set by *multiplying* each of the given numbers by 2. Find μ and σ for the new data set.
ANSWER $\mu = 20$, $\sigma = 8$.

The last exercise demonstrates that multiplying the numbers in a data set by 2 will multiply the average and the standard deviation by 2. In general:

|6| = 6

|−6| = 6

If c is a constant number, positive or negative, then adding c to every number in a given data set will add c to the average of the given set but will not change the standard deviation. However, multiplying or dividing every number in a given set by c will multiply or divide the mean by c and standard deviation by $|c|$. (*Note:* If c is negative, $|c|$ means to discard the minus sign. The symbol $|c|$ is called the *absolute value* of c.)

EXAMPLE If the mean wage rate for production employees is $3.50 per hour with a standard deviation of $0.20, what would be the effect on the mean and standard deviation of raising all rates by 10 percent?

SOLUTION Here the mean will increase by 10 percent to

$$\mu = 1.10(\$3.50) = \$3.85$$

Note, however, that a 10 percent increase is not a constant increase because higher wage rates are increased more than lower rates. That is, increasing by 10 percent is equivalent to *multiplying by* $c = 1.10$. Hence, the new standard deviation will be

$$\sigma = 1.10(\$0.20) = \$0.22$$

so the new wage rates (for which $\sigma = \$0.22$) will vary more than the old rates (for which $\sigma = \$0.20$).

EXERCISE See the last example. What would be the effect of increasing all rates by 35 cents per hour?

ANSWER The new mean would be $3.85, but the standard deviation would remain at $0.20.

4.12 OTHER VARIABILITY INDICATORS

Mean absolute deviation (MAD)

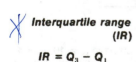

$$MAD = \frac{\Sigma|(x - \mu)|}{N}$$

Interquartile range (IR)

$$IR = Q_3 - Q_1$$

Range (R)

$$R = x_{max} - x_{min}$$

The Mean Absolute Deviation, Interquartile Range, and the Range

Analysts have a choice of methods for describing variability in a data set. One procedure starts as does the standard deviation calculation by finding the deviations $x - \mu$. Then minus signs are discarded and the deviations are averaged to obtain the *mean absolute deviation*—a measure which shows by how much, on the average, the numbers in a data set vary from their mean.

Another variability indicator is the difference between the third and first quartiles. This difference, $Q_3 - Q_1$, is called the *interquartile range*; it shows the interval width which contains the middle half of the data set.

The *range* of a data set—the difference between the largest and smallest number—also is an indicator of variability. I mention the foregoing because you may encounter them. However, statisticians prefer the standard deviation as a variability measure because of (1) its important role in statistical inference and (2) its applicability (as we have seen) to the problem of describing large data sets.

Relative Variability

The sizes of the variations in past prices of a stock are one indicator of the risk involved in buying the stock. If two stocks have average prices which are nearly the same, then the stock with the greater standard deviation would seem to be the riskier. However, if the average prices differ markedly, comparative risk is indicated by their *relative* variability as measured by their *coefficients of variation:*

$$\text{Coefficient of variation} = \frac{\sigma}{\mu}(100 \text{ percent})$$

This coefficient expresses σ as a percent of μ; so if the coefficient is, say, 30 percent, then σ is 30 percent as large as μ.

> **EXERCISE** The stock of Highprice, Inc., has been selling at a price averaging $\mu = \$250$ per share with $\sigma = \$40$. Lowprice, Inc., averages $\mu = \$20$ with $\sigma = \$5$. (a) Which stock has exhibited the greater variability? (b) Which stock seems to be the more risky?
>
> **ANSWER** (a) If we compare only standard deviations, then Highprice is much more variable than Lowprice. (b) The respective coefficients of variability for Highprice and Lowprice are 16 and 25 percent; so Lowprice appears to be the more risky stock.

4.13 PROBLEMS

1. (a) If μ and $\Sigma(x_i - \mu)$ are computed from all N numbers in a data set, what value will $\Sigma(x - \mu)$ have? (b) What is the relationship between the variance and the standard deviation?

2. Two companies reported net profit (percent of sales) for the last 5 years as follows:

Stable Co.	4.0	4.1	4.3	4.0	4.1
Gamble Co.	7.3	−3.7	8.4	−2.5	11.0

(a) Compute the average profit performance for each company. (b) What does comparison of the averages not disclose about the performances of the companies?

3. See Problem 2. Calculate the standard deviations for Stable Co. and Gamble Co. by the squared deviations method.

4. See Problem 2. Calculate the standard deviations for Stable Co. and Gamble Co. by the average of squares method.

5. Business experiences periods of expansion and contraction called business cycles. The National Bureau of Economic Research found that the durations of 10 cycles were 28, 36, 40, 64, 63, 88, 48, 58, 44, and 34 months. Compute the standard deviation of these cycle durations.

6. Salaries received by five graduates who had earned a master's degree

in accounting were, in thousands of dollars, 17, 18, 20, 21, and 24.
Compute the standard deviation of these salaries.

7. Weekly earnings of 50 manufacturing workers had a sum of $9000. The
sum of the squares of the 50 earnings was 1,643,408. Compute the
standard deviation of weekly earnings.

8. The data in Table A (arrayed in order of increasing size down the columns) were compiled from the 1975 issue of the *Statistical Abstract of
the United States*. (a) Compute μ and σ. (b) From the table, find what
percent of the numbers lie in the intervals $\mu \pm \sigma$, $\mu \pm 2\sigma$, $\mu \pm 3\sigma$. (c)
What percents are the normal percents for the intervals in (b)?

TABLE A
WEEKLY EARNINGS IN 110 METROPOLITAN AREAS (DOLLARS)

113	138	160	164	177	185	192	195	202	209	222
129	140	161	165	178	187	192	195	202	211	222
130	142	163	167	179	187	192	196	205	211	227
131	143	163	171	179	187	193	198	206	213	228
133	149	163	172	179	189	193	199	206	216	229
133	150	163	172	180	190	193	199	206	219	235
133	151	163	174	180	190	193	199	207	219	252
133	154	163	174	182	190	193	199	208	220	252
135	155	164	176	182	191	194	200	208	220	253
137	158	164	177	184	191	194	200	209	221	254

9. A bakery owner tabulated sales to 50 customers and obtained the distribution in Table B. Approximate the standard deviation of sales.

TABLE B

Sales in dollars	Number of customers
0.00–1.99	20
2.00–3.99	16
4.00–5.99	8
6.00–7.99	4
8.00–9.99	2

10. Mileage figures for 80 company-owned cars are shown in Table C.
Approximate the standard deviation of miles per gallon.

TABLE C

Miles per gallon	Number of cars
16.0–17.9	9
18.0–19.9	23
20.0–21.9	28
22.0–23.9	14
24.0–25.9	6

11. Weekly demand by a store's customers for Easy Crunch cereal averages 500 boxes, with a standard deviation of 100 boxes. Assuming the normal percents hold, describe the distribution of weekly demands.

12. A marketing consulting firm has in the past forecasted sales for hundreds of products. The firm states the average percent error in these forecasts was 1 percent. (a) Why might the reported average percent error be deceiving? (b) Suppose the standard deviation of the forecast errors was 5 percentage points. Assuming the normal percents hold, describe the distribution of forecast errors.

13. Gamma Company was concerned with the number of injuries to plant employees because summary data showed injuries were averaging $\mu = 5.2$ per 1000 labor-hours. Consequently, safety devices were installed on machines. In the following 1000 labor-hours there were 4 injuries, which implies that the devices have helped. What effect would the knowledge that the standard deviation of past injury ratios was 0.5 have upon the foregoing implication? Explain.

14. (a) State the Chebyshev inequality. (b) What is the advantage and the disadvantage of this inequality?

15. In the normal case, about 95 percent of the distribution lies in an interval extending 2 standard deviations on both sides of the mean. (a) What statement for this $\mu \pm 2\sigma$ interval can be made applying the Chebyshev inequality? (b) Does the Chebyshev statement allow for the chance that the $\mu \pm 2\sigma$ interval contains more than 95 percent of the population? Explain.

16. Salaries paid to professors in schools of management in a region of the country average $25,000 with a standard deviation of $4000. Assume no knowledge of the distribution of these salaries. Within what interval centered at the average did at least 50 percent of the salaries lie?

17. Property damage claims paid by a group of automobile insurance companies had a mean of $800 with a standard deviation of $400. Assuming no knowledge of the distribution of amounts paid, within what interval centered at the mean did at least two-thirds of the amounts fall?

18. Salaries paid last year to supervisors had a mean of $25,000 with a standard deviation of $2000. What will be the new mean and standard deviation if all salaries are (a) increased by $2500? (b) increased by 10 percent?

19. See Problem 18. If supervisors have been complaining about the disparity of salaries paid them, will a policy of raising all salaries by the same percent lessen the basis for this complaint? Explain.

20. (a) There are 1.609 km (kilometers) in a mile. Roadhug tires have tread lives averaging 22,000 miles and a standard deviation of 2000 miles. Express μ and σ in kilometers. (b) From (a) compute the coefficients of variability for tread life when expressed in miles and when expressed in kilometers.

21. A machine fills large and small boxes with rice. Amounts of fill for large

boxes average 907 grams with a standard deviation of 4 grams. Fills for small boxes average 227 grams with a standard deviation of 2 grams. (*a*) Compute the coefficients of variability for fills of large and small boxes. (*b*) Is the machine relatively more variable in filling large or small boxes?

4.14 SUMMARY

The *arithmetic mean* μ of a set of N values of x is

$$\mu = \frac{\Sigma x}{N}$$

The arithmetic mean is also called the arithmetic average, or simply the mean, or the average. The mean is the balance point of a frequency distribution graph. It has the total value property

$$\Sigma x = N\mu$$

Also, suppose one data set contains N_1 values with a mean of μ_1, and another data set contains N_2 values with mean μ_2. Next suppose the data sets are combined. Then

$$\mu \text{ (combined)} = \frac{N_1\mu_1 + N_2\mu_2}{N_1 + N_2}$$

If different values of x carry different weights w, the weighted average of the x values is

$$\mu(\text{weighted}) = \frac{\Sigma xw}{\Sigma w}$$

For grouped data—that is, data in a frequency distribution table—the class marks are taken as representative x values. The frequencies f are taken as weights. Then the average is approximated as

$$\mu(\text{grouped data}) \approx \frac{\Sigma fx}{\Sigma f}$$

The *median* is the 50-50 number in a data set. That is, about half the data numbers are below and half above the median. The median Md is determined by arraying a set of N data values in order of size. If N is odd, the median is the data value at position number $(N + 1)/2$ in the array. If N is even, the median is the average of the two middle numbers in the array.

For grouped data with a total frequency of N, the *median class* is the class in which the cumulative frequency first equals or exceeds $N/2$. The median is then approximated as

$$Md(\text{grouped data}) \approx L + \frac{r}{f}c$$

where L = lower limit of median class
  r = number of values needed from the median class to bring the cumulative frequency up to $N/2$
  f = frequency in the median class
  c = class interval

The mode Mo is the most frequently occurring number in a data set. Usually, the mode is computed from grouped data in which one class—the *modal* class—has the largest frequency. The formula is

$$Mo = L + \frac{d_1}{(d_1 + d_2)} c$$

where L = lower limit of the modal class
  d_1 = modal class frequency minus the frequency in the previous (smaller class limits) class
  d_2 = modal class frequency minus the frequency in the next (larger class limits) class
  c = class interval

The *geometric mean* (GM) is used to reduce the influence of large outliers in right-skewed distributions. The formula is

$$\text{GM} = \sqrt[N]{\text{product of } N \text{ values of } x} = (\text{product of } N \text{ values of } x)^{1/N}$$

The geometric mean should be used in computing an average period-to-period percent change, after each percent change has been converted to a growth factor.

The standard deviation σ of a data set measures the variability of the data values around their mean. The defining formula is

$$\sigma(\text{squared deviations method}) = \sqrt{\frac{\Sigma(x - \mu)^2}{N}}$$

Usually, it is easier to use the alternative formula

$$\sigma(\text{average of squares method}) = \sqrt{\frac{\Sigma x^2}{N} - \left(\frac{\Sigma x}{N}\right)^2}$$

For grouped data with class marks x and frequencies f, σ is approximated by

$$\sigma(\text{grouped data}) \approx \sqrt{\frac{\Sigma(fx^2)}{\Sigma f} - \left(\frac{\Sigma fx}{\Sigma f}\right)^2}$$

The square of the standard deviation of a data set σ^2 is called the *variance* of the data set.

For a normal distribution, the percents of all data values in the μ-centered intervals $\mu \pm \sigma$, $\mu \pm 2\sigma$, and $\mu \pm 3\sigma$ are, respectively, 68, 95, and 99.7 percent. These intervals and their percents also are used as approximate descriptive numbers for data sets which are unimodal (one mode) and not highly skewed.

Chebyshev's inequality can be used to describe any data set. It states that if we choose z to be a number which is 1 or greater, then the proportion of the data values falling in the interval $\mu \pm z\sigma$ is *at least* $1 - 1/z^2$.

4.15 REVIEW PROBLEMS

1. Write $\sum_{i=1}^{3} q_i$ in expanded form.
2. Write the indexed summation symbol representing

$$y_1 + y_2 + y_3 + \cdots + y_k$$

3. Given the (x_i, y_i) pairs (6, 3), (7, 4), (3, 2), (2, 1), compute (a) $\sum x_i$; (b) $\sum y_i^2$; (c) $(\sum y_i)^2$; (d) $\sum x_i y_i$.
4. Find the average time to assemble an engine if assembly times, in hours, for 10 engines were 3.2, 3.0, 2.8, 3.8, 2.7, 2.8, 3.1, 3.4, 2.5, 2.7
5. From Problem 4, find the median engine assembly time.
6. The average salary of the president and four vice presidents of a company is $50,000. The vice presidents' average salary is $45,000. What is the president's salary?
7. Average cost is $15 per unit when 99 units are produced and $15.40 when 100 units are produced. Find the marginal cost of the 100th unit.
8. A company which makes stereo receivers finds that average cost per unit decreases up to 3000 units produced, then increases. How must marginal cost behave? Explain.
9. A plumbing supply company has a pile of leftover scrap pipe ends weighing from 1 to 7 pounds each. (a) If the weights are uniformly distributed, what will be the median and average weights of the scrap ends? Why? (b) If a 1-pound piece and a 20-pound piece are added to the pile, what will happen to the average and median in (a)? Why?
10. A frequency distribution of balances of checking accounts in a bank is approximately exponential over the interval $0 to $5000. Would the median be less than, equal to, or greater than $2500? Why?
11. What is the connection between the fact that there is a minimum legal wage rate and the observation that wage distributions often are right-skewed?
12. A salesperson receives a year-end bonus if sales credited to that person average $50,000 per quarter or higher. The home office informs the salesperson that sales credited in the first three quarters have averaged $40,000 per quarter. What minimum sales must be credited in the fourth quarter if the bonus is to be received?
13. A student has grades of 68 on a 1-hour test and 65 on a 2-hour test. What grade does the student need on the 3-hour final to have a course grade of 80, assuming the course grade is computed as a weighted average using the hours allocated to the examinations as weights?
14. In 1 week a family buys 3 pounds of bananas at 30 cents per pound, 5 pounds of apples at 65 cents per pound, 4 pounds of citrus fruit at 70 cents per pound, and 2 pounds of miscellaneous fruit at 60 cents per pound. (a) Find the average price paid per pound of fruit bought. (b) In the next week, the price of bananas is down 20 percent, that of citrus fruit is up 20 percent, and other prices are the same. If the family buys the same quantities, find the average price per pound in the next week.

15. A company sells model 1 at $100 per unit, model 2 at $125 per unit, and model 3 at $175 per unit. Proportionate numbers of units sold are 0.5, 0.4, and 0.1, respectively, for models 1, 2, and 3. (*a*) Find the average selling price per unit. (*b*) Compute total dollar volume of sales if 1000 units (total, all models) are sold.

16. Suppose the company in Problem 15 raises the prices of models 1, 2, and 3 by 10, 15, and 20 percent, respectively, but proportionate sales remain the same. (*a*) Compute the new average selling price per unit. (*b*) Compute the percent change in average selling price per unit from the answers to Problems 15(*a*) and 16(*a*).

17. Approximate the average percent profit for companies in an industry from Table A.

TABLE A

Percent net profit	Number of companies
−3.00 and under −1.00	5
−1.00 and under 1.00	5
1.00 and under 3.00	25
3.00 and under 5.00	35
5.00 and under 7.00	15
7.00 and under 9.00	10
9.00 and under 11.00	5

18. Approximate the average amount of property damage per automobile accident from Table B.

TABLE B

Amount of property damage	Proportion of accidents
$ 0 and under $1000	0.60
1000 and under 2000	0.15
2000 and under 3000	0.09
3000 and under 4000	0.05
4000 and under 5000	0.05
5000 and under 6000	0.04
6000 and under 7000	0.02

19. Compute the average number of paid holidays per worker from Table C.

TABLE C

Number of paid holidays	Proportion of total workers having number of holidays
6	0.0750
7	0.0750
8	0.2500
9	0.2250
10	0.1875
11	0.1250
12	0.0625

20. Table D contains earnings per share for 55 corporations. (a) Find the median earnings per share. (b) Find the quartiles Q_1 and Q_3.

TABLE D

0.57	1.00	1.39	1.69	1.86	2.01	2.05	2.21	2.31	2.40	2.44
2.62	2.77	2.90	3.02	3.07	3.20	3.30	3.32	3.50	3.53	3.59
3.75	3.88	3.90	4.01	4.05	4.11	4.18	4.21	4.27	4.38	4.49
4.67	4.68	4.70	4.74	4.82	4.82	4.90	5.03	5.04	5.19	5.23
5.33	5.54	5.61	5.88	6.14	7.18	7.48	7.75	8.30	9.11	9.98

21. The durations of 12 business cycles in the United States from March 1919 to March 1974 were, in months, 28, 36, 40, 64, 63, 88, 48, 58, 44, 34, 117, and 52. Find the median duration of these cycles.

22. See Table A. Approximate the median percent net profit.

23. See Table A. Compute the mode for percent net profit.

24. A company's year-to-year percent changes in net profits were 30, −20, 40, 5, and 18 percent. (a) What are the growth factors corresponding to the percent changes? (b) Using the geometric mean of the growth factors, compute the average year-to-year percent change.

25. See Problem 21. Compute the standard deviation of the cycle durations.

26. The numbers of cars sold by a dealer in a 6-day period were 2, 8, 7, 8, 5, 10. Compute the standard deviation of car sales.

27. See Table A. Approximate the standard deviation of percent net profits.

28. See Table D. The sum of the numbers is 232.1. The sum of the squares of the numbers is 1183.0982. (a) Compute the standard deviation of the earnings per share. (b) What percent of the earnings per share lie in each of the following intervals: $\mu \pm \sigma$? $\mu \pm 2\sigma$? $\mu \pm 3\sigma$?

29. The wage rates paid production employees have a mean of $5.00 per hour and a standard deviation of $0.40 per hour. (a) Apply normal percents to describe the wage distribution. (b) Would $6.00 per hour be an unusually high wage rate? Explain.

30. Expenses of a company, as a percent of sales, have been fluctuating in a horizontal band with an average of 7.51 percent and a standard deviation of 0.3 percentage point. Would you, as an executive in charge of expense control, think that a current expense figure of 7.75 percent was high enough to warrant taking action? Explain.

31. Current wage rates average $\mu = \$5.00$ per hour with $\sigma = \$0.50$. What will be the new μ and σ if (a) all rates are increased by $0.40 per hour? (b) all rates are increased by 8 percent?

32. See Problem 31. (a) What is the current coefficient of variation? (b) What will be the resultant coefficient of variation if Problem 31(a) is carried out? (c) What will be the resultant coefficient of variation if Problem 31(b) is carried out?

33. Artificial diamonds made by a certain process have a mean weight of 1.2 carats with $\sigma = 0.4$ carat. According to the Chebyshev inequality, within what weight interval will at least 36 percent of the diamonds lie?

5

PROBABILITY

5.1 INTRODUCTION

Words implying probability, chance, or degrees of certainty and uncertainty abound in written and oral communication. Thus, on the evening newscast, the weather forecaster says there is a 60 percent chance of rain, but snow is virtually impossible. A commentator claims that political candidate Smith is almost certain to be elected. The sports announcer quotes odds of 7 to 5 that the Lions will win Saturday's football game, and the business analyst expresses the belief that there is an excellent chance that Smallfry Company will merge with Bigdeal Corporation.

Probability theory gives us methods of dealing with uncertainty—and uncertainty is an inherent part of the management decision-making process. For example, a decision to build a new manufacturing plant implies that the output of the plant can be sold in the quantity, and at a price, which will yield a satisfactory return on money invested. But the decision makers cannot be certain that their actions will prove to be correct. Managers who have a consistent record of correct decisions are said to have good judgment. And an important part of that good judgment is the ability to properly assess probabilities.

Probability comes into play when accountants test the adequacy of a firm's accounts receivable records by examining a small fraction of the thousands of accounts receivable; when contractors decide whether to assume the large cost of preparing a bid on a major contract which may be awarded to a competitor; when insurance companies establish the annual premium to be paid by the insured; when oil companies pay for the right to drill on a tract of land or sea bottom; when inspectors judge the quality of a plant's output after examining only a small fraction of its output; when personnel managers use tests in the selection of employees; when airlines predict what proportion of those who have made reservations will show up for the flight; when managers decide to introduce a new product; when sales are forecast; and so on and on. All the foregoing applications of probability, and others, will be discussed as we progress through the book.

In our study of probability, we shall concentrate most heavily on matters related to management. From time to time, however, we shall consider games of chance because they serve as an aid to understanding and they are fun. As a mental teaser, you may wish to think about the following game.

EXERCISE There are 30 students in a classroom (with no sets of twins). One student offers to bet $5 that at least two students in the room were born on the same day of the same month. What is the chance of winning this bet? (We shall solve this problem later in the chapter.)

5.2 MEANINGS AND SOURCES OF PROBABILITIES

Experiment and Event

To introduce some probability terms, suppose we plan to do something and we are not sure what the outcome will be. What we plan to do is called an

An **event** *is a possible outcome of an* **experiment.**

experiment. An outcome of an experiment is called an *event*. For example, suppose we plan to toss a coin and observe whether it lands heads up or tails up. If the coin lands on edge, it will be tossed again. Then the experiment is tossing a coin. One event is heads and the other event is tails. If the experiment is rolling a pair of dice and noting the sum of the spots on the two dice, the events are 2, 3, 4, . . . , 10, 11, 12.

Relative Frequency Definition of Probability

Most of us are comfortable with the idea that heads and tails have the same chance of occurring when a coin is tossed. We say heads and tails are *equally likely* because we assume they have the same chance of occurring. To convert the idea of equally likely into a numerical measure, we may say that there are two chances—one chance for heads and one chance for tails. Then heads (or tails) has one-half the total chances, and we measure this chance as the probability number

Equally likely *events have the same chance of occurring.*

$$\frac{1}{2} = 0.50 \quad \text{or} \quad 50 \text{ percent}$$

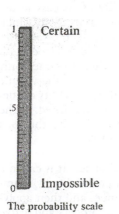

The probability scale

Statisticians usually express probabilities as decimal values or fractions. Managers, however, often use percents. Whatever the method of expression, the probability number scale is 0 through 1 (or, equivalently, 0 through 100 percent). The probability number 0 means impossible, and the number 1 means certain. Thus, getting both heads and tails in our coin-tossing experiment has a probability of 0—it is impossible. But getting either heads or tails has a probability of 1. The closer the probability of an event is to 1, the more likely it is to occur. The closer the probability of an event is to 0, the less likely it is to occur.

Each performance of an experiment is called a *trial*. Thus, one toss of a coin is a trial. The heads probability of 0.5 obviously does not tell us what will happen on a particular trial. What we mean by the 0.5 is that if a large number of trials is carried out, the proportion (relative frequency) of heads occurring will be very near 0.5. The "large number of trials" meaning is expressed by defining the probability of an event as the relative frequency of occurrence of the event "over the long run," that is, a very large number of trials.

Probabilities *may be computed as relative frequencies.*

In business, the relative frequency of an event in the past often is taken as the probability of that event. For example, suppose records show that on 180 of the past 200 selling days, a supermarket sold from 225 to 300 quarts of milk. Then the probability of the sales event "225 to 300 quarts" is taken as

$$\frac{180}{200} = 0.90$$

Again, suppose that 400 of 50,000 fire-insured houses had a fire. A fire insurance company would then take

$$\frac{400}{50,000} = 0.008$$

as the probability of fire.

The "relative frequency over the long run" meaning of probability has been in use for about 150 years. However, in the past few decades the decision-making thrust of statistics in business and other fields has given rise to a "degree-of-belief" meaning of probability. To distinguish between the two meanings, the term *objective* probability is used to refer to probabilities for games of chance, or probabilities computed from recorded data. Degree-of-belief probabilities are called *subjective* probabilities.

Subjective Probabilities

A problem with the long-run relative frequency definition of probability is that it seems to imply that probability can play no part in a chance situation that occurs only once. The fact of the matter, however, is that probability does play a part in one-time decisions. For example, suppose we have an opportunity to invest $50 in a venture which will yield a payoff of $1000 if it is successful. We would certainly consider the probability of success in deciding whether to make the investment, even if the opportunity is one which will not occur again. Most of us would be eager to make such an investment if we think there is a 50 percent chance of success. We would be less eager if the chance was smaller. Management decisions usually are of this once-only type. Thus, the decision to introduce a new product occurs in the unique environment of the time when the decision is made; if the probability of success is judged to be sufficiently high, the product will be marketed. If the product is not marketed, it may never be marketed. Clearly, this is a once-only type of decision in which probability plays a role.

A subjective probability is judgmental and expresses a degree of belief . . .

. . . but it may be the only information that is available.

The probability of success assessed by a marketing executive is an expression of the executive's degree of certainty or degree of belief. It is called a *subjective* probability. The executive arrives at such a probability by examining available information in the light of past experience, and then applying judgment. Another executive might follow the same process and arrive at a different probability. Executives use relative frequency (objective) probabilities when they are available. But often a decision situation is unique, so that objective probabilities are not available; then subjective probabilities have to be used. I hasten to add that the rules of probability which will be developed apply to both objective and subjective probabilities.

Probability and Odds

If we believe event A is twice as likely to occur as event B, we can express that belief by saying the "odds" are 2 to 1 for A. This corresponds to saying there are three chances—2 for A and 1 for B. Then,

$$\left[\text{Probability of } A = \frac{\text{chances for } A}{\text{total chances}} = \frac{2}{3} \right]$$

Similarly,

$$\text{Probability of } B = \frac{\text{chances for } B}{\text{total chances}} = \frac{1}{3}$$

$P(A) + P(B) = 1$

Odds of a to b mean
a probability of

$$\frac{a}{a+b}$$

Hence, if we call the odds numbers "chances," then odds can be converted to probabilities on the 0 to 1 scale by dividing the chances for the event by the total chances.

$0 \leq p \leq 1$

EXERCISE Suppose a person who has applied for a job believes the odds for getting the job are 10 to 1. What is the probability of getting the job?
ANSWER $^{10}/_{11}$, or about 0.91.

Many people find it easier to think first in terms of odds when assessing a subjective probability—and then convert to a probability. If you find it natural to think in terms of odds, you should be careful to distinguish between odds as we have just discussed them and *betting* odds. The betting odds in a commercial gambling establishment do not express a player's chances of winning and losing. Instead, they express the amount a player may win and the amount the player may lose. For example, betting odds of 7 to 1 mean that the player may win \$7 or lose \$1. Casinos and other gambling establishments set betting odds so that the establishment will make a profit. The probability of winning cannot be determined from betting odds.

Betting odds can't
be converted to a
probability.

EXERCISE What number would you assign as the probability that you will receive a grade of B minus, or higher, in statistics? Is this probability objective or subjective? Why?

5.3 PROBABILITY REQUIREMENTS

Mutually Exclusive, Collectively Exhaustive Events

(ayrık)

If only one of two or more events can occur, the events are called *mutually exclusive* events. For example, in our coin-tossing experiment, the two events, heads and tails, are mutually exclusive: if one occurs, the other cannot occur. On the other hand, the events "subscribe to *The New York Times*," "subscribe to *Fortune*," and "subscribe to *The National Geographic*" are not mutually exclusive—subscribing to one does not exclude subscribing to another.

When a set of events for an experiment includes every possible outcome, the set is said to be *collectively exhaustive*. Thus, heads and tails are a collectively exhaustive set of events for our coin-tossing experiment. One requirement we place on probability numbers is that the sum of the probabilities for a collectively exhaustive set of mutually exclusive events be equal to 1. Or, in everyday language, we could say that the sum of the probabilities for *all* the *different* events that can occur must be equal to 1. Another requirement is that a probability be a number on the scale from 0 through 1.

Probabilities that sum
to 1.

EXERCISE   A weather forecaster says the probability of rain tomorrow is 0.60. What must be the forecaster's probability that it will not rain?

ANSWER   0.40 because rain and not rain are mutually exclusive and collectively exhaustive—so the sum of the two probabilities must equal 1.

Simple Random Selection

A *population* consists of all *elements* of a specified type. For example, all the houses in a town constitute a population of houses; a particular house is an element of that population. Similarly, a 52-card bridge deck is a population of cards; a particular card is an element of that population. If we shuffle the deck of cards well, we assume that every card has the same chance of being the top card. The "same chance" assumption is called the assumption of *equal likelihood*. Because there are 13 spades in the deck, there are 13 chances in 52 chances that the top card of a shuffled deck will be a spade. The probability of the event "spade on top" then is

$$\frac{13}{52} = \frac{1}{4}$$

However, card players would hesitate to assign the ¼ probability unless the deck was shuffled thoroughly enough to make the equal-likelihood assumption reasonable.

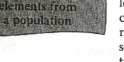

Key concept:

The random selection of elements from a population

A *selection process in which every element in a population has the same* probability of being chosen is called *simple random* selection. A common example is the card illustration above; another is mixing numbered lottery tickets and then selecting one ticket. Probability theory—and its applications—require that chance alone determines which element is selected from a population. Simple random selection is one way to ensure that chance determines selection. Usually, for brevity, we will use the word random by itself to mean simple random selection. For example, a worker selected "at random" will mean a worker chosen by simple random selection. You may think of the selection process as drawing from a well-shuffled deck of workers' personnel cards.

5.4 EVENT PROBABILITY SYMBOLS

We shall introduce probability symbols by reference to Table 5.1, which shows a classification of all workers in a firm (a population). The performance of each worker has been rated by a supervisor as high (H), average (A), or low (L). Additionally, employees have taken a job aptitude test and have been classified as qualify (Q) or fail (F). Table 5.1 shows that the total number of workers is 400. Classified by test result, 300 qualified and 100 failed. Classified by performance, 190 were high, 120 average, and 90 low. The upper left-hand corner entry shows that 150 workers were high performers and qualified on the test, and similarly for the other entries in the table. Later in this chapter we shall analyze such a table and draw conclu-

TABLE 5.1

TEST RESULT AND JOB PERFORMANCE FOR
400 WORKERS

Test result	Performance on job			
	High (*H*)	Average (*A*)	Low (*L*)	Total
Qualify (*Q*)	150	90	60	300
Fail (*F*)	40	30	30	100
Totals	190	120	90	400

sions about the usefulness of a test as a predictor of job performance, but our purpose here is simply to use the tabulated data to introduce probability terminology.

P(X) is the probability that event X will occur as the result of a single trial.

The symbol $P(\ )$ means the probability of the event specified in the parentheses. Thus, $P(A)$ is the probability that an employee selected at random is average in performance. Table 5.1 shows that 120 of the 400 are average; so

$$P(A) = \frac{120}{400} = 0.30$$

Similarly, $P(Q)$ is the probability that a randomly selected worker qualified on the test, and

$$P(Q) = \frac{300}{400} = 0.75$$

EXERCISE What does $P(H)$ mean for the data in Table 5.1? Compute $P(H)$.
ANSWER $P(H)$ is the probability that a randomly selected worker is a high performer. $P(H) = 0.475$.

5.5 JOINT EVENTS

If we draw a horizontal line through the second row of Table 5.1 and a vertical line down through the first column, the lines intersect at the entry 40. This is the number of workers who *both* failed on the test *and* are good workers. We shall use the symbol *FH* to mean both *F and H*. Notice that the intersection of *F* and *H* is the same as the intersection of *H* and *F*. Hence,

$$P(FH) = P(HF)$$

A joint event is the occurrence of two or more events in one trial.

We refer to·*FH* as the *joint* event *F* and *H*. We find

$$P(FH) = \frac{40}{400} = 0.10$$

Similarly,

$$P(QL) = \frac{60}{400} = 0.15$$

$P(QF) = 0 =)$

EXERCISE See Table 5.1. Write the symbol for, and the value of, the probability that a randomly selected worker will be a low performer and will have failed the test.

ANSWER $P(LF) = P(FL) = 0.075$.

5.6 MUTUALLY EXCLUSIVE EVENTS

Two mutually exclusive events cannot both occur in one trial.

Events which cannot happen together are called *mutually exclusive* events or *disjoint* events. Hence, for any two events X and Y,

If X and Y are mutually exclusive, then $P(XY) = 0$.

Notice that in Table 5.1 the "qualify" and "fail" rows do not intersect. A worker cannot both qualify on the test *and* fail the test. Therefore, Q and F are mutually exclusive; so

$$P(QF) = 0$$

EXERCISE If you toss two coins, you will get 0, 1, or 2 heads. Are 0, 1, or 2 heads mutually exclusive events? Why?

5.7 CONDITIONAL PROBABILITY

Suppose a supervisor tells us that a particular worker is a low performer. What then is the probability that this worker failed the test? In Table 5.1 we have now restricted our population to only those of the 400 workers who are low performers. There are 90 low performers. Of these, 30 failed the test; so the desired probability is $^{30}/_{90} = ^1/_3$. We describe the $^1/_3$ as the probability of failing *given* that the worker is a low performer, and symbolize *given* by a vertical line. Thus,

$$P(F|L) = \frac{30}{90} = \frac{1}{3} \quad \text{or about } 0.333$$

P(X|Y) is the probability that event X will occur, given that event Y has already occurred.

$P(F|L)$ is called the *conditional* probability of F given L because it is computed under the condition that L has occurred. On the other hand, the conditional probability of L given F is $P(L|F) = ^{30}/_{100} = 0.300$. Note that

$$P(L|F) = 0.300$$

and

$$P(F|L) = 0.333$$

are not equal. You could devise a table containing events X and Y where $P(X|Y)$ equals $P(Y|X)$; but usually $P(X|Y)$ does not equal $P(Y|X)$.

EXERCISE See Table 5.1. State the meaning, and compute the value, of $P(H|Q)$.

ANSWER $P(H|Q)$ is the probability that a worker is a high performer, given that the worker qualified on the test. $P(H|Q) = 0.50$.

5.8 THE PROBABILITY OF *X* OR *Y*

By the event *X* or *Y* we mean *X* or *Y* or both *X and Y*. For example, in Table 5.1, the event *Q* or *H* includes workers who qualified on the test, workers who were high performers, and workers who qualified *and* were high performers. The number of workers in the event *Q* or *H* is the number of *Q*'s (300), plus the number of *H*'s (190), minus the number at the intersection *QH* (150). The number at the intersection is subtracted because it has been counted twice—once with the *Q*'s and once with the *H*'s. Hence,

Is it true that P(H or Q) equals P(Q or H)? Try it.

$$ \cancel{X} \quad P(Q \text{ or } H) = \frac{300 + 190 - 150}{400} = \frac{340}{400} = 0.85 \qquad \overbrace{P(H \text{ and } Q)} $$

Of course, there are zero joint occurrences of mutually exclusive events; so, for example,

$$ P(H \text{ or } A) = \frac{190 + 120 - 0}{400} = \frac{310}{400} = 0.775 $$

EXERCISE See Table 5.1. (*a*) What is *P(Q or L)*? (*b*) What is *P(Q or F)*?
ANSWER (*a*) 0.825; (*b*) 1.

5.9 PROBLEMS

1. Distinguish between objective and subjective probabilities.
2. Cite an example of (*a*) an objective probability; (*b*) a subjective probability.
3. Convert the following odds to probabilities. (*a*) 4 to 1; (*b*) 7 to 9; (*c*) 11 to 9; (*d*) 7 to 4.
4. What is meant by betting odds?
5. All 600 employees of a firm were asked if they would favor cutting their lunch hour by $1/2$ hour so that they could leave work that much earlier. The results are shown in Table A, where we see, for example, that 204 employees were women who favored the proposal. Find the following probabilities. (*a*) *P(D)*; (*b*) *P(W)*; (*c*) *P(WF)*; (*d*) *P(FD)*; (*e*) *P(NM)*; (*f*) *P(MN)*; (*g*) *P(MW)*; (*h*) *P(F|M)*; (*i*) *P(M|F)*; (*j*) *P(D|W)*; (*k*) *P(W|N)*; (*l*) *P(M or F)*; (*m*) *P(F or D)*; (*n*) *P(M or W)*; (*o*) *P(W or N)*.

TABLE A

	Favor (F)	Disfavor (D)	Neutral (N)
Men (M)	84	12	24
Women (W)	204	180	96

6. See Table A. (*a*) If a randomly selected employee is a man, what is the probability that the employee is neutral? (*b*) What is the symbol for the probability in (*a*)?

5.10 A PROBABILITY TABLE

Applied probability problems are solved by means of a few basic rules for obtaining desired probabilities from available probabilities. Use of these rules also ensures that the probabilities in a problem are internally consistent, for example, that we do not get negative probabilities, or probabilities greater than 1, or different probabilities for the same event. In the coming sections we shall illustrate the relationships among probabilities by reference to Table 5.2. It contains the data of Table 5.1 in black print, and in color the probabilities obtained by dividing each black number by the overall total, 400. For example, Table 5.1 showed that 150 of the 400 qualified on the test and were high performers; this leads to $P(QH) = {}^{150}/_{400} = 0.375$ as shown in the upper left corner of Table 5.2.

TABLE 5.2
TEST RESULT AND JOB PERFORMANCE PROBABILITIES

Test result	Performance on job							
	High (H)		Average (A)		Low (L)		Total	
	No.	Prob.	No.	Prob.	No.	Prob.	No.	Prob.
Qualify (Q)	150	0.375	90	0.225	60	0.150	300	0.750
Fail (F)	40	0.100	30	0.075	30	0.075	100	0.250
Total	190	0.475	120	0.300	90	0.225	400	1.000

5.11 RULE FOR P(X OR Y)

Rule: $P(X \text{ or } Y) = P(X) + P(Y) - P(XY)$

Recall: X or Y means event X occurs, or event Y occurs, or both occur.

To illustrate this rule, refer to Table 5.2. Recall that the number of workers who fail *or* are low performers can be found by adding the total number who fail to the total number who are low, and then subtracting the doubly counted number who fail *and* are low. The net result divided by 400 is $P(F \text{ or } L)$. Thus,

$$P(F \text{ or } L) = \frac{100 + 90 - 30}{400}$$

Breaking the last fraction into parts, we have

$$P(F \text{ or } L) = \frac{100}{400} + \frac{90}{400} - \frac{30}{400}$$

$$= 0.250 + 0.225 - 0.075$$

$$= P(F) + P(L) - P(FL)$$

$$= 0.400$$

which illustrates that the probability of F or L is found by adding $P(F)$ to $P(L)$ and then subtracting the probability of the joint event, $P(FL)$.

For mutually exclusive events X and Y we have:

Rule (mutually exclusive events): $P(X \text{ or } Y) = P(X) + P(Y)$

Recall: For mutually exclusive events X and Y, we have P(XY) = 0.

For example, from Table 5.2,

$$P(H \text{ or } A) = P(H) + P(A) - P(HA)$$
$$= P(H) + P(A) - 0$$
$$= 0.475 + 0.300$$
$$= 0.775$$

EXAMPLE A political candidate runs for two offices, A and B. The candidate assesses the chance of winning A at 0.30, of winning B at 0.40, and of winning both at 0.10. What is the probability that the candidate wins office A or B?

SOLUTION We have

$$P(A \text{ or } B) = P(A) + P(B) - P(AB)$$
$$= 0.30 + 0.40 - 0.10$$
$$= 0.60$$

EXERCISE A contractor bids on two contracts, *A* and *B*, assessing the chances of winning at 0.5 and 0.6 for *A* and *B*, respectively, and the chance of winning both at 0.2. What is the chance of winning *A* or *B*?
ANSWER 0.90.

One reason for understanding probability rules is to ensure the internal consistency of probability assignments. For example, suppose the contractor of the last exercise had assessed probabilities for A, B, and both A and B at, respectively, 0.6, 0.8, and 0.2. Then $P(A \text{ or } B) = 0.6 + 0.8 - 0.2 = 1.2$, which would indicate that a reassessment is required because a probability cannot exceed 1.

Assessed probabilities are subjective probabilities.

5.12 RULES FOR CONDITIONAL AND JOINT EVENT PROBABILITIES

Conditional Probabilities

Rule: $P(Y|X) = \dfrac{P(XY)}{P(X)}$

The rule states that the probability of one event, given that another event has occurred, is the probability of the joint event divided by the probability of the given event.

Figure 5.1 will help you understand this rule. In this figure, called a *Venn diagram*, the probability of X is represented by the area of one circle and P(Y) by the area of the other. Here we see that if X has occurred, the total probability at hand is the area of the X circle. Then the chance that Y occurs, given X, is the fraction of X which is also Y, that is, P(XY)/P(X).

FIGURE 5.1
Venn diagram. Circles
are events, areas are
probabilities:

$$P(Y|X) = \frac{P(XY)}{P(X)}$$

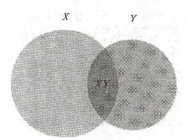

To illustrate the rule numerically, note in Table 5.2 that

$$P(L|F) = \frac{30}{100} = 0.30$$

or

$$P(L|F) = \frac{P(LF)}{P(F)} = \frac{0.075}{0.250} = 0.30$$

EXAMPLE In a firm, 20 percent of the employees have accounting backgrounds, while 5 percent of the employees are executives and have accounting backgrounds. If an employee has an accounting background, what is the probability that the employee is an executive?

SOLUTION Here we let A and E mean, respectively, accounting background and executive. We have P(A) = 0.20 and P(AE) = 0.05. We are looking for P(E given A). Hence,

$$P(E|A) = \frac{P(AE)}{P(A)} = \frac{0.05}{0.20} = 0.25$$

EXERCISE In the last example, suppose we know also that 8 percent of employees are executives. Write the symbolic rule for, and calculate the value of, the probability that an employee has an accounting background if the employee is an executive.
ANSWER P(A|E) = P(AE)/P(E), which is 0.625.

$$P(E|A) = \frac{P(AE)}{P(A)}$$

Joint Event Probabilities

If we take the rule

$$P(Y|X) = \frac{P(XY)}{P(X)}$$

and multiply both sides by $P(X)$, we get $P(Y|X)P(X) = P(XY)$. The last gives the rule for finding the probability of the joint event XY. Thus,

Rule: $P(XY) = P(X)P(Y|X)$

The rule says that the probability that both of two events occur is the probability that the first event occurs times the probability that the second event occurs given that the first has occurred. Recall also that $P(XY) = P(YX)$. Therefore,

$$P(XY) = P(YX) = P(Y)P(X|Y)$$

To illustrate the rule, note in Table 5.2 that

$$P(FL) = 0.075$$

We obtain the same result by applying the rule with $P(F) = 0.25$ and $P(L|F) = {}^{30}/_{100} = 0.30$. Thus,

$$P(FL) = P(F)P(L|F)$$
$$= (0.25)(0.30)$$
$$= 0.075$$

EXAMPLE   The probability that it will be colder tomorrow is 0.6 and the probability it will snow if it gets colder is 0.7. What is the probability that it will be colder and snow tomorrow?

SOLUTION   Letting S and C represent, respectively, snow and colder, we have $P(C) = 0.6$, $P(S|C) = 0.7$, and we want $P(SC)$, the probability of snow and colder. If we write

This is why you should remember that P(SC) = P(CS).

$$P(SC) = P(S)P(C|S)$$

we note that $P(S)$ and $P(C|S)$ are not available. Hence, we write

$$P(SC) = P(CS) = P(C)P(S|C)$$
$$= (0.6)(0.7) = 0.42$$

EXERCISE   A contractor has bid on two contracts, *A* and *B*. The probability of winning *A* is assessed at 0.5 and the probability of winning *B* if *A* is won is 0.7. Write the symbols for the rule, and compute the probability that the company wins both contracts.
ANSWER $P(AB) = P(A)P(B|A) = 0.35$.

EXAMPLE   A box contains 10 items, 3 of which are defective and 7 are good. Two items are selected. What is the probability that the *first* is good and the *second* defective?

To start, we have:

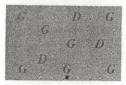

$P(G) = 7/10$
$P(D) = 3/10$

After a good is chosen, we have:

$P(G|G) = 6/9$
$P(D|G) = 3/9$

SOLUTION Here we could specify order by writing G_1D_2, letting the subscripts mean first good, second defective. More simply, we can let the sequence in which the symbols appear represent the order. Thus, GD means first good, second defective. Then, in the rule for the joint event,

$$P(GD) = P(G)P(D|G)$$

the right-hand side means the probability that the *first* is good times the probability that the *second* is defective *given* that the first is *good*. Inasmuch as there are 7 good in 10, the probability of the first being good is $7/10$. Given this has happened, there remain 9 items of which 3 are defective. So the probability of getting a defective if a good has been drawn, $P(D|G)$, is $3/9$. Hence,

$$P(GD) = \frac{7}{10} \cdot \frac{3}{9} = \frac{7}{30} = 0.233$$

The example is typical of a large class of problems in which joint probabilities are computed by chain multiplication of conditional probabilities. Thus, $P(GGG)$, the probability that three selected items all will be good, is computed by setting the probability that the first is good at $7/10$. Of the remaining 9, there are now 6 good; so the probability that the second is good if a good has been drawn is $6/9$. Of the remaining 8, 5 are good; so the probability that the third is good if two goods have been drawn is $5/8$. Hence,

$$P(GGG) = \frac{7}{10} \cdot \frac{6}{9} \cdot \frac{5}{8} = \frac{7}{24} = 0.292$$

Note that we can write $P(GGG)$ as

$$P(GGG) = P(G)P(G|G)P(G|GG)$$

EXERCISE A store receives 50 stereo sets from a supplier. Four of the sets, selected at random, are tested for defects. If all four are satisfactory (no defects), the store accepts the entire shipment of 50. Otherwise, the store returns the shipment to the supplier. Suppose the shipment contains 5 sets which have defects. (a) What is the probability that the shipment is accepted by the store? (b) What is the probability that, in the inspected sets, the first two inspected will have defects and the second two will not have defects?
ANSWER (a) 0.647; (b) 0.00716.

Independent and Dependent Events

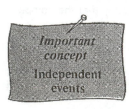

Important concept

Independent events

Two events are independent if the probability that one event occurs is not affected by the occurrence of the other event. In that case $P(Y|X)$ is the same as $P(Y)$, and $P(X|Y)$ is the same as $P(X)$. To illustrate this basic idea, suppose we select a card at random from a 52-card bridge deck. The deck has four kings; so the probability of a king is

$$P(K) = \frac{4}{52} = \frac{1}{13}$$

Now suppose someone selects a card and informs us that the card is black. There are 2 kings in the 26 black cards; so

$$P(K|B) = \frac{2}{26} = \frac{1}{13}$$

which is the same as $P(K)$. Thus, the information that the card was black (that is, given black) does not affect the probability that the card is a king. Hence, king and black are independent because

$$P(K|B) = P(K)$$

Also note that 26 of the 52 cards are black; so $P(B) = {}^{26}/_{52} = {}^{1}/_{2}$. Now if we are informed that a selected card is a king, there are 2 black kings among the 4 kings; so $P(B|K) = {}^{1}/_{2}$, which is the same as $P(B)$. Hence, black and king are independent because

$$P(B|K) = P(B)$$

The foregoing brings out the meaning of independence. That is, the probability that the chosen card is a king is not affected by knowing the card is black. And the probability that the card is black is not affected by knowing it is a king. However, the most useful rule for determining whether or not X and Y are independent—or for computing $P(XY)$ when X and Y are independent—is

Rule (independent events): $P(XY) = P(X)P(Y)$

To see where this rule comes from, write the general rule for the probability of XY as follows:

$$P(XY) = P(X)P(Y|X)$$

X and Y are independent if

$P(XY) = P(X)P(Y)$

or if

$P(X|Y) = P(X)$

Now if X and Y are independent, $P(Y|X) = P(Y)$. Then the last expression for $P(XY)$ becomes

$$P(XY) = P(X)P(Y)$$

The rule for independence can be used to test for independence. For example, refer to Table 5.2 and note that $P(A) = 0.30$, $P(F) = 0.250$, and $P(AF) = 0.075$. If we multiply $P(A)$ by $P(F)$, we obtain

$$P(A)P(F) = (0.30)(0.250) = 0.075$$

and 0.075 is $P(AF)$. Hence,

$$P(AF) = P(A)P(F)$$

so A and F are independent. This means that knowing a worker failed the test has no effect upon the probability that the worker is an average performer, and vice versa.

Events X and Y are *dependent* (not independent) if $P(XY)$ does not equal $P(X)P(Y)$. Thus, in Table 5.2, $P(F) = 0.25$, $P(H) = 0.475$, and $P(FH) = 0.100$. But

$$P(F)P(H) = (0.25)(0.475) = 0.11875$$

which is not the same as $P(FH) = 0.100$. Hence, fail the test and high performer are dependent. To see the nature of the dependence, note from Table 5.2 that

$$P(H) = 0.475$$

$$P(H|F) = \frac{40}{100} = 0.400$$

The last says the probability that a worker selected from the population of 400 is a high performer is 0.475. But if the worker failed the test, the probability of high performance is a lower value, 0.400.

EXERCISE See Table 5.2. State whether the following pairs of events are independent or dependent. If the events are dependent, describe the nature of the dependence. (a) A and Q. (b) L and F.

ANSWER (a) Independent. (b) Dependent. The probability of low performance is 0.225. But the probability of low performance given that the worker failed the test is a larger value, 0.300.

5.13 COMPLEMENTARY EVENTS

Meaning of Complementary Events

Venn diagram of all possible events

Let X' (X prime) mean the event "not X." Then in an experiment, X and X' complement each other in the sense that if one does not occur the other must occur. Hence, $P(X) + P(X') = 1$; so

$$P(X') = 1 - P(X) \qquad \text{or} \qquad P(X) = 1 - P(X')$$

The events X and X' are called *complementary* events. Thus, if the probability that it will rain is $P(R) = 0.80$, then the probability that it will not rain is

$$P(R') = 1 - P(R) = 1 - 0.80 = 0.20$$

EXERCISE Let S mean snow tomorrow and C mean colder tomorrow. (a) What would be meant by the event $S'C'$? (b) $S'C'$ is the complement of what event? That is, if $S'C'$ does not occur, what must occur?

ANSWER (a) Not snow *and* not colder. (b) If $S'C'$ does not occur, it must snow or get colder, or both. Thus, the complement of $S'C'$ is S or C, which contains SC, SC', and $S'C$.

	C	C'
S	SC	SC'
S'	$S'C$	$S'C'$

The Probability of at Least One Occurrence in Repeated Trials

Applied problems often involve experiments in which repeated trials are made and interest centers on the number of occurrences of some event. The numbers of occurrences are 0, 1, 2, 3, and so on. *At least one occurrence* means one or more occurrences, that is, 1, 2, 3, and so on occurrences. The complement of "at least one occurrence" is 0 occurrence. Hence,

$$P(\text{at least one occurrence}) = 1 - P(0 \text{ occurrence})$$

EXAMPLE Suppose we inspect four batteries selected at random from a box of 24 batteries. We will refuse to buy the box (reject it) if one or more of the inspected batteries is defective. Then suppose the box contains 3 defective and 21 good batteries. The probability of rejecting the box is

$$P(\text{at least one defective in 4}) = 1 - P(0 \text{ defective in 4})$$

Now, 0 defective in 4 means that all four are good, that is, GGGG. Hence,

Make sure you understand how I got P(GGGG).

$$P(\text{at least one defective}) = 1 - P(GGGG)$$

$$= 1 - \left(\frac{21}{24}\right)\left(\frac{20}{23}\right)\left(\frac{19}{22}\right)\left(\frac{18}{21}\right)$$

$$= 1 - 0.563$$

$$= 0.437$$

In the example, note that using the complement made it unnecessary to compute the probabilities of 1, 2, 3, or 4 defectives. Instead, we had only to compute the single probability $P(0) = P(GGGG)$ and subtract it from 1.

EXERCISE If three cards are dealt from a bridge deck, what is the probability that at least one will be an ace?
ANSWER 0.217.

Complementary Events Conditioned on the Same Event

In an experiment, Y or its complement Y' must occur. That is, $P(Y) + P(Y') = 1$. Even if we know that X has occurred, it remains true that either Y or Y' must occur. Hence,

Rule: $P(Y|X) + P(Y'|X) = 1$

If it's cloudy tomorrow, it will rain or it will not rain.

As an example, note in Table 5.2 that if it is given that a worker is a high performer (H), then the worker must either have qualified (Q) on the test or failed (F) the test. Fail (F) means not qualify; so Q' is the same as F. Computing, we find

$$P(Q|H) + P(Q'|H) = P(Q|H) + P(F|H) = \frac{0.375}{0.475} + \frac{0.100}{0.475} = 1$$

EXAMPLE The probability of finding oil in an area is 0.15 if the underlying stratum has a dome structure. What is the probability of not finding oil if there is a dome structure?

SOLUTION Letting F and D mean find oil and dome structure, respectively, we see that

$$P(F|D) + P(F'|D) = 1$$

$$P(F'|D) = 1 - P(F|D) = 1 - 0.15 = 0.85$$

Note carefully that the relation at hand refers to the probability of occurrence of an event or its complement, given the *same* event. In general, the value of $P(Y|X)$ tells us *nothing* about $P(Y|X')$. In the last example, the probability of finding oil if there is a dome structure tells us nothing about the probability of oil if there is not a dome structure. $P(F|D)$ and $P(F|D')$ need not sum to 1. In fact, geologists tell us that oil is less likely to be found if there is no dome structure; so $P(F|D')$ is less than 0.15, and $P(F|D) + P(F|D')$ is less than 1.

Usually, P(Y|X) + P(Y|X') does not equal 1.

> **EXERCISE** The probability of snow (S) tomorrow if it gets colder (C) is 0.6. (a) What is the probability it will not snow tomorrow if it is colder? (b) What is the probability that it will snow tomorrow if it does not get colder?
> **ANSWER** (a) 0.4. (b) Given only $P(S|C)$ it is not possible to determine $P(S|C')$.

5.14 TOTAL PROBABILITY AS THE SUM OF JOINT PROBABILITIES

Rule: The probability of event X occurring is the sum of the probabilities for all joint events in which X occurs. In particular,

$$P(X) = P(XY) + P(XY')$$

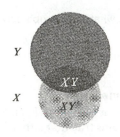

To see the meaning of this rule, refer to Table 5.2. The total probability of failing the test, $P(F) = 0.250$, is the sum of the probabilities of the joint events FH, FA, and FL, in which F appears. That is,

$$P(F) = P(FH) + P(FA) + P(FL)$$

or $0.250 = 0.100 + 0.075 + 0.075$

To illustrate the particular case of two events and their complements, let C mean colder and S mean snow, with C' and S' being the respective complements. From Table 5.3, we see that the total probability of snow is the sum of the probabilities of the joint events in which S appears. That is,

$$P(S) = P(SC) + P(SC')$$

TABLE 5.3
SUMS OF PROBABILITIES OF JOINT EVENTS

	Colder (C)	Not colder (C')	Total
Snow (S)	P(SC)	P(SC')	P(S)
Not snow (S')	P(S'C)	P(S'C')	P(S')
Total	P(C)	P(C')	1

EXERCISE · See Table 5.3. Write the probability of colder as the sum of probabilities of the joint events in which colder appears.
ANSWER $P(C) = P(SC) + P(S'C)$.

5.15 RULES FOR MORE THAN TWO EVENTS

Probability rules thus far have been stated in terms of two events, but they can be extended to more than two events. For example, for the *mutually exclusive* events A, B, and C,

$$P(A \text{ or } B \text{ or } C) = P(A) + P(B) + P(C).$$

And for the *independent* events X, Y, and Z,

$$P(X \text{ and } Y \text{ and } Z) = P(XYZ) = P(X)P(Y)P(Z)$$

The rules just stated—extended possibly to more than three events—are often used in the solution of probability problems.

It seems useful to pause at this point and permit you to fix in mind the rules presented thus far. The problems which follow have been designed for this purpose. After this set of problems a series of examples illustrating applications of the rules will be presented. Then you will be asked to work another set of problems patterned on the examples.

5.16 PROBLEMS

1. State the rule (a) for the probability of A or B; (b) for the probability of A or B if the events are mutually exclusive; (c) for the probability of B given that A has occurred; (d) for the probability of A and B; (e) for the probability of A and B if the events are independent.

2. The success S or failure S' of a contemplated expansion by a company depends upon whether competition increases, I, or not, I'. Executives have assessed the probabilities given in Table A. (a) Write the symbols for, and a word description of, the entry 0.08 in Table A. (b) Complete Table A by filling in the blanks. (c) In symbols, what probability rule is illustrated by adding the two first row entries of the completed table to get the row total? (d) In the completed table, find the ratio of each of the two first column entries to the column total. Add these ratios. In symbols, what probability rule is illustrated by the outcome of this addition? (e) Show numerically that $P(S|I)$ does not equal $1 - P(S|I')$.

TABLE A

	S	S'	Total
I	0.08		0.40
I'			
Total	0.50		

3. (a) An investor thinks the probability that stock A will rise in price is 0.7, and the corresponding probability for stock B is 0.4. The probability that both prices will rise is 0.3. Write the symbolic rule for, and calculate the probability that, A or B will rise. (b) Using A, B, A', and B' as classifications, make a complete table of probabilities as in the answer to Problem 2(b). (c) The answer to (a) is the sum of the probabilities of what joint events? (d) Verify that $P(A \text{ or } B) = 1 - P(A'B')$. Why would this relationship always hold for two events?

4. The probability that it will rain is 0.7. What is the probability that it will not rain?

5. An enclosed area has four smoke alarms. The probability that all four will fail to detect smoke when it is present is 0.005. What is the probability that at least one will detect smoke if it is present? Why?

6. Complete the following statements of conditional probability. (a) $P(X|A) = $; (b) $P(A|X) = $; (c) $P(Q|R) = $

7. Twenty-five percent of a college class graduated with honors, while 20 percent of the class were honors graduates and obtained good jobs. Letting H be honors and G be good job, write the symbolic probability rule for the probability that a person got a good job if the person graduated with honors. Compute this probability.

8. The probability that a job applicant will turn out to be a good worker, G, if he or she passes an aptitude test, P, is 0.75. (a) What is the probability that the person will not be a good worker if the test is passed? (b) Write the symbolic probability rule involved.

9. The probability of finding oil in an area where the underlying rock formation has a dome structure is 0.3. Based upon soundings, a geologist states the probability that a dome structure exists is 0.8. (a) What is the probability that the dome structure exists and oil will be found? (b) Using F and D, respectively, for find oil and dome exists, write the relevant symbolic probability rule for (a).

10. A box contains 12 items, of which 3 are defective, D, and 9 are good, G. (a) If two are selected, what is the probability that both are defective? (b) If two are selected, what is the probability the first is good and the second is defective? (c) Suppose the box is rejected (sent back to the supplier) if, in three selected items, at least one is defective. What is the probability that the box will be rejected?

11. Each of three independently operating fire alarms has a 0.95 probability of operating successfully, S, in the event of fire. (a) Write the symbols for the event that all three operate successfully. (b) Find the probability for the event in (a). (c) What word in the problem statement justifies the calculation procedure used in (b)? (d) Compute the probability that at least one operates successfully. (e) Explain the reasoning underlying the calculation in (d).

12. If A and B are mutually exclusive with $P(A) = 0.3$ and $P(B) = 0.4$, calculate $P(A \text{ or } B)$.

13. If A and B are independent with $P(A) = 0.3$ and $P(B) = 0.4$, calculate $P(A$ or $B)$. Explain the method used.

14. If $P(A) = 0.5$ and $P(AB) = 0.4$, calculate $P(B|A)$.

15. If $P(AB) = 0.2$ and $P(B|A) = 0.5$, calculate $P(A)$ and explain the reasoning used to obtain the answer.

16. If $P(A) = 0.3$ and $P(B) = 0.2$, what must be the value of $P(AB)$ if A and B are independent? Why?

17. If A and B are mutually exclusive and have nonzero probabilities, what must be the value of $P(B|A)$? Why?

18. Using X, X', Y, Y', list the joint events included in X or Y.

19. The probability of snow if it gets colder is 0.7. Is it possible that the probability of snow if it does not get colder could be 0.5? Explain.

20. The probability of snow if it gets colder is 0.7. Is it possible that the probability of no snow if it gets colder could be 0.5? Explain.

Note: In the following, if a statement is *always* true, mark it (T). Otherwise, mark it (F).

21. ( ) $P(A$ or $B) = P(A) + P(B)$.

22. ( ) $P(XY) = P(YX)$.

23. ( ) $P(RS) = P(S)P(R|S)$.

24. ( ) $P(B|A) = P(A|B)$.

25. ( ) If A and B have nonzero probabilities and are mutually exclusive, $P(AB) = P(A)P(B)$.

26. ( ) If A and B are mutually exclusive, $P(A$ or $B) = P(A) + P(B)$.

27. ( ) If R and S are independent, $P(R|S) = P(R)$.

28. ( ) If A and B are dependent with $P(A) = 0.3$ and $P(B) = 0.4$, then $P(AB) = 0.12$.

29. ( ) If R and S are not mutually exclusive and $P(R) = 0.3$ and $P(S) = 0.4$, then $P(R$ or $S)$ is less than 0.7.

30. ( ) $P(A$ or $B) = P(AB) + P(AB') + P(A'B)$.

31. ( ) $P(A$ or $B) = 1 - P(A'B')$.

32. ( ) $P(A) + P(A') = 1$.

33. ( ) If $P(RS) = 0.4$ and $P(S) = 0.5$, then $P(R|S) = 0.9$.

34. ( ) If $P(R) = P(S) = 0.3$, and $P(RS) = 0.1$, then R and S are dependent.

35. ( ) If R and S have nonzero probabilities and are mutually exclusive, then $P(R$ or $S)$ is greater than $P(R)$ and greater than $P(S)$.

36. ( ) The probability that A will win a contract if his competitor, B, does not bid is 0.8. It follows that the probability that A will win if B does bid is 0.2.

37. ( ) $P(R) = P(RS) + P(RS')$.

38. ( ) $P(R|S) = 1 - P(R'|S)$.

39. ( ) $P(R|S) + P(R|S') = 1$.

40. ( ) If X and Y have nonzero probabilities and are mutually exclusive, $P(Y|X) = 0$.

5.17 TREE DIAGRAMS

Tree diagrams often aid in understanding and solving probability problems. As an example, suppose that an arena has two hockey and two basketball games scheduled for a weekend. But to make time for repairs, only two games can be played.

These games are to be selected at random. The possible outcomes are represented on the tree diagram [Figure 5.2(a)]. Starting from the left, the

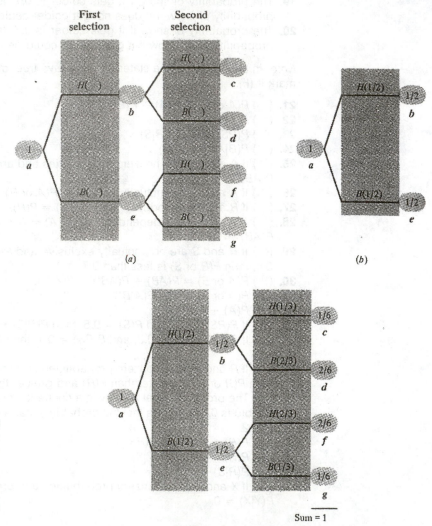

FIGURE 5.2

(a) Tree diagram for two selections with two choices per selection. (b) Tree diagram—first selection. (c) Tree diagram complete with probabilities.

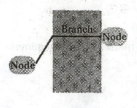

Branch Node
Node

diagram shows the outcome of the first selection as two *branches*, one for hockey (*H*), and one for basketball, (*B*). Each branch leads to an oval *node*, and each node again has two branches representing the possibilities for the second selection. A sequence of branches, such as that from *a* to *b* to *c*, is called a *path* through the tree.

In each oval at a node we shall insert the probability for the *joint* events on the path leading to the node. In the parentheses on a branch, we insert the conditional probability for the event on that branch, *given* that previous events on the path have occurred. The tree will allocate the total probability of 1, at *a*, to the paths, so that the sum of the probabilities at the ending nodes will be 1.

Here, P(H) = P(B) = ²/₄.

There are 2 hockey and 2 basketball games; so the probability of selecting hockey first and the probability of selecting basketball first are ¹/₂; these are inserted in Figure 5.2(*b*). In the top right ( ) of Figure 5.2(*c*) we want the conditional probability that hockey was the second selection *if* hockey was also the first selection. Now after selecting hockey once, the remaining

Finding branch probabilities

choice is from 1 hockey and 2 basketball games; so we have

$$P(H|H) = \frac{1}{3}$$

as shown at the top right of Figure 5.2(*c*).

The next path down is *HB*, which means hockey is selected first and basketball second. The second selection choice is again from 1 hockey and 2 basketball games; so

$$P(B|H) = \frac{2}{3}$$

as shown in Figure 5.2(*c*). The conditional probabilities for the two lower right branches of the figure are computed in a similar manner.

Finding node probabilities

To obtain the probability at node *c*, we multiply the probability at node *b*, ¹/₂, by the connecting branch probability, ¹/₃, to obtain

$$P(HH) = \left(\frac{1}{2}\right)\left(\frac{1}{3}\right) = \frac{1}{6}$$

which is the probability that both the first and second selections are hockey. Similarly, the probability for node *d* is

$$P(HB) = \left(\frac{1}{2}\right)\left(\frac{2}{3}\right) = \frac{2}{6}$$

which is the probability that the first selection is hockey and the second is basketball. You should now verify the probabilities at nodes *f* and *g*. Note that the sum of the probabilities at the ending nodes is 1.

The ending nodes contain the probabilities for all the joint events which can occur. Thus, the probability that 1 hockey and 1 basketball game will be played is the probability that either *HB* (path *abd*) or *BH* (path *aef*) occurs. These events are mutually exclusive; so we add their probabilities to obtain

This is P(HB or BH). $$P(HB) + P(BH) = \frac{2}{6} + \frac{2}{6} = \frac{4}{6} = \frac{2}{3}$$

EXERCISE See Figure 5.2c. What is the probability that both hockey games will be played?
ANSWER $P(HH) = \frac{1}{6}$.

The following rules apply to tree diagrams:
1. The probability at the beginning node of a branch times the (conditional) branch probability gives the probability at the end node of the branch.

   For example, on the branch *ae*, $(1)(\frac{1}{2}) = \frac{1}{2}$.
2. The sum of all the (conditional) probabilities on branches stemming from a node is 1.

   For example, the probabilities on the branches stemming from node *b* are $\frac{1}{3}$ and $\frac{2}{3}$. And $\frac{1}{3} + \frac{2}{3} = 1$.
3. The probability at a node is the sum of the probabilities at the ends of the branches stemming from the node.

   For example, the sum of the probabilities at the ends of the branches stemming from *b* is $\frac{1}{6} + \frac{2}{6} = \frac{3}{6} = \frac{1}{2}$, which is the probability at *b*.

EXAMPLE To finish a construction project, three phases, 1, 2, and 3, must be completed in sequence. The phases are to be done by contractors *A*, *B*, and *C*. To be on time the phases must be completed by June 1, August 15, and September 1, respectively. The probability that *A* will finish phase 1 on time is 0.8, and the completion date of September 1 cannot be met if *A* does not finish on time. If *A* finishes on time, the probability that *B* finishes phase 2 on time is 0.9. If *B* finishes on time, *C* is certain to finish phase 3 on time. In addition, *C* has a chance to call in extra help, and the probability that *C* finishes on time if *B* does not is 0.5. Find the probability that the project will be completed on time.

SOLUTION The tree diagram in Figure 5.3 shows the given probabilities. Note that a complete tree of all possible outcomes is not necessary because only the paths which lead to completion on time are needed. Hence, for example, we have excluded *A'*, as indicated by the symbol | |.

EXERCISE In Figure 5.3, (*a*) What are the values of the probabilities 1, 2, 3, 4, and 5? (*b*) What is the probability that the project will be completed on time?
ANSWER (*a*) (1) 0.72; (2) 0.72; (3) 0.1; (4) 0.08; (5) 0.04. (*b*) 0.76.

5.18 WORD PROBLEMS IN PROBABILITY

In this section we present a series of examples which you will find helpful for reference purposes. They also illustrate the "translation" of problems from

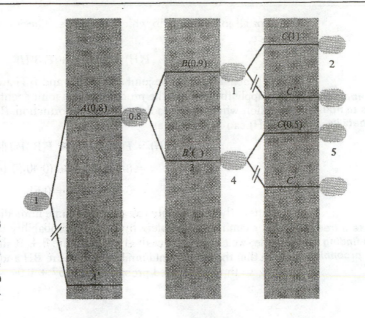

FIGURE 5.3
Construction project
tree diagram. $A = A$
finishes on time; $A' =$
A does not finish on
time.

words to probability symbols as a first step in the solution of real business problems.

EXAMPLE A product in the developmental stage has a probability of 0.60 of being a breakthrough (an innovative product), in which case it will have a 95 percent chance of capturing a high share of the market. If the product is not a breakthrough, the chance of capturing a high share of the market is only 10 percent. What is the probability that the product will capture a high share of the market?

***Symbolize the given
data.***
SOLUTION In this, as in many problems, it is helpful first to extract the pertinent data given in the problem and represent them symbolically. Thus, letting B mean breakthrough and H mean capturing a high share of the market, we have

$$P(B) = 0.60 \quad \text{so that} \quad P(B') = 0.40$$

$$P(H|B) = 0.95$$

$$P(H|B') = 0.10$$

***Determine what prob-
ability is to be found.***
Next, we must determine what is required to answer the question posed. Here it is clear that we want $P(H)$. Finally, having fixed the problem in mind, we either go directly to probability rules to compute the answer or use aids such as trees or tables to lead to the answer. In the present case, we can apply rules directly if we remember that $P(H)$ is the sum of the probabili-

ties of all joint events in which H occurs. These events are BH and $B'H$. Hence,

$$P(H) = P(BH) + P(B'H)$$

Use appropriate rules to find the probability . . .

The probabilities for the joint events BH and $B'H$ are not available, but we can apply the rule for the probability of a joint event twice to obtain an expression which involves the available information. Thus, $P(H) = P(BH) + P(B'H)$ can be written as

$$P(H) = P(B)P(H|B) + P(B')P(H|B')$$
$$= (0.60)(0.95) + (0.40)(0.10)$$
$$= 0.57 + 0.04 = 0.61$$

. . . or use a tree or a table in finding the probability.

Often, the appropriate rule does not come immediately to mind. We may then examine the problem by use of a probability table or a tree. For example, we can construct the tree in Figure 5.4. It should be clear immediately that the paths containing H, which are BH and $B'H$, are the ones desired, so that the desired probability is $0.57 + 0.04 = 0.61$.

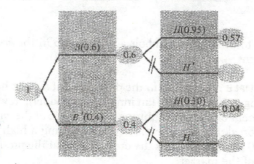

FIGURE 5.4
Market-share tree
diagram

EXAMPLE An assembled item contains five ball bearings, any one of which has a probability of 0.001 of being defective. An item is not acceptable if any one of its bearings is defective. What is the probability that an item is not acceptable?

SOLUTION Here we have only that

$$P(\text{bearing is defective}) = P(D) = 0.001$$

and we want to compute

$$P(\text{item is not acceptable}) = P(A')$$

P(at least one) = 1 − P(0) occurs often.

where A means acceptable and A' is the complement of acceptable. Noting that an item is not acceptable if *at least one* bearing is defective, we see that 0 defective is the complement of at least one defective. So we compute

$$P(A') = 1 - P(0 \text{ defective}) = 1 - P(\text{all five are good})$$

Since $P(D) = 0.001$, the probability that a bearing is good is 0.999. Hence,

$$P(A') = 1 - (0.999)(0.999)(0.999)(0.999)(0.999)$$
$$= 1 - 0.995$$
$$= 0.005$$

Note that in computing the joint probability for five good bearings, we used the same factor, 0.999 (which is $1 - 0.001$), each time because we take the problem statement that *any* bearing has $P(D) = 0.001$ to mean that the probability that one bearing is defective does not depend on whether other bearings are defective. Hence, *independence* is assumed. We may therefore use the probability rule for independent joint events.

EXAMPLE Shipments of perishable foods arrive from abroad by plane. Overall, 10 percent of the shipments have some spoilage. Records show that 3 percent of the shipments arrive on time and have some spoilage, and that 75 percent of all shipments arrive on time. What percent of the shipments which do not arrive on time have some spoilage?

SOLUTION Here we have

$$P(\text{spoilage}) = P(S) = 0.10$$

$$P(\text{arrive on time}) = P(T) = 0.75$$

$$P(\text{spoilage and arrive on time}) = P(ST) = 0.03$$

and we wish to find

$$P(\text{spoilage if shipment does not arrive on time}) = P(S|T')$$

A probability table often helps solve a two-event problem.   A table often aids in solving a problem in which only two events are involved. To make such a table, label the first row as one of the events, the second row as the complementary event, and the third row as total. Then label the first column as the other event, the second column as its complementary event, and the third column as total. Table 5.4*a* is a probability table for the events S and T. It contains the available probabilities. The sum of the probabilities for an event and its complement is 1.00; so the value 1.00 is also entered in the table.

TABLE 5.4a
PARTIAL PROBABILITY
TABLE FOR EVENTS S AND T

	T	T'	Total
S	0.03		0.10
S'			
Total	0.75		1.00

Row and column entries must sum to their respective totals; so you can easily fill in the blank spaces in Table 5.4a.

EXERCISE See Table 5.4a. Determine (a) $P(ST')$; (b) $P(S')$; (c) $P(S'T)$.
ANSWER (a) 0.07; (b) 0.90; (c) 0.72.

Proceeding in the manner of the exercise, we obtain Table 5.4b. From the data in the table we find the probability of spoilage given that a shipment does not arrive on time is

$$P(S|T') = \frac{0.07}{0.25} = 0.28, \text{ or 28 percent}$$

TABLE 5.4b
COMPLETED PROBABILITY TABLE
FOR EVENTS S AND T

	T	T'	Total
S	0.03	0.07	0.10
S'	0.72	0.18	0.90
Total	0.75	0.25	1.00

Suppose you want to solve the last problem by application of probability rules. Then, because you want $P(S|T')$, you would write the rule for conditional probability as

$$P(S|T') = \frac{P(ST')}{P(T')}$$

Look at the available information,

$$P(S) = 0.10 \qquad P(T) = 0.75 \quad \text{and} \quad P(ST) = 0.03$$

Rules will always work, but you have to determine which rules you need. You need $P(ST')$ and $P(T')$. Neither is available, but you can obtain $P(T')$ from $P(T)$ as

$$P(T') = 1 - P(T) = 1 - 0.75 = 0.25$$

The problem now is to determine $P(ST')$. You might take a nonproductive start here by writing $P(ST') = P(S)P(T'|S)$. But you do not have $P(T'|S)$. So, you try to think of a rule that involves $P(ST')$ and the available probabilities $P(S)$, $P(T)$, and $P(ST)$. The rule is that $P(S)$ is the sum of the probabilities of the joint events in which S appears. That is,

$$P(ST) + P(ST') = P(S)$$
$$0.03 + P(ST') = 0.10$$
$$P(ST') = 0.07$$

Finally, you compute

$$P(S|T') = \frac{P(ST')}{P(T')} = \frac{0.07}{0.25} = 0.28$$

Tree diagrams and tables often aid in solving probability problems, but at times a problem is best tackled by straightforward application of probability rules. Such is the case in the next example.

Do you think Pam has a better than 50 percent chance of winning?

EXAMPLE (The Birthday Problem) Pam, who is one of 30 guests at a party, bets $5 that at least two of the guests have the same birthday; that is, at least two were born on the same day of the same month. What is the probability that Pam wins?

SOLUTION In solving this problem, we shall assume for simplicity that none of the guests were born on February 29, there are no sets of twins, and all 365 birthdays are equally likely. If we approach the problem by thinking of the myriad of ways in which at least two could have the same birthday (2 could have the same birthday, or 3, or 4, or . . . , or all 30), it looks formidable. The key is to work with the complement, which would be that *no two* have the same birthday; that is, all have different birthdays. Now suppose Pam states her birthday, leaving 364 other birthdays for the next guest, so that

If there are many ways an event can happen, try working with the event's complement.

$$P(\text{second different from first}) = \frac{364}{365}$$

If the second is different from the first, there remain 363 different birthdays for the third; so the probability that the third is different from the first two, given that the first two are different, is

$$\frac{364}{365} \cdot \frac{363}{365}$$

EXERCISE What is the probability (a) that the first five have different birthdays? (b) that at least two of the first five have the same birthday?
ANSWER (a) (364/365)(363/365)(362/365)(361/365) = 0.973; (b) 1 − 0.973 = 0.027.

In the answer to part (a) of the exercise, note that in considering *five different birthdays*, we have four fractions, all with 365 as the denominator. The numerators start at 365 − 1 = 364 and end at 365 − (5 − 1) = 361. Similarly, for our example with 30 different birthdays, the numerators will start at 365 − 1 = 364 and end at 365 − (30 − 1) = 336. Hence, doing the computation on a calculator, we find

$$P\begin{pmatrix}\text{at least two have} \\ \text{the same birthday}\end{pmatrix} = 1 - P\begin{pmatrix}\text{no two have the} \\ \text{same birthday}\end{pmatrix}$$

$$= 1 - \frac{364}{365} \cdot \frac{363}{365} \cdot \frac{362}{365} \cdot \frac{361}{365} \cdots \cdot \frac{336}{365}$$

$$= 1 - 0.294$$

$$= 0.706$$

So, Pam's chances of winning are quite good—much better, in fact, than most people who have not done the calculation think they are.

5.19 BAYES' RULE

A First View of Bayes' Rule

The following conversation will introduce the idea involved in Bayes' rule.

Fran: The company newspaper says that sixty percent of our managers are business college graduates. I guess a business college education pays off.

Dan: It looks that way. Better than half of our managers had a business education.

Fran: Can the sixty percent be interpreted to mean that a business graduate hired by the company has a sixty percent chance of becoming a manager?

Dan: Come to think of it, I guess not. The newsletter refers to all of our managers, not to all business college graduates.

Fran: So the sixty percent has manager as given. Interpreted as a probability, that means the probability of business graduate given manager is sixty percent. If we let M be manager and B be business graduate, that will be the probability of B given M.

Dan: A student would be more interested in the chance that a business major will become a manager after graduation. That would be the probability of M given B.

Fran: Is there a relationship between the probability of M given B and the probability of B given M?

60 percent of managers (M) are business (B) college graduates means $P(B|M) = 0.60$.

The answer to Fran's question is yes. The relationship can be derived by writing the rule for the conditional probability $P(M|B)$, which is

$$P(M|B) = \frac{P(MB)}{P(B)}$$

Using the rule for the probability of a joint event, the numerator on the right is $P(MB) = P(M)P(B|M)$. So we may write

$$P(M|B) = \frac{P(M)P(B|M)}{P(B)}$$

$P(B|M)$ is the "reverse" of $P(M|B)$.

Note that $P(M|B)$ appears on the left, and the "reverse" conditional $P(B|M)$ appears on the right.

EXERCISE Write the equation relating $P(Y|X)$ to $P(X|Y)$.

ANSWER $P(Y|X) = \dfrac{P(Y)P(X|Y)}{P(X)}$

Bayes' rule usually is written in an expanded manner by converting the denominator of

$$P(Y|X) = \frac{P(Y)P(X|Y)}{P(X)} \tag{1}$$

to a form containing conditional probabilities—because problem statements often give conditional probabilities. To see how this is done, recall that $P(X)$ equals the sum of the probabilities of the joint events in which X occurs. In particular,

$$P(X) = P(YX) + P(Y'X)$$

Applying the rule for the probability of a joint event twice on the right gives

$$P(X) = P(Y)P(X|Y) + P(Y')P(X|Y')$$

To aid in memorizing the rule, the conditional probabilities are written first. That is,

$$P(X) = P(X|Y)P(Y) + P(X|Y')P(Y')$$

Substituting the last into the denominator of (1), we have

Bayes' rule
$$P(Y|X) = \frac{P(X|Y)P(Y)}{P(X|Y)P(Y) + P(X|Y')P(Y')}$$

The system for remembering Bayes' rule is illustrated by writing the expression for $P(B|A)$. We start with the "reverse" conditional probability, $P(A|B)$, and multiply it by $P(B)$ to get the numerator and the first term of the denominator. The second term of the denominator repeats the first, but with B' rather than B. Thus,

$$P(B|A) = \frac{P(A|B)P(B)}{P(A|B)P(B) + P(A|B')P(B')}$$

EXERCISE Write Bayes' rule for $P(W|S)$.

ANSWER $P(W|S) = \dfrac{P(S|W)P(W)}{P(S|W)P(W) + P(S|W')P(W')}$

The next example illustrates the application of Bayes' rule.

EXAMPLE In the past, the personnel department of a company has interviewed job applicants and based hiring decisions on judgments made as a result of the interviews. There are 400 people in the current workforce who have been hired by the personnel department. Supervisors have rated these workers and report that 280 are good, G, workers, and 120 are poor workers, G'. The personnel manager notes that $120/400$, or 30 percent, of the workers are rated G'. She decides to determine whether administering an aptitude test to workers who have had successful interviews would improve the selection procedure. To this end, the manager administers the test to present workers and compares the test results of good and poor workers. Test scores are symbolized by Q for qualify and Q' for not qualify. She finds that 168 of the 280 good workers qualified on the test, but only 24 of the 120 poor workers qualified. The manager reasons, properly, that

$$P(Q|G) = \frac{168}{280} = 0.6$$

$$P(Q|G') = \frac{24}{120} = 0.2$$

$$P(G) = \frac{280}{400} = 0.7$$

$$P(G') = 0.3$$

Comparison of $P(Q|G) = 0.6$ with $P(Q|G') = 0.2$ shows that good workers are much more likely to qualify on the test than poor workers. However, upon reflection, the manager realizes that this comparison does not provide the information needed, which is whether or not qualifying on the test is a useful criterion in selecting good workers. That is, the present interviewer technique has led to a workforce with $P(G) = 0.7$, or 70 percent, good workers. But how much improvement could be expected if workers were given the test, and only those qualifying on the test were hired? The relevant probability is $P(G|Q)$, the probability that an applicant will be a good worker if the applicant qualifies on the test. The manager applies Bayes' rule as follows:

The manager knows P(Q|G) but wants to know P(G|Q).

$$P(G|Q) = \frac{P(Q|G)P(G)}{P(Q|G)P(G) + P(Q|G')P(G')}$$

$$= \frac{(0.6)(0.7)}{(0.6)(0.7) + (0.2)(0.3)} = \frac{0.42}{0.42 + 0.06} = \frac{0.42}{0.48} = 0.875$$

Thus, the manager concludes that if job applicants are tested, and those who qualify are hired, 87.5 percent of those hired will be good workers. That result would be better than the present 70 percent good workers.

Observe that the information given in the foregoing example can be stated by saying (1) 70 percent of the present workers are good; (2) 60 percent of the good workers and 20 percent of the poor workers qualified on the test. We translate (1) into $P(G) = 0.70$, from which $P(G') = 0.30$. The information in (2) is $P(Q|G) = 0.60$ and $P(Q|G') = 0.20$.

Bayes' rule (and more) from a probability table

I shall now show you how to construct a complete probability table as a method of obtaining not only the "reverse" conditional probability $P(G|Q)$ but any other desired probability. We start with Table 5.5*a*, which contains the values for $P(G)$ and $P(G')$. We compute $P(QG)$ and $P(QG')$ at the right

TABLE 5.5a

	G	G'	Total	
Q				$P(QG)\ = P(G)P(Q|G)\ = (0.7)(0.6)\ = 0.42$
Q'				$P(QG') = P(G')P(Q|G') = (0.3)(0.20) = 0.06$
Total	0.70	0.30	1.00	

by the joint probability rule. If $P(QG) = 0.42$ is now entered in the upper left corner of Table 5.5a, we see that $P(Q'G) = 0.70 - 0.42 = 0.28$. Similarly, entering $P(QG') = 0.06$ yields $P(Q'G') = 0.30 - 0.06 = 0.24$. We now have the complete set of probabilities shown in Table 5.5b. From the table

TABLE 5.5b

	G	G'	Total
Q	0.42	0.06	0.48
Q'	0.28	0.24	0.52
Total	0.70	0.30	1.00

we can compute

$$P(G|Q) = \frac{0.42}{0.48} = 0.875$$

as before. Additionally, we can compute other probabilities, such as

$$P(G|Q') = \frac{0.28}{0.52} = 0.538, \text{ or about 54 percent}$$

The last statement is important because it implies that 54 percent of those not qualifying on the test (and therefore not hired) would be good workers. This would be a matter of concern to the personnel manager. To make this concern more explicit, suppose it is necessary to hire 50 new workers. Under the old procedure, the hiring project would be complete after 50 applicants had had successful interviews. Under the new procedure, the 50 now would be tested, and recalling from Table 5.5b that $P(Q') = 0.52$, 52 percent of the 50, or 26, would not qualify on the test and so would not be hired, leaving only 24 who would be hired. Moreover, $P(G|Q') = 0.538$ says that (0.538)(26), or about 14 of the 26 who did not qualify on the test and were not hired, would have been good workers.

A qualifying test can reject potentially good workers.

Viewing the last in a different light, let N be the number who have successful interviews. Then the number qualifying on the test will be $[P(Q)](N)$ or 0.48N. We want the number qualifying to be 50; so

$$0.48N = 50$$

$$N = \frac{50}{0.48} = 104.2$$

or about 104. Thus, use of the test will substantially increase the recruiting cost. Instead of securing 50 applicants with successful interviews, it will be necessary to secure about 104. Moreover, use of the test may deplete the available labor force to the point where fewer able workers apply, so that to obtain a given number who have successful interviews, increasing numbers will have to be interviewed; but there will be a higher percentage of good workers.

Probability arithmetic
gives "long-run"
answers . . . but the
answers are used in
making decisions.

. I should mention that the arithmetic I have been doing is "probability" arithmetic; so the results are "long-run" answers. That is, for example, the value $N = 104$ computed above means that on the average, for a very large number of applicants, about 104 will be needed to obtain 50 new employees. But even though 104 is a "long-run" figure, it is a figure required in deciding whether to use—or not use—the test.

EXERCISE From Table 5.5*b*, what are the symbols for, and the value of, the probability that an applicant will be a poor worker if the applicant does not qualify on the test?
ANSWER $P(G'|Q')$ is about 0.46.

Caution Commonly used language may disguise conditional probabilities and invite misinterpretation. For example, the statement that 50 percent of the executives, E, in a firm have marketing backgrounds, M, should be interpreted as the conditional probability $P(M|E) = 0.50$ because the statement applies to all executives but to executives only. That is, E is given; so it appears after the vertical. The statement does not apply to all who have marketing backgrounds; so it is *not* about $P(E|M)$, and it does *not* imply that an employee who has a marketing background has a 50 percent chance of being an executive. Moreover, the statement does *not* mean the joint probability $P(ME)$. In everyday language $P(ME)$ would be described as the probability that a person in the firm is an executive who has a marketing background. To clarify this, consider Table 5.6*a*, which shows that the company employs 400 people; 80 of these people are executives and 100 people have marketing backgrounds. The statement that 50 percent of the executives have marketing backgrounds means that 50 percent of the 80 executives, or 40, is the proper entry in the upper left corner of Table 5.6*a*. Entering the 40 makes it possible to fill in all the blanks, as shown in Table 5.6*b*.

"50 percent of the
executives" means
executive is given.

TABLE 5.6a

	E	E'	Total
M			100
M'			
Total	80		400

TABLE 5.6b

	E	E'	Total
M	40	60	100
M'	40	260	300
Total	80	320	400

EXERCISE From Table 5.6*b*, find the probability (*a*) that a person is an executive who has a marketing background; (*b*) that an executive has a marketing background.
ANSWER (*a*) 0.10; (*b*) 0.50.

EXERCISE Suppose that in the search for attributes of leadership, various characteristics of leaders L and nonleaders L' were studied. In the group studied, 15 percent were leaders. It was found that 60 percent of the leaders had a certain attribute A, whereas only 20 percent of the nonleaders had this attribute.

Find the probability that (a) a person having the attribute is a leader; (b) a person not having the attribute is a leader.

ANSWER (a) 0.35; (b) 0.08.

Another View of Bayes' Rule

This section is optional because it is not a prerequisite for further work in this text. However, I hope you will see the importance of the concept involved and be encouraged to pursue it later. The topic of interest is the reassessment of a probability after additional evidence has been obtained. We shall use an example which, though trivial, will introduce this important application of Bayes' rule. Let us suppose there are two boxes, identical in appearance, on a counter. One, which we will refer to as E, contains two excellent unflawed (U) diamonds. The other, which we refer to as M for mixed, contains one unflawed and one flawed (F) diamond. We do not know which box is M or which is E. We select one at random, with a resulting 50-50 chance of getting E. That is,

Box E contains UU, and box M contains UF.

$$P(E) = 0.5 \qquad P(M) = 0.5$$

Pick one box randomly, and select one diamond randomly.

We can afford to have only one diamond examined by an expert; so we take one at random from the box we selected, have it examined, and learn that it is unflawed. The problem is to determine the probability that the unexamined diamond is unflawed, that is, the probability that we selected box E.

We can easily determine the probability that the selected stone would be unflawed if we know which box we have. Thus, the probability of the sample stone being unflawed is $1/2$ *if* the selected box is M and 1 if the box is E. Symbolically,

$$P(U|M) = 0.5$$

$$P(U|E) = 1$$

If the selected diamond is U, what is the probability that box E was picked?

What is desired is the probability that we have box E *given* that the examined diamond is unflawed. This is

$$P(E|U)$$

We write Bayes' rule for the "reversed" conditional probability, keeping in mind that M is the same as E', and carry out the computation as shown next.

$$P(E|U) = \frac{P(U|E)P(E)}{P(U|E)P(E) + P(U|M)P(M)}$$

$$= \frac{(1)(0.5)}{(1)(0.5) + (0.5)(0.5)}$$

$$= \frac{0.50}{0.75} = \frac{2}{3}$$

Prior and posterior probabilities.

Now observe that *prior* to obtaining the additional information from the expert, the probability that we chose box E was 0.5. This is called the *prior* probability. After taking into account the additional information, the reassessed probability that we chose box E is the *posterior* probability, $2/3$.

EXERCISE A store has two identically appearing cases of canned vegetables, each containing 24 identically appearing cans. Case A has 12 cans each of peas and beans, while B has 16 cans of peas and 8 cans of beans. A case is selected at random, and a can is selected at random from that case. The can, when opened, is found to contain peas. What is the probability that case B was selected?

ANSWER $4/7$, or about 0.57.

In a context broader than our simple example, the concept we have introduced is that probabilities based upon available information may be altered when additional information is obtained. In so doing we use both the previously available and the additional information. Thus, a marketing executive who has strong reasons to believe that a new product will appeal to 75 percent of the potential customers will adjust this percent downward if a survey of a number of buyers shows only 50 percent of those surveyed found *Use sample information to adjust prior subjective probabilities.* the product appealing. However, if the analysis suggested by our example is carried out, the executive need not choose only between 75 and 50 percent as the result. The executive may make an adjustment to the 75 percent in the light of the survey information.

5.20 PROBLEMS

1. A lumberyard manager is expecting to receive two truckloads each of grade A and grade B pine lumber. Arriving at work on the day the trucks are due, the manager finds a note left by the night security guard, who is no longer available, relating that the supplier had called and said only two truckloads would arrive. What is the probability that one load is grade A and the other grade B?

2. Contractor A does the first part of a project, and B finishes the project. B cannot start until A is finished. If A finishes on time, B has a 90 percent chance of completing the project on time, but if A does not finish on time, B has only a 20 percent chance of completing the project on time. If A has a 65 percent chance of finishing on time, what is the probability that the project will be completed on time?

3. A salesperson has a policy of calling upon a customer a second time if she does not make the sale on the first call, and trying a third, and last, time if she fails on the first two calls. She has a probability of a sale on the first call of 0.3. If she fails on the first call, the probability of a sale on the second call is 0.2. If the first two calls are unsuccessful, her probability of success on the third call is 0.1. What is the probability that she makes the sale to a given customer?

4. A city has three independent reserve sources of electric power to use to prevent a blackout in the event that its regular source fails. The probability that any reserve source is available when the regular source fails is 0.8. What is the probability of not having a blackout if the regular source fails?

5. The probability of snow tomorrow is 0.6 and the probability that it will be colder is 0.7. The probability that it will not snow and not be colder is 0.1. What is the probability it will snow if it is colder tomorrow?

6. In a lottery, each digit of the winning four-digit number is determined by spinning a wheel having equally spaced digits (0, 1, . . . , 9) on its rim, and selecting the digit at a marking point when the wheel comes to rest. Tom bets a friend that the next winning four-digit number will contain a digit at least twice. For example, Tom wins if the number is 1315, 4224, 3335, 7777, and so on. What are Tom's chances of winning the bet?

7. A freshman class of 500 students entered a college in the fall of a year. At the end of the year, 75 percent were found to have been successful academically. Examining admissions data, an official of the college observed that 64 percent of those who were successful and 48 percent of those who were not successful had high ranks in their high school graduating class, where high was designated as being in the upper quarter of a class. (a) Find the probability that a student who had high rank had a successful first year at college. (b) Find the probability that a student who did not have high rank had a successful first year. (c) What percent of the college class of 500 had high rank? (d) If the college had admitted only those students who had high rank, how many of the 500 would not have been admitted? (e) See (d). Of those not admitted, how many would have been successful?

8. Dan's company has decided to add another vice president to the management group. Dan is wondering about his chances of getting the job if he applies for it. He thinks the chance of getting the job is $3/4$ if his associate, Fran, does not apply—but only $1/3$ if Fran does apply. Dan thinks the chance Fran will apply is $2/5$. What is the probability that Dan will get the job?

9. In trial by jury, four joint events may occur. That is, a defendant may be guilty, and the jury finding may be guilty or not guilty; or, a defendant may be innocent, and the jury finding may be guilty or not guilty. Use a prime to represent not guilty, with D' meaning defendant is not guilty and D meaning defendant is guilty. Similarly J' means jury finding is not guilty and J means a jury finding of guilty. Assume the following: (a) 80 percent of defendants brought to trial are guilty. (b) In 99.9 percent of cases when the defendant is not guilty, the jury finding is not guilty. (c) In 60 percent of the cases where the defendant is guilty, the jury finding is not guilty. If a jury finding is not guilty, what is the probability that the defendant is guilty?

10. A student taking courses A, B, C, and D assesses the respective probabilities of passing the courses at 0.8, 0.9, 0.7, and 0.5. Assuming independence, what is the probability that the student fails at least one course?

11. A company finds that 1 percent of the television sets it sells fail during the first month of use. Of those that do not fail in the first month, 0.5 percent ($1/2$ of 1 percent) fail during the next 5 months. Of those not failing by the end of the 6-month period, 0.1 percent fail by the end of the first year. The company replaces, free of charge, any set which fails during its warranty period. If 1000 sets are sold, how many will have to be replaced if (a) the warranty period is 6 months? (b) the warranty period is 1 year?

12. A die has six faces with spots representing the numbers 1, 2, 3, 4, 5, 6, each face being equally likely to occur when the die is rolled. If the die is rolled five times, what is the probability that the same number will occur at least twice?

13. Tennis players E and K are playing in a three-set championship match. The player winning two sets wins the match. Probabilities have been assigned as follows:

	Probability
E wins first set	0.60
E wins second set if E wins first set	0.70
E wins second set if E loses first set	0.30
E wins if the match goes to three sets	0.50

What is the probability that E wins the match?

14. In a study of its installment sales a furniture store accountant found that (a) 72 percent of its customers made a down payment on their purchases; (b) 33 percent were tardy in making payments; (c) 60 percent made down payments and were not tardy. Find the probability that a customer who does not make a down payment will be tardy in making payments.

15. In seeking the cause for below-standard power output which occurs on some of its station wagons, an automobile company's engineers have examined wagons with standard and below-standard outputs and checked engines for compression. The examination showed 75 percent had standard power, and of these, 84 percent had high engine compression. Only 40 percent of those with below-standard power had high compression. What is the probability that a wagon has below-standard power if it has low compression?

16. At a carnival booth, the operator of a game of "queens" has six cards: two kings, two queens, and two jacks. The operator shuffles the cards, spreads them face down before the player, and bets $1 even money that if the player selects two cards, at least one will be a queen. What is the probability that the operator wins?

17. Graduation exercises are to be held outdoors on a Friday if it does not rain. If it rains on Friday, the exercises will be postponed and held on Saturday—outdoors if it does not rain, and indoors if it rains. The probability of rain on Friday is 0.2, and if it rains on Friday the probability it will not rain on Saturday is 0.3. What is the probability that the exercises will be held outdoors?

18. An insurance company pays replacement costs if, in a hurricane, a building is damaged structurally or its contents are damaged by water. The probability of a hurricane during the year the building is insured is 0.01. In a hurricane, the probability is 0.2 that the building will be damaged structurally; if this happens, the probability is 0.4 that the contents will be damaged by water. But the probability that water damage will occur in a hurricane if there is no structural damage is 0.1. What is the probability that the insurance company will have to pay for structural or water damage during the year? (*Hint:* A tree diagram may help.)

19. A store has two identically appearing boxes each containing 12 sparkplugs. Box *A* has 2 defective plugs and *B* has 5 defective plugs. If a box is selected at random and a plug taken at random from the box is defective, what is the probability that *A* was the selected box?

5.21 SUMMARY

An objective probability is the relative frequency of occurrence of an event over the long run. A probability which expresses a person's degree of belief—or degree of certainty—is called a subjective probability.

Mutually exclusive events are events which cannot occur together,

The rules of probability are based on the following requirements: (1) elements must be selected randomly from a population; (2) the probability of an event must be a number on the scale from 0 through 1; (3) the sum of the probabilities for a collectively exhaustive, mutually exclusive, set of events (i.e., all possible different events) must be 1.

The event symbol XY means the occurrence of both event X and event Y. The event XY is called a *joint* event. The symbol $P(Y|X)$ means the probability that Y will occur given that X has occurred. Events X and Y are *independent* if the probability of occurrence of each of them is not affected by whether or not the other has occurred. Events which are not independent are dependent.

In general,

$$P(X \text{ or } Y) = P(X) + P(Y) - P(XY)$$

But if X and Y are mutually exclusive, then $P(XY) = 0$ and

$$P(X \text{ or } Y) = P(X) + P(Y)$$

In general,

$$P(Y|X) = \frac{P(XY)}{P(X)}$$

However, if X and Y are independent, then

$$P(Y|X) = P(Y) \quad \text{and} \quad P(X|Y) = P(X)$$

In general,

$$P(XY) = P(X)P(Y|X)$$

But if X and Y are independent, then

$$P(XY) = P(X)P(Y)$$

The last expression can be used as a test for the independence of X and Y. For *complementary* events X and X',

$$P(X) + P(X') = 1$$

In repeated trials of an event, zero occurrence is the complement of at least one occurrence; so

$$P(\text{at least one occurrence}) = 1 - P(\text{zero occurrence})$$

For an event X and its complement X', both conditioned on the same event Y,

$$P(X|Y) + P(X'|Y) = 1$$

The probability of an event X is the sum of the probabilities of all joint events in which X occurs. If the events are X, E_1, E_2, E_3, . . . , E_k, then

$$P(X) = P(XE_1) + P(XE_2) + P(XE_3) + \cdots + P(XE_k)$$

In particular,

$$P(X) = P(XY) + P(XY')$$

Bayes' rule shows that the conditional probability $P(Y|X)$ is related to $P(X|Y)$ as follows:

$$P(Y|X) = \frac{P(X|Y)P(Y)}{P(X|Y)P(Y) + P(X|Y')P(Y')}$$

5.22 REVIEW PROBLEMS

Note: In Problems 1 through 25, if the statement is *always* true, mark it (T); otherwise, mark it (F).

1. (   ) $P(R \text{ or } S) = 1 - P(R'S')$.
2. (   ) $P(R \text{ or } S) = P(R) + P(S)$.
3. (   ) $P(S) = 1 - P(S')$.
4. (   ) $P(R|S) = P(RS)/P(R)$.
5. (   ) $P(R) = P(RS)/P(S|R)$.

6. ( ) If R and S are independent, $P(R|S) = P(RS)/P(S)$.
7. ( ) If R and S are independent, $P(R|S) = P(R)$.
8. ( ) If R and S are independent, $P(RS) = P(R)P(S)$.
9. ( ) If R and S have nonzero probabilities, they cannot be mutually exclusive.
10. ( ) $P(R|S) = P(S|R)$.
11. ( ) $P(RS) = P(SR)$.
12. ( ) $P(R \text{ or } S) = P(RS) + P(RS') + P(R'S)$.
13. ( ) If no joint probability is zero, $P(R \text{ or } S)$ is greater than $P(R) + P(S)$.
14. ( ) If $P(RS) = 0.3$ and $P(S) = 0.4$, then $P(R|S) = 0.7$.
15. ( ) If $P(RS) = 0.36$ and $P(R|S) = 0.50$, then $P(S) = 0.18$.
16. ( ) $P(RS) + P(RS') = 1$.
17. ( ) $P(R|S) + P(R'|S) = 1$.
18. ( ) $P(R|S) + P(R|S') = P(R)$.
19. ( ) $P(R|S) + P(R|S') = 1$.
20. ( ) $P(RS) + P(RS') = P(R)$.
21. ( ) Odds of 13 to 7 are equivalent to a probability of 0.65.
22. ( ) Betting odds at a horse racetrack can be changed to an equivalent winning probability.
23. ( ) Betting odds of 4 to 1 at a horse racetrack can be changed to an equivalent winning probability of 0.8.
24. ( ) $P(R|S) = \dfrac{P(S|R)P(R)}{P(S|R)P(R) + P(S'|R)P(S')}$
25. ( ) $P(S|R) = \dfrac{P(RS)}{P(RS) + P(RS')}$
26. Convert the following odds to probabilities. (a) 8 to 5; (b) 7 to 3; (c) 1.3 to 1; (d) 11 to 5.
27. If an investment analyst says there is a 90 percent chance that Smallfry Company will merge with Bigdeal Company, is the stated number a subjective or an objective probability? Explain.
28. Workers in a plant were classified by age and by number of days absent. Table A shows, for example, that there were 144 young workers, and that 24 of these were in the high absentee class. Find the following probabilities. (a) $P(L)$; (b) $P(E)$; (c) $P(Y)$; (d) $P(ML)$; (e) $P(HE)$; (f) $P(ME)$; (g) $P(H|Y)$; (h) $P(H|E)$; (i) $P(M|L)$; (j) $P(Y \text{ or } M)$; (k) $P(M \text{ or } A)$; (l) $P(L \text{ or } E)$; (m) $P(L|A)$; (n) $P(Y')$; (o) $P(H')$.

TABLE A

Age class	Days absent			
	High (H)	Average (A)	Low (L)	Total
Young (Y)	24	36	84	144
Middle (M)	30	150	120	300
Elder (E).	6	114	36	156
Total	60	300	240	600

29. See Table A. (a) What relationship must be true if H and Y are independent? (b) Are H and Y independent? Show supporting numbers. (c) Are H and E independent? Show supporting numbers. (d) Are A and M independent? Show supporting numbers. (e) Is a young worker more likely to have high absenteeism

than a middle-aged or elder worker? Explain by showing the relevant numbers. (*f*) Are *M* and *E* mutually exclusive? Independent? Explain. (*g*) Are *Y* and *A* mutually exclusive? Independent? Explain. (*h*) Are *M* and *L* mutually exclusive? Independent? Explain.

30. An applicant judges the chance of getting a job to be 0.4. If a former employer has submitted a favorable recommendation, the chance of getting the job is 0.75. The chance that the employer has submitted a favorable recommendation is 0.5. Let *J* be gets the job and *F* be favorable recommendation. (*a*) Write the symbols for and calculate the probability of having a favorable recommendation and getting the job. (*b*) Fill in the following probability table, Table B. (*c*) What is the probability of getting the job if the recommendation is not favorable? (*d*) In symbols, what probability rule is illustrated by adding the two first column entries to obtain the column total? (*e*) In (*b*) find the ratio of each of the two first row entries to the row total. Add these ratios. In symbols, what probability rule is illustrated by the outcome of this addition? (*f*) Show numerically that $P(J|F) + P(J|F')$ does not equal 1.

TABLE B

	J	J'	Total
F			
F'	—	—	—
Total	—	—	—

31. In a plant, 40 percent of the workers are young, *Y*, while 30 percent are young and are good workers, *G*. Write the symbolic rule for, and calculate the probability that, a worker is good if the worker is young.
32. Given that *R* and *Q* are independent, complete the following. (*a*) $P(R|Q) =$; (*b*) $P(RQ) =$.
33. Given that *R* and *Q* are not independent, complete the following. (*a*) $P(R|Q) =$; (*b*) $P(Q|R) =$; (*c*) $P(QR) =$.
34. If a person makes an airline reservation, *R*, the probability that the person will show up, *S*, for the flight is 0.95. (*a*) If a person makes a reservation, what is the probability that the person will not show up for the flight? (*b*) Write the symbolic probability rule involved in (*a*).
35. A tire supplier has 10 tires in stock. Although they all look alike, two of them are retreads and eight are new. (*a*) If a buyer selects two at random, what is the probability that both are new? Both retreads? (*b*) If a buyer selects four, what is the probability that at least one is a retread?
36. The probability of finding oil when any well is drilled is 0.05. Assuming independence between the outcome of one drilling and another, what is the probability of finding oil at least once if four wells are drilled?
37. If $P(Q) = 0.24$ and $P(QS) = 0.06$, find $P(S|Q)$.
38. Given that *Q* and *S* are independent with $P(Q) = 0.4$ and $P(S) = 0.2$. Find $P(QS)$.
39. If $P(Q|S) = 0.25$ and $P(QS) = 0.1$, find $P(S)$.
40. *Q* and *R* have nonzero probabilities and $P(Q|R) = 0$. Must *Q* and *R* be mutually exclusive? Why?
41. Let *R*, *R'*, *Q*, *Q'* be two events and their complements. (*a*) What joint events

constitute R or Q? (b) What is the complement of R or Q? (c) Complete the following: $P(R \text{ or } Q) = 1 - P(\ )$.

42. Let S mean a new product will be successful, and F mean a favorable result in the marketing survey. Suppose that $P(S|F) = 0.8$. (a) Write the meaning of $P(S|F) = 0.8$. (b) Is it *possible* that the probability of not being successful if the survey is favorable could be 0.1? Explain. (c) Is it *possible* that the probability of success if the survey is unfavorable could be 0.9? Explain.

43. In a firm, 20 percent of all employees are executives. Records show that 80 percent of the executives and 30 percent of the nonexecutives are college graduates. What is the probability that an employee is an executive if the employee is a college graduate?

44. The A's and the B's are in a three-game playoff for the league championship, with the winner of two games becoming the champion. If the A's probability of winning any game is 0.6, independent of the outcome of previous games, what is the probability that A becomes the champion?

45. In a group of people, there are five who were born in the month of June. What is the probability that at least two of the five have the same birthday?

46. The stock of a company has been paying an annual dividend of $3 per share to stockholders. The price of a share of the stock has declined and an investor decides to buy some shares hoping that the $3 dividend will continue to be paid. Assume that the probability of continuing the $3 dividend is 0.9 if earnings are good, but only 0.2 if earnings are not good, and the probability that earnings will be good is 0.4. Find the probability that the investor will receive the $3 dividend.

47. By producing shock (seismic) waves and recording reflected sound, geologists can produce sketchy graphs of underground rock structures. A dome-shaped structure is an indicator of the possible presence of oil. Suppose that the probability of oil is 0.3 if a dome exists, but only 0.02 if a dome does not exist. After preliminary seismic tests in an area, a geologist says there is a 60 percent chance that a dome exists. What is the probability that there is oil in the area?

48. City A has its own electric power plant which supplies power adequate to meet demand except during extended summer heat waves when air conditioners are heavily used. If demand exceeds supply, A calls for aid from power plants B and C, which are in neighboring states. If B or C has excess supply, it can be diverted to A by operating switches. INC, a firm in city A, a heavy user of electricity, cannot operate without its full quota of power, and the city A power plant cannot supply this quota after several days of a heat wave unless it has aid from B or C.

    On the second day of a heat wave, Steve Holmes, the manager of INC, is concerned about the chance that the heat will continue the next day, A's capacity will be exceeded, B and C will not have excess capacity, so that INC will have to shut down. Steve thinks it is *certain* that city A's capacity will be exceeded if the heat continues, and the weather bureau states the probability it will continue is 70 percent. Steve then calls the chief engineer at the city A power plant and learns that the chance B will be able to aid if needed is 60 percent, and that if B is not able to help, the chance C can help is only 10 percent. Find the probability that INC will not have to shut down tomorrow.

49. An item is examined independently by two inspectors. The probability that inspector A will correctly classify the item as good or defective is $P(A) = 0.8$. Similarly, $P(B) = 0.9$. (a) State the meaning of the symbol $P(AB)$. (b) Compute $P(AB)$. (c) State the meaning of the symbol $P(A \text{ or } B)$. (d) Compute $P(A \text{ or } B)$. (e) What is the probability that at least one inspector will classify an item correctly?

(*f*) What is the meaning of $P(B|A)$? (*g*) What is the numerical value of $P(B|A)$? Why?

50. Suppose box A contains 9 unflawed and 1 flawed diamonds, while box *B* contains 6 unflawed and 4 flawed diamonds. A diamond selected at random from a box chosen at random is flawed. What is the probability that the selected box was *A*?

6

INTRODUCTION TO STATISTICAL DECISION ANALYSIS

6.1 INTRODUCTION

Usually, when a situation requires executive action, a choice has to be made from two or more available actions. The choice would be simple if each action had a single consequence and that consequence was known for certain, for then an executive would choose the action having the most desirable consequence. Again, however, in the usual situation an action may have various possible consequences; so an executive has to be concerned with the probabilities that these consequences will occur. In the first part of this chapter I introduce a measure called *expected monetary value*, which takes into account both the possible consequences of an action and the probabilities of these consequences. Then I discuss how decision problems may be solved by computing the expected monetary value for each available action and choosing the action having the highest expected monetary value. Next, I describe how to use *decision trees* to determine the action having the highest expected monetary value. Finally, recognizing that decision makers in different circumstances may view chancy situations differently, I consider how a particular decision maker can translate his or her own attitudes toward chances and consequences into a measure called *utility*. Then *expected utility value* can be used in place of expected monetary value in decision analysis.

6.2 EXPECTED VALUE

Formula for Expected Value

In this and later chapters we shall often use expected values. An expected value is simply a weighted average of the values X of outcomes of an experiment; the weight for each X is $P(X)$, the probability that X occurs. That is, the expected value of X is found by multiplying each of all the different values of X which may occur by its probability of occurrence $P(X)$, and then adding the products. Thus,

Formula for the expected value of X

$$\text{Expected value of } X = E(X) = \Sigma XP(X)$$

EXERCISE Generally, a weighted average is computed by (1) multiplying each X value by its weight and adding the products and then (2) dividing the sum of the products by the sum of the weights. Why is step (2) not shown in the definition $E(X) = \Sigma XP(X)$?

ANSWER The sum of the weights is the sum of the probabilities of all the different values of X which may occur. Hence, the sum of the weights is 1, and $\Sigma XP(X)$ divided by 1 is $\Sigma XP(X)$.

For all different events X,

$\Sigma P(X) = 1$

EXAMPLE A used-car dealer has sold as many as five cars in one day, and as few as none. The dealer has tabulated sales records for a large number of days and found that on 5 percent of the days $X = 0$ cars were sold. The dealer took 0.05 as the probability of zero sales in a day, as shown in Table 6.1. Probabilities for sales of 1, 2, 3, 4, and 5 cars were assigned in the same manner. The rightmost column lists $XP(X)$, which is number sold X

TABLE 6.1
COMPUTING THE EXPECTED VALUE
OF CAR SALES

Number of cars sold per day X	Probability for number sold P(X)	XP(X)
0	0.05	0.00
1	0.15	0.15
2	0.35	0.70
3	0.25	0.75
4	0.12	0.48
5	0.08	0.40
	1.00	2.48
Expected value of daily sales = $E(X)$ = 2.48		

weighted (multiplied) by the probability of selling this number $P(X)$, for each of the possible values of X. The expected value of daily sales is then

$$E(X) = \Sigma XP(X) = 2.48$$

E(X) is a long-run average expectation.

$E(X) = 2.48$ cars per day obviously does not mean 2.48 cars will be sold on a specific day, but rather how many cars per day will be sold on the average over the long run. Thus, if N is a large number of days, then expected sales for N days would be $NE(X)$. For example, for $N = 300$ days, a reasonably long run, expected sales would be estimated at about

$$NE(X) = 300(2.48) = 744 \text{ cars}$$

Similarly, if a coin is tossed, the number of heads appearing is either $X = 0$ or $X = 1$. Each value of X has a probability of 0.5; so the expected number of heads is

$$E(X) = \Sigma XP(X) = 0.5(0) + 0.5(1) = 0.5 \text{ head per toss}$$

Thus if the coin is tossed 150 times, the expected number of heads is $150E(X) = 150(0.5) = 75$.

EXERCISE A real estate agent sells 0, 1, or 2 houses each working week with respective probabilities of 0.5, 0.3, and 0.2. (a) Compute the expected value of the number of houses sold per week. (b) Compute expected sales for 40 weeks.
ANSWER (a) 0.7; (b) 28.

Use of Tree Diagrams

The next example shows the use of a tree diagram to convert an expected value problem into workable form.

EXAMPLE On the first visit with a customer, a salesperson sells either 2, 1, or 0 cases of a product with probabilities, respectively, of 0.2, 0.3, and 0.5. A second visit is made if 0 or 1 case was sold on the first visit, but not if 2 cases (a year's supply) were sold. Customers who bought 1 case on the first visit buy 1 or 0 on the second visit with respective probabilities of 0.4 and 0.6. Customers who bought 0 case on the first visit buy 2, 1, or 0 on the second visit with respective probabilities of 0.1, 0.3, and 0.6. No further visits are made. Find the expected number of cases sold per customer.

"Expected number of cases" means "expected value of the number of cases."

SOLUTION The tree of Figure 6.1 shows the numbers of cases that can be sold to a customer. On the top branch, 2 are sold on the first visit; so no second visit is made and the number sold is 2. If 1 is sold on the first visit and 1 on the second visit, the total also is 2, as shown by the second entry in the number sold column in the figure. The remaining entries are found by similar additions.

First visit	Second visit	Number sold
Sell 2		2
Sell 1	Sell 1	2
	Sell 0	1
Sell 0	Sell 2	2
	Sell 1	1
	Sell 0	0

FIGURE 6.1
Tree diagram for sales visits.

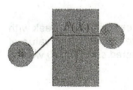

Use circles for nodes. Write probabilities on branches.

Figure 6.2 contains the probabilities given in the statement of the example, and the computed probabilities for the various numbers of cases that can be sold. The top branch, sell 2 on the first visit (no second visit), has the given probability, 0.2, which is the first entry in the $P(X)$ column. The event sell 1 on the first visit has the given probability 0.3 on its branch to node a. The two second visit branches from this node contain the conditional probabilities 0.4 and 0.6. These, when multiplied by the probability of 0.3 at their beginning node, lead to the joint probabilities 0.12 and 0.18 shown in the $P(X)$ column. The remaining $P(X)$ values are computed in the same manner. The rightmost column contains the $XP(X)$ products, and we find, by adding,

$$E(X) = \Sigma XP(X) = 1.07 \text{ cases per customer}$$

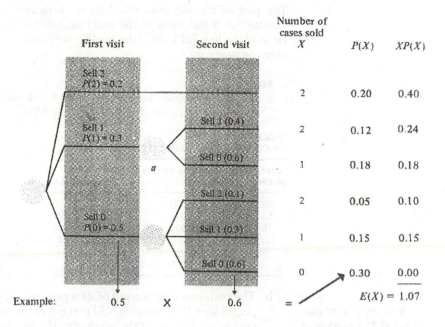

FIGURE 6.2
Calculating expected
sales.

		Number of cases sold X	P(X)	XP(X)
First visit	Second visit			
Sell 2 P(2) = 0.2		2	0.20	0.40
Sell 1 P(1) = 0.3	Sell 1 (0.4)	2	0.12	0.24
	Sell 0 (0.6)	1	0.18	0.18
	Sell 2 (0.1)	2	0.05	0.10
Sell 0 P(0) = 0.5	Sell 1 (0.3)	1	0.15	0.15
	Sell 0 (0.6)	0	0.30	0.00

Example: 0.5   X   0.6   = $E(X) = 1.07$

EXERCISE On Figure 6.2, change the first visit probabilities for sales of 2, 1,
and 0 to, respectively, 0.4, 0.4, and 0.2, and leave the second visit probabilities
unchanged. Compute expected sales per customer.
ANSWER 1.46.

Expected Monetary Value

*EMV: Expected mone-
tary value in dollars*

When the numbers being averaged are in monetary units, say, United States
dollars, expected value is often referred to as *expected monetary value* and
symbolized by EMV. It is computed in the same way as other expected values.

EXAMPLE A fire insurance company assigns a probability of 0.001 that a
particular type of building will be completely destroyed by fire during a year,
in which case the company will have to pay the insured 100 percent of the
value of the building. Similarly, the probabilities of 50 percent and 10 percent damage to the building are, respectively, 0.004 and 0.005. The company classifies all damage as being in one of these three categories. As a first
step in determining the amount to be paid for insurance on the building, the
company finds the expected monetary value of losses that will occur if the
building is damaged by fire. The amount to be paid by the buyer of the insurance is called the *premium*. The premium is larger than the expected loss
because the insurance company has to cover expenses and make a profit.

The part of the premium which is for expenses and profit is called the *loading*. (*a*) If the value of the building is $80,000, compute the expected value of the loss $E(L)$. (*b*) If the loading is 30 percent of the premium, compute the premium.

SOLUTION

a. Table 6.2 summarizes the given data and shows the computation of the expected value of the loss $E(L) = \$280$.

TABLE 6.2
CALCULATING THE EXPECTED LOSS

Loss, percent	Dollar value of loss L	P(L)	LP(L)
100	$80,000	0.001	$ 80
50	40,000	0.004	160
10	8,000	0.005	40
0	0	0.990	0
			$280

$$E(L) = \Sigma LP(L) = \$280$$

If loading is 30 percent (0.3), premium is

$$\frac{E(L)}{1 - 0.3}$$

b. The premium (100 percent of it) is part for loading and part for the expected loss. If the loading is 30 percent of the premium, $E(L)$ is 70 percent of (or 0.7 times) the premium. Hence,

$$0.7 \text{ (premium)} = E(L)$$

$$0.7 \text{ (premium)} = \$280$$

$$\text{Premium} = \frac{\$280}{0.7}$$

$$\text{Premium} = \$400$$

The difference between the premium, $400, and the expected loss, $280, is $120. Note that $120 is 30 percent of the $400 premium, as required.

EXERCISE Following the last example, (*a*) find the expected loss for a building valued at $20,000; (*b*) find the premium if the loading is 25 percent of the premium.

ANSWER (*a*) $70; (*b*) $93.33.

The game of queens

Two of six cards are queens

Expected value calculations may involve both gain and loss (negative gain) events.

EXAMPLE In the carnival game of queens, the operator shuffles six cards and places them face down on a table. Two of the cards are kings, two are queens, and two are jacks. The player, called the "mark" in carnival language, selects two cards. The operator bets the mark $5 even money that at least one of the selected cards is a queen. What is the mark's expected value in playing this game?

SOLUTION The bet means the mark wins $5 or loses $5. The outcomes for the mark are expressed as $5 and $-$5$. The mark wins if neither of the two selected cards is a queen. Because there are 4 nonqueens, the chance that the first card selected is not a queen is 4/6. Then if the first card is not a queen, the chance that the second is not a queen is 3/5. Hence, by the rule for the probability of a joint event,

$$P\text{(first card is not a queen } and \text{ second card is not a queen)} = \frac{4}{6} \cdot \frac{3}{5} = \frac{2}{5} = 0.4$$

The mark has a 0.4 probability of winning $5 and a $1 - 0.4 = 0.6$ probability of losing $5. Hence, the mark's expected value in playing the game is

A negative expected value is an expected loss.

$$\$5(0.4) + (-\$5)(0.6) = \$2 - \$3 = -\$1$$

On the average, the mark will lose $1 per play.

6.3 PROBLEMS

1. A retail store receives 3, 4, 5, or 6 telephone orders per hour with respective probabilities of 0.1, 0.4, 0.3, and 0.2. (a) Compute the expected number of calls per hour. (b) Estimate the number of calls received in a 50-hour business week.

2. A salesperson sells 0, 1, 2, 3, 4, 5, or 6 stereo systems a day with respective probabilities of 0.05, 0.10, 0.35, 0.25, 0.10, 0.08, and 0.07. (a) Compute the expected number of systems sold per day. (b) Estimate the number of systems sold in 70 days.

3. A retail store buys calculators for resale. It purchases these from time to time in lots of 50 calculators each. From experience, the store has found 98 percent of the lots contain no defective calculators; so the probability of 0 defective in a lot is assumed to be 0.98. Similarly, the probabilities for 1, 2, 3, and 4 defectives are, respectively, 0.010, 0.005, 0.003, and 0.002. Compute the expected number of defectives in a lot.

4. Seventy percent of the customers entering a doughnut shop buy one dozen doughnuts and leave. Thirty percent sit at the counter for coffee; two-thirds of these have one doughnut with their coffee, and one-third have two doughnuts. Forty percent of those who sit at the counter purchase a dozen doughnuts to carry out. Find the expected number of doughnuts sold per customer.

5. If an insured building is damaged by fire, the insurance company pays the insured 100 percent of the value of the building, or 80 or 60 or 40 or 20 percent, depending upon the extent of the damage. The probabilities of occurrence for the various percent damages in a year are, respectively, 0.001, 0.003, 0.004, 0.009, and 0.018. A building valued at

$120,000 is to be insured. (*a*) Calculate the expected monetary value of the insurance company's losses if the building is damaged by fire. (*b*) Calculate the premium the insured will pay if the insurance company's loading is one-third of the premium.

6. Contractor *A* spends $5000 to prepare a bid on a construction project which, after deducting expenses and the cost of bidding, will yield a profit of $25,000 if the bid is won. Contractor *A* thinks the chance of winning the contract is 10 percent. Compute the EMV of *A*'s profit.

7. Contractor *X* spends $10,000 to prepare a bid on a construction project which, after deducting expenses and the cost of bidding, will yield a profit of $50,000. Contractor *Y* is the only competitor who may also submit a bid. *X* thinks that his chance of winning if *Y* bids is only 0.10 but is 0.60 if *Y* does not bid, and that the chance that *Y* will bid is 0.8. Compute the EMV of *X*'s profit.

6.4 THE EMV DECISION CRITERION

The possible consequences of various courses of action are called *payoffs*. Medical doctors may use numbers of years of prolonged life as the possible payoffs for different methods of treating a disease. Political candidates may use numbers of votes as payoffs. Thus, what a decision maker considers as being payoffs depends upon the decision maker's objectives. In business decisions, payoffs are often expressed in terms of dollars of profit or loss. In what follows the term *payoff* will mean dollars.

Business payoffs are most often in dollars.

At the time that a choice is being made from available courses of action, a decision maker has to consider the events that may occur and the payoffs for each action if certain events do occur. Now suppose that the decision maker lists actions, events, event probabilities, and payoffs: Then the decision maker chooses the action which has the maximum (greatest) EMV. *Choosing the maximum EMV action is called using the EMV decision criterion.*

EMV decision criterion

To illustrate the EMV decision criterion in a simple manner, consider a simple example. Suppose that several months prior to the spring selling season, the buyer for a retail store has to decide whether to stock a large number or a small number of spring coats. The buyer will set the selling price at the beginning of the season, maintain this price if customer demand is high, but later put coats on sale at a lower price if demand is low. The buyer estimates that payoffs will be as shown in Table 6.3. They depend upon the action taken (buy large or small stock) and customer demand (high or low). Thus, for example, if the action taken is "buy a large stock" and demand turns out to be high, the profit payoff is $20,000. However, if demand turns out to be low, a loss of $6000 will be incurred. The decision maker has control over which action will be taken, but not over demand, which is a chance event. Table 6.3 is a *payoff* table for our example. In more general terms, a payoff table lists *all* the alternative action choices as column headings and all the uncontrollable chance events as row labels. The entries are the payoffs for each combination of an action and a chance event.

TABLE 6.3
PAYOFF TABLE

| | Actions, A | |
Events, E	A_1 Buy large stock	A_2 Buy small stock
High demand	$20,000	$10,000
Low demand	−6,000	5,000

The buyer next assesses the probabilities for high demand and for low demand at 0.6 and 0.4, respectively, then computes the EMV of each action. Thus, the EMV of action A_1 (buy large stock) is

$$EMV(A_1) = \binom{\text{payoff if}}{\text{high demand}} P(\text{high demand})$$

$$+ \binom{\text{payoff if}}{\text{low demand}} P(\text{low demand})$$

$$= (\$20,000)(0.6) + (-\$6000)(0.4)$$

$$= \$12,000 - \$2400$$

$$= \$9600$$

EXERCISE See Table 6.3. Compute the EMV of action A_2.
ANSWER $8000.

Observe that

$$EMV(\text{buy large stock}) = \$9600$$

$$EMV(\text{buy small stock}) = \$8000$$

EMV decision criterion: choose the action with the highest EMV.

If the buyer follows the EMV decision criterion, the action taken will be to buy a large stock.

EXERCISE Use the same payoffs as in the example just given, but change the probabilities of high and low demand to 0.4 and 0.6, respectively. (a) Find the EMVs of the two actions. (b) Which action would be decided upon according to the EMV criterion?
ANSWER (a) $4400 and $7000. (b) Buy a small stock.

Our buyer, of course, would have to consider many actions (numbers of coats that can be bought) and many chance events (numbers that might be sold). Many actions and many events complicate calculations; so the best way to learn decision analysis is to work with simplified situations.

EXAMPLE A publisher thinks demand for a book will be 100, 200, or 300 copies, with respective probabilities 0.4, 0.3, and 0.3. Total costs for printing

100, 200, and 300 copies are $250, $400, and $550. The books are sold at $5 per copy. The book is of short-term interest, so that copies unsold after 3 months are worthless. However, if demand exceeds the number printed, a second printing of 100 or 200 additional copies may be made to meet demand. Should the publisher decide on 100, 200, or 300 as the size of the initial printing?

SOLUTION Here,

Payoff accounting

$$\text{Payoff} = \text{sales income} - \text{cost of printing}$$

and three cases must be considered.

Case 1 Number demanded equals number initially printed. Suppose the demand is 200, and the initial printing is 200. Then,

Income	$5(200) = $1000
Cost	= $\underline{400}$
Payoff	$ 600

Case 2 Demand exceeds initial printing. Suppose the demand is 300, and the initial printing is 200. Then,

Income	$5(300) = $1500
Cost	
Initial 200	= $400
Additional 100	= $\underline{250}$
	= $\underline{650}$
Payoff	$ 850

Case 3 Demand is less than initial printing. Suppose the demand is 100, and the initial printing is 200. Then,

Income	$5(100) = $500
Cost of 200	= $\underline{400}$
Payoff	$100

EXERCISE Compute the payoff if (*a*) 100 are demanded, and the initial printing is 300; (*b*) 300 are demanded, and the initial printing is 100.
ANSWER (*a*) −$50; (*b*) $850.

Each payoff is computed from one action and one demand.

Calculations such as those above lead us to the payoffs in Table 6.4. Computing the EMV of the action "initial printing 100," we find

$$\text{EMV(print 100)} = 250(0.4) + 500(0.3) + 850(0.3)$$

$$= 100 + 150 + 255$$

$$= \$505$$

TABLE 6.4
BOOK DEMAND PAYOFF TABLE, WITH DEMAND
PROBABILITIES

		Action (number initially printed)		
Event D, number demanded	P(D)	100	200	300
100	0.4	$250	$100	− $ 50
200	0.3	500	600	450
300	0.3	850	850	950

EXERCISE Compute the EMV of (a) print 200; (b) print 300.
ANSWER (a) $475; (b) $400.

The EMVs for initial printings of 100, 200, and 300 are $505, $475, and $400, respectively. Applying the EMV decision criterion, the action chosen will be an initial printing of 100.

6.5 DECISION TREES FOR EMV CRITERION

is a decision node

is a chance node

The first step in analysis by a decision tree is to construct a "bare" tree. A bare decision tree is used to describe the sequence in which actions must be taken and chance events will occur. Let's use the earlier retail-store buyer example to introduce the procedure. Figure 6.3 shows the bare tree. We use a rectangle to represent a decision node. Action branches stem from a decision node. A circle represents a chance node. Event branches stem from a chance node. The action-event sequence in this example is simple. First a decision will be made; then a chance event will happen. However, buyers have to think "backward" when analyzing the situation; that is, they have to consider the payoffs and probabilities for the events before making a decision. It is for this reason that they draw the decision tree.

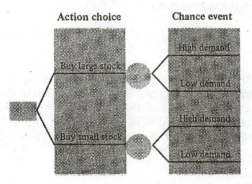

FIGURE 6.3
Bare decision-tree diagram. Rectangle = decision node; circle = chance node.

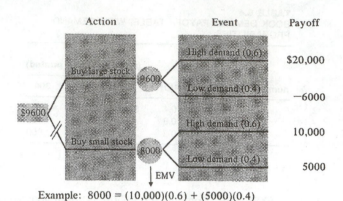

FIGURE 6.4
Decision tree with probabilities, payoffs, and EMV (expected monetary values).

Example: 8000 = (10,000)(0.6) + (5000)(0.4)

Figure 6.4 shows the tree with the payoffs and the event probabilities. Now the buyer computes the EMVs at the chance nodes ($9600 and $8000) and enters each EMV in its node. The buyer finds the "buy large stock" action has the higher EMV ($9600), and so cuts off the other action branch, as indicated by | | on Figure 6.4.

Procedure for using the EMV criterion with a decision tree

The tree approach to decision analysis is as follows:

1. Construct the bare tree to show the proper action-event sequence, from left to right.
2. Enter the payoffs at the ends of the rightmost branches.
3. Enter the event probabilities for the branches stemming from each chance node.
4. Work backward, from right to left: when a chance node is encountered, compute its EMV and enter it in the node. When a decision node is encountered, choose the action branch having the highest EMV, enter that EMV in the node, and cut off other action branches.
5. The leftmost decision node will contain the maximum EMV. The uncut branches are the maximum EMV actions.

EXERCISE Why is it that a decision maker can cut off an action branch but cannot cut off an event branch?

ANSWER The decision maker has control over actions, but not over the outcome at a chance node.

Now let's extend the tree procedure a little by considering another situation.

EXAMPLE (*Note:* To save excessive writing of zeros, all dollar values in this example are assumed to be in thousands of dollars.) Three months ago, the executive board of a company authorized the development of a new product. If marketed at its current stage of development, the product has probabilities of 0.50 of returning a large payoff ($200), 0.30 for a medium

($100) payoff, and 0.20 for a small ($20) payoff. These payoffs are net profit after expenses and first-stage development costs. The board believes that if an additional $30 is spent on second-stage development, reducing each payoff by $30, and the further development is successful, the probabilities of large, medium, and small payoffs will be changed to 0.80, 0.15, and 0.05, respectively. However, the first-stage probabilities will apply if further development is not successful. The board believes the probability is 0.60 that second-stage development will be successful. By tree diagram analysis, determine whether the board should authorize further development or market the product at its current stage of development.

Step 1 *Draw the bare tree.*

SOLUTION The decision to be made is between "further development" and "no further development," as shown in Figure 6.5. We now work on one

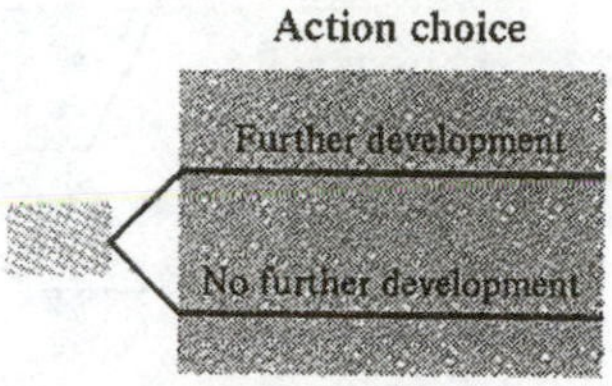

Action choice

Further development

No further development

FIGURE 6.5
Where to start.

of these branches, say the top one, and ask *then what* questions. For example, if further development is chosen, then what will happen? The answer is that the development may (chance node) be successful or not successful. Suppose it is successful, then what? Now the answer is that the payoff may (another chance node) be large, medium, or small. Figure 6.6 shows the analysis to this point.

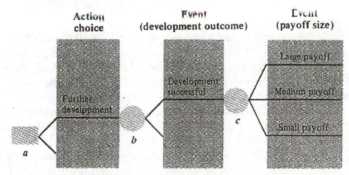

Action choice

Event (development outcome)

Event (payoff size)

Large payoff

Medium payoff

Small payoff

Development successful

Further development

c

b

FIGURE 6.6
Then what?

a

Next we start with "further development" and follow the incomplete (development not successful) branch from chance node *b* in Figure 6.6. The answers to "then what" would be large, medium, or small payoff. Finally, starting from the incomplete branch (no further development) from deci-

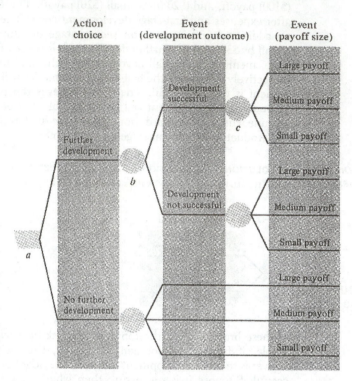

FIGURE 6.7
Completed executive
board bare decision
tree.

sion node *a*, the answer to "then what" is large, medium, or small payoff. The completed tree is shown in Figure 6.7.

Step 2   Enter the payoffs.

Now for the payoffs and probabilities. The example states that if the product is marketed at its present stage with no further development, large, medium, and small payoffs of $200, $100, and $20 have respective probabilities of 0.50, 0.30, and 0.20. The numbers in the last sentence are shown on the bottom three branches of Figure 6.8. Next, the example states that further development will cost $30, reducing the payoffs from $200, $100, and $20 to $170, $70, and −$10, respectively. The $170, $70, and −$10 occur for both successful and unsuccessful further development; so they appear at the ends of both the top three and the middle three branches of Figure 6.8. However, the example states that the respective payoff probabilities are 0.80, 0.15, and 0.05 for successful development but 0.50, 0.30, and 0.20 for unsuccessful development. The payoff probabilities in the last sentence are entered in order on the top six payoff branches of the figure. Then, noting from the example statement that further development has a probability 0.60 of being successful, we enter 0.60 and 1 − 0.60 = 0.40 on the branches from the chance node at *b*.

Step 3   Enter the probabilities.

Step 4   Compute and enter the EMVs.

Next we work our way backward (right to left) on Figure 6.8, computing EMVs at chance nodes as we go. Thus, at chance node *c*

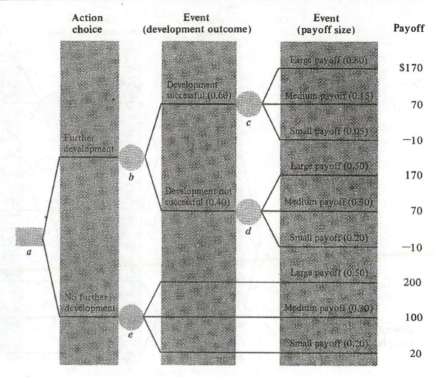

Action choice	Event (development outcome)	Event (payoff size)	Payoff

FIGURE 6.8
Executive board decision tree with payoffs and probabilities.

$$EMV = 0.80(170) + 0.15(70) + 0.05(-10) = 146$$

as shown in Figure 6.9 (on page 166).

EXERCISE Verify the entries 104 and 134 at chance nodes d, and e, respectively, in Figure 6.9.

For the chance node at b in Figure 6.9, we now find

$$EMV = 0.60(146) + 0.40(104) = 129.2$$

Step 5 *Note the maximum EMV action choice.*

Finally, from the *decision* node at a, the decision maker sees an EMV of $134 on the no further development branch and the smaller EMV, $129.2, on the further development branch. Consequently, the further development branch is cut off as shown by | | in Figure 6.9. The maximum EMV choice is no further development; its EMV, 134, is entered at a.

EXERCISE For practice assume that, in the foregoing example, probabilities for large, medium, and small markets are 0.90, 0.07, and 0.03, if further development is successful. (a) What is the EMV decision now? (b) What is the EMV of this decision?

ANSWER (a) Do further development before marketing the product. (b) $136.16.

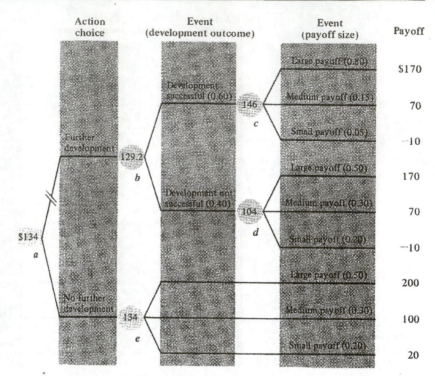

FIGURE 6.9
Executive board decision: No further development.

The next example involves a situation in which two decisions have to be made.

EXAMPLE (*Note:* All dollar values are in thousands of dollars.)   A company has decided to increase production facilities. Greg Jordan and his planning associates are trying to decide between two alternatives. The first is to build a plant large enough to satisfy high customer demand if it occurs; the second is to build a smaller plant first, and then expand it later if the outlook for high demand becomes favorable. The cost of the large plant is $100. The small plant costs $60, and an additional $60 would be required to expand it to large plant size. Jordan considers only two demand levels, high and low, leading, respectively, to gross profit (before deducting plant cost) of $300 and $100 for a large plant; small plant grosses for high and low demand are $150 and $100, *Assessing* respectively. In the light of information presently available, Jordan assesses *probabilities* the probability that the market outlook will be favorable or unfavorable at 0.50. He also takes 0.50 as the probability of high demand if he does not wait to determine the market outlook. On the other hand, if a small plant is built, the probability of high demand is 0.95 if the market outlook proves to be favorable but only 0.20 if the market outlook proves to be unfavorable. What decision should Jordan make?

SOLUTION We note that the first decision to be made is whether to build a small plant or a large plant. If the small plant is built, *then* a chance event (favorable or unfavorable market outlook) occurs, *after* which the decision to expand or not expand the plant must be made. Then a second chance event (high or low demand) occurs. The bare decision tree is shown in Figure 6.10.

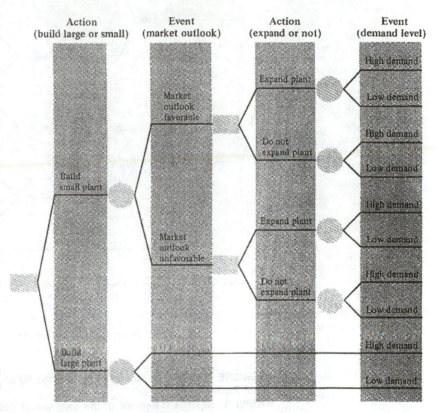

| Action (build large or small) | Event (market outlook) | Action (expand or not) | Event (demand level) |

FIGURE 6.10
Bare tree for plant-size decision.

Payoff accounting

Turning next to the payoffs, suppose the large plant is built at the stated cost, $100. If demand is high, the gross profit is $300. The net profit after deducting plant cost is $300 − $100 = $200, as shown at *i* on Figure 6.11 (on page 168). However, the gross for low demand is $100, and this value minus the $100 large plant cost leaves a payoff of $0 as shown at *j*.

If a small plant is built at a cost of $60, then expanded at the cost of another $60, the total cost is $120. The expanded plant can gross $300 for high demand, leaving a net payoff of $300 − $120 = $180, as shown at *a* on Figure 6.11. But if demand is low, the gross will be $100 and the net payoff will be $100 − $120 = − $20, as shown at *b*. The payoffs at *e* and *f* also are $180

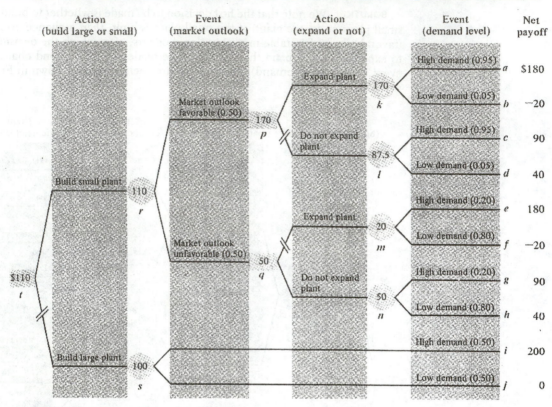

Action (build large or small)	Event (market outlook)	Action (expand or not)	Event (demand level)	Net payoff

FIGURE 6.11
Finding Jordan's decision.

and − $20 because actions again are to build a small plant and then expand it.

EXERCISE Explain the source of the payoffs 90 and 40 at *g* and *h*, respectively, of Figure 6.11.
ANSWER See the statement of the example. It costs $60 to build a small plant (but not expand it). The small plant can gross only $150 even if demand is high, leaving a net payoff of $150 − $60 = $90. If demand is low (gross $100), the net payoff will be $100 − $60 = $40.

Working backward through the tree

I leave it for you to verify that the probabilities entered on Figure 6.11 are those given in the statement of the example. Now we compute EMVs at the chance nodes, starting from the right and working to the left. Thus,

$$\text{EMV at } k = (0.95)(180) + (0.05)(-20) = 171 - 1 = 170$$

The EMVs at *l*, *m*, and *n* are found in the same manner.

Now move back to the *decision* node at *p*. Here we have a choice between actions with EMVs of 170 and 87.5; so we choose the action (expand plant) with the higher EMV and enter its EMV, 170, in the decision node; the other action branch (do not expand) is cut off. Similarly, we obtain the 50 entered in the decision node q.

Next, again moving backward, we compute the EMV at the chance node r

$$\text{EMV at } r = (0.50)(170) + (0.50)(50) = 110$$

Greg's EMV course of actions

The EMV at chance node s is found to be 100. Finally, moving back to the decision node t, we find the "build small plant" action branch has the higher EMV, 110; so we cut off the other action branch. The course of actions is specified by the parts of the tree which have not been cut off, as follows: Build a small plant; then if the market outlook is favorable, expand the plant—but if the outlook is unfavorable, do not expand the plant. The expected value of the payoff for this course of action is $110.

EXERCISE Although the maximum EMV is $110, Greg cannot earn $110 exactly. What possible payoffs could Greg earn by following the EMV course of actions?
ANSWER $180, −$20, $90, $40.

6.6 EMV MAY NOT BE A SATISFACTORY CRITERION

This section opens with a conversation which shows that a person may choose not to use the EMV criterion in making a decision. In following sections we shall discuss a procedure that can be used to solve a decision problem when EMV is not acceptable to the decision maker.

Fran: Dan, remember that law case I told you about? My lawyer says I have an eighty percent chance of being awarded fifty thousand dollars. She wants to know if I'd rather settle out of court. I've thought about it a lot, and I'd rather settle.

Dan: Why? Because of the hassle?

Fran: No. All I have to do is call the lawyer and she will handle things. So there's no hassle. But her fee is ten thousand is she goes to trial, so I'd be out the ten thousand if I lose.

Dan: If you win, you get fifty thousand less the ten thousand fee. If you lose, you are out ten thousand. So the chances are eighty percent for getting forty thousand and twenty percent for losing ten thousand. That gives an expected monetary value of thirty thousand.

Fran: That's right, but I don't like the chance of losing ten thousand, so I've decided I will settle for about twenty thousand even though the EMV is thirty. What would you do?

Dan: In my circumstances, with college bills and all, I'd be in a bad hole if I had to pay that ten grand fee. I'd settle for fifteen thousand. But your circumstances are different from mine—you have to make up your own mind. Would you settle for fifteen?

Fran: I don't like the thought of paying ten thousand if I lose, but I can handle that. And I don't expect to lose. After all, an eighty percent

Fran is indifferent to a $20,000 settlement and is taking her chances in court.

chance of winning is pretty high. As far as I am concerned, settling for twenty thousand or taking my chances in court are the same thing. I'd be willing to flip a coin to make that choice; or let someone else make the choice. But if I had to settle for fifteen or go to court, I'd rather go to court.

Fran, we note, did not apply the maximum EMV criterion in making her decision. Instead, she thought about the chances and the possible payoffs in the light of her own circumstances. Note also that she and Dan came up with different results; $20,000 for Fran and $15,000 for Dan. The variation illustrates the fact that attitudes toward chances and payoffs are affected by a decision maker's circumstances.

Circumstances affect attitudes toward chances and payoffs.

EXERCISE Your generous parents offer you the following choices: (1) Receive $200 or (2) toss a coin and receive $500 for heads but nothing for tails. Which choice would you make? Why?

I cannot answer the exercise for you. The EMV of the coin toss is 0.5($500) + 0.5($0) = $250, which is greater than the certain amount, $200. I would take the chance because a few hundred dollars is of little importance to me in my circumstances. However, a majority of my students say they would take the $200 for certain rather than the 50-50 chance at $500 or nothing.

We shall call a set of chances and payoffs a *chance situation* and refer to a decision maker's attitudes toward chances and payoffs as "attitudes toward chance situations." These attitudes, of course, reflect the decision maker's circumstances. We have seen that EMV does not take into account different attitudes toward chance situations. In what follows, we shall develop a procedure which allows these attitudes to be included in decision analyses.

Meaning of a chance situation

6.7 CERTAINTY EQUIVALENT FOR A CHANCE SITUATION

In the conversation recorded earlier, Fran said she would be willing to toss a coin to decide between a $20,000 settlement and going to court; she was indifferent to that choice. To Fran $20,000 for certain is the same as, or equivalent to, an 80-20 chance at $40,000 or −$10,000. We shall say that $20,000 is Fran's certainty equivalent for the chance situation.

Certainty equivalent for a chance situation

The *certainty equivalent* (CE) for a chance situation is the certain payoff (a payoff with probability 1) that a decision maker considers to be equivalent to the chance situation.

Figure 6.12 illustrates Fran's certainty equivalent for her chance situation. The certainty equivalence goes both ways; that is, the chance situation is equivalent to $20,000, and $20,000 is equivalent to the chance situation.

EXERCISE Suppose you had the happy choice of (a) an amount of money for certain or (b) a 50-50 chance at $1000 or nothing. What is your certainty

FIGURE 6.12
Fran's certainty equiva-
lent.

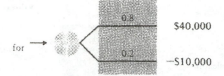

equivalent for the chance situation? Remember, you must be willing to let someone else decide whether you get your certainty equivalent or have to take the
chance.

6.8 UTILITY AND THE EXPECTED UTILITY CRITERION

Utility is a measure which quantitatively expresses a decision maker's attitudes toward chance situations. In this section we shall show how dollar
payoffs for decision problems can be converted to corresponding utility
measures. Then the choice of action can be determined by using expected
Using EUV instead of utility value EUV in place of expected monetary value.
EMV   To derive utility measures which reflect attitudes toward chance situations, a decision maker must first consider the best and worst circumstance
that might arise. Suppose, for example, that Bart Dart owns a small business. After careful thought about his circumstances, Bart concludes that the
best possible situation that could arise is one which would provide a certain
(probability 1) payoff of $60,000 and that the worst possible situation would
be one with a certain payoff of − $40,000 (a $40,000 loss). The best and worst
payoffs are called *reference values*. Bart's best possible situation has a certainty equivalent of $60,000, because it is $60,000 with probability 1 and
− $40,000 with probability 0. Similarly, Bart's worst possible situation has a
certainty equivalent of − $40,000.

Utility of a certainty   The *utility* of a certainty equivalent is defined as the probability for the
equivalent   *higher* reference value in the equivalent chance situation involving only the
reference values. Thus, Figure 6.13 shows that Bart's utility for $60,000 is 1.
Figure 6.14 (at the top of page 172) shows his utility for − $40,000 is 0. In
general, utilities for the best and worst payoffs are 1 and 0, respectively.

Our next objective is to determine Bart's utilities for dollar payoffs
between his reference values. To do this, we ask Bart to assign certainty

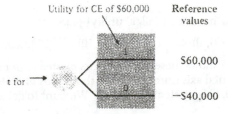

FIGURE 6.13
Bart's utility for
$60,000 is 1.

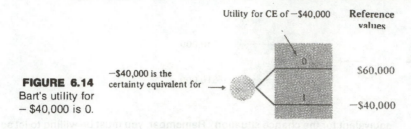

Utility for CE of −$40,000   Reference values

FIGURE 6.14
Bart's utility for
− $40,000 is 0.

−$40,000 is the
certainty equivalent for →

0    $60,000

1   −$40,000

Translation: I would pay $10,000 not to take equal chances of gaining $60,000 or losing $40,000.

equivalents for various chance situations involving his reference values. Suppose, for example, we ask him to assess his CE for a 50-50 chance at $60,000 and − $40,000. Bart considers the question and says he would pay to get out of the chance situation because a $40,000 loss could mean bankruptcy. After deliberating, Bart sets the CE at − $10,000; he would pay $10,000 to get out of the chance situation. The probability for the higher reference value is 0.5; so Bart's utility for − $10,000 is 0.5, as shown in Figure 6.15.

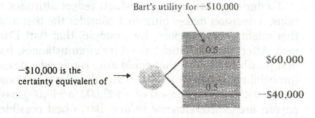

Bart's utility for −$10,000

FIGURE 6.15
Bart's utility for
− $10,000 is 0.5.

−$10,000 is the
certainty equivalent of →

0.5 $60,000

0.5   −$40,000

Translation: You would have to pay Bart $23,000 to buy his 75-25 chance of gaining $60,000 or losing $40,000.

EXERCISE See Figure 6.16. (a) What was Bart asked to do? (b) What was his response? (c) What is the resulting utility relationship?

ANSWER (a) To set his CE for a 75-25 chance at his reference values. (b) $23,000. (c) Bart's utility for $23,000 is 0.75.

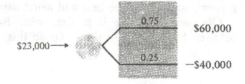

FIGURE 6.16
What did Bart do here?
(See exercise.)

$23,000 →

0.75 $60,000

0.25   −$40,000

We now have the (dollar, utility) pairs

(− $40,000, 0)   (− $10,000, 0.50)   ($23,000, 0.75)   ($60,000, 1)

Figure 6.17 shows these number pairs plotted as points on a graph. Note that the horizontal axis numbers are in thousands of dollars so that, for example, (− $40,000, 0) is plotted as (− 40, 0). We want to get enough points to make it

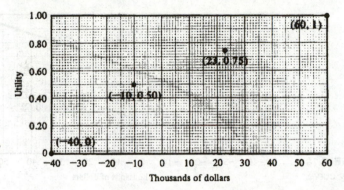

FIGURE 6.17
Some points on Bart's utility curve.

possible to sketch a smooth curve which will be Bart's utility curve. Consequently, we must ask Bart to assess certainty equivalents for more different chances at his reference values. Suppose Bart has done this, and provided the data in Table 6.5.

TABLE 6.5
POINTS ON BART'S UTILITY CURVE

Thousands of dollars	Utility
−40	0.00
−30	0.25
−20	0.40
−10	0.50
10	0.66
23	0.75
30	0.80
45	0.90
60	1.00

EXERCISE See Table 6.5. What do the numbers 45 and 0.90 on the next to the last line mean?
ANSWER Bart assigned a $45,000 certainty equivalent for a 90-10 chance at $60,000 and −$40,000.

Figure 6.18 (on page 174) contains the points of Table 6.5, with a smooth curve sketched through the points. This is Bart's utility curve. From the graph we can determine Bart's utility for any dollar amount. For example, as shown by the dashed lines on the figure, the utility of $5000 is found by drawing first a vertical line from $5000 to intersect the curve and then a horizontal line from the intersection point to the utility scale, where 0.62 is found as the utility of $5000.

After a utility curve has been drawn, utilities replace dollars and EUV re-

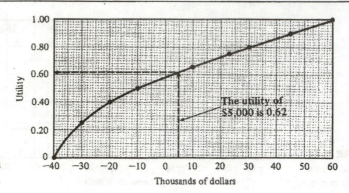

FIGURE 6.18
Bart's utility curve.

Steps: Utility decision analysis

places EMV. The steps in decision analysis using utilities are (1) construct the decision tree, then enter the final dollar payoffs and the probabilities; (2) replace the dollar payoffs by utilities read from the utility curve; (3) work backward through the tree. Compute *expected utility value* EUV at each chance node. At each decision node, select the action having the largest EUV and cut off other action branches. This three-step procedure will lead ultimately to the course of actions having the largest expected utility value.

The *EUV decision criterion* is to choose the course of action having the highest expected utility. As a simple illustration of the criterion, suppose Bart has the choice between two actions. Action A_1 has a payoff of $10,000 for certain. Action A_2 is a 55-45 chance with respective payoffs of $45,000 and −$30,000.

Figure 6.19 shows that the expected monetary value of the chance situa-

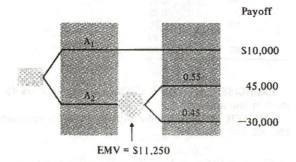

FIGURE 6.19
Bart's choices with
dollar payoffs.

tion A_2, $11,250, is greater than the $10,000 payoff for A_1. However, Bart will use his own utility curve to make the decision. He replaces the dollar payoffs of Figure 6.19 by their utilities, using his utility curve, to obtain Figure 6.20. Then he computes the expected utility of the chance situation by multiplying each utility by its probability and adding the products to obtain

$$EUV = (0.55)(0.90) + (0.45)(0.25) = 0.6075$$

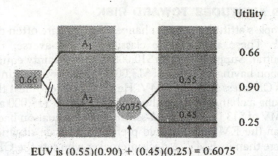

FIGURE 6.20
Bart's decision based
on utility.

EUV is $(0.55)(0.90) + (0.45)(0.25) = 0.6075$

*The decision is based
on the decision
maker's own evalua-
tion of chance situa-
tions*

Moving back to the decision node at the left, Bart will choose A_1 because its utility, 0.66, is greater than the expected utility, 0.6075, of A_2.

Now compare the last two figures. From Figure 6.19 we see that a decision maker using the EMV criterion would choose A_2. But Bart, after evaluating chance situations in the light of his circumstances and constructing his utility curve, chooses A_1. The EMV and the EUV courses of action often are the same, but there are important situations where they are different.

EXERCISE See Table 6.5 or Figure 6.18. Bart has to choose between action A_1, which is \$10,000 for certain, and A_2 which is a 75-25 chance at, respectively, \$30,000 or −\$20,000. (a) What is the utility of A_1? (b) What is the expected utility of A_2? (c) Which action will Bart choose?
ANSWER (a) 0.66; (b) 0.70; (c) A_2.

If you are skeptical about Bart's uncanny ability to provide certainty equivalents which led to the nice smooth curve in Figure 6.18—you should be. I contrived the example to make Bart consistent in his attitudes toward chance situations. In practice, a first attempt at assigning utilities generally will reveal inconsistencies which the decision maker will have to resolve. An obvious inconsistency would be to have the lower of two dollar payoffs have the higher utility. Utilities are personal assessments; so no rules can be stated for resolving inconsistencies. The resolution has to be made by the individual decision maker.

*Utility curves must
rise to the right—or
something is not
right.*

EXERCISE See Figure 6.18. The farther you go to the right on this curve, the higher the curve is. Should all utility curves rise as they move to the right? Explain.
ANSWER Yes, because logically the greater the dollar payoff, the higher should be its utility.

The exercise points out one common characteristic of utility curves; namely, such curves rise to the right.

6.9 ATTITUDES TOWARD RISK

People's attitudes toward chance situations are often called *attitudes toward risk*. These attitudes are classified as risk-averse, risk-seeking, and risk-neutral. Suppose Joe sets $10,000 as the certainty equivalent of a chance situation having an EMV of $13,000. Joe is *risk-averse* in this situation because his CE is *less* than the EMV. He would settle for less than the EMV to avoid taking a chance. Jill, on the other hand, sets $15,000 as the CE for the same EMV of $13,000. Jill is *risk-seeking* in this situation because her CE is *greater* than the EMV. She would prefer the chance situation unless she can get more than its EMV. A decision maker who sets the CE *equal* to the EMV of $13,000 is *risk-neutral* in this situation.

Recall (Table 6.5) that Bart's utility for $30,000 is 0.8. This means $30,000 is his CE for an 80-20 chance at $60,000 and $-$40,000. The EMV of the chance situation is

$$0.8(\$60,000) + 0.2(-\$40,000) = \$40,000$$

Bart's $30,000 CE is less than the $40,000 EMV; so he is risk-averse in this situation. Now turn to Figure 6.18 and connect the lower left-hand and upper right-hand corners with a straight line. Note that the utility curve lies *above* this line. This is because Bart is risk-averse in chance situations involving $-$40,000 and $60,000.

In general, pick any two points on a utility curve corresponding to dollar payoffs $X and $Y. Connect the points with a straight line. Then in chance situations involving these payoffs, the decision maker is (1) risk-averse if the curve lies above the line, (2) risk-neutral if the "curve" and the line coincide, and (3) risk-seeking if the curve lies below the line. The three attitudes toward risk are illustrated in Figures 6.21, 6.22, and 6.23.

Utility curves show risk aversion, neutrality, or seeking.

EXERCISE See Figure 6.18. Describe Bart's attitude toward chance situations involving dollar amounts (a) in the interval $-$40,000 to $-$10,000; (b) in the interval $20,000 to $60,000.

ANSWER (a) Risk-averse. (b) Just about risk-neutral because the "curve" is practically a straight line from $20,000 to $60,000.

The curve section of Figure 6.21 is said to be *concave downward*. The curve section of Figure 6.23 is said to be *concave upward*. Business executives usually are risk-averse; so their utility curves are concave downward. These downward concave curves usually tend to flatten out, becoming more like a straight line, as they move to the right; that is, executives tend toward a risk-neutral attitude as the payoffs move toward their higher reference values. However, there are utility curves which have both concave-upward and concave-downward sections. For example, in *Decisions under Uncertainty* (Harvard Business School, Cambridge, Mass., 1960, p. 304), C. J. Grayson notes that some of the oil wildcatters he interviewed had utility curves which started concave downward (risk-averse) at the left, then changed to concave

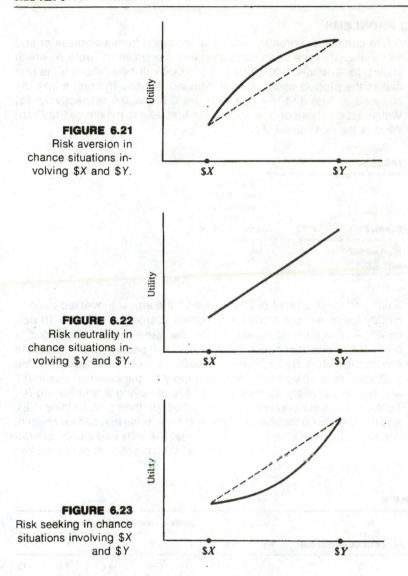

FIGURE 6.21
Risk aversion in chance situations involving $X and $Y.

FIGURE 6.22
Risk neutrality in chance situations involving $Y and $Y.

FIGURE 6.23
Risk seeking in chance situations involving $X and $Y

upward (risk-seeking). (An oil wildcatter is a person who puts up a large sum of money to drill a well in an area not known to contain oil.)

EXERCISE (a) What is your certainty equivalent for a 50-50 chance at $50 and −$20? (b) What is your attitude toward risk in this chance situation?

ANSWER (a) Enter your CE. (b) You are risk-averse, risk-neutral, or risk-seeking according as your CE is less than, equal to, or greater than $15.

6.10 PROBLEMS

1. A firm can make a product and sell it, or buy it from a wholesaler and sell it. Payoffs have been computed and are given in Table A, which shows, for example, that a profit of $50,000 will be realized if the firm makes the product and customer demand is high. The firm thinks the chances of high and low demands are 0.6 and 0.4 respectively. (a) Which action, make or buy, should the firm take to maximize EMV? (b) What is the maximum EMV?

TABLE A

Event, E	P(E)	Payoffs, thousands of dollars Make	Buy
High demand	0.6	50	35
Low demand	0.4	5	20

2. Smith can make a profit of 20 percent on the amount invested in commodity future A if commodity A becomes scarce but will lose 10 percent if A is in plentiful supply. Under the same supply conditions, a profit of 40 percent or a loss of 50 percent will occur if Smith invests in commodity future B. Smith has $50,000 to invest and assesses the probabilities of scarce and plentiful supply for the commodities at 0.7 and 0.3, respectively. Compute the EMVs of buying A and buying B.

3. Table B shows the events E which might occur, their probabilities P(E), and the payoffs (in thousands of dollars) for actions that can be chosen. For example, if the chosen action is to make 4 units and 2 units are demanded, the payoff is $11 thousand. (a) Which action should be taken if EMV is to be maximized? (b) What is the EMV of the action in (a)?

TABLE B

Event E, number of units demanded	P(E)	Action, number of units made 0	1	2	3	4	5
0	0.10	0	−7	−9	−11	−13	−15
1	0.15	0	5	3	1	−1	−3
2	0.25	0	5	15	13	11	9
3	0.30	0	5	15	25	23	21
4	0.15	0	5	15	25	35	33
5	0.05	0	5	15	25	35	45

4. Change the probabilities for demands of 0 through 5 in Problem 3 to 0.20, 0.30, 0.20, 0.15, 0.10, and 0.05, respectively. What action now has the maximum EMV? What is this EMV?

5. A wholesaler pays $100 per box for a perishable commodity and sells it at $160 per box during the 3 days the commodity is fresh. Any boxes remaining after 3 days are sold at $50 each. Possible demands during the first 3 days are 0, 1, 2, 3, 4, or 5 boxes, with respective probabilities of 0.01, 0.09, 0.20, 0.30, 0.20, and 0.20. The wholesaler must decide how many boxes to buy. (a) Make a payoff table showing profits and losses. (b) How many boxes should the wholesaler buy to maximize EMV? (c) What is the maximum EMV?

6. Suppose the wholesaler in Problem 5 can sell boxes remaining after 3 days at $80 each. What action now has the highest EMV, and what is this EMV?

Note: In answers to problems which require a decision tree, use the trees shown in the figures of this chapter as models. Include all pertinent labels and numerical values. Indicate branches to be cut off by the symbol | |.

7. Answer Problem 1 by constructing a decision tree.

8. Answer Problem 2 by constructing a decision tree.

9. A plant contributes $20,000 a day to company profit when operating but $0 when not operating. Occasionally, no electric power is available when workers arrive. In that case, partial wages must be paid, and a loss of $5000 is incurred. However, management may anticipate a power failure and order a tentative shutdown for the next day, telling workers to check the early morning newscast to find out whether they should report. In this case, if power is available tomorrow, workers will be called in. Then the plant will contribute $15,000 to company profit. If management thinks there is a 60 percent chance that power will be available tomorrow, should a tentative shutdown be ordered and workers told to check the morning newscast to find out if they should report to work? Answer by constructing and using a decision tree.

10. PC Company, the prime contractor in a development project, is considering having phases 1 and 2 of the development done by subcontractors A and B, respectively. PC is not set up to do these phases efficiently but could make a profit of $25,000 by doing the work. However, PC can realize a profit of $40,000 by subcontracting if both subcontractors complete their work on time. Smaller profits will occur if A and/or B do not finish on time as shown in Table C. The probability that A will finish on time is 0.7, and if this happens, B has a probability of 0.9 of finishing on time. However, if A is delayed, the probability that B will complete on time is 0.4. Should PC subcontract to A and B?

TABLE C

A	B	
	On time	Delayed
On time	$40,000	$30,000
Delayed	20,000	10,000

11. A company may proceed directly with the development and marketing of a proposed new product or first do a test market research study and then decide whether to abandon the product or proceed to develop and market it. The test market result may be favorable or unfavorable, and market demand may prove to be high or low. Make a tree for this decision problem.

12. (Use the tree constructed for Problem 11.) Gross profit (before costs) will be $240 thousand if demand is high and $10 thousand if demand is low. Costs, in thousands, are $65 for development and marketing and $25 for doing the test market study. If the product is developed and marketed without testing, the chances of high and low demands are 0.3 and 0.7, respectively, and these are also the respective chances for favorable and unfavorable reports from a test market study. The probabilities of high demand are 0.9 if the test market outcome is favorable and 0.05 if the outcome is unfavorable. (a) What are the EMVs of the initial action choices? (b) What procedure should the company follow according to the EMV criterion?

13. An investor can buy some property outright, running a 60-40 chance at a $100,000 profit or a $40,000 loss. Alternatively, she can pay $10,000 for an option to buy at the end of 6 months. During this period the outlook will become favorable or unfavorable, and the decision to buy or to drop the option can be based upon the outlook. The chance of a favorable outlook is the same as the chance taken if the property is purchased outright. If the property is purchased at the end of the option period, the chance of profit is 0.99 if the outlook is favorable and 0.2 if the outlook is unfavorable. (a) What are the possible dollar payoffs if the property is purchased at the end of the option period? (b) What is the payoff if the option to buy is taken but not exercised? (c) What action should be taken? What is the EMV of this action?

14. A fishing vessel may remain in its present area, 1, for the rest of the week or move to the captain's choice of a second area, 2. In either case, the fish supply may turn out to be plentiful or scarce. As a third possibility, the captain may hire a shore-based plane to fly out and look for a more promising location, 3. The pilot may or may not be successful in finding a new location. The captain will decide what to do after getting the pilot's report. A location 3, if found, may or may not have a plentiful fish supply. Make a tree diagram for the actions and events.

15. (See Problem 14.) The gross profit will be $20 thousand if fish are plentiful and $10,000 if fish are scarce. The cost of hiring the plane is $1000, and the cost of moving the boat to another location is $1000. The captain sets the chance of plentiful supply at 0.2 for location 1 and at 0.4 if the boat moves to 2. The chance that the pilot will be successful and find a location 3 is 0.7, and the chance of a plentiful supply at this location is 0.8. (a) According to the EMV criterion, what should the captain do? (b) Explain your answer to (a).

16. Nova Metals plans to spend $5 million to explore an area they think might contain a uranium ore deposit. If a promising location is found (probability 0.2), the value of the deposit may be $400 million (probability 0.2) or $200 million (probability 0.5) or $50 million (probability 0.3). They will carry out mining operations costing $20 million only if a promising location is found. Nova can decide to pay $10 million outright to landowners for exploration and mining rights, or they can offer to pay landowners $30 million only if mining operations are carried out. What should Nova do? Why?

17. (a) Suppose you were in the happy situation of being offered $1 for certain *or* a 50-50 chance at $5 or nothing. Would you take the $1 or take the chance? Why? (b) Suppose the payoffs in (a) were 100 times as large, that is, $100 for certain or a 50-50 chance at $500 or nothing. Which would you choose? Why? (c) Multiplying the payoffs in (b) by 10, consider $1000 for certain or a 50-50 chance at $5000 or nothing. Now which would you choose? Why? (d) If you did not always take the amount certain, or did not always choose the chance, why did you change your mind?

18. Jill's reference values are $10 million and − $2 million. She states that her certainty equivalent for a 50-50 chance at her reference values is $3 million. What is Jill's attitude toward risk in this situation? Explain.

19. Jim's reference values are $10 million and − $5 million. He has assessed a utility of 0.8 for $7 million. (a) What chance situation is involved in Jim's assessment? (b) What is Jim's attitude toward risk in this situation?

20. Sam's reference values are $50,000 and − $5000. Some points from his utility curve are given in Table D. Sam has to choose between actions A_1 and A_2. A_1 is a 60-40 chance at $35,000 or $10,000. A_2 has a payoff of $26,000 for certain. Which action should Sam choose? Why?

TABLE D
POINTS ON SAM'S UTILITY CURVE

Payoff, thousands of dollars	−5	0	4	7	10	14	19	26	35	43	50
Utility	0	0.1	0.2	0.3	0.4	0.5	0.6	0.7	0.8	0.9	1

21. (See Problem 20.) Sam has to choose between actions A_3 and A_4. A_3 has payoffs $26,000, $14,000, or − $5000 with chances of, respectively, 30, 20, and 50. A_4 is a 25-75 chance at $35,000 or $0. Which action should Sam choose?

22. (See Problem 20.) Table D shows Sam has a utility of 0.4 for $10,000. What does this mean?

23. Suppose Cleo has reference values of $200 and − $100, and suppose that she is always risk-neutral. (a) What is Cleo's certainty equivalent for a 10-90 chance at $200 and − $100? Why? (b) Find Cleo's CEs for the following chances at her reference values: 20-80; 40-60, 50-50;

60-40; 70-30; 80-20; 90-10. (c) Draw Cleo's utility curve. (d) Describe the shape of the curve in (c). State why the curve has this shape.

6.11 SUMMARY

The expected value of X, $E(X)$, is found by multiplying each of all the different possible values of X by its probability of occurrence and adding the products. Thus,

$$E(X) = \Sigma XP(X)$$

If the X's are monetary values such as dollars, then $E(X)$ is called *expected monetary value* EMV.

The *EMV decision criterion* for choosing an action from two or more available actions is to choose the action having the largest EMV.

A *payoff table* shows the payoff for each and every combination of an action and a chance event.

Decision problems involving a sequence of actions and chance occurrences are analyzed by making a *decision tree*. The bare tree is constructed first to show the proper sequence of decisions that must be made and chance nodes that will be encountered. After the tree has been constructed, payoffs are entered at the ends of the rightmost branches and probabilities are entered on the branches from the chance nodes. Then one works backward on the tree, as follows: (1) compute the EMV when a chance node is encountered; (2) choose the action branch with the highest EMV when a decision node is encountered, and cut off other action branches. When the backward process has been completed, the parts of the tree which remain specify the maximum EMV course of action.

A *chance situation* is a set of chances (for possible events) and payoffs. The *certainty equivalent* for a chance situation is the payoff (in dollars) for certain (probability 1) that the decision maker considers to be equivalent to the chance situation. The best and worst payoffs a decision maker thinks might be encountered are called, respectively, the higher and lower *reference values*. If $X is the certainty equivalent for a chance situation involving only the reference values, the probability of the higher reference value is called the decision maker's *utility* for $X. A *utility curve* shows a decision maker's utilities for payoffs ranging from the lower to the higher reference value.

A decision maker's circumstances affect his or her attitudes toward chance situations. Utilities take these attitudes into account. The *expected utility decision criterion* is to select the course of action which has the highest EUV (expected utility value). To apply the EUV criterion, a decision tree is constructed and ending dollar payoffs are replaced by their utilities. Then we work backward through the tree (as in EMV analysis), computing EUV at chance nodes and choosing the highest EUV branch at decision nodes. When the process has been completed, the parts of the tree which remain specify the maximum EUV course of action.

A decision maker is *risk-averse*, *risk-neutral*, or *risk-seeking* in a chance situation according as the decision maker's certainty equivalent is, respectively, less than, equal to, or greater than the EMV of the chance situation.

6.12 REVIEW PROBLEMS

1. During a 2-minute period the number of customers entering a bank is 0, 1, 2, 3, or 4. The respective probabilities for the numbers entering are 0.55, 0.35, 0.06, 0.03, and 0.01. (*a*) Find the expected value of the number entering in a 2-minute period. (*b*) Find the expected number entering in 6 hours.

2. In a five-number roulette bet, the player wins if any one of the five chosen numbers occurs on the spin of the wheel. There are 38 numbers which have equal probability of occurring. The betting odds are 6 to 1; that is, for each $1 bet the player either wins $6 or loses $1. Compute the expected monetary value of a five-number bet of $100.

3. Jones Company, which owns three buildings valued at $200,000, $100,000, and $50,000, applies for insurance which will pay the full value of any building destroyed by fire during a year. The insurance firm, after studying experience records, sets the probabilities of total loss for the buildings at 0.005, 0.008, and 0.011, respectively. The insurance company's loading is 30 percent of the premium which Jones Company will pay for the insurance. Compute the premium.

4. A company sells television sets at $600 each. Its warranty states that sets failing during the first year after purchase should be returned for a refund. The refund schedule is: (*a*) full refund of purchase price for failure during the first month; (*b*) refund of one-half for failure during the next 5 months; (*c*) one-fourth refund for failure during the remainder of the first year. Failure probabilities for (*a*), (*b*), and (*c*) are 0.006, 0.009, and 0.015. Because of the refunds the company does not net the full $600 per set sold. Compute the expected net amount received per set sold.

5. An investor buys 100 shares of Company A stock, thinking there is a 60 percent chance that A will merge with Company B. If A and B merge, the investor will make a profit of $5000. If the merger does not occur, the investor will lose $3000. Find the EMV of the investor's profit.

6. The controller of a company is trying to estimate the loss the company might suffer because of structural damage to a building and/or rain damage to its contents in a hurricane. Losses are estimated as follows: (*a*) $500,000 if there is structural and rain damage; (*b*) $400,000 if there is structural damage only; (*c*) $100,000 if there is rain damage only. The controller assigns 0.2 as the probability of structural damage but thinks that occurrence of rain damage is dependent on structural damage and sets 0.7 as the probability of rain damage if there is structural damage, but only 0.1 if there is no structural damage. Find the EMV of losses given that a hurricane occurs.

7. In roulette, each of 38 numbers is equally likely to appear on any play. Betting odds on a single number are 35 to 1. A player decides to make a $1 bet on a number and quit playing if she loses. If she wins, she leaves her $1 plus the $35 winnings on the number and plays again, quitting if she loses but leaving all money on the number for a third play if she wins. She quits after the third play, irrespective of the outcome. Compute the EMV of her winnings.

8. Without advertising, a company has a 50-50 chance at a large or small share of

the market, with respective payoffs of $50,000 and $20,000. By spending $5000 on advertising, the company can change the chances of large and small shares to 80-20. Which action, advertise or not advertise, has the higher EMV? What is this EMV?

9. Table A gives payoffs in thousands of dollars. It shows, for example, that if three units are made and two units are demanded, the payoff is $35,000. Probabilities for demands of 0, 1, 2, and 3 units are 0.1, 0.2, 0.3, and 0.4, respectively. Which action has the maximum EMV? What is this EMV?

TABLE A
PAYOFFS IN THOUSANDS OF DOLLARS

Event, number of units demanded	Action, number of units made			
	0	1	2	3
0	0	−5	−10	−15
1	0	20	15	10
2	0	20	40	35
3	0	20	40	60

10. In Problem 9, change the probabilities of demands for 0, 1, 2, and 3 to 0.4, 0.3, 0.2, and 0.1, and find which action now has the highest EMV. What is this EMV?

11. A store buys a product at $10 per unit and sells it at $15 per unit. All units not demanded by customers at the end of a month are sold at $6 per unit. During the month, the probabilities of demands of 0, 1, 2, 3, 4, and 5 units are, respectively. 0.10, 0.10, 0.20, 0.20, 0.30, and 0.10. What number of units should the store buy to maximize EMV? What is the maximum EMV?

Note: In answers to problems which require a decision tree, use trees shown in the figures of this chapter as models. Include all pertinent labels and numerical values. Indicate branches to be cut off by the symbol | |.

12. Answer Problem 8 by constructing a decision tree.

13. If a company spends $0 advertising a product, it has a 40-60 chance for large or small shares of the market with respective profits of $50,000 and $10,000. By spending $5000 on advertising, the chances for large and small shares can be improved to 60-40, and further improvement to 80-20 will result if $10,000 is spent. How much should be spent on advertising to maximize EMV? What is this EMV? Answer by constructing and using a decision tree.

14. CV Company can make and market a standard product which has a 60-40 chance at profits of $30,000 and $10,000. Alternatively, CV can spend $10,000 on R&D (research and development) which, if successful, will provide a product having an 80-20 chance at net profits (after R&D expenses) of $50,000 or $10,000. If R&D is not successful, CV will market the standard product with profits decreased by the cost of R&D. If the chance of successful R&D is 0.50, which action (perform R&D or market the standard product) has the higher EMV? What is this EMV? Answer by constructing and using a decision tree.

15. The owner of a ski resort has to decide in October whether to complete a new

trail that fall or wait until early winter, observe snow conditions, and then decide whether or not to rush completion during the early winter. The owner will not complete the trail in the winter if snow conditions are poor. The owner estimates high and low payoffs under various situations as shown in Table B. The chance of the high payoff is 0.9 if snow conditions are good and 0.5 if they are poor. The owner assesses the probability of good conditions at 0.6. What should the owner do to maximize EMV?

TABLE B

	Payoffs, thousands of dollars					
	Do not complete		Complete in fall		Complete in winter	
Snow conditions	High	Low	High	Low	High	Low
Good	30	20	70	60	50	40
Poor	25	15	10	4		

16. An investor will earn interest of $12,000 from funds in a bank account, and is considering withdrawing these funds and investing in a stock which has a 70-30 chance of yielding $20,000 or $5000 if the stock is bought now. If the investor waits, there is a 70-30 chance that the stock will begin to rise in price; if this happens, the investor will buy and there will be a 99-1 chance of yields of $18,000 or $3000. If the stock does not increase in price, the investor will leave the funds in the bank. Which action, leave funds in bank, invest now, or wait, has the highest EMV? What is this EMV? Answer by constructing and using a decision tree.

17. On the basis of a preliminary survey TX Company has located site A in an area which it thinks may contain (with probability 0.3) gas worth $200 million. The drilling cost is set at $10 million. TX can drill now at A or conduct an extensive survey costing $25 million to find a more favorable site, B. The chance of finding a site B is 0.4 and the chance of hitting gas worth $200 million at B is 0.8. TX has the choice of drilling now at A or exploring and drilling at B (if B is found), or at A (if B is not found). (a) According to the EMV criterion, should TX drill now or conduct the extensive survey? (b) What are the EMV's of the two alternative actions?

18. Delta Electronics Company has developed a product which Jane Sober, vice president for marketing, believes should be marketed. Sober states that the product has a 60 percent chance of a high demand, but the amount of the payoff will depend upon whether Delta makes the parts or has other companies make the parts (which Delta will then assemble into the final product). Consequently, a *make* or *buy* decision is at hand. Sober points out that the cost of carrying inventory, buying new machines, and so on, if Delta makes the parts, will be more than compensated for in payoff if market demand is high, but no profit would accrue if demand turns out to be low. Sober's estimates of payoffs are shown in Table C (at the top of page 186).

Irving Shaw, a business associate, agrees with Sober's percent chance of high demand but suggests it might be worthwhile to take a sample survey of con-

TABLE C

	Make parts and assemble	Buy parts and assemble
High demand	$210,000	$130,000
Low demand	0	90,000

sumers before deciding to make or buy. Survey results will be reported as favorable or unfavorable, and the cost of the survey is $10,000. If the survey report is favorable, the chance of high demand will rise to 0.85, but if the report is unfavorable the chance of high demand will fall to 0.15. Shaw sets the probability of a favorable survey report at 0.6. (a) According to the EMV criterion, what decision should be made? (b) What are the EMVs of the alternative actions?

19. (a) What is your certainty equivalent for a 50-50 chance at $20 or $0? (b) Should you be willing to let me decide whether you get your certainty equivalent or have to take the chance? (c) What is your attitude toward risk in this situation?

20. Bob's reference values are $200,000 and –$50,000. He says his certainty equivalent for a 60-40 chance at his higher and lower reference values is $100,000. (a) What is Bob's utility for $100,000? (b) What is Bob's attitude toward risk in this situation?

21. Pat has reference values of $900 thousand and –$200 thousand. Some points from her utility curve are given in Table D. (a) Pat has to choose between actions A_1 and A_2. A_1 has payoffs of $220,000, $40,000 or –$60,000 with respective chances of 30, 30, and 40. A_2 is a 50-50 chance at $700,000 or –$200,000. Which action should Pat choose? (b) Table D shows Pat has a utility of 0.6 for $500,000. What does this mean?

TABLE D
POINTS ON PAT'S UTILITY CURVE

Payoff, thousands of dollars	−200	−160	−110	−60	40	220	500	700	800	860	900
Utility	0	0.1	0.2	0.3	0.4	0.5	0.6	0.7	0.8	0.9	1

7

DISCRETE PROBABILITY DISTRIBUTIONS

7.1 INTRODUCTION

A surprisingly large number of applied probability problems involve simple situations in which a selection is made and one or the other of two outcomes must occur. For example, if a customer's account is selected, the account is overdue or it is not overdue; the two outcomes here are "overdue" and "not overdue." Similarly, a selected manufactured item may be classified as good or defective; or a selected person subscribes or does not subscribe to *The Wall Street Journal*. To have a general way of referring to the two outcomes, we shall refer to *the outcome of interest* as a "success" and the other outcome as a "failure." Note that a "success," the outcome of interest, need not be the more desirable outcome; for example, if we are interested in overdue credit accounts, an overdue account is a success.

The outcome of a single selection is either a success or a failure. In this chapter we shall be interested in the *number* of successes when the selection process is repeated. We shall also be interested in the probabilities of the various possible numbers of successes. You will learn how to compute the latter probabilities in different two-outcome situations by using special formulas called the binomial, Poisson, and hypergeometric probability formulas.

7.2 RANDOM VARIABLES

Meaning of Random Variable

Random variable A random variable is a variable whose value is determined by chance. For example, suppose we toss a coin twice (or toss two coins) and call heads on a toss a success. The number of successes then could be 0, 1, or 2. Which particular value occurs is a matter of chance; so the number of heads is a random variable. Let's give this random variable the general name X. Now note that there is a distinction between the name of the random variable, X, and the values 0, 1, or 2 which the random variable could have. If we are interested in the probability that X takes on the value 1, we could express this as

$$P(\text{number of heads} = 1)$$

or
$$P(X = 1)$$

However, the context of a discussion usually makes clear what the random variable is, and we shall usually simplify the symbolism by omitting the name of the random variable. Thus, in the context of tossing a coin twice and taking heads as a success,

$$P(1)$$

will mean the probability of exactly 1 success.

EXERCISE Suppose you take a 50-question multiple-choice exam, guessing every answer, and are interested in the number of correct answers obtained. (*a*)

What is the random variable? (b) What values might this random variable have? (c) What would P(40) mean?

ANSWER (a) The number of correct answers; (b) 0, 1, 2, 3, and so on through 50; (c) the probability that the number of correct answers (the random variable) is 40.

Types of Random Variables

A discrete random variable can take on only certain disconnected values in an interval.

When two coins are tossed, the random variable "number of heads" can take on only the values 0, 1, or 2. These values are separated, or *discrete*, and the variable "number of heads" is called a *discrete* random variable. Graphically, the values 0, 1, 2 are separated points, as in

0   1   2

A continuous random variable can take on any value in an interval.

If a random variable could have *any* value in some interval of values, it is called a *continuous* random variable. A continuous random variable which could have any value from, say, 0 through 5, would graph as a continuous straight line, as in

0   5

In this chapter we shall work with discrete random variables. In following chapters we shall work mainly with continuous random variables.

EXERCISE You are sitting in an airplane waiting for takeoff. The pilot announces a delay until some incoming planes land. For (a) and (b) which follow, state what the random variable is and whether it is discrete or continuous. (a) You are interested in how long it will be until takeoff. (b) You are interested in how many incoming planes there are.

ANSWER (a) Time (until takeoff) is continuous. (b) Number of planes is discrete.

7.3 DISCRETE PROBABILITY DISTRIBUTIONS

A discrete probability distribution is a list of all pairs [X, P(X)].

If we list all the mutually exclusive values a discrete random variable could have, together with the probability that each value occurs, the result is called a discrete *probability distribution*. Let's determine the probability distribution for the number of heads in two tosses of a coin. Now P(0) is the probability of zero heads, which means both tosses result in tails. We shall use TT to specify "first toss tails, second toss tails." The probability of tails on the first toss is 0.5. The outcome of the second toss is *independent* of what happened on the first toss; so

$$P(0) = P(TT) = P(T)P(T) = (0.5)(0.5) = 0.25$$

Next we want the probability of exactly one head in two tosses. If the two tosses result in either the order "first heads, second tails" or the order "first tails, second heads," we have 1 head. Therefore,

$$P(1) = P(HT) + P(TH)$$
$$= (0.5)(0.5) + (0.5)(0.5)$$
$$= 0.25 + 0.25$$
$$= 0.5$$

EXERCISE For the example at hand: (a) What does $P(2)$ mean? (b) What is the value of $P(2)$?
ANSWER (a) The probability of two heads; (b) 0.25.

Table 7.1 is the probability distribution for the number of heads in two tosses of a coin.

TABLE 7.1
PROBABILITY DISTRIBUTION FOR
NUMBER OF HEADS IN TWO TOSSES
OF A COIN

Random variable X, number of heads	$P(X)$, probability of number of heads
0	0.25
1	0.50
2	0.25
	Sum = 1.00

EXERCISE Why must the sum of the probabilities in a probability distribution always equal 1?
ANSWER A probability distribution includes *all* the mutually exclusive values the random variable could have. The total available probability, 1, must be completely *distributed* to the values of the random variable.

The answer to the exercise shows why Table 7.1 is called a probability distribution. It is because the table shows how much of the total probability, 1, is distributed among the values the random variable could have.

Figure 7.1 is a graph of the probability distribution in Table 7.1.

7.4 NUMBER OF ARRANGEMENTS, $\binom{n}{r}$

Let S and F represent, respectively, success and failure. Then

$$S\,S\,S\,F\,F$$

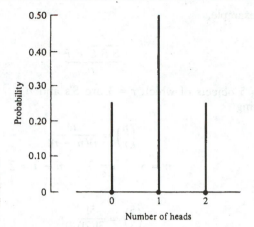

FIGURE 7.1
Probability distribution
for the number of
heads on two tosses of
a coin.

is one arrangement of three successes in five outcomes. Another arrangement of the three successes is

$$S S F S F$$

In determining $P(3)$, the probability of three successes, it is necessary to know how many arrangements of three successes and two failures there are. The number of arrangements can be computed from a formula which involves the factorial symbol, !, as in $n!$ which is read "n factorial." By definition

$$n! = n(n - 1)(n - 2)(n - 3) \cdot \cdot \cdot (3)(2)(1)$$
$$0! = 1$$

n!

For example,

$$6! = 6(5)(4)(3)(2)(1) = 720$$
$$10! = 10(9)(8)(7)(6)(5)(4)(3)(2)(1) = 3,628,800$$

Note that $n!$ gets large rapidly as n increases. Even 10! is quite large. The number 70!, if written out, would contain 100 digits.

EXERCISE Compute 3! and 7!.
ANSWER 6 and 5040.

The *counting formula* we need is as follows: The number of arrangements of n objects, of which r are of one type and the remaining $n - r$ are of another type, is symbolized as $\binom{n}{r}$, and computed as

**Number of distinct
arrangements of n
items of two types**

$$\binom{n}{r} = \frac{n!}{r!(n - r)!}$$

For example,

$$\overbrace{\underbrace{S\ S\ S}^{r}\ F\ F}_{n}$$

has $n = 5$ objects of which $r = 3$ are S's and $n - r = 5 - 3 =$ are F's. Evaluating

$$\binom{n}{r} = \frac{n!}{r!(n - r)!}$$

for $n = 5$ $r = 3$ $n - r = 2$

we have

$$\binom{5}{3} = \frac{5!}{3!(2!)}$$

$$= \frac{5(4)(3)(2)(1)}{3(2)(1)(2)(1)}$$

$$= 10$$

We can verify the count by listing the 10 arrangements as follows:

$$
\begin{array}{ll}
S\,S\,S\,F\,F & S\,F\,F\,S\,S \\
S\,S\,F\,S\,F & F\,F\,S\,S\,S \\
S\,F\,S\,S\,F & S\,F\,S\,F\,S \\
F\,S\,S\,S\,F & F\,S\,F\,S\,S \\
S\,S\,F\,F\,S & F\,S\,S\,F\,S
\end{array}
$$

All we shall need to know is the number of arrangements. The counting formula provides the desired number; so listing will not be necessary.

EXERCISE (a) How many different arrangements are there of two G's and two D's? (b) What is the numerical value of $\binom{n}{n}$? Why?

ANSWER (a) 6. (b) 1. Because n items, all alike, can be arranged in only one way. That's why 0! is defined to be 1.

Counting formula calculations can be simplified by breaking a factorial into parts. For example, we can write

$$10! = 10(9)(8)(7!)$$

then

$$\binom{10}{3} = \frac{10!}{3!7!} = \frac{10(9)(8)(\cancel{7!})}{3(2)(1)(\cancel{7!})} = 120$$

EXERCISE Compute $\binom{9}{2}$ and $\binom{9}{7}$.

ANSWER 36 in both cases.

The exercise illustrates the easily verified conclusion that

$$\binom{n}{r} = \binom{n}{n-r}$$

7.5 THE BINOMIAL PROBABILITY DISTRIBUTION

The Binomial Probability Formula

Probabilities for numbers of successes in special two-outcome situations are computed from special formulas. The most widely used formula is called the *binomial formula*. The type of situation in which the binomial formula applies can be illustrated by coin tossing. Calling each toss a *trial*, these characteristics are: (1) we are interested in the number of heads in a fixed number of trials; (2) each trial has only two possible outcomes, heads or tails; (3) the probability of heads is constant from trial to trial; (4) the occurrence of heads on one trial is independent of what happens on other trials. Trials having these characteristics are called *Bernoulli trials*. In general, the characteristics of Bernoulli trials are:

The binomial formula applies when these are true.

1. We are interested in the number of successes in a fixed number of trials.
2. Each trial has only two possible outcomes, success or failure.
3. The probability of success is constant from trial to trial.
4. All trials are independent.

Let's introduce the binomial formula by using an example.

EXAMPLE A student does not know the answers to five of the questions on a multiple-choice examination. Four choices are listed for each question; so the student rolls a die and takes the first choice if the die shows a one spot, the second choice if the die shows a two spot, and so on. If a five spot or a six spot shows, the die is rolled again. Let S represent a success (a correct response) and F represent a failure (an incorrect response). Then the probability of a correct response on a trial is 1 out of 4 or

$$P(S) = 0.25$$

Because each response is either correct or incorrect, the probability of an incorrect response is

$$P(F) = 0.75$$

Now consider

$$S\,S\,S\,F\,F$$

which is one arrangement of three successes in five trials; that is, three correct among the five answers. Because the trials are independent,

$$P(S\ S\ S\ F\ F) = P(S)P(S)P(S)P(F)P(F)$$

$$= (0.25)(0.25)(0.25)(0.75)(0.75)$$

$$= (0.25)^3(0.75)^2$$

Another arrangement of three successes in five trials is

$$S\ S\ F\ S\ F$$

and
$$P(S\ S\ F\ S\ F) = P(S)P(S)P(F)P(S)P(F)$$

$$= (0.25)(0.25)(0.75)(0.25)(0.75)$$

$$= (0.25)^3(0.75)^2$$

EXERCISE For the example at hand, what is $P(F\ F\ S\ S\ S)$?
ANSWER $(0.75)^2(0.25)^3$.

The foregoing calculations illustrate the fact that the probability of three successes in five trials is the same for all arrangements of the three S's and two F's. The number of arrangements is

$$\binom{5}{3} = \frac{5!}{3!2!} = 10$$

To find $P(3)$, the probability of three successes, we need the sum of the probabilities for the $\binom{5}{3}$ arrangements. But because the probabilities are the same, $P(3)$ can be computed by multiplying $\binom{5}{3}$ by the probability of one arrangement. That is,

$$P(3) = \binom{5}{3} P(S\ S\ S\ F\ F)$$

$$= 10(0.25)^3(0.75)^2$$

$$= 0.08789$$

Now let's change the symbols. The *binomial probability formula* states that

$$P(r) = \binom{n}{r} p^r q^{n-r}$$

Probability of r successes in n Bernoulli trials.

where r = exact number of successes
n = number of trials made
p = probability of success on a trial
$q = 1 - p$ = probability of failure on a trial

Applying the binomial formula to the previous example, we have

$$r = 3 \text{ successes (correct answers)}$$

$$n = 5 \text{ trials (questions)}$$

$$p = 0.25$$

$$q = 1 - p = 0.75$$

Hence, the probability of getting exactly three correct answers among the five questions is

$$P(r) = \binom{n}{r} p^r q^{n-r}$$

$$P(3) = \binom{5}{3} (0.25)^3 (0.75)^2$$

$$= 10(0.25)^3(0.75)^2$$

$$= 0.08789$$

as before.

EXERCISE For the example at hand, what is the probability of getting exactly one correct answer?
ANSWER 0.3955.

The complete probability distribution for our example, computed by using the binomial formula, is shown in Table 7.2 and in Figure 7.2 (at the top of page 196).

TABLE 7.2
BINOMIAL DISTRIBUTION FOR $n = 5$, $p = 0.25$

Number of correct answers r	**Probability of number of correct answers** $P(r)$
0	0.2373
1	0.3955
2	0.2637
3	0.0879
4	0.0146
5	0.0010
	Sum = 1.0000

The distribution has one pair [r, P(r)] for each possible value of r.

Probability distributions computed from the binomial formula are called *binomial distributions*. The binomial formula itself is called *the binomial distribution*. But you should understand that there is not just one binomial distribution. Rather, there is a different distribution for each different pair of *n, p* values.

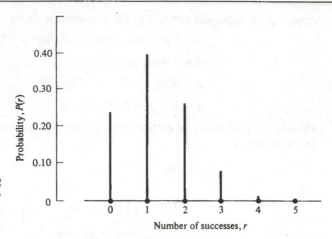

FIGURE 7.2
Binomial probability
distribution for $n = 5$,
$p = 0.25$.

Recall:

n = number of trials

*p = probability of
success on 1 trial*

Figures 7.3 through 7.5 show binomial distributions for $n = 6$ with different values of p. Figure 7.3 shows that with $p = 0.3$ (a 30 percent chance of success on a trial), the probabilities of getting 4, 5, or 6 successes in 6 trials are relatively small; so the distribution is skewed to the right. Figure 7.4,

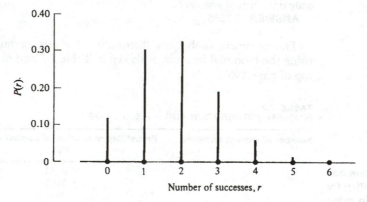

FIGURE 7.3
Binomial distribution
for $n = 6$, $p = 0.3$,
$q = 0.7$. Skewed to the
right.

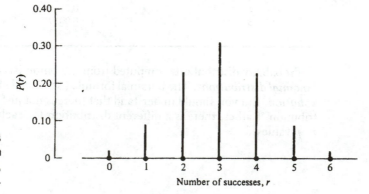

FIGURE 7.4
Binomial distribution
for $n = 6$, $p = 0.5$,
$q = 0.5$. Symmetrical.

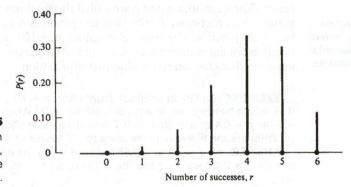

FIGURE 7.5

Binomial distribution
for $n = 6$, $p = 0.7$,
$q = 0.3$. Skewed to the
left.

which has $p = 0.5$ (a 50-50 chance of success on a trial), is symmetrical; three successes (50 percent of $n = 6$) has the highest probability; two and four successes are equally likely; one and five successes are equally likely; and zero and six successes are equally likely. Figure 7.5, which has $p = 0.7$, is skewed to the left.

The nearer p is to 0.5, the more nearly symmetrical is a binomial distribution. Moreover, even if p is not 0.5, the larger the value of n, the more nearly symmetrical is a binomial distribution. For example, Figure 7.6 shows the distribution for $p = 0.35$ and $n = 100$. The figure is nearly symmetrical. Note that the tops of the vertical probability lines outline a shape which is approximately the shape of a normal curve. We shall simplify problem solving in later chapters by using the normal distribution to approximate binomial distributions when n is large.

In a binomial distribution, the random variable is r, the number of suc-

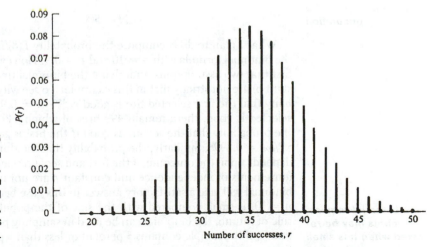

FIGURE 7.6

Binomial distribution
for $n = 100$, $p = 0.35$,
$q = 0.65$. Distribution
is nearly symmetrical
even though $p = 0.35$,
because $n = 100$ is
large.

The two parameters n and p are sufficient to specify a binomial distribution.

cesses. The quantities n and p are called the *parameters* of a binomial distribution. For a particular distribution, the parameters have constant values, as in $n = 6$, $p = 0.3$. The parameter values $n = 100$, $p = 0.35$ specify a different binomial distribution. In general, the parameters n and p are the numbers that characterize a binomial distribution.

EXERCISE (a) Which binomial distribution, $n = 50$, $p = 0.30$ or $n = 50$, $p = 0.65$, would be more nearly symmetrical? Why? (b) Which binomial distribution, $n = 30$, $p = 0.4$ or $n = 50$, $p = 0.4$, would be more nearly symmetrical? Why? (c) What are the binomial parameters for 25 tosses of a coin?
ANSWER (a) $n = 50$, $p = 0.65$ because it has the p value closer to 0.5. (b) $n = 50$, $p = 0.4$ because it has the larger n. (c) $n = 25$, $p = 0.5$.

Using the Binomial Formula

The binomial distribution is applied extensively in sampling problems. In these applications, it is customary to refer to the *size* of a sample rather than the number of trials. Suppose, for example, that a tire wholesaler has 500 Superbrand tires in stock, and that 50 tires with slightly damaged steel belting are randomly mixed in the stock. Suppose next that a retailer buys 10 of these tires. We want to know the probability that the retailer receives 8 good (undamaged) tires.

The number of tires bought by the retailer, 10, will be called a sample of size $n = 10$ from a *population* of 500 tires. Our interest is in the number of good tires, and there are 450 good tires (successes) in the population of 500 tires. Let R be the number of successes in the population of size N, so that here $R = 450$ and $N = 500$. *Before* any tires are taken, the proportion of good tires in the stock is

Calculating p for the population

$$\frac{R}{N} = \frac{450}{500} = 0.9$$

What I plan to do is compute the probability $P(8)$ for $r = 8$ good tires by the binomial formula with $n = 10$ and $p = 0.9$. However, I want to point out first that two assumptions underlying the binomial (independence and constant p) are not strictly met in this example. To see why, note that the probability that the first selected tire is good is $450/500 = 0.9$. However, if the first selected is good, there remain 499 tires of which 449 are good. Therefore, the probability that the second is good *if* the first is good is not $p = 0.9$ but $449/499 = 0.8998$. Similarly, the probability that the third selected tire is good depends upon the outcome of the first and second selections. Hence, the requirements of independence and constant p are not met. Nevertheless, the binomial will give a satisfactory answer in this case because the sample size, $n = 10$, is small compared with the size of the population, $N = 500$. As a rule of thumb, the binomial can be used in sampling problems if $n \leq 0.05N$, that is, if the sample contains 5 percent or less than 5 percent of the population.

The binomial requirements may be relaxed when n is small compared with N.

Now let's restate the example as follows, letting the statement "a large number of tires" mean the population is large enough so that we can use the binomial distribution to compute probabilities. The problem is to find the probability that there are eight good tires in a sample of 10 tires drawn from a large number of tires of which 90 percent are good. Then

$$n = 10 \qquad p = 0.9 \qquad q = 0.1 \qquad r = 8$$

$$P(r) = \binom{n}{r} (p)^r(q)^{n-r}$$

and
$$P(8) = \binom{10}{8} (0.9)^8(0.1)^2$$

$$= \frac{10!}{8!2!} (0.9)^8(0.1)^2$$

$$= 45(0.9)^8(0.1)^2$$

$$= 0.194$$

Note that the binomial formula does *not* involve the population size N. A problem statement may specify only n and p and that the population is "large," as in the next exercise. Or the statement may specify n, R, and N, in which case the binomial can be used with $p = R/N$ if $n \le 0.05N$. Finally, *Sampling* with *replacement* the binomial applies exactly if sampling *with replacement* is carried out, that is, if an element selected in one trial is replaced before the next trial is made. In sampling with replacement, the probability of a success remains constant from trial to trial.

EXERCISE If 60 percent of the voters in a large district prefer candidate Jordan, what is the probability that in a sample of 12 voters exactly 7 will prefer Jordan?
ANSWER 0.227.

Binomial Tables

The binomial formula gives the probability of *exactly* r successes. In many problems, however, we are interested in cumulative probabilities, such as the probability of at most three successes, or more than five successes. Suppose $n = 10$ and $p = 0.4$. Then the probability of at most three successes would be

$$P(0) + P(1) + P(2) + P(3)$$

which we can symbolize as

$$\sum_{r=0}^{3} P(r)$$

Similarly, the probability of more than five successes (that is, six or more) with $n = 10$ and $p = 0.4$ is

$$P(6) + P(7) + P(8) + P(9) + P(10) = \sum_{r=6}^{10} P(r)$$

Table 7.3 provides cumulative probabilities for the binomial distribution with $n = 10$, $p = 0.4$. The first cumulative probability is

$$P(0) = 0.00605$$

TABLE 7.3
CUMULATIVE BINOMIAL PROBABILITIES $n = 10$,
$p = 0.4$

Number of successes r	Cumulative probability $\sum_{0}^{r} P(r)$
0	0.00605
1	0.04636
2	0.16729
3	0.38228
4	0.63310
5	0.83376
6	0.94524
7	0.98771
8	0.99833
9	0.99990
10	1.00000

*cum P(r) = P(0) +
P(1) + · · · + P(r)*

The second row, for $r = 1$, means

$$P(0) + P(1) = \sum_{r=0}^{1} P(r) = 0.04636$$

The third row, for $r = 2$, means

$$P(0) + P(1) + P(2) = \sum_{r=0}^{2} P(r) = 0.16729$$

The probability for at most three successes is

*P(at most r) = cum
P(r)*

$$\sum_{r=0}^{3} P(r) = 0.38228$$

as shown in the fourth row of the table.

*P(less than r) = cum
P(r − 1)*

EXERCISE From Table 7.3, what is the probability of fewer than five successes?
ANSWER 0.63310.

Note that Table 7.3 cumulates from 0 success; that is, for example, the cumulative probability at $r = 5$ is

$$\sum_{r=0}^{5} P(r) = P(0) + P(1) + P(2) + P(3) + P(4) + P(5)$$

Now suppose we want the probability of *more* than five successes. With $n = 10$, more than 5 means 6, 7, 8, 9, 10; so

$$P(\text{more than } 5) = \sum_{r=6}^{10} P(r)$$

The table does not provide $P(\text{more than } 5)$, but it can be obtained easily by noting that, with $n = 10$,

$$\sum_{r=0}^{10} P(r) = 1$$

and 0 through 10 can be broken into the two parts, 0 through 5 and 6 through 10, as follows:

$$\sum_{r=0}^{10} P(r) = \sum_{r=0}^{5} P(r) + \sum_{r=6}^{10} P(r) = 1$$

From the last expression we have, by subtraction,

$$\sum_{r=6}^{10} P(r) = 1 - \sum_{r=0}^{5} P(r)$$

P(more than r) = 1 − cum P(r)

$$= 1 - 0.83376$$

$$= 0.16624$$

We can obtain the probability of *exactly* r successes from Table 7.3 by subtraction of successive cumulative probabilities. For example, the probability of exactly 3 successes is

$$[P(0) + P(1) + P(2) + P(3)] - [P(0) + P(1) + P(2)]$$

which is

$$\sum_{r=0}^{3} P(r) - \sum_{r=0}^{2} P(r) = 0.38228 - 0.16729 = 0.21499$$

P(r) = cum P(r) − cum P(r − 1)

In general, the probability of exactly r successes can be found by taking the cumulative probability for r and subtracting the preceding cumulative probability.

EXERCISE See Table 7.3. (a) Write the symbol for the probability of at least four successes. (b) What is the probability of at least four successes? (c) What is the probability of exactly six successes?
ANSWER (a) $\sum_{r=4}^{10} P(r) = 1 - \sum_{r=0}^{3} P(r)$; (b) 0.61772; (c) 0.11148.

Table I at the end of the book provides cumulative binomial probabilities for some combinations of n and p, to use in the problems you will encounter

*Using the table of cu-
mulative binomial
probabilities (Ap-
pendix Table I)*
in the text. The following example, and some problems you will be solving by use of Table I, refers to selecting a random sample from a *large lot* of manufactured items. The word *lot* means a number of items, and by a large lot we mean a number of items large enough so that the sample does not contain more than 5 percent of the lot. The lot size is the size of the population, and as stated earlier, the binomial distribution can be applied to two-outcome situations if the sample size *n* is not more than 5 percent of the size of the population.

EXAMPLE A buyer checks large lots of batteries by inspecting a sample of 10 batteries from each lot and classifying each inspected battery as good or defective. The buyer rejects the whole *lot*, and sends it back to the supplier, if the *sample* contains more than two defectives. Lots which are not rejected are accepted (not returned to the supplier). (*a*) If 5 percent of the batteries in the *lot* are defective, what is the probability that the lot will be accepted? (*b*) If a lot has 25 percent defective, what is the chance that it will be accepted?

*The sample is
inspected. The lot is
accepted or rejected.*

SOLUTION A lot is accepted if zero, one, or two defectives are found in the sample. Thus, the probability of acceptance is

$$\sum_{r=0}^{2} P(r)$$

where *r* is the number of defectives in the sample.

a. If the lot is 5 percent defective, then $p = 0.05$. From Table IA, with $n = 10$ and $p = 0.05$,

$$P(\text{acceptance}) = \sum_{r=0}^{2} P(r) = 0.9885$$

b. Here $p = 0.25$. Again from Table IA, with $n = 10$ and $p = 0.25$,

$$\sum_{r=0}^{2} P(r) = 0.5256$$

Acceptance Sampling

The example just given shows one approach to a procedure called *accept-ance sampling* which is widely applied in the area of quality control. The sampling plan is specified by two numbers, (n, a), where *n* is the number of items (the sample size) to be selected from a large lot and inspected, and *a*, called the *acceptance number*, means the maximum number of defectives permitted in the sample. That is, if the sample contains more than *a* defec-tives, the whole lot is rejected and some further action is taken (e.g., inspect the whole lot or return the lot to the supplier). If the number of sample de-fectives is *a* or less, the lot is accepted.

Sampling plan (n, a):

n = sample size

*a = maximum allow-
able number of de-
fectives in sample*

An acceptance sampling plan, (n, a), is an example of a statistical *decision rule.* As in all decisions based upon a sample, risk is involved in applying such a rule. If we think of acceptance sampling as being applied by a consumer (buyer) of lots made by a producer, the *consumer's risk* is the probability that the consumer will accept a low-quality lot. The *producer's risk* is the probability that a buyer will reject a high-quality lot. We will examine such risks more extensively later in our study of decision rules. To look at these risks in the context of the present sample, suppose that $p = 0.05$ (a 5 percent defective lot) is considered to be a high-quality lot. We found in our example that with $n = 10$ and $a = 2$

$$P(\text{accept}) = 0.9885$$

The producer's risk is the chance that the high-quality lot will be rejected by the buyer, which is

> **Meaning: In the long run, about 1 percent of the high-quality lots will be rejected.**

Producer's risk = $P(\text{reject}) = 1 - P(\text{accept}) = 1 - 0.9885 = 0.0115$

On the other hand, suppose that the 25 percent defective lot ($p = 0.25$) of the example is considered a low-quality lot. The consumer's risk is the chance that this lot will be accepted, which we found to be

> **Meaning: In the long run, about 53 percent of the low-quality lots will be accepted.**

Consumer's risk = $P(\text{accept}) = 0.5256$

The consumer, when learning this, may wish to reduce the risk by using a lower acceptance number, a, or a larger sample size, n, or both, as the following exercise shows.

EXERCISE Low-quality lots (25 percent defective) are received by a consumer. Find the consumer's risk for the following sampling plans: (a) $n = 10$, $a = 2$; (b) $n = 10$, $a = 1$; (c) $n = 20$, $a = 1$. (d) Suppose the producer sends a high-quality lot (1 percent defective) to a customer who uses the sampling plan $n = 10$, $a = 0$. Compute the producer's risk.
ANSWER (Use Tables IA and IB.) (a) 0.5256; (b) 0.2440; (c) 0.0243; (d) 1 − 0.9044 = 0.0956.

In the next example, we use Table I to find an acceptance number, a.

> **Here we have $n = 20$ and cum $P(r) = 0.15$; we want to find r.**

EXAMPLE In a sampling plan with $n = 20$, it is desired to hold the chance of accepting a 10 percent defective lot as close to 0.15 as possible. What acceptance number should be used?

SOLUTION We enter Table IB, for $n = 20$, in the 0.10 column. The first two entries, 0.1216 and 0.3917, straddle the desired 0.15, with 0.1216 being closer to 0.15. The value of r corresponding to 0.1216 is 0; so the acceptance number is $a = 0$.

EXERCISE A sampling plan with $n = 50$ is to be used to ensure that lots with a low percentage of defectives run a small chance of being rejected. It is desired that the probability of rejecting lots which are 1 percent defective be as close as possible to 0.02. What should a be?

ANSWER The chance of acceptance should be as close as possible to 1 − 0.02 = 0.98; so from Table IC we find $a = 2$,

The Mean and Standard Deviation of a Binomial Distribution

Asked how many heads are "expected" when 100 coins are tossed, most people answer 50, intuitively. Of course, every toss of 100 coins will not produce 50 heads. Instead, the number of heads will vary. What the 50 means is that over the long run (many tosses of 100 coins) the average number of heads is expected to be 50. The long-run average number of successes in binomial trials is called the *mean* of the binomial distribution. The mean is designated by the symbol μ, mu. The mean is also called the *expected value* of the number of successes, or the expected number of successes.

The formula for μ is

Formula for the mean of a binomial distribution

$$\mu = np$$

That is, given the parameter values n and p, the mean is simply the product of the parameters, n times p.

In tosses of 100 coins, $n = 100$ and the probability of heads is $p = 0.5$. Hence, the mean or expected number of heads is

$$\mu = np = 100(0.5) = 50$$

which is the answer obtained intuitively earlier.

EXERCISE Suppose 40 percent of the people entering a store make a purchase. If 10 people enter the store, find the expected number making a purchase.

ANSWER 4.

The mean μ of a binomial distribution can be calculated from the probability distribution itself, that is, from the numbers of successes and their probabilities. However, the calculation, if carried out, will only show that $\mu = np$. Similarly, the standard deviation σ of a binomial distribution can be calculated from the probability distribution, but the calculation now will show that

Formula for the standard deviation of a binomial distribution

$$\sigma = \sqrt{npq}$$

For our 100-coin-toss example,

$$n = 100 \qquad p = 0.5 \qquad q = 1 - p = 0.5$$

$$\sigma = \sqrt{npq} = \sqrt{100(0.5)(0.5)} = \sqrt{25} = 5 \text{ heads}$$

The standard deviation measures variability around the mean. In Chapter 4 you learned that, for normal distributions, about 95 percent of the distribution lies in the interval $\mu \pm 2\sigma$. Earlier in this chapter we saw (Figure 7.6) that the binomial distribution for $n = 100$ and $p = 0.35$ had a normal shape. Our 100-coin-toss example is a binomial with $n = 100$ and

$p = 0.5$, and the distribution of numbers of heads will have a normal shape.

No binomial can be exactly normal because binomials are discrete distributions and normal distributions are continuous. Nevertheless, the normal 95 percent will hold *approximately* for $n = 100$ and $p = 0.5$. With $\mu = 50$ and $\sigma = 5$,

$$\mu \pm 2\sigma = 50 \pm 2(5) = 50 \pm 10 \text{ heads}$$

and 50 ± 10 is the interval from 40 to 60 heads. Hence, the number of heads in tosses of 100 coins will be from 40 to 60 approximately 95 percent of the time. Or, we may say, the probability of getting from 40 to 60 heads when 100 coins are tossed is about 0.95.

A binomial distribution with n, p is approximated by a normal distribution with $\mu = np$ and $\sigma = \sqrt{npq}$.

The parameters of normal distributions are μ and σ; so values for these parameters are needed when working with a normal distribution. In later chapters we shall frequently approximate binomial distributions by normal distributions; so it is important to remember that in these approximations the mean number of successes is $\mu = np$ and $\sigma = \sqrt{npq}$.

7.6 PROBLEMS

1. Using the binomial formula, compute the probability of exactly r successes in n trials if (a) $r = 3, n = 5, p = 0.6$; (b) $r = 0, n = 4, p = 0.1$; (c) $r = 2, n = 6, p = 0.7$; (d) $r = 4, n = 8, p = 0.5$.

2. (a) Compute and tabulate the binomial distribution for $n = 4, p = 0.7$. (b) From the table for (a), compute the probability of at least two successes. (c) Make a graph of the distribution.

3. From Table IB, with $n = 20$ and $p = 0.75$, compute the probability of (a) less than 15 successes; (b) at least 15 successes; (c) at most 15 successes; (d) from 10 to 15 successes, inclusive; (e) exactly 13 successes.

4. A salesperson has a 10 percent chance of making a sale to any customer who is called upon. If 20 calls are made, what is the chance that (a) fewer than three sales are made? (b) at least one sale is made? (c) more than five sales are made.

5. A true-false test has 50 questions. To pass, a student must get 60 percent or more of the answers correct. What is the chance of passing if a student chooses the answer to each question by tossing a coin and checking true if heads appear and false if tails appear?

6. A town has three ambulances for emergency transportation to a hospital. The probability that any one of these will be available at a given time is 0.75. If a person calls for an ambulance, what is the probability that an ambulance will be available?

7. The probability that any inspector will properly classify a defective item as defective is 0.7. If a defective is examined independently by two inspectors, what is the chance that neither will classify it correctly?

8. A department store employs five clerks who take orders over the tele-

phone. Each clerk is busy taking an order 80 percent of the time. If three customers call at one time, what is the probability that, at that time, clerks will be available to take (a) all three orders? (b) only two orders?

9. A mail order firm sends out advertisements in batches of 50 at a time. The probability of receiving an order as a result of any one of the advertisements is 0.05. What is the probability of receiving (a) no orders from a batch? (b) three orders from a batch? (c) at most two orders from a batch? (d) more than four orders from a batch? (e) What is the expected number of orders per batch?

10. (a) How is an acceptance sampling plan with $n = 10$, $a = 2$ carried out? That is, what do $n = 10$ and $a = 2$ mean? (b) If $n = 10$, $a = 2$, what is the chance that a lot which is 10 percent defective will be accepted? (c) If $n = 10$, $a = 2$, what is the chance that a lot which is 25 percent defective will be rejected? (d) If $n = 20$, $a = 2$, what is the chance that a lot which is 25 percent defective will be rejected?

11. An acceptance sampling plan with $n = 50$ is to be used by a company which considers a lot having 1 percent defective to be a high-quality lot. The company wants the chance of accepting such a lot to be as close as possible to 0.99. What should the acceptance number be?

12. In acceptance sampling, what is meant by consumer's risk and producer's risk?

13. If 50 percent of all voters actually favor a political candidate, what is the chance that in a sample of $n = 50$ voters (a) exactly 50 percent (that is, 25) will favor the candidate? (b) less than 50 percent will favor the candidate?

14. Seventy-five percent of the production workers hired by Griggs Company are good workers. If Griggs hires 20 workers, what is the probability that (a) exactly 15 are good workers? (b) at least 15 are good workers? (c) all 20 are good workers?

15. A space shuttle has independently functioning computers. All four must be operating properly before the shuttle will be cleared for lift-off. If the probability of proper operation is 0.995 for each computer, what is the probability that improper computer operation will delay lift-off?

16. If a coin is tossed 20 times: (a) What is the expected number of heads? (b) What is the probability that the number of heads will turn out to be the expected number?

17. Suppose a binomial distribution has $n = 4$ and $p = 0.3$. (a) What is the mean of the distribution? (b) What is the standard deviation of the distribution?

18. Table A shows the binomial distribution for $n = 4$ and $p = 0.3$.

TABLE A

r	0	1	2	3	4
$P(r)$	0.2401	0.4116	0.2646	0.0756	0.0081

(a) The expected value of r, μ, is the weighted average of the r's. Each r is weighted (multiplied) by its probability and the products are summed to give

$$\mu = \Sigma[rP(r)]$$

It is not necessary to divide by the sum of the weights $\Sigma P(r)$ because this sum equals 1. Compute μ from Table A and verify that the result is the answer to Problem 17(a). (b) The standard deviation of the values of r is

$$\sigma = \sqrt{\Sigma(r - \mu)^2 P(r)}$$

Compute σ for Table A and verify that the result is the answer to Problem 17(b).

7.7 THE POISSON PROBABILITY DISTRIBUTION

The Poisson distribution is named for its originator, Siméon D. Poisson. It is a discrete probability distribution, that is, a probability distribution for a discrete random variable which could have the values 0, 1, 2, 3, and so on. One form of the distribution, the *Poisson binomial approximation formula*, can be used to approximate binomial probabilities in certain situations. A different form, the *Poisson process formula*, can be used to compute probabilities for numbers of arrivals, for example, probabilities for numbers of customers arriving at a bank during the noon hour.

The Poisson Binomial Approximation Formula

Use the Poisson approximation when $n \geq 20$ and $p \leq 0.05$.

The Poisson formula can be used to approximate the probability of r successes in n binomial trials in situations where n is large and the probability of success p is small. The rule of thumb followed by most statisticians is that n is large enough and p is small enough if n is 20 or more and p is 0.05 or less; that is, $n \geq 20$ and $p \leq 0.05$. In general, the larger n is and the smaller p is, the better will be the approximation.

The conditions of large n and small p are often encountered in applied work. For example, examination of 100 bank balances would bring to light very few, if any, erroneous balances, because the probability that a particular balance is in error is very small. Again, a sample of a large number of homeowners would contain few owners whose home had a major fire last year because the probability of such a fire is very small.

The Poisson formula is easier to use than the binomial formula. Another important advantage is that Poisson probabilities can be tabulated more efficiently than binomial probabilities. The Poisson formula for approximating $P(r)$, the number of successes in n binomial trials, is

Poisson formula for approximating the binomial P(r)

$$P(r) = \frac{e^{-\mu}\mu^r}{r!}$$

where $\mu = np$

$\quad\quad e \approx 2.71828$

The only new quantity in the Poisson formula is the constant number e, which, rounded to six digits, is 2.71828. To evaluate the Poisson formula, we need values of e to negative powers. Values for some of these powers can be found in Table II at the end of the book. There you can verify that

$$e^{-2} = 0.1353 \quad\quad e^{-3.2} = 0.0408 \quad\quad e^{-0.8} = 0.4493$$

Some hand calculators have a key which provides values of e to a power. Of course, these powers can also be found on any calculator which has a power key. For example,

$$e^{-2} \approx (2.71828)^{-2} \approx \frac{1}{(2.71828)^2} \approx 0.1353$$

rounded to four digits. Hand calculators are easier to use than a table, and provide more accurate values for many more powers than a table.

EXAMPLE Two hundred passengers have made reservations for an airplane flight. If the probability that a passenger who has a reservation will not show up is 0.01, what is the probability that exactly three will not show up?

SOLUTION Here a "no show" is a success. We assume that the 200 reservations constitute a sample from a large population (size unspecified) of reservations. Moreover, for the population, $p = 0.01$ is the probability of success.

Step 1 *Make sure* $n \geq 20$ *and* $p \leq 0.05$. Note that $n = 200$ is large enough and $p = 0.01$ is small enough to satisfy the rule of thumb that n should be at least 20 and p should not be greater than 0.05. We first find

Step 2 *Calculate* $\mu = np$.

$$\mu = np = 200(0.01) = 2$$

Then, with $r = 3$ successes and $\mu = 2$, we have

$$P(r) = \frac{e^{-\mu}\mu^r}{r!}$$

Step 3 *Calculate* $P(r)$.

$$P(3) = \frac{e^{-2}(2)^3}{3!}$$

From Table II, we find e^{-2} is 0.1353; so

$$P(3) = \frac{(0.1353)(8)}{6} = 0.1804$$

For comparison, let's compute $P(3)$ for the example by the binomial formula

$$P(r) = \binom{n}{r} p^r q^{n-r}$$

We have $n = 200$, $p = 0.01$, $q = 1 - p = 1 - 0.01 = 0.99$. Then

$$P(3) = \binom{200}{3} (0.01)^3 (0.99)^{197}$$

$$= \frac{200!}{3!(197!)} (0.01)^3 (0.99)^{197}$$

$$= \frac{200(199)(198)(197!)}{6(197!)} (0.01)^3 (0.99)^{197}$$

$$= 0.1814$$

Observe that the Poisson approximation, 0.1804, is nearly the same as the binomial value, 0.1814.

It is clear that the Poisson calculation is simpler than the binomial calculation. However, a greater advantage of the Poisson formula, if it is applicable, is that it has only one parameter, μ, whereas the binomial distribution has two parameters, n and p; consequently, Poisson probabilities can be tabulated more compactly than binomial probabilities. For example, the Poisson probability $P(3)$ is the same for $n = 200$, $p = 0.01$ as it is for $n = 100$, $p = 0.02$, and for any other pair of n and p values whose product is $\mu = np = 2$. Therefore, all Poisson distributions with the same value of μ can be tabulated in a single column of a table. An illustrative tabulation of the probabilities of exactly r successes for various values of μ is provided in Table IIIA at the end of the book. In this table, the entry for the airplane reservation example, where $\mu = 2$ and $r = 3$, is found to be the Poisson value, 0.1804, computed in the example.

See Appendix Table IIIA for Poisson probabilities of exactly r successes.

As stated earlier, the Poisson formula provides good approximations of binomial distributions when $n \geq 20$ and $p \leq 0.05$. Table 7.4 and Figure 7.7 (at the top of page 210) compare the binomial-Poisson probabilities for $n = 20$ and $p = 0.05$. As noted in Table 7.4, with $n = 20$, more than six successes are possible, but the probabilities for more than six successes are very small. Moreover, it should be noted that with $n = 20$, it is impossible to have

TABLE 7.4
COMPARISON OF BINOMIAL AND POISSON
PROBABILITIES FOR $n = 20$ AND $p = 0.05$

Number of successes r	P(r) Binomial	P(r) Poisson
0	0.358	0.368
1	0.377	0.368
2	0.189	0.184
3	0.060	0.061
4	0.013	0.015
5	0.002	0.003
6	0.000	0.001
*	Sum = 1.000*	1.000*

* More than 6 successes are possible, but the probabilities for more than 6 successes are less than 0.0005.

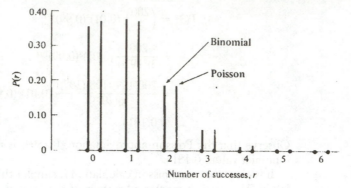

FIGURE 7.7
Comparison of Poisson
and binomial probabil-
ities for $n = 20$ and
$p = 0.05$. Poisson
probabilities are close
to binomial probabili-
ties.

more than 20 successes. However, the Poisson formula, if applied with r
larger than 20, will give a very small nonzero probability—so small that for
practical purposes it is zero. In fact, the Poisson formula will give a nonzero
probability for any value of r, no matter how large; but, again, only 0, 1, 2, 3,
and a small additional number of r values have probabilities large enough to
be of practical significance.

EXERCISE (a) Five percent of the items in a large lot are defective. A sample
of 60 is inspected. Write the Poisson expression for the probability that the
sample contains exactly four defectives, and calculate this probability by the
Poisson formula. (b) Verify your answer to (a) by referring to Table IIIA. (c) Calculate the probability of exactly four defectives if 4 percent of the items in the
lot are defective.
ANSWER (a) $P(4) = [e^{-3}(3)^4]/4! = 0.1680$; (b) 0.1680; (c) 0.125.

See Appendix Table   Table IIIB at the end of the book contains cumulative Poisson probabili-
IIIB for cumulative   ties,
Poisson probabilities.

$$\sum_{r=0}^{r} P(r)$$

for selected values of μ to be used in problems.

EXAMPLE The manager of Music, Inc., is planning to stock and advertise
a very expensive stereo system. The manager expects to draw 250 interested
customers and assesses the probability of selling a system to a customer at
0.02. Suppose the manager decides to stock six systems. What then would be
the probability of (a) being able to satisfy customer demand? (b) not being
able to satisfy customer demand?

SOLUTION Here we have $n = 250$, $p = 0.02$; so

$$\mu = np = 250(0.02) = 5$$

is the mean or expected value of the number demanded.

a. The probability of being able to satisfy demand is the probability that demand will be from 0 through 6 systems. From Table IIIA, with $\mu = 5$, this is

$$\sum_{r=0}^{6} P(r) = 0.7622$$

b. The probability of *not* being able to satisfy demand is the probability that demand is more than 6, that is, 7 or 8 or 9 and so on. Demands from 0 through 6, and demands of more than 6, include all possible demands; so

$$P(\text{demand 0 through 6}) + P(\text{demand more than 6}) = 1$$

$$P(\text{demand more than 6}) = 1 - P(\text{demand 0 through 6})$$

$$= 1 - \sum_{r=0}^{6} P(r)$$

$$= 1 - 0.7622$$

$$= 0.2378$$

EXERCISE In the last example, there is a rather high probability, 0.2378, of not being able to satisfy demand. What would be the probability of not being able to satisfy demand if nine stereo systems were in stock?
ANSWER 0.0318.

The Poisson Process Formula

We next consider the Poisson distribution in a context much broader than that of binomial approximation. To set the stage, suppose it is the busy Friday noon hour at a bank, and we are interested in the number of customers who might arrive during that hour, or during a 5-minute or a 10-minute interval in that hour; that is, our interest centers on time *intervals* and numbers of *arrivals*. The Poisson process formula provides probabilities for the number of arrivals in a time interval if the arrival process has the following characteristics:

P(x arrivals in t units of time)

1. The average arrival rate per unit of time is constant.

Characteristics of a Poisson process

In our setting, this would mean that if the average arrival rate for the noon-hour period is, say, 72 per hour, then this rate holds for any time interval in the noon hour; that is, the rate can be changed to an average of 36 per $\frac{1}{2}$ hour, 1.2 per minute, and so on.

2. The number of arrivals in a time interval does not depend on (is independent of) what happened in previous time intervals.

The idea here is often expressed by saying a Poisson process has "no memory," so what happens from now on is independent of what happened previously. In our setting, this would mean, for example, that the chance of an arrival in the next minute is the same no matter what minute we are considering.

3. It is extremely unlikely that there will be more than one arrival in a very short interval of time; the shorter the interval, the closer to zero is the probability of more than one arrival.

In our setting, this would mean that it is impossible for more than one customer to get through the revolving entrance door in a fraction of a second.

When referring to Poisson processes, it is conventional to use the Greek letter lambda, λ, to denote the average arrival rate per unit of time, such as $\lambda = 72$ arrivals per hour. A typical question then is: If arrivals average $\lambda = 72$ per hour, what is the probability of $x = 4$ arrivals in $t = 3$ minutes? The answer is provided by the *Poisson process formula*

Poisson process formula

$$P(x) = \frac{e^{-\lambda t}(\lambda t)^x}{x!}$$

where t = number of units of time

x = number of arrivals in t units of time

λ = average arrival rate per unit of time

In the question at hand, $\lambda = 72$ arrivals per *hour*; so 1 hour or 60 minutes is the unit of time. Consequently, 3 minutes is $^3/_{60} = {}^1/_{20}$ unit of time; so $t = {}^1/_{20}$. Then

$$\lambda t = 72 \left(\frac{1}{20}\right) = 3.6$$

The value $\lambda t = 3.6$ means that the average of 72 arrivals per 60 minutes is an average of 3.6 arrivals per 3 minutes. Then

$$P(x) = \frac{e^{-\lambda t}(\lambda t)^x}{x!}$$

so the probability that $x = 4$ arrivals in 3 minutes is

$$P(4) = \frac{e^{-3.6}(3.6)^4}{4!}$$

From Table II, $e^{-3.6} = 0.0273$; so

$$P(4) = \frac{(0.0273)(168.0)}{24} = 0.191$$

Hence, if the arrivals are arrivals of customers at a bank, there is a 19.1 percent chance that exactly four customers will arrive in the next 3 minutes.

This is a problem involving cumulative probabilities in a Poisson process.

EXAMPLE A machine has to be shut down for repairs an average of two times in 24 days. When more than four shutdowns occur in 24 days, the production schedule cannot be attained. If shutdowns are a Poisson process, what is the probability that the production schedule cannot be attained?

SOLUTION The number of shutdowns is from 0 through 4, or it is more than 4. Hence,

$$P(0 \text{ through 4 shutdowns}) + P(\text{more than 4 shutdowns}) = 1$$

so the probability that the schedule cannot be met is

$$P(\text{more than 4 shutdowns}) = 1 - P(0 \text{ through 4 shutdowns})$$

$$= 1 - \sum_{x=0}^{4} P(x)$$

The problem states $\lambda = 2$ per 24 days; so 24 days is the unit of time. Also, we are interested in the number of shutdowns in 24 days; so $t = 1$ unit of time. With $\lambda t = 2(1) = 2$, we can find $\sum_{x=0}^{4} P(x) = 0.9473$ from Table IIIB because λt takes the place of μ in the Poisson binomial approximation formula. Hence,

$P(x > 4) = 1 - cum$
$\qquad P(4)$

$$P(\text{more than 4 shutdowns}) = 1 - \sum_{x=0}^{4} P(x)$$

$$= 1 - 0.9473$$

$$= 0.0527$$

so there is only about a 5 percent chance that the schedule will not be attained.

EXERCISE Calls at a telephone switchboard follow a Poisson process and occur at an average rate of six calls per 10 minutes. The operator leaves for a 5-minute coffee break. (a) What is the value of λt? (b) What is the probability that exactly two calls come in (and so go unanswered) while the operator is away? (c) What is the probability that more than three calls go unanswered?
   ANSWER (a) 3; (b) 0.2240; (c) 0.3528.

EXAMPLE Brad Smith is waiting for a taxicab at an intersection at a time when an average of nine empty cabs pass by in 30 minutes. If cab arrivals are a Poisson process: (a) What is the probability that Brad will get a cab in the next 6 minutes? (b) Does it make any difference in the probability calculation whether Brad is waiting at the beginning or the middle of the 30-minute period? Explain. (c) What is the probability that Brad will wait from 6 to 10 minutes to get a cab?

SOLUTION
a. The key to answering this question is to recognize first that Brad will get his cab if *at least one* cab arrives in 6 minutes. Second, either 0 cab arrives, or at least 1 cab arrives, in 6 minutes; so

$P(x \text{ is at least 1}) =$
$\qquad 1 - P(x = 0)$

$$P(0 \text{ cab}) + P(\text{at least one cab}) = 1$$

$$P(\text{at least one cab}) = 1 - P(0 \text{ cab})$$

We have $\lambda = 9$ and the unit of time is 30 minutes. Hence, 6 minutes is $6/30 = 1/5$ unit of time; so $t = 1/5$ and

$$\lambda t = 9 \left(\frac{1}{5}\right) = 1.8$$

Then,

$$P(x) = \frac{e^{-\lambda t}(\lambda t)^x}{x!}$$

and with $\lambda t = 1.8$, the probability of $x = 0$ cab is

$$P(0) = \frac{e^{-1.8}(1.8)^0}{0!} = \frac{e^{-1.8}(1)}{1} = e^{-1.8} = 0.1653$$

Hence,

$$P(\text{at least one cab}) = 1 - P(0 \text{ cab})$$
$$= 1 - 0.1653$$
$$= 0.8347$$

so Brad has a good chance, about 83 percent, of getting a cab in 6 minutes.

b. It makes no difference in the probability calculation whether Brad is waiting at the beginning or the middle of the 30-minute period if the arrival process is Poisson because a Poisson process has no memory. The idea here is the same as in coin tossing; that is, the probability of getting, say, two heads in the next five tosses does not depend upon whether these are the first five tosses, or the second five tosses, or any other five tosses: the coin has "no memory."

A Poisson process is "memoryless."

c. Brad will wait from 6 to 10 minutes if 0 cab arrives in the next 6 minutes *and* at least one cab arrives in the following 4 minutes. We have already calculated

$$P(0 \text{ cab in 6 minutes}) = 0.1653$$

Next we find that for 4 minutes, $t = 4/30$ and $\lambda t = 9(4/30) = 1.2$. Then

$$P(\text{at least 1 cab in 4 minutes}) = 1 - P(0 \text{ cab in 4 minutes})$$
$$= 1 - \frac{e^{-1.2}(1.2)^0}{0!}$$
$$= 1 - e^{-1.2}$$
$$= 1 - 0.3012$$
$$= 0.6988$$

We want

$$P(0 \text{ cab in 6 minutes } and \text{ at least 1 cab in 4 minutes})$$

Recall: For independent events A and B,

$$P(AB) = P(A)P(B)$$

Because of the independence characteristic of Poisson processes, the last probability is the product of the two probabilities,

$$P(0 \text{ cab in 6 minutes}) P(\text{at least 1 cab in 4 minutes})$$

which is

$$P(\text{wait from 6 to 10 minutes}) = (0.1653)(0.6988)$$

$$= 0.1155$$

Other types of rates may be considered as Poisson arrival processes.

The Poisson process formula also has been used in problems involving occurrence rates that are not arrivals per unit of time. For example, suppose a truck averages three breakdowns per 20,000 miles of use. Then $\lambda = 3$ and the unit of distance is 20,000 miles. To find the probability of, say, two breakdowns in 10,000 miles, 10,000 miles would be expressed as

$$t = \frac{10,000}{20,000} = 0.5 \text{ unit of distance}$$

Then $\lambda t = 3(0.5) = 1.5$, and assuming that breakdowns are a Poisson process, we have

$$P(2 \text{ breakdowns in 10,000 miles}) = \frac{e^{-1.5}(1.5)^2}{2!}$$

$$= \frac{(0.2231)(2.25)}{2}$$

$$= 0.251$$

so there is about a 25 percent chance of two breakdowns in 10,000 miles.

7.8 PROBLEMS

1. Find the value of (a) e^{-9}; (b) $e^{-8.0}$; (c) $e^{-2.6}$.
2. (a) State the rule of thumb for circumstances where binomial probabilities can be approximated by the Poisson formula. (b) In 100 binomial trials with $p = 0.015$, the probability of exactly three successes, computed from the binomial formula, is 0.1260. Compute the Poisson approximation of this binomial probability.
3. Use the Poisson formula to compute the approximate values of the binomial probability of r successes if (a) $n = 150, p = 0.01, r = 2$; (b) $n = 60, p = 0.005, r = 4$; (c) $n = 1000, p = 0.0057, r = 5$; (d) $n = 50, p = 0.0025, r = 0$.
4. If 1.25 percent of a bank's account balances are in error and a sample of 200 accounts is selected, approximate by the Poisson formula the probability that (a) none of the 200 accounts is in error; (b) exactly one account is in error; (c) more than one account is in error.
5. If 0.4 percent of a bank's account balances are in error and a sample of 200 accounts is selected, find from the appropriate table the approxi-

mate probability that (a) none of the 200 balances is in error; (b) exactly one balance is in error; (c) at least three balances are in error; (d) the number of balances in error is from two to five, inclusive; (e) fewer than four balances are in error.

6. For $n = 50$, $p = 0.01$, find from the cumulative tables: (a) the binomial probability of fewer than three successes; (b) the Poisson probability of fewer than three successes; (c) the difference between the answers to (a) and (b). (d) What rule of thumb does the foregoing illustrate?

7. If 1 in 1000 manufactured ball bearings is defective, what is the chance that a purchaser of 500 of these bearings will receive one or more defective bearings? (Use the Poisson approximation.)

8. "Lots" of 500 transistors are purchased by the Main Frame Computer Company. Company inspectors test a sample of 24 transistors from each lot and return the lot to the supplier if more than two defective transistors are found in the sample. Suppose a lot containing 25 defective transistors is purchased and inspected. (a) What are the values of n and p? (b) What is the probability that this lot will be returned to the supplier?

9. One percent of the oysters found by native divers off Palm Tree Atoll contain a pearl. If Captain Cruiser buys 40 oysters, what is the probability that he will obtain at least three pearl-bearing oysters?

10. The chance of winning a bet on a number in roulette is $1/38$; so by binomial calculation the probability of winning at least once in 38 plays is $1 - (37/38)^{38} = 0.6370$. What is the Poisson approximation of this probability?

11. A computer system in a company has a breakdown once in 25 days, on the average. Assuming breakdowns are a Poisson process, what is the probability of (a) exactly one breakdown in the next 10 days? (b) more than one breakdown in the next 10 days?

12. Operators of a telephone switchboard can handle up to three incoming calls per minute before putting callers on "hold." If incoming calls average 120 per hour, what is the probability that in any minute at least one caller will be put on hold? (Assume a Poisson process.)

13. On the average, there is one major oil spill off a certain coastline every 5 years. What is the chance that there will be at least one such spill next year if oil spills are a Poisson process?

14. A manufacturer delivers refrigerators to a retail appliance store once a month. The number of refrigerators demanded by the store's customers averages three per month. Assume demand is a Poisson process. (a) Find the probability that the store will be out of stock during a month if it has three refrigerators in stock at the beginning of the month. (b) How many refrigerators should the store have in stock at the beginning of a month if it wishes to hold the chance of not being able to satisfy demand as close as possible to 0.05?

15. A sport fishing boat catches an average of three tuna fish in 5 days. Assuming catches are a Poisson process, what is the probability of

catching (*a*) exactly two tuna in 3 days? (*b*) at least three tuna in 2 days?

16. (See Problem 15.) What is the probability that the next catch will be made within the next 2 days?

17. (See Problem 15.) A businessperson charters the boat for 5 days but will return home on the evening of the day the first tuna is caught. (*a*) What is the probability that no tuna will be caught in 2 days? (*b*) What is the probability that at least one tuna will be caught in 2 days? (c) Using the answers to (*a*) and (*b*) and the appropriate probability rule, find the probability that the businessperson will fish from 2 to 4 days before returning home.

18. An airline reservation desk clerk services an average of 18 customers per hour. Sue Myer, a customer, is the fifth in line waiting for service. What is the probability that Sue will wait more than 10 minutes for service?

19. An investment manager receives an average of 10 calls per 8-hour day from clients. Assuming calls are a Poisson process, what is the probability that the manager will not be interrupted by a call during a meeting lasting 2 hours?

20. A secretary types 75 words per minute and averages six errors per hour of typing. Assuming error occurrences are a Poisson process, what is the probability that a 225-word letter will be typed without error?

7.9 THE HYPERGEOMETRIC PROBABILITY DISTRIBUTION

The hypergeometric distribution is used when the binomial requirements cannot be relaxed.

Earlier we noted that the binomial formula can be applied in two-outcome sampling situations where the sample size *n* was not more than 5 percent of the population size *N*. When *n* is greater than 5 percent of *N*, the hypergeometric formula should be used. Before stating the formula, an example will be given to show what is involved in hypergeometric calculations.

EXAMPLE A store has 50 seemingly identical Super XX tires in stock. There are 10 tires with slightly damaged steel belting mixed randomly in the stock. A customer buys a set of five tires. Compute the probability distribution for the number of good (undamaged) tires obtained by the customer.

SOLUTION There are *N* = 50 tires, of which 40 are good (G) and 10 are damaged (D). The sample size is *n* = 5 tires. The probability of zero good tires is the probability that all five are damaged; that is,

$$P(0 \text{ good}) = P(D\ D\ D\ D\ D)$$

Sampling without replacement

The probability that the first selected tire is damaged is $^{10}/_{50}$. When a tire is taken from stock, it is not replaced before the next tire is taken; so we say the sample of five tires is selected *without replacement*. Consequently, if the first selected tire is damaged, there remain 49 tires of which nine are damaged. Hence, the probability that the second tire is damaged *if* the first tire is damaged is $9/49$. The change from $10/50$ to $9/49$ in the probability of selecting a damaged tire occurs because the population is sampled without replacement: and the change in probability is the reason the binomial distribution is not applicable.

The probability that the third tire is damaged *if* the first two are damaged is $8/48$. Similarly, the probability that the fourth is damaged if the first three are damaged is $7/47$, and so on. Hence,

$$P(0) = P(D\,D\,D\,D\,D) = \frac{10}{50}\left(\frac{9}{49}\right)\left(\frac{8}{48}\right)\left(\frac{7}{47}\right)\left(\frac{6}{46}\right) = 0.0001$$

Next, for one good, we note that one arrangement of one good and four damaged is

$$G\,D\,D\,D\,D$$

and there are

Recall:

$$\binom{n}{r} = \frac{n!}{r!\,(n-r)!}$$

$$\binom{5}{1} = 5$$

arrangements of one G and four D's. Hence,

$$P(1\text{ good}) = \binom{5}{1} P(G\,D\,D\,D\,D)$$

$$= 5 \left(\frac{40}{50}\right)\left(\frac{10}{49}\right)\left(\frac{9}{48}\right)\left(\frac{8}{47}\right)\left(\frac{7}{46}\right)$$

$$= 0.0040$$

Similarly, the probability of two good is

$$P(2\text{ good}) = \binom{5}{2} P(G\,G\,D\,D\,D)$$

$$= 10 \left(\frac{40}{50}\right)\left(\frac{39}{49}\right)\left(\frac{10}{48}\right)\left(\frac{9}{47}\right)\left(\frac{8}{46}\right)$$

$$= 0.0442$$

EXERCISE In the example at hand, what is the probability of (a) three good? (b) five good?
ANSWER (a) 0.2098; (b) 0.3106.

The complete probability distribution for the number of good tires is shown in Table 7.5 and Figure 7.8.

The distribution of Table 7.5 is called a *hypergeometric* probability distribution. Hypergeometric distributions can be computed by the *hypergeometric probability formula*

Hypergeometric formula

$$P(r) = \frac{\binom{R}{r}\binom{N-R}{n-r}}{\binom{N}{n}}$$

TABLE 7.5
PROBABILITY DISTRIBUTION FOR NUMBER
OF GOOD TIRES

Number of good tires r	Probability of number of good tires $P(r)$
0	0.0001
1	0.0040
2	0.0442
3	0.2098
4	0.4313
5	0.3106
	Sum = 1.0000

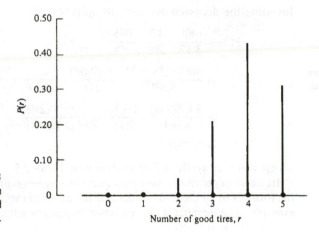

FIGURE 7.8
Probability distribution
for number of good
tires.

where N = population size
n = sample size
R = number of "successes" in the population
r = number of "successes" in the sample

Of course, the number of successes in the sample, r, cannot exceed either the sample size n or R, the number of successes in the population.

In the last example

N = 50 tires

The hypergeometric requires more information than the binomial or Poisson, and . . .

n = 5 tires

R = 40 good tires in the population

r = 0, 1, 2, 3, 4, 5

Applying the hypergeometric formula to find the probability of $r = 3$ good tires (3 successes), we have $N - R = 50 - 40 = 10$ and $n - r = 5 - 3 = 2$.

$$P(r) = \frac{\binom{R}{r}\binom{N-R}{n-r}}{\binom{N}{n}}$$

$$P(3) = \frac{\binom{40}{3}\binom{10}{2}}{\binom{50}{5}}$$

$$= \frac{\dfrac{40!}{3!37!} \cdot \dfrac{10!}{2!8!}}{\dfrac{50!}{5!45!}}$$

Inverting the denominator and multiplying give

$$P(3) = \frac{40!}{3!37!} \cdot \frac{10!}{2!8!} \cdot \frac{5!45!}{50!}$$

. . . is more tedious
to compute by hand.

$$= \frac{40(39)(38)(37!)}{3!37!} \cdot \frac{10(9)(8!)}{2!8!} \cdot \frac{5!45!}{50(49)(48)(47)(46)(45!)}$$

$$= \frac{40(39)(38)}{3(2)(1)} \cdot \frac{10(9)}{2(1)} \cdot \frac{5(4)(3)(2)(1)}{50(49)(48)(47)(46)}$$

$$= 0.2098$$

which you may verify is $P(3)$ as shown in Table 7.5.

In hand calculations, you may compute hypergeometric probabilities by the formula or by the more direct and meaningful method of the original tire example. The formula is chosen when hypergeometric calculations are carried out on a computer.

EXERCISE Suppose there are 15 seemingly identical tires in stock, and five are slightly damaged. What is the probability that a customer who buys four tires will obtain two damaged tires?
ANSWER 0.330.

Use the binomial if n
is not too large.

When the binomial formula is used in sampling problems, it is often being used to approximate hypergeometric results. The approximations are good enough for practical purposes when the sample size n is not more than 5 percent of N, the population size or, to put it another way, when $n \le 0.05N$. Binomial probabilities are easier to compute than hypergeometric probabilities. Because the condition $n \le 0.05N$ is often satisfied when large populations are sampled, the binomial formula is encountered much more frequently than the hypergeometric formula.

Use the hypergeo-
metric only when you
have to—or on a
computer.

Earlier, you learned that the Poisson approximation to the binomial formula works well when $n \ge 20$ and $p \le 0.05$. Suppose that the Poisson is used to approximate the binomial which, in turn, is being used to approxi-

**Better yet, use the
Poisson wherever you
can.**

mate the hypergeometric. Then the Poisson is being used to approximate the hypergeometric. Putting two approximation conditions together, the rule of thumb is that the Poisson can be used to approximate the hypergeometric when $n \leq 0.05N$, $n \geq 20$, and $p \leq 0.05$.

7.10 PROBLEMS

1. A box contains 10 seemingly identical resistors, seven of which are good and three are defective. Two resistors are selected. Compute the probability distribution for the number of defectives in the sample of two.

2. A box contains 10 items, seven of which are good and three are defective. A sample of four items is to be selected. (a) Compute the probability distribution for the numbers of defectives. (b) Both Problems 1 and 2 have $N = 10$ and $R = 3$. Why are the probability distributions different?

3. Sable Company is expanding. The personnel manager has hired 12 new secretaries, of whom seven are trained in the use of a special word-processing typewriter. After discussion with the vice president, the manager decides to assign the secretaries at random to executives. Dot Stone, an executive who will get three secretaries, is interested in how many of the three can use the word-processing typewriter. (a) To Dot, what is a "success"? (b) Determine the probability distribution for Dot's numbers of successes. (c) What is the probability that Dot gets at least two secretaries who can use the word-processing typewriter?

4. Oil-drilling rights at 25 sites on government-owned property have been sold to oil companies. The sites are to be assigned at random to the companies. Oil Ventures, Inc., which has purchased leases for four sites, has a preference for three of the 25 sites. What is the probability that Oil Ventures gets at least two of its preferred sites?

5. Bill Raus owns Raus Trading Co., a company which buys and sells stamps, coins, and other collectors' items. Bill keeps 60 stamps, each in an opaque envelope, in a black bag. Ten of the stamps are worth $20 each, and the others are worthless. Bill charges $4 per stamp, sight unseen, as a sales promotion idea. Suppose a customer buys five stamps. (a) What is the probability that all five stamps are worthless? (b) What is the probability that the customer just breaks even?

6. A deck of cards contains 52 cards, of which 13 are spades. If five cards are dealt and all are spades, the outcome is called a *spade flush*. What is the probability of dealing a spade flush?

7.11 SUMMARY

A *random* variable is a variable whose value depends on chance. A *discrete* random variable is one that may have only certain distinct separated values. A *continuous* random variable is one which may have any value in an interval of values.

The *probability distribution* of a discrete random variable can be defined as (1) a listing of all the different values that the random variable may take on, together with the probability of each value—or (2) a formula from which the probabilities of values of the random variable can be computed.

In two-outcome situations, the outcome of interest is called a "success" and the other outcome is called a "failure." Binomial trials are two-outcome situations, as in coin tossing, in which (1) the probability of success is the same on every trial and (2) the outcome of any trial is independent of outcomes on other trials. The *binomial probability formula* is

$$P(r) = \binom{n}{r} p^r q^{n-r}$$

where r = number of successes
$\quad n$ = number of trials
$\quad p$ = probability of success on each trial
$\quad q = 1 - p$ = probability of failure on each trial

Each particular binomial distribution is characterized by its parameters n and p.

The mean (average or expected) number of successes in n binomial trials is

$$\mu = np$$

The standard deviation of the number of successes in n trials is

$$\sigma = \sqrt{npq}$$

In sampling problems, n is the size of a sample drawn from a population of size N. If $n \leq 0.5N$, the binomial formula (which does not involve N) can be used to calculate success probabilities. In such problems, the value of p is usually given, and N is not given. If R (the number of successes in the population) and N are given, then $p = R/N$.

Binomial probabilities can be approximated by a Poisson formula when $n \geq 20$ and $p \leq 0.05$. The *Poisson binomial approximation formula* is

$$P(r) = \frac{e^{-\mu}\mu^r}{r!}$$

where r = number of successes
$\quad \mu = np$

Poisson distributions have only one parameter, μ.

The *Poisson process* formula can be used to compute probabilities for the numbers of arrivals in an interval of time, if the arrivals have the following characteristics of a Poisson process: (1) the average arrival rate per unit of time is constant, (2) arrivals in an interval are independent of what happened previously, (3) it is extremely unlikely that there will be more than one arrival in a very short time interval. The *Poisson process formula* is

$$P(x) = \frac{e^{-\lambda t}(\lambda t)^x}{x!}$$

where t = number of units of time

x = number of arrivals in t units of time

λ = average arrival rate per unit of time

The formula can also be used for Poisson processes involving rates which are not arrivals per unit of time, such as the average number of truck breakdowns per 10,000 miles traveled.

In two-outcome situations where samples are drawn without replacement from a population of size N, exact success probabilities are computed by the following *hypergeometric probability formula*:

$$P(r) = \frac{\binom{R}{r}\binom{N-R}{n-r}}{\binom{N}{n}}$$

where r = number of successes in the sample

R = number of successes in the population

N = size of the population

n = size of the sample

The binomial formula, which does not involve N, can be used to approximate hypergeometric success probabilities when $n \le 0.05N$. The Poisson binomial approximation formula can be used to approximate hypergeometric success probabilities when $n \le 0.05N$ and $n \ge 20$ and $p \le 0.05$.

7.12 REVIEW PROBLEMS

1. Using the binomial formula, compute the probability of exactly r successes in n trials if (a) $r = 0$, $n = 5$, $p = 0.2$; (b) $r = 2$, $n = 4$, $p = 0.4$; (c) $r = 3$, $n = 7$, $p = 0.8$; (d) $r = 5$, $n = 5$, $p = 0.5$.

2. (a) Compute and tabulate the binomial probability distribution for the number of heads appearing if four coins are tossed. (b) Make a graph of the distribution for (a).

3. The probability of success on a binomial trial is 0.10. For $n = 50$ trials, find the probability that the number of successes will be (a) less than five; (b) at least five; (c) at most five; (d) more than three; (e) at least two, but less than seven; (f) from zero to five, inclusive; (g) exactly six; (h) at least 10.

4. A motel has 45 rooms available on a particular night. Inasmuch as 10 percent of the large population of those making motel reservations fail to show up, the motel makes 50 reservations for this particular night. Use the binomial distribution to find the probability that rooms will be available for all those who do show up.

5. If the true vote nationwide for two political candidates is split exactly 50-50, what is the chance that in a sample of 50 voters, one candidate would receive less than 46 percent of the votes?

6. A lottery ticket has four randomly selected digits printed on it and open to view. Another four concealed random digits are exposed by the buyer of a ticket. A prize is won if the digit in any *position* of the exposed number matches the digit in the corresponding position of the number printed on the ticket. Compute the probability that the number of matches is 0, 1, 2, 3, or 4.

7. (a) How is an acceptance sampling plan with $n = 20$, $a = 3$ carried out? That is, what do $n = 20$ and $a = 3$ mean? (b) If $n = 20$, $a = 3$, what is the chance of accepting a large lot which is 1 percent defective? (c) If $n = 20$, $a = 3$, what is the chance of rejecting a large lot which is 10 percent defective? (d) If $n = 50$, $a = 3$, what is the chance of accepting a large lot which is 1 percent defective? (e) If $n = 50$, $a = 3$, what is the chance of rejecting a large lot which is 10 percent defective? (f) Repeat (d) and (e) using $a = 4$, and by comparison of results state what happens to the chance of accepting a good lot (1 percent defective) and the chance of rejecting a poor lot (10 percent defective) when a is increased from 3 to 4.

8. In an acceptance sampling application, a 1 percent defective lot is a high-quality lot and 10 percent defective is a low-quality lot. If the plan has $n = 50$, $a = 3$, compute (a) consumer's risk; (b) producer's risk.

9. A student carries a circular card with four equal sectors marked a, b, c, d to a multiple-choice test on which each question has four responses from which to make a selection. The card has a metal arrow attached by a pivot at its center. Whenever the student can't answer a question, he spins the arrow and uses the letter at which its point comes to rest as the response. If this process is used on 10 questions, what is the chance of getting (a) more than three correct? (b) more than five correct?

10. Jay Patterson, a buyer for Patterson Produce Company, is examining a 5-acre field of watermelons. Jay will select 20 melons at random and cut them open. If 18 or more of the 20 are of high quality (ripe, red, and sweet), Jay will buy the whole crop. Suppose 90 percent of the melons are of high quality. What is the probability that Jay will buy the crop?

11. Use the Poisson binomial approximation formula to compute the probability of r successes in n trials if (a) $n = 100$, $p = 0.025$, $r = 3$; (b) $n = 350$, $p = 0.002$, $r = 1$.

12. When its production process is running properly, 1.6 percent of the thousands of rolls of film made by Quality Film, Inc., are of inferior quality. Examination of a random sample of 100 rolls of recently produced film revealed five rolls of inferior quality. Dave Hardman, the production manager, stated that the sample results were unexpectedly poor, and that something should be done about the situation. If the process is running properly, then in a sample of 100: (a) What is the expected number of rolls of inferior-quality film? (b) What is the probability that the sample would have five or more inferior-quality rolls?

13. Over many years, a college has found that 4 percent of newly accepted graduate students do not register for classes at the college. Next fall's class list has 125 newly admitted graduate students. What is the probability that at least 120 register for classes?

14. Three percent of the large number of tires made by a manufacturer are defective. If a store buys 100 of these tires, what is the probability that the number of defectives received is (a) zero? (b) less than three? (c) more than six?

15. An area has a hurricane once in 10 years, on the average, and hurricane arrivals are a Poisson process. What is the probability that in the next 4 years there will be (a) exactly one hurricane? (b) at least two hurricanes?

16. (See Problem 15.) What is the probability that the next hurricane will arrive during the next 5 years?

17. The accident emergency staff of C. B. Schwartz, Inc., employs a doctor and two paramedics. Accident arrivals at the clinic are a Poisson process with an average

of four arrivals in 8 hours. What is the probability that the emergency staff will have to attend to more than three accident cases in a 4-hour period?

18. (See Problem 17.) What is the probability that it will be an hour or more before the next accident arrival?

19. A doctor receives an average of three telephone calls from 9 p.m. until 9 a.m. the next morning. Assuming Poisson arrivals of calls, what is the probability that the doctor will not be disturbed by a call if she goes to bed at midnight and arises at 6 a.m.?

20. On a canal, locks which move small boats from one level to another are operated when 10 boats have assembled in the waiting area. Assume boat arrivals are Poisson with an average arrival rate of 1 boat in 30 minutes. What is the probability that the ninth boat arriving will have to wait from 15 to 30 minutes before the locks are operated? (*Hint:* You have to find two probabilities and then apply a probability rule to obtain the answer.)

21. Five of the 24 seemingly identical diamonds on display at Short's Jewelers are of excellent (flawless) quality, and the remainder have slight imperfections. Jan Long purchased four randomly selected diamonds to store in a safe-deposit box as an investment. Compute the probability distribution for the numbers of excellent diamonds Jan purchased.

22. A bird arose early one morning and ate five of the 20 cherries remaining on a cherry tree. Four of the 20 cherries contained a worm. What is the probability that the early bird got three or more worms?

23. A population has $N = 500$, of which $R = 10$ are "successes." Suppose a random sample of $n = 25$ is selected. We want the probability of $r = 1$ success, $P(1)$. (*a*) Write the hypergeometric factorial expression for $P(1)$. (*b*) Reduce the factorials in (*a*) by cancellation, and compute $P(1)$ to three decimal places. (You will want a hand calculator for this computation.) (*c*) Let p be the proportion of successes in the population and approximate $P(1)$ by the binomial formula. (*d*) Let p be the proportion of successes in the population and approximate $P(1)$ by the Poisson binomial approximation formula. (*e*) Which approximation, the binomial (*c*) or the Poisson (*d*), is more accurate?

8

THE NORMAL DISTRIBUTION AND OTHER CONTINUOUS PROBABILITY DISTRIBUTIONS

8.1 INTRODUCTION

About 200 years ago, scientists discovered that large numbers of measurements often exhibit bell-shaped frequency distribution patterns. The bell shape was encountered in many situations and came to be called the *normal* pattern. The graph of the pattern is called the normal curve. The normal curve was introduced in Chapter 3 as a smooth curve used to describe frequency distribution histograms, as illustrated in Figure 8.1.

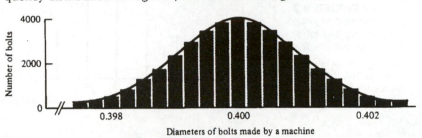

FIGURE 8.1
Normal curve describing a frequency distribution histogram.

In addition to its role in describing a frequency distribution pattern, the normal curve is used extensively in solving probability problems, and in statistical inference. In this chapter you will learn how to use the normal curve to solve a variety of problems in probability. In later chapters you will learn how to use the normal curve to solve problems in statistical inference, that is, problems arising when information about a population has to be inferred from a sample of the population.

After a detailed study of the continuous normal probability distribution, we shall consider two other continuous distributions, the uniform distribution and the exponential distribution.

8.2 CONTINUOUS PROBABILITY DISTRIBUTIONS

The random variable "number of successes" of the last chapter may take on the values 0, 1, 2, 3, and so on; it is a discrete random variable. The values of a discrete random variable are graphed as separated points, and probabilities as the lengths of vertical line segments, as illustrated in Figure 8.2 (at the top of page 228). A probability distribution contains all possible values of the random variable; so the sum of all the probabilities (the sum of the lengths of the vertical segments in Figure 8.2) must be 1.

A continuous random variable can take on any value in an interval of values. A continuous variable in the interval from 0 to 8 could have the value 3.4685, or 5.217849, or any value from 0 to 8. The possible values for a continuous random variable are graphed as a line or line segment, but now we cannot draw a vertical line to represent the probability of each value of the variable. Instead, the *probability for an interval is graphed as an area*, as illustrated in Figure 8.3 (at the bottom of page 228). Because a probability distribution must include all values of the random variable, the sum of the probabilities (the total shaded area in Figure 8.3) must be 1. I did not put a vertical

The probability of an interval is represented by the area above the interval.

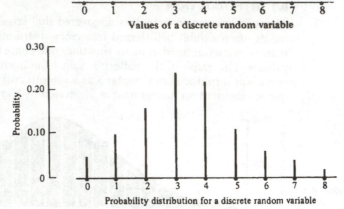

Values of a discrete random variable

FIGURE 8.2
A discrete random
variable and its proba-
bility distribution. The
sum of the lengths of
the vertical line seg-
ments for the distribu-
tion is 1.

Probability distribution for a discrete random variable

axis or a vertical scale on Figure 8.3 because a vertical distance tells us what
the height of the curve is, and that is not what we want. We want areas under
segments of curves. We will get these areas from tables prepared by mathematical statisticians, or by evaluating formulas.

EXERCISE See the probability distribution of Figure 8.3. What is the probability of the interval 4 to 8? Why?
ANSWER 0.40 because the total shaded area must be 1.

It is important to remember that a line segment has no area (zero area),
because a line has no width. Thus, the vertical segment at 4 in the distribution of Figure 8.3 has an area of zero. This means the probability of 4 is zero.

*For any number a, in
the continuous case,
P(exactly a) = 0.*

In general, the probability for an exact (single) value of a continuous
random variable is zero. Consequently, the probability of an interval is the
same whether the endpoints are included or not—because the endpoints
have a probability of zero.

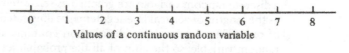

Values of a continuous random variable

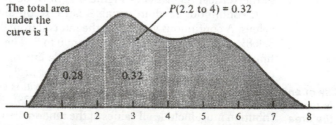

The total area
under the
curve is 1

$P(2.2 \text{ to } 4) = 0.32$

0.28   0.32

FIGURE 8.3
A continuous random
variable and its proba-
bility distribution.

Probability distribution for a continuous random variable
(the probability of a horizontal interval is the area over the interval)

EXERCISE What would we add to $P(2 \text{ to } 4)$ to obtain $P(2 \text{ to } 8)$ (a) if we have a discrete random variable (Figure 8.2)? (b) if we have a continuous random variable (Figure 8.3)?
ANSWER (a) $P(5 \text{ to } 8)$; (b) $P(4 \text{ to } 8)$.

8.3 PARAMETERS OF NORMAL PROBABILITY DISTRIBUTIONS

μ and σ are parameters of a normal distribution.

The parameters, or characteristics, of normal distributions are the mean and the standard deviation. A particular normal distribution is specified by its mean, say, $\mu = 50$, and its standard deviation, say, $\sigma = 5$. Different normal distributions (the number of them is unlimited) have different means or different standard deviations. In Figure 8.4, distributions A and B have the same mean; A is comparatively narrow and tall because it has a smaller

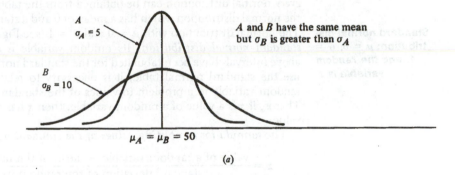

(a)

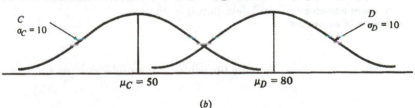

(b)

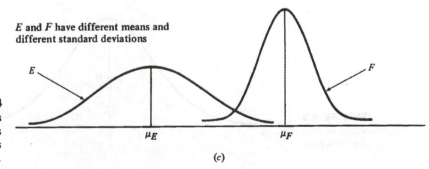

FIGURE 8.4
Normal distributions with various values of the parameters μ and σ.

(c)

standard deviation than B. B is comparatively broad and low because it has a larger standard deviation than A. Curves C and D have the same standard deviations, but D has a larger mean than C.

EXERCISE See Figure 8.4, curves E and F. Which has (a) the larger standard deviation? (b) the larger mean?
ANSWER (a) E; (b) F.

8.4 THE STANDARD NORMAL PROBABILITY DISTRIBUTION

The Standard Normal Variable z

Because the number of possible values for μ and σ is unlimited, the number of different normal distributions is unlimited. However, probabilities for *every* normal distribution can be obtained from the table of probabilities for the normal distribution which has a mean of 0 and a standard deviation of 1. The normal distribution with $\mu = 0$ and $\sigma = 1$ (see Figure 8.5) is called the *standard normal distribution*. Its random variable is called z. The areas above intervals have been tabulated for the standard normal distribution. To use the standard normal table, it is necessary to relate the values of the random variable in a problem to values of the standard normal variable z. That is, if x is a value of a random variable, then x has to be changed to a z value.

Standard normal distribution: $\mu = 0$, $\sigma = 1$, and the random variable is z.

The *formula for computing values of the standard normal variable is*

$$z = \frac{\text{value of a random variable} - \text{mean of the random variable}}{\text{standard deviation of the random variable}}$$

This formula relates values x of the random variable to values z in Appendix Table V.

Thus, if x is a value of a random variable whose mean is μ, and whose standard deviation is σ, then

$$z = \frac{x - \mu}{\sigma}$$

Suppose the values x in a problem have a normal distribution with $\mu = 50$

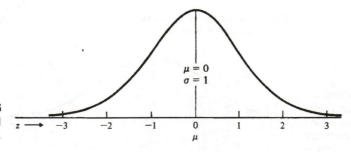

FIGURE 8.5
The standard normal distribution.

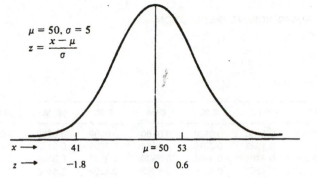

FIGURE 8.6
Changing an x value to
its z value.

and $\sigma = 5$, as shown in Figure 8.6. At the bottom of the figure is a scale for x and, under that, a scale for the corresponding values of z.

At $x = 41$, we find

$$z = \frac{x - \mu}{\sigma}$$

$$z = \frac{41 - 50}{5} = \frac{-9}{5} = -1.8$$

At $x = 50$,

$$z = \frac{x - \mu}{\sigma}$$

$$z = \frac{50 - 50}{5} = \frac{0}{5} = 0$$

Thus, at $x = 50$, which is the mean, the z value is 0. From the definition of z, which has $x - \mu$ in the numerator, you can see that z always will be zero when $x = \mu$.

At $x = 53$,

$$z = \frac{x - \mu}{\sigma}$$

$$z = \frac{53 - 50}{5} = \frac{3}{5} = 0.6$$

EXERCISE See Figure 8.6. What is z at (a) $x = 56.2$? (b) $x = 48$?
ANSWER (a) 1.24; (b) −0.4.

Table of Probabilities for the Standard Normal Distribution

Table V at the end of the book contains probabilities (areas) for the standard normal distribution. Table 8.1 is part of Table V. The figure in the heading

TABLE 8.1
AREAS FOR THE STANDARD NORMAL DISTRIBUTION

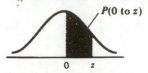

z	0.00	0.01	0.02	0.03	0.04	0.05	0.06	0.07	0.08	0.09
0.0	0.0000	0.0040	0.0080	0.0120	0.0160	0.0199	0.0239	0.0279	0.0319	0.0359
0.5	0.1915	0.1950	0.1985	0.2019	0.2054	0.2088	0.2123	0.2157	0.2190	0.2224
1.0	0.3413	0.3438	0.3461	0.3485	0.3508	0.3531	0.3554	0.3577	0.3599	0.3621
1.5	0.4332	0.4345	0.4357	0.4370	0.4382	0.4394	0.4406	0.4418	0.4429	0.4441
2.0	0.4772	0.4778	0.4783	0.4788	0.4793	0.4798	0.4803	0.4808	0.4812	0.4817
2.5	0.4938	0.4940	0.4941	0.4943	0.4945	0.4946	0.4948	0.4949	0.4951	0.4952
3.0	0.4987	0.4987	0.4987	0.4988	0.4988	0.4989	0.4989	0.4989	0.4990	0.4990

P(0 to z) means the probability for the interval from 0 to the value of z.

shows that the table provides areas only for intervals starting at $z = 0$ (where $x = \mu$) and ending at a positive value of z. For example, if $z = 1.56$, we find the row where $z = 1.5$, then move across that row to the column headed 0.06 to find the entry 0.4406 for $z = 1.56$. Using $P(0$ to $z)$ to mean the probability of the interval 0 to z, we may write

$$P(0 \text{ to } 1.56) = 0.4406$$

Normal distributions are symmetrical, with the left half being a mirror image of the right half. Consequently it is not necessary to tabulate probabilities for negative values of z (values to the left of $z = 0$). That is, $P(0$ to $z)$ is

P(0 to −z) = P(0 to z).

the same whether the particular value of z is positive or negative. For example,

$$P(0 \text{ to } -1.56) = P(0 \text{ to } 1.56) = 0.4406$$

EXERCISE From Table 8.1, find (a) $P(0$ to 2); (b) $P(0$ to 0.09); (c) $P(0$ to $-2.57)$.
ANSWER (a) 0.4772; (b) 0.0359; (c) 0.4949.

Using the Standard Normal Table

The following examples illustrate the use of the table of areas for the standard normal distribution. In each example, values of the random variable in the problem statement are converted to z values; then needed probabilities are obtained from Table V at the end of the book. A statement that a variable is "normally distributed" means that the variable has a normal probability distribution.

EXAMPLE A filling machine is set to pour 952 ml (milliliters) of wine into bottles. The amounts of fill are normally distributed with a mean of 952 ml and a standard deviation of 4 ml. Use the standard normal table to find the probability that a bottle contains between 952 and 956 ml.

SOLUTION   Figure 8.7 is a sketch showing the information given in the

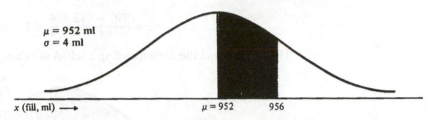

μ = 952 ml
σ = 4 ml

FIGURE 8.7
Sketch containing information given in the example.

x (fill, ml) ⟶   μ = 952   956

Step 1   Calculate the appropriate z values.

example. We want to find the area above the interval 952 to 956 ml. Before going to Table V, the x values must be changed to z values using the formula

$$z = \frac{x - \mu}{\sigma}$$

At x = 952, which is the mean, we compute

$$z = \frac{952 - 952}{4} = \frac{0}{4} = 0$$

Thus, as always, z = 0 at the mean. At x = 956, we find

$$z = \frac{956 - 952}{4} = \frac{4}{4} = 1$$

Step 2   Find the areas (probabilities) in the table.

Hence, the x interval 952 to 956 becomes the z interval from 0 to 1. From Table V, we find

$$P(0 \text{ to } 1) = 0.3413$$

Step 3   Interpret your results.

which is the probability that a bottle contains between 952 and 956 ml. Put another way, 34.13 percent of filled bottles will contain between 952 and 956 ml. Figure 8.8 shows the example solution graphically.

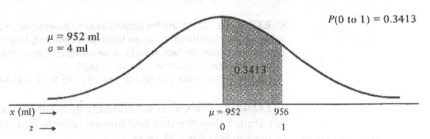

P(0 to 1) = 0.3413

μ = 952 ml
σ = 4 ml

0.3413

FIGURE 8.8
Sketch showing example solution.

x (ml) ⟶   μ = 952   956
z ⟶   0   1

EXAMPLE   For the foregoing example, find what percentage of filled bottles will contain between 948 and 956 ml.

SOLUTION With $\mu = 952$ and $\sigma = 4$, we have for $x = 948$

$$z = \frac{948 - 952}{4} = \frac{-4}{4} = -1$$

For $x = 956$,

$$z = \frac{956 - 952}{4} = \frac{4}{4} = 1$$

The x values and the corresponding z values are shown in Figure 8.9. From

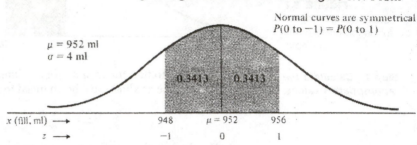

Normal curves are symmetrical
$P(0 \text{ to } -1) = P(0 \text{ to } 1)$

$\mu = 952$ ml
$\sigma = 4$ ml

0.3413   0.3413

x (fill, ml) ——→   948 $\mu = 952$ 956
z ——→   −1   0   1

FIGURE 8.9
Probability for 948 to
956 ml.

*Here we use the sym-
metry of the normal
curve.*

Table V, we find $P(0 \text{ to } 1)$ is 0.3413. Because of symmetry, $P(0 \text{ to } -1)$ also is 0.3413. Hence,

$$P(-1 \text{ to } 1) = 0.3413 + 0.3413 = 0.6826$$

Consequently, 68.26 percent of the bottles will contain between 948 and 956 ml.

In Chapter 4 we used μ, σ, and the "normal percents" in describing frequency distributions. These percents come from areas of the standard normal distribution. Note in Figure 8.9 that the interval from 948 ml to the mean, 952 ml, is 4 ml, and 4 ml is one standard deviation. Also, from the mean to 956 ml is one standard deviation. Thus, the interval 948 to 956 ml extends from one standard deviation to the left of μ to one standard deviation to the right of μ, and contains 68.26 percent, or about 68 percent, of the area. Hence, the normal percent for the interval $\mu \pm 1\sigma$ is about 68 percent, as you learned earlier.

About 68% of
the total area

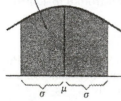

σ μ σ

★ **EXERCISE** (a) In the foregoing example, what would be the lower and upper values of x, in milliliters, for an interval extending from two standard deviations below the mean to two standard deviations above the mean? (b) What is the "normal percent" for the interval in (a)?
   ANSWER · (a) 944 to 960 ml; (b) $2P(0 \text{ to } 2) = 0.9544$, or about 95 percent.

EXAMPLE Test scores are normally distributed with mean 70 and standard deviation 8. Use the standard normal table to find the percent of test scores in the interval from 54 to 84.

*Make a sketch,
showing x and z val-
ues, for each
problem; it helps.*

SOLUTION The problem solution is shown graphically in Figure 8.10. As the figure shows, at $x = 54$

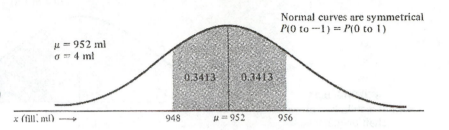

Normal curves are symmetrical
$P(0 \text{ to } -1) = P(0 \text{ to } 1)$

$\mu = 952$ ml
$\sigma = 4$ ml

0.3413   0.3413

FIGURE 8.10
Normal distribution of
test scores.

x (fill, ml) ⟶   948 $\mu = 952$ 956

$$z = \frac{54 - 70}{8} = \frac{-16}{8} = -2$$

and at $x = 84$,

$$z = \frac{84 - 70}{8} = \frac{14}{8} = 1.75$$

From the standard normal table we find

$$P(0 \text{ to } -2) = P(0 \text{ to } 2) = 0.4772$$

$$P(0 \text{ to } 1.75) = 0.4599$$

Here we add proba-
bilities to find the
total probability.

The sum of the shaded areas in Figure 8.10 is the desired probability.
It is

$$P(0 \text{ to } -2) + P(0 \text{ to } 1.75) = 0.4772 + 0.4599$$

$$= 0.9371$$

Hence, 93.71 percent of the scores are in the interval from 54 to 84.

EXERCISE In the last example, what percent of the scores are in the interval
from 52 to 76?
ANSWER 76.12 percent.

The parts of the next example show various addition and subtraction procedures which arise in the use of Table V.

EXAMPLE Assume that the diameters of the shafts made by an automatic
machine are normally distributed with a mean of 25 mm and a standard deviation of 0.5 mm.
  a. What is the probability that a shaft will have a diameter between 25.2
     and 25.9 mm? We show the problem solution graphically in Figure
     8.11. First we compute the z values.
     At $x = 25.2$, we have

$$z = \frac{25.2 - 25}{0.5} = \frac{0.2}{0.5} = 0.4$$

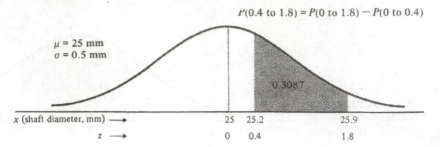

FIGURE 8.11
Normal distribution of
shaft diameters.

At $x = 25.9$,

$$z = \frac{25.9 - 25}{0.5} = \frac{0.9}{0.5} = 1.8$$

From Table V, we find

$$P(0 \text{ to } 0.4) = 0.1554 \quad \text{and} \quad P(0 \text{ to } 1.8) = 0.4641$$

It is important to remember that Table V gives areas for intervals which have one end at $z = 0$. The interval of interest in this problem, from $z = 0.4$ to $z = 1.8$, does not have one end at $z = 0$. Consequently, to get $P(0.4 \text{ to } 1.8)$ we start with $P(0 \text{ to } 1.8)$ and subtract $P(0 \text{ to } 0.4)$. Thus,

*Here we subtract
probabilities to
find the required
probability.*

$$P(0.4 \text{ to } 1.8) = P(0 \text{ to } 1.8) - P(0 \text{ to } 0.4)$$
$$= 0.4641 - 0.1554$$
$$= 0.3087$$

The probability that a shaft has a diameter between 25.2 and 25.9 mm is 0.3087.

b. What proportion of the shafts have diameters of 25 mm or less? At 25 mm, which is the mean, $z = 0$. Figure 8.12 shows the desired probability is the area to the left of $z = 0$. Because of symmetry, half (0.5) of the area lies to the left of $z = 0$, and half lies to the right. The mathematical normal curve extends indefinitely to the left and right, as indicated by the infinity symbols $-\infty$ and ∞ in Figure 8.12. The symbol

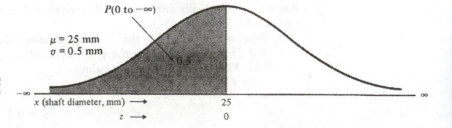

FIGURE 8.12
The area to the left of
μ is 0.5.

$P(0 \text{ to } -\infty)$ represents the shaded area of Figure 8.12. We have

$$P(0 \text{ to } -\infty) = 0.5$$

so the proportion of shafts with diameters of 25 mm or less is 0.5.

The fact that the normal curve extends from $-\infty$ to ∞ causes no difficulty in applied problems because almost all the area is in the interval from $z = -3$ to $z = 3$. That is,

$$P(-3 \text{ to } 3) = 2P(0 \text{ to } 3)$$
$$= 2(0.4987)$$
$$= 0.9974$$

There is very little probability beyond $\mu \pm 3\sigma$.

Thus, 99.74 percent of the area lies in the interval from $z = -3$ to $z = 3$. Also, rounded to four decimal places, the area from $z = -4$ to $z = 4$ is 1.0000; so, for practical purposes, 100 percent of the area is in the interval $z = -4$ to $z = 4$.

c. If 1000 shafts are made, how many would be expected to have diameters of 24.07 mm or less? At $x = 24.07$, we compute

$$z = \frac{24.07 - 25}{0.5} = \frac{-0.93}{0.5} = -1.86$$

We want the left *tail* area in Figure 8.13, the area to the left of 24.07. This may be found as the total area to the left of the mean, which is an area of 0.5, less the area over the interval 0 to -1.86. Hence,

$$P(-1.86 \text{ to } -\infty) = 0.5 - P(0 \text{ to } -1.86)$$
$$= 0.5 - P(0 \text{ to } 1.86)$$
$$= 0.5000 - 0.4686$$
$$= 0.0314$$

If 1000 shafts are made, the number expected to have diameters of 24.07 mm or less is

$$1000(0.0314) = 31.4$$

or about 31 shafts.

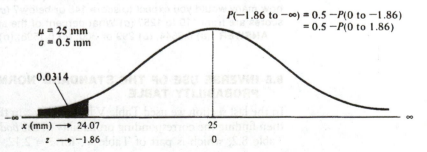

FIGURE 8.13
A left-tail area.

$\mu = 25$ mm
$\sigma = 0.5$ mm

0.0314

x (mm) $\longrightarrow$ 24.07   25
$z \longrightarrow$ -1.86 0

$P(-1.86 \text{ to } -\infty) = 0.5 - P(0 \text{ to } -1.86)$
$= 0.5 - P(0 \text{ to } 1.86)$

d. What percent of the shafts made will have diameters of 24.56 mm or more? At $x = 24.56$ mm we compute

$$z = \frac{24.56 - 25}{0.5} = \frac{-0.44}{0.5} = -0.88$$

The desired area, shown in Figure 8.14, is the sum of the area from 0

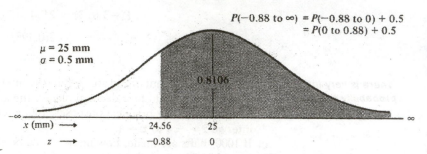

FIGURE 8.14
Area for an interval
from the left of μ to ∞.

to -0.88, and the area of 0.5 to the right of the mean. Hence, we compute

$$P(24.56 \text{ to } \infty) = P(-0.88 \text{ to } \infty)$$
$$= P(0 \text{ to } 0.88) + 0.5$$
$$= 0.3106 + 0.5$$
$$= 0.8106$$

so 81.06 percent of the shafts will have diameters of 24.56 mm or more

It is time now for you to practice the procedures illustrated in the foregoing examples. You will do much better on the next exercise if you draw a figure for each part.

EXERCISE Aptitude test scores of job applicants are normally distributed, with a mean of 140 and a standard deviation of 20. (a) What is the probability that a score will be in the interval 100 to 180? (b) If 500 applicants take the test, how many would you expect to score 145 or below? (c) What proportion of the scores are from 110 to 125? (d) What percent of the scores exceed 183?
ANSWER (a) 0.9544; (b) 299 or 300; (c) 0.1598; (d) 1.58 percent.

8.5 INVERSE USE OF THE STANDARD NORMAL PROBABILITY TABLE

In the last section we used Table V by locating z in the left and top *margins*, then finding the corresponding probability in the *body* of the table. Thus, in Table 8.2, which is part of Table V, for $z = 2.12$, we find $P(0 \text{ to } 2.12)$ is

TABLE 8.2

AREAS FOR THE STANDARD
NORMAL DISTRIBUTION

z	0.00	0.01	0.02	0.03
2.0	0.4772	0.4778	0.4783	0.4788
2.1	0.4821	0.4826	0.4830	0.4834
2.2	0.4861	← 0.4864	0.4868	0.4871
2.3	0.4893	0.4896	0.4898	0.4901
2.4	0.4918	0.4920	0.4922	0.4925
2.5	0.4938	0.4940	0.4941	0.4943

Inverse use of the table: *Given a probability, find the corresponding value of z.*

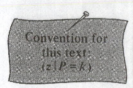

Convention for this text: $(z|P = k)$

0.4830. *Inverse* use of the table means to find the value of z (in the margins) which corresponds to a given probability in the body of the table. For example, given the probability $P = 0.4864$, what is the corresponding value of z? To find out, we scan the *body* of the table and find 0.4864, shown in a box in Table 8.2. The corresponding numbers in the left and top margins are 2.2 and 0.01; so $z = 2.21$.

We shall symbolize the inverse use of Table V by writing

$$(z|P = k)$$

which means *the value of z given that* $P(0$ to $z) = k$. Thus, in the last example,

$$(z|P = 0.4864) = 2.21$$

EXERCISE From Table 8.2, find $(z|P = 0.4922)$.
ANSWER 2.42.

A given probability P may not appear in a standard normal table. In that case, take the closest probability listed in the table and write its z value. For example, suppose we want

$$(z|P = 0.4780)$$

The probability closest to 0.4780 in Table 8.2 is 0.4778; so write $z = 2.01$. Of course, the given probability may be exactly halfway between two tabulated values. In that case, I will use the z value which ends in an *even* digit. If you do the same, you will be able to check your answers against mine. For example, from Table 8.2, I would write

$$(z|P = 0.4828) = 2.12$$

and

$$(z|P = 0.4942) = 2.52$$

EXERCISE From Table 8.2, find (a) $(z|P = 0.4786)$; (b) $(z|P = 0.4919)$.
ANSWER (a) 2.03; (b) 2.40.

When solving problems where we had to find probabilities, an x value of the problem was changed to a corresponding z value, and then the probability was looked up. To work inversely, given a probability, we first look up the z value, then change this z value to an x value in the problem. To see what is involved, note that

$$z = \frac{x - \mu}{\sigma}$$

can be written as

$$z\sigma = x - \mu$$

Finding x when you know z, μ, and σ   so that $$x = \mu + z\sigma$$

But *remember* that z is the negative of the value in Table V when x is to the left of the mean; that is, z is negative when $x < \mu$.

For example, suppose that the x values of a problem have $\mu = 100$ and $\sigma = 10$, and we want to find the x value such that $P(0 \text{ to } x) = 0.45$. Figure

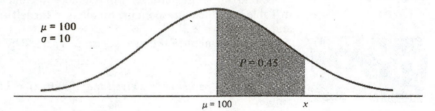

$\mu = 100$
$\sigma = 10$

$P = 0.45$

FIGURE 8.15
Problem statement for
finding x.

$\mu = 100$ x

8.15 shows the given information: x is to the right of μ; so z is positive. From Table V we find that

$$(z|P = 0.4500) = 1.64$$

so $z = 1.64$. Therefore,

$$x = \mu + z\sigma$$
$$= 100 + (1.64)(10) = 116.4$$

EXERCISE   See Figure 8.16. What is the value of x for which the *left tail* area is 0.05? Why?
ANSWER   83.6. The left tail area is 0.05; so $P(0 \text{ to } z) = 0.45$ and $(z|P = 0.45) = 1.64$. But x is to the left of μ; so $z = -1.64$. Hence, $x = 100 - 1.64(10) = 83.6$.

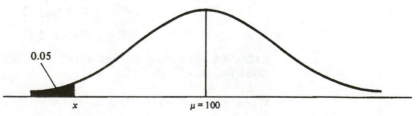

0.05

FIGURE 8.16
Finding x, given μ, σ,
and a probability.

x $\mu = 100$

You should make a sketch when solving a problem involving the inverse use of Table V. Read the problem carefully. Put x on the proper side of the mean. Put the given probability on the sketch.

EXAMPLE   Weekly demand for a liquid reagent stocked by Masanto Chemical Supply Company is normally distributed. The mean is 250 gallons and the standard deviation is 80 gallons. How many gallons should be available for a week if Masanto wants to ensure that the probability of running out of stock does not exceed 0.02?

Why is x to the right of μ?

SOLUTION   Figure 8.17 shows the given information. Note that if demand is greater than x, the amount available, Masanto will run out of stock. The

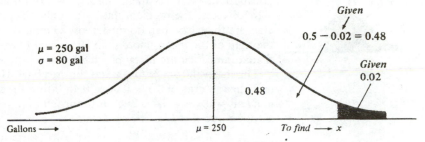

FIGURE 8.17
Masanto's demand
problem.

Remember: Table V does not give tail areas.

given probability, 0.02, is the probability that demand is greater than x. Because 0.02 is a tail area, the interval from 250 to x has an area of $0.5 - 0.02 = 0.48$. From Table V, we find

$$(z|P = 0.48) = 2.05$$

Why is z positive?   Hence,

$$x = \mu + z\sigma$$

$$= 250 + 2.05(80) = 414 \text{ gallons}$$

Masanto should have 414 gallons (or more) available.

EXERCISE   Assume that scores on an aptitude test are normally distributed. If the mean score is 140 points and $\sigma = 25$ points, find the cutoff passing grade such that 67 percent of those taking the test will pass.
ANSWER   129 points.

Finding μ when x, σ, and area are given

EXAMPLE   An automatic machine makes cylinders whose diameters are normally distributed. The mean diameter of the cylinders is the diameter that the machine is set to produce. If the standard deviation of the diameters is 0.5 millimeter (mm), at what mean value μ should the machine be set to ensure that only 4 percent of the cylinders have diameters of 25 mm or less?

SOLUTION   We start with Figure 8.18, which shows μ at the center of the

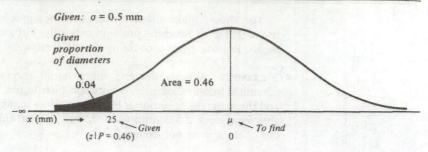

FIGURE 8.18
Finding μ.

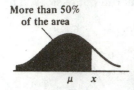

More than 50% of the area

distribution. We mark the diameter $x = 25$ mm at a point to the *left* of μ. Why? Because the problem states that only 4 percent (or 0.04) of the diameters are to be *less* than (to the left of) 25 mm. If x was incorrectly placed to the right of the mean, more than 50 percent of the diameters would be less than x mm. (See the marginal sketch.)

The interval from 25 to $-\infty$ has the area 0.04. Hence, the interval from μ to 25 has an area of $0.5 - 0.04 = 0.46$. From the standard normal table we find $(z|P = 0.46) = 1.75$. But x is to the left of μ; so $z = -1.75$. Hence, substituting into $x = \mu + z\sigma$, we obtain

$$25 = \mu - 1.75(0.5)$$

$$25 + 1.75(0.5) = \mu$$

$$25.875 \text{ mm} = \mu$$

The machine setting should be 25.875 mm.

EXERCISE   The cylinder-making machine has $\sigma = 0.5$ mm. At what mean value μ should the machine be set to ensure that only 2.5 percent of the cylinders have diameters of 25.48 mm or more?
ANSWER $\mu = 24.5$ mm.

Finding the interval when μ and σ are given

EXAMPLE   The machine of the last example has $\sigma = 0.5$ mm. If the machine is set at $\mu = 25$ mm, within what interval of values centered at the mean will the diameters of 80 percent of the cylinders lie?

SOLUTION   Figure 8.19 shows the interval centered at μ which contains 80 percent (or 0.8) of the cylinder diameters. The interval extends from x_1 to x_2. Half of the 80 percent (or 0.4) is on each side of the mean; so we find

$$(z|P = 0.4) = 1.28$$

The point x_2 is to the right of μ; so $z = 1.28$ at this point. Hence,

$$x_2 = \mu + z\sigma$$

$$= 25 + 1.28(0.5) = 25.64 \text{ mm}$$

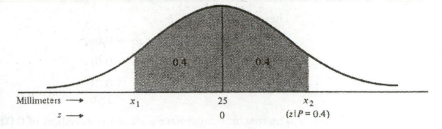

FIGURE 8.19

Finding the endpoints of an interval centered at μ.

The point x_1 is to the left of μ; so $z = -1.28$ at this point. Therefore,

$$x_2 = 25 - 1.28(0.5) = 24.36 \text{ mm}$$

Thus, 80 percent of the diameters will lie between 24.36 and 25.64 mm.

EXERCISE Assume that aptitude test scores are normally distributed. The mean is 140 and $\sigma = 25$ points. Within what interval (x_1 to x_2) centered at the mean will 95 percent of the test scores lie?
ANSWER Between $x_1 = 91$ points and $x_2 = 189$ points.

Finding the standard deviation when an area and an interval are given.

EXAMPLE A machine is to be designed so that only 2.5 percent of the lengths of bolts made are more than 0.01 mm above the mean μ and only 2.5 percent are more than 0.01 mm below the mean. What standard deviation must the machine have to meet these objectives?

SOLUTION Figure 8.20 shows the given information and the derived area,

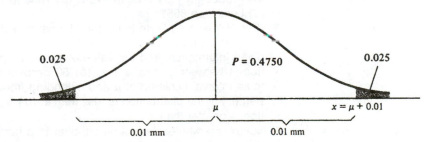

FIGURE 8.20

Finding the value of σ.

$0.5 - 0.025 = 0.4750$. We want to find the value of σ that results in the areas shown. First we must find

$$(z|P = 0.4750) = 1.96$$

so $z = 1.96$. Since $x = \mu + z\sigma$ and, as shown on the figure, $x = \mu + 0.01$, it follows that

$$\mu + z\sigma = \mu + 0.01$$

Therefore,

$$z\sigma = 0.01$$

so

$$1.96\sigma = 0.01$$

$$\sigma = \frac{0.01}{1.96} = 0.005 \text{ mm}$$

The machine must have a standard deviation of 0.005 mm.

EXERCISE What must be the standard deviation of the bolt-making machine if 94 percent of the bolt lengths are to be in an interval extending from 0.0047 mm to the left of the mean to 0.0047 to the right of the mean?
ANSWER $\sigma = 0.0025$ mm.

8.6 PROBLEMS

1. (a) Explain why there are an unlimited number of different normal distributions. (b) What makes it possible to use one probability table for all normal distributions? (c) Write the defining expression or formula for z.
2. Write the symbol for, and the value of, the probability that z is (a) in the interval 1 to 2; (b) less than 1; (c) more than 1.57.
3. Write the symbol for, and the value of, z for which the probability for the interval 0 to z is (a) 0.3944; (b) 0.4610; (c) 0.4933.
4. A random variable takes on values symbolized by x. If the variable is normally distributed with a mean of 1000 and a standard deviation of 100, what is the probability that x will be in the following intervals? (Make a normal curve sketch for each part, showing μ, the interval, and the probability.) (a) 1000 to 1155? (b) 1050 to 1140? (c) 925 to 1075? (d) Less than 865?
5. (See Problem 4.) State the value of a which satisfies the following requirement. (Make a normal curve sketch for each part showing μ, the given information, and the value of a.) (a) 20 percent of the distribution is between μ and $\mu + a$. (b) 50 percent of the distribution lies in an interval centered at μ and extending from $\mu - a$ to $\mu + a$. (c) 2 percent of the distribution is less than a. (d) 5 percent of the distribution is greater than a.
6. Gulfex is a wholesale fuel oil supplier in a northeastern state. Gulfex stores large quantities of oil and sells it to tank truckers who, in turn, sell and distribute to retail customers. In the period from December through the following February, Gulfex sells (truckers demand) an average of 80 thousand gallons per day with a standard deviation of 10 thousand gallons per day. Assuming demand is normally distributed, what is the probability that demand per day, in thousands of gallons, will be (a) from 80 to 95? (b) from 90 to 100? (c) in the interval $\mu \pm$ 12.5? (d) less than 100? (e) more than 66.5? (f) from 75 to 90? (g) less than 72? (h) more than 3 standard deviations above the mean?
7. (See Problem 6.) If Gulfex has a supply of 92.5 thousand gallons avail-

able at the start of the day, what is the probability that the day's demand will exceed the supply?

8. (See Problem 6.) How many gallons should Gulfex have on hand at the start of a day if it is desired to have a probability of only 0.025 of not being able to satisfy the day's demand?

9. Forecast, Inc., is a market research firm that forecasts sales of products for its client companies. Forecast, Inc., measures errors made in past forecasts by obtaining actual product sales data from client companies and computing the percent difference between actual and forecast sales. For example, if sales of a product were forecast at 220 units and actual sales turned out to be 200 units, the error would be 20 in 200, or 10 percent. Similarly, if forecast and actual were 460 and 500, respectively, the error would be -40 in 500, or -8 percent. Forecast, Inc., states that its errors average 2 percent with a standard deviation of 4 percentage points. Assuming errors are normally distributed, what is the probability that the error percent in a forecast was (a) from -3 to 2? (b) from -1 to 3? (c) more than 2? (d) from 5 to 10? (e) more than 8? (f) less than -10? (g) greater than 0?

10. (See Problem 9.) (a) Within what interval centered at the mean did 50 percent of the forecast errors lie? (b) If Forecast wishes to state that 95 percent of its errors were in the interval $2 \pm a$ percentage points, what value should a have?

11. The average time before the gear train of a certain make of automobile needs a major overhaul is 56 months, with a standard deviation of 16 months. The manufacturer wishes to warranty these gear trains, offering to make any necessary overhaul free of charge if the buyer of a new automobile has a gear-train breakdown before a certain number of months of ownership have elapsed. Assume that the number of months before an overhaul is required is normally distributed. For how many months should the manufacturer warrant gear trains to limit the number of warranty overhauls to no more than 2.28 percent of the automobiles sold?

12. In normal distributions having $\sigma = 5$, what must μ be if the following condition is to be satisfied? (a) 1.5 percent of the distribution is to be less than 40. (b) 33 percent of the distribution is to be greater than 100. (c) 99.8 percent of the distribution is to be greater than 20.

13. The engineering department of Superflex, a tire manufacturing company, plans to make batches of tires and wear them out on test equipment. They will increase the amount of rubber on the tire treads in successive batches until the average wear life is acceptable. The standard deviation of wear lives is fairly constant at 2500 miles from batch to batch. If the company wants 80 percent of their tires to have a wear life of at least 25,000 miles, what is the lowest acceptable average wear life that must be achieved by the engineering department? Assume wear life is normally distributed.

14. (See Problem 13.) What should μ be if the probability that a tire will wear out in less than 20,000 miles is to be 0.01?

15. In a normal distribution with $\mu = 200$, what must σ be if 96 percent of the distribution is to be greater than 165?

16. In a normal distribution in which the variable is measured in ounces, what must σ be if 95 percent of the distribution is to be in an interval of width 19.6 ounces centered at the mean?

17. American Automation buys precision parts for a control device from United Machine. Each part has a specified mean dimension μ. A part having a dimension which differs from μ by more than 0.25 mm is classified as a defective part. American requires that no more than 1 percent of parts may be defective. If United Machine is to satisfy the requirement, what is the maximum variability (standard deviation) that can be permitted for dimensions of parts made for American? Assume the dimensions of parts made are normally distributed.

18. The manager of Texas Sales, Inc., has received complaints from some customers about the excessive time taken by company employees to service their requests. The manager has data collected and finds that the average time to service requests is 6.6 days, but that 20 percent of requests took 15 days or longer before service was provided. Assuming time to service is normally distributed, (a) what is the present standard deviation of the service times? (b) What would σ have to be if at least 80 percent of requests are to be serviced within 10 days, assuming μ remains at 6.6 days? (c) Refer to the answer to (a). Suppose that by increasing the number of employees, service time for each order can be reduced by 25 percent. What then will be the values of μ and σ? Why? (d) See (c). If service time for each order is decreased by 25 percent, what then will be the percent of customers for whom service time would be 15 days or longer?

19. After an airplane has discharged its passengers, it takes crew A an average of 15 minutes ($\sigma = 4$ minutes) to complete its task of handling baggage and loading food and other supplies. Crew B fuels the plane and does maintenance checks, taking an average of 16 minutes ($\sigma = 2$ minutes) to complete its task. Assume the crews work independently and times to complete tasks are normally distributed. What is the probability that both crews will complete their tasks soon enough for the plane to be ready for takeoff within 20 minutes?

20. A mail-order company obtains a quick estimate of the day's dollar volume of orders by weighing the mail received early in the morning of each business day. It has been found that if the weight is W pounds, the dollar volume of orders in the mail is normally distributed with mean $160W$ and standard deviation $20W$. Find the probability that on a day when the mail weight is 150 pounds, the dollar volume of orders is (a) between $21,000 and $27,000; (b) more than $28,500.

21. When a dispensing machine is set to pour a certain number of ounces of coffee or a soft drink into a container, the amounts poured are normally distributed with μ being the machine setting. The amounts poured by a particular machine have a standard deviation of 0.4 ounce and are distributed normally. (a) Suppose 8-ounce coffee cups are to be filled. At what number of ounces should the machine be set if not more than 5 percent of the cups are to be overfilled? (b) A sign on a machine states that the amount to be poured into each container is 12 ounces. At what number of ounces should the machine be set to ensure that no more than 10 percent of the containers are underfilled?

8.7 NORMAL APPROXIMATION OF BINOMIAL PROBABILITIES

Binomial distributions (see Chapter 7) are discrete probability distributions for the number of "successes" in n trials, or the number of successes in a sample of size n. The parameters of a binomial distribution are n, the number of trials, and p, the probability of success on a trial. Thus, probabilities for the numbers of heads in 16 coin tosses are computed from the binomial formula using $n = 16$ and $p = 0.5$.

Binomial formula calculations can be very time-consuming; so tables such as Table I at the end of the book have been prepared for a fairly large selection of values of n and p. However, a binomial table including n values of, say 2, 3, 4, . . . , 1998, 1999, 2000 and p values of 0.01, 0.02, 0.03, . . . , 0.97, 0.98, 0.99 would have thousands of pages. No such table exists, because when n is sufficiently large, binomial probabilities can be closely approximated using one table, the standard normal probability table. In this section you will learn how to make such approximations, and how large n should be for close approximations.

Approximating Heights by Areas

Figure 8.21 shows the probabilities for the numbers of heads in 16 coin tosses. Note that the probability of 10 heads is 0.122. In the figure, $P(10) = 0.122$ is represented by the height of the vertical line segment for 10 heads. But we represent normal-distribution probabilities with areas. To approximate a binomial probability, we will first represent the probability as the area

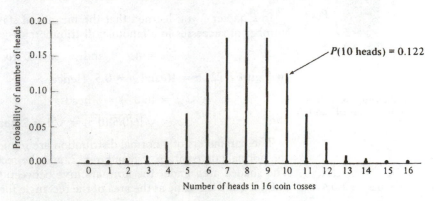

FIGURE 8.21
Binomial probability distribution for number of heads in 16 coin tosses: $n = 16$, $p = 0.5$.

$P(10 \text{ heads}) = 0.122$

Number of heads in 16 coin tosses

of a rectangle, and then approximate the area of the rectangle with a normal curve area.

In Figure 8.22, the "ten" rectangle has a base extending from 9.5 to

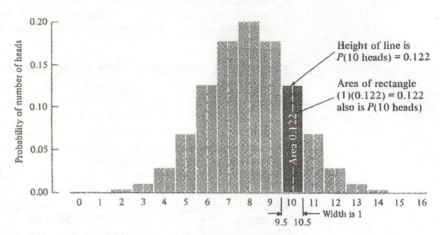

FIGURE 8.22
Representing probabilities of a discrete variable by areas of rectangles: $n = 16$, $p = 0.5$.

Number of heads in 16 coin tosses

We represent the "binomial" height

$P(x)$

x

10.5, with 10 at the center; the base width of the rectangle is 1. The height of the rectangle is $P(10) = 0.122$; that is, the dashed vertical line at 10 is the same as the vertical line at 10 in Figure 8.21. The area of the rectangle is

$$\text{\ast} \quad (\text{Base})(\text{height}) = (1)(0.122) = 0.122$$

so the area of the rectangle also is the probability of 10 heads. Thus, the rectangular areas in Figure 8.22 equal the probabilities shown by the lengths of the vertical segments in Figure 8.21.

As this "binomial" area

$P(x)$

$x - 0.5 \quad x + 0.5$

EXERCISE What is the total area of all the rectangles in Figure 8.22? Why?
ANSWER 1. You should know by now.

In Chapter 7 you learned that the mean and standard deviation of the number of successes in a binomial distribution are

$$\mu = np \quad \text{and} \quad \sigma = \sqrt{npq}$$

And then approximate it with this "normal" area

In Figure 8.22, $n = 16$ and $p = 0.5$. Hence,

$$\mu = 16(0.5) = 8 \text{ heads}$$

and

$$\sigma = \sqrt{16(0.5)(0.5)} = \sqrt{4} = 2 \text{ heads}$$

$x - 0.5 \quad x + 0.5$

The parameters of a normal distribution are μ and σ. Figure 8.23 shows the normal curve with $\mu = 8$ and $\sigma = 2$, and the rectangles of Figure 8.22. The shaded area under the normal curve between 9.5 and 10.5 is almost but not quite the same as the area of the rectangle for 10 heads. The normal

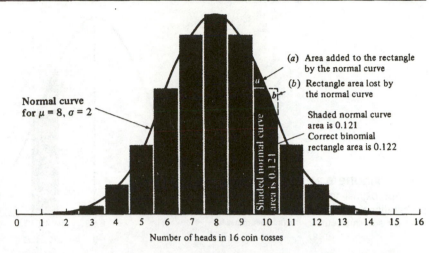

(a) Area added to the rectangle by the normal curve

(b) Rectangle area lost by the normal curve

Normal curve for $\mu = 8$, $\sigma = 2$

Shaded normal curve area is 0.121
Correct binomial rectangle area is 0.122

Shaded normal curve area is 0.121

Number of heads in 16 coin tosses

FIGURE 8.23
Approximating a rectangular area by a normal curve area.

curve area adds the area shown as a, and subtracts the area b, from the area of the rectangle. The net result is that the normal curve area is 0.121, which is 0.001 less than the correct rectangle area.

Computing the Approximation

We have seen how the vertical line segment giving the exact probability for a value of a discrete variable (Figure 8.21) is represented by the area of a rectangle (Figure 8.22). Then (Figure 8.23) the rectangle area is approximated by a normal curve area. In the change from the single point, 10 heads, to a rectangle, 10 is replaced by an interval extending 0.5 to the left and right of 10. That is, as shown in Figure 8.23, 10 becomes the interval 9.5 to 10.5. With $\mu = 8$ and $\sigma = 10$, we find the normal curve area for the interval 9.5 to 10.5 in the usual manner, as shown next.

Step 1   Find the x values by adding +0.5 or −0.5 to the binomial values.

To obtain the z values, we find that at $x = 9.5$

Step 2   Transform the x values to z values.

$$z = \frac{x - \mu}{\sigma}$$

$$z = \frac{9.5 - 8}{2} = 0.75$$

Then at $x = 10.5$

$$z = \frac{10.5 - 8}{2} = 1.25$$

Step 3   Proceed as usual.

The shaded area in Figure 8.24 is

$$P(0 \text{ to } 1.25) - P(0 \text{ to } 0.75) = 0.3944 - 0.2734 = 0.1210$$

The approximate probability of 10 heads in 16 coin tosses is 0.1210, as shown

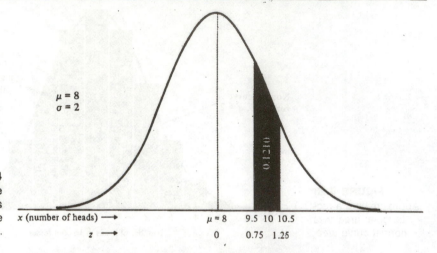

FIGURE 8.24
Approximating the
probability of 10 heads
by a normal curve
area.

$\mu = 8$
$\sigma = 2$

0.121

x (number of heads) ⟶ $\mu = 8$ 9.5 10 10.5

z ⟶   0   0.75 1.25

in Figure 8.24. The exact value (see Figure 8.21) is 0.122; so the error is

Approximate value − exact value = 0.121 − 0.122 = −0.001

The error in this case is so small that it would be of no consequence in most
applied problems.

EXERCISE The exact probability for nine heads in 16 coin tosses is 0.1746.
(a) What is the normal approximation of the probability of nine heads? (b) What
is the error in the approximation?
ANSWER (a) 0.1747; (b) 0.0001.

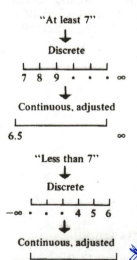

"At least 7"

↓

Discrete

7 8 9 • • • ∞

↓

Continuous, adjusted

6.5   ∞

"Less than 7"

↓

Discrete

−∞ • • • 4 5 6

↓

Continuous, adjusted

−∞   6.5

Note carefully that in using a normal curve probability (which is a probability for an *interval*) we had to substitute an interval for a discrete point.
The 0.5 used in making the substitution is called a *continuity adjustment*.
Adjusted for continuity, a discrete value x becomes the interval from $x − 0.5$
to $x + 0.5$. Thus, the discrete value 7, adjusted, means 6.5 to 7.5. The interval *at least* 7 includes 7; so it starts at 6.5 and extends indefinitely (to ∞);
that is, at least 7 becomes the interval 6.5 to ∞. On the other hand, *less than*
7 means 6 or less; so this interval extends from 6.5 downward indefinitely;
that is, less than 7 becomes the interval 6.5 to −∞.

EXERCISE In using normal areas to approximate binomial probabilities,
what interval would be used to find the probability of the following numbers of
successes: (a) From 4 to 10, inclusive? (b) More than 4 but less than 10? (c) At
least 5? (d) More than 5? (e) Less than 12?
ANSWER (a) 3.5 to 10.5; (b) 4.5 to 9.5; (c) 4.5 to ∞; (d) 5.5 to ∞; (e) 11.5
to −∞.

EXAMPLE Two percent of the account balances of customers of High
Grade Stores contain errors. Suppose a random sample check of 500 ac-

counts is made. What is the probability that the number of incorrect account balances in the sample will be (a) less than 5? (b) 6 to 13, inclusive?

SOLUTION

a. The given 2 percent of all accounts is the probability of success $p = 0.02$. The sample size is n; so $n = 500$. Then

$$\mu = np = 500(0.02) = 10$$

and
$$\sigma = \sqrt{npq} = \sqrt{500(0.02)(0.98)} = 3.13$$

"Less than 5" does not include 5.

The set of discrete values (numbers of accounts) less than 5 is replaced by the interval 4.5 to $-\infty$, as shown in Figure 8.25.

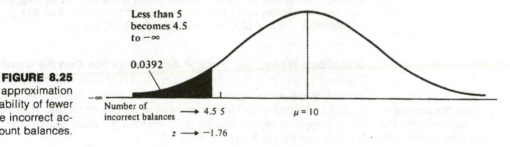

FIGURE 8.25
Normal approximation of probability of fewer than five incorrect account balances.

At $x = 4.5$,

$$z = \frac{4.5 - 10}{3.13} = -1.76$$

The desired tail probability is

$$0.5 - P(0 \text{ to } 1.76) = 0.5 - 0.4608 = 0.0392$$

The probability of less than 5 incorrect balances is approximately 0.0392.

"6 to 13, inclusive," must include both 6 and 13.

b. The set of discrete values, 6 to 13, inclusive, is replaced by the interval 5.5 to 13.5 as shown in Figure 8.26.
At $x = 5.5$,

$$z = \frac{5.5 - 10}{3.13} = -1.44$$

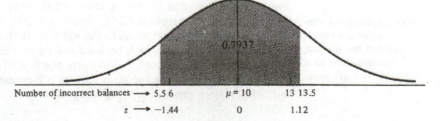

FIGURE 8.26
Probability of 6–13 incorrect balances.

At $x = 13.5$,

$$z = \frac{13.5 - 10}{3.13} = 1.12$$

The shaded area is

$$P(0 \text{ to } 1.44) + P(0 \text{ to } 1.12) = 0.4251 + 0.3686 = 0.7937$$

The probability of 6 to 13 defective accounts is approximately 0.7937.

EXERCISE Over a long period of time, a company has hired thousands of workers and has found that 70 percent of those applying for jobs are satisfactory. Suppose 84 workers apply for jobs. (a) Compute μ and σ for the number of satisfactory workers in the 84 workers. What is the probability that the number who are satisfactory is (b) from 50 through 60? (c) more than 50?
ANSWER (a) $\mu = 58.8$, $\sigma = 4.2$; (b) 0.6418; (c) 0.9761.

Situations Where the Normal Approximation Can Be Used

The nearer p is to 0.5, and the larger the value of n, the more closely will normal curve areas approximate binomial probabilities. The farther p is from 0.5, the larger should be the value of n. The usual rule of thumb is that normal approximations will be good enough for most practical purposes if both np and nq are greater than 5.

Use the normal to approximate the binomial when both np and nq are larger than 5.

In Figure 8.23, we saw that the normal approximation was very close for the binomial having $n = 16$, $p = 0.5$; that's because 0.5 is the most favorable value of p; and

$$np = 16(0.5) = 8$$

$$nq = 16(0.5) = 8$$

so np and nq both exceed 5. However, if n is 16 and p is 0.1, the binomial probability of 3 successes is $P(3) = 0.142$: The normal approximation of the binomial probability is 0.170, which is a poor approximation. Note that with $n = 16$ and $p = 0.1$, np is 1.6, which is not greater than 5; so the rule of thumb tells us not to use the normal approximation in this situation.

Many probability distributions tend toward the normal distribution as n increases.

It is instructive, both for current purposes and for later work, to observe how the normal distribution emerges from a binomial distribution as n increases. Figures 8.27(a) through 8.27(d) all have $p = 0.1$, a value far from the ideal value 0.5. There is no suggestion of a normal curve shape in Figure 8.27(a), where $n = 10$. In Figures 8.27(b) and 8.27(c), which have respective n values of 20 and 50, we see the normal shape emerging, but there is right skewness. In Figure 8.27(d), where $n = 100$, we see a near normal shape, with only slight skewness to the right. Note that Figure 8.27(d) is the only one of the four for which both np and nq exceed 5 (np is 10, and nq is 90). Figures 8.27(a) through 8.27(d) give the first of several examples you will see of "tendency toward normality as n increases." Tendency toward normality plays a major role in statistical inference.

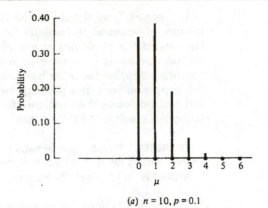

(a) $n = 10, p = 0.1$

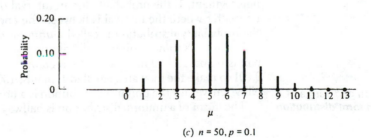

(b) $n = 20, p = 0.1$

(c) $n = 50, p = 0.1$

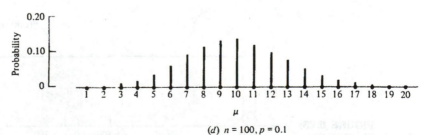

FIGURE 8.27
Binomial probabilities
(heights of points).

(d) $n = 100, p = 0.1$

In Chapter 7, we stated that the Poisson distribution gave good approximations of binomial probabilities for $n \geq 20$ *and* $p \leq 0.05$. We could also have stated the conditions as $n \geq 20$ and $p \geq 0.95$. The Poisson approximation works best for very small and very large values of p. The normal approximation, on the other hand, works better the closer p is to 0.5. The two approximations thus partially complement each other; that is, when n and p do not satisfy the conditions for one of the approximations, they may satisfy the conditions for the other.

EXERCISE Which approximation of binomial probabilities, Poisson or normal, should be used (a) if $n = 40$ and $p = 0.3$? (b) if $n = 40$ and $p = 0.04$?
ANSWER (a) Normal; (b) Poisson.

There are, of course, many values of n and p for which neither a normal nor a Poisson approximation of binomial probabilities is suitable; those values of n and p are the ones which appear in tables of binomial probabilities.

8.8 TWO MORE CONTINUOUS PROBABILITY DISTRIBUTIONS

Many continuous probability distributions are used in statistical work. Two simple distributions are described in this section. Others will be introduced in later chapters as the need arises.

The Uniform Distribution

Suppose we have a continuous random variable that can take on values on a line segment. If the probability for an interval of a given length is the same no matter where the interval is between the endpoints of the line segment, the probability distribution is called a *uniform* distribution.

Figure 8.28 shows a uniform distribution over the line segment with endpoints 0 and 1000. The base of the rectangle is 1000; so its height must be 0.001 to make the total area equal to 1; that is, $1000 \times 0.001 = 1$. The probability "curve" for the uniform distribution is a horizontal line at height 0.001.

Mean *and* range of a uniform distribution

The *mean* of a uniform distribution is halfway between its endpoints. The

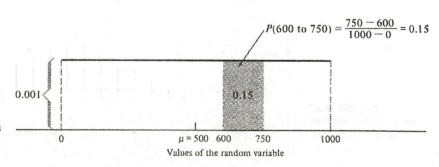

$$P(600 \text{ to } 750) = \frac{750 - 600}{1000 - 0} = 0.15$$

FIGURE 8.28
A uniform distribution.

0.001

0.15

0          $\mu = 500$ 600   750   1000
Values of the random variable

range of a uniform distribution is the difference between its endpoints. In Figure 8.28, the mean and range are, respectively, 500 and 1000. In the figure, any interval between 0 and 1000 which has a width of 100 will have $^{100}/_{1000}$, or one-tenth, of the area. In general, for a uniform distribution, the probability for an interval is the width of the interval divided by the range. Thus, for the interval from *a* to *b*, whose width is $b - a$, the *uniform distribution probability* formula is

Probability of an interval for a uniform distribution

$$P(a \text{ to } b) = \frac{b - a}{\text{range}}$$

In the formula, both *a* and *b* must be between, or at, the endpoints. Any part of an interval which is outside the endpoints has a probability of zero.

For example, for Figure 8.28,

$$P(600 \text{ to } 750) = \frac{750 - 600}{1000} = 0.15$$

EXAMPLE Suppose that the weight of maple sugar obtained by boiling down a tank of maple-tree sap is uniformly distributed with a mean of 10 pounds and a range of 1.8 pounds. (*a*) What are the smallest and largest weights of sugar obtained from a tank of sap? (*b*) What is the probability that a tank of sap will boil down to between 9 and 10.5 pounds?

SOLUTION

a. The mean, 10, is the center point of a line segment whose length is the range, 1.8 pounds. Hence, the line segment extends $^1/_2(1.8) = 0.9$ pound to the left and to the right of 10, that is, from 9.1 to 10.9 pounds.

b. Dividing the length of the interval by the range gives

$$P(9 \text{ to } 10.5) = \frac{10.5 - 9}{1.8} = 0.833$$

as the probability that a tankful will boil down to between 9 and 10.5 pounds of sugar.

EXERCISE (*a*) See the last example. What is the probability that a tankful will boil down to more than 9.5 pounds of sugar? (*b*) What is the height of the rectangle representing the distribution of the example?
ANSWER (*a*) 0.778; (*b*) 1/1.8, or about 0.5556.

a   *b*

Range = $b - a$

$\mu = \dfrac{a + b}{2}$

Height = $\dfrac{1}{b - a}$

Area = 1

Uniform distributions are sometimes used in problem situations where we are almost totally without information about the probability distribution for a continuous random variable. Then we may choose to assume that all intervals of a given length are equally likely, that is, we assume the distribution is uniform. Also, as you will find out in the next chapter, uniform distributions are used to demonstrate some important conclusions about the behavior of samples drawn from a population.

The Exponential Distribution

A Poisson process (see Chapter 7) generates "arrivals" during a period of time. The single parameter of a Poisson process probability distribution is λ, lambda, the average arrival rate per unit of time. For example, if taxicab arrivals at an intersection during the 3 to 5 p.m. period average 18 per hour, λ = 18, and the unit of time is 1 hour. In Chapter 7 we were interested in the discrete variable, number of arrivals: There we computed probabilities for the number of arrivals in t units of time. In this section we are interested in the probability that the *next* arrival will occur in t units of time. Calling the time interval of interest (t units of time) 0 to t, we want to determine $P(0$ to $t)$, the probability that the next arrival will occur in t units of time. The random variable t is continuous. *For a Poisson process,*

P(0 to t) means the probability that the next arrival occurs in t units of time.

$P(0$ to $t)$ = probability that next arrival will occur between now and t time units from now

$$P(0 \text{ to } t) = 1 - e^{-\lambda t}$$

where λ = average arrival rate per unit of time
        t = continuous random variable; number of units of time

EXAMPLE Suppose taxicab arrivals from 3 to 5 p.m. are a Poisson process. If the cabs arrive at an average rate of 18 per hour, what is the probability that a person will have to wait up to 5 minutes for a cab?

SOLUTION Here, λ = 18 per hour; so the unit of time is 1 hour. Five minutes is $5/60 = 1/12$ hour; that is, $1/12$ of the time unit for λ. Hence $t = 1/12$. Then

1 hour (60 minutes) is the unit of time; so 5 minutes is t = 5/60 unit of time.

$$\lambda t = 18 \left(\frac{1}{12}\right) = 1.5$$

and $P(0$ to 5 minutes$) = P(0$ to $1/12$ hour$)$. From the formula,

$$P(0 \text{ to } t) = 1 - e^{-\lambda t}$$

$$P(0 \text{ to } 1/12) = 1 - e^{-1.5}$$

$$= 1 - 0.2231$$

$$= 0.7769$$

The probability of getting a cab within 5 minutes is 0.7769.

Figure 8.29 illustrates the solution of the example. The expression $P(0$ to $t) = 1 - e^{-\lambda t}$ is called the *exponential* probability distribution. All exponential probability curves have a shape like that of the curve in the figure; that is, the curve has its highest point at the left ($t = 0$) and falls to the right, forming a curve shaped something like a ski jump.

Here, again, the total area under the curve is 1.

EXERCISE See the last example. By subtraction of probabilities, find the probability that a person will have to wait between 5 and 10 minutes for a cab.
ANSWER 0.173.

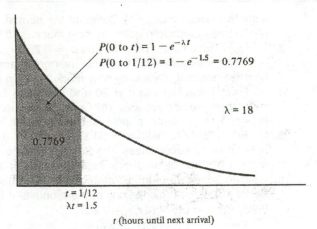

$$P(0 \text{ to } t) = 1 - e^{-\lambda t}$$
$$P(0 \text{ to } 1/12) = 1 - e^{-1.5} = 0.7769$$

$\lambda = 18$

0.7769

FIGURE 8.29
Exponential distribu-
tion for time until next
taxi arrives.

$t = 1/12$
$\lambda t = 1.5$

t (hours until next arrival)

8.9 PROBABILITY DISTRIBUTIONS, A RECAPITULATION

In Chapter 7 we introduced three discrete probability distribution formulas: These are the binomial formula, the Poisson process formula for the number of arrivals in an interval of time, and the hypergeometric formula. In this chapter we discussed three continuous probability distributions: These are the normal distribution, the uniform distribution, and the Poisson process distribution for the time from now until the next arrival. Tabulated probabilities for the normal distribution and other continuous distributions yet to be introduced will play a major role in the coming study of statistical inference. Frequently, you will find, continuous distributions are used to approximate discrete distributions. The normal approximation of the binomial is an example. We use approximations for two reasons: (1) Exact values of discrete probabilities are not needed in applied problems; the approximations are close enough. (2) Tabulated probabilities for continuous distributions usually are much easier to use than formulas for discrete probability distributions.

The link between this chapter and the next is the demonstration of "tendency toward normality as n increases." Figures 8.27(a) through 8.27(d) showed the tendency toward normality of the probability distribution for the discrete random variable "number of successes." Because many other random variables also exhibit tendency toward normality, the normal distribution has been called the most important of all probability distributions.

8.10 PROBLEMS

1. In normal approximations of binomial probabilities, what continuous interval would represent the discrete set of numbers (a) less than 20? (b) more than 20? (c) exactly 20? (d) at least 20? (e) 15 through 25? (f) exactly μ?

2. (a) From Table IB, with $n = 20$ and $p = 0.25$, find the probability of ex-

actly five occurrences. (b) Compute the normal approximation of (a). (c) To three decimal places, by how much is (b) in error?

3. (a) From Table IC, with $n = 50$ and $p = 0.25$, find the probability of exactly 12 occurrences. (b) Compute the normal approximation of (a). (c) To three decimal places, by how much is (b) in error?

4. (a) From Table IB, with $n = 20$ and $p = 0.25$, find the probability of fewer than five occurrences. (b) Compute the normal approximation of (a). (c) To three decimal places, by how much is (b) in error?

5. (a) From Table IC, with $n = 50$ and $p = 0.25$, find the probability of fewer than 12 occurrences. (b) Compute the normal approximation of (a). (c) To three decimal places, by how much is (b) in error?

6. Following the rule of thumb stated in the chapter, how large should n be for normal approximations of the binomial if (a) $p = 0.10$? (b) $p = 0.90$? (c) $p = 0.50$? (d) $p = 0.25$?

Note: Use the normal approximation of the binomial in Problems 7 to 12.

7. If 55 percent of the voters in an area favor a particular candidate, what is the probability that, in a sample of 200 voters, less than half would favor the candidate?

8. Some people who make reservations for air travel do not show up for their scheduled flight. Airlines may make allowances for these "no-shows" by booking reservations for more persons than can be accommodated on a flight. If 4 percent of the large population of reservations turn out to be no-shows, and 350 reservations are made for a particular flight on a plane seating 340, what is the probability that seats will be available for all those who do show up for the flight?

9. In an audit of accounts of Jordan-Holtman, a large department store, it is decided first to check a sample of 1000 accounts, and then to carry out a more detailed study if the number of sample accounts in error exceeds 15. One percent of all Jordan-Holtman accounts contain errors. What is the probability that the sample audit results will lead to a more detailed study?

10. A charitable organization seeks volunteer aid by making requests via telephone. If 15 percent of the population of potential volunteers agree to help, what is the probability that 100 calls will enlist at least 20 volunteers?

11. The quality-control manager for Alisson Products Company has a staff of inspectors who test each of the approximately 4000 transformers made each week by the company. The staff inspects transformers as they are made and discards any they find to be defective. Transformers made and inspected during a week are assembled and given an identifying "lot" number. On the last Friday of each month, after the plant closes, Jan Berger, who is the supervisor of inspectors, tests a sample of 200 transformers selected at random from the week's lot as a check on the work done by the inspection staff during the week. Jan expects that some inspection errors will occur, but if she finds more than four defectives in her sample, she will, in the following week, have each

staff inspector's work assembled in sublots. At the end of the week, each sublot will be checked to identify inspectors who are not doing a good job. Suppose that 3 percent of a week's lot of transformers are defective. What is the probability that Jan will be checking sublots next week?

12. Suds, Inc., sponsors a weekly television program. Al Smith, Suds' advertising vice president, has a random sample of 1000 viewers in the television audience (population) interviewed each week. If fewer than 500 of the sample viewers saw Suds' program, Al will cancel the program. Suppose that, one week, 54 percent of the total audience saw the program. What is the probability that Al will cancel?

13. Assume that wheat yields, in bushels per acre, are uniformly distributed over the interval 25 to 40 bushels per acre. What is the probability that an acre yields (a) from 30 to 35 bushels? (b) 30 bushels or more?

14. Assume that gasoline mileage, in miles per gallon, for a certain model of automobile is uniformly distributed with a mean of 16 and a range of 8. What proportion of the automobiles obtain (a) from 18 to 20 miles per gallon? (b) 15 or fewer miles per gallon?

15. Assume a distribution is uniform over the interval 0 to 50. (a) What will be the height of the rectangle representing the distribution? Why? (b) What is the mean of the distribution?

16. On Tuesday afternoons, customer arrivals at the Tenth National Bank are a Poisson process. Arrivals average three customers per 5 minutes. (a) What is the probability that the next customer will arrive within 2 minutes? (b) What is the probability that the time until the next customer arrives will be from 1 to 3 minutes? (c) What is the probability that it will be more than 5 minutes before the next customer arrives?

17. An investment manager for Penner-Fish receives an average of 12 telephone calls per 8-hour day from major investors. Assuming calls are a Poisson process, what is the probability that the manager will not be interrupted by a call during a meeting lasting 1 hour?

18. Fordhart Casualty Co. insures a large number of buildings for fire damage. On the average, Fordhart has to pay eight damage claims of over $1 million each year. The company is short of cash and will have to sell some of its securities to get cash if it has to pay a damage claim of more than $1 million during the next 3 months. Assuming damage claims over $1 million are a Poisson process, what is the probability that Fordhart will have to sell securities?

8.11 SUMMARY

A continuous random variable can have any value in a specified interval of values. Values of a continuous variable graph as a line or a line segment. The probability for a single value of a continuous random variable is zero. An interval of values has a nonzero probability represented by the area under the probability curve for that interval.

Normal distributions have two parameters, μ (the mean) and σ (the standard deviation). The *standard* normal distribution has $\mu = 0$ and $\sigma = 1$. Areas (probabilities) for the standard normal distribution are given in Table V at the end of the book. Table V can be used for other normal distributions by transforming to values of the standard normal variable

$$z = \frac{x - \mu}{\sigma}$$

where x = value of the random variable
   μ = mean of the given normal distribution
   σ = standard deviation of the given normal distribution

Table V provides probabilities for a z interval starting at 0 ($z = 0$ at the mean). Tabulated values are for $P(0 \text{ to } z)$. Figure 8.30 shows a selection of normal probability areas which can be determined by using Table V.

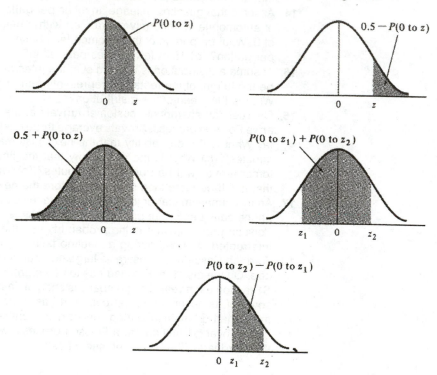

FIGURE 8.30
Normal curve areas.

Inverse use of the standard normal probability table means to use the table to find the value of z when the probability is known. The symbol $(z|P = k)$ means the value of z for which $P(0 \text{ to } z) = k$, as illustrated in Figure 8.31.

Binomial probabilities can be approximated closely by normal curve areas if the binomial parameters n and p are such that both np and nq are greater than 5. The relevant parameters for the normal approximation are

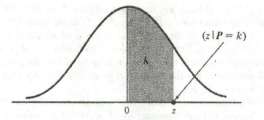

FIGURE 8.31
Meaning of $(z|P = k)$.

$$\mu = np \quad \text{and} \quad \sigma = \sqrt{npq}$$

The binomial variable is discrete. Consequently a *continuity adjustment* is made to a stated value of x before the z value is computed. The adjustment is made by adding 0.5 to, or subtracting 0.5 from, the stated value of x. Whether to add or subtract 0.5 depends on the problem at hand. Normal approximations of binomial probabilities are better the nearer p is to 0.5; however, if p is not 0.5, normal approximations become better the larger n is.

In general, binomial distributions become more "normal" as n increases. The "tendency toward normality as n increases" holds for distributions other than the binomial. Because of this tendency, the normal distribution has been called the most important of all probability distributions.

In a *uniform* probability distribution, the probability for an interval of a given length is the same no matter where that interval is between the endpoints. The endpoints are the smallest and largest values for the random variable. The mean is halfway between the endpoints. The range is the difference between the endpoints. For random variable values a and b which are between or at the endpoints, the probability for the interval from a to b in a *uniform distribution* is

$$P(a \text{ to } b) = \frac{b - a}{\text{range}}$$

For a Poisson process, the time from now until time t is written as 0 to t. The probability that the time until the next arrival will be from 0 to t is given by the *exponential distribution formula*

$$P(0 \text{ to } t) = 1 - e^{-\lambda t}$$

where λ = average arrival rate per unit of time
t = number of units of time

8.12 REVIEW PROBLEMS

1. Write the symbol for, and the value of, the normal probability that z is (a) in the interval 1.5 to 2; (b) below -0.8; (c) more than 1.23.
2. Write the symbol for, and the value of, z for which the normal probability for the interval 0 to z is (a) 0.4850; (b) 0.4840; (c) 0.3000.
3. A random variable takes on values symbolized by x. If the variable is normally distributed with a mean of 50 and a standard deviation of 4, what is the probabil-

ity that x will be in the following intervals? (*a*) 50 to 54? (*b*) 45 to 54? (*c*) 53 to 58? (*d*) more than 60? (*e*) less than 45? (*f*) more than 45?

4. (See Problem 3.) State the values of a which satisfy the following conditions: (*a*) 30 percent of the distribution is between μ and $\mu + a$. (*b*) 10 percent of the distribution is less than a. (*c*) 4 percent of the distribution is greater than a. (*d*) 75 percent of the distribution is in an interval centered at μ and extending from $\mu - a$ to $\mu + a$.

5. The average time it takes a four-person crew to build the frame of a certain type of house is two 40-weeks, or (4 workers)(2 weeks)(40 hours per week) = 320 labor-hours. The standard deviation is 50 labor-hours. If framing time is normally distributed, what is the probability that the time to frame a house is (*a*) more than 320 labor-hours? (*b*) from 280 to 360 labor-hours? (*c*) more than 260 labor-hours? (*d*) from 260 to 300 labor-hours? (*e*) less than 250 labor-hours? (*f*) from 300 to 350 labor-hours?

6. (See Problem 5.) If the company employing the crew promises to frame a house in 350 labor-hours or less and agrees to pay a penalty of $40 for each additional labor-hour spent, what is the probability that the company will pay a penalty of $1000 or more?

7. (See Problem 5.) If the company promises to frame a house within an agreed-upon number of labor-hours and wishes to have a 90 percent chance of fulfilling the promise, what should be the agreed-upon number of labor-hours?

8. (See Problem 5.) If two equally proficient four-person crews each start a house at the same time and work independently, what is the chance that (*a*) both houses will be framed in less than 350 labor-hours? (*b*) at least one of the two will be framed in less than 350 labor-hours?

9. (See Problem 5.) By using a five-person crew, framing time for every house can be reduced by 60 hours. (*a*) What will μ and σ be for a five-person crew? (*b*) What is the probability that a five-person crew will frame a house in less than 300 labor-hours?

10. A company has an automatic machine which makes shafts whose average diameter is the value at which the machine is set. Diameters are normally distributed with a standard deviation of 0.125 mm (millimeter). If the machine is set at 12.70 mm, what proportion of the shafts will have diameters (*a*) from 12.45 to 12.95 mm? (*b*) above 12.85 mm? (*c*) from 12.50 to 12.80 mm? (*d*) from 12.50 to 12.60 mm? (*e*) more than 12.65 mm? (*f*) Shafts with diameters less than 12.55 mm are unacceptable and are thrown into a scrap bin. If 1000 shafts are made, how many may be expected to end up in the scrap bin?

11. In a normal distribution with $\sigma = 10$, what must be the value of μ if the following condition is to be satisfied? (*a*) 5 percent of the distribution is to be below 70. (*b*) 25 percent of the distribution is to be greater than 80. (*c*) 99 percent of the distribution is to be less than 100.

12. (See Problem 10.) An important customer of the company requires that shafts must have diameters in the specification range 12.55 to 12.85 mm. Those below 12.55 mm are scrapped and those above 12.85 are reworked to bring their diameters into the specification range. Scrapping an undersized shaft is more costly than reworking an oversized one; so the machine is to be set at a μ such that only 5 percent of the shafts will have to be scrapped. (*a*) To the nearest thousandth of a millimeter, what should μ be? (*b*) If 1000 shafts are made at the setting of μ in (*a*), how many may be expected to need reworking?

13. (See Problem 12.) The company finds that the cost of scrap and reworking

(which is reflected in the unit price quoted to the customer) is too high, and faces the possibility of losing this customer to a competitor. Inasmuch as the customer accounts for a substantial part of the company's total sales volume, management decides to invest in a new, more precise, machine. If 95 percent of the shafts made by the new machine are to be in the specification range 12.55 to 12.85 mm when the machine is set at $\mu = 12.70$ mm, how precise must the machine be? That is, what is the maximum allowable standard deviation?

14. A regional sales firm which represents a number of national manufacturers of hydraulic equipment pays its sales personnel an annual salary. The firm is considering paying a bonus to those whose sales are in the upper 15 percent of all sales personnel. If sales per salesperson are normally distributed with a mean of $200 thousand per year and a standard deviation of $25 thousand, what level of sales should be announced as the minimum level for receiving the bonus?

15. Super Tread tires have wear lives which are normally distributed with a mean of 20,000 miles and a standard deviation of 2500 miles. Within what interval centered at the mean will the wear lives of 60 percent of the tires lie?

16. (See Problem 15.) The mean wear life of the tires is to be increased so that 67 percent of the tires last more than 20,000 miles. If σ remains at 2500 miles, what must be the new mean?

17. Computer hardware procedures: After the placing of an order for a computer system, the time it takes for delivery, installation, checking, and training of operators is normally distributed with $\mu = 180$ days, $\sigma = 20$ days. Software procedures: The time it takes to write computer programs to replace former data processing methods is normally distributed with $\mu = 220$ days, $\sigma = 50$ days. If hardware and software procedures start at the same time and proceed independently, what is the probability that both procedures will be completed within 200 days?

18. When asked if grades are "curved," a professor replies that she uses the normal curve as a guide in assigning letter grades to large classes. She first finds the average numerical grade and the standard deviation of the numerical grades, and then assigns letter grades as follows:

Numerical grade (x) interval	Grade
$x \geq \mu + 1.5\sigma$	A
$\mu + 0.5\sigma \leq x < \mu + 1.5\sigma$	B
$\mu - 0.5\sigma \leq x < \mu + 0.5\sigma$	C
$\mu - 1.5\sigma \leq x < \mu - 0.5\sigma$	D
$x < \mu - 1.5\sigma$	F

(a) In a class of 500, approximately how many students will receive each letter grade? Round to the nearest whole number, rounding 0.5 upward. (b) The professor finds that the class average is 72, with a standard deviation of 8. What is the lowest passing numerical grade, that is, the lowest grade between 0 and 100 that will receive a D?

19. In the normal approximation of binomial probabilities, what continuous interval would represent the discrete set of values (a) exactly 50? (b) less than 50? (c) more than 40? (d) at least 40? (e) exactly μ? (f) 40 through 50?

20. (a) From Table IC with $n = 50$, $p = 0.75$, find the probability of at least 40

occurrences. (b) Compute the normal approximation of (a). (c) To three decimal places, by how much is (b) in error?

21. (a) From Table IC with $n = 50$, $p = 0.05$, find the probability of fewer than three occurrences. (b) Compute the normal approximation of (a). (c) By how much is (b) in error? (d) Why is the error so large? (e) How large should n be if binomial probabilities are to be approximated by applying the normal distribution and $p = 0.05$?

Note: Use the normal approximation of the binomial in Problems 22 to 26.

22. Five percent of the toasters made by Toastpoaster Company are defective. What is the probability that a store buying 200 of these toasters will obtain at least 15 defective toasters?

23. Fifty-three percent of the stockholders in Bim, Inc., are in favor of a merger with Big Deal, Inc. What is the probability that in a sample of 100 stockholders less than half will be in favor of the merger?

24. If 7 percent of the workers in an area are unemployed, what is the probability that in a sample of 150 workers more than 15 will be unemployed?

25. On the average, 80 percent of people making dinner reservations actually attend the dinners. A dinner is to be held in a room seating 100 people. If 120 reservations are taken, what is the probability that seats will be available for all who attend?

26. A test has 25 true-false questions. A student flips a coin for each question and checks true if heads show and false if tails show. If 17 or more correct is passing, what is the chance that this student will pass?

27. Would you use the Poisson or normal distribution to approximate a binomial distribution with $n = 80$ and $p = 0.045$? Why?

28. Assuming the contents of bottles of snake-oil filled by a machine are uniformly distributed over the interval 450 to 460 cc (cubic centimeters), what proportion of bottles will contain (a) from 452 to 457 cc? (b) more than 453.6 cc?

29. Assuming mileages obtained by a certain brand of tire are uniformly distributed with a mean of 25,000 miles and a range of 10,000 miles, (a) what are the upper and lower limits of tire mileages? (b) What is the probability that a tire will last 26,000 miles or more?

30. Mary McCarthy invests money in new companies that are set up to make and sell innovative products. Mary waits for "good deals" because such investments are very risky. Mary has $500,000 available to invest. However, 6-month bank certificates of deposit (CDs) currently are paying the highest interest rate ever, about 15 percent. If Mary puts her money into CDs, it will be tied up for 6 months. But if she holds the money in her checking account waiting for a good deal, she will receive only about 5 percent interest. Mary wants to know the probability that a good deal will show up in 6 months. Compute this probability, assuming arrivals of good deals are a Poisson process, and good deals arrive on an average of 3 in 5 years.

31. Bill Peters has observed that when he leaves the office at the end of the day, he has to wait an average of 4 minutes to get an elevator. Assume elevator arrivals are a Poisson process. (a) What is the value of λ? What is the unit of time? (b) What is the probability that Bill will have to wait from 2 to 4 minutes for an elevator? (c) What is the probability that Bill will have to wait more than 8 minutes for an elevator?

9

SAMPLING METHODS AND SAMPLING DISTRIBUTIONS

9.1 INTRODUCTION

Suppose you open a can of mixed nuts, scoop out a handful, and find that you have some cashews, filberts, and peanuts. All the nuts in the can are a population of nuts. Your handful is a sample of the population. The sample provides some information about the population. Similarly, 500 television viewers in the Los Angeles metropolitan area are a sample of the area's population of viewers. The viewer sample provides some information about the viewer population.

The basic unit of a population is called an *element* of the population. Each nut is an element of the can-of-nuts population; each television viewer is an element of the viewer population. Thus, a population is the totality of elements being studied, and a sample is part of the population. Gathering information from part of a population is called *sampling*. Gathering information from all elements in a population is called taking a *census*, or making a *complete enumeration*.

Decision makers need information about populations, that is, census information. However, census taking often is unnecessarily (or prohibitively) expensive, or too time-consuming to provide information when it is needed. Additionally, it is not feasible to include the whole population when determining burning lives of bulbs, bursting pressures of tires, and in general, when elements are destroyed to obtain information. Consequently, sampling is used extensively to provide information needed by decision makers.

In the first part of the chapter, I will describe some methods that are used to select samples.

In the second part of the chapter we will consider how information obtained from samples can vary from the corresponding information for the population. The facts and formulas that you learn will serve as the foundation for our discussion of statistical inference which starts in the next chapter. At this point, you should, and probably do, understand that larger samples give more precise results. Thus, in estimating the proportion of the viewer population who watched a television show, a sample of 2000 gives a more precise estimate than a sample of 1000. In the next chapter you will learn a formula that relates precision to sample size. For now, let's agree that a sample of "adequate" size means a sample large enough to provide the precision needed for decision-making purposes.

9.2 RANDOM SAMPLES

Meaning of Random Sample

Random sample: Every element has a known, nonzero chance of being selected.

Statistical sampling theory provides the methods used to solve applied problems. The theory is based upon random samples. A *random* sample, also called a *probability* sample, is a sample selected in a way such that every element of a population has a known chance (not zero) of being included in the sample. Note that the definition of a random sample really is the definition of a selection procedure. Once a sample has been selected, there is no way to check it to determine definitely whether or not it is a random sample. Thus, we call a sample random if the selection procedure guarantees a known, nonzero, chance of selection for each population element.

It should be noted that random, in the statistical sense of the word, does not mean haphazard, nor does it mean the absence of a selection procedure. However, you should know that in everyday language people use the word random in the nonstatistical senses just noted. For example, suppose a reporter interviews students he meets on a college campus during a 1-hour visit; then, in reporting his findings, he says he interviewed "a random sample" of students. What he did was interview students who happened to be available. An obvious reason for saying the reporter's sample is not random, in the statistical sense, is that students in class at the time of the visit had a zero chance of being in the sample.

In statistics, we use samples that satisfy the definition of a random sample. Four types of random samples are discussed in what follows. In practice, precision and the cost of sampling are determining factors when a method of sampling is to be chosen.

Simple Random Samples

Simple random sample: Every element has the same chance of being selected, as does every sample of size n.

A sample containing *n* elements selected from a population is called a sample of size *n*. A *simple random sample* is a sample selected in such a way that (1) every element in the population has the same chance of being chosen *and* (2) every sample of size *n* has the same chance of being chosen.

To illustrate the definition, suppose that Bert, Cathy, Donna, and Ed are an office staff population. All four want the same vacation period, but only two can be away at the same time. Consequently, chips lettered *B*, *C*, *D*, and *E* (for Bert, Cathy, Donna, and Ed) are shaken in a container, and the office manager (blindfolded) draws out two chips. The possible samples of size 2 from the *B, C, D, E* population are

$$BC \qquad BD \qquad BE \qquad CD \qquad CE \qquad DE$$

Note that *B* appears in three of the six samples; so

$$P(B) = \frac{3}{6} = \frac{1}{2}$$

Similarly, $P(C) = P(D) = P(E) = 1/2$; so (1) each element of the population has the same chance, $1/2$, of being chosen to have the desired vacation period. Moreover, (2) each of the six possible samples has the same chance, $1/6$, of being selected. Consequently, the selection method satisfies parts (1) and (2) of the definition and provides a simple random sample.

The example shows that simple random selection corresponds to the common practice of picking lottery winners by selecting tickets from a container in which all the lottery tickets have been mixed. Some lotteries use a rotating wheel in selecting winners. The wheel (Figure 9.1) has equal segments on its rim, one for each of the digits 0 through 9. Lottery tickets are numbered, and winning numbers are selected by spinning the wheel. For

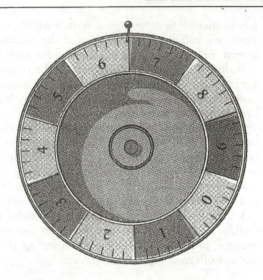

FIGURE 9.1

Lottery wheel.

example, suppose the tickets have five-digit numbers. A ticket number then would be selected by spinning the wheel five times and recording the digit which appears at the pointer each time the wheel stops. If the digit sequence generated is 30081, then ticket number 30081 is a winner.

We could, of course, spin the wheel a million times and record the digits in a table. Then we could dispense with the wheel, and use the table to select winners. Statisticians use tables in selecting simple random samples. However, computers, not wheels, are used to generate the tables, which are called *random-digit* tables or *random-number* tables. Published tables contain as many as a million random digits. I will use Table 9.1, which contains only 500 digits, to show how a random-digit table is applied in simple random sampling.

TABLE 9.1

500 RANDOM DIGITS

36861	12020	16351	37957	70926	13592	59320	44966	58651	31772
44815	75794	23268	34193	79473	21839	51234	27384	26091	56945
87459	25129	62329	04157	90554	25734	16695	04732	57324	01437
88299	31664	23219	75346	41733	65662	62032	01716	93425	12363
16466	22600	36826	66048	15805	47479	17184	17124	21563	40137
37488	32990	46299	89130	91961	74012	84151	15469	17099	20559
36569	21645	06617	67783	47946	32059	51247	18625	24431	44110
39937	30705	29773	50682	46178	55086	24633	08529	48970	22874
60620	.00577	36139	68962	20100	96971	07889	41046	88774	31398
15016	39816	28154	86012	48631	17409	89026	78276	34586	81916

Suppose a company has 500 employees. A simple random sample of 25 employees is to be selected. Each employee in the sample will be interviewed to obtain the employee's opinion about the company's vacation policy. In order to select the sample, each of the 500 employees must have, or be assigned, an identification number. Suppose these numbers are 001, 002, . . . , 499, 500. Now we go to Table 9.1 and pick an arbitrary starting point, say, the upper left-hand corner number 36861. The employee numbers in our example have only three digits; so let's take the first three, 368. Employee number 368 is in the sample. Next we proceed in some methodical way through the table to obtain more numbers. Let's go across rows, left to right, taking the first three digits in each of the five-digit groups. The second group in the first row is 12020; so employee number 120 is in the sample. Similarly, numbers 163 and 379 are in the sample. The next group of five digits (the 70926 in the fifth column) has 709 as the first three digits: we discard this group because the largest employee number is 500. We also discard any number previously selected.

The employee sample is simple random because Table 9.1 is simple random.

EXERCISE For the employee example, what employee numbers would be obtained from the second row of Table 9.1?
ANSWER 448, 232, 341, 218, 273, and 260.

Table 9.2 shows the identification numbers of the 25 employees who will be in the simple random sample selected as described above.

TABLE 9.2
**IDENTIFICATION NUMBERS OF A
SIMPLE RANDOM SAMPLE OF
25 EMPLOYEES**

368	120	163	379	135
449	317	448	232	341
218	273	260	251	041
257	166	047	014	316
417	017	123	164	226

Simple random sampling can be used when (1) the population has been numbered, or can be numbered at a low cost, and (2) the sample elements are easily accessible (that is, accessible at a low cost). Both are true for our company example.

Systematic Random Samples

Systematic random sample: The first element is chosen randomly, the remainder systematically.

A systematic random sample is a sample which contains every ith element of a population. For example, suppose we have the 15-element population

$$A\ B\ C\ D\ E\ F\ G\ H\ I\ J\ K\ L\ M\ N\ O$$

and every fifth ($i = 5$) element is to be in the sample. We need to start with one of the first five elements A, B, C, D, E. We number these, respectively, 1, 2, 3, 4, 5 and obtain a random starting point from a table of random digits. Let's agree (before looking) to take the first usable digit (1, 2, 3, 4, or 5) from the numbers starting in the fourth row, ninth column of Table 9.1. Now look: the digit sequence is 93425. The 9 is not usable, but the 3 is. So element 3, which is C, is in the sample. Starting with C and taking every fifth population element provides the systematic random sample C H M.

The sample C D E could not be chosen in this systematic random selection.

In the process just described, every element has a known, nonzero, chance (1 in 5) of being selected, because the starting point is selected at random. Consequently, we have a random sample. However, most of the samples that could arise in simple random sampling cannot occur in systematic selection; so simple and systematic selection are different random sampling methods.

EXERCISE Which samples that can occur in simple random sampling cannot occur when a systematic sample containing every tenth population item is selected?

ANSWER Every sample that contains more than one element from any group of 10 successive elements.

Systematic sampling can be used for populations that are in some kind of order, such as listed populations or populations of records in a file. If a population is in order, only the first i elements need to be numbered to give the starting element for systematic selection. For example, suppose interviews are to be conducted at 100 of the population of 1000 houses in a residential area. That's a sample of 1 in 10; so a starting point in the first 10 is selected from a table of random digits. Suppose the starting number is 7. An interviewer can now go to the seventh house on one side of the first street in the area. That's the first house in the sample. The interviewer then proceeds down one side of the first street, up the other side; then down one side of the next street and up the other side, and so on. Interviews are conducted at every tenth house along the interviewer's serpentine path. Note that in the procedure just described, it was not necessary to have a listing of the 1000-house population.

Systematic selection may result in a nonrepresentative sample.

Systematic selection can produce an error that is not present in simple random selection. To see why, suppose that the residential survey just described sought to determine how many of the residents expected to buy a high-priced new car in the next 6 months. Suppose also that every tenth house happened to be a corner house on a double lot (an expensive house). People who live in the more expensive houses probably will buy more high-priced cars than others. Consequently, in this situation, buying expectations for the sample could be substantially higher than population expectations.

The advantages of systematic selection, when it can be used, are that it is easy to carry out, and it is not costly.

Stratified Random Samples

Dividing a population into nonoverlapping groups is called *stratification*. If a population is first stratified, and then a random sample is selected from

**Stratified random
sample:** *A random
sample is chosen
from each distinct
group within the
population.*

each stratum, the procedure is called *stratified random sampling*. One reason for selecting samples from each stratum rather than selecting the sample from the whole population is to ensure that samples of adequate size are obtained from each stratum. Suppose, for example, that unemployment information is wanted for the nation (the whole population) and for each state. If a simple random sample of the nation is selected, it could happen that the sample in one or more states would be too small to provide the precision desired. However, if the nation is first stratified by state, sample sizes for the states can be decided on in advance, and not left to chance as they are in simple random sampling of the nation. Therefore, one reason for

*Stratification ensures
adequate strata
representation in
the sample.*

using stratified random sampling is to ensure that samples of adequate size are obtained from each of the strata.

Stratification is used also to improve sample estimates of population characteristics. The general principle is that a stratified random sample gives

*Stratification can im-
prove precision.*

more precise results than a simple random sample *if* differences between strata are greater than differences within strata. To see why, look at Figure 9.2, which shows a 10-chip population. The population total (the sum of the

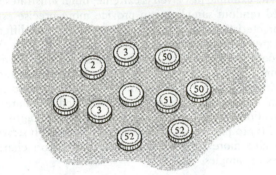

FIGURE 9.2
Ten-chip population.

numbers on the chips) is 265. This total is to be estimated by selecting a random sample of 2 chips, then multiplying the sum of the two chip numbers by 5 (5 times 2 chips is 10 chips). If we take a simple random sample, we can get any pair of chips. Some pairs of two will give very poor estimates of the population total. For example, chips numbered 1 and 2 estimate the total (265) as

$$5(1 + 2) = 15$$

Now suppose we stratify the population as shown in Figure 9.3 and draw one chip at random from the low stratum L and one from the high stratum H. Stratifying, then sampling each stratum, makes it impossible to get two small numbers or two large numbers. The smallest estimate of the population total, 265, arises if the sample is 1 and 50, the smallest number in each stratum. This estimate is

$$5(1 + 50) = 255$$

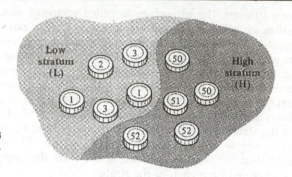

FIGURE 9.3
Stratified 10-chip pop-
ulation.

EXERCISE What is the largest estimate of the population total that could arise in our stratified random sample?
ANSWER 275.

The example just given is extreme, but it illustrates the principle that stratified random sampling can provide more precise estimates of population characteristics than simple random sampling if differences between strata are greater than differences within strata. Thus, the superiority of stratified random sampling in the example occurs because the differences of numbers from stratum L to stratum H are greater than the differences of the numbers in either stratum. Stratified random sampling is used extensively in sampling human populations. Samples are stratified by characteristics such as age, educational level, sex, income level, and geographic area. Stratification is used (1) to provide an adequate sample for each stratum and (2) because it can give more precise estimates of population characteristics than other types of samples.

Random Cluster Samples

**Random cluster
sampling: *Select a
random sample of
groups; then select
all—or a random
sample of—elements
from each group.***

Cluster sampling means selecting groups (clusters) of population elements. After clusters have been selected, all, or part of, the elements in each cluster are included in the sample.

As an example, suppose information about attitudes on working conditions is wanted for workers in the factories of a large industrial area. A list of the many thousands of workers is not available and would be costly to compile. However, it is easy to compile the relatively small list of all factories. Each factory contains a cluster of workers. We may then select a simple random sample of *factories* (clusters), and interview a random sample of the workers in these factories. The procedure described is called *two-stage* sampling. The first stage was selecting a sample of clusters. The second stage was selecting a sample of elements in each cluster. Alternatively, of course, all the workers in the selected clusters could be included in the sample.

Cluster sampling is used mainly because it is economical. However, the cost of sampling has to be weighed against the precision of results. The goal of sampling is to achieve a desired degree of precision at the lowest cost. In cluster sampling, only a fraction (often a small fraction) of the clusters in a population are sampled. The remaining clusters are ignored. Precision will suffer little if the ignored clusters are similar to the sampled clusters. Consequently, cluster samples work best for homogeneous populations, that is, populations which have uniform composition throughout. Thus, after a sample sip of a bottle of wine we know whether the whole bottle is sour or not because the population (the bottleful) is homogeneous. Sampled populations usually are not completely homogeneous. However, stratification can lead to strata which are reasonably homogeneous. Consequently, if cluster sampling is to be used for populations which have different strata, the strata should be delineated first; then sample clusters should be selected from each stratum. For example, suppose information about income, or factors related to income, is desired for a city. The city (population) would first be stratified into, say, high, medium, and low income strata—perhaps by neighborhood —then a sample of several city blocks (clusters) would be selected from each stratum.

Cluster sampling from a stratified population gives a more representative sample.

9.3 NONRANDOM SAMPLES

Nonrandom samples are called *judgment* samples. As the term implies, judgment, rather than chance alone, determines which population elements are selected for a sample. The degree of judgment applied in selecting elements for a judgment sample varies greatly. Little judgment is used when a sample is selected simply because it is convenient. On the other hand, a company that test markets a new product in a single city will use the best judgment available in selecting the test city and the stores where the product will be offered for sale.

Quota-controlled sample: The objective is to make the sample represent known facts about the population.

In a *quota-controlled* judgment sample, various segments of a population have the same percentage representation in the sample as they have in the population. For example, suppose the population percentages of low-, medium-, and high-income families in a city are, respectively, 35, 45, and 20 percent. Then, in a sample of 1000 families, the sample would be controlled to obtain about 350 (35 percent of 1000) low-income families, 450 middle-income families, and 200 high-income families. Similarly, the percentages of various ethnic groups in the sample, and other sample percentages, are controlled to make them correspond to population percentages. However, the elements (families) in the sample are not selected randomly. Interviewers, or their supervisors, using judgment, select the families; their job is to fill the quotas. .

The precision of the information obtained from a judgment sample may be lower than, as high as, or higher than that obtained from a random sample. The disadvantage of judgment samples is that there is no objective method for determining how precise the results are. Statisticians use random samples because there is an objective method for determining their precision. The background you will need to understand the method will be given after the problem set.

9.4 PROBLEMS

1. Mel Barkin, controller of West Manufacturing Company, wants to check vouchers to make sure that they have been recorded correctly in company accounting ledgers. Vouchers are filed in consecutive voucher order number, starting with 0000, in a drawer file. There are 3400 vouchers for the year to date. Mel wants to check a random sample of 340 vouchers. Describe how he can select the sample.

2. (See Problem 1.) Suppose the vouchers are filed by date. Explain how Mel can obtain the sample.

3. Hops Brewery has a bottle-filling machine with 50 filling stations. Fifty empty bottles are loaded on the machine; then all 50 are filled and capped. Next, the bottles from filling stations 1 to 50 are loaded in order on a conveyor belt and taken to the shipping department. The whole process is automatic. The machine operates 16 hours, then is shut down for cleaning and maintenance. Each time the machine starts up, a random number from 1 to 200 is used to determine the first bottle to be inspected. Thereafter, every 200th bottle is inspected to determine whether it is properly filled and capped. (a) What type of sampling is being used? (b) What problem could arise?

4. (See Problem 3.) Twice a day, the Hops Brewery manager looks at bottles coming along the conveyor and picks out an occasional bottle that appears to be underfilled or improperly capped. An inspector checks the selected bottles and reports what he finds to the manager. About 80 percent of the bottles selected by the manager are properly filled and capped. (a) Does the manager have a random sample? Explain. (b) Should the manager conclude that 20 percent of the bottles from the machine are underfilled or improperly capped? Why?

5. Bess Donahue is chairperson of the Gould for Mayor Committee. Bess wants to devise campaign literature that will convince voters that Gould will solve their problems. But Bess does not know which problems the voters consider to be the most important. Suppose she instructs 20 volunteer workers to make telephone calls and ask voters about problems. Each volunteer is to continue calling until 10 responses have been obtained. Will Bess then have a random sample of 200 responses? Explain.

6. Each month the government releases figures on the number and percentage of employed and unemployed persons in the nation. Do you think these figures are derived from a sample or a census? Why?

7. Gerry Bight received a letter from Jones and Jones, a bank auditing firm, stating that she had $975.62 in her bank account. The letter asked whether her records agreed with the bank's figure. Gerry's friends who had accounts at the same bank did not receive a letter. What do you suppose is taking place?

8. Under what circumstances will a stratified random sample of a given size give more precise results than a simple random sample of the same size?

9. Lou Galiano is inventory supervisor for Halsey Hydraulics. In the inventory are hydraulic cylinders made in Halsey's two plants, North Plant and South Plant. Customers have registered complaints about faulty cylinders. Lou has been directed to make a sample check and estimate the number of faulty cylinders in the inventory. Should Lou use a simple random sample or a stratified random sample? Why?

10. What is a cluster sample?

11. Why are cluster samples used?

12. The Bureau of the Census has divided the nation into small sections called census enumeration tracts. Suppose a map showing the tracts in a large suburban area is prepared, and the low-, middle-, and high-income parts of the area are delineated. Next suppose the tracts in the area are numbered, and a table of random numbers is used (as we used Table 9.1) to select a sample of tracts from each part. Finally interviews are conducted at all residences in the sample of tracts. (a) What sampling methods have been used? (b) Is it necessary to have a list of all the residences in the area to carry out the described procedure? Explain.

Population **p**arameter

Sample **s**tatistic

Complete notation: For a sample of size n

$$\bar{x} = \frac{\Sigma_{i=1}^{n}\, x_i}{n}$$

9.5 PARAMETERS AND STATISTICS

A *parameter* is a characteristic of a population. A *statistic* is a characteristic of a sample. Thus, the mean of a population is a population parameter. If a sample is drawn from a population, the mean of the sample is a statistic. The symbol $\bar{x}$ (x bar) is used to denote a sample mean, and as we know, μ is used to denote a population mean. The *formula for the sample mean* is

$$\bar{x} = \frac{\Sigma x}{n}$$

where the values x are the numbers in the sample, and n is the size of the sample.

Suppose we have a population which contains only the five numbers

$$0 \quad 3 \quad 6 \quad 3 \quad 18$$

We will use the symbol μ_x to denote the mean of a population of values of x. Thus,

$$\mu_x = \frac{0 + 3 + 6 + 3 + 18}{5} = 6$$

The population parameter has the single value, $\mu_x = 6$.

Next, suppose we draw a sample of size $n = 3$ from the population. If the sample contains the numbers 6, 3, 18, then

$$\bar{x} = \frac{\Sigma x}{n}$$

$$= \frac{6 + 3 + 18}{3} = 9$$

Sample statistics
are
random variables!

However, the sample 0, 3, 3, which could have been drawn, has $\bar{x} = 2$. And other possible samples have other means. Thus, for a given population, the parameter μ_x is a single number, but the statistic $\bar{x}$ is a random variable whose value depends upon which sample is drawn. Similarly, the proportion of Republicans in the population of voters is a parameter that has a single value at a given time; but the proportion of Republicans in a random sample is a statistic whose value depends upon which sample is drawn.

In what follows, we will be interested in how far a sample statistic could be from the corresponding population parameter. That depends, in part, upon the type of sample that is selected. From here on in this book we will use *simple random samples*. For brevity, I shall often write only the words *random sample*, or sometimes only the word *sample*. Please note, therefore, that random sample, or sample, means simple random sample.

9.6 THE SAMPLING DISTRIBUTION OF THE MEAN

Definition of sampling distribution

A sampling distribution is a probability distribution of a sample statistic. Thus, the *sampling distribution of the mean* is the probability distribution of the means $\bar{x}$ of all simple random samples of a given size that can be drawn from a population. The sampling distribution of the mean is also called the *distribution of $\bar{x}$*. In this section the definition will be illustrated by determining the probability distribution of the mean for samples of size $n = 3$ drawn from a population that has $N = 5$ elements. The elements are designated, for reference, by the letters A, B, C, D, and E. The elements and their values are

$$
\begin{array}{ccccc}
A & B & C & D & E \\
0 & 3 & 6 & 3 & 18
\end{array}
$$

One sample of $n = 3$ that can be drawn from the population is ABC. The sample mean is

$$\bar{x} = \frac{0 + 3 + 6}{3} = 3$$

Another sample is ABD; its mean is

$$\bar{x} = \frac{0 + 3 + 3}{3} = 2$$

The number of samples that can be drawn from a population depends on whether we sample with replacement or without replacement. In sampling *with replacement*, a selected element is returned to the population before another selection is made. The almost universal practice, which we shall

Sample without replacement

follow, is to sample without replacement; consequently, it will be impossible for us to get a sample in which an element appears more than once.

The number of simple random samples of size n that can be drawn without replacement from a population of size N is

$$\binom{N}{n} = \frac{N!}{n!(N-n)!}$$

With $N = 5$ and $n = 3$, so that $N - n$ is 2,

$$\binom{5}{3} = \frac{5!}{3!2!} = 10$$

The 10 samples that can be drawn from our population, and their means $\bar{x}$, are given in Table 9.3.

TABLE 9.3

GENERATING SAMPLE MEANS $\bar{x}$ FROM POPULATION VALUES

	Population values	Sample	Sample values	Sample mean $\bar{x}$
This contains a list of	A = 0	ABC	0, 3, 6	3
all possible samples	B = 3	ABD	0, 3, 3	2
of size 3 and their	C = 6	ABE	0, 3, 18	7
means.	D = 3	ACD	0, 6, 3	3
	E = 18	ACE	0, 6, 18	8
		ADE	0, 3, 18	7
		BCD	3, 6, 3	4
		BCE	3, 6, 18	9
		BDE	3, 3, 18	8
		CDE	6, 3, 18	9
				60

Table 9.4 is a frequency distribution of the sample means in Table 9.3.

TABLE 9.4

FREQUENCY DISTRIBUTION OF THE SAMPLE MEANS IN TABLE 9.3

	Sample mean $\bar{x}$	Frequency f
This is a list of all	2	1
possible means (for	3	2
n = 3) and their	4	1
frequencies.	7	2
	8	2
	9	2
		10

Next we compute the probabilities (relative frequencies) of the $\bar{x}$ values in Table 9.4 by dividing each frequency by the total frequency, 10. The result is the sampling distribution of the mean for samples of size 3, shown in Table 9.5.

TABLE 9.5
SAMPLING DISTRIBUTION
OF THE MEAN FOR
SAMPLES OF SIZE $n = 3$
FROM THE POPULATION
OF TABLE 9.3

Value of $\bar{x}$	Probability of $\bar{x}$
2	0.1
3	0.2
4	0.1
7	0.2
8	0.2
9	0.2
	1.0

This is a list of all possible means (for $n = 3$) and their probabilities (relative frequencies).

Table 9.5 illustrates that the *sampling distribution of the mean is the probability distribution for the means of all samples of a given size that can be drawn from a population*. I will sometimes call the sampling distribution of the mean the "distribution of $\bar{x}$" or the "distribution of sample means." Whatever the terminology used, the word *distribution* serves to emphasize that we are referring to more than one, and usually very many, sample means.

EXERCISE (a) How many samples of size 4 can be drawn from the population 0, 3, 6, 3, 18? (b) Compute the sampling distribution of the mean.
ANSWER (a) 5. (b) The $\bar{x}$ values are 3, 6, 6.75, and 7.5, with respective probabilities of 0.2, 0.2, 0.4, and 0.2.

9.7 RELATIONSHIPS BETWEEN THE POPULATION AND THE SAMPLING DISTRIBUTION OF THE MEAN

In this section you will learn the relationships of the mean and standard deviation of the distribution of $\bar{x}$ to the mean and the standard deviation of the population. The following symbols will be used:

You know the first four symbols.

N = population size

μ_x = population mean

σ_x = population standard deviation

n = sample size

$\mu_{\bar{x}}$ and $\sigma_{\bar{x}}$ are new symbols.

$\mu_{\bar{x}}$ = mean of the distribution of $\bar{x}$

$\sigma_{\bar{x}}$ = standard deviation of the distribution of $\bar{x}$

The subscript x on μ_x and σ_x means that these symbols represent population parameters. The subscript $\bar{x}$ on $\mu_{\bar{x}}$ and $\sigma_{\bar{x}}$ means that these symbols refer to the distribution of the sample statistic $\bar{x}$.

Population and Sampling Distribution Means

People generally find it intuitively reasonable to expect that if a population has a mean of μ_x, then the mean of the means of all samples (of a given size) that can be drawn from the population will equal μ_x. That is, the mean $\mu_{\bar{x}}$ of the distribution of $\bar{x}$ will equal μ_x. Intuition is correct. It is always true that

$$\mu_{\bar{x}} = \mu_x$$

To illustrate, recall that the mean of the population in Table 9.3, which has $N = 5$ elements, is

This population mean equals . . .

$$\mu_x = \frac{0 + 3 + 6 + 3 + 18}{5} = 6$$

The 10 sample means in the table have a sum of 60; so

. . . this mean of sample means.

$$\mu_{\bar{x}} = \frac{60}{10} = 6$$

(It works every time.)

and $\mu_{\bar{x}} = \mu_x$. The mean of all the sample means equals the population mean.

Population and Sampling Distribution Standard Deviations

The standard deviation of sample means $\sigma_{\bar{x}}$ is called the *standard error of the mean*. The relationship between the standard error of the mean $\sigma_{\bar{x}}$ and the population standard deviation σ_x is not intuitively obvious. The *formula relating $\sigma_{\bar{x}}$ to σ_x* is

$$\sigma_{\bar{x}} = \frac{\sigma_x}{\sqrt{n}} \sqrt{\frac{N - n}{N - 1}}$$

Let's illustrate the formula using our example. First we shall compute the standard error of the mean $\sigma_{\bar{x}}$, which is the standard deviation of the 10 sample means in Table 9.3. The mean of these means is $\mu_{\bar{x}} = 6$, as shown in Table 9.6 (at the top of page 280). The deviations of the $\bar{x}$ values from their mean are in the second column. The squares of the deviation are in the third column. The standard deviation is the square root of the average of the squared deviations (see Chapter 4). It is

$$\sigma_{\bar{x}} = \sqrt{6.6} = 2.569$$

EXERCISE (a) Compute the standard deviation of the population 0, 3, 6, 3, 18. (b) What is the symbol for the standard deviation in (a)?
ANSWER (a) $\sqrt{39.6} = 6.293$; (b) σ_x.

Now let's apply the formula and compute $\sigma_{\bar{x}}$ from the value $\sigma_x = 6.293$ determined in the exercise. We start with $\sigma_x = 6.293$, $n = 3$, and $N = 5$. The formula says

$$\sigma_x = \frac{\sigma_x}{\sqrt{n}} \sqrt{\frac{N - n}{N - 1}}$$

TABLE 9.6
COMPUTATION OF $\sigma_{\bar{x}}$

$\bar{x}$	$\bar{x} - 6$	$(\bar{x} - 6)^2$
3	−3	9
2	−4	16
7	1	1
3	−3	9
8	2	4
7	1	1
4	−2	4
9	3	9
8.	2	4
9	3	9
Sum = 60		66

Here we compute $\sigma_{\bar{x}}$ from the 10 sample means.

$$\sigma_{\bar{x}} = \sqrt{\frac{\Sigma(\bar{x} - 6)^2}{10}}$$

$$= \sqrt{\frac{66}{10}}$$

$$= \sqrt{6.6}$$

$$= 2.569$$

Mean $= \mu_{\bar{x}} = \dfrac{60}{10} = 6$

Here we compute $\sigma_{\bar{x}}$ from the formula relating σ_x and $\sigma_{\bar{x}}$.

Substituting, we find

$$\sigma_{\bar{x}} = \frac{6.293}{\sqrt{3}} \sqrt{\frac{5 - 3}{5 - 1}}$$

$$= \frac{6.293}{1.732} \sqrt{0.5}$$

Eureka!

$$= 2.569$$

which is the value of $\sigma_{\bar{x}}$ computed in Table 9.6.

A standard deviation measures variability. Except in the rare case where $\sigma_x = 0$ (so $\sigma_{\bar{x}} = 0$), averages vary less than the population values from which the averages are computed. Thus, in our example, population variability is $\sigma_x = 6.293$, but the variability of sample averages is the smaller number $\sigma_{\bar{x}} = 2.569$. Averaging reduces variability, and the larger the sample size (that is, the greater the number of population values used in computing averages), the smaller $\sigma_{\bar{x}}$ will be. Hence, except in the rare case where all population numbers are equal (so $\sigma_x = \sigma_{\bar{x}} = 0$),

Sample means vary less than population values.

1. $\sigma_{\bar{x}}$ is less than σ_x.
2. The larger n is, the smaller $\sigma_{\bar{x}}$ is.

EXERCISE A population of 100 numbers has a mean of 19.2 and a standard deviation of 1.0. (a) What are the symbols for, and the values of, the mean and standard deviation of the sampling distribution of the mean for samples of size 10? (b) What is the standard error of the mean for samples of size 25?
ANSWER (a) $\mu_{\bar{x}} = 19.2$, $\sigma_{\bar{x}} = 0.302$; (b) $\sigma_{\bar{x}} = 0.174$.

In the exercise, note that $\sigma_{\bar{x}}$ is less than σ_x in both parts, *and* $\sigma_{\bar{x}}$ for $n = 25$ is less than $\sigma_{\bar{x}}$ for $n = 10$.

In the formula for the standard error of the mean,

$$\sigma_{\bar{x}} = \frac{\sigma_x}{\sqrt{n}} \sqrt{\frac{N-n}{N-1}}$$

The rightmost square root expression is called the *finite population multiplier*. If the population size N is large and the sample size n is relatively small, the multiplier can be omitted, leading to the simpler formula for the standard error,

Approximate formula when N is large and n is small

$$\sigma_{\bar{x}} = \frac{\sigma_x}{\sqrt{n}}$$

To illustrate why the finite population multiplier can sometimes be omitted, suppose N is 10,000 and n is 100. Then

$$\sqrt{\frac{N-n}{N-1}} = \sqrt{\frac{10,000 - 100}{10,000 - 1}}$$

$$= 0.995 \approx 1$$

The point is that with large N and small n, the multiplier is almost 1; so we may as well call it 1. Then, for practical purposes, $\sigma_{\bar{x}}$ is equal to $\sigma_x/\sqrt{n}$.

As a rule of thumb, we can omit the multiplier when $n < 0.05N$, that is, when the sample contains less than 5 percent of the population. In applications, n usually is less than 5 percent of N; so we will usually apply the simpler formula in computing the standard error of the mean.

9.8 SUMMARY OF SECTIONS 9.6 AND 9.7

A population contains N values. For the population, the mean is μ_x and the standard deviation is σ_x. The sampling distribution of the mean (also called the distribution of $\bar{x}$) is the probability distribution of the means $\bar{x}$ of all samples of a given size n that can be drawn from the population. For the sampling distribution, the mean is $\mu_{\bar{x}}$ and the standard deviation, called the standard error of the mean, is $\sigma_{\bar{x}}$. The following relationships hold:

$$\mu_{\bar{x}} = \mu_x$$

$$\sigma_{\bar{x}} = \frac{\sigma_x}{\sqrt{n}} \sqrt{\frac{N-n}{N-1}}$$

If the sample contains less than 5 percent of the population (a common situation), the simpler formula

Use when n < 0.05N (as it often is).

$$\sigma_{\bar{x}} = \frac{\sigma_x}{\sqrt{n}}$$

can be used to compute the standard error of the mean.

I illustrated the definitions and relationships stated in the foregoing summary by using a small population of $N = 5$ values. There are only 10 samples of size $n = 3$ that can be drawn from a population of $N = 5$. For the populations and sample sizes arising in applications, the number of samples is astronomical. For example, if $N = 100$ and $n = 10$, then the number of samples is

$$\binom{N}{n} = \binom{100}{10} \approx 17{,}310{,}309{,}000{,}000$$

FIGURE 9.4

Angry magazine reports on samples of size 10 drawn from a population of size 100.

rounded to the nearest million. That number is more than 17 trillion; so there are more than 17 trillion samples that can be drawn. Even so, as Secret Agent X Bar in the cartoon (Figure 9.4) well knows, the relationships between $\mu_{\bar{x}}$ and μ_x, and that between $\sigma_{\bar{x}}$ and σ_x, hold true.

EXERCISE Upon what did Secret Agent X Bar base his deductions?
ANSWER The agent does not disclose his sources of information.

9.9 NORMAL DISTRIBUTIONS OF $\bar{x}$

For a normal population: *The sample means are normally distributed.*

The term *population distribution* means the probability distribution of a random variable. Suppose, for example, that scores on a college entrance examination have a normal probability distribution. Then we could say, and have said, the scores are normally distributed; or, as we shall say, the test score population is normal. This section illustrates two statements that you will use extensively in this and later chapters. They are: (1) If a population has a normal distribution, the distribution of $\bar{x}$ is normal for all sample sizes.

For any large population: *The sample means are nearly normally distributed for $n > 30$.*

(2) The distribution of $\bar{x}$ is practically normal if the sample size n is greater than 30, for all populations usually encountered in business problems. The statements are based upon mathematical results obtained by working with infinite populations, that is, populations with a limitless number of elements. However, the statements apply closely enough for populations of modest size, say, 1000 or more. The usual reason for sampling in business problems is that it is too costly to obtain information for the entire population, because the population is very large; consequently, statement (2) is usually applicable.

Figure 9.5 (on page 284) starts with a normal population, having $\sigma_x = 10$. The distribution of $\bar{x}$ for samples of $n = 4$ also is normal, because the population is normal, but the standard error of the mean is

$\sigma_{\bar{x}}$ is less than σ_x.

$$\sigma_{\bar{x}} = \frac{\sigma_x}{\sqrt{n}}$$

$$= \frac{10}{\sqrt{4}} = 5$$

The larger n is, the smaller $\sigma_{\bar{x}}$ is —and the taller and thinner is the distribution of the means.

so the sampling distribution has less variability than the population. With $n = 16$, the distribution of $\bar{x}$ again is normal, because the population is normal; but now the standard error of the mean is

$$\sigma_{\bar{x}} = \frac{\sigma_x}{\sqrt{n}}$$

$$= \frac{10}{\sqrt{16}} = 2.5$$

The distribution of $\bar{x}$ is normal for all sample sizes if the population is normal, and the larger the sample size n the smaller will be the standard error $\sigma_{\bar{x}}$.

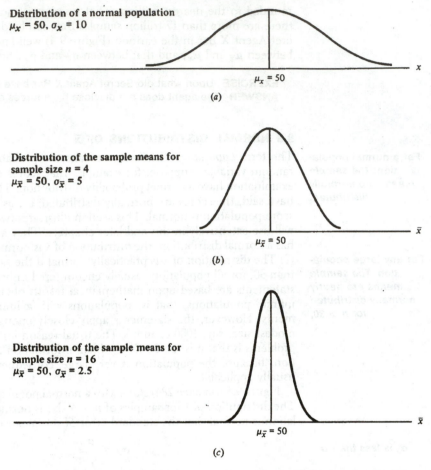

Distribution of a normal population
$\mu_x = 50$, $\sigma_x = 10$

$\mu_x = 50$

x

(a)

Distribution of the sample means for
sample size $n = 4$
$\mu_{\bar{x}} = 50$, $\sigma_{\bar{x}} = 5$

$\mu_{\bar{x}} = 50$

$\bar{x}$

(b)

Distribution of the sample means for
sample size $n = 16$
$\mu_{\bar{x}} = 50$, $\sigma_{\bar{x}} = 2.5$

$\mu_{\bar{x}} = 50$

$\bar{x}$

(c)

FIGURE 9.5
For a normal popula-
tion, distributions of
sample means are
normal.

In Chapter 8, we saw that probabilities for the numbers of successes in n binomial trials (or a sample of size n) tended toward normal curve probabilities as the sample size n increased. This behavior was called "tendency toward normality as n increases." This tendency also occurs for distributions of $\bar{x}$. The *central limit theorem* (CLT) proves that if simple random samples are drawn from an infinite population that has a mean and standard deviation, then the distribution of $\bar{x}$ always tends toward normality as the sample size n increases. The important point is that the CLT is not restricted to normal populations. The tendency occurs for all populations usually encountered. Figure 9.6 contains some graphs that illustrate this tendency. At the left is a "triangular" population, whose left skewness is still apparent in the distributions of $\bar{x}$ for $n = 2$ and $n = 5$; but the distribution for $n = 30$ is nearly normal. Similarly, the distributions of $\bar{x}$ for $n = 30$ for the uniform (middle) and exponential (right) populations in Figure 9.6 are nearly normal.

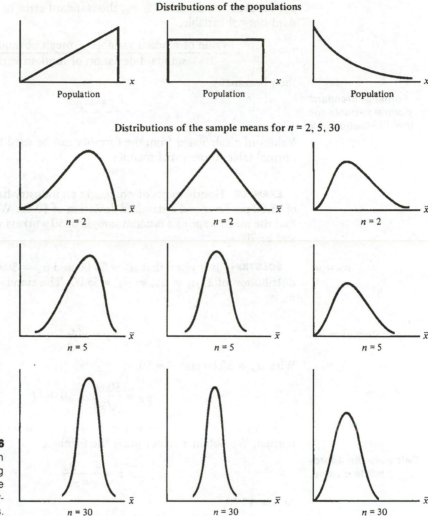

Distributions of the populations

Population   Population   Population

Distributions of the sample means for n = 2, 5, 30

$n = 2$ $n = 2$ $n = 2$

$n = 5$ $n = 5$ $n = 5$

$n = 30$ $n = 30$ $n = 30$

FIGURE 9.6
Look down a column
and see the sampling
distribution of the
mean approach nor-
mality as n increases.

IMPORTANT
Do not forget

Figure 9.6 illustrates the tendency toward normality of the distributions of $\bar{x}$ for distinctly nonnormal populations. In applied problems, we will take as a rule of thumb that, *for $n > 30$, the distribution of $\bar{x}$ is normal with $\mu_{\bar{x}} = \mu_x$ and $\sigma_{\bar{x}} = \sigma_x/\sqrt{n}$.*

9.10 USING THE DISTRIBUTION OF $\bar{x}$

To make use of the fact that a distribution is normal, we need to know its mean and standard deviation. If the normally distributed random variable is $\bar{x}$, then the mean of $\bar{x}$ is $\mu_{\bar{x}}$ which, of course, equals the population mean

μ_x; the standard deviation is $\sigma_{\bar{x}}$, the standard error of the mean. The standard normal variable,

$$z = \frac{\text{value of random variable} - \text{mean of random variable}}{\text{standard deviation of random variable}}$$

then becomes

Formula: *Standard normal variable for the distribution of $\bar{x}$*

$$z = \frac{\bar{x} - \mu_{\bar{x}}}{\sigma_{\bar{x}}}$$

Values of z calculated from the formula can be used to enter the standard normal table in the usual manner.

EXAMPLE Hourly wages of workers in an industry have a mean wage rate of $5.00 per hour and a standard deviation of $0.60. What is the probability that the mean wage of a random sample of 50 workers will be between $5.10 and $5.20?

$\mu_{\bar{x}} = \mu_x$

SOLUTION It is given that $\mu_x = \$5.00$ and $\sigma_x = \$0.60$. For the sampling distribution of $\bar{x}$, $\mu_{\bar{x}} = \mu_x$; so $\mu_{\bar{x}} = \$5.00$. The standard error of the mean $\sigma_{\bar{x}}$ is

Calculate $\sigma_{\bar{x}}$.

$$\sigma_{\bar{x}} = \frac{\sigma_x}{\sqrt{n}}$$

With $\sigma_x = \$0.60$ and $n = 50$,

$$\sigma_{\bar{x}} = \frac{\$0.60}{\sqrt{50}} = \$0.0849$$

Because $n = 50$ satisfies the $n > 30$ rule, the distribution of $\bar{x}$ will be normal. We obtain z values using the formula

Calculate the appropriate z value.

$$z = \frac{\bar{x} - \mu_{\bar{x}}}{\sigma_{\bar{x}}}$$

At $\bar{x} = \$5.10$,

$$z = \frac{5.10 - 5.00}{0.0849} = 1.18$$

At $\bar{x} = \$5.20$,

$$z = \frac{5.20 - 5.00}{0.0849} = 2.36$$

Use a sketch and Table V to solve the problem.

Figure 9.7 shows our results thus far: Note carefully that the horizontal axis shows $\bar{x}$ as the variable because we are working with a distribution of sample means. The solution is the area from $z = 1.18$ to $z = 2.36$. This area is

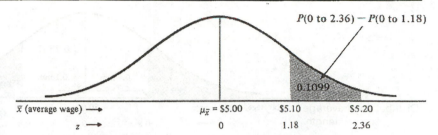

FIGURE 9.7
Distribution of average
wage.

$$P(0 \text{ to } 2.36) - P(0 \text{ to } 1.18) = 0.4909 - 0.3810 = 0.1099$$

The probability that the sample mean wage is between \$5.10 and \$5.20 is 0.1099.

EXERCISE In the last example, which has $\mu_x = \$5.00$ and $\sigma_x = \$0.60$, what is the probability that the mean wage of a sample of 36 workers will be from \$5.10 to \$5.20?
ANSWER 0.1359.

EXAMPLE Valve stems made by an automatic machine have lengths which are normally distributed with a mean of 50 mm and a standard deviation of 0.25 mm. What is the probability that the mean length of a sample of four stems will be more than 0.10 mm from the population mean length of 50 mm?

σ_x is given. We have
to calculate $\sigma_{\bar{x}}$.

SOLUTION The population of lengths is normally distributed; so the distribution of $\bar{x}$ will be normal for any sample size. From the given population standard deviation $\sigma_x = 0.25$ mm, we compute the standard error of the mean for samples of size $n = 4$ to be

$$\sigma_{\bar{x}} = \frac{\sigma_x}{\sqrt{n}}$$

$$= \frac{0.25}{\sqrt{4}}$$

$$= 0.125 \text{ mm}$$

The mean of the distribution of $\bar{x}$ is $\mu_{\bar{x}} = \mu_x = 50$ mm. If a sample average $\bar{x}$ is 0.1 mm from $\mu_{\bar{x}}$, then $\bar{x} - \mu_{\bar{x}}$ equals 0.1. Hence,

$$z = \frac{\bar{x} - \mu_{\bar{x}}}{\sigma_{\bar{x}}}$$

$$= \frac{0.1}{0.125}$$

$$= 0.8$$

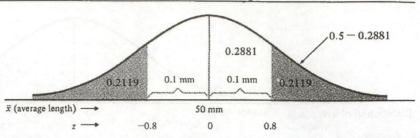

FIGURE 9.8
Distribution of average
length.

**Recall: *Table V does
not give tail areas.***

Figure 9.8 shows our results thus far. The problem asks for the probability that $\bar{x}$ will be "more than" 0.1 mm from 50 mm. This probability consists of two equal tail areas. The area of each tail is

$$0.5 - P(0 \text{ to } 0.8) = 0.5 - 0.2881 = 0.2119$$

The area of the two tails is

$$2(0.2119) = 0.4238$$

Hence, the probability that the mean length of a sample of four parts will be more than 0.1 mm from the population mean is 0.4238.

9.11 SAMPLING DISTRIBUTION OF THE PROPORTION

***p* is a parameter.**   We shall use p to mean the parameter *population proportion of successes*. Our population of $N = 5$ numbers

$$0 \quad 3 \quad 6 \quad 3 \quad 18$$

contains three even numbers, 0, 6, and 18, and two odd numbers, 3 and 3. The population *proportion* of even numbers ("successes") is

$$p = \frac{3}{5} = 0.6$$

Now consider a sample of size $n = 3$, say, the first three population numbers, 0, 3, and 6. Two of the numbers in the sample are even. Hence, the sample proportion of even numbers is

$$\bar{p} = \frac{2}{3}$$

$\bar{p}$ is a statistic.   The bar on $\bar{p}$ means the symbol represents the sample proportion. Thus, $\bar{p}$ is a *statistic*; it can have different values in different samples. For example, the sample 0, 3, 3 has $\bar{p} = \frac{1}{3}$, and the sample 0, 6, 18 has $\bar{p} = 1$.

Ten samples of size $n = 3$ can be drawn from a population of $N = 5$. The $\bar{p}$ values for all 10 samples of 3 are

$$\frac{2}{3} \quad \frac{1}{3} \quad \frac{2}{3} \quad \frac{2}{3} \quad 1 \quad \frac{2}{3} \quad \frac{1}{3} \quad \frac{2}{3} \quad \frac{1}{3} \quad \frac{2}{3}$$

Three of the 10 are $\frac{1}{3}$; so the probability for $\bar{p} = \frac{1}{3}$ is $\frac{3}{10}$, or 0.3. Similarly, for $\bar{p} = \frac{2}{3}$ and $\bar{p} = 1$, the respective probabilities are 0.6 and 0.1. Hence, we have the sampling distribution of the proportion (also called the distribution of $\bar{p}$) shown in Table 9.7.

TABLE 9.7
SAMPLING DISTRIBUTION OF
THE PROPORTION

Sample proportion $\bar{p}$	Probability of $\bar{p}$
$\frac{1}{3}$	0.3
$\frac{2}{3}$	0.6
1	0.1
	$\overline{1.0}$

The sampling distribution of the proportion is all pairs [$\bar{p}$, P($\bar{p}$)].

Now return to the 10 values of $\bar{p}$ listed above. I computed the mean and standard deviation of these 10 numbers and obtained 0.6 for the mean and 0.2 for the standard deviation. That is, using the subscript $\bar{p}$ to designate sample proportions,

$$\mu_{\bar{p}} = 0.6$$

$$\sigma_{\bar{p}} = 0.2$$

The symbol $\mu_{\bar{p}}$ represents the mean of the distribution of $\bar{p}$. Note that $\mu_{\bar{p}} = 0.6$ and the population proportion p is also 0.6. This equality always holds; that is,

Proportion distribution mean equals population proportion.

$$\mu_{\bar{p}} = p$$

The symbol $\sigma_{\bar{p}}$ is called the *standard error of the proportion*. It is the standard deviation of all possible sample proportions. Let p be *any given* population proportion, and $q = 1 - p$; then for samples of size n from a population of size N,

Formula for the standard error of the proportion

$$\sigma_{\bar{p}} = \sqrt{\frac{pq}{n}} \sqrt{\frac{N - n}{N - 1}}$$

Thus, for our example, which has $p = 0.6$ (so $q = 0.4$), $n = 3$, and $N = 5$, we can compute

$$\sigma_{\bar{p}} = \sqrt{\frac{(0.6)(0.4)}{3}} \sqrt{\frac{5 - 3}{5 - 1}} = \sqrt{0.04} = 0.2$$

which is the value I computed for $\sigma_{\bar{p}}$ using the 10 sample proportions.

Note the presence of the finite population multiplier (the rightmost square root) in the formula for $\sigma_{\bar{p}}$. When n is less than 5 percent of N, as it usually is in applications, the multiplier can be omitted. Hence, *we will usually compute $\sigma_{\bar{p}}$ by the formula*

Approximate but simpler formula for the standard error of the proportion

$$\sigma_{\bar{p}} = \sqrt{\frac{pq}{n}}$$

When we discussed the binomial distribution, p was called the probability of success. In this section, and afterward, we will call p the proportion of successes or the population proportion. Thus, in our example, there are three successes (even numbers) in the population of $N = 5$; so the population proportion is $p = 0.6$. Now recall from Chapter 8 that success probabilities for binomial trials can be approximated by normal curve probabilities under certain conditions. The same holds true for the distribution of sample proportions. Specifically, we will take as a rule of thumb that *sample proportions $\bar{p}$ are normally distributed when both np and nq are greater than 5*. We will always, from now on, have np and nq greater than 5. Consequently, we will solve problems involving sample proportions by using a normal distribution whose mean and standard deviation are

When np > 5 and nq > 5,

sample proportions are nearly normally distributed

with this mean and this standard deviation.

$$\mu_{\bar{p}} = p$$

$$\sigma_{\bar{p}} = \sqrt{\frac{pq}{n}}$$

Figure 9.9 illustrates the concept of the sampling distribution of the proportion. The population has 320 circles (elements); $p = 0.6$ is the population proportion of solid circles, and $q = 1 - 0.6 = 0.4$ is the proportion of open circles. The sample size is $n = 16$. The number of samples, $\binom{320}{16}$, is astronomical. Each sample has a proportion of solid circles $\bar{p}$. The sampling distribution of the proportion is the probability distribution of all the sample proportions; it is represented by the normal distribution, which has

$$\mu_{\bar{p}} = p \quad \text{and} \quad \sigma_{\bar{p}} = \sqrt{\frac{pq}{n}}$$

The normal curve at the bottom of the figure has

$$\mu_{\bar{p}} = 0.6 \quad \text{and} \quad \sigma_{\bar{p}} = 0.122$$

EXAMPLE Suppose 55 percent ($p = 0.55$) of the television audience population watched a particular program one Saturday evening. What is the probability that, in a random sample of 100 viewers, less than 50 percent of the sample watched the program?

SOLUTION The random variable is $\bar{p}$. Its mean is

Step 1 $\mu_{\bar{p}}$ is the given value p.

$$\mu_{\bar{p}} = p = 0.55$$

The standard error of $\bar{p}$ is

Step 2 Calculate $\sigma_{\bar{p}}$.

$$\sigma_{\bar{p}} = \sqrt{\frac{pq}{n}}$$

$$= \sqrt{\frac{(0.55)(0.45)}{100}}$$

$$= 0.0497$$

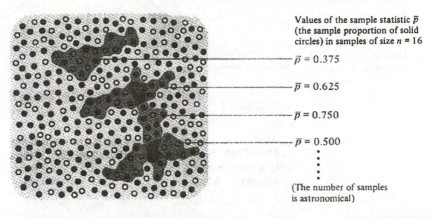

Population: N is 320
Proportion of solid circles is $p = 0.6$
Proportion of open circles is $q = 1 - p = 0.4$

Values of the sample statistic $\bar{p}$
(the sample proportion of solid
circles) in samples of size $n = 16$

$\bar{p} = 0.375$

$\bar{p} = 0.625$

$\bar{p} = 0.750$

$\bar{p} = 0.500$

$\vdots$

(The number of samples
is astronomical)

The distribution of the sample proportions

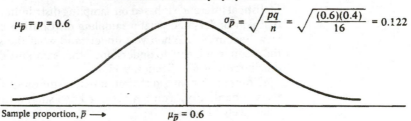

$\mu_{\bar{p}} = p = 0.6$ $\qquad\qquad \sigma_{\bar{p}} = \sqrt{\dfrac{pq}{n}} = \sqrt{\dfrac{(0.6)(0.4)}{16}} = 0.122$

FIGURE 9.9
Distribution of the
sample proportion.   Sample proportion, $\bar{p} \longrightarrow$ $\qquad\qquad \mu_{\bar{p}} = 0.6$

The general standard normal variable is

$$z = \frac{\text{value of random variable} - \text{mean of random variable}}{\text{standard deviation of random variable}}$$

The statistic $\bar{p}$ is our random variable; so

**Step 3   Calculate z
by this formula.**

$$z = \frac{\bar{p} - \mu_{\bar{p}}}{\sigma_{\bar{p}}} = \frac{\bar{p} - p}{\sigma_{\bar{p}}}$$

The 50 percent stated in the example is $\bar{p} = 0.50$. For this value of $\bar{p}$ we find

$$z = \frac{0.50 - 0.55}{0.0497} = -1.01$$

as shown in Figure 9.10. We want the probability that $\bar{p}$ is less than 0.50.
This probability is the tail area

**Step 4   Proceed as
usual with the stan-
dard normal table.**

$$0.5 - P(0 \text{ to } 1.01) = 0.5 - 0.3438 = 0.1562$$

Thus, if 55 percent of the viewer population saw the program, there is a

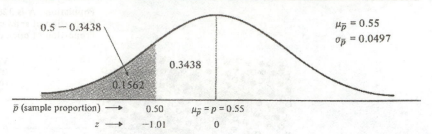

FIGURE 9.10
Distribution of $\bar{p}$ for
television audience
samples.

probability of 0.1562 that less than 50 percent of the sample saw the program.

> **EXERCISE** See the last example. If a random sample of 500 viewers is taken, what is the probability that less than 50 percent of the sample saw the program?
> **ANSWER** 0.0122.

9.12 THE IMPORTANCE OF SAMPLING DISTRIBUTIONS AND STANDARD ERRORS

Statistical inference is based on sampling distributions. If you are not certain that you understand what a sampling distribution is, now is the time to review Section 9.6. When you understand what the sampling distribution of the mean is, it is easy to understand other sampling distributions, such as the distribution of $\bar{p}$ in Section 9.11.

Different sampling distributions have different formulas for computing the standard error. You have learned two such formulas, which we will use extensively. They are

$$\sigma_{\bar{x}} = \frac{\sigma_x}{\sqrt{n}} \quad \text{and} \quad \sigma_{\bar{p}} = \sqrt{\frac{pq}{n}}$$

Again, if you are not certain that you understand what $\sigma_{\bar{x}}$ is, now is the time to review Section 9.7. When you understand what $\sigma_{\bar{x}}$ is, it is easy to understand the meaning of other standard errors, such as $\sigma_{\bar{p}}$. We will need additional standard error formulas as we go on. Each will be given when the need for it arises.

9.13 PROBLEMS

1. (*Note:* You do not have to compute sampling distributions to solve problems. However, the best way to make sure you understand the concept is to compute a sampling distribution.) Given the population

    2   4   8   8   10   10

    (a) How many samples of size $n = 2$ can be drawn from the population? (b) Compute and tabulate the sampling distribution of the mean for samples of size $n = 2$.

2. (a) What does σ_x mean? (b) What does $\sigma_{\bar{x}}$ mean? (c) For a given population, which is larger, σ_x or $\sigma_{\bar{x}}$?

3. The Dow Jones industrial average is an average of the prices of 30 stocks. The average varies from day to day. Suppose 100 stocks were used in computing the average. Would you expect the 100-price average to have greater or smaller variations than the 30-price average? Why?

4. The Palm Tree Vacation Resort advertises that it has ideal weather with an average (mean) temperature of 70°F. In a random sample of 35 days, what is the probability that mean temperature will be 68°F or lower if the standard deviation of daily temperatures is (a) 4 degrees? (b) 9 degrees?

5. An automatic machine made by Global Dispensers pours an average (mean) of 15.85 ounces into bottles whose contents are supposed to be 16 ounces. The standard deviation of the amounts of fill is 0.3 ounce, and amounts of fill are normally distributed. If a random sample of nine bottles is selected, what is the probability that the sample mean amount of fill will be 16 ounces or more?

6. The mean number of Synchrons sold by Synchronics, Inc., is 210 per day, and the standard deviation is 30 Synchrons per day. In a random sample of 36 selling days, what is the probability that mean daily Synchron sales will be 200 or more?

7. A quality-control inspector for National Shafts checks automatic machine operations in National's manufacturing plant. One machine has been set to make shafts that are supposed to have a diameter of 50 mm (millimeter). Machine output is normally distributed, and shaft diameters have a standard deviation of 0.02 mm. Periodically, the inspector selects a random sample of four shafts, measures them, and then computes the sample mean diameter. If the sample average is below 49.98 mm, or above 50.02 mm, the inspector has the machine stopped and reset. Suppose the mean diameter of shafts being produced is 50 mm. What is the probability that, after computing a sample mean, the operator will have to reset the machine?

8. Gen Green, an executive of the United Manufacturers Association, wants to estimate the mean daily wage in a large industry by using the mean wage of a random sample of 100 workers. Gen's objective is to have the sample mean differ from the industry mean by $1 or less. If the standard deviation of daily wages is $4 per day, what is the probability that Gen achieves her objective?

9. Wheat Products has appropriated funds to sample Massachusetts (population about 5 million) and Rhode Island (population about 1 million) to estimate average (mean) product consumption for each state. It is assumed that product consumption variability σ_x is the same for each state. Money is available to obtain a total sample size of 1200. Suppose the sample is proportioned 5 to 1, as are the state populations. (a) What will be the sample size for each state? (b) After the samples

have been taken, would you expect the Rhode Island sample mean would be as close to its population (state) mean as the Massachusetts sample mean is to its state mean? Why?

10. (See Problem 9.) Suppose the sample size for each state is 600. Would you expect the Massachusetts sample mean to be as close to its state mean as the Rhode Island sample mean is to its state mean? Why?

11. The formula $\sigma_{\bar{x}} = \sigma_x/\sqrt{n}$ is used in many applied situations even though it is not mathematically correct. (a) Why isn't the formula correct? (b) Why is the formula used if it is not correct?

12. (a) Is the formula $\sigma_{\bar{x}} = \sigma_x/\sqrt{n}$ applicable in Problems 9 and 10? Explain. (b) N does not appear in the formula $\sigma_{\bar{x}} = \sigma_x/\sqrt{n}$. What relationship does the absence of N have to the answers to Problems 9 and 10?

13. Suppose that in the Saturday night 8 to 9 p.m. hour, 100 million people watched television. Forty million watched a show called Nifty Tricks. (a) Compute the proportion who watched Nifty Tricks. What is the symbol for this proportion? (b) Now consider random samples of size 2500. Compute the value for $\sigma_{\bar{p}}$. (c) The number of samples of size 2500 is astronomical, but suppose you had all of them. How would $\sigma_{\bar{p}}$ be computed using the information in the samples?

14. (See Problem 13.) (a) What is the probability that, in a random sample of 2500, more than 41 percent of the sample watched Nifty Tricks? (b) What is the proportion symbol for the 41 percent in (a)?

15. Ten percent of the 1-pound boxes of sugar in a large warehouse operated by Sweet Company are underweight. Suppose a retailer buys a random sample of 144 of these boxes. What is the probability that at least 5 percent of the sample boxes will be underweight?

16. Final tabulation of election results showed candidate Bronson to be the winner with 51 percent of the vote. Candidate Landson received the other 49 percent of the vote. During the voting, a random sample of voters leaving the polls was asked which candidate they had voted for. Of the 125 voters in the sample, 60, or 48 percent, had voted for Bronson. Hence, the sample conclusion was that Bronson had lost, and this conclusion turned out to be incorrect. The error was 3 percentage points, or 0.03. (a) In the situation described, what is the probability of making an error as large as, or larger than, 0.03? (b) Which number, 0.51 or 0.48, should be used in computing $\sigma_{\bar{p}}$? Why?

9.14 SUMMARY

A *random sample* is a sample selected in a way such that every element in the population has a known chance, not zero, of being included in the sample. In a *simple random sample* of size n, (1) every element in the population has an equal probability of being included in the sample, and (2) every sample of size n has an equal probability of being the selected sample. In a *systematic random sample*, every ith element in the population is selected; the starting point in the first i elements is obtained randomly. In a *stratified random sample*, a population is first divided into strata; then a random sample is selected from each stratum. In a *random cluster sample*, the population is first divided into small sections called clusters; then a random sample of clusters is selected and all, or a sample of, the elements in the chosen clusters are included in the final sample.

Nonrandom samples are called *judgment* samples. Judgment samples include those selected haphazardly or for convenience, as well as those in which judgment rather than chance determines the elements selected. In the *quota-controlled* judgment sample, samples are constructed to have the same percentage composition as the population with respect to properties such as sex, age, or economic status.

A *statistic* is a characteristic of a sample; the corresponding population characteristic is called a *parameter*. The mean of a population μ_x and the standard deviation σ_x are population parameters. The sample mean, designated by $\bar{x}$, is a statistic. The formula for $\bar{x}$ is

$$\bar{x} = \frac{\Sigma x}{n}$$

where the x values are the sample values, and n is the number of values in the sample.

A population has one mean, μ_x. The statistic $\bar{x}$ for samples of size n drawn from the population can have different values in different samples. The *sampling distribution of the mean* is the probability distribution for the means of all samples of a given size that can be drawn from the population. The mean of all the sample means $\mu_{\bar{x}}$ equals the population mean μ_x. The formula usually applied in calculating the standard deviation of all the sample means $\sigma_{\bar{x}}$ is

$$\sigma_{\bar{x}} = \frac{\sigma_x}{\sqrt{n}}$$

where σ_x is the population standard deviation and n is the sample size. If the sample contains 5 percent, or more than 5 percent, of the population, $\sigma_x/\sqrt{n}$ in the last formula should be multiplied by the *finite population multiplier*

$$\sqrt{\frac{N-n}{N-1}}$$

The standard deviation of all sample means $\sigma_{\bar{x}}$ is called the *standard error of the mean*.

If the population distribution is normal, the sampling distribution of the mean is normal for any sample size. If the population distribution is not normal, the sampling distribution of the mean is nearly normal if the sample size is more than 30.

The proportion of "successes" in a population is the population parameter p. The proportion of successes $\bar{p}$ in a sample is a statistic. The *sampling distribution of the proportion* is the probability distribution of the values of $\bar{p}$ in all samples of a given size that can be drawn from the population. The mean of the sampling distribution is

$$\mu_{\bar{p}} = p$$

The *standard error of the proportion* (the standard deviation of the sample proportions $\bar{p}$) $\sigma_{\bar{p}}$ is usually calculated by applying the formula

$$\sigma_{\bar{p}} = \sqrt{\frac{pq}{n}}$$

where p is the population proportion, $q = 1 - p$, and n is the sample size. If the sample size is 5 percent, or more than 5 percent, of the population size, the right side of the last formula should be multiplied by the finite population multiplier. The sampling distribution of the proportion is nearly normal if both np and nq are greater than 5.

9.15 REVIEW PROBLEMS

1. Snow and Sale, a bank auditing firm, wants to check a random sample of 500 of the accounts of the Last National Bank. Letters will be sent to a sample of the bank's depositors asking them to verify Last National's record of their account balances. How should Snow and Sale select the sample?
2. (See Problem 1.) How should Snow and Sale select the sample if they want to take into account the fact that 70 percent of Last National's depositors have small account balances and 30 percent have large balances?
3. Why do statisticians use random samples?
4. A haphazard sample is not a random sample. Why not?
5. Describe how you would obtain a systematic random sample of 200 from a population list of 8000 elements.
6. Why is it that tasting a very small sample of a chunk of cheese is enough to determine whether or not you buy the chunk?
7. For what kind of population will cluster sampling work well?
8. Why are populations sometimes stratified before selecting clusters?
9. Given the six-element population

$$0 \quad 3 \quad 6 \quad 12 \quad 15 \quad 18$$

(a) What are the symbols for, and the values of, the population mean and standard deviation? (b) What are the symbols for, and the values of, the mean and standard deviation of the sampling distribution of the mean for samples of size 3? (c) How many samples of size 3 are there? (d) Compute the sampling distribution of the mean for samples of size 3. Present the distribution in a table. (e) Compute the values of $\mu_{\bar{x}}$ and $\sigma_{\bar{x}}$ from (d).
10. Suppose a friend says, "I know the formula for computing the standard error of the mean, but I don't understand what the standard error really is." Write a note to your friend explaining what the standard error really is.
11. The error in a sample proportion $\bar{p}$ is the difference between $\bar{p}$ and the population parameter p. Why would you expect the error to be larger the larger $\sigma_{\bar{p}}$ is?
12. (See Problem 11.) The United States government currently uses a sample of about 50,000 families (about 1 family per 1000 families in the population) to esti-

mate the nation's unemployment rate and other population parameters. Assume that 50,000 is adequate to provide estimates of sufficient precision for decision-making purposes. Now suppose the size of the population doubled. Would a sample of 100,000 families then be needed to provide sufficient precision? Explain.

13. Consolidated Grinding Supply makes and sells artificial diamonds in boxes of 50. Each box is a random sample of Consolidated's output. Diamonds in the output population have a mean weight of 2 carats and a standard deviation of 0.2 carat. Gary Abrasive Company bought one box. What is the probability that the mean weight of the 50 diamonds in Gary's box is between 1.95 and 2.05 carats?

14. Corporate Testing Services has found that the mean score made by job applicants on its Personality Scan test is 250, and the standard deviation of the scores is 50. The scores are normally distributed. If a random sample of 10 applicants takes the test, what is the probability that the sample mean score will be greater than (a) 250? (b) 270?

15. Moor's Distilling Corporation has an automatic beer bottle filling machine. The machine can be set to pour various amounts up to 36 ounces into bottles. The amounts poured have a mean which is the machine setting. Amounts poured are normally distributed with a standard deviation of 0.12 ounce. If a random sample of 12 bottles is selected, what is the probability that the sample mean amount of fill is more than 0.1 ounce below the machine setting?

16. If the percent of unemployed workers in a large region actually is 8 percent, what is the probability that the percent unemployed in a random sample of 850 workers would be higher than 9 percent?

17. Suppose that a random sample of 500 television viewers is taken. George Jorge argues that the percent watching a particular program could easily be 5 percentage points, or more, away from the actual (population) percent watching the show. If 35 percent of the population watched the show, what is the probability that the sample percent will differ by 5 percentage points or more from 35 percent?

10

STATISTICAL INFERENCE: ESTIMATION

10.1 INTRODUCTION

An increase of 1 percentage point in the nation's unemployment rate from, say, 6.9 to 7.9 percent, can, among other things, influence stock-market prices, trigger the transfer of millions of dollars to high-unemployment areas, and cause difficulty for an incumbent President of the United States who is seeking reelection. The fact is, however, that no one knows what the actual value of this important rate is. The figure we read and hear for the latest unemployment rate is obtained from a sample survey. The value is a sample *estimate* of a population parameter, the percent unemployed in the worker population. An error of one percentage point in estimating the rate would be intolerable. But how large might the error be? You will learn how to answer that question in this chapter. You will also learn to determine how large the error could be if the sample statistic $\bar{x}$ is used to estimate a population mean μ.

The sampling distribution of the mean (Chapter 9) shows how far sample means could be from a *known* population mean. Similarly, the sampling distribution of the proportion shows how far sample proportions could be from a *known* population proportion. Our problem in this chapter is to determine how far an *unknown* population mean could be from the mean of a simple random sample selected from that population; or how far an *unknown* population proportion could be from a sample proportion: Those are the concerns of *statistical inference*, in which a statement about an *unknown* population parameter is derived from information contained in a random sample selected from the population. The facts and formulas you learned in Chapter 9 play a major role in solving problems in statistical inference. In this chapter, as in the discussion of sampling distributions, the term random sample means a simple random sample.

10.2 POINT AND INTERVAL ESTIMATES OF POPULATION PARAMETERS

Point Estimates

An *estimator* is a sample statistic that is used to estimate an unknown parameter. A *point estimate* is a single value of an estimator. Thus, the sample average $\bar{x}$ is an estimator of the population mean μ. Suppose we have the following random sample of $n = 6$ elements from a population whose parameter values are not known:

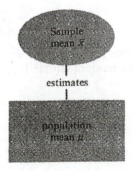

$$1 \quad 2 \quad 4 \quad 5 \quad 7 \quad 11$$

The sample mean is

$$\bar{x} = \frac{\Sigma x}{n} = \frac{30}{6} = 5$$

The estimator is $\bar{x}$, and 5 is a point estimate of the unknown population mean.

Next, note that our sample of $n = 6$ elements contains two even

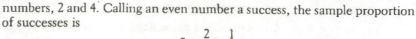
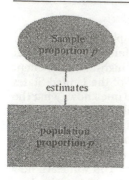

numbers, 2 and 4. Calling an even number a success, the sample proportion of successes is

$$\bar{p} = \frac{2}{6} = \frac{1}{3}$$

The statistic $\bar{p}$ is an estimator of the unknown population proportion of successes; and $\frac{1}{3}$ is a point estimate of the population proportion.

We shall use the symbol s_x to mean an estimator of the unknown population standard deviation σ_x. The estimator s_x, called the *sample standard deviation*, is defined by the formula

$$s_x = \sqrt{\frac{\Sigma(x - \bar{x})^2}{n - 1}}$$

where $\bar{x}$ = sample average
n = sample size

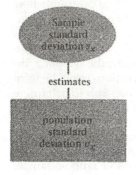

Note the divisor $n - 1$ (sample size minus 1) in the formula. Earlier, we used the divisor N when computing a population standard deviation σ_x. Why, then, do we use $n - 1$ rather than n when computing s_x? Two reasons are: (1) In order to compute a value for the estimator s_x, we have to use the value of one other estimator, $\bar{x}$: (2) s_x is used in making inferences about how far the unknown population mean μ might be from the sample mean $\bar{x}$—and these inferences are more likely to be correct if $n - 1$ rather than n is used in computing s_x.

EXERCISE For the random sample 1, 2, 4, 5, 7, 11, write the symbol for, and compute the value of, the sample standard deviation.
ANSWER $s_x = 3.633$.

$\sigma_{\bar{x}}$ is the standard deviation of the distribution of sample means—$\sigma_{\bar{x}}$ is called the standard error of the mean.

Next, recall (Chapter 9) that the standard error of the mean is computed by the formula $\sigma_{\bar{x}} = \sigma_x/\sqrt{n}$ when the sample size is less than 5 percent of the population size. In our work, the sample will be less than 5 percent of the population, and we will use $s_x/\sqrt{n}$ to estimate the standard error $\sigma_{\bar{x}}$. The symbol $s_{\bar{x}}$ is called the *sample standard error of the mean*. The formula for $s_{\bar{x}}$ is

$$s_{\bar{x}} = \frac{s_x}{\sqrt{n}}$$

where s_x = sample standard deviation
n = sample size

Thus, s_x is our estimator for σ_x, and $s_{\bar{x}}$ is our estimator for $\sigma_{\bar{x}}$.

In the last exercise, you computed $s_x = 3.633$ for the random sample 1, 2, 4, 5, 7, 11. The sample standard error of the mean is

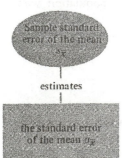

$$s_{\bar{x}} = \frac{s_x}{\sqrt{n}}$$

$$= \frac{3.633}{\sqrt{6}} = 1.483$$

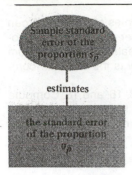

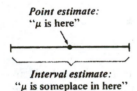

Soon you will learn that the estimator $s_{\bar{x}}$ plays a dominant role in determining how far an unknown population mean might be from a sample mean. Similarly, you will learn that the *sample standard error of the proportion* $s_{\bar{p}}$ plays a dominant role in determining how far an unknown population proportion might be from a sample proportion. We will use $s_{\bar{p}}$ as our estimator of $\sigma_{\bar{p}}$, the standard error of the proportion. The formula for $s_{\bar{p}}$ is

$$s_{\bar{p}} = \sqrt{\frac{\bar{p}\bar{q}}{n}}$$

where $\bar{p}$ = sample proportion of successes
$\bar{q} = 1 - \bar{p}$
n = sample size

EXERCISE Let an even number be a success, and suppose a sample of 200 numbers selected randomly from a population contains 120 even numbers. Write the symbol for, and compute the value of, the point estimate of the standard error of the proportion.
ANSWER $s_{\bar{p}} = 0.0346$.

Interval Estimates

An interval estimate describes a range of values within which a parameter might lie. For example, suppose we have the sample

1   2   4   5   7   11

Point estimate:
"μ is here"

Interval estimate:
"μ is someplace in here"

selected randomly from a population whose mean μ is unknown. The sample mean $\bar{x} = 5$ is our point estimate of μ. On the other hand, if we state that μ is between $\bar{x} - 1 = 4$ and $\bar{x} + 1 = 6$, the range of values from 4 to 6 is an interval estimate of μ. The interval just used for the estimate is 5 ± 1. Alternatively, we may write

$$4 \leq \mu \leq 6$$

which says that μ is between 4 and 6. The narrow part of the symbol $<$ points toward the smaller number. Thus, reading from the middle, the last statement says that μ is greater than or equal to 4, and μ is less than or equal to 6. You will learn how to construct interval estimates for μ after the following set of problems.

10.3 PROBLEMS

1. Distinguish between (a) $\bar{x}$ and μ; (b) s_x and σ_x; (c) $s_{\bar{x}}$ and $\sigma_{\bar{x}}$; (d) $\bar{p}$ and p; (e) $s_{\bar{p}}$ and $\sigma_{\bar{p}}$.

2. Write the symbol for (a) the point estimator of a population standard deviation; (b) the point estimator of the standard error of the mean; (c) the point estimator of the standard error of the proportion.

3. The standard error of the mean was defined in Chapter 9 as the standard deviation of the means of all simple random samples of size *n* that can be selected from a population. Usually, the number of samples is astronomically large. Can the standard error of the mean be estimated from the elements in *one* of these samples? If so, how is the estimate computed?

4. The elements in a random sample are 4, 10, 11, 13, 16, and 18. Compute the following point estimates: (*a*) the estimate of the population mean; (*b*) the estimate of the population standard deviation; (*c*) the estimate of the standard error of the mean.

5. In a random sample of size $n = 50$,

$$\Sigma(x - \bar{x})^2 = 449$$

Estimate the standard error of the mean.

6. In a random sample of 1600 voters, 480 voters were independents. Estimate the standard error of the proportion of independents.

7. A point estimate is correct if it is equal to the actual value of the parameter being estimated. An interval estimate is correct if the actual value of the parameter is in the interval. Which has the greater chance of being correct, a point estimate or an interval estimate?

8. (See Problem 7.) If two interval estimates, $10 \le \mu \le 12$ and $8 \le \mu \le 14$, are made from the same sample, which has the greater chance of being correct? Why?

10.4 CONFIDENCE INTERVAL ESTIMATES OF A POPULATION MEAN

Meaning of the Confidence Interval Estimate

An interval estimate of μ is an interval of values *a* to *b* within which an unknown population mean is expected to lie. The interval is an inference based upon (1) the value of the mean $\bar{x}$ of a simple random sample selected from the population, and (2) known facts about the sampling distribution of the mean (Chapter 9). We cannot be 100 percent certain that such an in-

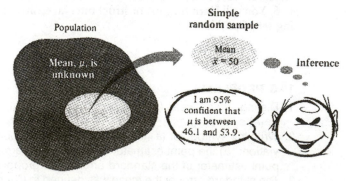

FIGURE 10.1
A statistical inference.

terval is correct (contains the unknown μ) because the sample is only part (and usually a very small part) of the population. A *confidence interval estimate of μ* is an interval estimate, together with a statement of how confident (e.g., 90 percent, 95 percent) we are that the interval is correct. Figure 10.1 illustrates the confidence interval concept. The choice of method used in constructing a confidence interval for μ depends upon whether or not the population is normal and whether the population standard deviation σ_x is known or unknown.

Confidence Interval Estimate of μ, Normal Population, σ_x Known

Suppose we have a normal population whose mean and standard deviation are μ and σ_x. Then (from Chapter 9) the sampling distribution of the mean will be normal with a mean of μ and a standard error of $\sigma_{\bar{x}} = \sigma_x/\sqrt{n}$. For the sampling distribution of the mean, the standard normal variable is

$$z = \frac{\bar{x} - \mu}{\sigma_{\bar{x}}}$$

At the point where $\bar{x} = \mu + 1.96\sigma_{\bar{x}}$, shown in Figure 10.2,

$$z = \frac{(\mu + 1.96\sigma_{\bar{x}}) - \mu}{\sigma_{\bar{x}}} = \frac{1.96\sigma_{\bar{x}}}{\sigma_{\bar{x}}} = 1.96$$

The z value 1.96 also appears in the figure.

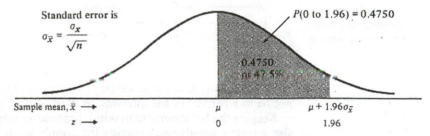

Standard error is

$$\sigma_{\bar{x}} = \frac{\sigma_x}{\sqrt{n}}$$

$P(0 \text{ to } 1.96) = 0.4750$

0.4750
or 47.5%

FIGURE 10.2
Sampling distribution of the mean.

Sample mean, $\bar{x} \longrightarrow$ μ $\mu + 1.96\sigma_{\bar{x}}$

$z \longrightarrow$ 0   1.96

From the standard normal probability table (Table V)

$$P(0 \text{ to } 1.96) = 0.4750$$

so 47.5 percent of the sample means fall in the interval from μ to $\mu + 1.96\sigma_{\bar{x}}$. Also, 47.5 percent of the sample means fall in the interval from μ to $\mu - 1.96\sigma_{\bar{x}}$. Thus, as shown in Figure 10.3, 95 percent fall in the interval $\mu \pm 1.96\sigma_{\bar{x}}$, that is the interval from $\mu - 1.96\sigma_{\bar{x}}$ to $\mu + 1.96\sigma_{\bar{x}}$.

Because 95 percent of the sample means are within $\pm 1.96\sigma_x$ of μ, it is also true that *μ is within $\pm 1.96\sigma_{\bar{x}}$ of 95 percent of the sample means*. To see the meaning of the last sentence, suppose we have the mean of one sample $\bar{x}_1$, and we write the interval

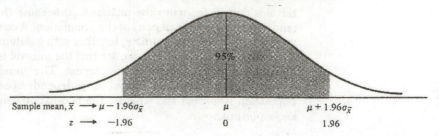

FIGURE 10.3
Ninety-five percent of
sample means are in
the interval
$\mu \pm 1.96\,\sigma_{\bar{x}}$.

Sample mean, $\bar{x}$ ⟶ $\mu - 1.96\sigma_{\bar{x}}$ μ $\mu + 1.96\sigma_{\bar{x}}$

z ⟶ -1.96 0 1.96

$$\bar{x}_1 - 1.96\sigma_{\bar{x}} \text{ to } \bar{x}_1 + 1.96\sigma_{\bar{x}}$$

shown in Figure 10.4. Now consider another sample whose mean is $\bar{x}_2$ and

FIGURE 10.4
A 95 percent confi-
dence interval.

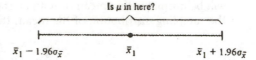

Is μ in here?

$\bar{x}_1 - 1.96\sigma_{\bar{x}}$ $\bar{x}_1$ $\bar{x}_1 + 1.96\sigma_{\bar{x}}$

write the interval

$$\bar{x}_2 - 1.96\sigma_{\bar{x}} \text{ to } \bar{x}_2 + 1.96\sigma_{\bar{x}}$$

shown in Figure 10.5. We could continue writing intervals using other

FIGURE 10.5
Another 95 percent
confidence interval.

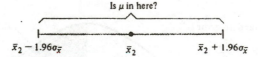

Is μ in here?

$\bar{x}_2 - 1.96\sigma_{\bar{x}}$ $\bar{x}_2$ $\bar{x}_2 + 1.96\sigma_{\bar{x}}$

sample means $\bar{x}_3$, $\bar{x}_4$, and so on. The question in each case is "Is μ in this interval?" The answer is that μ will be in 95 percent of the intervals, and μ will not be in 5 percent of the intervals, as illustrated in Figure 10.6.

Keeping the last statement in mind, suppose we select only *one* sample of size n from a population, compute the sample mean $\bar{x}$, then state that μ is between $\bar{x} - 1.96\sigma_{\bar{x}}$ and $\bar{x} + 1.96\sigma_{\bar{x}}$. The statement is either correct (μ is in the interval), or incorrect (μ is not in the interval). However, we are quite confident that the statement is correct because 95 percent of such statements are correct.

The *proportion of correct statements* (0.95 in our illustration) *is called the confidence coefficient C*. The number $100C$ percent (95 percent in our illustration) *is called the confidence level*. The *proportion of incorrect statements is symbolized by the Greek letter α (alpha)*. The sum of the proportions of correct and incorrect statements is 1; so

$$C + \alpha = 1 \qquad \text{or} \qquad \alpha = 1 - C$$

We can describe C as the chance that a confidence interval is correct, and α as the chance that an interval is incorrect.

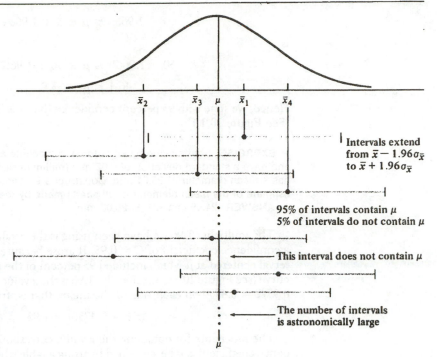

Intervals extend
from $\bar{x} - 1.96\sigma_{\bar{x}}$
to $\bar{x} + 1.96\sigma_{\bar{x}}$

95% of intervals contain μ
5% of intervals do not contain μ

This interval does not contain μ

The number of intervals
is astronomically large

FIGURE 10.6
Ninety-five percent of
the intervals contain μ.

*See Figure 10.2 for
the relation between
$1.96\sigma_{\bar{x}}$ and 95
percent.*

·The interval from $\bar{x} - 1.96\sigma_{\bar{x}}$ to $\bar{x} + 1.96\sigma_{\bar{x}}$ is called a 95 percent confidence interval (CI) estimate of μ because the z value is 1.96. We can express this interval as $\bar{x} \pm 1.96\sigma_{\bar{x}}$, or as

$$95 \text{ percent CI: } \bar{x} - 1.96\sigma_{\bar{x}} \leq \mu \leq \bar{x} + 1.96\sigma_{\bar{x}}$$

Reading from μ, the expression states that μ is greater than or equal to $\bar{x} - 1.96\sigma_{\bar{x}}$, and less than or equal to $\bar{x} + 1.96\sigma_{\bar{x}}$.

EXAMPLE A normal population has a standard deviation of 10. A random sample of size 25 has a mean of 50.0. Construct a 95 percent confidence interval estimate of the population mean.

SOLUTION The information given is

$$\sigma_x = 10 \qquad n = 25 \qquad \bar{x} = 50$$

Step 1 *Compute $\sigma_{\bar{x}}$.* First, we must compute the standard error of the mean $\sigma_{\bar{x}}$. It is

$$\sigma_{\bar{x}} = \frac{\sigma_x}{\sqrt{n}}$$

$$= \frac{10}{\sqrt{25}} = 2$$

Step 2 *Find the interval $\bar{x} \pm 1.96\sigma_{\bar{x}}$.* The 95 percent confidence interval,

$$\bar{x} - 1.96\sigma_{\bar{x}} \le \mu \le \bar{x} + 1.96\sigma_{\bar{x}}$$

is

$$50 - 1.96(2) \le \mu \le 50 + 1.96(2)$$

$$46.1 \le \mu \le 53.9$$

Hence, we state with 95 percent confidence that μ is between 46.1 and 53.9. (See Figure 10.1.)

EXERCISE Shafts made by an automatic machine are normally distributed and have a standard deviation of 0.02 mm (millimeter). A sample of four shafts has a mean diameter of 25.01 mm. Construct a 95 percent confidence interval estimate of the mean diameter of all shafts made by the machine.
ANSWER 24.99 mm $\le \mu \le$ 25.03 mm.

The multiplier 1.96 we have been using is the z value that corresponds to a confidence coefficient of $C = 0.95$. It arose because we started with an interval centered at μ which included 95 percent of the area under the normal curve (see Figure 10.3). Specifically, 1.96 is the z value which gives an area of $0.95/2 = 0.4750$ on each side of the mean; that is, from Table V

$$(z|P = 0.4750) = 1.96$$

The procedure for obtaining the z value corresponding to a stated confidence coefficient can be simplified by using a table which gives the value of z for a specified one-tail area. Suppose, for example, that we want C to be 0.99. Then, as shown in Figure 10.7, 0.99 is the central area, and the area in the two tails is

$$1 - C = 1 - 0.99 = 0.01$$

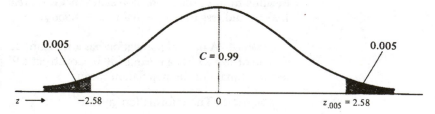

FIGURE 10.7
For a one-tail area of
0.005, z is 2.58.

Half of the·two-tail area, 0.005, is in each tail. Now refer to Table 10.1, which is part of Table VI at the end of the book. The entries in the margins are one-tail areas; the numbers in the body of the table are z values corresponding to the right-tail areas. Thus, for our right-tail area of 0.005, the z value is 2.58. We will use a subscript on z to mean the positive z value for the right-tail area corresponding to the subscript. Thus, $z_{0.005}$ means z for a right-tail area of 0.005, and (from Table 10.1)

TABLE 10.1
z VALUES FOR ONE-TAIL AREAS
(See also Table VI)

	Area	0.000	0.001	0.002	0.003	0.004	0.005	0.006
For a right-tail area	0.00		3.09	2.88	2.75	2.65	2.58	2.51
of 0.005,	0.01	2.33	2.29	2.26	2.23	2.20	2.17	2.14
	0.02	2.05	2.03	2.01	2.00	1.98	1.96	1.94
z = 2.58	0.05	1.64	1.64	1.63	1.62	1.61	1.60	1.59

$$z_{0.005} = 2.58$$

Similarly, for $C = 0.95$ (95 percent confidence interval) the area of the two tails is 0.05; so the right-tail area is

$$\frac{0.05}{2} = 0.025$$

Hence, from Table 10.1,

$$z_{0.025} = 1.96$$

is the z value we used earlier in constructing 95 percent confidence intervals.

EXERCISE Use Table 10.1 to find the z value that corresponds to a 96 percent confidence interval.
ANSWER 2.05.

The one-tail area subscript we have used for z is $\alpha/2$. To illustrate, suppose that $C = 0.95$ (confidence level 95 percent). Then, since $C + \alpha = 1$,

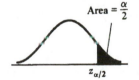

Area $= \frac{\alpha}{2}$

$z_{\alpha/2}$

$$\alpha = 1 - C$$
$$= 1 - 0.95$$
$$= 0.05$$

The α value, 0.05, is the two-tail area. The right-tail area that we need to enter Table 10.1 (or Table VI) is

$$\frac{\alpha}{2} = \frac{0.05}{2} = 0.025$$

Then

$$z_{\alpha/2} = z_{0.025} = 1.96$$

For a 98 percent interval

$\alpha = 1 - 0.98 = 0.02$,

In general the z value to use for a confidence coefficient of C is found by first computing

$$\alpha = 1 - C$$

Next, compute

and $\dfrac{\alpha}{2} = 0.01$. $$\frac{\alpha}{2} = \frac{1 - C}{2}$$

Then the z value to be used is $z_{\alpha/2}$, which can be found in Table VI. Figure 10.8 shows the relationship between a stated confidence coefficient C and the $z_{\alpha/2}$ value to be used in constructing the confidence interval.

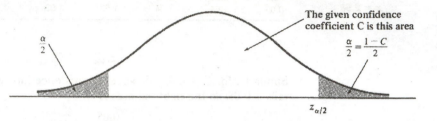

FIGURE 10.8
$z_{\alpha/2}$ is the z value for a one-tail area of $\alpha/2$.

If we want a 90 percent confidence interval ($C = 0.90$) we first compute

$$\alpha = 1 - C$$

$$= 1 - 0.90 = 0.10$$

$$\frac{\alpha}{2} = 0.05$$

Then, from Table 10.1 (or Table VI), we find

$$z_{\alpha/2} = z_{0.05} = 1.64$$

A 90 percent confidence interval therefore would be

$$\bar{x} - 1.64\sigma_{\bar{x}} \leq \mu \leq \bar{x} + 1.64\sigma_{\bar{x}}$$

Or, because $\sigma_{\bar{x}} = \sigma_x/\sqrt{n}$, we can write

$$\bar{x} - 1.64\frac{\sigma_x}{\sqrt{n}} \leq \mu \leq 1.64\frac{\sigma_x}{\sqrt{n}}$$

In general, we have

$$\bar{x} - z_{\alpha/2}\frac{\sigma_x}{\sqrt{n}} \leq \mu \leq \bar{x} + z_{\alpha/2}\frac{\sigma_x}{\sqrt{n}}$$

where $\bar{x}$ = sample mean
$\alpha = 1 - C$
σ_x = population standard deviation
n = sample size
μ = unknown population mean

Confidence interval estimate of μ: normal population; σ_x known, confidence coefficient C

The procedure followed in constructing the confidence interval is shown in Figure 10.9.

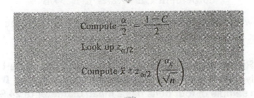

FIGURE 10.9
Confidence interval estimate of μ, normal population σ_x known.

EXAMPLE A normal population has a standard deviation of 10. A random sample of size 15 selected from the population has a mean of 52.50. Construct the 80 percent confidence interval estimate of the population mean.

SOLUTION The given information is

$$\sigma_x = 10 \qquad n = 15 \qquad \bar{x} = 52.50 \qquad C = 0.80$$

Step 1 *Compute $\alpha/2$ from the confidence coefficient.* First we find

$$\alpha = 1 - C$$
$$= 1 - 0.80 = 0.20$$

Then

$$\frac{\alpha}{2} = \frac{0.20}{2} = 0.10$$

Step 2 *In Table VI, find the z value for that $\alpha/2$.* and, from Table VI, $z_{\alpha/2}$ is

$$z_{0.10} = 1.28$$

The confidence interval,

Step 3 Construct the confidence interval.

$$\bar{x} - z_{\alpha/2}\frac{\sigma_x}{\sqrt{n}} \le \mu \le \bar{x} + z_{\alpha/2}\frac{\sigma_x}{\sqrt{n}}$$

is

$$52.50 - 1.28\frac{10}{\sqrt{15}} \le \mu \le 52.50 + 1.28\frac{10}{\sqrt{15}}$$

$$52.50 - 3.30 \le \mu \le 52.50 + 3.30$$

so that

$$80 \text{ percent CI: } 49.2 \le \mu \le 55.8$$

Thus, with 80 percent confidence, we can say the unknown population mean is between 49.2 and 55.8.

EXERCISE Bolts made by an automatic machine have lengths which are normally distributed with a standard deviation of 0.02 mm (millimeter). A random sample of four bolts has a mean diameter of 24.98 mm. Construct the 98 percent confidence interval for the mean diameter of all bolts made by the machine.
ANSWER $24.96 \le \mu \le 25.00$ mm.

Precision, Confidence, and Sample Size We say that the narrower a confidence interval is, the more *precise* it is; and the wider the interval, the less precise is the interval. For example, the interval $9 \le \mu \le 11$ is more precise (narrower) than the interval $6 \le \mu \le 14$. The endpoints of a confidence interval for μ are

A narrower confidence interval is more precise.

$$\bar{x} \pm z_{\alpha/2}\frac{\sigma_x}{\sqrt{n}}$$

The smaller the value of

$$z_{\alpha/2}\frac{\sigma_x}{\sqrt{n}}$$

the more precise (narrower) is the confidence interval. Consequently, the smaller $z_{\alpha/2}$ and σ_x are, and the larger n is, the more precise will be the interval; that's because $z_{\alpha/2}$ and σ_x are in the numerator of the last expression and n is in the denominator. (The smaller the numerator and the larger the denominator, the smaller is the value of a fraction.)

Larger samples give more precise estimates.

We conclude that the larger the sample size, the more precise is an interval estimate. That makes sense because, for example, a sample of 100 should provide a more precise estimate than a sample of 50. Also, the smaller the population variability, which is measured by σ_x, the more precise will be an interval estimate. The point of the last sentence is that if the numbers in a population are close to μ, so σ_x is small, the numbers in a random sample also will be close to μ, so the sample mean will be close to μ. Finally, the lower the confidence coefficient, the smaller $z_{\alpha/2}$ will be; for ex-

Smaller variability leads to more precise estimates.

Lower confidence coefficients C allow us to construct more precise estimates.

ample, if $C = 0.99$, $z_{\alpha/2} = 2.58$, but if $C = 0.90$, $z_{\alpha/2} = 1.64$; consequently, the lower the confidence level, the more precise will be an interval estimate. That makes sense because it says we have low confidence in very precise estimates, and higher confidence in less precise estimates; for example, we would have less confidence in the estimate $9.9 \leq \mu \leq 10.1$ than in the estimate $6 \leq \mu \leq 14$.

We can control the precision of an interval estimate by our choice of sample size and confidence level. We cannot control the variability of a population; σ_x is what it is; the less variable a population is, the more precise will be an interval estimate of its mean.

EXERCISE Assume populations are normal. (a) Suppose the mean of a random sample of $n = 25$ is $\bar{x} = 50$. Construct the 95 percent confidence interval for μ if $\sigma_x = 10$. (b) Suppose $n = 100$ and $\bar{x} = 50$. Construct the 90 percent confidence interval estimate of μ if $\sigma_x = 4$. (c) Which interval estimate, (a) or (b), is more precise? Why?
ANSWER (a) $46.1 \leq \mu \leq 53.9$. (b) $49.3 \leq \mu \leq 50.7$. (c) (b) is more precise (narrower) because, compared with (a), population variability is smaller, the confidence level is lower, and the sample size is larger.

Confidence Interval Estimate of μ, Normal Population, σ_x Unknown

If we know that the population is normal, and we know the population standard deviation σ_x, the confidence interval for μ should be constructed in the manner already shown, using the normal curve $z_{\alpha/2}$ value. Usually, however, if μ is unknown, σ_x also is unknown; then σ_x must be estimated from the sample. The estimator, as discussed earlier, is the sample standard deviation

When σ_x is unknown, use s_x in place of σ_x.

$$s_x = \sqrt{\frac{\Sigma(x - \bar{x})^2}{n - 1}}$$

Then the standard error of the mean $\sigma_{\bar{x}} = \sigma_x/\sqrt{n}$ is estimated by the sample standard error of the mean

$s_x/\sqrt{n}$ is an estimator of $\sigma_x/\sqrt{n}$.

$$s_{\bar{x}} = \frac{s_x}{\sqrt{n}}$$

When σ_x is known, so that $\sigma_{\bar{x}}$ can be computed, the confidence interval we developed earlier was based on the fact that the variable

$$z = \frac{\bar{x} - \mu}{\sigma_x}$$

has the standard normal distribution; that's why we used $z_{\alpha/2}$ (z for normal) in constructing intervals. However, if $\sigma_{\bar{x}}$ is estimated by $s_{\bar{x}}$, the variable

The distribution of t is not a normal distribution.

$$t = \frac{\bar{x} - \mu}{s_{\bar{x}}}$$

does not have a normal distribution. In the early 1900s, W. S. Gosset, an employee of the Guinness Brewery in Dublin, Ireland, studied the distribution of t. Gosset published his results under the pen name of "Student." Consequently the t distribution is often referred to as Student's t distribution.

There is a different t distribution for each sample size. The distributions are symmetrical but have higher tails than the standard normal distribution. Figure 10.10 shows a standard normal distribution, and t distributions for

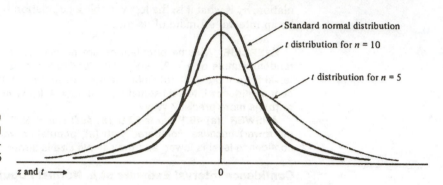

FIGURE 10.10
The standard normal distribution and t distributions for $n = 5$ and $n = 10$.

sample sizes $n = 5$ and $n = 10$. The smaller the sample size, the higher are the tails of the t distribution. Thus, the t distribution for $n = 5$ has higher tails than the one for $n = 10$, and both have higher tails than the normal distribution. Consequently, the t value for a given right tail area is greater than the z value for the same area. For example, Figure 10.11 shows $z_{0.025} = 1.96$,

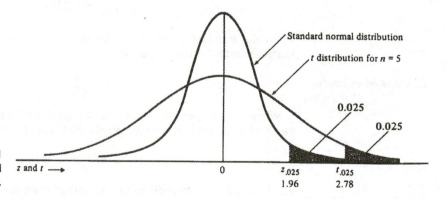

FIGURE 10.11
For the same right-tail area, t is larger than z.

the point such that the normal curve tail area is 0.025. The t tail starting from the point 1.96 contains more than 0.025. To reduce the t tail area to 0.025, we must move to the right of 1.96 to the larger value, 2.78.

Tail areas for t distributions are tabulated according to a parameter called

v means "degrees of freedom."

degrees of freedom. We shall use the symbol v for degrees of freedom. In this chapter

$$\text{Degrees of freedom} = v = n - 1$$

that is, v is the sample size minus 1. It will help here, and in other chapters where v is something other than $n - 1$, to think of degrees of freedom in the following way: Consider a set of $n = 5$ numbers whose mean is $\bar{x} = 8$, so that the sum of the 5 numbers must be $5(8) = 40$. Suppose we want to construct such a set of numbers. Then we are *free* to choose any four numbers, arbitrarily. But we are not free to choose the fifth number, because it must be the number which will make the sum of the five numbers equal to 40. For example, suppose we write any four numbers, say

$$-4 \quad 12 \quad 8 \quad 10$$

The sum of the four numbers is

$$-4 + 12 + 8 + 10 = 26$$

so the fifth number *must* be 14 to make the sum equal to 40. Thus, if 5 numbers are constrained by the condition that their sum must equal 40, we can choose 4 numbers freely; so we have $5 - 1 = 4$ degrees of freedom. In general, if n numbers are constrained to have a given sum (or mean), the constraint results in the loss of one degree of freedom, and we have $n - 1$ degrees of freedom.

One degree of freedom is lost when the mean is specified.

Table VII at the end of the book provides t values for one-tail areas of t distributions. Table 10.2 shows part of Table VII.

TABLE 10.2
STUDENT'S t DISTRIBUTION (t VALUES FOR SELECTED ONE-TAIL AREAS)
(See also Table VII)

Degrees of freedom	Tail area		
v	0.05	0.025	0.01
5	2.02	2.57	3.36
15	1.75	2.13	2.60
30	1.70	2.04	2.46
60	1.67	2.00	2.39
∞	1.64*	1.96*	2.33*

* These are z values for the one-tail areas.

When n is large, the t distribution is almost the standard normal distribution.

In Table 10.2, observe that the t values in each of the tail area columns decrease as v increases; and the bottom-line entry (*) is the normal curve z value. Thus, t distributions approach the standard normal distribution as degrees of freedom v increase. Or, since $v = n - 1$, we can say that t distributions approach normality as n increases. We see again the "tendency toward normality as n increases." Tables for t values usually contain all degrees of freedom from 1 to 30, but few, if any, for more than 30 degrees of freedom. That's because statisticians generally use the normal (z) table for sample sizes of greater than 30.

To use the t table, we need to know two numbers, the tail area and the degrees of freedom. We shall use the symbol

$$t_{\alpha/2,v}$$

Meaning of $t_{\alpha/2,v}$ to mean the t value for a one-tail area of $\alpha/2$ and v degrees of freedom. For example, if α is 0.05 and the sample size is $n = 16$, so that

$$\frac{\alpha}{2} = \frac{0.05}{2} = 0.025$$

and

$$v = 16 - 1 = 15$$

then

$$t_{\alpha/2,v} = t_{0.025,15} = 2.13$$

from Table 10.2 (or Table VII).

The formula for confidence interval estimates of μ with σ_x known was

$$\bar{x} - z_{\alpha/2} \frac{\sigma_x}{\sqrt{n}} \le \mu \le \bar{x} + z_{\alpha/2} \frac{\sigma_x}{\sqrt{n}}$$

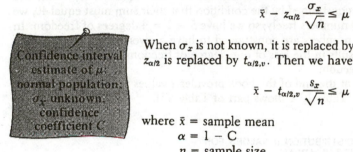

When σ_x is not known, it is replaced by s_x (computed from the sample), and $z_{\alpha/2}$ is replaced by $t_{\alpha/2,v}$. Then we have

$$\bar{x} - t_{\alpha/2,v} \frac{s_x}{\sqrt{n}} \le \mu \le \bar{x} + t_{\alpha/2,v} \frac{s_x}{\sqrt{n}}$$

Confidence interval estimate of μ; normal population; σ_x unknown; confidence coefficient C

where $\bar{x}$ = sample mean
$\alpha = 1 - C$
n = sample size
$v = n - 1$ (degrees of freedom)
s_x = sample standard deviation
μ = unknown population mean

The procedure followed in constructing the confidence interval is shown in Figure 10.12.

EXAMPLE The environmental protection officer of a large industrial plant sought to determine the mean daily amount of sulfur oxides (a pollutant) emitted by the plant. Because measurement costs were high, only a random sample of 10 days' measurements were obtained: These were, in tons per day,

8   7   10   15   11   6   8   5   13   12

Suppose emissions per day are normally distributed. Estimate μ, the mean amount of sulfur oxides emitted per day, using a confidence interval with a confidence coefficient of 0.95.

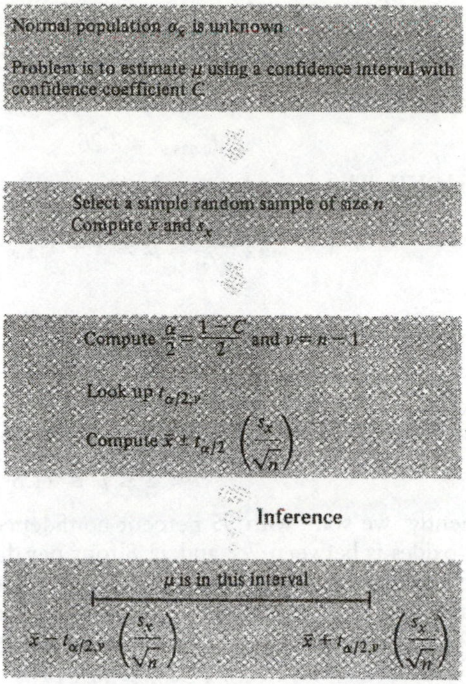

Normal population σ_x is unknown

Problem is to estimate μ using a confidence interval with confidence coefficient C

Select a simple random sample of size n
Compute $\bar{x}$ and s_x

Compute $\frac{\alpha}{2} = \frac{1-C}{2}$ and $\nu = n - 1$

Look up $t_{\alpha/2,\nu}$

Compute $\bar{x} \pm t_{\alpha/2} \left(\frac{s_x}{\sqrt{n}} \right)$

Inference

FIGURE 10.12
Confidence interval for μ, normal population, σ_x unknown.

μ is in this interval

$$\bar{x} - t_{\alpha/2,\nu} \left(\frac{s_x}{\sqrt{n}} \right) \qquad \bar{x} + t_{\alpha/2,\nu} \left(\frac{s_x}{\sqrt{n}} \right)$$

Step 1 *Compute $\bar{x}$.*

SOLUTION First we compute the sample mean

$$\bar{x} = \frac{8 + 7 + 10 + 15 + 11 + 6 + 8 + 5 + 13 + 12}{10} = \frac{95}{10}$$

$$= 9.5 \text{ tons per day}$$

Next we estimate σ_x by

Step 2 *Compute s_x.*

$$s_x = \sqrt{\frac{\Sigma(x - \bar{x})^2}{n - 1}}$$

For our sample we compute

$$s_x = \sqrt{\frac{(8 - 9.5)^2 + (7 - 9.5)^2 + (10 - 9.5)^2 + \cdots + (13 - 9.5)^2 + (12 - 9.5)^2}{10 - 1}}$$

$$= \sqrt{\frac{94.5}{9}} = 3.24 \text{ tons per day}$$

The confidence level is 95 percent; so $C = 0.95$ and

$$\alpha = 1 - C$$

$$= 1 - 0.95 = 0.05$$

Step 3 *Compute $\alpha/2$ and ν.*

$$\frac{\alpha}{2} = \frac{0.05}{2} = 0.025$$

Next we compute $v = n - 1$,

$$v = 10 - 1 = 9$$

Step 4 Look up $t_{\alpha/2,v}$. Then we find

$$t_{0.025,9} = 2.26$$

from Table VII. The desired interval

Step 5 Construct the confidence interval.

$$\bar{x} - t_{\alpha/2,v} \frac{s_x}{\sqrt{n}} \leq \mu \leq \bar{x} + t_{\alpha/2,v} \frac{s_x}{\sqrt{n}}$$

is

$$9.5 - (2.26) \frac{3.24}{\sqrt{10}} \leq \mu \leq 9.5 + (2.26) \frac{3.24}{\sqrt{10}}$$

$$9.5 - 2.3 \leq \mu \leq 9.5 + 2.3$$

so that

$$7.2 \leq \mu \leq 11.8$$

Consequently, we state with 95 percent confidence that the mean output of sulfur oxides is between 7.2 and 11.8 tons per day.

In the example, if we had known σ_x, and it was 3.24 tons per day, we would have used $z_{0.025} = 1.96$ rather than $t = 2.26$ in construction of the interval. The result would have been the more precise (narrower) interval

$$7.5 \leq \mu \leq 11.5$$

In general, interval estimates of μ are more precise when we know σ_x than when we do not know σ_x and have to estimate it from a sample.

EXERCISE See the last example. Suppose that for another random sample, this time with $n = 16$ days, the sample mean emission is 10.3 tons per day and the sample standard deviation is 3 tons per day. Construct a 90 percent confidence interval estimate of μ.
ANSWER $9.0 \leq \mu \leq 11.6$ tons per day.

Approximate Confidence Interval Estimates of μ

In the usual situation encountered in practice, we do not know the value of σ_x and we are not sure the population is normally distributed. However, we do know (Chapter 9) that for samples of more than 30 ($n > 30$), the distribution of sample means is nearly normal even though the population is not normal. Second, experimentation has shown t distributions for $n > 30$ provide good approximations of confidence intervals for skewed (nonnormal) populations which are unimodal (have one peak). Third, as we saw in Table 10.2, t distributions are nearly normal when n is more than 30. Statisticians have used the foregoing three facts to formulate a rule of thumb, which is as **When $n > 30$, use normal (z) values.** follows: When σ_x is not known, but $n > 30$, estimate σ_x by s_x, but use the normal (z value) tail areas in constructing approximate interval estimates of a population mean. Thus,

Approximate confidence interval estimate of μ: $n > 30$, confidence coefficient C

$$\bar{x} - z_{\alpha/2}\frac{s_x}{\sqrt{n}} \le \mu \le \bar{x} + z_{\alpha/2}\frac{s_x}{\sqrt{n}}$$

where $\bar{x}$ = sample mean
$\alpha = 1 - C$
n = sample size
s_x = sample standard deviation
μ = unknown population mean

The procedure followed in constructing the confidence interval is shown in Figure 10.13.

Any population σ_x is unknown

Problem is to estimate μ using a confidence interval with confidence coefficient C

Select a simple random sample of size $n > 30$
Compute $\bar{x}$ and s_x

Compute $\dfrac{\alpha}{2} = \dfrac{1 - C}{2}$

Look up $z_{\alpha/2}$

Compute $\bar{x} \pm z_{\alpha/2}\left(\dfrac{s_x}{\sqrt{n}}\right)$

Inference

μ is in this interval

$\bar{x} - z_{\alpha/2}\left(\dfrac{s_x}{\sqrt{n}}\right)$ $\bar{x} + z_{\alpha/2}\left(\dfrac{s_x}{\sqrt{n}}\right)$

FIGURE 10.13
Confidence interval for μ, $n > 30$, any population, σ_x unknown.

In the problems which follow, use the z table when $n > 30$. When $n \le 30$ and σ_x *is not known*, use the t table. If the population is normal and σ_x is *known*, use the z table for any sample size.

10.5 PROBLEMS

1. (a) What is the numerical value of $z_{0.01}$? (b) What is the meaning of the value in (a)?

2. With reference to confidence intervals, what is the meaning of α?
3. A time study has been carried out at a manufacturing plant owned by Target Industries, Inc., to determine how long it takes, on the average, to assemble a gyroscope. Random sample times, in hours, were

$$3.6 \quad 4.2 \quad 4.0 \quad 3.5 \quad 3.8 \quad 3.1$$

Suppose the population of assembly times has a normal distribution whose standard deviation is 0.3 hour. Construct a 98 percent confidence interval for the population mean assembly time.
4. The standard deviation of the amounts poured into bottles by an automatic filling machine is 1.8 ml (ml means milliliter). The amounts of fill in a random sample of bottles, in ml, were

$$481 \quad 479 \quad 482 \quad 480 \quad 477 \quad 478 \quad 481 \quad 482$$

Suppose the population of amounts of fill is normal. Construct a 90 percent confidence interval for the mean amount in all bottles filled by the machine.
5. (a) What is the meaning of $t_{0.01,5}$? (b) Write the expression for a 90 percent confidence interval estimate of μ based on a random sample of size 10 selected from a normal population.
6. (See Problem 3.) Suppose you think the standard deviation, 0.3 hour, is incorrect. Construct the confidence interval using the sample estimate of σ_x.
7. (See Problem 4.) Suppose you think the standard deviation, 1.8 ml, is incorrect. Construct the confidence interval using the sample estimate of σ_x.
8. Jacobs Media Research, Inc., paid respondents in a random sample of 100 households in the New England states to record TV viewing times in diaries. The sample mean number of hours per respondent spent viewing programs on the VBC network during the 6 to 7:30 p.m. period each day was 35 minutes, and the sample standard deviation was 10.2 minutes. Construct the 95 percent confidence interval for mean VBC viewing time per household in the New England states.
9. (See Problem 8.) Fifteen of the respondents in the sample are from Maine. Their reported numbers of minutes spent viewing VBC programs are shown in Table A. Suppose that viewing times are normally distributed. Construct the 95 percent confidence interval for mean viewing time per household in Maine.

TABLE A

90	24	24	15	18
42	30	10	15	45
15	42	50	0	30

10. (See Problem 9.) In checking the diaries, it was found that the first

listed item (the 90 in Table A) was listed for some other network. Replace the 90 with a zero, and then recompute the 95 percent confidence interval.

11. A random sample of regular gas prices at 36 stations in Los Angeles had a mean of $1.60 per gallon; the sample standard deviation was 0.9 cent per gallon. Construct confidence intervals for the mean gas price at all Los Angeles stations with confidence coefficient (a) 0.90; (b) 0.998. (c) Refer to your answers for (a) and (b). State which is the more precise interval, and why that interval is the more precise of the two intervals.

12. The manager of the Dallas regional sales office of Multiform, Inc., a national company, is required to prepare a forecast of regional sales of the company products in the coming year. The manager selected a random sample of 36 customers (companies) in the Dallas region. Then the manager obtained estimates of next year's purchases of Multiform products from the purchasing agent in each of the sample companies. The sample mean for product X2B was 50 units per company, and the standard deviation was 12 units per company. Construct the 98 percent confidence interval for mean purchases of X2Bs per company for all customer companies in the region.

13. (See Problem 12.) There are 2000 Multiform customers in the Dallas region. (a) If you knew μ, the population mean purchase of X2Bs, how would you compute total purchases? (b) Construct a 98 percent confidence interval for total purchases of X2Bs in the Dallas region.

14. A jar contains 1000 marbles which look alike to the eye. However, their weights vary but are normally distributed. A random sample of 2 marbles is selected. One weighs 4.60 grams and the other weighs 4.50 grams. (a) Construct the 50 percent confidence interval estimate of the mean weight per marble for all the marbles in the jar. (b) If you knew the mean weight of all the marbles μ, how would you compute the total weight of all the marbles? (c) Construct the 50 percent confidence interval for the weight of all the marbles in the jar. (d) Construct the 98 percent confidence interval for the weight of all the marbles in the jar.

15. A quality-control inspector for Baum Machine Tool Co. selects frequent random samples of size $n = 6$ from the output of an automatic lathe to check on the average diameter μ of parts being made. Diameters are normally distributed. One sample of six had a mean diameter of 2.0016 inches and a standard deviation of 0.0012 inch. Construct the 99 percent confidence interval for μ.

16. Fran and Dan estimated sales of a new product from data obtained in a random sample of customers. They used the same data and their calculations were correct. Both used the z table in constructing an interval estimate of total product sales. Nevertheless, Fran's estimate was more precise than Dan's. (a) What is the meaning of the statement that Fran's estimate was more precise than Dan's? (b) Why was Fran's estimate more precise than Dan's?

17. Suppose a normal population has a known (fixed) standard deviation. (a) What will determine the precision of a 95 percent confidence interval estimate of the population mean constructed from a sample? (b) How can the precision of a 95 percent confidence interval be increased?

18. A random sample of 50 stocks traded on the New York Stock Exchange had a mean price of $57.42; the sample standard deviation was $6.28. Construct a 90 percent confidence interval estimate of the mean price of all stocks traded on the NYSE.

19. A normal population has a standard deviation of 8. The mean of a random sample of size 5 selected from the population is 60. Construct the 95 percent confidence interval estimate of μ.

10.6 APPROXIMATE CONFIDENCE INTERVAL ESTIMATE OF A POPULATION PROPORTION

Often we wish to estimate an unknown population proportion, such as the proportion of television viewers who watched a particular program. The symbol p represents the population proportion of "successes," and $q = 1 - p$. Thus, a television program viewer is a success and p is the population proportion of viewers; $q = 1 - p$ is the proportion of the population who did not watch the program.

If a simple random sample of size n is selected from a population that has p as the proportion of successes, the sample proportion of successes is symbolized as $\bar{p}$; and $\bar{q} = 1 - \bar{p}$. The formulas are

$$\bar{p} = \frac{\text{number of successes in a sample of size } n}{n}$$

$$\bar{q} = 1 - \bar{p}$$

The hypergeometric distribution or the binomial distribution (Chapter 7) is the correct probability distribution to use in constructing confidence interval estimates of p, but the calculations are complicated and time-consuming; so we will base our interval estimates on the normal distribution.

This is another normal approximation of a distribution that "tends to normality."

You learned in Chapter 9 that the sampling distribution of p is nearly normal if n, the sample size, is "sufficiently" large. In Chapter 9 the rule of thumb was that n is sufficiently large if both np and nq are greater than 5. That rule assumes that we know the value of p. Here we will use $\bar{p}$ as the estimator of p, and the *rule of thumb we shall follow is that both $n\bar{p}$ and $n\bar{q}$ should be greater than 15* $(n\bar{p} \geq 15$ and $n\bar{q} \geq 15)$.

The sampling distribution of p (Chapter 9) has a mean of p and a standard error of

$$\sigma_{\bar{p}} = \sqrt{\frac{pq}{n}}$$

When constructing a confidence interval for the unknown value of p, we use the estimator $\bar{p}$ in place of p in the formula. Next we compute the sample standard error of the proportion,

$$s_{\bar{p}} = \sqrt{\frac{\bar{p}\bar{q}}{n}}$$

and use $s_{\bar{p}}$ as the estimator of $\sigma_{\bar{p}}$. Then we have

$$\bar{p} - z_{\alpha/2}\sqrt{\frac{\bar{p}\bar{q}}{n}} \le p \le \bar{p} + z_{\alpha/2}\sqrt{\frac{\bar{p}\bar{q}}{n}}$$

> **Approximate confidence interval for p: $n\bar{p} > 15$, $n\bar{q} > 15$, confidence coefficient C**

where $\bar{p}$ = sample proportion of successes
$\bar{q} = 1 - \bar{p}$
$\alpha = 1 - C$
n = sample size

Note that the interval statement just written has the same form as the statement for estimating μ; but now we use $\bar{p}$ rather than $\bar{x}$, and $s_{\bar{p}} = \sqrt{\bar{p}\bar{q}/n}$ rather than $s_{\bar{x}} = s_x/\sqrt{n}$. The procedure followed in constructing the confidence interval is shown in Figure 10.14.

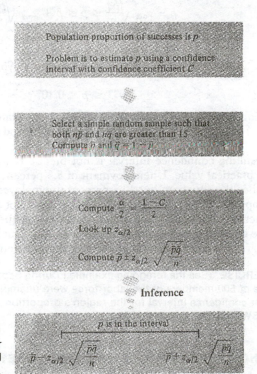

FIGURE 10.14
Confidence interval for p, $n\bar{p} > 15$, and $n\bar{q} > 15$.

EXAMPLE Last July, a random sample of 400 members of the labor force in a five-state region showed that 32 were unemployed. Construct the 95 percent confidence interval for the proportion unemployed in the region.

Step 1 *Compute $\bar{p}$.*

SOLUTION First we compute the sample proportion unemployed,

$$\bar{p} = \frac{32}{400} = 0.08$$

Then, with $C = 0.95$ (95 percent), we have

$$\alpha = 1 - C$$
$$= 1 - 0.95 = 0.05$$

Step 2 *Compute $\alpha/2$.*

$$\frac{\alpha}{2} = 0.025$$

and, from Table VI, we find

Step 3 *Look up $z_{\alpha/2}$.*

$$z_{0.025} = 1.96$$

Consequently, the interval

Step 4 *Construct the interval.*

$$\bar{p} - z_{\alpha/2} \sqrt{\frac{\bar{p}\bar{q}}{n}} \le p \le \bar{p} + z_{\alpha/2} \sqrt{\frac{\bar{p}\bar{q}}{n}}$$

is

$$0.08 - 1.96 \sqrt{\frac{(0.08)(0.92)}{400}} \le p \le 0.08 + 1.96 \sqrt{\frac{(0.08)(0.92)}{400}}$$

so that $$0.053 \le p \le 0.107$$

Consequently, with 95 percent confidence, we state that the population (region) proportion unemployed is between 0.053 and 0.107, that is, between 5.3 and 10.7 percent. Observe that even with a sample as large as $n = 400$, the resulting confidence interval is not precise (narrow) enough to be of much practical value. Unemployment of 5.3 percent would indicate a relatively healthy situation, but 10.7 percent unemployed would indicate quite the opposite. Thus, the interval estimate does not settle the question of whether the situation is good or bad. To settle the question, we need a more precise interval; and that would require a sample much larger than 400. You will learn how large a sample to use in the next section.

A large sample is needed to get a precise confidence interval for p.

EXERCISE (See the foregoing example.) During September, 35 of a random sample of 500 members of the labor force were unemployed. Construct the 90 percent confidence interval for the region's proportion unemployed.
ANSWER $0.051 \le p \le 0.089$.

10.7 HOW LARGE SHOULD THE SAMPLE BE?

The reason for taking a sample from a population is that it would be too costly to gather data for the whole population. But collecting sample data

Larger samples give more precise results . . . .

. . . . . but smaller samples cost less

also costs money; and the larger the sample, the higher the cost. To hold cost down, we want to use as small a sample as possible. On the other hand, we want the sample to be large enough to provide "good" estimates of population parameters. Consequently, the question is "How large should the sample be?" The answer depends on three factors: (1) How precise (narrow) do we want a confidence interval estimate to be? (2) How confident do we want to be that the interval estimate is correct (e.g., that p is in a stated interval)? (3) How variable is the population being sampled? In general, the higher the desired precision or level of confidence, the larger (more costly) will be the sample; also, for a given precision and level of confidence, the larger population variability is, the larger (more costly) will be the sample.

Sample Size for Estimating a Population Proportion

The confidence interval for p is

$$\bar{p} - z_{\alpha/2} \sqrt{\frac{\bar{p}\bar{q}}{n}} \le p \le \bar{p} + z_{\alpha/2} \sqrt{\frac{\bar{p}\bar{q}}{n}}$$

That interval extends from

$$\bar{p} - z_{\alpha/2} \sqrt{\frac{\bar{p}\bar{q}}{n}} \quad \text{to} \quad \bar{p} + z_{\alpha/2} \sqrt{\frac{\bar{p}\bar{q}}{n}}$$

so we can express it as

$$\bar{p} \pm z_{\alpha/2} \sqrt{\frac{\bar{p}\bar{q}}{n}}$$

The interval will be more precise (narrower) the smaller is the term following $\pm$. We shall call that term the *error* term, and symbolize it by e. Thus, here we have

$$e = z_{\alpha/2} \sqrt{\frac{\bar{p}\bar{q}}{n}}$$

so we can express the confidence interval as

$$\bar{p} \pm e$$

The interval width is $2e$, that is, a distance of e on both sides of $\bar{p}$.

For example, suppose a 95 percent confidence interval for p is expressed as

$$0.42 \pm 0.03$$

Confidence interval for p:

The number 0.42 is $\bar{p}$, the sample proportion. The error term, ± 0.03, means that if the interval is correct (we have 95 percent confidence that it is), the point estimate could be "off" by as much as 0.03 one way or the other; that is, the population proportion is within 0.03 of the sample estimate. The width of the confidence interval, $2e = 0.06$, measures the precision of the interval estimate. The smaller the error term, the higher is precision; and the larger the error term, the lower is precision.

If we square both sides of

$$e = z_{\alpha/2} \sqrt{\frac{\bar{p}\bar{q}}{n}}$$

we obtain

$$e^2 = z_{\alpha/2}^2 \frac{\bar{p}\bar{q}}{n}$$

which, after rearrangement, becomes ·

$$n = \frac{z_{\alpha/2}^2 \bar{p}\bar{q}}{e^2}$$

We are trying to determine how large our sample should be; so we do not have values for $\bar{p}$ and $\bar{q}$ because the sample has not yet been taken. Of course, p would be a better value than $\bar{p}$ to use in the formula for n because $\bar{p}$ is only an estimate of p. But we don't know the value of p either. We will have to make a guess; so we might as well guess what p is. Using our guessed value of p, the formula for n_p, *the sample size needed in estimating a population proportion with confidence coefficient C,* is

Sample size needed to estimate p to within ± e with confidence coefficient C.

$$n_p = \frac{z_{\alpha/2}^2 pq}{e^2}$$

where $\alpha = 1 - C$.

The product pq is in the numerator of the formula; so the larger pq is, the larger will be n_p. If we guess $p = 0.5$, then $q = 1 - p = 0.5$, and $pq = (0.5)(0.5) = 0.25$. If we guess $p = 0.4$ ($q = 0.6$), then pq is the smaller value 0.24. If you try various pq values, you will find out that $p = 0.5$ gives the maximum value of pq, 0.25. Hence, the safest (largest) sample size is computed using $p = 0.5$.

Suppose we want to estimate a population proportion to within ± 0.04 ($e = 0.04$), and we want a confidence coefficient of $C = 0.90$. Then

$$\alpha = 1 - C$$
$$= 1 - 0.90 = 0.10$$

$$\frac{\alpha}{2} = 0.05$$

$$z_{0.05} = 1.64$$

Substituting $e = 0.04$ and $z_{\alpha/2} = 1.64$ into the formula

$$n_p = \frac{z_{\alpha/2}^2 pq}{e^2}$$

gives

$$n_p = \frac{(1.64)^2 pq}{(0.04)^2}$$

Next, suppose we guess that $p = 0.5$. Then

$$n_p = \frac{(1.64)^2(0.5)(0.5)}{(0.04)^2} = 420.25$$

so (rounding to the next whole number) a sample size of about 421 will be required. However, this is the largest sample size because we used $p = 0.5$. If we believe, say, from previous sampling, that p is about 0.20, then the indicated sample size is

$$n_p = \frac{(1.64)^2(0.20)(0.80)}{(0.04)^2} = 268.96$$

Guess at p based on all the information you have.

or about 269. This sample size, 269, is smaller (less costly) than the $n_p = 421$ we obtained by guessing $p = 0.5$. The point is this: If you have some information (past experience, say) about p, use it because it will prevent taking larger (more costly) samples than you need. Guessing $p = 0.5$ leads to the safest (largest) sample size. If your information leads you to believe that p is between two values, proceed as follows to obtain the safer sample size: if both values are on the same side of 0.5, choose p as the value closer to 0.5; but if 0.5 is between the two values, use 0.5 for p.

EXERCISE An advertising executive thinks that the proportion of consumers who have seen his company's advertising in newspapers is somewhere between 0.65 and 0.85. The executive wants to estimate the consumer population proportion to within ± 0.05 and have 98 percent confidence in the estimate. How large a sample should be taken? State the safer sample size.
   ANSWER 495.

If the executive in the last exercise had required that the estimate be good to within ± 0.01 ($e = 0.01$), then

$$n_p = \frac{(2.33)^2(0.65)(0.35)}{(0.01)^2} = 12,351$$

That's a large sample. It is much larger than the exercise answer, 495, because $e = 0.01$ is much smaller than the $e = 0.05$ in the exercise. In general, if the error term is to be as small as, or smaller than, 0.01, large samples are required. It is not difficult to find situations where we would want e to be less than 0.01. For example, if national unemployment is running about 7 percent of the labor force, a useful estimate of the population proportion would require that the population proportion should be within, say, $e = 0.001$ of the sample proportion. The Bureau of Labor Statistics estimates the proportion unemployed from information obtained in a national sample that includes about 47,000 *households*. The number of workers included in the sample is over 100,000. In round numbers, the sample contains 1 worker for each 10,000 workers in the civilian labor force. That is a large sample, but as noted in the introduction to this chapter, an error as large as 1 percentage point ($e = 0.01$) in the sample estimate of the population proportion unemployed would be intolerable.

Why doesn't the needed sample size n.. depend on the population size N?

We know that the larger the sample size n, the smaller will be the error term. Call e_n the error term for a sample of size n. Then

$$e_n = z_{\alpha/2} \sqrt{\frac{pq}{n}}$$

Note that e_n is inversely proportional to $\sqrt{n}$. That is, if we let e_{kn} be the error term for a sample of size kn, then

$$e_{kn} = \frac{1}{\sqrt{k}} \, e_n$$

A k-fold increase in the sample size reduces the error to $\frac{1}{\sqrt{k}}$ times its original value.

For example, if we increase our sample fourfold, we decrease our error by only one-half, because

$$e_{4n} = \frac{1}{\sqrt{4}} \, e_n = \frac{1}{2} \, e_n$$

The question then is whether the one-half reduction in error is worth the fourfold increase in the sample size. And it is important to answer that question because sampling cost (excluding planning costs and other fixed costs) for a simple random sample is directly proportional to sample size. Thus, a fourfold increase in sample size quadruples sampling cost but reduces error by only one-half.

EXERCISE How will the error for a sample of size 2000 compare with the error for a sample size of 1000?

· **ANSWER** The error for 2000 will be 0.707 times the error for 1000; that is, the error for 2000 is 70.7 percent as great as, or 29.3 percent less than, the error for 1000.

Sample Size for Estimating a Population Mean

The confidence interval estimate of μ,

$$\bar{x} - z_{\alpha/2} \frac{\sigma_x}{\sqrt{n}} \le \mu \le \bar{x} + z_{\alpha/2} \frac{\sigma_x}{\sqrt{n}}$$

can be expressed as

$$\bar{x} \pm z_{\alpha/2} \frac{\sigma_x}{\sqrt{n}}$$

The last is of the form $\bar{x} \pm e$, where

$$e = z_{\alpha/2} \frac{\sigma_x}{\sqrt{n}}$$

Squaring both sides, we have

$$e^2 = \frac{z_{\alpha/2}^2 \sigma_x^2}{n}$$

Solving for n, we have

$$n = \frac{z_{\alpha/2}^2 \sigma_x^2}{e^2} = \left(\frac{z_{\alpha/2}\sigma_x}{e}\right)^2$$

To use this formula, we must guess a value for σ_x. Using the guessed value for σ_x, the *formula for the sample size needed in estimating* μ is

Sample size needed to estimate μ to within $\pm$ e with confidence coefficient C.

$$n_\mu = \left(\frac{z_{\alpha/2}\sigma_x}{e}\right)^2$$

In the formula, we see that the larger σ_x is, the larger is the required sample size; that is, the more variable the population, the larger the sample size. We do not have a value for σ_x or its estimator s_x prior to selecting the sample. Sometimes we can base our guess at σ_x on a standard deviation obtained in a sample survey (or census) carried out in the past. Or, because we plan to take a sample anyway, we can take a small subsample, compute its standard deviation s_x, and use that standard deviation as our guess for σ_x; then we can determine the size for the complete sample from the formula for n_μ. Another method, which I have used occasionally, is to try to determine what would be unusually large and small values for a particular population. Such information usually can be obtained from people concerned with the population parameter of interest. For example, even though a plumbers' union official may not think in terms of standard deviations, the official probably has a good idea of what would be unusually large and small plumber salaries. Now recall that about 95 percent of a normal distribution lies in an interval extending $2\sigma_x$ on each side of the population mean. That interval is $4\sigma_x$ in width, and its endpoints are unusually high and low values. Consequently, I would guess that the difference between the official's high and low values is about $4\sigma_x$; that is,

$$4\sigma_x \approx \text{official's high value} - \text{official's low value}$$

and

$$\sigma_x \approx \frac{\text{official's high value} - \text{official's low value}}{4}$$

EXAMPLE A sample is to be taken to estimate the mean salary of plumbers to within $\pm\$500$ ($e = \$500$), with a confidence coefficient of 0.99. A plumbers' union official states that $\$40,000$ and $\$26,000$ would be unusually large and small salaries for plumbers in the union. What should the sample size be?

SOLUTION With $C = 0.99$, $\alpha = 0.01$; so $\alpha/2 = 0.005$, and

$$z_{0.005} = 2.33$$

Step 1 Use expert opinion to obtain an estimate of σ_x.

Taking the official's statement as the opinion of an expert, we guess that

$$\sigma_x \approx \frac{\text{high value} - \text{low value}}{4}$$

$$\sigma_x \approx \frac{\$40{,}000 - \$26{,}000}{4} = \$3500$$

Then

Step 2   Calculate n_μ.

$$n_\mu = \left(\frac{z_{\alpha/2}\sigma_x}{e}\right)^2$$

$$n_\mu = \left[\frac{2.33(\$3500)}{\$500}\right]^2 = 266.02$$

or, rounding to the next whole number, the sample size should be 267.

> **EXERCISE**   You want to estimate workers' mean weekly income to within ± $2 with a confidence coefficient of 0.95. Past sample surveys indicate that the standard deviation of weekly incomes is somewhere between $8 and $10. (a) To obtain the safer (larger) sample size, should $8 or $10 be used in the formula for n_μ? Why? (b) What is the safer sample size?
> **ANSWER**   (a) $10, because the greater the population variability, the larger is the required sample size. (b) 97.

It is always a good idea to determine how large a sample is needed before taking the sample. Such planning makes us think carefully about the relationship between the error we can tolerate and the cost of obtaining the sample information. We do have to guess a value for the standard deviation, or for p if the parameter of interest is a population proportion. However, these guesses usually can be informed guesses. Moreover, whether we guess well or not, we can use the sample data to construct a confidence interval estimate of the population parameter of interest. If our guess leads to an unnecessarily large sample, the error will be smaller than we planned on; and if our guess leads to a smaller sample than required for our purposes, the error will be larger than we planned on. But the point is this: if we do not plan the sample size, we can easily end up with a sample which is either much more costly than we need, or a sample which is almost useless because the error term is too large.

10.8 PROBLEMS

1. Before entering into full-scale production and marketing of Brightglow, a new hair shampoo, the developer, Polette Co., makes enough bottles of Brightglow in its laboratory to stock the shelves in a random sample of stores. In these stores, a random sample of 400 customers were observed as they purchased shampoo; and 80 bought Brightglow. Using a confidence coefficient of 0.954, construct a confidence interval estimate of Brightglow's market share (the proportion of all shampoo buyers who will select Brightglow).
2. Auditors employed by Myer and Smith want to estimate the proportion of Last National Bank's customer accounts which may be in error. The auditors mail the bank's recorded balance to a random sample of 500

depositors. A return envelope is enclosed, and the depositors are asked whether or not they agree with the bank's record. All depositors respond, and 25 disagree with the bank's record. Construct a 95 percent confidence interval estimate of the proportion of all Last National's depositors who disagree with the bank's record.

3. In a random sample of 300 voters, 120 expressed a preference for candidate Pauline McGowan. Using a confidence coefficient of 0.90, construct the confidence interval estimate of the proportion of all voters who prefer McGowan.

4. In a random sample of 1200 television viewers, 456 watched the Nifty Tricks program. Construct the 99 percent confidence interval estimate of the proportion of all viewers who watched Nifty Tricks.

5. Suppose that in a random sample of 400 purchases of men's shirts, 300 purchases were made by women. Construct a 95 percent confidence interval for the proportion of men's shirt purchases that are made by women.

6. Big Deal Mergers, Inc., is considering the purchase of Small Fry Co. Small-Fry makes and sells electric fryers. Small Fry claims it has 30 percent of the total electric fryer market. Big Deal plans to check this claim by conducting a sample survey. What should the sample size be if Big Deal wants to estimate Small Fry's market share (proportion of total market) to within ±0.025 with 90 percent confidence?

7. What is the largest sample size that would be needed in estimating a population proportion to within ±0.02, with a confidence coefficient of 0.95?

8. To gauge the effect of its advertising, Brush and Sons wants to learn what proportion of consumers know the company's product slogan. The slogan has been used in many newspaper and television advertisements. Marketing experts think the proportion could be as low as 0.15 or as high as 0.45. The proportion is to be estimated to within ±0.05 with a confidence coefficient of 0.95. What should the sample size be if Brush and Sons wants to be on the safe (larger sample) side?

9. From time to time, the popularity of the President of the United States is gauged, by sampling, to determine what proportion of the public favors the President. In past samples, the proportion has varied from 0.40 to 0.65. How large a sample should be taken, to be on the safe side, if the proportion is to be estimated to within ±0.05 with 90 percent confidence?

10. By what percent is the error term e in a confidence interval estimate reduced if the sample size is increased by 50 percent?

11. A random sample is to be taken to estimate the average (mean) amount of time per evening television viewers spend watching programs on the QBC network during the 6 to 10 p.m. period. The population mean is to be estimated to within ±5 minutes, with 99 percent confidence. (a) What should the sample size be if past samples indicate that the standard deviation of viewing times is about 40 minutes? (b) What would the sample size be if the standard deviation was 20 minutes?

12. To check the adjustable setting on an automatic machine, frequent random samples of output are selected and measured. After a sample has been selected, the mean diameter $\bar{x}$ of the sample parts is computed. Then the mean diameter for all parts being made is estimated by using the interval $\bar{x} \pm 0.008$ mm. If the diameter specified in the blueprints does not fall in this interval, the machine is shut down for readjustment. The standard deviation of diameters is about 0.024 mm. What sample size should be used if the interval $\bar{x} \pm 0.008$ is to be (a) a 90 percent confidence interval? (b) a 99 percent confidence interval?

13. Suppose the standard deviation of prices charged for unleaded gas in the Chicago Metropolitan area is about 1 cent per gallon. What size sample should be used to estimate the average (mean) price per gallon for all stations in the area to within ± 0.2 cent per gallon, with a confidence coefficient of 0.95?

14. Executive Placement Services wants to estimate the mean monthly rent charged for three-bedroom condominiums in a large upper-income suburban area. A random sample is to be taken and used to estimate the mean to within $\pm \$50$ per month, with a confidence level of 90 percent. The best information EPS can obtain indicates that $1500 and $2500 per month would be unusually low and high rentals. What should the sample size be?

15. Suppose you guessed a value for σ_x and used it to determine the sample size n needed to construct a 95 percent confidence interval for an unknown mean μ to within ± 50. Then you obtained the sample of size n, computed the standard deviation s_x, and found it to be larger than the value you guessed for σ_x. Would that mean you could not construct a 95 percent confidence interval? If not, how would the confidence interval you construct differ from the one you planned to construct?

10.9 SUMMARY

An *estimator* is a sample statistic that is used to estimate an unknown population parameter. A *point estimate* is a single value of an estimator. The sample mean

$$\bar{x} = \frac{\Sigma x}{n}$$

is used as the estimator of the population mean μ. The sample standard deviation

$$s_x = \sqrt{\frac{\Sigma(x - \bar{x})^2}{n - 1}}$$

is used as the estimator of the population standard deviation σ_x. The sample standard error of the mean

$$s_{\bar{x}} = \frac{s_x}{\sqrt{n}}$$

is the estimator of the standard error of the mean $\sigma_{\bar{x}}$. The estimator of the population proportion of successes p is the sample proportion of successes

$$\bar{p} = \frac{\text{number of successes in a sample of size } n}{n}$$

A confidence interval estimate is a range of values within which we state a population parameter lies. The proportion of confidence intervals that are correct (that is, that contain the population parameter) is called the *confidence coefficient* C; the *confidence level* is C expressed as a percent. The proportion of incorrect intervals is symbolized as α;

$$\alpha = 1 - C \quad \text{and} \quad \frac{\alpha}{2} = \frac{1 - C}{2}$$

The symbol $z_{\alpha/2}$ means the z value for which the one-tail area of the standard normal curve is $\alpha/2$. The confidence interval (with confidence coefficient C) for the mean of a normal population whose standard deviation is σ_x is

$$\bar{x} - z_{\alpha/2} \frac{\sigma_x}{\sqrt{n}} \leq \mu \leq \bar{x} + z_{\alpha/2} \frac{\sigma_x}{\sqrt{n}}$$

If σ_x is estimated by s_x, and sample size $n > 30$, the approximate confidence interval for μ is

$$\bar{x} - z_{\alpha/2} \frac{s_x}{\sqrt{n}} \leq \mu \leq \bar{x} + z_{\alpha/2} \frac{s_x}{\sqrt{n}}$$

If the sample is drawn from a normal population whose standard deviation is unknown, and $n \leq 30$, we use the Student t value (rather than z) in constructing a confidence interval for μ. The t value depends on $\alpha/2$ and the *number of degrees of freedom* v. For the methods discussed in this chapter, $v = n - 1$. The symbol $t_{\alpha/2,v}$ means the t value for a one tail t distribution area of $\alpha/2$, with v degrees of freedom. The confidence interval for μ, with confidence coefficient C, is

$$\bar{x} + t_{\alpha/2,v} \frac{s_x}{\sqrt{n}} \leq \mu \leq \bar{x} + t_{\alpha/2,v} \frac{s_x}{\sqrt{n}}$$

When both $n\bar{p}$ and $n\bar{q}$ are greater than 15, the approximate confidence interval for a proportion of successes (with confidence coefficient C) is

$$\bar{p} - z_{\alpha/2} \sqrt{\frac{\bar{p}\bar{q}}{n}} \leq p \leq \bar{p} + z_{\alpha/2} \sqrt{\frac{\bar{p}\bar{q}}{n}}$$

The sample size needed to estimate an unknown population parameter to within $\pm e$ depends upon (1) the value of e, (2) the confidence coefficient C, and (3) the population variability. To compute the sample size n_μ for estimating a population mean, first decide on the value to be used for e, and the confidence coefficient desired, C. Next guess a value for σ_x, the population standard deviation. Then

$$n_\mu = \left(\frac{z_{\alpha/2}\sigma_x}{e}\right)^2$$

To compute the sample size n_p for estimating a population proportion, first establish values for e and C. Next, guess the value of the proportion p. Then

$$n_p = \frac{z_{\alpha/2}^2 pq}{e^2}$$

For given values of e and C, sample sizes are larger (1) the larger is the guessed value of σ_x used in computing n_μ or (2) the closer the guessed value of p used in computing n_p is to 0.5.

10.10 REVIEW PROBLEMS

1. Compute s_x and $s_{\bar{x}}$ for the following samples: (a) 2, 3, 4; (b) 2, 3, 4, 5, 16.
2. (a) What is the meaning of $z_{0.05}$? (b) What is the value of $z_{0.05}$? (c) What is the value of $z_{\alpha/2}$ for a confidence interval with a confidence coefficient of 0.93?
3. Amcar Motor Company has test-driven a random sample of 35 new Amcars. Gasoline mileage figures for the sample cars, in miles per gallon, are given in Table A. Construct a 95 percent confidence interval for mean miles per gallon for all new Amcars.

TABLE A

15.4	18.3	19.1	20.4	21.0	21.8	19.3
16.3	18.7	19.4	20.5	21.3	21.8	20.8
16.7	18.7	19.4	20.6	21.4	22.5	22.0
17.2	19.0	19.8	20.9	21.5	23.2	20.1
18.1	19.0	20.4	21.0	21.6	25.0	17.8

4. Amcar Motors (Problem 3) has introduced a new Mini Amcar which has greater fuel economy than the regular-sized Amcar. A random sample of 50 Mini Amcars averaged 30 miles per gallon, and had a standard deviation of 3 miles per gallon. Construct a 95 percent confidence interval for mean miles per gallon for all Mini Amcars.
5. The mean price of a nationally distributed brand of coffee in a random sample of 100 stores is $2.75 per pound. The sample standard deviation is $0.10 per pound. Construct the confidence interval for the mean price in all stores with a confidence coefficient of (a) 0.95; (b) 0.99.
6. High Gloss Wax Company has determined that there are 6500 potential customers for wax in a particular region. In a random sample of 40 customers, the mean amount of wax used per customer was 14.2 pounds per month, and the standard deviation was 1.8 pounds per month. (a) Construct the 95 percent confidence interval for mean monthly wax consumption in the region. (b) Construct the 95 percent confidence interval for total monthly wax consumption in the region.
7. On the basis of information in a random sample of $n = 35$, a market analyst obtains $40 \le \mu \le 50$ as a 95 percent confidence interval. When asked what the interval means, the analyst replies that there are many other samples of 35 which might have been selected, but in 95 percent of the various samples, μ would be

between 40 and 50. This reply is incorrect. (*a*) Why is the reply incorrect? (*b*) Write the correct reply.

8. Under what circumstances is Student's *t* distribution the correct distribution to use when constructing a confidence interval estimate of the population mean?

9. (*a*) What is the meaning of $t_{\alpha/2,v}$? (*b*) For a sample of size 10 and a confidence coefficient of 0.95, what is the value of $t_{\alpha/2,v}$?

10. Borg Company makes Super Grow lights. The lights are fluorescent tubes that radiate light similar to outdoor daylight; they are used by florists and other plant growers. A random sample of 20 tubes were left on until they burned out. The sample mean burning life was 925 hours, and the standard deviation was 34.6 hours. Suppose burning lives are normally distributed. Construct a 95 percent confidence interval estimate of the mean life of all Super Grow lights.

11. A cattle raiser selected a random sample of 10 steers, all of the same age, and fed them a special mixture of grains and other ingredients. After a period of time, weight gains were recorded. The sample mean weight gain, per steer, was 142.6 pounds, and the standard deviation was 10.4 pounds. Suppose weight gains are normally distributed. Construct a 90 percent confidence interval for the population mean weight gain per steer.

12. A supervisor wishes to check the time employees spend on the 10-minute coffee breaks allowed in the union-management contract. The supervisor observes a random sample of 15 employees and notes the time, in minutes, spent by each for the coffee break. The times are 14, 14, 8, 12, 13, 10, 14, 10, 11, 13, 9, 10, 15, 12, 15. Suppose times spent are normally distributed. Construct the 95 percent confidence interval for the mean time per employee spent by all employees who take coffee breaks.

13. The diameters of ball bearings made by an automatic machine are normally distributed and have a standard deviation of 0.02 mm. The mean of a random sample of four ball bearings is 6.01 mm. Construct the 95 percent interval for the mean diameter of all ball bearings being made by the machine.

14. North American Oil is considering sites for new gas stations. An estimate of the mean traffic flow (average number of passing cars per day) at each site is to be determined by taking a traffic count for a random sample of days. The mean μ for each site is to be estimated to within ± 50 cars per day, with 95 percent confidence. Experience at existing sites indicates that the standard deviation of numbers of cars passing in a day could be as low as 70 or as high as 100. To be on the safe (larger sample) side, what sample size should be used?

15. To determine whether fares collected on a bus line are in reasonable agreement with the number of passengers carried, the Short Line Bus Co. needs an estimate of the mean number of passengers per bus trip. The mean μ is to be estimated to within ± 2 passengers, with 95 percent confidence. Past records indicate that the standard deviation is about 6 passengers per trip. People not known to company employees will make trips on the line at randomly assigned times, and record the number of passengers. How many sample trips should be made?

16. Interviewers called a random sample of 300 homes while the Joystick TV special was being shown; 105 respondents said they were watching the special. Construct the 95 percent confidence interval for the proportion of all homes where the special was being watched.

17. In a 6-month period, half of a random sample of 40 stocks traded on the New York Stock Exchange had a greater percent increase than the Dow Jones average of 30 industrial stock prices. Construct the 95 percent confidence in-

terval for the proportion of all NYSE stocks that had a higher percent increase than the Dow Jones average.

18. The proportion of unemployed workers in a 10-state region is to be estimated to within ± 0.005, with a confidence coefficient of 0.95. If the proportion is thought to be around 0.10, what sample size should be used?

19. The proportion of all consumers favoring a new product might be as low as 0.20 or as high as 0.60. A random sample is to be used to estimate the proportion of consumers who favor the product to within ± 0.05, with a confidence coefficient of 0.90. To be on the safe (larger sample) side, what sample size should be used?

20. What is the largest sample size needed to estimate a population proportion to within ± 0.02 with a confidence coefficient of 0.90?

21. How is the precision of a confidence interval estimate related to a confidence coefficient used in constructing the interval?

22. (a) What is the error term in the following confidence interval formula?

$$\bar{x} - z_{\alpha/2} \frac{s_x}{\sqrt{n}} \leq \mu \leq \bar{x} + z_{\alpha/2} \frac{s_x}{\sqrt{n}}$$

(b) By what percent will the error term be reduced if the sample size is increased by 60 percent?

11

STATISTICAL INFERENCE: HYPOTHESIS TESTING

11.1 INTRODUCTION

In Chapter 10, we used the information obtained in a simple random sample to construct a confidence interval estimate of the *unknown* value of a population parameter. In this chapter we shall start with an assumed value of a population parameter: then we shall use sample evidence to decide whether the assumed value is unreasonable and should be rejected, or whether it should be accepted.

The assumptions we make about the values of population parameters are called hypotheses. Sample evidence is used to test the reasonableness of hypotheses; hence, the statistical inferences made in this chapter are referred to as hypothesis testing. The following dialogue illustrates the kind of reasoning involved in hypothesis testing. The dialogue is fiction, but it was prompted by an article that appeared in a large city newspaper.

> Fran: *This article says that the city's inspector of weights and measures road-tested ten rental cars. He used a special device that measures distance traveled very precisely. The inspector wanted to see if the mileage recorded by rental-car mileage gauges—odometers—exceeded actual miles, so that car renters might be overcharged. All ten odometers registered more than the actual miles traveled. But the inspector said that the excesses were within reasonable limits, since odometers are expected to show some variability. The inspector's conclusion was that rental cars do not show more than the actual miles traveled.*
>
> Dan: *I rent cars often, and I've wondered about the mileages I have been charged for. But it's hard to see that any conclusion can be reached by testing only ten cars.*
>
> Fran: *Maybe not, but the inspector's conclusion doesn't seem to jibe with what he found out. After all, every one of the ten odometers showed excessive mileage.*
>
> Dan: *That is peculiar. Odometers do vary, as the inspector said. But if they are properly adjusted you would expect some to be on the low side and some on the high side—maybe fifty-fifty.*
>
> Fran: *The test is sort of like tossing a coin ten times and getting ten heads in a row. That does happen once in a while, but it's very unusual.*
>
> Dan: *Let's figure it this way. The chance of heads is one-half, so the chance of two heads in two tosses is one-half times one-half, which is one out of four, and if you keep on multiplying, the chance of ten heads in a row is—let me see—less than one in a thousand. . . .*
>
> Fran: *I think the road test showed that more than fifty percent of the odometers record excess mileage. I could be wrong, but after all, one out of a thousand!*
>
> Dan: *Maybe I'll write a letter to the editor.*
>
> Fran: *Maybe I'll stop renting cars.*

The line of reasoning in the dialogue goes like this. First, assume (state the hypothesis) that the population proportion p of odometers that register excessive mileage is 0.5 (that is, Dan's 50-50 hypothesis). Then, based on the sample evidence, decide whether the hypothesis $p = 0.5$ is unreasonable and should be rejected, or should be accepted. In the sample, 10 out of 10 cars (sample proportion $\bar{p} = 1.00$ or 100 percent) showed excessive mileage: Fran and Dan decided that the hypothesis $p = 0.5$ was unreasonable; so it was rejected. The conclusion was that p is greater than 0.5; that is, more than 50 percent of odometers register excessive mileage.

Fran concluded that the hypothesis (assumption) that $p = 0.5$ was unreasonable because of Dan's probability calculation; that calculation showed that if $p = 0.5$, the chance of getting a random sample in which 10 out of 10 cars showed excessive mileage was only about 0.001 (1 out of 1000). Consequently, Fran was convinced by the sample evidence that the hypothesis $p = 0.5$ had a very small chance of being true. Or, to put it the other way, Fran was convinced by the sample evidence that the hypothesis $p = 0.5$ had a very high chance of being false.

11.2 NULL AND ALTERNATIVE HYPOTHESES

H_0: the null hypothesis (to be tested)

H_a: the alternative hypothesis (true if H_0 is false)

In this chapter we shall test hypotheses about values of unknown population parameters. In each test there will be two hypotheses. One is called the *null* hypothesis, and the other is called the *alternative* hypothesis. The null hypothesis is designated as H_0 (H sub zero) and the alternative hypothesis is designated by H_a. The hypotheses are written in a form like

$$H_0: \mu \geq 16 \text{ ounces}$$

$$H_a: \mu < 16 \text{ ounces}$$

Here the null hypothesis is that the population mean is greater than or equal to 16 ounces, and the alternative hypothesis is that the population mean is less than 16 ounces. As another example, consider

$$H_0: p = 0.2$$

$$H_a: p \neq 0.2$$

Here the null hypothesis is that the population proportion is 0.2 and the alternative is that the proportion does not equal 0.2; that is, the proportion is either less than or greater than 0.2.

11.3 TYPE I AND TYPE II ERRORS

Sample evidence is used to test the null hypothesis H_0. If the sample evidence convinces us that H_0 has only a small chance of being true (a large chance of being false), we say H_0 is unreasonable and reject it. If the sample evidence does not convince us that H_0 is unreasonable, we accept H_0. Our test conclusion, therefore, will be to accept or reject H_0.

We cannot be sure that the conclusion we reach from a test is correct because the conclusion is an inference based upon sample evidence. A conclu-

Type I error:
Reject a true H_0.

Type II error:
Accept a false H_0.

sion is correct if a true null hypothesis is accepted, or if a false null hypothesis is rejected. An error is made if a true H_0 is rejected, or if a false H_0 is accepted. Rejecting a true H_0 is called a *Type I error*. Accepting a false H_0 is called a *Type II error*. For example, suppose the null hypothesis is that the population mean is at least 16 ounces so that we have

$$H_0: \mu \geq 16 \text{ ounces}$$

$$H_a: \mu < 16 \text{ ounces}$$

We do not know whether or not H_0 is true. But suppose, unknown to us, that $\mu = 16$ ounces, *so that H_0 is true*. The sample evidence we would use to test H_0 is the mean $\bar{x}$ of a simple random sample selected from the population. We know from our study of sampling distributions that if μ is 16 (H_0 is true), sample $\bar{x}$ values can differ from 16. Now suppose that the sample mean we obtain happens to be so far below 16 that we decide H_0 is an unreasonable hypothesis: so we reject H_0. We would have then rejected a true H_0 and

A Type I error   committed a Type I error.

EXERCISE Suppose in the example that μ (unknown to us) is 15.6 ounces, but that the sample mean is so close to 16 ounces that we do not think $\mu \geq 16$ is unreasonable: so we accept H_0. What error would we have committed? Explain.
ANSWER A Type II error because μ is 15.6 ounces, so $H_0: \mu \geq 16$ ounces is

A Type II error   false; and we accepted a false hypothesis.

It is possible to commit a Type I error only when H_0 is rejected. It is possible to commit a Type II error only when H_0 is accepted. If a false H_0 is rejected, or a true H_0 is accepted, the correct conclusion has been drawn, and neither error has been committed.

A legal analogy will help you fix Type I and Type II errors in mind. In trial by jury in the United States, the accused (the defendant) is presumed to be

H_0: The defendant is innocent.

innocent at the start of the trial. We may think of the presumption of innocence as being a kind of null hypothesis that is to be accepted or rejected. The jury listens to the evidence presented during the trial. Afterward, the jury reaches its conclusion. Now suppose that the defendant really is innocent, but the jury's finding is guilty. The jury has rejected a true null hypothesis (innocence) and committed a Type I error. On the other hand, if the defendant actually is guilty and the jury's finding is innocent, the jury has accepted a false null hypothesis and committed a Type II error.

11.4 PROBABILITIES OF TYPE I AND TYPE II ERRORS

We would, of course, like to avoid Type I and Type II errors entirely. But we cannot avoid the possibilities of making these errors when inferences about unknown values of population parameters are based on sample information. The next most desirable objective would be to set the chances of both types of error at low values, but that usually would require sample sizes which are larger than we can afford to obtain. Consequently, what is usually done is to

α is the probability of making a Type I error.

β is the probability of making a Type II error.

set the chance of a Type I error at a low value (0.10 or less). As you will learn soon, chances of Type I errors are tail areas of sampling distributions; so we will use the symbol α to designate probabilities for Type I errors. Setting α at a low value means that the decision maker wants most to avoid the error of rejecting a true H_0 (Type I error) and has less concern about the chance of accepting a false H_0 (Type II error). The decision maker determines what value α shall have.

The probability of accepting a false H_0 (Type II error) is designated by β (beta). When α is set at a low value, β can be quite high. There is a trade-off between α and β. This does not mean $\alpha + \beta = 1$; rather, it means that the smaller α is, the larger will be β, and the larger α is, the smaller will be β.

An analogy will help you understand the trade-off between the two types of errors. Let's say that a good college applicant is one who is capable of doing college work and graduating and that a poor applicant is one who is not capable of doing college work. Suppose the admissions officer at a college assumes that an applicant is good unless the applicant's aptitude test scores and other information convince the officer that the assumption is unreasonable, and the applicant should be rejected. The assumption of "good applicant" is a kind of null hypothesis H_0. If the officer applies very low standards in the selection of students to be admitted, the chance of rejecting a good student (rejecting a true H_0) will be small; but the chance of accepting a poor student will be large. The chance of rejecting a good student is α, and the chance of accepting a poor student is β. Low admissions requirements make α small, but β will be large.

Next, suppose that admissions standards are raised. This makes it more difficult for both good and poor students to gain admittance. The chance α that a good student will be rejected will be larger and the chance β that a poor student will be accepted will be smaller. Thus, the higher the admissions standards, the larger will be α, and the smaller will be β; and the lower the admissions standards, the smaller will be α, and the larger will be β.

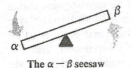

The $\alpha - \beta$ seesaw

11.5 THE RATIONALE OF HYPOTHESIS TESTING

Forms of the hypotheses

The procedure involved in testing hypotheses depends upon (1) the form of the hypotheses and (2) the decision maker's attitude about the importance of Type I and Type II errors. In this chapter we will (1) use the generally applicable hypotheses forms in which H_0 contains an equality sign, as in $=$, $\leq$, or $\geq$. If H_0 contains the strict equality sign $=$, H_a will contain the not-equal sign $\neq$; if H_0 has the weak inequality sign $\leq$, H_a will have the strict inequality sign $>$; and if H_0 contains $\geq$, H_a will contain $<$. Examples are

$$H_0: p = 0.25 \qquad H_a: p \neq 0.25$$

$$H_0: p \leq 0.25 \qquad H_a: p > 0.25$$

Set the chance of rejecting a true H_0 at a low value α.

and

$$H_0: p \geq 0.25 \qquad H_a: p < 0.25$$

Also, we will (2) formulate the hypotheses so that, to the decision maker, rejecting a true H_0 is the worst error that can be made, and set a low value α as the chance of making that worst error.

The value of α will be associated with the = sign in H_0. For example, suppose we have $\alpha = 0.05$ and

Associate α with the = sign in H_0.

$$H_0: p \leq 0.25 \qquad H_a: p > 0.25$$

Then we will take $\alpha = 0.05$ as the chance of rejecting the true equality part of H_0, $p = 0.25$. We shall do this because (1) the chance α of rejecting H_0 depends upon what the value of p is. Consequently, if α is to be a specific number such as 0.05, p has to have a specific value such as $p = 0.25$. We cannot associate a specific value of α with an indefinite null hypothesis such as $p < 0.25$. Also (2) if we reject the equality $p = 0.25$ (and accept $H_a: p > 0.25$) we are automatically rejecting all values of p that are less than 0.25. That is, if we conclude $p > 0.25$, then we would reject both $p = 0.25$ and $p < 0.25$, which means rejecting $H_0: p \leq 0.25$.

EXAMPLE Suppose the sponsor of the Nifty Tricks television program states that the program should be canceled if there is convincing evidence (obtained from a random sample of the TV audience) that the program's share of the viewing audience is less than 25 percent. The sponsor also states (1) that the worst error would be to cancel the program if its audience share is 25 percent or more and (2) the chance of making the worst error is to be only 5 percent. A sample of 1250 TV viewers will be interviewed, and the sample proportion $\bar{p}$ of viewers who watch Nifty Tricks will be used to decide whether or not the program is canceled. Now suppose there are 260 Nifty Tricks viewers in the sample. Then the sample proportion of viewers is

$$\bar{p} = \frac{260}{1250} = 0.208$$

Should the sponsor cancel the program?

How to identify H_0 and H_a.

SOLUTION First we identify H_0 and H_a. The easiest way to do this is to take the sponsor's strict inequality statement "less than 25 percent" as H_a. That makes $H_a: p < 0.25$; so we have $H_0: p \geq 0.25$. Or, take the sponsor's "25 percent or more" statement (which means ≥ 0.25, and contains the equality) as $H_0: p \geq 0.25$; then, as before, the alternative hypothesis is $H_a: p < 0.25$. But note also that $H_0: p \geq 0.25$ and $\alpha = 0.05$ are the translation of the sponsor's statement that the chance of canceling the program if the show has 25 percent or more of the audience (the worst error) is to be 5 percent. So we have

$$H_0: p \geq 0.25 \qquad H_a: p < 0.25$$

Next we want a rule, called a *decision rule*, for the sponsor to use to determine whether to accept or to reject H_0. If H_0 is accepted, the sponsor will continue the program. If H_0 is rejected, the sponsor will accept $H_a: p < 0.25$ and cancel the program. The sponsor would not, of course, reject H_0 if the sample proportion $\bar{p}$ of viewers is 0.25 or more, because such values of $\bar{p}$ support H_0: $p \geq 0.25$. But a $\bar{p}$ value less than 0.25 raises doubt about the truth of H_0: and if $\bar{p}$ is much smaller than 0.25, the sponsor should reject H_0.

We want to associate $\alpha = 0.05$ with the equality part of H_0, $p = 0.25$. To do so, we need the sampling distribution of $\bar{p}$, and that is easily determined; it is a normal distribution that has

$$\mu_{\bar{p}} = p = 0.25$$

and, with $n = 1250$,

$$\sigma_{\bar{p}} = \sqrt{\frac{pq}{n}} = \sqrt{\frac{(0.25)(0.75)}{1250}} = 0.0122$$

The distribution is shown in Figure 11.1. It has a tail area of 0.05 extending

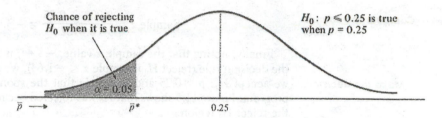

FIGURE 11.1
Distribution of $\bar{p}$ when
$p = 0.25$.

to the left of a sample $\bar{p}$ designated as $\bar{p}^*$. Now if the sponsor rejects H_0 for any sample $\bar{p}$ value that is less than $\bar{p}^*$, a true null hypothesis will be rejected; that's because H_0: $p \geq 0.25$ is true when, as in the figure, $p = 0.25$. Moreover, the chance of rejecting the true H_0 is the tail area $\alpha = 0.05$.

To establish the decision rule we must determine the value of $\bar{p}^*$ in Figure 11.1, or the value of z associated with $\bar{p}^*$. We will use the z value in the decision rule. For the tail area $\alpha = 0.05$ (in the figure) the value of z associated with $\bar{p}^*$ (which is to the left of the mean) is $-z_{0.05} = -1.64$. The decision rule is

**State the decision
rule in terms of the
sample z value.**

Reject H_0 if sample $z < -1.64$

The rule is equivalent to rejecting H_0 if the sample p is less than $\bar{p}^*$, as shown in Figure 11.2 (at the top of page 342).

Now we must compute the value of the sample z that is associated with the sample $\bar{p}$ value

$$\bar{p} = \frac{260}{1250} = 0.208$$

It is

$$\text{Sample } z = \frac{\bar{p} - p}{\sigma_{\bar{p}}}$$

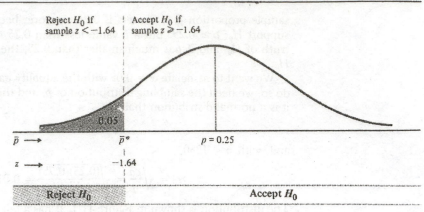

FIGURE 11.2
A decision rule.

With $\sigma_{\bar{p}} = 0.0122$ (computed earlier) and $p = 0.25$, we compute

Compute the sample z value.

$$\text{Sample } z = \frac{0.208 - 0.25}{0.0122} = -3.44$$

Finally, noting that the sample z value, -3.44, is less than the -1.64 in the decision rule (reject H_0 if sample $z < -1.64$), we reject H_0. That means

Make the decision.

we accept H_a: $p < 0.25$ and conclude that the sponsor should cancel the program. Figure 11.3 shows that H_0 was rejected because the sample z lies in the reject H_0 region.

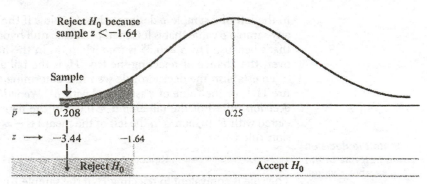

FIGURE 11.3
Rejecting H_0.

11.6 PERFORMING A HYPOTHESIS TEST

The quantity we compute using sample information to test a hypothesis is called a *test statistic*. In the television sponsor example of the last section, the test statistic was the *sample z value*. I shall use the instruction "perform a hypothesis test" to mean

Hypothesis test procedure

1. State the hypotheses.
2. State the decision rule.
3. Compute the value of the test statistic.
4. Reject H_0 or accept H_0.

When tests are performed in a management decision context, I may also ask you to state what is implied by the conclusion in step (4). An implication is not part of a formal test, but it should be stated because a test result often is used in making decisions.

The statement of the television sponsor example led to the hypotheses

1. Hypotheses

$$H_0: p \geq 0.25 \qquad H_a: p < 0.25$$

The sponsor's requirement that the probability of rejecting a true null hypothesis be 0.05 means that $\alpha = 0.05$. Using $\alpha = 0.05$, we formed the decision rule

2. Decision rule

$$\text{Reject } H_0 \text{ if sample } z < -1.64$$

In general, the decision rule form is $z < -(\ )$ when H_a contains the $<$ sign. Next, we obtained the sample and computed the sample test statistic

3. Test statistic

$$\text{Sample } z = -3.44$$

The value of the test statistic, $z = -3.44$, lies in the rejection region of the decision rule. Consequently, we

4. Accept or reject

$$\text{Reject } H_0$$

The implication of the test result in this management decision problem is that the program should be canceled.

EXAMPLE A company has developed a new hair shampoo named Brightglow. The company's marketing executive has obtained figures for the costs of plant expansion and new product advertising. Taking these costs into account, the executive thinks it would be a mistake to market Brightglow unless there is substantial evidence that more than 20 percent of shampoo buyers would choose Brightglow rather than a competitive shampoo. The executive wants the chance of marketing Brightglow to be 0.01 (quite low) if it does not have more than 20 percent of the market. The plan is to stock a random sample of stores with Brightglow, and have a random sample of 500 customers observed as they select a shampoo to purchase. (*a*) Perform a hypothesis test if 110 of the customers in the sample purchased Brightglow. (*b*) What is implied by the test result?

SOLUTION Let's use the words Brightglow's *market share* to mean the proportion of shampoo buyers who choose Brightglow.

a. The executive wants substantial evidence that Brightglow's market share p is greater than 0.20; that is, $p > 0.20$. The strict inequality $p > 0.20$ is the alternative hypothesis. The null hypothesis is $p \leq 0.20$. Hence,

**1. Hypotheses
(from the problem
statement)**

$$H_0: p \leq 0.20 \qquad H_a: p > 0.20$$

The executive wants the chance of rejecting H_0 if it is true to be $\alpha = 0.01$. Substantial evidence that $p > 0.20$ (so H_0 should be rejected) would be a sample proportion $\bar{p}$ which is substantially *higher* than 0.20. That means that H_0 will be rejected if the value of the test statistic (the sample z) is greater than $z_{0.01}$. From Table VI, we find $z_{0.01} = 2.33$. Therefore, we state the decision rule

2. Decision rule (from Table VI)

$$\text{Reject } H_0 \text{ if sample } z > 2.33$$

The $>$ sign in $H_a: p > 0.20$ is the reason for using $>$ in the decision rule.

Next we have to compute the value of the sample z by the formula

$$\text{Sample } z = \frac{\bar{p} - p}{\sigma_{\bar{p}}}$$

As explained earlier, only the equality part of H_0, $p = 0.20$, is used in the test. With $p = 0.20$ ($q = 0.80$) and $n = 500$, the distribution of $\bar{p}$ is normal and has the standard error

$$\sigma_{\bar{p}} = \sqrt{\frac{pq}{n}}$$

$$\sigma_{\bar{p}} = \sqrt{\frac{(0.2)(0.8)}{500}} = 0.0179$$

In the sample, 110 of the 500 customers purchased Brightglow. Hence,

$$\bar{p} = \frac{110}{500} = 0.22$$

Now we compute

3. Test statistic (computed)

$$\text{Sample } z = \frac{\bar{p} - \text{p}}{\sigma_{\bar{p}}}$$

$$= \frac{0.22 - 0.20}{0.0179} = 1.12$$

The decision rule is to reject H_0 if the sample z is greater than 2.33. Our sample z, 1.12, is not greater than 2.33; so we do not reject H_0. Instead, we conclude

4. Accept or reject (by comparing results in 2 and 3)

$$\text{Accept } H_0$$

b. The conclusion means we accept the statement that Brightglow's market share is 20 percent or lower. The implication is that Brightglow should not be marketed.

Figure 11.4 illustrates the hypothesis test just performed. The rejection region corresponds to a *right*-tail area because the alternative hypothesis $H_a: p > 0.20$ is a "greater than" inequality. For a right-tail area, z is positive; so the rule is to

$$\text{Reject } H_0 \text{ if sample } z > 2.33$$

In the test, the sample proportion was $\bar{p} = 0.22$, but we accepted

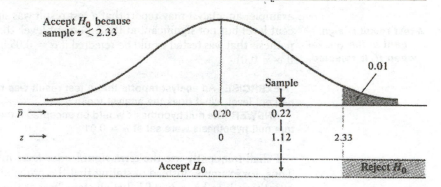

FIGURE 11.4
Accepting H_0.

We accept

H_0: *p* $\leq$ *0.20*

even though $\bar{p}$ is
greater than 0.20.

the null hypothesis H_0: $p \leq 0.20$. Of course, a sample proportion of $\bar{p} = 0.22$, which is greater than 0.20, is evidence that H_0 is false. However, the evidence is not substantial enough to lead us to reject H_0 when $\alpha = 0.01$. The point to keep in mind is that when the chance of rejecting a true H_0 is set at a low level α, H_0 will be accepted unless the sample shows substantial evidence that H_0 is false.

EXERCISE A group of dissident stockholders claim that a high proportion of all stockholders are against company management policies. The directors think the proportion against is less than 0.30. The dissidents agree to abandon their claim if a random sample of 200 stockholders provides substantial evidence that the proportion is less than 0.30. The dissidents and the directors agree that the chance of concluding incorrectly that p is less than 0.30 is to be set at 0.10. (a) Perform a hypothesis test if 46 of the 200 stockholders in the sample are against management policies. (b) What is implied by the test result?
ANSWER (a) 1. $H_0: p \geq 0.30$; $H_a: p < 0.30$. 2. Reject H_0 if sample $z < -1.28$. 3. Sample $z = -2.16$. 4. Reject H_0. (b) The dissidents should abandon their claim.

11.7 THE LEVEL OF SIGNIFICANCE

The symbol α denotes the chance of committing a Type I error; that is the probability of rejecting a true null hypothesis. α is called the *significance level* of a test. When the value of a test statistic (z in our work to date) leads to rejection of H_0, we say that the value is *statistically significant*. For example, in the last exercise the sample z, -2.16, led us to reject $H_0: p \geq 0.30$; so we say that the sample z is statistically significant. The sample z, -2.16, shows us that the sample proportion

$$\bar{p} = \frac{46}{200} = 0.23$$

is "substantially" less than 0.30. Or, we may say, 0.23 is *significantly* less than 0.30, enough less to convince us that the null hypothesis $H_0: p \geq 0.30$ should be rejected.

Significance levels often are used by analysts in reporting test results. For

*A test result is signifi-
cant at the α level
when H_0 is rejected.*

example, an analyst may report that a test result was significant at the 5 percent level but not significant at the 1 percent level: that means the null hypothesis that was tested would be rejected if $\alpha = 0.05$ but would be accepted
if $\alpha = 0.01$.

EXERCISE An analyst reports that a test result was not significant at the 1
percent level. What does the analyst mean?
ANSWER The null hypothesis would be accepted if the chance of rejecting a
true null hypothesis were set at $\alpha = 0.01$.

I shall frequently use the term *significance level* in problem statements.
Thus, for example, instead of stating that the probability of rejecting a true
hypothesis is to be, say, 0.02, I shall state "test at the 2 percent level."

11.8 TWO-TAIL TEST OF A POPULATION PROPORTION

When H_0 contains only the = sign, H_a will contain the $\neq$ (not equal) sign.
The test then is called a *two-tail test* because the rejection region consists of
two tails of the sampling distribution.

EXAMPLE During a year-end audit, discrepancies were found in a company's invoice ledger. Consequently, the controller had all invoices for the
year checked to determine if they were correctly recorded in the ledger. The
proportion of incorrectly recorded invoices was found to be 0.04. The controller instituted a new procedure for processing invoices. Subsequently, a
random sample of 500 invoices was checked to determine whether the proportion incorrectly recorded had *changed* from 0.04. (*a*) Perform a hypothesis test at the 5 percent level if 11 of the sample invoices were recorded
incorrectly. (*b*) What is implied by the test result?

SOLUTION

a. The population proportion of incorrectly recorded invoices has
changed from 0.04 if it is either less than or greater than 0.04. Consequently, the hypotheses are $p = 0.04$ and $p \neq 0.04$, where $p \neq 0.04$
means p is either less than or greater than 0.04. The null hypothesis is
the equality and the alternative hypothesis is the inequality. Hence,

*This type of hy-
pothesis leads to a
two-tail test.*

1. $H_0: p = 0.04 \qquad H_a: p \neq 0.04$

H_0 will be rejected if the sample proportion leads to a sample z which is
in either of the two tails of Figure 11.5. The figure is drawn for a true
H_0; that is, the mean is $p = 0.04$. If H_0 is true, and if the sample z
happens to fall in either of the two rejection regions, a true null hypothesis will be rejected and a Type I error committed. The probabil-

*In a two-tail test, half
the rejection area α
is apportioned to
each tail.*

ity of a Type I error is to be 0.05 (significance level 5 percent). Since
there are two rejection regions, half of $\alpha = 0.05$ is assigned to each
tail. The z value for a tail area of $\frac{1}{2}(0.05) = 0.025$ is

$$z_{\alpha/2} = z_{0.025} = 1.96$$

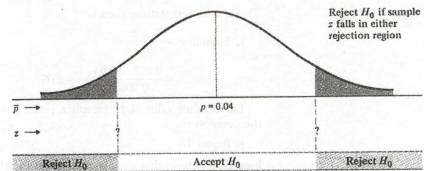

FIGURE 11.5
A two-tail test.

Figure 11.6 illustrates the decision rule we need. It is to reject H_0 if the sample z is less than -1.96 (the left ? in Figure 11.5), or if it is greater than 1.96 (the right ? in Figure 11.5). A simple way to express the rule

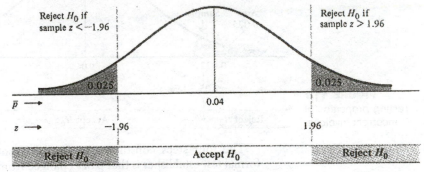

FIGURE 11.6
A two-tail test with $\alpha = 0.05$.

is to state that H_0 will be rejected if the *absolute value* of the sample z, designated by $|z|$, is greater than 1.96. Thus, for example, if the sample z is -2.3, then $|-2.3| = 2.3$, so H_0 would be rejected; and if the sample z is 2.3, $|2.3| = 2.3$, so H_0 would be rejected. The decision rule is

This is a two-tail decision rule.

2. Reject H_0 if |sample z| > 1.96

We need the standard error of the proportion to compute the value of the z test statistic. It is

$$\sigma_{\bar{p}} = \sqrt{\frac{pq}{n}}$$

With $p = 0.04$ (from H_0), so that $q = 0.96$ and $n = 500$,

$$\sigma_{\bar{p}} = \sqrt{\frac{(0.04)(0.96)}{500}} = 0.00876$$

The sample proportion of incorrectly recorded invoices (11 out of 500) is

$$\bar{p} = \frac{11}{500} = 0.022$$

The sample test statistic then is

3. Sample $z = \dfrac{\bar{p} - p}{\sigma_{\bar{p}}}$

$$= \dfrac{0.022 - 0.04}{0.00876} = -2.05$$

The absolute value of the sample z, $|-2.05| = 2.05$, exceeds 1.96; so the decision is

4. Reject H_0

Figure 11.7 shows that we rejected H_0 because the sample z value is in the rejection region.

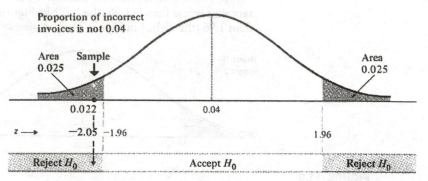

FIGURE 11.7
Testing proportion of incorrect invoices.

The four steps constitute the formal hypothesis test. What the formal test establishes is that p has changed from 0.04, or, we may say, p is significantly different from 0.04. The fact that the sample proportion is $\bar{p} = 0.022$ suggests not only that p differs from 0.04 but that p is less than 0.04. However, the logic of hypothesis testing does not permit us to start with a two-tail test and draw a one-tail (less than or greater than) conclusion. Nevertheless, we can, and should, state the implication of the test result.

b. H_0: $p = 0.04$ was rejected. The sample proportion $\bar{p} = 0.022$ implies that the new procedure instituted by the controller should be continued because it reduced the proportion of incorrectly recorded invoices.

The wording of a situation indicates when a two-tail test is needed.

We performed a two-tail test in the example because the controller was interested in whether or not the proportion had *changed*. The word *change* or the word *different* indicates that a two-tail test is to be performed.

11.9 PROBLEMS

1. (a) Define Type I error. (b) Define Type II error.
2. (a) What is meant by the statement that the significance level of a test is $\alpha = 0.05$? (b) What is meant by the symbol β?

3. A good college applicant is one who is capable of doing college-level work and graduating; a poor applicant is one who is not capable of doing college-level work. Suppose that a college adheres to the presumption that an applicant is a good applicant unless there is convincing evidence to the contrary. Should the college have high or low admissions requirements if α is to be small? Why?

4. Microchip Company makes chips used in electronic circuits. A random sample of 125 chips is to be selected from those produced. Production is to be halted for careful inspection if the sample percent of defective chips is significantly higher than normal, where normal is taken as 5 percent or less defective. It is required that the chance of halting normal production is to be only 0.02. (a) Perform a hypothesis test if the sample contains 10 defective chips. (b) What is implied by the test result?

5. In considering a proposed new personnel policy, executives of Portia Company feel it would be a mistake to institute the policy if 25 percent or more of company employees oppose it. The executives want the chance of making this mistake to be 0.10. (a) Perform a hypothesis test if 38 of a random sample of 200 employees oppose the policy. (b) What is implied by the test result?

6. Sparrow and Sons (S & S) manufactures papermaking machinery. S & S is considering whether or not to buy space and advertise in a trade journal. S & S is interested in the proportion of all engineers in papermaking companies who subscribe to the journal. Executives of S & S feel that it would be a mistake to advertise if the proportion of engineers who subscribe is 0.30 or lower, and want the chance of making that mistake to be 0.05. Members of the sales staff of S & S have interviewed a random sample of 100 engineers and found that 40 subscribe to the journal. (a) Perform a hypothesis test. (b) What is implied by the result?

7. Mogan, Inc., sponsors a television program called Guess Who. Mogan thinks it would be a mistake to cancel Guess Who if the program captures 40 percent or more of the audience. Mogan wants the chance of making that mistake to be 0.03. (a) Perform a hypothesis test if 178 of a random sample of 500 viewers watched Guess Who. (b) What is implied by the test result?

8. Pleasant Valley Company, a wine maker, buys thousands of boxes of grapes each year. Pleasant Valley's buyer visits vineyards and samples grapes on the vines. If the sample convinces the buyer that less than 20 percent of the total crop of a vineyard is of poor wine-making quality, the buyer purchases the entire crop. (a) Perform a hypothesis test at the 1 percent level of significance if a random sample of 500 grapes contains 75 poor-quality grapes. (b) What is implied by the test result?

9. A governmental agency will grant unemployment aid to a region if a sample shows substantial evidence that more than 7.5 percent of the region's workers are unemployed. (a) Perform a hypothesis test at the 2 percent level of significance if there are 170 unemployed in a random sample of 2000 workers. (b) What is implied by the test result?

10. An environmentalist claims that at least 30 percent of the fish in a large body of water are contaminated with mercury, and are not safe to eat. An opponent states that the claim is an exaggeration. (*a*) Perform a hypothesis test at the 1 percent level if 41 of a random sample of 200 fish are contaminated. (*b*) What is implied by the test result?

11. Trade association compilations showed that Pickers Peanuts, Inc., had 42 percent of the total peanut market in the past year. Pickers has made some changes in marketing policy and wants to determine if its market share has changed from 42 percent. Perform a hypothesis test at the 1 percent level of significance if 180 of a random sample of 400 customers buy Pickers Peanuts.

12. A test at the 5 percent level of significance is to be made to determine if the proportion of uncommitted voters in a state differs from 0.40. (*a*) Perform a hypothesis test if 175 voters in a random sample of 500 voters are uncommitted. (*b*) What is implied by the test result?

13. A chain store has been buying hot dogs from a meat-processing company which was sold recently and now is under new management. In the past, 90 percent of all hot dogs purchased were of high quality. The chain wants to determine whether the percentage is different under the new management. (*a*) Perform a test at the 1 percent level of significance if 238 of a random sample of 250 hot dogs are of high quality. (*b*) What is implied by the test result?

14. It is asserted that because no real coin can be exactly symmetrical, the proportion *p* of heads for a coin will differ from 0.50. Perform a hypothesis test of the assertion at the 5 percent level for a coin which showed 475 heads in 1000 tosses.

11.10 ONE-TAIL AND TWO-TAIL TESTS OF A POPULATION MEAN

Forms of Hypotheses

Let's use μ_h to mean a hypothesized value of a population mean. Three possible null hypotheses about a population mean, and their corresponding alternative hypotheses, are

$$
\begin{array}{ccc}
(a) & (b) & (c) \\
H_0: \mu \leq \mu_h & H_0: \mu \geq \mu_h & H_0: \mu = \mu_h \\
H_a: \mu > \mu_h & H_a: \mu < \mu_h & H_a: \mu \neq \mu_h
\end{array}
$$

The first two lead to a one-tail test; (*a*) is a right-tail test and (*b*) is a left-tail test. Test (*c*) is a two-tail test. In each case, the test will be made by obtaining a simple random sample of size *n* and computing the sample mean $\bar{x}$. Then $\bar{x}$ will be used in computing a test statistic. Depending upon the value of the test statistic, H_0 will be accepted or rejected.

The Test Statistic

We know from Chapter 9 that for a normal population having a mean of μ_h and a known standard deviation σ_x the distribution of sample means $\bar{x}$ is normal: the sampling distribution has a mean of μ_h and a standard error of

$$\sigma_{\bar{x}} = \frac{\sigma_x}{\sqrt{n}}$$

Test statistic for mean of normal population, σ_x known.

Then the statistic

$$z = \frac{\bar{x} - \mu_h}{\sigma_{\bar{x}}}$$

has the standard normal distribution. Consequently, the sample z value is the test statistic for testing a hypothesis about the mean of a normal population whose standard deviation is known.

If the standard deviation of the population σ_x is unknown, then we estimate σ_x by the sample standard deviation s_x; and we estimate the standard error of the mean by $s_{\bar{x}}$, where

$$s_{\bar{x}} = \frac{s_x}{\sqrt{n}}$$

If the population is normal, the statistic

Test statistic for mean of normal population, σ_x unknown.

$$t = \frac{\bar{x} - \mu_h}{s_{\bar{x}}}$$

has the Student t distribution with $n - 1$ degrees of freedom. Consequently, the sample t value is the test statistic for testing a hypothesis about the mean of a normal population whose standard deviation is unknown.

·Finally, recall the rule of thumb (Chapter 9) which states that the sampling distribution of $\bar{x}$ can be assumed to be normal even for nonnormal populations if the sample size is greater than 30 ($n > 30$). Following that rule of thumb, we will use the test statistic

Test statistic for mean of any population, $n > 00$.

$$? = \frac{\bar{x} - \mu_h}{\text{standard error of the mean}}$$

to test a hypothesis about the mean of any population (normal or not). In the last formula, the standard error of the mean is $\sigma_{\bar{x}}$ if the population standard deviation is known, but is $s_{\bar{x}}$ if the population standard deviation is unknown. To summarize, in testing a population mean we will

1. Use the sample z test statistic when (*a*) the population is normal and σ_x is known, or (*b*) the sample size is greater than 30 ($n > 30$).
2. Use the sample t test statistic when the population is normal, σ_x is not known, and $n \leq 30$.

One-Tail Test of a Population Mean

"The mean is at least 32 ounces . . ."

EXAMPLE The president of a chain of stores selling dairy products asserts that the mean content of the store's 32 fluid ounce (1 quart) milk containers is at least 32 ounces. Perform a hypothesis test at the 1 percent level of significance if the mean content of a random sample of 60 containers is 31.98 ounces and the sample standard deviation is 0.10 ounce.

SOLUTION The assertion that the mean is at least 32 ounces is the null hypothesis $\mu \geq 32$. Hence, we have

. . . means H_0:
$\mu \geq 32$

1. $H_0: \mu \geq 32 \quad H_a: \mu < 32$

The test will be *left*-tailed because H_a states μ is *less* than 32. The sample size, 60, is greater than 30; so the test statistic is the sample z.

If $\mu = 32$, so that H_0 is true, the chance of rejecting this true hypothesis (committing a Type I error) is to be $\alpha = 0.01$, the significance level of the test. Figure 11.8 shows the acceptance and rejection regions for a test which

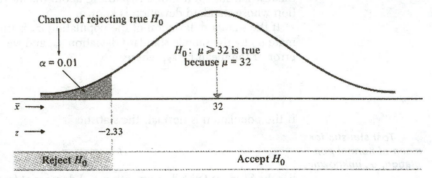

FIGURE 11.8
Distribution of $\bar{x}$ when H_0 is true.

will have a probability of 0.01 of rejecting H_0 if $\mu = 32$. Since $z_{0.01} = 2.33$, we have the decision rule

2. Reject H_0 if sample $z < -2.33$

The test statistic is

$$\text{Sample } z = \frac{\bar{x} - \mu_h}{\sigma_{\bar{x}}}$$

where $\mu_h = 32$ ounces. The sample mean is $\bar{x} = 31.98$ ounces. We need a value for the standard error of the mean $\sigma_{\bar{x}}$. The example statement provides the sample standard deviation $s_x = 0.10$ ounce. We estimate $\sigma_{\bar{x}}$ by the sample standard error of the mean,

We must compute $s_{\bar{x}}$, and use it to estimate the unknown $\sigma_{\bar{x}}$.

$$s_{\bar{x}} = \frac{s_x}{\sqrt{n}}$$

The sample size is $n = 60$; so

$$s_{\bar{x}} = \frac{0.10}{\sqrt{60}} = 0.0129$$

Next we compute

$$\text{Sample } z = \frac{\bar{x} - \mu_h}{s_{\bar{x}}}$$

$$= \frac{31.98 - 32}{0.0129} = -1.55$$

Hence,

3. Sample $z = -1.55$

The sample z, -1.55, is not less than -2.33; so we

4. Accept H_0

Thus, we accept the president's assertion that the mean content of the containers is at least 32 ounces. Figure 11.9 shows that H_0 was accepted because the sample z value lies in the acceptance region of the test.

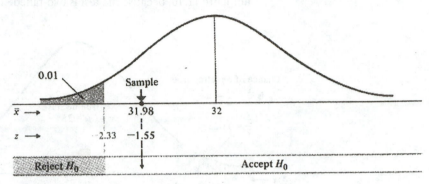

FIGURE 11.9
One-tail test of a population mean.

EXERCISE During contract negotiations with officials of Stone Company, union officials claim that the mean hourly wage paid by other companies in the region is higher than the mean hourly wage of $4.50 paid by Stone Company. Perform a hypothesis test at the 5 percent level of significance if the mean wage of a random sample of 49 workers in other companies is $4.65 and the sample standard deviation is $0.56.

    ANSWER 1. H_0: $\mu \leq 4.50$; H_a: $\mu > 4.50$. 2. Reject H_0 if sample $z > 1.64$. 3. Sample $z = 1.88$. 4. Reject H_0.

Two-Tail Test of a Population Mean

In a two-tail test of a population mean, we proceed as we did in the two-tail test of a population proportion.

    EXAMPLE When properly adjusted, an automatic machine should produce parts that have a mean diameter of 25 millimeters (mm). Part diameters are normally distributed. The mean diameter of a sample of 10 parts is to be used to check whether or not the machine is running properly. (*a*) Perform a hypothesis test at the 5 percent level if the mean of the sample is 25.02 mm and the sample standard deviation is 0.024 mm. (*b*) What is implied by the test result?

    SOLUTION

    a. The machine is running properly if the mean diameter of parts is $\mu =$

25 mm. If μ is either less than or greater than 25 mm ($\mu \neq 25$ mm) the machine is not running properly. Hence, we have a two-tail test with

Recall:
We use the t statistic
for a normal popula-
tion, σ_x unknown,
$n \leq 30$.

1. $H_0: \mu = 25$ mm $H_a: \mu \neq 25$ mm

We know that part diameters are normally distributed, but their standard deviation σ_x is unknown. Therefore, σ_x must be estimated from the sample, and the test statistic is the sample t value. The chance of rejecting $H_0: \mu = 25$ when it is true is to be 0.05 (the significance level). We place half of this chance, 0.025, in each tail, as shown in Figure 11.10, because the test is two-tailed. To determine the t value

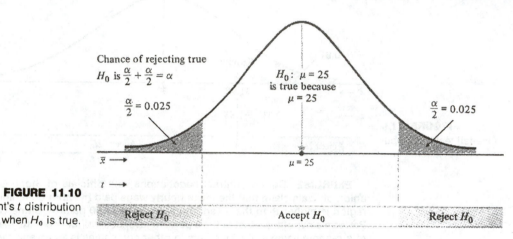

FIGURE 11.10
Student's *t* distribution
when H_0 is true.

for a one-tail area of 0.025, we need to know the number of degrees of freedom v. In testing a hypothesis about a population mean, the number of degrees is one less than the sample size. That is,

$$v = n - 1 = 10 - 1 = 9$$

The t value for a one-tail area of 0.025 and 9 degrees of freedom is found to be

$$t_{0.025,9} = 2.26$$

from Table VII. H_0 will be rejected if the sample t value is less than -2.26 or greater than 2.26; that is,

2. Reject H_0 if |sample t| > 2.26

Next we need the sample t value,

$$\text{Sample } t = \frac{\bar{x} - \mu_h}{s_{\bar{x}}}$$

The example states that the sample standard deviation s_x is given as

0.024 mm. The sample standard error of the mean $s_{\bar{x}}$ is computed by the formula

$$s_{\bar{x}} = \frac{s_x}{\sqrt{n}}$$

With $n = 10$ and $s_x = 0.024$, we compute

$$s_{\bar{x}} = \frac{0.024}{\sqrt{10}} = 0.00759$$

The sample mean is $\bar{x} = 25.02$ mm; so

$$\text{Sample } t = \frac{\bar{x} - \mu_h}{s_{\bar{x}}}$$

$$= \frac{25.02 - 25}{0.00759} = 2.64$$

Consequently,

3. Sample $t = 2.64$

Because |sample t| = |2.64| = 2.64 is greater than the 2.26 in the decision rule, we

Hypothesis testing is as easy as 1, 2, 3, 4.

4. Reject H_0

Figure 11.11 shows that $H_0: \mu = 25$ was rejected because the sample z lies in the rejection region of the test.

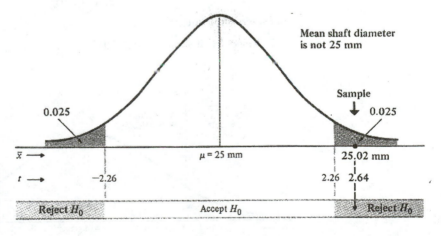

FIGURE 11.11
Testing the mean diameter of shafts made on a lathe.

b. The result of the test and the fact that the sample mean, 25.02 mm, is greater than the proper mean, 25 mm, imply that the population mean is greater than 25 mm. Therefore, the machine setting should be adjusted to a smaller diameter.

EXERCISE In the last example, where the significance level is 5 percent, suppose that the machine's standard deviation was *known* to be 0.024 mm. What then would have been the decision rule?
ANSWER Reject H_0 if |sample z| > 1.96.

The exercise calls attention to the fact that when σ is known, the decision rule makes use of the normal z value rather than the t value.

11.11 TYPE II ERROR PROBABILITIES

P(Type II error) = β

Accepting a false null hypothesis is a Type II error. The probability of a Type II error is designated as β. In this section we will compute values of β.

EXAMPLE Suppose a sugar refinery ships 454-gram (1-pound) boxes of sugar to wholesalers in railroad carload lots. The weights of boxes are normally distributed and have a standard deviation of $\sigma_x = 8$ grams. Before a carload is shipped, a random sample of $n = 25$ boxes is weighed. Then a hypothesis test is performed at the 2 percent level to determine whether the mean weight for the carload is less than 454 grams. The hypotheses are

1. $H_0: \mu \geq 454$ $H_a: \mu < 454$

If H_0 is rejected, the carload is removed to an inspection station and checked more extensively. If H_0 is accepted, the carload is dispatched to the wholesaler.

The test is a left-tail test. With $\alpha = 0.02$, z_α is

$$z_{0.02} = 2.05$$

so the decision rule is

Decision rule in terms of z

2. Reject H_0 if sample $z < -2.05$

as shown in Figure 11.12.

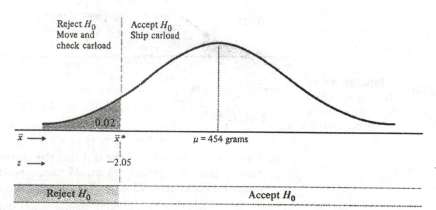

FIGURE 11.12
Using $\bar{x}$ instead of z in a decision rule.

To compute β, we need the decision rule in terms of x̄. Our purpose is to compute values of β. For that purpose it is necessary to express the decision rule in terms of $\bar{x}$, the sample mean. From the definition

$$z = \frac{\bar{x} - \mu}{\sigma_{\bar{x}}}$$

we obtain

$$\bar{x} = \mu + z\sigma_{\bar{x}}$$

With $\sigma_x = 8$ and $n = 25$, we compute

$$\sigma_{\bar{x}} = \frac{\sigma_x}{\sqrt{n}} = \frac{8}{\sqrt{25}} = 1.6$$

Consequently, the $\bar{x}$ corresponding to $z = -2.05$ is

$$\bar{x}^* = \mu + z\sigma_{\bar{x}} = 454 - 2.05(1.6) = 450.72$$

Hence, the rule to reject H_0 if the sample z is less than -2.05 is equivalent to the rule to reject H_0 if the sample mean is less than 450.72 grams. The rule is illustrated in Figure 11.13. A Type II error can be committed only if a false

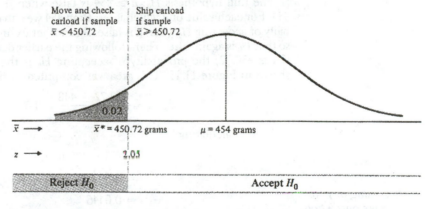

FIGURE 11.13
Accept H_0 if sample mean is equal to or greater than 450.72 grams.

H_0 is accepted; so let's express the decision rule as

Acceptance rule in terms of x̄

$$\text{Accept } H_0 \text{ if } \bar{x} \geq 450.72$$

$H_0: \mu \geq 454$ will be false if μ is any value less than 454. Suppose μ is 452, so that H_0 is false. Then β is the probability of accepting H_0 when $\mu = 452$. In Figure 11.14, the shaded area is the probability β of accepting H_0, following the rule derived earlier to accept if $\bar{x} \geq 450.72$. The figure shows $\beta = 0.7881$. To calculate β, we first find the z value for 450.72. With $\sigma_{\bar{x}} = 1.6$, we have

$$z = \frac{450.72 - 452}{1.6} = -0.8$$

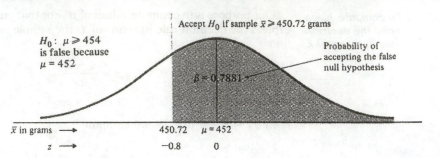

FIGURE 11.14
Probability β of accepting a false null hypothesis: $\alpha = 0.02$.

The shaded area is

$$\beta = 0.5 + P(0 \text{ to } 0.8)$$

This value of β applies only when $\mu = 452$.

From Table V, $P(0 \text{ to } 0.8)$ is 0.2881; so

$$\beta = 0.5 + 0.2881 = 0.7881$$

Thus, there is a fairly high probability, $\beta = 0.7881$, of accepting $H_0: \mu \geq 454$ when actually $\mu = 452$.

The null hypothesis $H_0: \mu \geq 454$ is false when μ is any value less than 454. For each value of μ which is less than 454 we can compute β, the probability of accepting H_0 when it is false. As another example, suppose $\mu = 448$, so that H_0 is again false. Then, following the earlier derived rule to accept H_0 if $\bar{x} \geq 450.72$, the probability of accepting H_0 is the shaded area, 0.0446, shown in Figure 11.15. This area was computed by first calculating

$$z = \frac{450.72 - 448}{1.6} = 1.7$$

and then calculating

$$\beta = 0.5 - P(0 \text{ to } 1.7)$$

$$= 0.5 - 0.4554$$

This value of β applies only when $\mu = 448$.

$$= 0.0446$$

Thus, the probability of accepting $H_0: \mu \geq 454$ when $\mu = 448$ (so that H_0 is false) is the rather small value 0.0446.

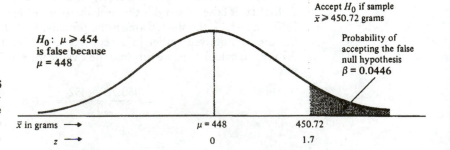

FIGURE 11.15
Probability β of accepting another false null hypothesis: $\alpha = 0.02$.

EXERCISE For the example, compute β if (a) $\mu = 449$; (b) $\mu = 451$.
ANSWER (a) Using $z = 1.08$, $\beta = 0.1401$; (b) using $z = -0.18$, $\beta = 0.5714$.

The β probabilities we calculated for the μ values 448, 449, 451, and 452 are plotted in Figure 11.16. Thus, as shown on the figure, if $\mu = 452$, so that

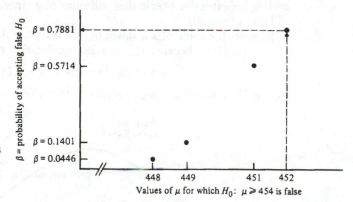

FIGURE 11.16
Probabilities β of accepting false null hypotheses.

$H_0: \mu \geq 454$ is false, β is 0.7881. By calculating β for other values of μ which are less than 454, we can obtain more points and sketch the curve shown in Figure 11.17. The curve is called an *operating characteristic* (OC) *curve*. The

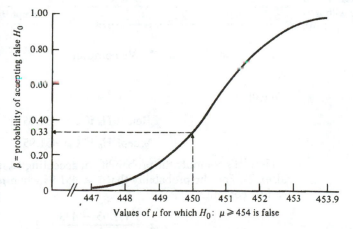

The closer the actual mean is to the hypothesized mean, the larger β is.

FIGURE 11.17
Operating characteristic curve for a left-tail test.

OC curve for a decision rule shows the probability of accepting H_0 for all values of the parameter (μ in our example) where H_0 is false.

An OC curve is of help in determining whether or not a specified hypothesis test is adequate for the purpose at hand. Thus, in our example, the refinery management may feel that it is unwise to ship a carload that has a mean weight of 450 grams (rather than 454 grams, or more). But the OC curve in Figure 11.17 shows that the chance of doing so is about 0.33. If the refinery executives decide this chance is too high, then there are three ways in which it can be lowered. They can increase α (now $\alpha = 0.02$) or increase the sample size (now $n = 25$) or both. Increasing α results in a higher chance of rejecting H_0: $\mu \geq 454$ when it is true. In decision terms, increasing α means a higher chance of unnecessarily removing the carload and making an extensive check; that will raise cost. Increasing the sample size will also raise cost.

Suppose the value of α is raised to $\alpha = 0.10$, but the sample size remains at $n = 25$. Then, because $z_{0.10} = 1.28$, the decision rule is to

$$\text{Reject } H_0 \text{ if sample } z < -1.28$$

Figure 11.18 shows the decision rule in terms of $z = -1.28$ and the corre-

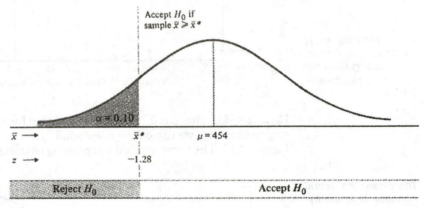

Accept H_0 if sample $\bar{x} \geq \bar{x}^*$

$\alpha = 0.10$

$\bar{x} \longrightarrow$ $\bar{x}^*$ $\mu = 454$

$z \longrightarrow$ -1.28

Reject H_0 Accept H_0

FIGURE 11.18
Decision rule with $\alpha = 0.10$.

sponding sample mean $\bar{x}^*$. We compute

$$\bar{x}^* = \mu + z\sigma_{\bar{x}} = 454 - 1.28(1.6) = 451.95$$

We will

$$\text{Reject } H_0 \text{ if } \bar{x} < 451.95$$

$$\text{Accept } H_0 \text{ if } \bar{x} \geq 451.95$$

Now let's compute the probability of accepting H_0 if $\mu = 448$ (so that H_0 is false). To find the probability that $\bar{x} \geq 451.95$ when μ is 448, and $\sigma_{\bar{x}} = 1.6$, we first compute

$$z = \frac{451.95 - 448}{1.6} = 2.47$$

The desired probability is

$$\beta = 0.5 - P(0 \text{ to } 2.47)$$
$$= 0.5 - 0.4932$$
$$= 0.0068$$

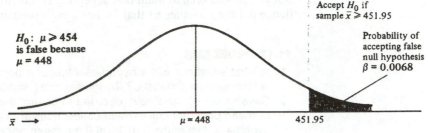

Accept H_0 if
sample $\bar{x} \geq 451.95$

H_0: $\mu \geq 454$
is false because
$\mu = 448$

Probability of
accepting false
null hypothesis
$\beta = 0.0068$

$\bar{x} \longrightarrow$ $\mu = 448$ 451.95

FIGURE 11.19
Probability β of accepting a false null hypothesis with $\alpha = 0.10$. (Compare with Figure 11.15.)

as shown in Figure 11.19. Earlier (see Figure 11.15) we found that $\beta = 0.0446$ when $\mu = 448$; but then α was 0.02, not 0.10. Thus, increasing α from 0.02 to 0.10 lowered β from 0.0446 to 0.0068. In general, for a given sample size, the larger α, the smaller will be the values of β; and the smaller α is, the larger will be the values of β. Thus, as stated early in the chapter, there is a trade-off between α and β.

A larger α leads to a smaller β.

EXERCISE In the example, which has H_0: $\mu \geq 454$, H_a: $\mu < 454$, and $\sigma_x = 8$, suppose $\alpha = 0.02$ and $n = 100$. (a) What is the value of $\sigma_{\bar{x}}$? (b) What values of the sample $\bar{x}$ will result in accepting H_0? (c) Compute β if $\mu = 452$.
ANSWER (a) 0.8; (b) $\bar{x} \geq 452.36$, (c) $\beta = 0.3264$.

In the original example, with $\alpha = 0.02$ and $n = 25$, β was 0.7881 when $\mu = 452$ (see Figure 11.14). In the last exercise, the larger sample size (100) reduced β to 0.3264 when $\mu = 452$. The hypothesis test of the exercise does a better job than the test in the original example because β is smaller. Statisticians say that the exercise hypothesis test is the more powerful of the two tests; they define the *power* of a test as $1 - \beta$. Since β is the chance of accepting a false H_0, $1 - \beta$ is the chance of rejecting a false H_0. Hence, the *power of a hypothesis test*, $1 - \beta$, *is the chance of rejecting a false null hypothesis*. In the last exercise, β is 0.3264; so the power of the test is

A larger sample size leads to a smaller β.

Power of test = $1 - \beta$

$$1 - 0.3264 = 0.6736$$

or about 67 percent.

Type I error, rejecting a true H_0, is usually considered to be more serious than a Type II error, accepting a false H_0. Consequently, decision makers set the chance of a Type I error α at a low value (usually 0.10 or lower). Then if H_0 is rejected, the decision maker is convinced that there is a high probability that H_0 is false. However, if H_0 is accepted, it would not be correct to say there is a high probability that H_0 is true: that's because our β calculations show that the probability of accepting a false H_0 can be high. In some decision problems, managers replace "reject H_0 or accept H_0" by "reject H_0 or do not reject H_0." Then, if H_0 is not rejected, judgment is deferred; and more sample information is obtained before deciding whether or not to accept H_0. However, in problems where the implications of tests are used in determining courses of action, judgment cannot be deferred; so the decision has to be to reject H_0 or accept H_0. In this book, we shall accept or reject H_0;

but you should keep in mind that accepting H_0 means only that sample evidence did not convince us that H_0 has a high probability of being false.

11.12 PROBLEMS

1. In what situations will a hypothesis test of a population mean employ (a) the sample z statistic? (b) the sample t statistic?

2. Government officials have decided to control the price of a product if its mean price per unit in retail outlets rises above $2.50. (a) Perform a hypothesis test at the 0.01 level if the mean price in a random sample of 40 outlets is $2.52 and the sample standard deviation is $0.10. (b) What is implied by the test result?

3. Safe-Fly Company makes parachutes. Safe-Fly has been buying snap links from a manufacturing firm which recently merged with Big Deal Corporation. Safe-Fly is concerned that the quality of snap links they receive from Big Deal might not be up to specifications. Specifically, Safe-Fly wants to be convinced that the links will withstand a mean breaking force of more than 5000 pounds. (a) Perform a hypothesis test at the 0.005 (0.5 percent) level if the mean breaking force for a random sample of 50 links is 5100 pounds and the sample standard deviation is 221 pounds. (b) What is implied by the test result?

4. Food Machinery Supplies (FMS) manufactures automatic cola-dispensing machines that are supposed to pour 8 ounces into a cup. Before shipping a machine, FMS makes a sample check to determine if the mean amount poured by the machine is at least 8 ounces. (a) Perform a hypothesis test at the 0.05 level if a random sample of 60 filled cups had a mean fill amount of 7.92 ounces and a standard deviation of 0.16 ounce. (b) What action is implied by the test result?

5. Seniors in the high schools of a city have in the past had a mean score of 490 on a standardized mathematics test. A teacher suggests that seniors will have a higher mean score if they attend tutorial sessions before taking the test. (a) Perform a hypothesis test at the 0.05 level if the scores of a random sample of 35 tutored seniors who take the standardized test have a mean of 510 and a standard deviation of 85. (b) What is implied by the test?

6. The Super Tread Tire Company requires that the tires it makes should withstand a mean pressure of more than 150 psi (pounds per square inch) before bursting. From each large batch of tires made, a random sample of 10 tires is selected and subjected to increasing pressures until they burst. Bursting pressures have been found to be normally distributed. Only batches of tires that meet the psi requirement are sold under the Super Tread brand name. (a) Perform a hypothesis test at the 1 percent level for a batch in which the sample mean psi is 154 and the sample standard deviation is 3.7 psi. (b) What is implied by the test result?

7. (See Problem 6.) What would the decision rule be if it is known that the standard deviation is $\sigma_x = 3.7$ psi?

8. Consumer Protection, Inc., rates vacuum cleaners as having a satisfactory noise level if their mean noise level is less than 60 decibels. Noise levels are normally distributed. (a) Perform a hypothesis test at the 0.05 level if a random sample of six cleaners have a mean noise level of 56 decibels and a standard deviation of 5 decibels. (b) What is implied by the test result?

9. Expensive test borings were made in an oil shale area to determine if the mean yield of oil per ton of shale rock is greater than 4.5 barrels. Five borings, made at randomly selected points in the area, indicated the following numbers of barrels per ton

4.8   5.4   3.9   4.9   5.5

Suppose barrels per ton are normally distributed. Perform a hypothesis test at the 5 percent level.

10. The environmental protection officer of a large industrial plant wants to determine whether the mean amount of sulfur oxides emitted by the plant exceeds 7 tons per day. Suppose emission amounts are normally distributed. Perform a hypothesis test at the 5 percent level if, for a random sample of 10 days, tons of emission per day are

8   7   10   15   11   6   8   5   13   12

11. The standard assembly rate for a product is 50 units per worker per day. To keep track of worker performance, the production manager finds the mean output of a random sample of 32 workers. The manager wants to determine if the mean output for all workers differs from 50. (a) Perform a hypothesis test at the 5 percent level if the sample mean is 52 and the sample standard deviation is 5. (b) What is implied by the test result?

12. The sales manager of Amcar Motors asserts that Amcars average 30 miles per gallon of gas. The marketing vice president wants to determine if the average is different from 30. (a) Perform a hypothesis test at the 10 percent level if a random sample of 40 Amcars had an average of 28.2 miles per gallon and a standard deviation of 2 miles per gallon. (b) What is implied by the test result?

13. Auto Instruments Company (AIC) manufactures automobile mileage gauges (odometers). AIC asserts that when their gauges are installed in cars, they will record 100 miles, on the average, when cars are driven 100 miles. Amcar Motors is considering installing AIC odometers in their new cars but will not do so if the mean differs from 100 miles. Assume odometer recordings are normally distributed. (a) Perform a hypothesis test at the 5 percent level if the mean for a random sample of 15 odometers is 100.6 miles and the standard deviation is 1.2 miles. (b) What is implied by the test result?

14. (See Problem 13.) Change the significance level to 10 percent. (a) Perform the hypothesis test. (b) What is implied by the test result?

15. If the null hypothesis is H_0: $\mu \le 30$, when would a Type II error be made?

16. Given H_0: $\mu \leq 30$, H_a: $\mu > 30$, $n = 35$, $\alpha = 0.06$, $\sigma_x = 2.1$. (a) For what values of the sample mean $\bar{x}$ will H_0 be accepted? (b) Compute β if μ is actually 30.8. (c) Compute β if μ is actually 30.2.

17. If the null hypothesis is H_0: $\mu \geq 500$, when would a Type II error be made?

18. Given H_0: $\mu \geq 500$, H_a: $\mu < 500$, $n = 36$, $\alpha = 0.055$, $\sigma_x = 60$. (a) For what values of the sample mean $\bar{x}$ will H_0 be accepted? (b) Compute β if μ is actually 485. (c) Compute β if μ is actually 470.

19. Suppose the force required to break parachute snap links should average 5000 pounds. In performing a hypothesis test with a small α, would you use H_0: $\mu \geq 5000$ pounds or H_0: $\mu \leq 5000$ pounds? Why?

20. Suppose you are a milk distributor and have been accused of under-filling 16-fluid-ounce containers. In performing a hypothesis test with a small α, would you prefer to test H_0: $\mu \geq 16$ or H_0: $\mu \leq 16$? Why?

11.13 TESTS OF THE DIFFERENCE IN TWO POPULATION PROPORTIONS

The Distribution of the Differences in Sample Proportions

If the proportion of successes in a population is p, then (Chapter 9) we can

Consider two populations, and a proportion in each.

assume that the distribution of sample proportions $\bar{p}$ is normal if both np and nq exceed 5. In this section we shall use samples large enough so that we can assume sampling distributions are normal. Suppose we have two populations, 1 and 2, with respective success proportions p_1 and p_2. Then sample proportions $\bar{p}_1$ for samples of size n_1 from population 1 are normally distributed; and sample proportions $\bar{p}_2$ for samples of size n_2 from population 2 are normally distributed.

Let's use the symbol dist ( ) to mean the distribution of the sample statistic inside the ( ). Thus dist ($\bar{p}_1$) means the distribution of $\bar{p}_1$. Dist ($\bar{p}_1$) is

For each population, the distribution of sample proportions (where n is large enough) is normal.

normal. Its mean is the population proportion p_1; that is,

$$\mu_{\bar{p}_1} = p_1$$

The standard error of the proportion is

$$\sigma_{\bar{p}_1} = \sqrt{\frac{p_1 q_1}{n_1}}$$

Similarly, for dist ($\bar{p}_2$),

$$\mu_{\bar{p}_2} = p_2$$

$$\sigma_{\bar{p}_2} = \sqrt{\frac{p_2 q_2}{n_2}}$$

Now take a sample from each population, and form the difference $\bar{p}_1 - \bar{p}_2$.

Now suppose (Figure 11.20) we select a sample of size n_1 from population 1 and compute the sample proportion of successes $\bar{p}_1$. Then we select a sample of size n_2 from population 2 and compute $\bar{p}_2$. Next we compute the difference between the sample proportions $\bar{p}_1 - \bar{p}_2$. The number of samples

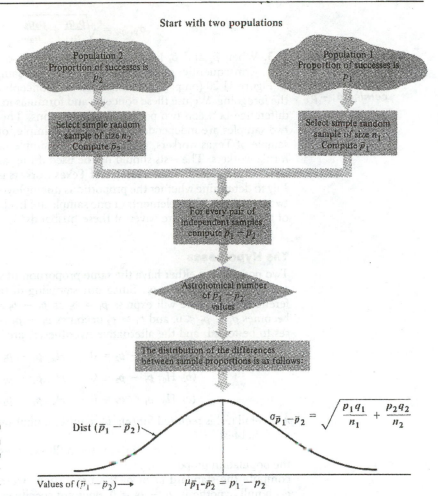

Start with two populations

Population 2
Proportion of successes is
p_2

Population 1
Proportion of successes is
p_1

Select simple random
sample of size n_2
Compute $\bar{p}_2$

Select simple random
sample of size n_1
Compute $\bar{p}_1$

For every pair of
independent samples,
compute $\bar{p}_1 - \bar{p}_2$

Astronomical number
of $\bar{p}_1 - \bar{p}_2$
values

The distribution of the differences
between sample proportions is as follows:

Dist $(\bar{p}_1 - \bar{p}_2)$

$$\sigma_{\bar{p}_1 - \bar{p}_2} = \sqrt{\dfrac{p_1 q_1}{n_1} + \dfrac{p_2 q_2}{n_2}}$$

Values of $(\bar{p}_1 - \bar{p}_2) \longrightarrow$ $\mu_{\bar{p}_1 - \bar{p}_2} = p_1 - p_2$

FIGURE 11.20
Sampling distribution
of the difference
between two propor-
tions.

that can be drawn from each population is astronomically large. Consequently, the number of differences $\bar{p}_1 - \bar{p}_2$ is astronomically large. We will be working with the sampling distribution of the $\bar{p}_1 - \bar{p}_2$ values, dist $(\bar{p}_1 - \bar{p}_2)$. Mathematicians have proved the following facts about dist $(\bar{p}_1 - \bar{p}_2)$:

The distribution of all values $\bar{p}_1 - \bar{p}_2$ has these properties.

1. The mean of dist $(\bar{p}_1 - \bar{p}_2)$, denoted by $\mu_{\bar{p}_1 - \bar{p}_2}$, is the difference between the population means; that is,

$$\mu_{\bar{p}_1 - \bar{p}_2} = p_1 - p_2$$

2. If the samples are independent, the variability (standard error) of the $\bar{p}_1 - \bar{p}_2$ values is greater than the variability of the $\bar{p}_1$ values, and greater than the variability of the $\bar{p}_2$ values. The formula for the standard error of dist $(\bar{p}_1 - \bar{p}_2)$ is

$$\sigma_{\bar{p}_1 - \bar{p}_2} = \sqrt{\frac{p_1 q_1}{n_1} + \frac{p_2 q_2}{n_2}}$$

We may therefore use z values to test hypotheses concerning $\bar{p}_1 - \bar{p}_2$.

3. When $\bar{p}_1$ and $\bar{p}_2$ have normal distributions, dist $(\bar{p}_1 - \bar{p}_2)$ is normal. Consequently, our test statistic will be the sample z value.

Figure 11.20 (on page 365) illustrates the concepts and formulas stated in the foregoing. We use these concepts and formulas in developing tests of the difference between two population proportions. The tests assume that the two samples are independent; that is, for example, one is a simple random sample of Texas workers, and the other is a simple random sample of California workers. The tests should not be used if the samples are related, that is, for example, if the same sample of Texas workers is surveyed in June and July to determine whether the proportions unemployed are different in these two months; or if the elements of one sample are husbands and the elements of the other sample are wives of these husbands.

The Hypotheses

Two populations either have the same proportion of successes, so that $p_1 = p_2$, or $p_1 < p_2$, or $p_1 > p_2$. Since our sampling distribution is for the difference $p_1 - p_2$, we will express $p_1 = p_2$ as $p_1 - p_2 = 0$; similarly, $p_1 < p_2$ becomes $p_1 - p_2 < 0$, and $p_1 > p_2$ becomes $p_1 - p_2 > 0$. The null hypotheses to be tested, and the alternative hypotheses, are

$$(a) \ H_0: p_1 - p_2 = 0 \qquad H_a: p_1 - p_2 \neq 0$$

$$(b) \ H_0: p_1 - p_2 \leq 0 \qquad H_a: p_1 - p_2 > 0$$

$$(c) \ H_0: p_1 - p_2 \geq 0 \qquad H_a: p_1 - p_2 < 0$$

A two-tail test is required for (a); (b) requires a right-tail test, and (c) requires a left-tail test.

In the test of a single proportion, the null hypothesis includes a value for the population proportion, as in $H_0: p \geq 0.25$. Then we use the value of p to compute the standard error of the proportion. Here, the equality part of each null hypothesis, $p_1 - p_2 = 0$, does not specify values for p_1 and p_2. Instead, $p_1 - p_2 = 0$ means that the proportions have the same value but does not say what the value is. In addition, $p_1 = p_2$ implies that *we should assume $p_1 = p_2$ until sample evidence convinces us that the assumption is unreasonable*.

Sample Estimate of the Standard Error

The formula for the standard error, given earlier, is

We need the standard error of dist $(\bar{p}_1 - \bar{p}_2)$ to compute z values.

$$\sigma_{\bar{p}_1 - \bar{p}_2} = \sqrt{\frac{p_1 q_1}{n_1} + \frac{p_2 q_2}{n_2}}$$

But we should assume $p_1 = p_2$ until convinced otherwise. Consequently, we assume p_1 and p_2 have the same value, and that value is p_c. Then we have

$$\sigma_{\bar{p}_1 - \bar{p}_2} = \sqrt{\frac{p_c q_c}{n_1} + \frac{p_c q_c}{n_2}}$$

or

$$\sigma_{\bar{p}_1 - \bar{p}_2} = \sqrt{p_c q_c \left(\frac{1}{n_1} + \frac{1}{n_2}\right)}$$

Since we do not know what the common value p_c is, we estimate it from the samples, and call the estimator $\bar{p}_c$. Then the sample standard error of dist $(\bar{p}_1 - \bar{p}_2)$ is

We'll use this formula to estimate
$\sigma_{\bar{p}_1 - \bar{p}_2}$ . . .

$$s_{\bar{p}_1 - \bar{p}_2} = \sqrt{\bar{p}_c \bar{q}_c \left(\frac{1}{n_1} + \frac{1}{n_2}\right)}$$

Now, how shall we compute $\bar{p}_c$ from the samples? We assume, until convinced otherwise, that the population proportions are equal. Consequently, it is reasonable to *combine* the samples and compute

. . . and this one to compute $\bar{p}_c$.

$$\bar{p}_c = \frac{\text{sum of successes in two samples}}{n_1 + n_2}$$

Thus, the subscript c on $\bar{p}_c$ means the *combined* sample proportion of successes. For example, suppose there are 43 unemployed in a sample of $n_1 = 500$ workers in Texas and 20 unemployed in a sample of $n_2 = 400$ workers in California, then

$$\bar{p}_c = \frac{\text{sum of numbers unemployed}}{n_1 + n_2}$$

$$= \frac{43 + 20}{500 + 400} = 0.07$$

$$\bar{q}_c = 1 - \bar{p}_c = 0.93$$

Now we can compute

$$s_{\bar{p}_1 - \bar{p}_2} = \sqrt{\bar{p}_c \bar{q}_c \left(\frac{1}{n_1} + \frac{1}{n_2}\right)}$$

$$= \sqrt{(0.07)(0.93)\left(\frac{1}{500} + \frac{1}{400}\right)}$$

$$= 0.0171$$

EXERCISE Suppose there are 69 unemployed in a random sample of 600 Indiana workers, and 64 unemployed in a random sample of 800 Michigan workers. (a) Compute $\bar{p}_c$. (b) Compute $s_{\bar{p}_1 - \bar{p}_2}$.
ANSWER (a) 0.095; (b) 0.0158.

Sample Size

Large samples usually are required for tests of the difference between two proportions. To determine how large the samples should be, proceed as follows: Guess which of the values p_1, q_1, p_2, q_2 is the smallest proportion, and guess its value. Then both n_1 and n_2 should exceed 5 divided by the smallest proportion. For example, if you guess p_2 is the smallest proportion, and that p_2 is about 0.04, both n_1 and n_2 should exceed 125 because $5/0.04 = 125$.

The Test Statistic

Dist $(\bar{p}_1 - \bar{p}_2)$ has a mean of $p_1 - p_2$. In tests we use the equality part of H_0, $p_1 - p_2 = 0$; so the mean of dist $(\bar{p}_1 - \bar{p}_2)$ will be 0, as shown in Figure 11.21.

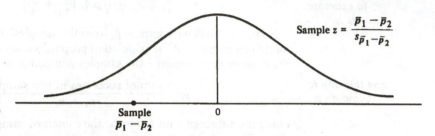

Sample $z = \dfrac{\bar{p}_1 - \bar{p}_2}{s_{\bar{p}_1 - \bar{p}_2}}$

Sample
$\bar{p}_1 - \bar{p}_2$ 0

FIGURE 11.21
Formula for sample z in tests of difference between proportions.

The difference in the sample proportions is $\bar{p}_1 - \bar{p}_2$. The z value for the difference is

$$z = \frac{\text{sample difference} - \text{mean}}{s_{\bar{p}_1 - \bar{p}_2}}$$

But the mean is 0. Hence, the formula for the test statistic is

We'll use this formula to compute z values.

$$\text{Sample } z = \frac{\bar{p}_1 - \bar{p}_2}{s_{\bar{p}_1 - \bar{p}_2}}$$

Performing Tests

Now that we have the necessary formulas, hypothesis tests of $p_1 - p_2$ are routine.

EXAMPLE Random samples of 1600 workers in region 1 and 1400 workers in region 2 have been obtained to determine whether the population proportions unemployed in the two regions are different. Perform a hypothesis test at the 5 percent level if the numbers unemployed in the samples were 120 in region 1 and 84 in region 2.

SOLUTION The word *different* in the statement of the example means $p_1 \neq p_2$, or $p_1 - p_2 \neq 0$. Hence, we have the hypotheses

1. The hypotheses $H_0: p_1 - p_2 = 0$ $H_a: p_1 - p_2 \neq 0$

The test is two-tailed, with $\frac{1}{2}(0.05) = 0.025$ in each tail; because $z_{0.025} = 1.96$, we have the decision rule

2. The decision rule   Reject H_0 if |sample z| > 1.96

That is, we will reject H_0 if the sample z is less than -1.96, or if it is greater than 1.96.

We need $\bar{p}_c$ to use in computing $s_{\bar{p}_1 - \bar{p}_2}$. It is

$$\bar{p}_c = \frac{\text{sum of numbers unemployed in the two samples}}{n_1 + n_2}$$

$$= \frac{120 + 84}{1600 + 1400}$$

$$= 0.068$$

Next we compute

$$s_{\bar{p}_1 - \bar{p}_2} = \sqrt{\bar{p}_c \bar{q}_c \left(\frac{1}{n_1} + \frac{1}{n_2} \right)}$$

$$= \sqrt{(0.068)(0.932) \left(\frac{1}{1600} + \frac{1}{1400} \right)}$$

$$= 0.00921$$

Now it is time to determine whether the difference between the sample proportions is large enough to convince us that $H_0: p_1 = p_2$ is false. To obtain the sample proportions, we note that, in region 1, 120 of 1600 were unemployed; so

$$\bar{p}_1 = \frac{120}{1600} = 0.075$$

In region 2, 84 of 1400 were unemployed; so

$$\bar{p}_2 = \frac{84}{1400} = 0.060$$

The test statistic is

$$\text{Sample } z = \frac{\bar{p}_1 - \bar{p}_2}{s_{\bar{p}_1 - \bar{p}_2}}$$

For our data

$$\text{Sample } z = \frac{0.075 - 0.060}{0.00921} = \frac{0.015}{0.00921} = 1.63$$

Hence,

3. The test statistic   Sample $z = 1.63$

Because $z = 1.63$ is not greater than the value $z = 1.96$ specified in the decision rule, we

4. Accept or reject   Accept H_0

Thus, we accept the hypothesis that the proportions unemployed are equal because the samples do not provide convincing evidence that they are different. Figure 11.22 shows that H_0 is accepted because the sample z value, 1.63, lies in the accept H_0 region.

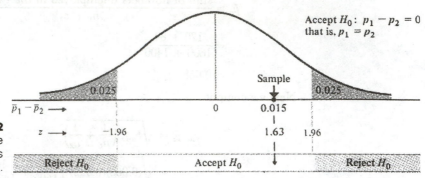

FIGURE 11.22
Testing the difference between proportions unemployed.

EXAMPLE Continuing with the last example, suppose that at a later time independent random samples, both of size 1500, are taken and show 74 unemployed in region 1 and 129 unemployed in region 2. Perform a hypothesis test at the 5 percent level to determine whether the proportion unemployed in region 1 is less than the proportion unemployed in region 2.

SOLUTION The words less than mean $p_1 < p_2$, or $p_1 - p_2 < 0$. Hence, we have the hypotheses

1. $H_0: p_1 - p_2 \geq 0$ $H_a: p_1 - p_2 < 0$

This is a left-tail test.   With $\alpha = 0.05$, we use $z_{0.05} = 1.64$. The $<$ in H_a specifies a left-tail test; so our decision rule is

2. Reject H_0 if sample $z < -1.64$

The combined sample proportion is

$$\bar{p}_c = \frac{74 + 129}{1500 + 1500} = 0.0677$$

$$\bar{q}_c = 1 - \bar{p}_c = 0.9323$$

Next we compute

$$s_{\bar{p}_1 - \bar{p}_2} = \sqrt{\bar{p}_c \bar{q}_c \left(\frac{1}{n_1} + \frac{1}{n_2}\right)}$$

$$= \sqrt{(0.0677)(0.9323)\left(\frac{1}{1500} + \frac{1}{1500}\right)} = 0.00917$$

The sample proportions unemployed are

$$\bar{p}_1 = \frac{74}{1500} = 0.0493$$

$$\bar{p}_2 = \frac{129}{1500} = 0.0860$$

Hence,

$$\bar{p}_1 - \bar{p}_2 = 0.0493 - 0.0860 = -0.0367$$

Next, we compute

$$\text{Sample } z = \frac{\bar{p}_1 - \bar{p}_2}{s_{\bar{p}_1 - \bar{p}_2}}$$

$$= \frac{-0.0367}{0.00917} = -4.00$$

So,

3. Sample $z = -4.00$

The sample z, -4.00, is less than the value -1.64 in the decision rule; so we

4. Reject H_0

When we reject H_0,
we accept H_a.

Rejection of H_0 means we conclude that $p_1 - p_2 < 0$, or $p_1 < p_2$; that is, the proportion unemployed in region 1 is smaller than the proportion unemployed in region 2. Figure 11.23 shows that H_0 is rejected because the sample z lies in the reject H_0 region.

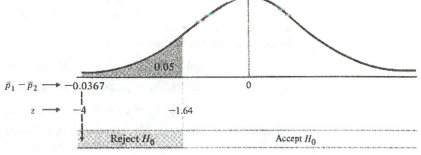

FIGURE 11.23
Left-tail test of the difference between two proportions.

EXERCISE Random samples of 500 men and 500 women have been selected to determine whether the proportion of women favoring a political candidate is greater than the proportion of men favoring the candidate. Carry out a hypothesis test at the 1 percent level if, in the samples, 40 women and 20 men favor the candidate.

ANSWER Let subscripts 1 and 2 designate, respectively, women and men. 1. $H_0: p_1 - p_2 \leq 0$; $H_a: p_1 - p_2 > 0$. 2. Reject H_0 if sample $z > 2.33$. 3. Sample $z = 2.66$. 4. Reject H_0.

11.14 TESTS OF THE DIFFERENCE BETWEEN TWO POPULATION MEANS: INDEPENDENT SAMPLES

Large Sample Tests

"Large sample" means $n_1 > 30$ and $n_2 > 30$.

Suppose we start with two normal populations. Population 1 has a mean of μ_1 and a standard deviation of σ_1. Population 2 has a mean of μ_2 and a standard deviation of σ_2. Next we draw independent samples of sizes n_1 and n_2 from the respective populations and compute the difference $\bar{x}_1 - \bar{x}_2$ between the means of all pairs of samples. Then it can be proved mathematically that the distribution of the difference between means, dist $(\bar{x}_1 - \bar{x}_2)$, is normal, as illustrated in Figure 11.24: it will have a mean of

$$\mu_{\bar{x}_1 - \bar{x}_2} = \mu_1 - \mu_2$$

and a standard error of

$$\sigma_{\bar{x}_1 - \bar{x}_2} = \sqrt{\frac{\sigma_1^2}{n_1} + \frac{\sigma_2^2}{n_2}}$$

With large samples we can use the z statistic . . .

Usually we do not know the values of σ_1 and σ_2; so we estimate them by the sample standard deviations s_1 and s_2. If both sample sizes are greater than 30, then we can assume dist $(\bar{x}_1 - \bar{x}_2)$ is normal, and we may use the *sample standard error of the difference between means,*

. . . with this standard error.

$$s_{\bar{x}_1 - \bar{x}_2} = \sqrt{\frac{s_1^2}{n_1} + \frac{s_2^2}{n_2}}$$

to estimate the standard error of dist $(\bar{x}_1 - \bar{x}_2)$.

We will test hypotheses about $\mu_1 - \mu_2$, the difference between population means. The difference is equal to, less than, or greater than zero. Hence, the hypotheses are

(a) $H_0: \mu_1 - \mu_2 = 0$ $H_a: \mu_1 - \mu_2 \neq 0$

(b) $H_0: \mu_1 - \mu_2 \geq 0$ $H_a: \mu_1 - \mu_2 < 0$

(c) $H_0: \mu_1 - \mu_2 \leq 0$ $H_a: \mu_1 - \mu_2 > 0$

Figure 11.25 (on page 374) shows the distribution of $\bar{x}_1 - \bar{x}_2$ when the equality part of H_0, $\mu_1 - \mu_2 = 0$, is true. The value of z for a sample point is

$$z = \frac{(\bar{x}_1 - \bar{x}_2) - (\mu_1 - \mu_2)}{s_{\bar{x}_1 - \bar{x}_2}}$$

But $\mu_1 - \mu_2 = 0$; so the test statistic is

$$\text{Sample } z = \frac{\bar{x}_1 - \bar{x}_2}{s_{\bar{x}_1 - \bar{x}_2}}$$

Start with two normal populations

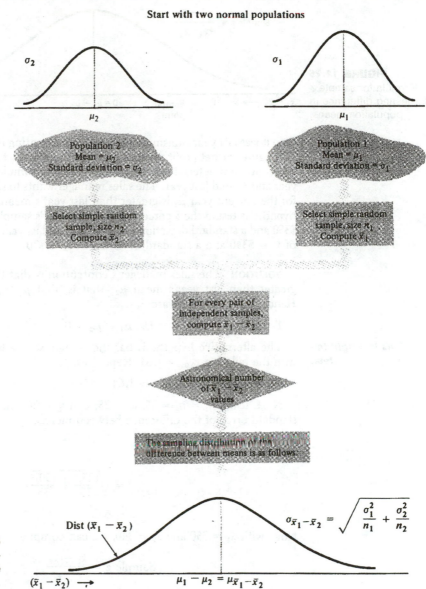

FIGURE 11.24
The sampling distribution of the difference between two means.

Dist $(\bar{x}_1 - \bar{x}_2)$

$$\sigma_{\bar{x}_1-\bar{x}_2} = \sqrt{\frac{\sigma_1^2}{n_1} + \frac{\sigma_2^2}{n_2}}$$

$(\bar{x}_1 - \bar{x}_2) \longrightarrow$ $\mu_1 - \mu_2 = \mu_{\bar{x}_1-\bar{x}_2}$

EXAMPLE The president of a large automobile sales agency tells his sales manager that he is pleased with the increase over last year in the number of cars sold per day but not pleased with the net profit per car sold. The sales manager contends that the mean net profit per car sold this year is higher

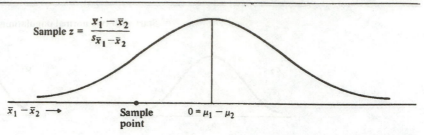

FIGURE 11.25
Formula for sample z
for testing difference in
population means.

than it was last year. Inasmuch as detailed accounting is required to obtain a firm figure for net profit realized on a particular sale, the sales manager has an accountant determine this profit for random samples of 35 cars sold this year and 35 sold last year. The sales manager wants to show that mean profit for the current year μ_1 is greater than last year's mean profit μ_2. Perform a hypothesis test at the 5 percent level if this year's sample has a mean of $\bar{x}_1 = \$350$ and a standard deviation of $s_1 = \$25$, and last year's sample has a mean of $\bar{x}_2 = \$340$ and a standard deviation of $s_2 = \$30$.

SOLUTION The sales manager's contention is that this year's mean μ_1 is greater than last year's mean μ_2, that is, that $\mu_1 > \mu_2$, or $\mu_1 - \mu_2 > 0$. Hence, the hypotheses are

1. $H_0: \mu_1 - \mu_2 \le 0$ $H_a: \mu_1 - \mu_2 > 0$

This is a right-tail test. The alternative hypothesis has the $>$ sign; so the test is a right-tail test with the tail area $z_{0.05} = 1.64$. Hence, we

2. Reject H_0 if sample $z > 1.64$

Next, using $n_1 = n_2 = 35$, $s_1 = 25$, and $s_2 = 30$, we compute the sample standard error of the difference between means,

$$s_{\bar{x}_1 - \bar{x}_2} = \sqrt{\frac{s_1^2}{n_1} + \frac{s_2^2}{n_2}}$$

$$= \sqrt{\frac{(25)^2}{35} + \frac{(30)^2}{35}}$$

$$= 6.60$$

Now, with $\bar{x}_1 = 350$ and $\bar{x}_2 = 340$, we can compute

$$\text{Sample } z = \frac{\bar{x}_1 - \bar{x}_2}{s_{\bar{x}_1 - \bar{x}_2}}$$

$$= \frac{350 - 340}{6.60}$$

$$= 1.51$$

Therefore,

3. Sample $z = 1.51$

The sample z, 1.51, is not greater than the 1.64 of the decision rule. Hence, we

4. Accept H_0

Since H_0 is accepted, we conclude that the sales manager has not produced convincing evidence that this year's mean profit is greater than last year's mean profit. Figure 11.26 shows H_0 was accepted because the sample z lies in the acceptance region.

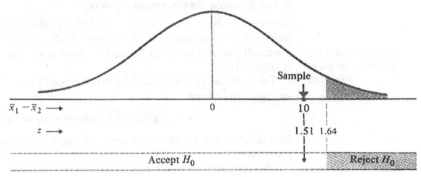

FIGURE 11.26
Net profit test.

The key words here (and in every hypothesis test) are "convincing evidence."

Thus, even though the sample mean profit of $350 this year is above the sample mean of $340 for last year, the sales manager does not have convincing evidence that this year's population mean profit is greater than last year's population mean profit.

Suppose the sales manager had set out to determine whether this year's mean profit *differed* from last year's. Then we would have

1   $H_0: \mu_1 - \mu_2 = 0$ $H_a: \mu_1 - \mu_2 \neq 0$

The test is two-tailed. With a significance level of 5 percent, $\alpha/2 = 0.025$ and $z_{0.025} = 1.96$; so the decision rule is

2. Reject H_0 if |sample z| > 1.96

The sample z is computed by the same formula for one-tail and two-tail tests; so, from the foregoing,

3. Sample $z = 1.51$

And the conclusion is

4. Accept H_0

The samples do not provide convincing evidence that this year's mean profit differs from last year's mean profit.

EXERCISE Either method 1 or method 2 can be used in assembling a product. Fifty assemblies are made by each method to determine if mean assembly times are different. (a) Perform a hypothesis test at the 1 percent level if the method 1 sample has a mean of 10 hours and a standard deviation of 0.45 hour, compared with a mean of 9.6 hours and a standard deviation of 0.40 hour for the method 2 sample. (b) What is implied by the test result?
ANSWER (a) 1. $H_0: \mu_1 - \mu_2 = 0; H_a: \mu_1 - \mu_2 \neq 0$. 2. Reject H_0 if |sample z| > 2.58. 3. Sample z = 4.70. 4. Reject H_0. (b) Method 2 should be used because it has the lower mean assembly time.

Small Sample Tests when $\sigma_1 = \sigma_2$

As usual, we use the t statistic for small samples.

Suppose we have two normal populations whose standard deviations are unknown but are equal. If the independent samples used in testing means are small (30 or less), then the test is based upon the Student t distribution (Chapter 10).

The decision rule is formed from the value (Table VII) of $t_{\alpha,v}$ (or $t_{\alpha/2,v}$ for a two-tail test) where

$$v = \text{degrees of freedom} = n_1 + n_2 - 2$$

In this two-sample test, two degrees of freedom are lost (the -2 in the formula for v).

The test statistic

$$\text{Sample } t = \frac{\bar{x}_1 - \bar{x}_2}{s_{\bar{x}_1 - \bar{x}_2}}$$

has the same symbols we used for the large sample (greater than 30) z test statistic; but now, for small samples, the assumption that $\sigma_1 = \sigma_2$ leads to a different formula for computing $s_{\bar{x}_1 - \bar{x}_2}$: the formula is

$$s_{\bar{x}_1 - \bar{x}_2} = \sqrt{\frac{(n_1 - 1)s_1^2 + (n_2 - 1)s_2^2}{n_1 + n_2 - 2} \left(\frac{1}{n_1} + \frac{1}{n_2} \right)}$$

EXAMPLE A rancher wants to test two food mixtures, mix 1 and mix 2, on random samples of steers to determine if there is a difference in mean weight gains for the mixtures. The sample mean weight gains, $\bar{x}_1$ and $\bar{x}_2$, and other sample data are

Mix 1: n_1 = 12 steers $\bar{x}_1$ = 140 pounds s_1 = 6 pounds

Mix 2: n_2 = 15 steers $\bar{x}_2$ = 124 pounds s_2 = 5 pounds

(a) Perform a hypothesis test at the 2 percent level. (b) What is implied by the test result?

SOLUTION

a. A test to determine if there is a difference between means is a two-tail test. The hypotheses are $\mu_1 = \mu_2$ and $\mu_1 \neq \mu_2$ or, expressed as differences,

1. $H_0: \mu_1 - \mu_2 = 0$ $H_a: \mu_1 - \mu_2 \neq 0$

Since the test is two-tailed with $\alpha = 0.02$, we use the $0.02/2 = 0.01$ column of Table VII to obtain the t value for the decision rule. We need v, the number of degrees of freedom. With $n_1 = 12$ and $n_2 = 15$,

$$v = n_1 + n_2 - 2$$

$$= 12 + 15 - 2 = 25$$

In Table VII, in the 0.01 column and the $v = 25$ row, we find $t_{0.01,25}$ is 2.49. Hence,

2. Reject H_0 if $|$sample $t| > 2.49$

Next we compute the standard error of the difference between means,

$$s_{\bar{x}_1 - \bar{x}_2} = \sqrt{\frac{(n_1 - 1)s_1^2 + (n_2 - 1)s_2^2}{n_1 + n_2 - 2}\left(\frac{1}{n_1} + \frac{1}{n_2}\right)}$$

$$= \sqrt{\frac{(12 - 1)(6)^2 + (15 - 1)(5)^2}{12 + 15 - 2}\left(\frac{1}{12} + \frac{1}{15}\right)}$$

$$= \sqrt{4.476} = 2.116$$

Now we can compute the value of the test statistic

$$t = \frac{\bar{x}_1 - \bar{x}_2}{s_{\bar{x}_1 - \bar{x}_2}}$$

$$= \frac{140 - 124}{2.116} = 7.56$$

so that

3. Sample $t = 7.56$

The sample t, 7.56, is greater than the value 2.49 in the decision rule; so we

4. Reject H_0

b. Because the mix 1 sample mean weight gain is greater than the mix 2 mean, the test result implies that steers should be fed mix 1.

EXERCISE Costly road testing of random samples of cars was carried out to determine if mean mileage (mpg) is greater for model 1 cars than for model 2 cars. The sample data were as follows:

Model 1: $n_1 = 8$ $\bar{x}_1 = 26.0$ $s_1 = 1.4$

Model 2: $n_2 = 10$ $\bar{x}_2 = 23.6$ $s_2 = 1.2$

(a) Perform a hypothesis test at the 5 percent level. (b) What is implied by the test result?
ANSWER 1. $H_0: \mu_1 - \mu_2 \leq 0$; $H_a: \mu_1 - \mu_2 > 0$. 2. Reject H_0 if sample $t > 1.75$. 3. Sample $t = 3.92$. 4. Reject H_0. (b) Model 1 has greater mean mileage than model 2.

11.15 PAIRED DIFFERENCE TESTS OF TWO POPULATION MEANS

Thus far, we have used independent samples in testing means. However, we may want to use samples that are not independent. For example, suppose we want to determine if a training program will increase worker output. To do so, we would record before-training output of a random sample of workers, train these workers, and then record their after-training output. The before and after pair of numbers for a worker are not independent. The set of sample pairs is called a *paired sample*.

A single pair might be (54, 60). Its difference d is 6.

The difference between the two numbers in a matched pair is d. The mean of the sample d values is $\bar{d}$. The population mean difference D is the mean of the population of d values. We will use $\bar{d}$ to test hypotheses about D. The symbols that will be used are

$$D = \text{population mean difference}$$

$$n = \text{number of sample differences}$$

$$d = \text{difference between a sample pair}$$

$$\bar{d} = \text{sample mean difference}$$

$$s_d = \text{standard deviation of the } d\text{'s}$$

$$s_{\bar{d}} = \text{standard error of } \bar{d}$$

The formulas for $\bar{d}$, s_d, and $s_{\bar{d}}$ are

$$\bar{d} = \frac{\Sigma d}{n}$$

$$s_d = \sqrt{\frac{\Sigma(d - \bar{d})^2}{n - 1}}$$

$$s_{\bar{d}} = \frac{s_d}{\sqrt{n}}$$

We will assume the d's are normally distributed. Then the test statistic is the sample t value with $n - 1$ degrees of freedom. The equality part of H_0 will be that $D = 0$; that is, the population mean difference is zero. The formula for the test statistic then is

$$\text{Sample } t = \frac{\bar{d}}{s_{\bar{d}}}$$

"Greater after than before" translates as D > 0.

EXAMPLE Productivity (units produced per day) for a random sample of 10 workers was recorded before and after training. The following data pairs were obtained; the first number in each pair is the "before" output and the second is the "after" output: (54, 60); (56, 59); (50, 57); (52, 56); (55, 56); (52, 58); (56, 62); (53, 55); (53, 54); (60, 64). Perform a hypothesis test at the 1 percent level to determine if mean productivity is greater after training than before training.

SOLUTION If mean productivity is greater after than before training, then the population mean "after minus before" difference D is greater than 0. Hence, $D > 0$ is the alternative hypothesis; so we have

1. $H_0: D \le 0$ $H_a: D > 0$

The test is one-tailed with $\alpha = 0.01$. There are $n = 10$ differences; so the number of degrees of freedom is

$$v = n - 1$$
$$= 10 - 1 = 9$$

From Table VII, $t_{0.01,9} = 2.82$. Hence,

2. Reject H_0 if sample $t > 2.82$

To compute the sample t, we need $\bar{d}$ and $s_{\bar{d}}$. Table 11.1 shows the computations of the sample differences d, their mean $\bar{d}$, and the numbers needed to compute s_d; s_d is used in computing $s_{\bar{d}}$.

TABLE 11.1
COMPUTATIONS FOR PAIRED SAMPLES

Worker	Units produced per day Before	After	Difference d (after minus before)	$d - \bar{d}$	$(d - \bar{d})^2$
1	54	60	6	2	4
2	56	59	3	-1	1
3	50	57	7	3	9
4	52	56	4	0	0
5	55	56	1	-3	9
6	52	58	6	2	4
7	56	62	6	2	4
8	53	55	2	-2	4
9	53	54	1	-3	9
10	60	64	4	0	0
			$\Sigma d = \overline{40}$		$\Sigma(d - \bar{d})^2 = \overline{44}$
			$\bar{d} = 4$		

The sample mean difference is

$$\bar{d} = \frac{\Sigma d}{n}$$

$$= \frac{40}{10} = 4$$

The sample standard deviation of the d's is

$$s_d = \sqrt{\frac{\Sigma(d - \bar{d})^2}{n - 1}}$$

$$= \sqrt{\frac{44}{10 - 1}} = 2.21$$

Now we can compute the standard error of $\bar{d}$,

$$s_{\bar{d}} = \frac{s_d}{\sqrt{n}}$$

$$= \frac{2.21}{\sqrt{10}} = 0.699$$

Then,

$$\text{Sample } t = \frac{\bar{d}}{s_{\bar{d}}}$$

$$= \frac{4}{0.699} = 5.72$$

3. Sample $t = 5.72$.

The sample t, 5.72, exceeds the value 2.82 in the decision rule. Hence, we

4. Reject H_0

We conclude that $D > 0$, that is, that after-training productivity is greater than before-training productivity.

EXERCISE Use the following (before, after) data pairs: (12, 10); (8, 14); (9, 9); (10, 15); (11, 12). Perform a hypothesis test at the 10 percent level to determine if the "after" population mean differs from the "before" mean.
ANSWER 1. $H_0 : D = 0$; $H_a : D \neq 0$. 2. Reject H_0 if |sample t| > 2.13. 3. Sample $t = 1.32$. 4. Accept H_0.

11.16 PROBLEMS

1. Random samples of 500 men and 500 women are selected to determine whether the proportions of men and women favoring a political candidate are different. (a) Perform a hypothesis test at the 5 percent level if, in the samples, 225 men and 275 women favor the candidate. (b) What is implied by the test result?

2. Officials in city 1, citing the fact that city 2 has been granted unemployment aid, claim their city should also receive aid because it has a higher proportion of unemployed than city 2. Random samples of 4950 workers in city 1 and 5625 in city 2 have been obtained. (a) Perform a hypothesis test at the 2 percent level if, in the samples, the numbers unemployed are 396 for city 1 and 387 for city 2. (b) What is implied by the test result?

3. The production manager of Electric Products Company wants to determine if the proportions of defective assemblies made by shift 1 and shift 2 workers are different. Random samples of 500 shift 1 assemblies and 400 shift 2 assemblies have been obtained. (a) Perform a hy-

pothesis test at the 10 percent level if the shift 1 assemblies had 72 defectives and the shift 2 assemblies had 36 defectives. (b) What is implied by the test result?

4. The maker of Amcar automobiles has hired Research, Inc., a marketing research company, to survey a sample of car owners. If the sample gives convincing evidence that the proportion of dissatisfied Amcar owners is less than the proportion of dissatisfied owners of other cars, Amcar will feature the survey outcome in its advertising. (a) Perform a hypothesis test at the 5 percent level if, in a random sample of 1000 owners, there are 200 Amcar owners, of whom 40 are dissatisfied, and 800 owners of other makes, of whom 200 are dissatisfied. (b) What is implied by the test result?

5. Amcar has been buying brand 1 tires to mount on new cars. A representative of a competing tire company selling brand 2 tires claims that mean mileage for brand 2 is greater than mean mileage for brand 1. Amcar submits random samples of 50 of each brand to simulated road wear until they wear out. (a) Perform a hypothesis test at the 5 percent level if the sample brand 1 tires had a mean of 30,000 miles and a standard deviation of 3000 miles, while brand 2 sample tires had a mean of 32,000 miles and a standard deviation of 4000 miles. (b) What is implied by the test result?

6. Executive Search, Inc. (ESI) finds people to fill executive openings. Clients frequently ask about housing costs. ESI wants to determine if the mean rent for three-bedroom apartments in section 1 of a city differs from the mean rent in section 2 of the city. Random samples of 35 rents will be obtained for each section. (a) Perform a hypothesis test at the 5 percent level if the section 1 sample has a mean of $770 and a standard deviation of $65, while the section 2 sample has a mean of $730 and a standard deviation of $55. (b) What is implied by the test result?

7. A retired executive who is interested in vegetable gardening tests different seeds to see which do well in her soil. In one experiment, she planted 50 hills of corn variety 1 and 50 hills of variety 2. Each hill was thinned, leaving the same number of plants per hill. She wants to determine if the mean yields per hill for the varieties are different. (a) Perform a hypothesis test at the 10 percent level if the variety 1 sample had a mean yield of 13.1 ounces per hill and a standard deviation of 3 ounces, while the variety 2 sample had a mean yield of 12 ounces per hill and a standard deviation of 2 ounces. (b) What is implied by the test result?

8. Moor's Brewery makes brand 1 beer. Moor's claims that brand 1 contains fewer calories per can than competitive brand 2. The calorie contents for random samples of 40 cans of each brand are obtained. (a) Perform a hypothesis test at the 1 percent level if the brand 1 sample has a mean of 79 calories and a standard deviation of 3 calories, while the brand 2 sample has a mean of 81 calories and a standard deviation of 2 calories. (b) What is implied by the test result?

9. The fire chief of Dunsboro is considering which fire station to assign to alarms coming from a certain section of the city during the afternoon rush hour. The chief wants to determine if the mean times to reach the section are different for stations 1 and 2. Samples of seven trial runs from station 1 and nine from station 2 were made at randomly selected times. The samples provided the following data:

Station 1: $n_1 = 7$ $\bar{x}_1 = 15.1$ minutes $s_1 = 1.6$ minutes

Station 2: $n_2 = 9$ $\bar{x}_2 = 12.0$ minutes $s_2 = 2.4$ minutes

(a) Perform a hypothesis test at the 10 percent level. (b) What is implied by the test result?

10. Eastern States Farmers (ESF) is a cooperative serving member farmers. ESF wants to determine if the mean amount of active ingredient in fertilizers purchased from supplier 1 is greater than the mean for supplier 2. Random samples of 10 bags of fertilizer have been obtained from each supplier. Chemical analyses of the sample bags provided the following data:

Supplier 1: $n_1 = 10$ $\bar{x}_1 = 9.1$ pounds $s_1 = 0.2$ pound

Supplier 2: $n_2 = 10$ $\bar{x}_2 = 9.2$ pounds $s_2 = 0.3$ pound

Perform a hypothesis test at the 1 percent level.

11. The capacities of brand 1 and brand 2 window air conditioners are rated the same. Capacities of random samples of six units of each brand were determined. The sample data, in thousands of Btu (British thermal units), were

Brand 1: 6.1   6.4   5.6   6.2   6.4   5.9

Brand 2: 4.8   5.2   5.3   5.1   5.0   5.2

Perform a hypothesis test at the 5 percent level to determine whether mean Btu consumptions for the two brands differ.

12. Pat Strong is president of Strong Realty Company. Pat has available the services of two reputable house-value appraisers. She prefers appraiser 1, but in the interest of her clients, she will choose appraiser 2 if the latter places higher values on houses. Pat selects a random sample of 10 houses and has them valued by both appraisers, making sure that neither appraiser knows the other has made an appraisal. The results, in thousands of dollars, are shown in Table A. (a) Perform a hypothesis

TABLE A

House number	1	2	3	4	5	6	7	8	9	10
Appraiser 1	60	50	40	35	90	55	70	65	45	80
Appraiser 2	62	53	39	37	92	53	68	67	47	82

test at the 5 percent level to determine if the mean difference in appraisal values (appraiser 2 minus appraiser 1) is greater than zero. (b) What is implied by the test result?

13. Typing rates (words per minute) were recorded for a random sample of 15 secretaries using standard model 1 typewriters, at which they were proficient. Then the secretaries practiced with model 2 typewriters: after they reached proficiency, typing rates were again recorded. For each secretary, the difference d = (model 2 rate − model 1 rate) was computed. It was found that, in words per minute, Σd = −110, and the sample standard deviation of the d's was 5. Perform a hypothesis test at the 5 percent level to determine if the mean rate of typing is lower on model 2 than on model 1.

14. Hackwood's is a large multidepartment retail store. Hackwood's plans to rent time from a computer service bureau to process various programs on the bureau's computer. Hackwood's prefers bureau 1. However, bureaus charge a high rate per minute to process programs; so Hackwood's will choose bureau 2 if its mean run time for processing programs is less than the mean processing time for bureau 1. Time was purchased to run a random sample of eight of Hackwood's programs at each bureau. In the following pairs of minutes of processing times, the first number is the time for a given program at bureau 1; the second number is the time for the same program at bureau 2. The sample data are (1.5, 1.3); (2.1, 2.0); (1.9, 2.4); (2.1, 1.9); (4.5, 5.1); (2.7, 3.1); (2.2, 2.4); (2.4, 2.8). (a) Perform a hypothesis test at the 5 percent level. (b) What is implied by the test result?

11.17 SUMMARY

In this chapter, null hypotheses about values of population parameters are tested against alternative hypotheses. The chance α of rejecting a true null hypothesis is set by the decision maker and used to establish a rule for deciding whether to reject or accept a null hypothesis. The value of α is called the significance level of a test. The steps in a test are

1. State the null and alternative hypotheses.
2. State the decision rule.
3. Compute the value of the sample test statistic.
4. Reject or accept the null hypothesis.

The tests presented in the chapter are listed below.

Tests of a Proportion

Let p_h be the hypothesized value of the population proportion, and $q_h = 1 - p_h$. Then the sample size n should be such that both np_h and nq_h exceed 5.

The hypotheses and their decision rules are

$H_0: p \geq p_h$ $\qquad$ $H_a: p < p_h$ $\qquad$ Reject H_0 if sample $z < -z_\alpha$

$H_0: p \leq p_h$ $\qquad$ $H_a: p > p_h$ $\qquad$ Reject H_0 if sample $z > z_\alpha$

$H_0: p = p_h$ $\qquad$ $H_a: p \neq p_h$ $\qquad$ Reject H_0 if |sample $z| > z_{\alpha/2}$

The sample test statistic is

$$\text{Sample } z = \frac{\bar{p} - p_h}{\sigma_{\bar{p}}}$$

where $\sigma_{\bar{p}} = \sqrt{\dfrac{p_h q_h}{n}}$

$q_h = 1 - p_h$

$\bar{p} = \dfrac{\text{number of successes in sample}}{n}$

Tests of Difference between Two Proportions (Independent Samples)

Populations 1 and 2 have unknown proportions p_1 and p_2. Samples from the respective populations have sizes n_1 and n_2. Let $q_1 = 1 - p_1$ and $q_2 = 1 - p_2$. Guess which of the values p_1, q_1, p_2, q_2 is the smallest proportion, and guess its value. Then both n_1 and n_2 should exceed 5 divided by the smallest proportion.

The hypotheses and their decision rules are

$H_0: p_1 - p_2 \geq 0$ $\qquad$ $H_a: p_1 - p_2 < 0$ $\qquad$ Reject H_0 if sample $z < -z_\alpha$

$H_0: p_1 - p_2 \leq 0$ $\qquad$ $H_a: p_1 - p_2 > 0$ $\qquad$ Reject H_0 if sample $z > z_\alpha$

$H_0: p_1 - p_2 = 0$ $\qquad$ $H_a: p_1 - p_2 \neq 0$ $\qquad$ Reject H_0 if |sample $z| > z_{\alpha/2}$

The sample test statistic is

$$\text{Sample } z = \frac{\bar{p}_1 - \bar{p}_2}{\sqrt{\bar{p}_c \bar{q}_c \left(\dfrac{1}{n_1} + \dfrac{1}{n_2} \right)}}$$

where $\bar{p}_c = \dfrac{\text{sum of successes in the two samples}}{n_1 + n_2}$

$\bar{q}_c = 1 - \bar{p}_c$

$\bar{p}_1 = \dfrac{\text{number of successes in sample 1}}{n_1}$

$\bar{p}_2 = \dfrac{\text{number of successes in sample 2}}{n_2}$

Large Sample Tests of a Mean

Let μ_h be the hypothesized value of the population mean. The sample size n should exceed 30.

The hypotheses and their decision rules are

$H_0: \mu \geq \mu_h$ $H_a: \mu < \mu_h$ Reject H_0 if sample $z < -z_\alpha$

$H_0: \mu \leq \mu_h$ $H_a: \mu > \mu_h$ Reject H_0 if sample $z > z_\alpha$

$H_0: \mu = \mu_h$ $H_a: \mu \neq \mu_h$ Reject H_0 if |sample $z| > z_{\alpha/2}$

Sample values are denoted by x. The sample test statistic is

$$\text{Sample } z = \frac{\bar{x} - \mu_h}{s_{\bar{x}}}$$

where $\bar{x} = \dfrac{\Sigma x}{n}$

$s_x = \sqrt{\dfrac{\Sigma(x - \bar{x})^2}{n - 1}}$

$s_{\bar{x}} = \dfrac{s_x}{\sqrt{n}}$

Large Sample Tests of the Difference between Two Means (Independent Samples)

Populations 1 and 2 have respective means of μ_1 and μ_2. Respective sizes of samples drawn from the populations are n_1 and n_2. Both n_1 and n_2 should exceed 30. The symbols x_1 and x_2 denote values of sample elements drawn from the respective populations.

The hypotheses and their decision rules are

$H_0: \mu_1 - \mu_2 \geq 0$ $H_a: \mu_1 - \mu_2 < 0$ Reject H_0 if sample $z < -z_\alpha$

$H_0: \mu_1 - \mu_2 \leq 0$ $H_a: \mu_1 - \mu_2 > 0$ Reject H_0 if sample $z > z_\alpha$

$H_0: \mu_1 - \mu_2 = 0$ $H_a: \mu_1 - \mu_2 \neq 0$ Reject H_0 if |sample $z| > z_{\alpha/2}$

The sample test statistic is

$$\text{Sample } z = \frac{\bar{x}_1 - \bar{x}_2}{s_{\bar{x}_1 - \bar{x}_2}}$$

where $\bar{x}_1 = \dfrac{\Sigma x_1}{n_1}$

$\bar{x}_2 = \dfrac{\Sigma x_2}{n_2}$

$s_1 = \text{sample 1 standard deviation} = \sqrt{\dfrac{\Sigma(x_1 - \bar{x}_1)^2}{n_1 - 1}}$

$s_2 = \text{sample 2 standard deviation} = \sqrt{\dfrac{\Sigma(x_2 - \bar{x}_2)^2}{n_2 - 1}}$

$s_{\bar{x}_1 - \bar{x}_2} = \sqrt{\dfrac{s_1^2}{n_1} + \dfrac{s_2^2}{n_2}}$

Small Sample Tests of a Mean

This test is used when a sample of $n \leq 30$ is drawn from a normal population whose standard deviation is unknown. The test statistic is Student's t with

$v = n - 1$ degrees of freedom. Let μ_h be the hypothesized value of the population mean.

The hypotheses and their decision rules are

$H_0: \mu \geq \mu_h$ $H_a: \mu < \mu_h$ Reject H_0 if sample $t < -t_{\alpha,v}$

$H_0: \mu \leq \mu_h$ $H_a: \mu > \mu_h$ Reject H_0 if sample $t > t_{\alpha,v}$

$H_0: \mu = \mu_h$ $H_a: \mu \neq \mu_h$ Reject H_0 if $|$sample $t| > t_{\alpha/2,v}$

The sample test statistic is

$$\text{Sample } t = \frac{\bar{x} - \mu_h}{s_{\bar{x}}}$$

where $\bar{x} = \dfrac{\Sigma x}{n}$

$s_x = \sqrt{\dfrac{\Sigma(x - \bar{x})^2}{n - 1}}$

$s_{\bar{x}} = \dfrac{s_x}{\sqrt{n}}$

Small Sample Tests of Difference between Two Means (Independent Samples)

Normal populations 1 and 2 have respective means of μ_1 and μ_2. The population standard deviations, while unknown, are equal. Sample sizes are $n_1 \leq 30$ and $n_2 \leq 30$. The symbols x_1 and x_2 denote values of sample elements drawn from the respective populations. The test statistic is Student's t with $v = n_1 + n_2 - 2$ degrees of freedom.

The hypotheses and their decision rules are

$H_0: \mu_1 - \mu_2 \geq 0$ $H_a: \mu_1 - \mu_2 < 0$ Reject H_0 if sample $t < -t_{\alpha,v}$

$H_0: \mu_1 - \mu_2 \leq 0$ $H_a: \mu_1 - \mu_2 > 0$ Reject H_0 if sample $t > t_{\alpha,v}$

$H_0: \mu_1 - \mu_2 = 0$ $H_a: \mu_1 - \mu_2 \neq 0$ Reject H_0 if $|$sample $t| > t_{\alpha/2,v}$

The sample test statistic is

$$\text{Sample } t = \frac{\bar{x}_1 - \bar{x}_2}{s_{\bar{x}_1 - \bar{x}_2}}$$

where $\bar{x}_1 = $ sample 1 mean $= \dfrac{\Sigma x_1}{n_1}$

$\bar{x}_2 = $ sample 2 mean $= \dfrac{\Sigma x_2}{n_2}$

$s_{\bar{x}_1 - \bar{x}_2} = \sqrt{\dfrac{(n_1 - 1)s_1^2 + (n_2 - 1)s_2^2}{n_1 + n_2 - 2} \left(\dfrac{1}{n_1} + \dfrac{1}{n_2} \right)}$

$s_1 = $ sample 1 standard deviation $= \sqrt{\dfrac{\Sigma(x_1 - \bar{x}_1)^2}{n_1 - 1}}$

$s_2 = $ sample 2 standard deviation $= \sqrt{\dfrac{\Sigma(x_2 - \bar{x}_2)^2}{n_2 - 1}}$

Paired Difference Test of Two Means

The sample consists of n *pairs* of related elements (x_1, x_2). A pair difference $x_1 - x_2$ is denoted by d; that is, $d = x_1 - x_2$. D denotes the population mean difference. The test statistic is Student's t with $n - 1$ degrees of freedom.

The hypotheses and their decision rules are

$$H_0: D \geq 0 \qquad H_a: D < 0 \qquad \text{Reject } H_0 \text{ if sample } t < -t_{\alpha,v}$$

$$H_0: D \leq 0 \qquad H_a: D > 0 \qquad \text{Reject } H_0 \text{ if sample } t > t_{\alpha,v}$$

$$H_0: D = 0 \qquad H_a: D \neq 0 \qquad \text{Reject } H_0 \text{ if } |\text{sample } t| > t_{\alpha/2,v}$$

The sample test statistic is

$$\text{Sample } t = \frac{\bar{d}}{s_{\bar{d}}}$$

where $\bar{d} = \dfrac{\Sigma d}{n}$

$s_{\bar{d}} = \dfrac{s_d}{\sqrt{n}}$

$s_d = \sqrt{\dfrac{\Sigma(d - \bar{d})^2}{n - 1}}$

11.18 REVIEW PROBLEMS

1. The purchasing agent for Wholesale Farm Products does not want to buy a freight carload of oranges unless the percent of substandard oranges is less than 15 percent. (*a*) Perform a hypothesis test at the 2 percent level if a random sample of 250 oranges contains 225 high-quality oranges. (*b*) What is implied by the test result?

2. Two years ago, tax officials paid a consulting firm to assess the value of every house in their town. The firm found that 18 percent of the houses were undervalued; that is, the value used in computing real estate taxes was below the market value. The officials think the present figure is greater than 18 percent. Perform a hypothesis test at the 1 percent level if 36 of a random sample of 150 houses assessed are found to be undervalued.

3. Central Electronics, Inc. (CEI) makes transistors. CEI's quality-control personnel have a standard of 5 percent defective. From time to time, they inspect a random sample of 300 transistors to determine whether the percentage of defective transistors being produced differs from 5 percent. (*a*) Perform a hypothesis test at the 5 percent level if the sample contains six defectives. (*b*) What is implied by the test result?

4. The superintendent of schools in city 1 asserts that the proportion of high school seniors with poor reading skills in his city is less than the proportion in city 2. Random samples of 200 seniors from each city are given a reading skills examination. Perform a hypothesis test at the 5 percent level if the sample numbers with poor reading skills are 32 in city 1 and 58 in city 2.

5. The president of Arman Industries has a proposal to present to the stockholders but does not want to present it to all stockholders unless more than 50 percent favor the proposal. Attitudes toward the proposal are secured from a random

sample of 100 stockholders. (a) Perform a hypothesis test at the 1 percent level if 59 of the sample favor the proposal. (b) What is implied by the test result?

6. The manufacturer of Jetcar automobiles uses a random sample of 500 car owners to determine if the proportion of satisfied car owners is different for Jetcar than for other cars. (a) Perform a hypothesis test at the 5 percent level if the sample contained 100 Jetcar owners, of whom 70 were satisfied, and 400 other car owners, of whom 320 were satisfied. (b) What is implied by the test result?

7. Grain Cereal Products checks a random sample of 40 boxes of cereal to determine if the mean content of boxes is at least 8 ounces. Perform a hypothesis test at the 2 percent level if the sample mean is 7.98 ounces and the sample standard deviation is 0.11 ounce.

8. Precision Metals Company has an automatic lathe that makes shafts. When the lathe is running properly, the shafts produced have a mean diameter of 5 mm (millimeters). The diameters of a random sample of 40 shafts have been obtained to determine if the machine is running properly. (a) Perform a hypothesis test at the 5 percent level if the sample shafts have a mean diameter of 5.0021 mm and a standard deviation of 0.0049 mm. (b) What is implied by the test result?

9. The mean base wage rate at Bushe Company is $8.25 per hour. Labor union officials claim that the mean base rate in other companies in the region is higher than $8.25. Perform a hypothesis test at the 10 percent level if a random sample of 50 workers in other companies has a mean of $8.40 per hour and a standard deviation of $1.05 per hour.

10. At the end of October, the mean price of all stocks listed on a stock exchange was $55.30 per share. In November, a random sample of 35 stocks was selected to determine if the mean price per share for all stocks had changed from $55.30. Perform a hypothesis test at the 5 percent level if the sample mean is $56.10 per share and the sample standard deviation is $4.86 per share.

11: A city inspector wants to determine whether odometers in rental cars register excess mileage. She rents a random sample of 15 cars and drives each over a measured distance of 10 miles. (a) Perform a hypothesis test at the 5 percent level if the sample mean registered mileage is 10.21 miles and the standard deviation is 0.32 mile. (b) What do you conclude about odometers from the test result?

12. Random samples are used to determine whether the mean rents paid for similar apartments in two cities are different. Random samples of 35 rents are obtained for each city. Perform a hypothesis test at the 5 percent level if the city 1 sample mean is $300 per month and the sample standard deviation is $25 per month, while the city 2 sample mean is $290 per month and the sample standard deviation is $20 per month.

13. The Chamber of Commerce of city 1 claims that the mean hourly wage rate paid in the city is higher than the mean rate paid in city 2. Random samples of 50 workers are obtained for each city. Perform a hypothesis test at the 10 percent level if the city 1 sample has a mean of $6.38 per hour and a standard deviation of $1.23 per hour, whereas the city 2 sample mean is $6.19 per hour and the standard deviation is $1.11 per hour.

14. Universal Baking, Inc., purchases bags of flour which vary somewhat in weight. The bakery wants to determine if the mean weights per bag purchased from two suppliers are different. Random samples of 36 bags from each supplier are weighed. (a) Perform a hypothesis test at the 10 percent level if the supplier 1 sample mean is 49.74 pounds and the sample standard deviation is 0.49 pound, whereas the supplier 2 sample mean is 50.08 pounds and the standard deviation is 0.58 pound. (b) What is implied by the test result?

15. National Oil Affiliates (NOA) is considering mining oil-bearing shale in a region.

NOA will start mining if the mean yield of oil in the shale exceeds 3 barrels of oil per ton of shale. Oil yields per ton of shale are obtained from eight randomly selected parts of the region. (a) Perform a hypothesis test at the 1 percent level if the sample mean yield per ton of shale is 5.32 barrels and the standard deviation is 0.4 barrel. (b) What should NOA conclude about oil yields from the test result?

16. The research laboratory of Brown Industrial Products is trying to perfect a process which will make artificial industrial-quality diamonds whose mean weight is greater than 0.5 carat. (a) Perform a hypothesis test at the 5 percent level if a random sample of five diamonds produced by the process has the following weights (in carats): 0.7, 0.8, 0.6, 0.9, 0.5. (b) What do you conclude from the test result?

17. A supervisor wishes to determine whether the mean time employees spend on the 10-minute coffee break allowed in the union-management contract differs from 10 minutes. She observes a random sample of 15 employees and notes the time, in minutes, spent by each for a coffee break. (a) Perform a hypothesis test at the 5 percent level if the sample times are 14, 14, 8, 12, 13, 10, 14, 10, 11, 13, 9, 10, 15, 12, 15. (b) What is implied by the test result?

18. Dataflow, a large computer manufacturer, is considering whether method 1 or method 2 should be adopted for training technicians who must find and correct problems arising in its computer systems. Method 1 relies heavily on a checklist process of elimination, while method 2 concentrates more on teaching fundamentals of the functions and the interrelations of component parts. A random sample of 10 workers is trained by method 1 and another random sample of 10 workers is trained by method 2. After training, technicians in each sample are exposed to the same series of problems. The sample mean times to correct the problems will be used to determine whether the mean times to solve a problem by the two methods are different. (a) Perform a hypothesis test at the 5 percent level if the method 1 sample has a mean of 3.2 hours and a standard deviation of 0.6 hour, whereas the method 2 sample has a mean of 3.8 hours and a standard deviation of 0.5 hour. (b) What is implied by the test result?

19. Richco, Inc., uses an expensive ingredient, Goldpowder, in one of its products. Goldpowder is purchased in boxes containing 100 grams, but there is some variation from box to box. Richco's supplier has announced a large price increase, and two competing suppliers offer a lower price. Richco prefers supplier 1 but will buy from supplier 2 if the mean weight per box for supplier 2 is greater than the mean weight for supplier 1. Richco obtains a random sample of six boxes from each supplier and sends the boxes to a laboratory for weight measurement. The sample weights in grams are:

Supplier 1:	96	100	99	98	97	101
Supplier 2:	103	100	102	99	103	102

Perform a hypothesis test at the 10 percent level.

20. Amcar has a new car which will be sold with the option of a gasoline or a diesel fuel engine. Amcar is interested in whether mean mileages (mpg's) for the two options are different. Random samples of cars with each option yield the following miles per gallon data:

Gasoline engine:	26	24	25	22	23		
Diesel engine:	27	26	29	28	30	24	25

(a) Perform a hypothesis test at the 10 percent level. (b) What is implied by the test result?

21. A random sample of 10 high school students who had taken the college board mathematics examination in the fall were tutored, and then took the examination given in the following spring. Scores for each student, shown in the form (fall, spring) are as follows: (500, 515); (610, 590); (425, 470); (520, 510); (450, 475); (420, 445); (570, 595); (480, 485); (530, 555); (440, 455). The question of interest is whether tutoring raises the mean test score. Perform a hypothesis test at the 10 percent level.

22. A random sample of 15 executives undertook a physical exercise program to determine if exercise results in weight reduction. The difference between weight at the end of the program and weight at the start of the program (ending weight minus starting weight) was computed for each executive. The sample mean difference is minus 3.9 pounds, and the standard deviation of the sample differences is 4.7 pounds. Perform a hypothesis test at the 5 percent level.

23. If the null hypothesis is $H_0: \mu \geq 200$, when would a Type II error be committed?

24. Given $H_0: \mu \geq 200$, $H_a: \mu < 200$, $n = 100$, $\alpha = 0.023$, $\sigma_x = 25$. (a) For what values of the sample mean $\bar{x}$ will H_0 be accepted? (b) Compute β if μ is actually 191. (c) Compute β if μ is actually 198. (d) What is the power of the test in (b)? What does it mean?

12

SIMPLE LINEAR REGRESSION AND CORRELATION

12.1 INTRODUCTION

Regression and correlation analyses are used to study relationships among variables. Simple regression analysis provides an equation that can be used to estimate or predict the value of one variable from a given value of another. Thus, simple regression relates two variables. In simple *linear* regression, the estimating equation has a graph which is a straight line. The estimating equation is determined by performing calculations on observed data. For example, suppose data on retail sales and population size are collected for 50 cities. By regression analysis of these data, we obtain an equation that relates retail sales to population size. Then if we know the population of some city but do not know the city's retail sales, we can use the equation to estimate retail sales from the size of the city's population.

The purpose of simple linear correlation analysis is to determine whether or not two variables are related, that is, whether one variable tends to be larger (or smaller) as the other variable gets larger. Statisticians use the word correlation (co-relation) to emphasize that the existence of a relationship does not necessarily—or even usually—mean that changes in one variable are the cause of changes in the other variable. Thus, two variables may be correlated, but not causally related. The outcome of correlation analysis is not an estimating equation but a conclusion that there is, or is not, a relationship (a correlation) between the variables. Often, two variables are correlated, but an estimating (regression) equation does a poor job of predicting the value of one variable from the known value of the other variable. Nevertheless, the fact that the variables are correlated can aid in making decisions.

Applications of regression and correlation analyses exist in all areas of business. Executives want to know the relationship between company sales and advertising expenditures, personnel officers want to know the relationship between various aptitude test scores and worker performance, investors want to know which of the sets of financial data available in company reports are related to the values (or potential prices) of the company's common stock, and so on.

Applied regression and correlation analysis on large data sets involves tedious calculations. We will start with small data sets so that your attention can be focused on concepts rather than on repetitious calculations. After the first set of problems, the results of preliminary calculations will be provided so your attention can be directed to applications and to making inferences from more extensive data sets.

12.2 SIMPLE LINEAR EQUATIONS

A simple linear equation has two variables which we shall call x and y; the form of the equation is

General form of the simple linear equation

$$y = a + bx$$

By convention, x is called the *independent* variable and y is called the *dependent* variable. The letters a and b are numbers, not variables. The constant a is the value of y when x equals 0; a is called the y intercept. The number b is called the slope of the line; b is the amount y changes when x increases by 1.

Suppose the cost of renting a car for 1 day is $25 plus a charge of $0.30 (30 cents) for each mile the car is driven. Then the rental cost for a day, in dollars, is

$$\text{Cost} = 25 \text{ plus } 0.30 \text{ times (number of miles driven)}$$

Letting y represent cost and x represent miles driven, we have the linear equation

$$y = 25 + 0.30x$$

Comparing $y = 25 + 0.30x$ with $y = a + bx$, we see that the constant term (the y intercept) is $a = 25$; that means the $25 cost is incurred no matter how many miles the car is driven. Also, the slope of our line is $b = 0.30$; that means that the total cost for a day's rent increases by $0.30 for each additional mile driven.

Simple linear equations have graphs which are straight lines. It is easy to plot the graph of a linear equation because two different points completely determine a unique straight line. To plot a line, we choose two values for x, arbitrarily. Next, we compute y values by substituting the x values into the equation. Then we plot each (x, y) pair as a point on a graph and draw the line through the points. For example, for our line

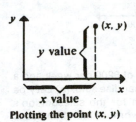

y value

x value

Plotting the point (x, y)

$$y = 25 + 0.30x$$

we choose $x = 100$ and $x = 400$, arbitrarily. Next we compute the y values:

At $x = 100$ $y = 25 + 0.30(100) = 55$

At $x = 400$ $y = 25 + 0.30(400) = 145$

so we have the (x, y) pairs (100, 55) and (400, 145). Now we plot these points and draw a line through them, as shown in Figure 12.1. The negative parts

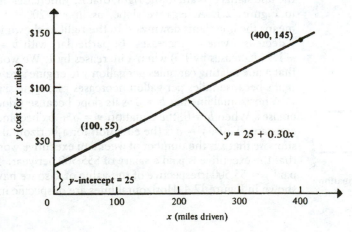

FIGURE 12.1
Car rental cost.

of the x and y axes have not been included in Figure 12.1 because the variables in this example cannot have negative values.

And *all points on the line satisfy the equation.*

The number of (x, y) pairs we can obtain by substituting x values into a given linear equation is limitless: but all the (x, y) pairs that satisfy the equation are points on one straight line, as illustrated in Figure 12.2.

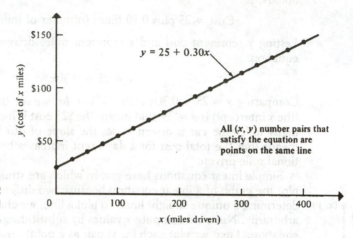

FIGURE 12.2
Points on the rental
cost line.

EXERCISE Suppose a salesperson receives a salary of $200 per week and a commission of 3.5 percent of the dollar amount of merchandise sold. (a) Let y be weekly pay and x be amount sold. Write the equation for the salesperson's weekly pay. (b) What is the pay for a week when $4000 worth of merchandise is sold? (c) What is the pay for a week when the salesperson is ill at home? (d) Make a graph of the linear equation.
ANSWER (a) $y = 200 + 0.035x$; (b) $340; (c) $200. (d) Plot the points (4000, 340) and (0, 200); then draw a line through the points.

A positive slope, such as $b = 0.30$ in our car rental example, means that the line slants upward to the right; that is, y increases as x increases as shown in Figure 12.1. A negative slope, as in $y = 200 - 1.5x$ where $b = -1.5$, means the line slants downward to the right as shown in Figure 12.3; that is, y decreases when x increases. In particular, with $b = -1.5$, y changes by -1.5 (decreases by 1.5) when x increases by 1. We would find, for example, that a line relating car miles per gallon y to engine size x has a negative slope; that's because miles per gallon decreases as engine size increases.

A horizontal line has $b = 0$ as its slope because y does not change as x increases. When $b = 0$, the equation $y = a + bx$ becomes $y = a$, where a is a constant. Thus, $y = a$ is the equation for a horizontal line. As an example, suppose that x is the number of weeks an executive works during a year, and that the executive is paid a salary of $55,500 per year. Then the executive is paid $y = 55,500$ irrespective of the value of x; so we have the horizontal line shown in Figure 12.4. Horizontal lines are of specific interest in the study of

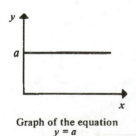

Graph of the equation
$y = a$

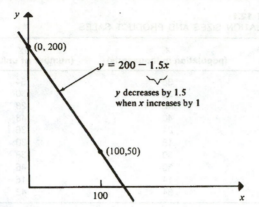

FIGURE 12.3
A line with a negative slope.

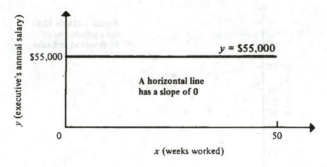

FIGURE 12.4
A horizontal line.

relationships because a horizontal line means that y is not related to x; in our example, the executive's salary is not related to the number of weeks worked.

12.3 ESTIMATING EQUATIONS

In statistical studies, we collect pairs of data numbers, called *observations*, rather than generate them from a given mathematical equation. For example, the data in Table 12.1 are observations on population sizes x and product sales y in 10 sales regions.

If the number pairs in Table 12.1 [such as (36, 54), (26, 30), and so on] are plotted, we obtain the points shown in Figure 12.5. The figure is aptly called a *scatter plot·* or a scatter diagram. The points do not all lie on the same straight line, but there is a tendency for the points to rise as we move to the right. That is, sales tend to be higher in regions of higher population. We want to describe this tendency with a straight-line equation. One way to do this is to stretch a piece of thread along the central region of the scatter of points, and adjust the thread until it seems to balance off the points above and below it, as shown in Figure 12.6. After tacking down the thread, we

Fitting a line "by eye"
to a scatter plot

TABLE 12.1
POPULATION SIZES AND PRODUCT SALES

Sales region	x (population in thousands)	y (number of units sold)
1	36	54
2	26	30
3	12	28
4	40	48
5	24	36
6	18	30
7	30	38
8	30	46
9	14	16
10	34	42

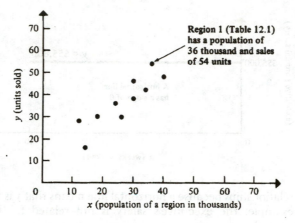

FIGURE 12.5
Scatter plot of sales versus population.

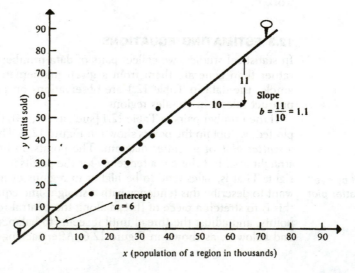

FIGURE 12.6
Fitting a line to a scatter plot.

Finding the equation of the fitted line

measure the *y* intercept and find it is $a = 6$. Next, as shown at the upper right of the figure, we draw a right triangle which has any section of the line as its hypotenuse. The slope of the straight line is obtained by measuring the sides of the triangle, and then dividing the length of the vertical side by the length of the horizontal side. For our example, we obtain

$$\text{Slope} = b = \frac{11}{10} = 1.1$$

Thus, we have $a = 6$ and $b = 1.1$. The equation of the estimating line can be written as $y = 6 + 1.1x$. However, we use the symbol $\hat{y}$ (read as "*y* hat") instead of *y* when writing estimating equations. That is, $\hat{y}$ means the vertical coordinate of a point *on the estimating line*, whereas *y* (Table 12.1) is the vertical coordinate of *an observed point*.

The line in Figure 12.6 has the equation

$$\hat{y} = 6 + 1.1x$$

Table 12.1 does not have sales for a region with a population of 20 thousand, but we can use the equation to estimate what they would be. If we substitute $x = 20$ into the equation, we obtain

$$\hat{y} = 6 + 1.1(20)$$

$$= 28$$

y-hat is an estimate of *y*.

Thus, we estimate sales of 28 units for a region having a population of 20 thousand. Of course, if a sales outlet is set up in a new region which has a population of 20 thousand, actual (observed) sales probably will be above or below 28 units; that is, 28 units is only an estimated, or predicted, value for sales.

EXERCISE For the example, estimate sales for a region having a population of 28 thousand.
ANSWER 36.8 or, rounded, 37 units.

Scatter plots are a helpful tool in the study of relationships. A scatter plot may exhibit no pattern which suggests a relationship between two variables: in that case, an estimating equation is worthless. For example, the points in Figure 12.7 exhibit no apparent pattern; number of days absent does not appear to be related to worker age. On the other hand, Figure 12.8 does exhibit a pattern—but the pattern suggests the relationship is curved: In this case, the straight-line method of estimating relationships that we develop in this chapter should not be applied; instead, a curve should be fitted to the data.

12.4 FITTING A STRAIGHT LINE BY THE LEAST-SQUARES METHOD

If you had made a thread-line fit to describe the linear tendency of the points in the scatter plot of Figure 12.6, the chances are that your line would differ from the one I drew. Whether your line or my line or some other line is the

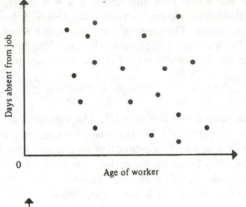

FIGURE 12.7
Absenteeism and worker age. The scatter plot shows no apparent relationship between worker age and number of days absent.

Days absent from job

Age of worker

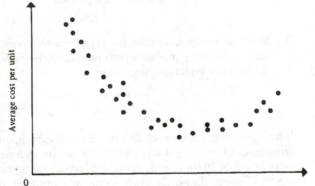

FIGURE 12.8
Average cost per unit versus number of units made. The relationship is curvilinear.

Average cost per unit

Number of units made

The eyeball is not the best line-fitting tool.

"best" line depends on how we define what is meant by the best-fitting line. Statisticians define the best-fitting line to be that line for which the sum of the squares of the errors has the smallest possible value. Figure 12.9 illus-

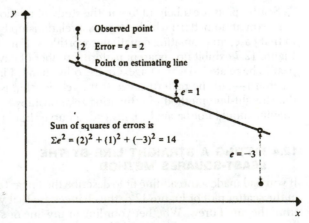

y

Observed point

2 Error = $e = 2$

Point on estimating line

$e = 1$

Sum of squares of errors is
$$\Sigma e^2 = (2)^2 + (1)^2 + (-3)^2 = 14$$

$e = -3$

FIGURE 12.9
The sum of the squares of the errors.

x

trates what is meant by the "sum of the squares of the errors." An error is a vertical distance between an actual observed point and the point directly below (or above) it on the estimating line. Thus, the leftmost observed point is 2 units above the line; so the error is $e = 2$. The middle observed point is 1 unit above the line; so $e = 1$. The rightmost point is 3 units below the line; its error is $e = -3$. The sum of the squares of the errors is

$$\Sigma e^2 = (2)^2 + (1)^2 + (-3)^2 = 14$$

Notice in Figure 12.9 that the sum of the errors is zero. That is,

$$\Sigma e = 2 + 1 - 3 = 0$$

Consequently, Σe is not a satisfactory measure of the total error because negative and positive errors are still errors, and a negative error should not offset a positive error; that's why statisticians take Σe^2, in which an e^2 cannot be negative, rather than Σe, as a measure of total error.

Now suppose we leave the observed points as they are in Figure 12.9 but draw a different line as shown in Figure 12.10. The new line comes closer to

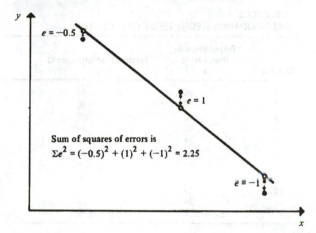

FIGURE 12.10
A smaller sum of squares of errors.

the points than the line of Figure 12.9. The new line has

$$\Sigma e^2 = (-0.5)^2 + (1)^2 + (-1)^2 = 2.25$$

We say the new line is a better "fit" for the observed data because its Σe^2, 2.25, is smaller than the $\Sigma e^2 = 14$ in Figure 12.9.

The line with the smallest Σe^2 is the best fit.

For a given set of observed data, different lines have different values of Σe^2. The *best-fitting* line is defined as the one having the smallest possible Σe^2. This best-fitting line is called the *least-squares* line. The least-squares line can be determined by calculations performed on the observed (x, y) data pairs. The calculations lead to a value for the slope b and a value for the intercept a. After a and b have been computed, their values are substituted into $\hat{y} = a + bx$ to obtain the estimating equation. For historic reasons that are not relevant here, the line is called the least-squares *regression* line. The slope of the regression line b is often called the *regression coefficient*, and the y intercept a is often called the *constant*.

By mathematical analysis (calculus) it has been proved that a and b for a least-squares regression line can be computed with the formulas

$$\hat{y} = a + bx \qquad \left\{ \begin{array}{l} \rightarrow \quad b = \dfrac{n(\Sigma xy) - (\Sigma x)(\Sigma y)}{n(\Sigma x^2) - (\Sigma x)^2} \\[2em] \rightarrow \quad a = \dfrac{\Sigma y - b(\Sigma x)}{n} \end{array} \right\}$$

where b = slope of the regression line
$\quad a$ = y intercept of the regression line
$\quad n$ = number of pairs of data
$\quad$ all sums are computed from the observed (x, y) data pairs

Let's illustrate the calculations involved by computing b and a for the population and sales data of Table 12.1. First we set up a table with the column headings shown in Table 12.2. Next, for each (x, y) pair we compute the

TABLE 12.2
LEAST-SQUARES REGRESSION CALCULATIONS

Region	Population in thousands x	Number of units sold y	xy	x^2
1	36	54	1944	1296
2	26	30	780	676
3	12	28	336	144
4	40	48	1920	1600
5	24	36	864	576
6	18	30	540	324
7	30	38	1140	900
8	30	46	1380	900
9	14	16	224	196
10	34	42	1428	1156
	$\Sigma x = 264$	$\Sigma y = 368$	$\Sigma xy = 10556$	$\Sigma x^2 = 7768$

product xy and the square of x, x^2, as shown; then we find the sum of each column. The values of b and a are computed from the column sums, and the value of n, which is 10. (Remember, n is the number of data *pairs*.) We have

Compute b first . . .

$$b = \frac{n(\Sigma xy) - (\Sigma x)(\Sigma y)}{n(\Sigma x^2) - (\Sigma x)^2}$$

$$= \frac{10(10,556) - (264)(368)}{10(7768) - (264)^2}$$

$$= \frac{8408}{7984}$$

$$= 1.053106$$

Next we compute

*. . . because b is
used in computing a.*

$$a = \frac{\Sigma y - b(\Sigma x)}{n}$$

$$= \frac{368 - (1.053106)(264)}{10}$$

$$= 8.998002$$

Rounded, $a = 9.00$. Notice that I wrote the value $b = 1.053106$ with six decimal places. I did so because if I had rounded it to, say, 1.05 and then used 1.05 in computing a, the result would have been $a = 9.08$, not the more correct figure, $a = 9.00$. In general, you should not use a rounded value of b when computing a. However, after a has been found, it is appropriate to round both a and b to three or four significant digits when writing the regression equation. Thus, we write the regression equation as

$$\hat{y} = 9.00 + 1.05x$$

We can draw the least-squares regression line by assigning two arbitrary values to x, say $x = 0$ and $x = 50$. Then we compute $\hat{y}$ from the equation

$$\hat{y} = 9.00 + 1.05x$$

Thus,

At $x = 0$ $\qquad\qquad \hat{y} = 9.00 + 1.05(0) = 9.00$

At $x = 50$ $\qquad\qquad \hat{y} = 9.00 + 1.05(50) = 61.5$

We next plot (0, 9.00) and (50, 61.5), then draw the least-squares regression line through the two points, as shown in Figure 12.11.

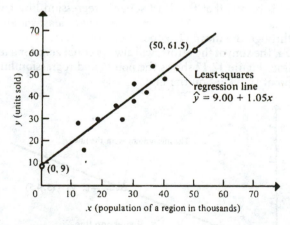

FIGURE 12.11

A least-squares regression line.

The least-squares regression line $\hat{y} = 9.00 + 1.05x$ differs from the equation $\hat{y} = 6 + 1.1x$ obtained by the thread-line fit in Figure 12.6. The for-

UNCONDITIONAL
GUARANTEE

Least-squares is
the best fit or
your money back.

mulas we applied in computing a and b for the least-squares line guarantee that $\hat{y} = 9.00 + 1.05x$ has the smaller sum of squares of errors because the least-squares line has the smallest possible Σe^2.

EXERCISE Given the observations (2, 2), (4, 5), (6, 4), and (8, 7), (a) find b and a for the least-squares regression line; (b) write the regression equation; (c) plot the observed data and the regression line.

ANSWER (a) $b = 0.7$, $a = 1$; (b) $\hat{y} = 1 + 0.7x$. (c) See Figure 12.12.

For the data given in the exercise, the mean value of x is

$$\bar{x} = \frac{\Sigma x}{n} = \frac{2 + 4 + 6 + 8}{4}$$

$$= 5$$

The mean value of y is

$$\bar{y} = \frac{\Sigma y}{n} = \frac{2 + 5 + 4 + 7}{4}$$

$$= 4.5$$

Thus, the mean point is $(\bar{x}, \bar{y}) = (5, 4.5)$. Moreover, $(\bar{x}, \bar{y})$ satisfies the regression equation

$$\hat{y} = 1 + 0.7x$$

That is, if we substitute $\bar{x} = 5$ for x, we get

$$\hat{y} = 1 + 0.7(5) = 4.5$$

$$= \bar{y}$$

One point on every least-squares line is $(\bar{x}, \bar{y})$.

This means that this least-squares regression line goes through $(\bar{x}, \bar{y})$, the mean data point. More generally, every least-squares regression line goes through the mean $(\bar{x}, \bar{y})$ point of the observations. And, as a consequence, Σe, the sum of the errors, will always equal zero for a least-squares regression line. Figure 12.12 shows the points and regression line of the exercise. The point $(\bar{x}, \bar{y})$ lies on the line.

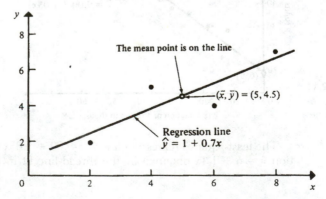

FIGURE 12.12

The mean point is on the least-squares line.

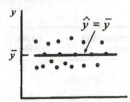

A horizontal regression line (or b = 0) means y is not related to x.

Suppose the computed regression coefficient b in $\hat{y} = a + bx$ turns out to be zero. Then the regression equation is $\hat{y} = a$. Its graph is a horizontal line. Moreover, because the regression line passes through $(\bar{x}, \bar{y})$, the value of a will equal $\bar{y}$; so the least-squares regression equation when b is zero is

$$\hat{y} = \bar{y}$$

Then the estimates $\hat{y}$ are the same for all values of x, or we may say that y is not related to x. Thus, we interpret $b = 0$ to mean that y is not related to x.

12.5 PROBLEMS

1. Plot the graphs of (a) $y = 3 + 2x$; (b) $y = 25 - 0.5x$; (c) $y = -2 + 1.5x$.

2. It costs $2000 to prepare the plates and set up the presses before printing copies of a book. The cost per book for printing and binding is $3. (a) Write the equation for the total cost y of producing x books. (b) Find the total cost of producing 5000 books.

3. Now, at $x = 0$ year, Volta Company pays $10,000 for a new machine and records the purchase price as the beginning book value of the machine. The book value y declines at the rate of $1000 per year. (a) Write the equation for the book value y after x years. (b) What is the book value after 5.5 years?

4. Table A shows assets and sales for 16 large corporations. (a) Make a scatter plot of the data, taking assets as the independent (x) variable. (b) Does the scatter plot indicate that sales and assets are related?

TABLE A

Assets (billions)	Sales (billions)	Assets (billions)	Sales (billions)
$7.8	$9.2	$3.6	$5.5
8.8	8.5	4.2	5.4
7.0	8.4	1.8	4.7
6.0	8.0	4.6	4.4
4.1	6.5	4.3	4.3
6.6	6.4	3.3	3.9
5.3	6.2	2.8	3.9
4.3	5.8	1.5	3.7

5. Table B (on page 404) shows numbers of employees and sales for 16 large corporations. (a) Make a scatter plot of the data, taking number of employees as the independent (x) variable. (b) Does the scatter plot indicate that number of employees and sales are related?

6. Table C (on page 404) shows engine sizes and miles per gallon for 18 manual-shift cars. (a) Make a scatter plot of the data, taking engine size as the independent (x) variable. (b) Does the scatter plot indicate that engine size and miles per gallon are related?

TABLE B

Number of employees (thousands)	Sales (billions)	Number of employees (thousands)	Sales (billions)
32	$9.2	98	$5.5
27	8.5	16	5.4
133	8.4	67	4.7
44	8.0	97	4.4
52	6.5	37	4.3
113	6.4	113	3.9
161	6.2	7	3.9
151	5.8	52	3.7

TABLE C

Engine size (cubic inches)	Miles per gallon	Engine size (cubic inches)	Miles per gallon
85	33	225	19
140	30	232	23
151	30	231	21
140	28	250	20
98	30	231	19
122	24	305	19
182	17	305	18
140	26	318	14
200	24	350	15

7. Table D shows number of units produced by a new worker and the number of days the worker has been employed. (*a*) Make a scatter plot of the data, taking number of days worked as the independent (*x*) variable. (*b*) What type of relationship between the variables is indicated by the scatter plot?

TABLE D

Number of days on job	Number of units produced	Number of days on job	Number of units produced
1	7	11	27
2	8	12	28
3	10	13	30
4	12	14	29
5	16	15	31
6	19	16	31
7	21	17	32
8	23	18	31
9	24	19	33
10	26	20	32

8. For the (*x*, *y*) points (4, 3), (8, 5), and (12, 9): (*a*) Find *a* and *b*, and then write the equation of the least-squares regression line. (*b*) Plot the points and the regression line. (c) Show that the point $(\bar{x}, \bar{y})$ is on the regression line.

9. For the (x, y) points $(1, 4)$, $(2, 2)$, and $(3, 3)$: (a) Find a and b, and then write the equation of the least-squares regression line. (b) Plot the points and the regression line. (c) Show that the point $(\bar{x}, \bar{y})$ is on the regression line.

10. For the (x, y) points $(3, 8)$, $(2, 4)$, $(4, 10)$, $(3, 6)$, $(2, 10)$, $(4, 4)$: (a) Find a and b and then write the equation of the least-squares regression line. (b) Plot the points and the regression line. (c) Compute $\bar{y}$ for the data and verify that the regression equation for these data is $\hat{y} = \bar{y}$.

11. The Springfield Home Mortgage Bank wants to estimate the number of foreclosures per 1000 houses sold. Bank officials think that the number of foreclosures y is related to the size of the down payment made by house buyers. Table E contains foreclosure and down payment data. (a) Let x be the down payment percent. Compute a and b, and then write the regression equation. (b) Use the regression equation to estimate foreclosures per 1000 houses sold if the down payment is 15 percent.

TABLE E

Down payment (percent of purchase price)	Number of foreclosures per 1000 houses
10	36
12	25
14	28
16	16
18	12
20	9

12. Table F contains data on assets and sales for eight large corporations. (a) Let x be assets. Compute a and b, and then write the equation of the regression line. (b) Use the regression equation to estimate sales of a corporation whose assets are $5 billion.

TABLE F

Assets (billions)	Sales (billions)	Assets (billions)	Sales (billions)
$7.8	$9.2	$4.2	$5.4
7.0	8.4	4.6	4.4
4.1	6.5	3.3	3.9
5.3	6.2	1.5	3.7

13. Tasty Grain Products varied the amount of shelf space allotted for displaying its cereal in a supermarket. Table G contains data on space allotment and sales. (a) Let x be space allotment. Find a and b, and then

write the equation of the regression line. (*b*) Using the regression equation, estimate sales for a space allotment of 7 square feet.

TABLE G

Space allotted (square feet)	Sales (number of boxes)
2	20
4	36
6	38
8	38
10	52
12	54

14. Clair Heating Oil Company wants to determine the relationship between its sales of heating oil and daily temperature. Table H contains sales and temperature data. Let *x* be the average daily temperature. Compute *a* and *b*, and then write the equation of the regression line.

TABLE H

Average daily temperature (degrees Fahrenheit)	Sales (thousands of gallons)
2	44
7	35
12	33
14	26
19	26
22	19
25	17
30	10
35	8
44	4

12.6 POPULATION AND SAMPLE REGRESSION LINES

Usually the (x, y) data we obtain and analyze are only a sample of all the observations that exist. The totality of observation pairs is called the *population*. From now on, a regression equation written with small letters, as in

$$\hat{y} = a + bx$$

will mean a sample regression equation, that is, a regression equation computed from a random sample of observations. We will use

$$\mu_Y = A + BX$$

to denote a population regression equation. The symbol μ_Y reminds us that

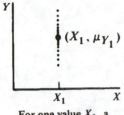

For one value X_1, a population contains many Y values. Their mean is μ_{Y_1}.

even if we know the population regression equation, the best we can do with the equation is to determine the mean value μ_Y for a given value of X; that's because population points scatter about the population regression line as illustrated in Figure 12.13.

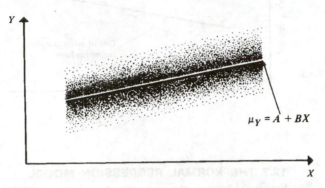

FIGURE 12.13
A population regression line.

An astronomical number of samples of size, say, $n = 35$ observations, can be drawn from the population of Figure 12.13. One sample is shown, with the sample regression line, in Figure 12.14. This line, $\hat{y} = a + bx$, is an

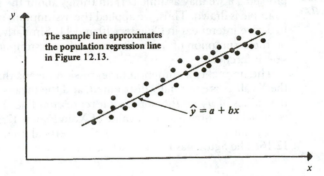

FIGURE 12.14
A sample regression line.

approximation of the population regression line $\mu_Y = A + BX$ in Figure 12.13. The sample constant term a is an estimate of the population constant term A; and the sample slope b is an estimate of the population slope B. A and B are population regression parameters. Our sample regression line is not the same as the population regression line; Figure 12.15 shows a population regression line and one of the many possible sample regression lines.

Usually we have to work with sample estimates of population regression lines because we cannot obtain observations for the whole population. For example, it would be prohibitively costly to obtain engine sizes and gas mileages (miles per gallon) for the population of all existing cars. However, that population does exist; so we can select a sample of cars and use the sample regression equation to estimate the population relationship between gas mileage and engine size.

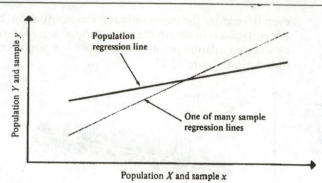

FIGURE 12.15
Population and sample
regression lines.

12.7 THE NORMAL REGRESSION MODEL

We have ŷ = a + bx.
We want to use it to
make inferences
about $\mu_1 = A + BX$.

Statistical inference comes into play when a sample regression line is used to estimate a population regression line. For example, we may want to construct a confidence interval for the population slope B or we may want to test a hypothesis about the value of B. We can solve statistical inference problems if we may assume certain things about the population from which a sample is drawn. Thus, we applied the assumption of normality extensively to derive inferences in Chapters 10 and 11. Similarly, statisticians often rely on the assumption of normality, and other assumptions, in deriving regression inferences.

The normality assumption in regression means that for every value of X, the Y values are normally distributed; and the means of the distributions are the values of μ_Y on the population regression line. For example, suppose a vertical line is drawn at an X value of X_1 in Figure 12.13; and then we make a histogram of all the values of Y on that vertical line, as illustrated in Figure 12.16. The figure has been drawn as if it were being viewed at an angle. You

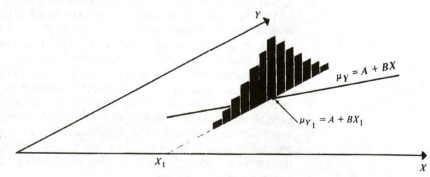

FIGURE 12.16
Histogram of Y values
at $X = X_1$.

should visualize the histogram as standing perpendicular to the book page.

Normality assumption The normality assumption means that the histogram can be represented as a normal distribution with a mean of μ_{Y_1}, where μ_{Y_1} is the mean value of Y when $X = X_1$, as shown in Figure 12.17. Also shown on the figure is the

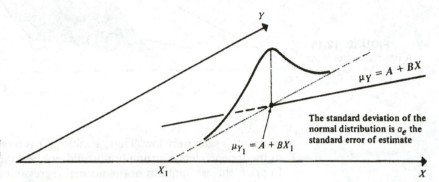

FIGURE 12.17
Normal distribution of
Y values when $X = X_1$.

symbol σ_e, which is the standard deviation of the normal distribution. σ_e is called the standard error of estimate (the e subscript serves well because e is the first letter in both *error* and *estimate*).

Now suppose we take another value of X, say, X_2. Then we consider all values of Y for this value of X. The mean of the Y values is

$$\mu_{Y_2} = A + BX_2$$

The normal regression model assumes that the distribution of the Y values for $X = X_2$ is normal, with a mean of μ_{Y_2}, and has the same standard error σ_e as the distribution of the Y's when $X = X_1$. Similarly, the model assumes that for every value of X, the distribution of the Y's is normal; that the mean of the Y's is the point on the population regression line; and that every such

Equal-standard-error assumption normal distribution has the same standard deviation σ_e. Consequently, the normal regression model can be pictured as a surface in three dimensions, as illustrated in Figure 12.18. Every cross-sectional slice of the surface is a normal distribution of Y values for one X value.

The standard error formulas we will use in making regression inferences are based upon the assumption that any one value of Y is independent of every other value. For example, suppose gas mileage (Y) for one car is independent of (not related to) gas mileage of any other car; then the assumption

Independence assumption of independence would be valid. On the other hand, suppose the Y variable is the monthly production of steel or some other product which responds to changes in general business activity: then, in a period of high activity, a month's sales will tend to be high if the previous month's sales were high; and, in a period of low activity, a month's sales will tend to be low if the pre-

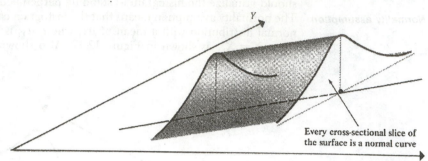

FIGURE 12.18
A normal regression
surface.

Every cross-sectional slice of
the surface is a normal curve

vious month's sales were low. Thus, a value of Y is related to other values of Y; so the independence assumption would not be valid.

In brief, the assumptions of the normal regression model are that the Y values for every X are independent and normally distributed; and that every distribution has the same standard deviation σ_e.

In a sample regression line, $\hat{y} = a + bx$, a and b are, respectively, estimates of the population constant term A and the population slope B. In simple linear regression inferences, a consequence of using the two sample estimators a and b is that two degrees of freedom are lost. Thus, if we have n data points, the number of degrees of freedom is

> *Two degrees of freedom are lost when two estimators are used.*

$$v = n - 2$$

12.8 THE SAMPLE STANDARD ERROR OF ESTIMATE

We will need a value for σ_e in deriving regression inferences. This population value is a standard deviation which measures variations of points above and below the population regression line. Since we do not know the value of σ_e, we estimate it by s_e, the *sample standard error of estimate*. The number s_e is a standard deviation which measures the variations of sample points above and below the sample regression line. Specifically, s_e is the standard deviation of the errors e we discussed earlier in the chapter. The formula defining s_e is

> *s_e is an estimator for σ_e, derived from the sample.*

$$s_e = \sqrt{\frac{\Sigma(e - \bar{e})^2}{n - 2}}$$

The divisor is $n - 2$ because, as stated in the last paragraph, two degrees of freedom are lost in simple linear regression inferences.

Each error e is the difference between an observed y value and the $\hat{y}$ on the regression line directly above or below y, as illustrated in Figure 12.19. That is,

$$e = y - \hat{y}$$

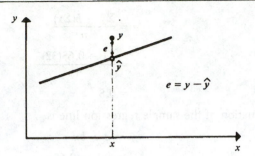

FIGURE 12.19
Error is $y - \hat{y}$.

Since $\bar{e} = 0$ (because $\Sigma e = 0$), (all the values are on the line)

$$\Sigma(e - \bar{e})^2 = \Sigma e^2 = \Sigma(y - \hat{y})^2$$

Therefore, we could compute s_e by the formula

We could compute s,
by this formula . . .

$$s_e = \sqrt{\frac{\Sigma(y - \hat{y})^2}{n - 2}}$$

But, to do so, we would first have to calculate $\hat{y}$ (from the regression equation) for each observed value of x. We will use a simpler formula to compute s_e. It is

. . . but we will use
this simpler formula.

$$s_e = \sqrt{\frac{\Sigma y^2 - a\Sigma y - b\Sigma xy}{n - 2}}$$

Table 12.3 contains the calculation results needed to obtain both a and b

TABLE 12.3
CALCULATIONS NEEDED TO OBTAIN a, b, AND s,

x	y	xy	x²	y²
4	3.0	12	16	9.00
6	5.5	33	36	30.25
10	6.5	65	100	42.25
12	9.0	108	144	81.00
$\Sigma x = 32$	$\Sigma y = 24.0$	$\Sigma xy = 218$	$\Sigma x^2 = 296$	$\Sigma y^2 = 162.50$

for the least-squares regression line, and the sample standard error of estimate s_e. First we obtain

$$b = \frac{n(\Sigma xy) - (\Sigma x)(\Sigma y)}{n(\Sigma x^2) - (\Sigma x)^2}$$

$$= \frac{4(218) - (32)(24)}{4(296) - (32)^2}$$

$$= 0.65$$

Next,

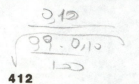
$$a = \frac{\Sigma y - b(\Sigma x)}{n}$$

$$= \frac{24 - 0.65(32)}{4}$$

$$= 0.8$$

The equation of the sample regression line is

$$\hat{y} = a + bx$$

$$= 0.8 + 0.65x$$

We now proceed to compute

$$s_e = \sqrt{\frac{\Sigma y^2 - a\Sigma y - b\Sigma xy}{n - 2}}$$

$$= \sqrt{\frac{162.5 - 0.8(24) - 0.65(218)}{4 - 2}}$$

$$= \sqrt{\frac{1.6}{2}}$$

$$= 0.894$$

The value just obtained, $s_e = 0.894$, is the sample standard error of estimate.

EXERCISE Given the data pairs (1, 2), (2, 4), and (3, 3), (a) calculate a and b; then write the equation of the regression line. (b) Calculate s_r.
ANSWER (a) $\hat{y} = 2 + 0.5x$; (b) 1.225.

The larger s_r is, the less accurate are the $\hat{y}$ estimates.

The sample standard error of estimate s_e measures the amount of variation of the sample points above and below the regression line. If s_e equals zero, all the sample points lie on the regression line, as illustrated in Figure 12.20. Usually, s_e is not zero, and the larger s_e is, the less accurate are the es-

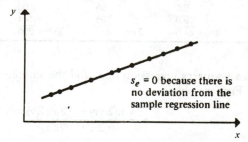

$s_e = 0$ because there is no deviation from the sample regression line

FIGURE 12.20
All sample points are on the regression line.

timates $\hat{y}$ obtained by substituting x values into $\hat{y} = a + bx$. In the next few sections, you will learn that s_e plays a principal role in deriving regression inferences.

(handwritten notes in top margin) (βαγε'nin defter) $N > 30 \Rightarrow z$ $N < 30 \Rightarrow t$

12.9 INFERENCES ABOUT THE SLOPE OF THE POPULATION REGRESSION LINE

In Chapters 9 and 10 we discussed inferences of two kinds, confidence intervals and hypothesis testing. In this section we shall first test hypotheses about the population slope B; then we shall construct confidence intervals for B.

Testing Hypotheses about B

An astronomical number of samples can be selected from a population; so the number of sample slopes is astronomical. Each sample slope b is an estimate of the population slope B. The sample slopes will vary around the value of B; so we need a measure of slope variation. This measure is denoted by s_b, and it is called the *sample standard error of the slope*; statisticians compute s_b with the formula

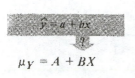

$$s_b = \frac{s_e}{\sqrt{\Sigma x^2 - \frac{(\Sigma x)^2}{n}}}$$

where s_e = sample standard error of estimate
n = sample size

Also, for the normal regression model, mathematicians have proved that the statistic

Test statistic for hypotheses concerning B

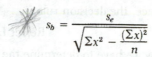

$$t = \frac{b - B}{s_b}$$

has the Student t distribution with $v = n - 2$ degrees of freedom. Consequently, we will use the t distribution of Table VII at the back of the book (or the normal z in Table VI if $v > 30$) in testing hypotheses about the population slope B.

Slight change: We use the normal z if v ⊃ 30.

One hypothesis is that $B = 0$; that is, the variables are not related. Or, a hypothesis could be that $B = 1$, or $B = k$, where k is zero or some other constant number. The hypotheses we can test, with their decision rules at significance level α, follow (remember that $v = n - 2$):

$$H_0: B = k \qquad H_a: B \neq k \qquad \text{Reject } H_0 \text{ if } |\text{sample } t| > t_{\alpha/2, v}$$

or $\qquad H_0: B \leq k \qquad H_a: B > k \qquad \text{Reject } H_0 \text{ if sample } t > t_{\alpha, v}$

or $\qquad H_0: B \geq k \qquad H_a: B < k \qquad \text{Reject } H_0 \text{ if sample } t < -t_{\alpha, v}$

EXAMPLE On 10 occasions, machinists made varying numbers of gears. On each occasion, records were kept of the number of labor-hours spent x and the number of gears made y. The following sums were computed from the sample data:

$$\Sigma x = 320 \qquad \Sigma y = 250 \qquad \Sigma xy = 9415 \qquad \Sigma x^2 = 12{,}400 \qquad \Sigma y^2 = 7230$$

At the 5 percent level of significance, perform a test of the hypothesis that the slope of the population regression line is greater than 0.5.

SOLUTION The hypothesis that the population slope B is greater than 0.5 is H_a; that is, H_a is $B > 0.5$ and H_0 is $B \le 0.5$. Thus

1. State the hypotheses.
$$H_0: B \le 0.5 \qquad H_a: B > 0.5$$

The test is one-tailed. There are $n = 10$ sample points; so the number of degrees of freedom is

$$\nu = n - 2$$
$$= 10 - 2 = 8$$

From Table VII, with $\alpha = 0.05$ and $\nu = 8$, we find

$$t_{\alpha,\nu} = t_{0.05,8} = 1.86$$

Hence, the decision rule is

2. State the decision rule.
$$\text{Reject } H_0 \text{ if sample } t > 1.86$$

Now we have to determine the value of the sample test statistic

$$t = \frac{b - B}{s_b}$$

$$= \frac{b - 0.5}{s_b}$$

To compute the sample t, we must calculate, in order, first b, then a, then s_e, then s_b, and finally, t. From the sums provided in the example, we calculate

2 1/2. Compute b.
$$b = \frac{n(\Sigma xy) - (\Sigma x)(\Sigma y)}{n(\Sigma x^2) - (\Sigma x)^2} = \frac{10(9415) - (320)(250)}{10(12,400) - (320)^2}$$

$$= \frac{14,150}{21,600} = 0.65509$$

Then,

2 3/4. Compute a.
$$a = \frac{\Sigma y - b\Sigma x}{n} = \frac{250 - (0.65509)(320)}{10} = 4.0371$$

Next,

2 7/8. Compute s_e.
$$s_e = \sqrt{\frac{\Sigma y^2 - a\Sigma y - b\Sigma xy}{n - 2}}$$

$$= \sqrt{\frac{7230 - (4.0371)(250) - (0.65509)(9415)}{10 - 2}}$$

$$= \sqrt{\frac{53.05}{8}} = 2.575$$

Then,

2 15/16. Compute s_b.

$$s_b = \frac{s_e}{\sqrt{\Sigma x^2 - \frac{(\Sigma x)^2}{n}}}$$

$$= \frac{2.575}{\sqrt{12,400 - \frac{(320)^2}{10}}} = \frac{2.575}{\sqrt{2160}}$$

$$= 0.05541$$

Rounding to three significant digits, we have

$$b = 0.655$$

$$s_b = 0.0554$$

Hence, with $B = 0.5$ (the 0.5 in H_0: $B \le 0.5$), we compute the value of the test statistic

3. Compute the sample statistic (at last!).

$$t = \frac{b - B}{s_b} = \frac{0.655 - 0.5}{0.0554}$$

$$= 2.80$$

So we have

$$\text{Sample } t = 2.80$$

Because the sample t, 2.80, exceeds the value 1.86 in the decision rule we

4. Accept or reject H_0.

$$\text{Reject } H_0$$

In this case, rejecting H_0: $B \le 0.5$ means that the sample shows convincing evidence, at the 5 percent level of significance, that the population slope is greater than 0.5. Now recall that the slope b is the change in y (number of gears made) when x (number of labor-hours) increases by 1. The test shows that, for the population, the number of gears made per additional labor-hour is greater than 0.5.

Earlier in the chapter you learned that if $b = 0$, the sample regression line is the horizontal line $\hat{y} = \bar{y}$. When $b = 0$, the sample indicates that there is no relationship between y and x. If the population slope B is zero, there is no relationship between Y and X in the population. If $B = 0$, a regression equation is useless; so before using a regression equation as an estimating equation, statisticians test the hypotheses

Test B = 0 to see if X and Y are related.

$$H_0: B = 0 \qquad H_a: B \ne 0$$

This test is two-tailed. With a sample size of n and significance level α, the decision rule is

$$\text{Reject } H_0 \text{ if } |\text{sample } t| > t_{\alpha/2, v}$$

where, as before, the number of degrees of freedom is $v = n - 2$. With $B = 0$, the statistic

$$t = \frac{b - B}{s_b}$$

becomes the sample test statistic

$$t = \frac{b}{s_b}$$

If $H_0: B = 0$ is rejected, the conclusion is that the two variables are related; but if H_0 is accepted, the conclusion is that the variables are not related.

EXERCISE The following sums were calculated for $n = 50$ sample points (x is the number of items listed on an order and y is the cost of processing the order): $\Sigma x = 80$, $\Sigma y = 95$, $\Sigma xy = 400$, $\Sigma x^2 = 438$, $\Sigma y^2 = 475$. The sample regression equation is $\hat{y} = 0.62 + 0.8x$. Perform a test at the 1 percent level to determine if there is a relationship between the number of items on an order and the cost of processing the order.

ANSWER 1. $H_0: B = 0$; $H_a: B \neq 0$. 2. (Note that $v > 30$.) Reject H_0 if |sample z| > 2.58. 3. Sample $z = 9.95$. 4. Reject H_0 and conclude that processing time is related to the number of items on an order.

Confidence Intervals for a Population Slope

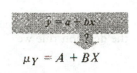

$$\mu_Y = A + BX$$

A test of a hypothesis about B starts with a hypothesized value of the population slope, as in $H_0: B \geq 0.5$. A confidence interval starts with b, the sample estimate of B. Then we derive an inference which states that B is between two values calculated from the sample data. Recall that, in Chapter 10, the confidence interval for the population mean is expressed as

$$\bar{x} - t_{\alpha/2, v}s_{\bar{x}} \leq \mu \leq \bar{x} + t_{\alpha/2, v}s_{\bar{x}}$$

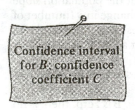

Confidence interval for B; confidence coefficient C

A confidence interval for B has the same form, with b replacing $\bar{x}$ and s_b replacing $s_{\bar{x}}$. Thus, we have

$$b - t_{\alpha/2, v}s_b \leq B \leq b + t_{\alpha/2, v}s_b$$

where $v = n - 2$
$\alpha/2 = (1 - C)/2$

In the last example, where $n = 10$, we computed

Step 1 *Compute b and s_b.*

$$b = 0.655$$

$$s_b = 0.0554$$

To construct a 95 percent ($C = 0.95$) confidence interval for B, we first compute

$$\frac{\alpha}{2} = \frac{1 - 0.95}{2} = 0.025$$

and $v = n - 2 = 10 - 2$

$$= 8$$

Next, from Table VII, we find

Step 2   Look up $t_{\alpha/2,v}$. $t_{0.025,8} = 2.31$

The desired confidence interval

$$b - t_{\alpha/2,v}s_b \leq B \leq b + t_{\alpha/2,v}s_b$$

is

**Step 3   Form the
confidence interval.** $0.655 - (2.31)(0.0554) \leq B \leq 0.655 + (2.31)(0.0554)$

$$0.527 \leq B \leq 0.783$$

The result, in the context of the example, means that we have 95 percent confidence that the number of gears made per additional labor-hour is between 0.527 and 0.783.

EXERCISE   In the last exercise, $n = 50$, $b = 0.8$, and $s_b = 0.0804$. Construct a 99 percent confidence interval for the population slope.
ANSWER $0.59 \leq B \leq 1.01$.

12.10 CONFIDENCE INTERVALS FOR μ_Y GIVEN A VALUE OF X

Once we have computed a sample regression line $\hat{y} = a + bx$, we use it as an estimate of the population regression line $\mu_Y = A + BX$. A value of $\hat{y}$ computed by substituting a value of x into the sample regression equation is an estimate of the population mean μ_Y for the value $X = x$. Of course, sample estimates $\hat{y}$ will vary from the population value μ_Y, and we need a measure of that variation to construct confidence intervals for μ_Y. The measure is called *the standard error of estimating μ_Y, given X*, and it is denoted by the symbol $s(\mu_Y|X)$. For the normal regression model, we use the following formula to compute $s(\mu_Y|X)$:

$\hat{y} = a + bx$

$\mu_Y = A + BX$

$$s(\mu_Y|X) = s_e \sqrt{\frac{1}{n} + \frac{(X - \bar{x})^2}{\Sigma x^2 - (\Sigma x)^2/n}}$$

where s_e = sample standard error of estimate
        n = sample size
        X = value of X for which μ_Y is to be estimated
        $\bar{x} = \Sigma x/n$

Confidence interval
for μ_Y, given a
value of X;
confidence
coefficient C

The *confidence interval formula for μ_Y, given a value of X*, is

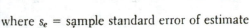

$$\hat{y} - t_{\alpha/2,v}s(\mu_Y|X) \leq \mu_Y \leq \hat{y} + t_{\alpha/2,v}s(\mu_Y|X)$$

where $\hat{y} = a + bX$
$\alpha/2 = (1 - C)/2$
$v = n - 2$

EXAMPLE In the example we have been using, on 10 occasions machinists made varying numbers of gears y during different numbers of labor-hours x. The regression equation is $\hat{y} = 4.037 + 0.6551x$; the standard error of estimate is $s_e = 2.575$; also $\Sigma x = 320$ and $\Sigma x^2 = 12,400$. Construct a 95 percent confidence interval for the mean number of gears made in 50 labor-hours.

SOLUTION For $X = 50$ labor-hours we substitute $x = 50$ into

$$\hat{y} = 4.037 + 0.6551x$$

and obtain

Step 1 *Compute $\hat{y}$.*

$$\hat{y} = 4.037 + 0.6551(50)$$
$$= 36.8$$

as our point estimate of μ_Y. We need $\bar{x}$ to compute $s(\mu_Y|X)$. With $\Sigma x = 320$ and $n = 10$,

Step 2 *Compute $\bar{x}$.*

$$\bar{x} = \frac{\Sigma x}{n} = \frac{320}{10}$$
$$= 32$$

Next we compute the standard error of estimating μ_Y, given X, as follows:

Step 3 *Compute $s(\mu_1|X)$.*

$$s(\mu_Y|X) = s_e \sqrt{\frac{1}{n} + \frac{(X - \bar{x})^2}{\Sigma x^2 - (\Sigma x)^2/n}}$$

$(\Sigma x)^2/n$ is called a shilling fraction. It means $\dfrac{(\Sigma x)^2}{n}$

$$= (2.575) \sqrt{\frac{1}{10} + \frac{(50 - 32)^2}{12,400 - (320)^2/10}}$$

$$= (2.575) \sqrt{0.1 + 0.15} = (2.575)(0.5)$$

$$= 1.29$$

For a 95 percent confidence interval, $C = 0.95$

$$\frac{\alpha}{2} = \frac{1 - C}{2} = \frac{1 - 0.95}{2}$$
$$= 0.025$$

Also,

$$v = n - 2 = 10 - 2$$
$$= 8$$

From Table VII, we find $t_{\alpha/2,v}$ is

Step 4 *Find $t_{\alpha/2,v}$.*

$$t_{0.025,8} = 2.31$$

Hence, the desired confidence interval is

Step 5 *Construct the confidence interval.*

$$\hat{y} - t_{\alpha/2,v}s(\mu_Y|X) \le \mu_Y \le \hat{y} + t_{\alpha/2,v}s(\mu_Y|X)$$

$$36.8 - (2.31)(1.29) \le \mu_Y \le 36.8 + (2.31)(1.29)$$

$$33.8 \le \mu_Y \le 39.8$$

Thus, with 95 percent confidence, we may say that the mean number of gears produced in 50 labor-hours will be between 33.8 and 39.8. Figure 12.21

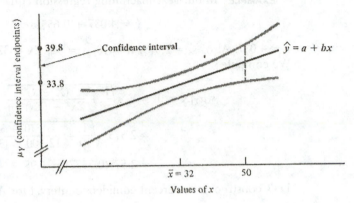

FIGURE 12.21
Confidence interval for μ_Y, given $X = 50$.

shows the confidence interval; it also shows that confidence intervals for μ_Y given a value of X are more precise (narrower) the closer X is to the sample mean $\bar{x}$. That's because the quantity $(X - \bar{x})^2$ in the formula for $s(\mu_Y|X)$ is smaller, and $s(\mu_Y|X)$ is smaller, the closer X is to $\bar{x}$; and the smaller $s(\mu_Y|X)$ is, the narrower (more precise) will be the confidence interval.

> **EXERCISE** In a previous exercise, the regression equation computed for $n = 50$ observations is $\hat{y} = 0.62 + 0.8x$. Here, x is the number of items on an order and y is the cost, in dollars, of processing the order. Sample calculations showed that $\Sigma x = 80$, $\Sigma x^2 = 438$, and $s_e = 1.415$. Construct a 90 percent confidence interval estimate of the mean cost of processing orders for four items.
> **ANSWERS** $3.36 \le \mu_Y \le$ $4.28.

Confidence Interval for the Population Constant Term

The constant term A in

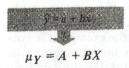

$$\mu_Y = A + BX$$

is the value of μ_Y when $X = 0$. Therefore, the confidence interval for A is the confidence interval for μ_Y when $X = 0$. The point estimate of A is the constant a in the sample regression equation

$$\hat{y} = a + bx$$

The standard error of estimating A is $s(\mu_Y|X = 0)$. Hence, we can construct the confidence interval

$$a - t_{\alpha/2,v}s(\mu_Y|X = 0) \leq A \leq a + t_{\alpha/2,v}s(\mu_Y|X = 0)$$

where a = the constant in the sample regression equation
$\alpha/2 = (1 - C)/2$
$v = n - 2$

EXAMPLE In our gear-machining regression equation

$$\hat{y} = 4.037 + 0.6551x$$

$a = 4.037$. Also, $s_e = 2.575$, $n = 10$, $\bar{x} = 32$, $\Sigma x = 320$, and $\Sigma x^2 = 12{,}400$. We compute

$$s(\mu_Y|X = 0) = s_e \sqrt{\frac{1}{n} + \frac{(X - \bar{x})^2}{\Sigma x^2 - (\Sigma x)^2/n}}$$

$$= 2.575 \sqrt{\frac{1}{10} + \frac{(0 - 32)^2}{12{,}400 - (320)^2/10}}$$

$$= 2.575(0.7577) = 1.95$$

Let's construct a 90 percent confidence interval for A. Then

$$\frac{\alpha}{2} = \frac{1 - 0.9}{2} = 0.05$$

and $v = n - 2$; so

$$t_{\alpha/2,v} = t_{0.05,8} = 1.86$$

Hence, the confidence interval

$$a - t_{\alpha/2,v}s(\mu_Y|X = 0) \leq A \leq a + t_{\alpha/2,v}s(\mu_Y|X = 0)$$

is

This interval for A is imprecise (wide) because X = 0 is far from $\bar{x}$ = 32.

$$4.037 - (1.86)(1.95) \leq A \leq 4.037 + (1.86)(1.95)$$

$$0.41 \leq A \leq 7.66$$

In the regression equation of the example,

$$\hat{y} = 4.037 + 0.6551x$$

The constant a (or A) must be interpreted for the situation at hand.

$a = 4.037$ is the estimate of labor-hours spent when $x = 0$ gears are made; that could mean that some labor-hours are spent before machining starts ($x = 0$) to set up the machines. So, in the context of the example, the constant term may have the meaning of setup time. If so, the interval estimate of setup time is from 0.41 to 7.66 hours. Often, however, the constant term has no meaning. For example, in the last exercise, x is the number of items listed on an order and y is the cost of processing the order. It is unlikely that there are orders listing x = 0 items; so the constant term probably is meaningless in this situation.

12.11 INTERVAL PREDICTION OF Y GIVEN A VALUE OF X

Note: Prediction intervals—not confidence intervals— for Y.

Population values Y, given a value of X, are values of a random variable; they are not constants like the parameters A and B, or a value of μ_Y given a value of X. We construct a *prediction* interval for values of a random variable.

The formula for the *standard error of predicting Y given X* is

$$s(Y|X) = s_e \sqrt{1 + \frac{1}{n} + \frac{(X - \bar{x})^2}{\Sigma x^2 - (\Sigma x)^2/n}}$$

Prediction interval for Y, given a value of X: confidence coefficient C

The 1 under the square root symbol does not appear in the formula for $s(\mu_Y|X)$. Its presence makes $s(Y|X)$ larger than $s(\mu_Y|X)$; so the prediction interval for Y given X is wider than the confidence interval for μ_Y given the same value of X. The *formula for predicting Y given a value of X* is

$$\hat{y} - t_{\alpha/2,v}s(Y|X) \leq Y \leq \hat{y} + t_{\alpha/2,v}s(Y|X)$$

where $\hat{y} = a + bx$

$\alpha/2 = 1 - C/2$

$v = n - 2$

Let's use our gear-making example one more time. The regression equation for number of gears y and number of labor-hours x is

$$\hat{y} = 4.037 + 0.6551x$$

The sample size is n = 10, Σx = 320, Σx^2 = 12,400, and s_e = 2.575. The sample mean is $\bar{x}$ = $^{320}/_{10}$ = 32. To construct a 95 percent prediction interval for Y, given X = 50, we first compute

$$\hat{y} = 4.037 + 0.6551(50) = 36.8$$

Next we need the value of the standard error of predicting Y given X; it is

$$s(Y|X) = s_e \sqrt{1 + \frac{1}{n} + \frac{(X - \bar{x})^2}{\Sigma x^2 - (\Sigma x)^2/n}}$$

Is 12,400 divided by the 10 in the shilling fraction?

$$= 2.575 \sqrt{1 + \frac{1}{10} + \frac{(50 - 32)^2}{12,400 - (320)^2/10}}$$

$$= 2.575 \sqrt{1.25} = 2.88$$

With 95 percent confidence and $n = 10$

$$t_{0.025,8} = 2.31$$

So we have the interval

$$\hat{y} - t_{\alpha/2,v}s(Y|X) \le Y \le \hat{y} + t_{\alpha/2,v}s(Y|X)$$

$$36.8 - 2.31(2.88) \le Y \le 36.8 + 2.31(2.88)$$

$$30.1 \le Y \le 43.5$$

Thus we predict with 95 percent confidence that the number of gears made in 50 labor-hours will be between 30.1 and 43.5. Recall that in the previous example we estimated μ_Y more precisely; that is, we estimated with 95 percent confidence that the *mean* number of gears μ_Y made in 50 labor-hours will be between 33.8 and 39.8.

EXERCISE See the last exercise. Construct a 90 percent prediction interval for the cost of processing an order for four items.
ANSWER $\$1.46 \le Y \le \$6.18$.

12.12 PROBLEMS

1. Collette McNess, manager of the Cross Roads Hotel, collected sample data on x, the number of people who made room reservations before arriving at the hotel, and y, the number of these people who registered at the hotel. The data are given in Table A. The computed regression equation is $\hat{y} = -1.0093 + 0.8514x$. (a) Compute the standard error of estimate. (b) Compute the standard error of the slope. (c) At the 1 percent level of significance, test the hypothesis that the slope of the population regression line is zero.

TABLE A

Number of reservations x	Number who registered y
14	8
22	22
37	27
62	57
80	64

2. Arne Nielsen, owner of Nielsen's Farms, collected data on the number of bags of fertilizer x applied to a section of corn-seeded land, and the corn yield y, in bushels, from the section. All land sections were of the same size. The data are shown in Table B. The regression equation is $\hat{y} = 23.7333 + 5.8857x$. (a) Compute the standard error of estimate. (b) Compute the standard error of the slope. (c) At the 10 percent level of significance, test the hypothesis that the increase in yield per additional bag of fertilizer equals 5 bushels.

TABLE B

Bags of fertilizer applied x	Yield in bushels y
1	24
2	44
3	42
4	40
5	60
6	56

3. Rex Canby bought two precision thermometers. One thermometer was calibrated in degrees Celsius (°C) and the other in degrees Fahrenheit (°F). Table C contains corresponding readings on the thermometers at different temperatures. (a) Find b and a, and then write the regression equation. (b) Compute s_e. (c) What does the value of s_e mean with respect to the observations in Table C?

TABLE C

Degrees Celsius x	Degrees Fahrenheit y
5	41
10	50
20	68
40	104
50	122

4. Joyce Laplace, an executive of Market Advice, Inc., wanted to determine the relationship between y, the amount of money a family spends, and x, the amount of income the family receives. She expressed both x and y in thousands of dollars. For a sample of 12 families, Joyce computed the regression line $\hat{y} = 6.0785 + 0.6078x$. She also computed $\Sigma x = 390$, $\Sigma x^2 = 13,400$, and $s_e = 4.2243$. (a) Perform a hypothesis test at the 1 percent level to determine whether spending and income are related; that is, test the hypothesis that the slope of the population regression line equals zero. (b) Construct the 95 percent confidence interval estimate of the slope of the population regression line. (c) Construct the 95 percent prediction interval estimate for the amount spent by a family having an income of $40 thousand. (d) Construct the 95 percent confidence interval estimate for the mean amount spent by families whose income is $40 thousand. (e) At the 5 percent level, perform a hypothesis test to determine whether the increase in the amount spent from an additional $1 thousand of income is greater than $0.5 thousand.

5. Pat Beaumont, president of Beauty Products Company, recorded 12 observations on advertising expenditure x and sales y. Pat recorded both expenditures and sales in thousands of dollars. Each observation was for a 3-month period. The regression equation is $\hat{y} = 40 + 2.8x$. Also, $\Sigma x = 96$, $\Sigma x^2 = 854$, and the standard error of estimate is 2.4. (a) At the 5 percent level, test the hypothesis that the slope of the population regression line is greater than 2. (b) What does the result of the test in (a) mean about the sales-advertising relationship? (c) Construct the 95 percent confidence interval estimate of the population slope. (d) Construct the 90 percent prediction interval estimate of sales for a 3-month period when advertising expenditure is 10 thousand dollars. (e) Construct the 90 percent confidence interval estimate of mean sales in 3-month periods when advertising expenditure is 10 thousand dollars.

6. R. C. Cory, Inc., a large mail-order company, has a staff of people who work on both inventory management and customer order filling. At the beginning of each working day it is necessary to assign a certain number of these people to do order filling. For this purpose, a quick estimate of the number of orders in the early morning mail is needed. It was suggested that the estimate might be calculated from the weight of the mail. Consequently, a sample of 20 days' mail was selected and, for each day, a tabulation was made of the mail weight x, in hundreds of pounds, and the number of orders in the mail y, in thousands. Regression calculation yielded $\Sigma x = 210$, $\Sigma y = 530$, $\Sigma xy = 7225$, $\Sigma x^2 = 2870$, $\Sigma y^2 = 18,190$, $a = 0.28948$, $b = 2.49624$, and $s_e = 0.263$. (a) Construct the 95 percent prediction interval estimate of the number of orders in the mail on a day when the weight of the mail is 15 hundred pounds. (b) Construct a 90 percent confidence interval estimate of the mean number of orders on days when the mail weighs 15 hundred pounds. (c) At the 5 percent level of significance, perform a test of the hypothesis that the slope of the regression line is less than 3.

7. In this problem, x is the Environmental Protection Agency (EPA) gas mileage (mpg) of a car in highway driving, and y is mpg for the car in city driving. Calculations for 18 observations (cars) provided the following data: $\Sigma x = 520$, $\Sigma y = 375$, $\Sigma xy = 11,250$, $\Sigma x^2 = 15,680$, and $\Sigma y^2 = 8150$. The regression line is $\hat{y} = 2.5337 + 0.6334x$. The standard error of estimate is 2.14 mpg. (a) At the 1 percent level of significance, test the hypothesis that the slope of the regression line is greater than zero. (b) Construct a 99 percent confidence interval estimate of the slope of the population regression line. (c) Construct the 95 percent prediction interval estimate of the city mpg for a car getting 30 mpg in highway driving. (d) Construct the 95 percent confidence interval estimate of mean city mpg for cars which get 30 mpg in highway driving.

8. In this problem, x is city mpg and y is combined city and highway mpg. For 18 cars, $\Sigma x = 375$, $\Sigma y = 435$, $\Sigma xy = 9430$, $\Sigma x^2 = 8150$, $\Sigma y^2 = 10,920$, $\hat{y} = 1.4812 + 1.0889x$, and $s_e = 0.678$ mpg. (a) At the 5 percent level of significance, test the hypothesis that the slope of the population regression line is less than 1. (Hint: Be careful when you decide

whether to accept or reject H_0.) (b) Construct a 95 percent confidence interval estimate of the slope of the population regression line. (c) Construct a 95 percent prediction interval estimate of combined mpg for a car getting 15 mpg in city driving. (d) Construct a 95 percent confidence interval estimate of mean combined mpg for cars getting 15 mpg in city driving.

9. Security analysts often are interested in the "beta" of a stock. Beta (β) is the slope of a population regression line relating the performance of a particular stock to general stock-market performance. That is, β is an alternative symbol for B in $\mu_Y = A + BX$. For some stock funds, analysts want to select stocks for which beta (or B) is greater than 1. Suppose that x is the measure of a particular stock's performance, and y is the measure of general stock-market performance. Suppose also that for $n = 15$ (x, y) observations, $\Sigma x = 360$, $\Sigma y = 435$, $\Sigma xy = 11,600$, $\Sigma x^2 = 9670$, $\Sigma y^2 = 14,200$. (a) Calculate a and b for the least-squares regression line. (b) Calculate the standard error of estimate. (c) Calculate the standard error of the slope. (d) At the 5 percent level of significance, perform a hypothesis test to determine whether the population slope is greater than 1. (e) Is the performance of the stock related to general stock-market performance? To answer the question, test the hypothesis that $B = 0$ at the 5 percent level of significance.

10. An accountant for a retail store obtained 15 observations of weekly store sales in thousands of dollars x and store expenses in thousands of dollars y. The sample regression equation was $\hat{y} = 4.9 + 0.73x$. Also, $\Sigma x = 330$, $\Sigma x^2 = 11,500$, and $s_e = 0.65$. (a) Construct the 95 percent confidence interval for the constant term A of the population regression line $\mu_Y = A + BX$. (b) Interpret the interval in (a).

11. In Problem 6, does the constant term a have any meaning? Why or why not?

12. In Problem 10, does the constant term a have any meaning? Why or why not?

12.13 CORRELATION ANALYSIS

Regression analysis is carried out to obtain an estimating equation. Often, however, analysts want to know only whether or not two variables are related or, as we shall say, whether or not two variables are correlated. Then the analyst wants a measure of correlation rather than an estimating equation. The two commonly computed measures are the *coefficient of determination* and the *correlation coefficient*.

The Coefficient of Determination

Figure 12.22 shows sample pairs (x, y).

To get an intuitive understanding of the coefficient of determination, let's consider family incomes and expenditures, as illustrated in the scatter plot of Figure 12.22. We see that some points are higher than others, that is, that

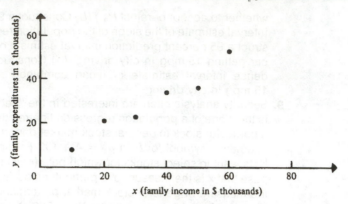

FIGURE 12.22

Family incomes and expenditures.

some families spend more than others. That's expected, we say, because family income determines, in part, how much the family can spend. Consequently, some variation in spending is expected because of the relationship between spending and income. Statisticians usually call the expected variation the variation that is "explained" by the relationship between y and x. The sample coefficient of determination, denoted by r^2 (r-square), is the proportion of the total variation in y that is explained by the relationship between y and x. The coefficient r^2 will be 0 if none of the variation in y is explained by the relationship; r^2 will be 1 if all the variation in y is explained; and r^2 will be between 0 and 1 (e.g., 0.78) if only part of the variation in y is explained by the relationship. Hence,

|————————————————|
0   1

r^2 is between 0 and 1, inclusive.

$$0 \leq r^2 \leq 1$$

that is, r^2 is a number in the interval 0 to 1, inclusive.

The coefficient of determination can, and will be, computed without determining the equation of the regression line. But reference to the regression line will help you understand the number r^2. What we want to do now is to measure two quantities. First we want to measure the total variation in y. Second, we want to measure the variation in y that is explained by (or expected because of) the relationship between y and x. Then

Meaning of r^2

$$r^2 = \frac{\text{explained (or expected) variation}}{\text{total variation in } y}$$

Figure 12.23 contains the scatter plot of Figure 12.22, and a horizontal line at the mean expenditure $\bar{y}$. The variation of an observed y value is expressed as the difference $y - \bar{y}$, as illustrated for the rightmost point in the figure. Statisticians use

$$\Sigma(y - \bar{y})^2$$

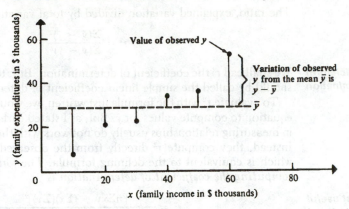

FIGURE 12.23
The total variation in y is $\Sigma(y - \bar{y})^2$.

"Total variation in y" means variation from the mean $\bar{y}$.

to measure the total variation in y. They do not use $\Sigma(y - \bar{y})$ because that sum is always zero.

Figure 12.24 shows the regression line for the (x, y) = (income, expendi-

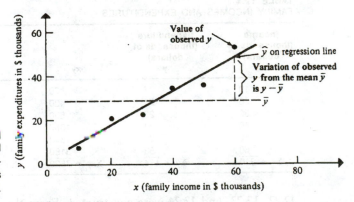

FIGURE 12.24
The variation explained by the relationship between y and x is $\Sigma(\hat{y} - \bar{y})^2$.

ture) points of our example. For the rightmost plotted point, the expected value for y is the value on the regression line $\hat{y}$. The difference $\hat{y} - \bar{y}$ is the variation expected because of, or explained by, the relationship described by the regression line. Statisticians measure the total explained variation by $\Sigma(\hat{y} - \bar{y})^2$. Again they do not use $\Sigma(\hat{y} - \bar{y})$ because that sum is always zero for a least-squares regression line. Also, as stated earlier, we use the term "explained" variation rather than expected variation. Hence, we have

"Explained variation" means demonstrated by the least-squares regression line.

$$\text{Explained variation} = \Sigma(\hat{y} - \bar{y})^2$$

$$\text{Total variation} = \Sigma(y - \bar{y})^2$$

The ratio, explained variation divided by total variation, is

$$r^2 = \frac{\Sigma(\hat{y} - \bar{y})^2}{\Sigma(y - \bar{y})^2}$$

Coefficient of dete r^2 mination We shall call r^2 the coefficient of determination. But, to be more accurate, r^2 should be called the simple linear coefficient of determination.

To evaluate r^2 with the formula just written, we would need the regression equation to compute values for $\hat{y}$. But, as I stated earlier, analysts interested in measuring relationships usually do not work with the regression equation. Instead, they compute r^2 directly from the observed data with a formula which is equivalent to the defining formula. The *formula we shall use for computing the coefficient of determination is*

The most useful formula for r^2

$$r^2 = \frac{[n\Sigma xy - (\Sigma x)(\Sigma y)]^2}{[n\Sigma x^2 - (\Sigma x)^2][n\Sigma y^2 - (\Sigma y)^2]}$$

The formula looks a bit complex, but it allows us to compute r^2 from the same column sums we calculate in regression analysis.

Table 12.4 contains the income and expenditure data from which Figures

TABLE 12.4
FAMILY INCOMES AND EXPENDITURES

Income (thousands of dollars) x	Expenditure (thousands of dollars) y	xy	x^2	y^2
10	7	70	100	49
20	21	420	400	441
30	23	690	900	529
40	34	1360	1600	1156
50	36	1800	2500	1296
60	53	3180	3600	2809
$\Sigma x = 210$	$\Sigma y = 174$	$\Sigma xy = 7520$	$\Sigma x^2 = 9100$	$\Sigma y^2 = 6280$

12.22, 12.23, and 12.24 were constructed. From the column sums in the table we compute, with $n = 6$,

$$r^2 = \frac{[n\Sigma xy - (\Sigma x)(\Sigma y)]^2}{[n\Sigma x^2 - (\Sigma x)^2][n\Sigma y^2 - (\Sigma y)^2]}$$

$$= \frac{[6(7520) - (210)(174)]^2}{[6(9100) - (210)^2][6(6280) - (174)^2]}$$

$$= \frac{(8580)^2}{[54,600 - 44,100][37,680 - 30,276]}$$

$$= \frac{(8580)^2}{(10,500)(7404)}$$

$$= 0.95$$

The interpretation of r² is loose but customary.

The value $r^2 = 0.95$ means that the total squared expected variation $\Sigma(\hat{y} - \bar{y})^2$ is 95 percent as large as the total squared variation $\Sigma(y - \bar{y})^2$. We interpret $r^2 = 0.95$ by saying that 95 percent of the variation in spending is explained by the relationship between spending y and income x. Of course, income dollars do not actually explain spending dollars—so saying 95 percent of spending variation is explained by income variation is an imprecise use of words. Nevertheless, r^2 is usually interpreted in this way.

EXERCISE Compute the coefficient of determination for the (x, y) observations $(1, 2)$, $(3, 7)$, $(4, 6)$, and $(5, 9)$.
ANSWER 0.86.

When the observed points do not all lie on the regression line, and the regression line is not horizontal, r^2 will be between 0 and 1; this is the case in our spending example, as shown in Figure 12.24. For these points we found $r^2 = 0.95$. Now suppose all the observed points fall on the regression line, and the line is not horizontal. Then, as shown in Figure 12.25, for every

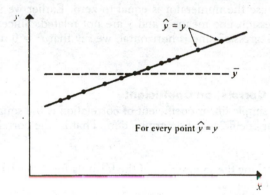

FIGURE 12.25
Every observed data point is on the regression line, so $r^2 = 1$.

For every point $\hat{y} = y$

point the observed y is the same as $\hat{y}$ on the line; so

$$\hat{y} = y$$

and

$$\hat{y} - \bar{y} = y - \bar{y}$$

and

$$\Sigma(\hat{y} - \bar{y})^2 = \Sigma(y - \bar{y})^2$$

Consequently

$$r^2 = \frac{\Sigma(\hat{y} - \bar{y})^2}{\Sigma(y - \bar{y})^2} = 1$$

Meaning of r² = 1

because the numerator is equal to the denominator. Thus, $r^2 = 1$ means all observed points are on the regression line.

Figure 12.26 shows a horizontal regression line; its equation is

$$\hat{y} = \bar{y}$$

Hence, for every point

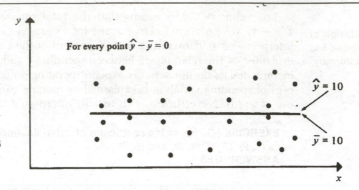

For every point $\hat{y} - \bar{y} = 0$

$\hat{y} = 10$

$\bar{y} = 10$

FIGURE 12.26
Regression line is horizontal: $r^2 = 0$.

$$\hat{y} - \bar{y} = 0$$

and

$$r^2 = \frac{\Sigma(\hat{y} - \bar{y})^2}{\Sigma(y - \bar{y})^2} = 0$$

Meaning of $r^2 = 0$

because the numerator is equal to zero. Earlier we said that a horizontal regression line means x and y are not related. Since r^2 will be zero when the regression line is horizontal, we say that $r^2 = 0$ means x and y are not related.

The Correlation Coefficient

The simple linear coefficient of correlation is the square root of the simple linear coefficient of determination. That is, the correlation coefficient r is

Coefficient of correlation

$$r = \sqrt{r^2}$$

Or, taking the square root of the formula for r^2, we have the *formula for the correlation coefficient*

The formula for r

$$r = \frac{n\Sigma xy - (\Sigma x)(\Sigma y)}{\sqrt{[n\Sigma x^2 - (\Sigma x)^2][n\Sigma y^2 - (\Sigma y)^2]}}$$

The coefficient of determination r^2 is a square; so its value always is positive or zero. The largest possible value of r^2 is 1. Therefore

$$r = \sqrt{1} = \pm 1$$

so r is in the interval -1 to 1, inclusive. Thus,

$$-1 \leq r \leq 1$$

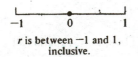

r is between -1 and 1, inclusive.

The coefficient of correlation is positive if the numerator of the formula for r,

$$n\Sigma xy - (\Sigma x)(\Sigma y)$$

is positive, and negative if this numerator is negative. The numerator of r is the same as the numerator of b, in the formula for the slope of the regression line

$$b = \frac{n\Sigma xy - (\Sigma x)(\Sigma y)}{n\Sigma x^2 - (\Sigma x)^2}$$

The sign of r is that of the slope of the regression line.

Consequently r is positive when b is positive; that is, r is positive when the regression line (if it is drawn) rises to the right. We say that the correlation is *positive* when r is positive. Similarly, we say that the correlation is negative if r is negative. If the regression line is horizontal ($b = 0$), then $r^2 = 0$ and $r = 0$. When $r = 0$ we say there is no correlation between the variables. Figure 12.27 shows some illustrative values of r. Panels (a) and (b) show, respec-

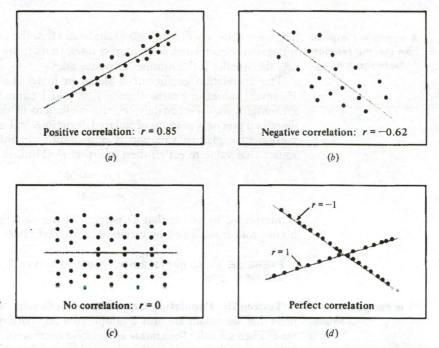

Positive correlation: $r = 0.85$

(a)

Negative correlation: $r = -0.62$

(b)

No correlation: $r = 0$

(c)

$r = -1$

$r = 1$

Perfect correlation

(d)

FIGURE 12.27
Some correlation coefficients.

Perfect correlation: $r = 1$ *or* $r = -1$

tively, a positive and a negative correlation. Panel (c) exhibits no correlation and $r = 0$. Panel (d) exhibits the two cases of *perfect* correlation; here, in each case, the observed points all fall on a line; so we have $r = -1$ for one case, $r = 1$ for the other case, and $r^2 = 1$ in both cases.

EXAMPLE The research director of the Dubarry Savings and Loan Bank collected 24 observations of mortgage interest rates x and number of house sales y at each interest rate. The director computed $\Sigma x = 276$, $\Sigma y = 768$, $\Sigma xy = 8690$, $\Sigma x^2 = 3300$, and $\Sigma y^2 = 25,000$. Compute the correlation coefficient.

SOLUTION Substituting into the formula

$$r = \frac{n\Sigma xy - (\Sigma x)(\Sigma y)}{\sqrt{[n\Sigma x^2 - (\Sigma x)^2][n\Sigma y^2 - (\Sigma y)^2]}}$$

we have, with $n = 24$,

$$r = \frac{24(8690) - (276)(768)}{\sqrt{[24(3300) - (276)^2][24(25,000) - (768)^2]}}$$

$$= \frac{-3408}{\sqrt{[3024][10,176]}}$$

$$= -0.61$$

A negative r implies an inverse relation between x and y. The correlation coefficient, -0.61, indicates that the number of house sales is negatively correlated with interest rates; that is, the higher interest rates are, the smaller is the number of house sales.

The correlation coefficient is stated in many studies of relationships. However, values of r other than -1, 0, and 1 cannot be interpreted in a meaningful way. Fortunately, r^2, the coefficient of determination, can be described precisely in terms of squared deviations and interpreted as the proportion of explained variation. Consequently, to interpret a value of r, square that value to get r^2, then interpret r^2. Thus, in the last example,

$$r = -0.61$$

$$r^2 = 0.37$$

is interpreted by saying that 37 percent of the variation in the number of houses sold is explained by variation in interest rates.

EXERCISE Compute r for the (x, y) observations $(1, 2)$, $(3, 7)$, $(4, 6)$, and $(5, 9)$.
ANSWER 0.93.

r is computed for a sample. **Testing the Population Correlation Coefficient** Usually, the observations that we obtain are only a sample of a population of observations that exist. Then we call r the *sample* correlation coefficient. The unknown population correlation coefficient is denoted by ρ (rho). Now suppose that the population variables (X, Y) are uncorrelated; that is, X and Y are not related; then $\rho = 0$. An astronomical number of samples can be drawn from a population—so the number of possible sample r values is astronomical. These sample r values will be distributed around the value 0 of the population correlation coefficient ρ. Some r values will be positive (greater than zero); others will be negative (less than zero). Thus, there is a sampling distribution of r. Mathematicians have proved that if X and Y are normally distributed and $\rho = 0$, then, and only then, the statistic

p is the unknown population correlation coefficient.

Test statistic for the null hypothesis $\rho = 0$.

$$t = r\sqrt{\frac{n - 2}{1 - r^2}}$$

has the Student t distribution with $v = n - 2$ degrees of freedom. Consequently, we can use Table VII (or Table VI if $v > 30$) to test the hypothesis that X and Y are not correlated, that is, to test the hypothesis $H_0: \rho = 0$ against the alternative hypothesis, $\rho \neq 0$. If H_0 is accepted, we conclude that X and Y are not correlated. If we reject H_0, we conclude that X and Y are correlated.

EXAMPLE In the last example x is the mortgage interest rate and y is the number of houses sold. At the 5 percent level, perform a test of the hypothesis that interest rate and house sales are not correlated.

SOLUTION The hypotheses are

1. $H_0: \rho = 0 \qquad H_a: \rho \neq 0$

The test is two-tailed with $\alpha/2 = 0.05/2 = 0.025$. The sample size is $n = 24$, so that $v = 24 - 2 = 22$ degrees of freedom. From Table VII

$$t_{0.025,22} = 2.07$$

so we have the decision rule

2. Reject H_0 if |sample t| > 2.07

Next we compute the sample test statistic

$$t = r\sqrt{\frac{n-2}{1-r^2}}$$

With $r = -0.61$ and $n = 24$,

$$t = -0.61\sqrt{\frac{24-2}{1-(0.61)^2}}$$

$$= -3.61$$

So,

3. Sample $t = -3.61$

The absolute value of the sample t, $|-3.61| = 3.61$, exceeds the 2.07 of the decision rule. Hence, we

4. Reject H_0

The result of the test, reject H_0, means that number of house sales and mortgage rates are correlated. We say that the correlation coefficient, -0.61, is significant at the 5 percent level. Because $r = -0.61$ is negative, the test result implies that house sales are negatively correlated with mortgage rates.

If we want to test for positive or for negative correlation, the test is one-tailed. The hypotheses and decision rule in testing for positive correlation at significance level α are, with $v = n - 2$,

$$H_0: \rho \leq 0 \qquad H_a: \rho > 0 \qquad \text{Reject } H_0 \text{ if } t > t_{\alpha,v}$$

The hypotheses and decision rule in testing for negative correlation are

*In a one-tail test of ρ,
H_a is*

$$H_0: \rho \geq 0 \qquad H_a: \rho < 0 \qquad \text{Reject } H_0 \text{ if sample } t < -t_{\alpha,v}$$

        $\rho > 0$

or $\rho < 0$

EXERCISE A sample of 20 stocks was analyzed to determine whether the dividend paid to the holder of a share of stock is positively correlated with the price of a share of stock. Perform a hypothesis test at the 5 percent level if the sample correlation coefficient is 0.78.

    ANSWER 1. $H_0: \rho \leq 0$; $H_a: \rho > 0$. 2. Reject H_0 if sample $t > 1.73$. 3. Sample $t = 5.29$. 4. Reject H_0. Stock price is positively correlated with stock dividend. The correlation coefficient 0.78 is significant at the 5 percent level.

One reason investors buy stocks is to obtain dividends. Consequently, we would expect stock dividends to be positively correlated with stock prices; that is, we would expect to find a tendency for the dividend to be larger for higher-priced stocks. The last exercise bears out our expectation. But the fact that the dividend-price correlation is significant does not tell us how close is the relation between dividend and price. Regression analysis is needed to examine the closeness of a relationship. For example, I did a regression analysis for the observations that led to $r = 0.78$ in the exercise. I found the 95 percent prediction interval estimate of the dividend for a stock price of $50 was from $0.25 to $4.21: that estimate is not precise enough to be of any predictive use. The point is that, in general, a significant value of r means only that there is strong evidence that a relationship exists. But neither the value of r nor the value of r^2 tells us whether the relationship is close enough to provide predictions or estimates that are precise enough to be of practical use.

The value of r (or r^2) is not a measure of the precision of estimates.

12.14 REGRESSION AND CORRELATION CORRESPONDENCES

When the regression line is horizontal, its slope is $b = 0$ and the correlation coefficient is 0. Thus, $b = 0$ and $r = 0$ both mean that the variables are not correlated; and in this case, of course, r^2, the coefficient of determination, is also 0. On the other hand, if all observed points are on the regression line, the standard error of estimate (computed in regression analysis) is 0 and the correlation is perfect. Therefore, $s_e = 0$ means that $r = 1$ or $r = -1$ and, of course, $r^2 = 1$.

12.15 CAUTIONS TO OBSERVE IN REGRESSION AND CORRELATION ANALYSES

Many questions about relationships arise in practical problems. Consequently, regression and correlation analyses are extensively used statistical tools. However, you should keep the following points in mind when working with these tools, because it is easy to misuse them.

Assumptions

No assumptions are involved in the calculation of a regression equation. That's because the least-squares criterion is generally accepted as being a

Assumptions of the
normal regression
model:
—*Normality*
—*Equal σ,'s*
—*Independence*

good criterion. But the assumptions of the normal regression model are involved when we draw statistical inferences, that is, when we construct confidence interval estimates or test hypotheses about the slope of the regression line. So before you accept statistical regression inferences in a particular analysis, you should question whether the data at hand could reasonably be expected to have the characteristics of the normal regression model.

Extrapolation

Extrapolation means applying a computed regression equation outside the interval of observed data. For example, suppose we collect data on car engine size x and gas mileage y, and suppose the smallest and largest engine sizes observed are 150 and 350 cubic inches. Then we compute the regression equation. If we now apply the equation to estimate gas mileage for a car with a 500 cubic inch engine, the estimate is an extrapolation. It can be difficult to judge whether available observed data have a linear tendency and conform reasonably well with the normal regression model, but the sample data provide no basis for making a judgment outside the region of observations. For example, what appears to be a linear tendency in the observed interval could look more like a curve if a wider interval were obtained.

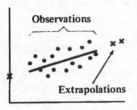

Observations

Extrapolations

Approach with caution!

When a regression equation is used to make an extrapolation (and they are so used), you should realize that the extrapolation contains an unknown element not present when the equation is used to make estimates within the observed data interval. This caution is particularly appropriate when a confidence interval estimate of the constant term A is constructed. That's because in $\hat{y} = a + bx$, we set $x = 0$ to obtain a, the point estimate of A, and usually the interval of observed x values does not extend to 0.

Relevancy of Historical Data

The data we analyze are past data. They are history, recent or more distant. Relationships may (and many do) change over time. Therefore, it is wise to question whether it is reasonable in current circumstances to apply a relationship determined from data that relate to circumstances of the past.

Misleading Interpretations of the Correlation Coefficient

Interpreting small and large values of r, say, $r = 0.20$ and $r = 0.70$, as indicating "weak" and "strong" correlation can be misleading; that's because even a small value of r can be significant at the 1 percent level, but a larger value of r may not be significant at even the 5 percent level. You should state the value of r and the level at which it is, or is not, significant. You should also understand that significant does not mean the relationship is of any practical value; rather, significant means only that the sample provides convincing evidence that a relationship exists. You have to carry out regression calculations to obtain the equation of the relationship and determine whether confidence interval estimates are precise enough to be of practical use.

Correlation, Cause, and Nonsense

The existence of a significantly high correlation between two variables tells us nothing about why the correlation exists. In particular, the correlation does not tell us that one variable is the cause and the other is the effect. Also, correlations often exist because the variables selected for analysis are only two of a number of interrelated variables. For example, we would expect to find a positive correlation between the number of schoolteachers in various cities and liquor consumption in these cities because both number of teachers and liquor consumption are related to population size. Finally, it should be noted that if you look at enough sets of data pairs, you will occasionally find a set that contributes to the supply of "significant correlations" (or regression equations that give close estimates) that make no sense at all. I call these nonsense correlations. An example of such nonsense would be a "significant correlation" between daily temperatures at the North Pole and daily newspaper sales in Houston, Texas.

12.16 PROBLEMS

1. R. C. Corey, Inc., a large mail-order company, tabulated the weight of the early morning mail x in hundreds of pounds and the number of orders in the mail y, in thousands. Calculations for $n = 20$ days provided $\Sigma x = 210$, $\Sigma y = 530$, $\Sigma xy = 7225$, $\Sigma x^2 = 2870$, and $\Sigma y^2 = 18,190$. (a) Compute r. (b) Compute and interpret r^2. (c) At the 1 percent level, test the hypothesis that the number of orders is positively correlated with the weight of the mail.

2. Jeanette Peters, a security analyst for Peters, Peters, and Paul, wanted to determine whether earnings of companies are positively correlated with inventory turnover. Jeanette measured the inventory turnover rate x by dividing sales by inventory value, and she let y be earnings expressed as a percent of sales. For 19 companies, Jeanette found $\Sigma x = 100$, $\Sigma y = 222$, $\Sigma xy = 1212$, $\Sigma x^2 = 540$, and $\Sigma y^2 = 2808$. (a) Compute r. (b) Compute and interpret r^2. (c) At the 1 percent level, test the hypothesis that earnings are positively correlated with inventory turnover rate.

3. Short Run Transportation Company found the correlation between the price of a bus ticket x and the number of tickets sold y to be -0.82. The sample size was $n = 12$. (a) At the 1 percent level, test the hypothesis that ticket sales are negatively correlated with the price of tickets. (b) Compute and interpret r^2.

4. Professor Jan Henkel of the University of Georgia obtained information from 272 college graduates who majored in accounting and took the certified public accountant (CPA) examination. He found the correlation between the number of college accounting courses taken by the graduates and success on CPA exams was 0.09. At the 5 percent level, test the hypothesis that success on the CPA exam is positively correlated with number of accounting courses taken.

5. The personnel manager of Boise Corrugated Box Company obtained the data in Table A. At the 5 percent level, test the null hypothesis that age x and days absent y are not correlated.

TABLE A

Employee age	Number of days absent	Employee age	Number of days absent
30	5	35	6
20	3	55	9
40	4	25	9
65	11	50	7
45	10	60	6

6. Vota Company designs and builds special systems for controlling the operations of machines. Anita Smith, the cost estimator for Vota, wondered whether the cost of designing and building a system is correlated with the number of transistors in the system. Anita obtained the data in Table B. (a) Compute and interpret r^2. (b) At the 1 percent level, test the hypothesis that number of transistors and system cost are positively correlated.

TABLE B

System	Number of transistors	Cost (thousands of dollars)	System	Number of transistors	Cost (thousands of dollars)
A	89	16	D	189	26
B	106	24	E	212	34
C	142	25	F	280	40

7. What is the value of s_e if $r = -1$? Why?
8. What is the slope of the regression line if $r = 0$?
9. Suppose $n = 2000$ in a correlation analysis. Then, at the 5 percent level, would $r = 0.05$ be significantly different from 0? That is, would you reject the null hypothesis that $\rho = 0$?
10. Calculations with five observations on the number of sperm whales caught x and the Standard & Poor's stock price index y provided the following sums: $\Sigma x = 131$, $\Sigma y = 445$, $\Sigma xy = 11,612$, $\Sigma x^2 = 3447$, $\Sigma y^2 = 39,795$. (a) At the 5 percent level, test the hypothesis that stock prices are negatively correlated with the number of whales caught. (b) What do you think the test result in (a) implies?
11. Suppose you took temperature readings at different temperatures. At each temperature you recorded the readings in degrees Fahrenheit x and degrees Celsius y. Then suppose you computed the correlation coefficient. What do you expect the value of r would be? Why?
12. Table C contains data on number of employees x and sales y for 16

large corporations. At the 5 percent level test the hypothesis that sales are positively correlated with number of employees.

TABLE C

Number of employees (thousands)	Sales (billions)	Number of employees (thousands)	Sales (billions)
32	$9.2	98	$5.5
27	8.5	16	5.4
133	8.4	67	4.7
44	8.0	97	4.4
52	6.5	37	4.3
113	6.4	113	3.9
161	6.2	7	3.9
151	5.8	52	3.7

12.17 SUMMARY

In studying the relationship between two variables x and y, each of n observed (x, y) data pairs is plotted as a point on a graph to obtain a *scatter plot*. If the scatter plot indicates a linear tendency, we fit a straight-line equation of the form

$$\hat{y} = a + bx$$

to the n data points as follows: first compute the slope (regression coefficient) b with the formula

$$b = \frac{n(\Sigma xy) - (\Sigma x)(\Sigma y)}{n(\Sigma x^2) - (\Sigma x)^2}$$

Next, compute the constant term (the y intercept) a with the formula

$$a = \frac{\Sigma y - b(\Sigma x)}{n}$$

Then write the equation by substituting the computed values of a and b into the expression $\hat{y} = a + bx$.

The expression $\hat{y} = a + bx$ is called an estimating equation, or a *regression equation*. A given value of x, when substituted into the equation, provides an estimated or predicted value of y denoted by $\hat{y}$. The mean point $(\bar{x}, \bar{y})$ of the observed data always is on the regression line. If b is 0, x and y are not related; the regression line is horizontal and has the equation $\hat{y} = \bar{y}$.

Usually the observed (x, y) data points are not all on the fitted line. The variation of the points from the line is measured by s_e, the *standard error of estimate*; s_e is computed with the formula

$$s_e = \sqrt{\frac{\Sigma y^2 - a(\Sigma y) - b(\Sigma xy)}{n - 2}}$$

If all the data points fall on the regression line, $s_e = 0$.

The sample slope b is an estimate of an unknown population slope B. The *sample standard error of the slope* s_b is computed with the formula

$$s_b = \frac{s_e}{\sqrt{\Sigma x^2 - (\Sigma x)^2/n}}$$

The t table (Table VII) with $v = n - 2$ degrees of freedom (or the normal z table, Table VI, if $v > 30$) is used to test hypotheses about the value of B. The test statistic is

$$t = \frac{b-B}{s_b}$$

where B is some hypothesized value of the slope of the population regression line.

The *confidence interval for B*, with confidence coefficient C, is

$$b - t_{\alpha/2,v}s_b \leq B \leq b + t_{\alpha/2,v}s_b$$

where $\alpha/2 = (1 - C)/2$
$v = n - 2$

Letting μ_Y be the mean value of Y for a given value of X, the *standard error of estimating μ_Y, given X*, is

$$s(\mu_Y|X) = s_e \sqrt{\frac{1}{n} + \frac{(X - \bar{x})^2}{\Sigma x^2 - (\Sigma x)^2/n}}$$

The *confidence interval for μ_Y given X* is, with confidence coefficient C,

$$\hat{y} - t_{\alpha/2,v}s(\mu_Y|X) \leq \mu_Y \leq \hat{y} + t_{\alpha/2,v}s(\mu_Y|X)$$

where $\hat{y}$ is the value computed from the regression equation $\hat{y} = a + bx$ by substituting the given X for x. When X is taken as 0, the interval obtained is the confidence interval for the population constant term A.

The *standard error of predicting Y, given X*, is

$$s(Y|X) = s_e \sqrt{1 + \frac{1}{n} + \frac{(X - \bar{x})^2}{\Sigma x^2 - (\Sigma x)^2/n}}$$

The *prediction interval for Y, given X*, with confidence coefficient C, is

$$\hat{y} - t_{\alpha/2,v}s(Y|X) \leq Y \leq \hat{y} + t_{\alpha/2,v}s(Y|X)$$

Correlation analysis is carried out when interest centers on whether or not a relationship exists, rather than on obtaining an estimating (regression) equation. Then the sample *correlation coefficient*

$$r = \frac{n(\Sigma xy) - (\Sigma x)(\Sigma y)}{\sqrt{[n\Sigma x^2 - (\Sigma x)^2][n\Sigma y^2 - (\Sigma y)^2]}}$$

is computed. The population correlation is denoted by ρ (rho). The sample r value is used to test whether X and Y are not correlated ($\rho = 0$), or whether X and Y are positively correlated ($\rho > 0$), or whether X and Y are negatively correlated ($\rho < 0$). Table VII with $v = n - 2$ (or Table VI if $v > 30$) is used to test hypotheses about ρ. The sample test statistic is

$$t = r \sqrt{\frac{n - 2}{1 - r^2}}$$

The *coefficient of determination* is

$$r^2 = \frac{[n(\Sigma xy) - (\Sigma x)(\Sigma y)]^2}{[n(\Sigma x^2) - (\Sigma x)^2][n(\Sigma y^2) - (\Sigma y)^2]}$$

The coefficient of determination is interpreted by saying that r^2 is the proportion of the variation in the dependent variable that is explained by the variation in the independent variable.

12.18 REVIEW PROBLEMS

1. Peg Orville of Supermarket Research, Inc., obtained the following (x, y) data pairs. The x value is the radius, in miles, of the central circular trading area of a supermarket; the y value is supermarket sales in millions of dollars: (1, 2), (2, 4), (4, 5), (3, 5), (5, 7), (3, 4), (5, 8), and (6, 10). (*a*) Make a scatter plot of the data. (*b*) Compute a and b; then write the equation of the regression line. (*c*) Plot the regression line on the scatter plot in (*a*).

2. Joe Brown collected data on car weights in thousands of pounds x and miles per gallon y. The (x, y) data pairs are (2.0, 33), (2.4, 30), (2.8, 28), (3.2, 23), and (3.6, 19). (*a*) Make a scatter plot of the data. (*b*) Compute a and b; then write the equation of the regression line. (*c*) Plot the regression line on the scatter plot in (*a*).

3. A publisher received the price quotations shown in Table A from a printer. Let x be the number of books and y be the price. (*a*) Compute the standard error of estimate. (*b*) Interpret the outcome in (*a*).

TABLE A

Thousands of books printed	Price (thousands)
1	$ 4
2	6
5	12
10	22

4. Jim Baxter, a cost accountant for Carvar Machine Company, compiled the data in Table B. (*a*) Make a scatter plot of the points in Table B. (*b*) Compute a and b; then write the equation of the regression line. (*c*) Plot the regression line on the scatter plot in (*a*). (*d*) At the 1 percent level, test the hypothesis that the slope of the population regression line equals 1. (*e*) What is implied by the outcome of the test in (*d*)? (*f*) Construct a 99 percent confidence interval for the number of shafts made per additional labor-hour worked. (*g*) Construct a 95 percent confi-

dence interval for the mean number of shafts made in 40 labor-hours. (*h*) Construct a 95 percent prediction interval for the number of shafts made in 40 labor-hours.

TABLE B

Labor-hours spent x	Number of shafts made y
20	21
25	27
30	31
10	9
10	8
50	54
50	55
45	52
45	51
35	39

5. Sybil Thresher, chief accountant for Barlow's department store, estimates that for each 6-day week of operations, fixed (constant) expenses are $2.25 thousand, and that other expenses (cost of goods sold, selling expenses, and so on) amount to $0.75 per $1 of sales. Write Sybil's equation for total expenses *y* for a week when sales are *x* thousand dollars.

6. (See Problem 5.) Sybil compiled the data for 12 weeks of operations in Table C. (*a*) Compute *a* and *b*, and then write the regression equation. (*b*) At the 1 percent level, perform a test of the hypothesis that the slope of the population regression line is 0.75. (*c*) Construct a 99 percent confidence interval for the slope of the population regression line. (*d*) Construct a 95 percent confidence interval for mean total expenses for weeks when sales are $35 thousand. (*e*) Construct the 95 percent confidence interval for fixed expenses, that is, the interval for μ_Y when $X = 0$. (*f*) Construct the 95 percent prediction interval for total expenses for a week when sales are $35 thousand.

TABLE C

Sales (thousands)	Total expense (thousands)	Sales (thousands)	Total expense (thousands)
$32	$25	$23	$21
30	25	30	23
20	13	22	19
37	31	32	27
24	21	25	23
41	33	20	19

7. Regression calculations were carried out to determine the relationship between the price of a share of Your Mutual Transportation Fund *y* and the Dow Jones average price of 20 transportation stocks *x*. Results for $n = 23$ observations were $\Sigma x = 5410$, $\Sigma y = 548$, $\Sigma xy = 140,740$, $\Sigma x^2 = 1,388,100$, $\Sigma y^2 = 14,391$, and $\hat{y} =$

$-0.27259 + 0.10245x$. (a) Compute the standard error of estimate. (b) At the 1 percent level, perform a test of the hypothesis that the slope of the population regression line is greater than 0.10. (c) Construct the 95 percent confidence interval for the population slope. (d) Construct the 95 percent prediction interval for the price of a share of the mutual fund when the Dow Jones average is 250.

8. Regression calculations were carried out to determine the relationship between car engine size x, measured in cubic inches of displacement, and gas mileage (mpg). For 18 cars the results were $\Sigma x = 3634$, $\Sigma y = 435$, $\Sigma xy = 82,118$, $\Sigma x^2 = 819,132$, $\Sigma y^2 = 10,917$, and $\hat{y} = 37.6 - 0.0667x$. (a) Compute the sample standard error of estimate. (b) At the 5 percent level, perform a test of the hypothesis that the slope of the population regression line is less than -0.05. (c) Construct the 95 percent confidence interval for the population slope. (d) Construct the 95 percent confidence interval estimate of the mean mileage for a fleet of cars having 205 cubic inch engines. (e) What is the meaning of the value of the constant term 37.6 in the regression equation?

9. (See Problem 1.) Compute and interpret the coefficient of determination.

10. (See Problem 2.) Compute and interpret the coefficient of determination.

11. (See Problem 7.) Compute and interpret the coefficient of determination.

12. (See Problem 8.) Compute and interpret the coefficient of determination.

13. In Table D, x is the number of years until the amount paid for a bond is returned to the bond buyer; y is the percent interest yield received by the buyer. (a) Compute the sample coefficient of correlation. (b) Perform a test at the 5 percent level to determine whether yield is positively correlated with the number of years until money is returned.

TABLE D

Years x	Interest yield y, %
4	10.0
7	11.1
10	11.4
12	9.9
14	6.7
16	10.2
18	15.3
20	14.7

14. The controller of a chain of 215 stores obtained the data in Table E. x is the amount, in hundreds of dollars, spent on inventory protection; y is the amount, in thousands of dollars, of inventory lost or stolen. (a) Would you expect the correlation between x and y to be positive or negative? Why? (b) Compute the correlation coefficient. (c) Perform a hypothesis test at the 5 percent level to determine whether your expectation in (a) is confirmed.

15. Dr. Mildred Cohen, staff physician at the McNiel Company, obtained observations on 60 executives. Dr. Cohen found the correlation between executive salaries and their diastolic blood pressure to be 0.31. (a) Perform a test at the 2 percent level to determine whether blood pressure and salary are, or are not, correlated. (b) What is implied by the result of the test in (a)?

TABLE E

Amount spent on protection (hundreds) x	Amount of inventory lost or stolen (thousands) y
$30	$12
18	10
24	6
20	16
24	6
38	8
22	12
32	6
26	14
14	16

16. Alvin Theodore, personnel manager at Borgia Enterprises, obtained observations of days absent and distance from home to job for 50 employees. He found the correlation coefficient for days absent and distance to be 0.46. (a) Perform a test at the 1 percent level to determine whether days absent and distance are, or are not, correlated. (b) What is implied by the result of the test in (a)?

13

MULTIPLE AND CURVILINEAR REGRESSION

13.1 INTRODUCTION

Simple regression equations have one independent variable, x. Multiple regression equations have two or more independent variables. Regression analysis with two or more independent variables is called *multiple regression analysis*. For example, suppose we want to determine the relationship among the number of responses to a newspaper advertisement, newspaper circulation (numbers of copies sold), and the size (in column inches) of the advertisement. After obtaining data, we would derive a multiple regression equation relating number of responses, the dependent variable, to the two independent variables, circulation and advertisement size.

In this chapter you will learn (1) how to fit a linear equation with two independent variables to sample data; (2) how to interpret computer-generated multiple regression results, and use the results to make statistical inferences; and (3) how to fit a curvilinear equation to sample data.

13.2 MULTIPLE LINEAR REGRESSION EQUATIONS

The form of the simple linear regression equations of Chapter 12 is

$$\hat{y} = a + bx$$

The simple linear equation has one independent variable, designated as x. If we have two independent variables, we designate them by x_1 and x_2. That is, x means independent variable, and x_1 and x_2 are two different independent variables. Also, b is our symbol for regression coefficient, and b_1 and b_2 are two different regression coefficients. The form of the linear multiple regression equation with two independent variables is

b is called a regression coefficient (not the slope) in multiple regression analysis.

$$\hat{y} = a + b_1x_1 + b_2x_2$$

Similarly,

$$\hat{y} = a + b_1x_1 + b_2x_2 + b_3x_3$$

is the multiple linear regression equation with three independent variables, and

General form of the multiple linear regression equation

$$\hat{y} = a + b_1x_1 + b_2x_2 + b_3x_3 + \cdots + b_px_p$$

is the form when there are p independent variables.

In simple regression, a data point is an (x, y) number pair such as $(6, 2)$. With two independent variables, a data point is an (x_1, x_2, y) number triple, such as $(6, 2, 1)$; and similarly for data points when there are more than two independent variables.

EXERCISE Suppose (7, 2, 3, 5) is a data point. (a) How many independent variables are there? (b) What is the value of y in the data point?
ANSWER (a) 3; (b) 5.

The constant a and the regression coefficients are obtained from calculations made with the observed data points. Suppose the results of the calculations are $a = 3$, $b_1 = 1.2$, $b_2 = -0.4$, and $b_3 = 1.8$. Then the regression equation is

$$\hat{y} = 3 + 1.2x_1 - 0.4x_2 + 1.8x_3$$

Next, suppose one of the data points involved in the calculations is (5, 10, 15, 34); that is,

$$x_1 = 5 \qquad x_2 = 10$$
$$x_3 = 15 \qquad y = 34$$

If we substitute the observed values of x_1, x_2, and x_3 into

$$\hat{y} = 3 + 1.2x_1 - 0.4x_2 + 1.8x_3$$

we obtain

$$\hat{y} = 3 + 1.2(5) - 0.4(10) + 1.8(15)$$
$$= 32$$

Thus, the estimated value for y is $\hat{y} = 32$. But the observed value is $y = 34$; so the error e is

Error equals observed minus estimated:

$$e = y - \hat{y}$$

$$e = y - \hat{y}$$
$$= 34 - 32 = 2$$

EXERCISE Use the foregoing regression equation. Compute e for the data point (10, 15, 5, 15).
ANSWER -3.

As in simple regression, the least-squares criterion defines the equation that best fits the observed data. It is, again, the equation for which the sum of the squares of the errors

The least-squares criterion minimizes Σe^2.

$$\Sigma(y - \hat{y})^2$$

has the smallest possible value. Mathematicians have derived formulas for the constant term and the regression coefficients in the least-squares equation. We will work with some of these formulas in the next section.

13.3 MULTIPLE LINEAR REGRESSION WITH TWO INDEPENDENT VARIABLES

Calculating a, b_1, and b_2

In this section we will fit an equation of the form

$$\hat{y} = a + b_1x_1 + b_2x_2$$

to a set of n observed data points, each of which is a number triple (x_1, x_2,

CAUTION: Dangerous equations approaching

y). The formulas for computing a, b_1, and b_2 from the observed data, derived from the least-squares criterion, are

$$b_1 = \frac{[n\Sigma x_1 y - (\Sigma x_1)(\Sigma y)][n\Sigma x_2^2 - (\Sigma x_2)^2] - [n\Sigma x_1 x_2 - (\Sigma x_1)(\Sigma x_2)][n\Sigma x_2 y - (\Sigma x_2)(\Sigma y)]}{[n\Sigma x_1^2 - (\Sigma x_1)^2][n\Sigma x_2^2 - (\Sigma x_2)^2] - [n\Sigma x_1 x_2 - (\Sigma x_1)(\Sigma x_2)]^2}$$

$$b_2 = \frac{[n\Sigma x_2 y - (\Sigma x_2)(\Sigma y)][n\Sigma x_1^2 - (\Sigma x_1)^2] - [n\Sigma x_1 y - (\Sigma x_1)(\Sigma y)][n\Sigma x_1 x_2 - (\Sigma x_1)(\Sigma x_2)]}{[n\Sigma x_1^2 - (\Sigma x_1)^2][n\Sigma x_2^2 - (\Sigma x_2)^2] - [n\Sigma x_1 x_2 - (\Sigma x_1)(\Sigma x_2)]^2}$$

$$a = \frac{\Sigma y - b_1 \Sigma x_1 - b_2 \Sigma x_2}{n}$$

RELAX!
Help is here.

The formulas are complicated; so let's break the calculations into parts to simplify our work.

First we will calculate the sum of the observations for each variable, Σx_1, Σx_2, and Σy; the sum of the products of each pair of numbers in an observation, $\Sigma x_1 y$, $\Sigma x_2 y$, and $\Sigma x_1 x_2$; and the sum of the squares of the observations for each variable, Σx_1^2, Σx_2^2, and Σy^2. Next, with the sums just calculated and n, the number of data points, we compute

$$A = n\Sigma x_1 y - (\Sigma x_1)(\Sigma y)$$

$$B = n\Sigma x_2^2 - (\Sigma x_2)^2$$

$$C = n\Sigma x_1 x_2 - (\Sigma x_1)(\Sigma x_2)$$

$$D = n\Sigma x_2 y - (\Sigma x_2)(\Sigma y)$$

$$E = n\Sigma x_1^2 - (\Sigma x_1)^2$$

$$F = EB - C^2$$

Then we compute b_1, b_2, and a from the values of A, B, C, D, E, and F, by the formulas

$$b_1 = \frac{AB - CD}{F}$$

$$b_2 = \frac{DE - AC}{F}$$

$$a = \frac{\Sigma y - b_1 \Sigma x_1 - b_2 \Sigma x_2}{n}$$

Finally, we substitute the values for b_1, b_2, and a into

$$\hat{y} = a + b_1 x_1 + b_2 x_2$$

to obtain the multiple regression equation.

EXAMPLE An advertising executive wanted to determine the relationship between the number of responses to an advertisement and the two independent variables, size of advertisement and newspaper circulation. The executive obtained the data in Table 13.1. We need the column sum for

TABLE 13.1
ADVERTISEMENT SIZE, CIRCULATION, AND NUMBER OF RESPONSES

Size of advertisement (number of column-inches) x_1	Newspaper circulation (thousands) x_2	Number of responses (hundreds) y
1	2	1
8	8	4
3	1	1
5	7	3
6	4	2
10	6	4

Step 1 Tabulate the data points.

each variable, the sum of the products of all pairs of variables, and the sum of the squares for each variable. These are calculated in Table 13.2 for the $n = 6$ data points.

Step 2 Tabulate the products of each variable with every variable, including itself . . .

TABLE 13.2
REGRESSION CALCULATIONS WITH TWO INDEPENDENT VARIABLES

x_1	x_2	y	$x_1 y$	$x_2 y$	$x_1 x_2$	x_1^2	x_2^2	y^2
1	2	1	1	2	2	1	4	1
8	8	4	32	32	64	64	64	16
3	1	1	3	1	3	9	1	1
5	7	3	15	21	35	25	49	9
6	4	2	12	8	24	36	16	4
10	6	4	40	24	60	100	36	16
33	28	15	103	88	188	235	170	47

. . . and find the totals.

Next with the column sums and $n = 6$, we compute

$$A = n\Sigma x_1 y - (\Sigma x_1)(\Sigma y) = 6(103) - (33)(15)$$
$$= 123$$
$$B = n\Sigma x_2^2 - (\Sigma x_2)^2 = 6(170) - (28)^2$$
$$= 236$$

Step 3 Use the formulas to compute A, B, C, D, E, and F.

$$C = n\Sigma x_1 x_2 - (\Sigma x_1)(\Sigma x_2) = 6(188) - (33)(28)$$
$$= 204$$
$$D = n\Sigma x_2 y - (\Sigma x_2)(\Sigma y) = 6(88) - (28)(15)$$
$$= 108$$
$$E = n\Sigma x_1^2 - (\Sigma x_1)^2 = 6(235) - (33)^2$$
$$= 321$$
$$F = EB - C^2 = (321)(236) - (204)^2$$
$$= 34,140$$

Now we calculate

Step 4 *Use A–F to compute b_1, b_2, and a.*

$$b_1 = \frac{AB - CD}{F} = \frac{(123)(236) - (204)(108)}{34,140}$$

$$= \frac{6996}{34,140} = 0.204921$$

$$b_2 = \frac{DE - AC}{F} = \frac{(108)(321) - (123)(204)}{34,140}$$

$$= \frac{9576}{34,140} = 0.280492$$

and

$$a = \frac{\Sigma y - b_1 \Sigma x_1 - b_2 \Sigma x_2}{n}$$

$$= \frac{15 - (0.204921)(33) - (0.280492)(28)}{6}$$

$$= 0.063972$$

The multiple regression equation

$$\hat{y} = a + b_1 x_1 + b_2 x_2$$

is, after rounding a, b_1, and b_2,

Step 5 *Write the linear multiple regression equation.*

$$\hat{y} = 0.0640 + 0.2049 x_1 + 0.2805 x_2$$

where $\hat{y}$ = number of responses in hundreds
x_1 = advertisement size in column-inches
x_2 = newspaper circulation in thousands

We can apply the equation to estimate the number of responses to, say, an $x_1 = 4$ column-inch advertisement in a newspaper that has a circulation of $x_2 = 5$ thousand. The estimate is

$$\hat{y} = 0.0640 + 0.2049(4) + 0.2805(5)$$

$$= 2.286 \text{ hundred responses}$$

or about 229 responses.

The Standard Error of Estimate

In Chapter 12 you learned that the standard error of estimate s_e in simple regression is the standard deviation of the errors e, and the number of degrees of freedom used in computing s_e is $n - 2$ because two sample estimates a and b are needed to compute s_e. In multiple regression, s_e is the standard deviation of the errors, but with p independent variables we need p regression coefficients and the constant term a to calculate s_e; so we need $p + 1$ sample estimates to compute s_e, and we lose $p + 1$ degrees of freedom. Hence, *the number of degrees of freedom in multiple linear regression with p indepen-*

dent variables is

**Degrees of freedom v
for multiple
regression**

or

$$v = n - (p + 1)$$

$$v = n - p - 1$$

EXERCISE We are analyzing 20 data points, each of which is a set of values (x_1, x_2, x_3, x_4, y). How many degrees of freedom are there?
ANSWER 15.

The formula for s_e in multiple linear regression is

*Here, again, s, will
enter into many of
our calculations.*

$$s_e = \sqrt{\frac{\Sigma y^2 - a\Sigma y - b_1\Sigma x_1 y - b_2\Sigma x_2 y - b_3\Sigma x_3 y - \cdots - b_p\Sigma x_p y}{n - p - 1}}$$

With $p = 2$ independent variables, $v = n - p - 1 = n - 3$ degrees of freedom, and

$$s_e = \sqrt{\frac{\Sigma y^2 - a\Sigma y - b_1\Sigma x_1 y - b_2\Sigma x_2 y}{n - 3}}$$

For the advertising example we have from Table 13.2 and the regression calculations

$$\Sigma y^2 = 47 \qquad a = 0.063972$$
$$\Sigma y = 15 \qquad b_1 = 0.204921$$
$$\Sigma x_1 y = 103 \qquad b_2 = 0.280492$$
$$\Sigma x_2 y = 88 \qquad n = 6$$

Hence

$$s_e = \sqrt{\frac{\Sigma y^2 - a\Sigma y - b_1\Sigma x_1 y - b_2\Sigma x_2 y}{n - 3}}$$

$$= \sqrt{\frac{47 - (0.063972)(15) - (0.204921)(103) - (0.280492)(88)}{6 - 3}}$$

$$= \sqrt{\frac{0.250261}{3}} = 0.29$$

In the example, y is the number of hundreds of responses to an advertisement; so $s_e = 0.29$ means the standard error is 0.29 hundred, or 29 responses. The standard error is needed to derive regression inferences that will be discussed later in the chapter. However, for present purposes, it will be helpful to interpret s_e in terms of normal percents. Recall that, in a normal distribution, about 68 percent of the values are within plus or minus one standard deviation of the mean. In regression, the corresponding statement is that about 68 percent of the actual y values are within plus or minus one standard error of their estimated values $\hat{y}$. The last statement is correct for a normal regression population which has a standard error of σ_e. We, of course, have a sample regression equation and s_e is the sample standard error of estimate. Nevertheless, for interpretive purposes, we shall take as a

*About 68 percent of
observed y have val-
ues between $\hat{y} - s$,
and $\hat{y} + s$,.*

rule of thumb that about 68 percent of observed y have values that are within $\pm s_e$ of estimates computed from the regression equation. Thus, for the advertising example, which has $n = 6$ observed y values, about 68 percent of 6, or 4, of the values are within $s_e = 0.29$ of values computed by substituting the associated x_1 and x_2 into the regression equation. (I computed $\hat{y}$ for each observed x_1 and x_2 and found that actually there are 5 rather than 4 observed values that are in the $\hat{y} \pm s_e$ interval.)

When s_e is large, the regression equation may be of little or no use in prediction or estimation. The rule of thumb just stated aids in judging how closely actual y values can be estimated by the $\hat{y}$ values computed from a regression equation. But more extensive calculations, discussed later, are needed to obtain the prediction intervals used in statistical inference.

The Coefficient of Multiple Determination

In multiple regression, the coefficient of multiple determination r^2 is interpreted as the proportion (or percent) of the variation in the dependent variable that is explained by its relation to the independent variables. As was the case in simple regression, the defining formula is

r^2 is, again. the proportion of "explained" variation.

$$r^2 = \frac{\Sigma(\hat{y} - \bar{y})^2}{\Sigma(y - \bar{y})^2}$$

However, to compute r^2 in the case of two independent variables we will use the following alternative *formula for the coefficient of multiple linear determination:*

Formula for r^2 (two independent variables)

$$r^2 = \frac{n(a\Sigma y + b_1\Sigma x_1 y + b_2\Sigma x_2 y) - (\Sigma y)^2}{n\Sigma y^2 - (\Sigma y)^2}$$

In the advertising example,

$$n = 6 \qquad a = 0.063972 \qquad \Sigma y = 15 \qquad b_1 = 0.204921$$

$$\Sigma x_1 y = 103 \qquad b_2 = 0.280492 \qquad \Sigma x_2 y = 88 \qquad \Sigma y^2 = 47$$

Thus,

$$r^2 = \frac{6[(0.063972)(15) + (0.204921)(103) + (0.280492)(88)] - (15)^2}{6(47) - (15)^2}$$

$$= \frac{55.50}{57}$$

$$= 0.97$$

Thus, 0.97, or 97 percent, of the variation in number of responses is explained by advertisement size and newspaper circulation.

The square root of r^2, which is r, is called the coefficient of multiple correlation. Positive and negative signs for r, which had meanings in simple regression, do not have meanings in multiple regression: The coefficient of multiple correlation is always written as a positive number (or zero). In this chapter we will not explore multiple correlation analysis. But we will com-

r^2 has the same meaning as in simple linear regression.

pute r^2 because this number aids in describing the results of a multiple regression analysis. As in simple regression, $r^2 = 0$ means that there is no relationship (no correlation) between the dependent variable and the independent variables; and $r^2 = 1$ means that all the observed points satisfy the regression equation exactly; that is, the error e for every point is 0. Also, since all the e's are 0 when $r^2 = 1$, s_e equals 0 when $r^2 = 1$. Usually, r^2 is between 0 and 1, and s_e is not zero.

In the problems that follow, the number of observations n is small so that you will not be burdened with extensive calculations. Larger values of n (30 or more if possible) are needed to obtain reliable estimates of the constant term and the regression coefficients.

13.4 PROBLEMS

1. Use the data in Table A. (a) Compute a, b_1, and b_2; then write the regression equation. (b) Compute the value of s_e. (c) Compute the value of r^2. (d) What do the answers to (b) and (c) mean in terms of the data points and the regression equation?

TABLE A

x_1	x_2	y
0	1	6
0	3	0
1	2	5
2	1	20
2	3	8

2. The Northeast Ski Association obtained data for five ski areas. The association wants to use the lift capacity (number of skiers who can be accommodated in a day) and the number of miles of ski trails to estimate the number of customers at an area. The data are given in Table B. (a) Compute a, b_1, and b_2; then write the regression equation. (b) Estimate the number of customers for an area which has a lift capacity of 5 thousand and 12 miles of trails (c) Compute the value of s_e; then state the rule-of-thumb interpretation of that value. (d) Compute and interpret the value of r^2.

TABLE B

Lift capacity (thousands) x_1	Number of miles of trails x_2	Number of customers (hundreds) y
2	10	20
1	3	6
4	15	30
2	7	12
6	22	47

3. Arctic Delivery transports produce in refrigerated trucks. The owner, Herman Arctic, collected the data in Table C to derive an equation for estimating the percent of spoiled produce. The independent variables are truck temperature in degrees Celsius and the number of miles that produce was transported. (a) Compute a, b_1, and b_2; then write the regression equation. (b) Estimate the percent of spoiled produce for a truck temperature of 8° and a distance of 4 hundred miles. (c) Compute the value of s_e; then state the rule-of-thumb interpretation of that value. (d) Compute and interpret the value of r^2.

TABLE C

Truck temperature (degrees Celsius) x_1	Number of miles (hundreds) x_2	Spoiled produce (percent) y
6	1	6
10	2	8
12	3	13
4	5	5
11	6	12
5	8	7

4. George Ryan of the Federal Steel Company collected the data in Table D. George wants to estimate the supervisor rating of an employee from the scores that the employee makes on test 1 and test 2. (a) Compute a, b_1, and b_2; then write the regression equation. (b) Estimate the supervisor's rating for an employee whose scores were 85 on test 1 and 75 on test 2. (c) Compute the value of s_e; then state the rule-of-thumb interpretation of that value. (d) Compute and interpret the value of r^2.

TABLE D

Test 1 score x_1	Test 2 score x_2	Supervisor rating y
97	70	92
80	67	61
86	57	70
91	80	81
78	58	51
81	93	75

5. Paula Higgins is chief cost analyst for Economy Drive, a car rental business. Paula wants to estimate gas mileage (mpg) for a car from the car's engine size and weight. She collected the data in Table E. (a) Compute a, b_1, and b_2; then write the regression equation. (b) Estimate gas mileage for a car that has a 2.8 hundred cubic inch engine and

weighs 3 thousand pounds. (c) Compute the value of s_e; then state the rule-of-thumb interpretation of that value. (d) Compute and interpret the value of r^2.

TABLE E

Engine size (hundreds of cubic inches) x_1	Car weight (thousands of pounds) x_2	Miles per gallon y
1.0	2.0	32
1.4	2.6	28
2.0	3.0	24
3.0	3.6	15
2.3	2.9	21
2.5	3.5	20
1.5	2.7	30
2.3	3.4	19

6. Clair Oil Co. collected the data in Table F. They want to use outside average temperature and the thickness of insulation to estimate fuel consumption for a house during a 30-day period. (a) Compute a, b_1, and b_2; then write the regression equation. (b) Estimate fuel consumption when the average temperature is 5 degrees, for a house with 6 inches of insulation. (c) Compute the value of s_e; then state the rule-of-thumb interpretation of that value. (d) Compute and interpret the value of r^2.

TABLE F

Average outside temperature (degrees Celsius) x_1	Thickness of insulation (inches) x_2	30-day oil consumption (hundreds of gallons) y
15	3	1.8
−10	4	4.2
2	5	2.7
18	6	1.0
10	7	1.5
7	8	1.6
−5	9	2.9
−15	10	3.4

7. Consumer Products Company (CPC) wants to estimate sales of a product in various regions of the country. The independent variables are population and income per capita. CPC collected the data in Table G. (a) Compute a, b_1, and b_2; then write the regression equation. (b) Estimate sales in a region that has a population of 3 hundred thousand,

and a per capita income of 5.5 thousand dollars. (c) Compute the value of s_e; then state the rule-of-thumb interpretation of that value. (d) Compute and interpret the value of r^2.

TABLE G

Population (hundreds of thousands) x_1	Per capita income (thousands of dollars) x_2	Product sales (hundreds of thousands of dollars) y
2.7	4.4	1.7
1.8	5.2	1.3
3.8	6.8	2.1
2.0	4.8	1.4
0.9	4.3	0.7
2.6	5.7	1.8
1.0	5.0	0.6
3.3	4.4	2.1
2.0	3.9	1.2
0.5	4.0	0.5

8. The Diners' Association wants to determine the relationship between restaurant sales and two independent variables, the number of restaurant employees and restaurant floor area. The association collected the data in Table H. (a) Compute a, b_1, and b_2; then write the regression equation. (b) Estimate sales for a restaurant that has nine employees and 8 thousand square feet of floor area. (c) Compute the value of s_e; then state the rule-of-thumb interpretation of that value. (d) Compute and interpret the value of r^2.

TABLE H

Number of employees x_1	Floor area (thousands of square feet) x_2	Sales (thousands of dollars) y
15	10	30
8	5	22
12	10	16
7	3	7
10	2	14

9. Fran's Real Estate Agency analyzed the prices of lots in a lakeshore development. They obtained the data in Table I. (a) Compute a, b_1, and b_2; then write the regression equation. (b) Estimate the price of a lot that has 1 hundred feet of shoreline and contains 10 thousand square feet of land. (c) Compute the value of s_e; then state the rule-of-thumb interpretation of that value. (d) Compute and interpret the value of r^2.

TABLE I

Shore frontages (hundreds of feet) x_1	Lot size (thousands of square feet) x_2	Lot price (thousands of dollars) y
0.5	18	30
0.8	8	35
1.0	6	50
1.2	20	60
1.5	15	80
1.7	16	80
2.2	21	95

10. Which number, r^2 or s_e, measures the predictive accuracy of a regression equation?

13.5 MULTIPLE REGRESSION ON A COMPUTER

In this section we will have a computer do regression calculations for us. Our job will be to derive regression inferences from the results of the calculations. It is not necessary to know how a computer does calculations, but you should know what calculations are being carried out.

The first step in regression analysis is to calculate products and squares for each $(x_1, x_2, x_3, \ldots, x_p, y)$ data point, where the subscript p on x_p means the number of independent variables is p. For each data point there will be $p(p + 1)/2$ products and $(p + 1)$ squares.

After products and squares have been computed, all sums of products (e.g., $\Sigma x_1 x_2$) and all sums of squares (e.g., Σx_1^2) must be calculated. Next, formulas using these sums must be evaluated to obtain b_1, b_2, b_3, $\ldots$, b_p, the constant term a, the standard error of estimate s_e, the coefficient of determination r^2, and the standard errors needed to derive regression inferences.

In broad overview, then, all that is required in regression computations is the calculation of products and squares, and the evaluation of formulas. But with large data sets and several (say, 4 or more) independent variables, a vast amount of calculation is required. Fortunately, computers can do millions of calculations in a few seconds; specially written instructions, called programs, make it easy for you to command a computer to do regression analyses for you. Here's how it works: The program is stored in a computer, ready for use. All you have to do is supply the computer with the program name and the data set you want analyzed. For example, I often use the Interactive Data Analysis (IDA) regression program. To do so, I type RUN IDA on a typewriter (called a *terminal*) that is connected to the computer, and supply the data. Then I can command the computer to do all the regression calculations for me and print out the results. What I supply to the computer is called *input*, and what the computer supplies to me is called *output*.

Programmers (the people who write programs) have developed sets of programs for doing a variety of statistical analyses; a set of these programs is called a *statistical package*. IDA is a statistical package that, among other

Computer
+
program
+
data
↓
a lot less tedious work for the statistician

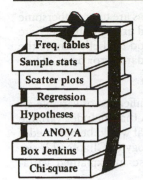

Freq. tables

Sample stats

Scatter plots

Regression

Hypotheses

ANOVA

Box Jenkins

Chi-square

things, does regression calculations, computes standard d and correlation coefficients, makes frequency tables and s putes values of various sample test statistics, and so on. Other packages include the Statistical Package (STATPACK), the Statistical Package for the Social Sciences (SPSS), MINITAB, and the Biomedical Computer Programs (BMDP). Each package has its own special attributes, but they all perform regression calculations.

Inferences from Computer Output

The Regression Equation, r^2, and s_e Let's work with the $n = 6$ data points of Table 13.1, where

$$x_1 = \text{size of advertisement (column-inches)}$$

$$x_2 = \text{newspaper circulation (thousands)}$$

$$y = \text{number of responses to an advertisement (hundreds)}$$

I supplied the data of Table 13.1 to a computer and commanded it to perform regression calculations. The computer output that will be discussed first is given in Table 13.3. The numbers on the first line are $r^2 = 0.974$ and

TABLE 13.3
COMPUTER REGRESSION OUTPUT

r^2 and s_e → **Multiple r-square = 0.974**		**Standard error = 0.28883**
Variable	**Coefficient**	**Standard error coefficient**
$x_1, b_1,$ and s_{b_1} → 1	0.20492	0.05882
$x_2, b_2,$ and s_{b_2} → 2	0.28049	0.06860
a →	Constant term = 0.06397	

$s_e = 0.28883$. The numbers 1 and 2 under "Variable" mean that the variables are x_1 and x_2; their regression coefficients are given under "Coefficient." They are

$$b_1 = 0.20492 \quad \text{and} \quad b_2 = 0.28049$$

The constant term is

$$a = 0.06397$$

Consequently, we can write the regression equation from the computer output; it is

$$\hat{y} = 0.06397 + 0.20492x_1 + 0.28049x_2$$

Testing the Independent Variables All the Table 13.3 values referred to thus far are the same, except for rounding, as the corresponding values we computed earlier by hand. But the computer supplied some standard errors that we did not compute by hand (because the formulas are too cumbersome for hand calculation). The numbers under "Standard error coefficient" are the standard errors of the regression coefficients b_1 and b_2. Let's denote the regression coefficient of variable x_i by b_i, and its standard error by s_{b_i}. Then

$$s_{b_1} = 0.05882 \qquad s_{b_2} = 0.06860$$

The value of s_{b_i} is used in a hypothesis test of the significance of variable x_i. The test determines whether the regression equation that includes variable x_i is a significant "improvement" over the equation that would be obtained if x_i were not included in the analysis. In the terminology of Chapter 12, significant "improvement" means a significant increase in explained variation.

The hypotheses of the test, stated briefly, are

Note the unusual (words only) hypotheses . . .

H_0: variable x_i does not improve the regression equation

H_a: variable x_i improves the regression equation

The regression coefficient test statistic is

. . . and the very simple test statistic.

$$\text{Sample } t = \frac{b_i}{s_{b_i}}$$

The decision rule at significance level α is

$$\text{Reject } H_0 \text{ if } |\text{sample } t| > t_{\alpha/2, v}$$

where, with n data points and p independent variables,

$$v = n - p - 1$$

Let's test at $\alpha = 0.05$ to determine if x_1, size of advertisement, improves the regression equation that would be obtained if only x_2, circulation, was included in the analysis. The hypotheses are

1. Hypotheses

H_0: variable x_1 does not improve the equation

H_a: variable x_1 does improve the equation

We have $n = 6$ and $p = 2$; so

$$v = n - p - 1 = 6 - 2 - 1$$
$$= 3$$

degrees of freedom. With $\alpha/2 = 0.05/2 = 0.025$, we find $t_{0.025,3} = 3.18$ in Table VII. The decision rule is

2. Decision rule

$$\text{Reject } H_0 \text{ if } |\text{sample } t| > 3.18$$

From Table 13.3, $b_1 = 0.20492$ and $s_{b_1} = 0.05882$. Next we compute

$$\text{Sample } t = \frac{b_i}{s_{b_i}} = \frac{b_1}{s_{b_1}}$$
$$= \frac{0.20492}{0.05882} = 3.48$$

Thus,

3. Test statistic

$$\text{Sample } t = 3.48$$

The sample $t = 3.48$ exceeds the 3.18 in the decision rule; so we

4. Accept or reject

$$\text{Reject } H_0$$

Rejecting H_0 means that x_1 does improve the regression equation; that is, the regression equation computed from the (x_1, x_2, y) data points is an improvement over the equation that would be obtained using the pairs (x_2, y) as data points.

EXERCISE In the advertising example, does variable x_2 (circulation) improve the regression equation? Why? (Test at $\alpha = 0.05$.)
ANSWER Yes, because sample $t = 4.09$ exceeds $t_{0.025,3}$, which is 3.18.

Accepting H_0 in a t test of variable x_i means that x_i does not improve the regression equation. So when H_0 is accepted, an analyst may eliminate x_i from the analysis. Often, however, retaining variables for which H_0 is accepted will have little effect upon the precision of predictions made from the regression equation.

Confidence Intervals and Prediction Intervals In Chapter 12 you learned how to construct confidence intervals and prediction intervals. The interval formulas contained

$s(\mu_Y|X) = $ standard error of estimating the mean value of Y, given a value of X

and $s(Y|X) = $ standard error of predicting Y, given a value of X

In multiple regression with p independent variables, the corresponding standard error symbols are

$$s(\mu_Y|X_1, \ldots, X_p)$$

and $$s(Y|X_1, \ldots, X_p)$$

Some regression programs can be commanded to calculate these standard errors. We have to supply the values of $X_1, \ldots, X_p$. Also, we have to set the confidence coefficient C, and construct the interval. The *confidence interval formula for μ_Y* is

Recall:
A confidence interval
for μ_1 . . .

$$\hat{y} - t_{\alpha/2,v}[s(\mu_Y|X_1, \ldots, X_p)] \leq \mu_Y \leq \hat{y} + t_{\alpha/2,v}[s(\mu_Y|X_1, \ldots, X_p)]$$

The *prediction interval formula for Y* is

. . . and a prediction
interval for Y

$$\hat{y} - t_{\alpha/2,v}[s(Y|X_1, \ldots, X_p)] \leq Y \leq \hat{y} + t_{\alpha/2,v}[s(Y|X_1, \ldots, X_p)]$$

where $\alpha/2 = (1 - C)/2$

Let's construct 90 percent confidence and prediction intervals for the advertising example. The observations (Table 13.1) do not include a 4 column-inch advertisement in a newspaper with a circulation of 5 thousand. I want

TABLE 13.4
STANDARD ERRORS FOR ESTIMATION
AND PREDICTION

"Let $x_1 = 4$" →	Value of variable 1 = 4
"Let $x_2 = 5$" →	Value of variable 2 = 5
$\hat{y}$ →	Estimated Y = 2.2861
$s(\mu_Y|4, 5)$ →	Standard error for estimating mean = 0.15875
$s(Y|4, 5)$ →	Standard error for predicting Y = 0.32958

to estimate the mean number of responses, and predict the number of responses, for $X_1 = 4$, $X_2 = 5$. I supplied the values $X_1 = 4$ and $X_2 = 5$ to the computer and obtained the output shown in Table 13.4. The *estimated Y* value is

$$\hat{y} = 2.2861$$

The computer calculated this value by substituting $x_1 = 4$ and $x_2 = 5$ into the regression equation

$$\hat{y} = 0.06397 + 0.20492x_1 + 0.28049x_2$$

The *standard error for estimating mean* is

$$s(\mu_Y|4, 5) = 0.15875$$

Similarly, the *standard error for predicting Y* is

$$s(Y|4, 5) = 0.32958$$

Calculation of the confidence interval for μ_Y with computer-generated $\hat{y}$ and standard error

The standard error estimating μ_Y is always the smaller of the two because means of sample values of a random variable vary less than do the values of the random variable.

For a 90 percent confidence interval, $C = 0.90$, and

$$\frac{\alpha}{2} = \frac{1 - C}{2} = \frac{1 - 0.90}{2}$$

$$= 0.05$$

First calculate $\alpha/2$ and v; then find $t_{\alpha/2,v}$ . . .

As before, with $n = 6$, $p = 2$,

$$v = n - p - 1 = 6 - 2 - 1$$

$$= 3$$

In Table VII, we find

$$t_{\alpha/2,v} = t_{0.05,3} = 2.35$$

The confidence interval for μ_Y,

. . . and construct the interval.

$$\hat{y} - t_{\alpha/2,v}[s(\mu_Y|4, 5)] \leq \mu_Y \leq \hat{y} + t_{\alpha/2,v}[s(\mu_Y|4, 5)]$$

is

$$2.2861 - (2.35)(0.15875) \leq \mu_Y \leq 2.2861 + (2.35)(0.15875)$$

$$1.91 \leq \mu_Y \leq 2.66$$

Responses are in hundreds, so the interval is

$$191 \leq \mu_Y \leq 266$$

Thus, the estimated mean number of responses to 4 column-inch advertisements in papers having circulations of 5 thousand is from 191 to 266.

The method for constructing a prediction interval for the value (not the mean value) of Y is the same as that just shown, except that the standard error for predicting Y has to be used.

EXERCISE Construct the 90 percent prediction interval for the number of responses Y to a 4 column-inch advertisement in a newspaper with a circulation of 5 thousand.

ANSWER $151 \leq Y \leq 306$.

13.6 PROBLEMS

1. Write the multiple regression equation which has $a = 10$, $b_1 = 2.5$, $b_2 = -1.4$, and $b_3 = 0.2$.
2. How many degrees of freedom are there in a regression analysis of thirty $(x_1, x_2, x_3, x_4, x_5, y)$ data points?
3. Clair Oil Company did a regression analysis to study the relationship between monthly consumption of heating oil in 15 homes, temperature, and thickness of home attic insulation. The variables were

    $x_1 =$ average monthly temperature in degrees Fahrenheit

    $x_2 =$ number of inches of attic insulation

    $y =$ monthly consumption of oil in gallons

    Answer the following by using the computer output in Table A. (a) Write the regression equation. (b) From the equation in (a), estimate consumption of oil during a month when temperature averages 30 degrees, for a home with 8 inches of insulation. (c) Interpret the value of r^2. (d) State the rule-of-thumb interpretation of the value of the standard error of estimate. (e) How many degrees of freedom are there in this problem? (f) Test the independent variables for significance at the 5 percent level. What do you conclude from these tests?

TABLE A

Multiple r-square = 0.966		Standard error = 25.970
Variable	Coefficient	Standard error coefficient
1	−5.446	0.3356
2	−20.010	2.3385
	Constant term = 562.44	

4. International Products, Inc., did a regression study on data obtained for 20 manufacturing plants. The variables were

x_1 = plant operating rate (percent of capacity)

x_2 = raw material and labor costs (dollars per unit)

y = manufacturing cost (dollars per unit)

Answer the following by using the computer output in Table B. (a) Write the regression equation. (b) From the equation in (a), estimate manufacturing cost per unit for a plant operating at 80 percent of capacity if raw material and labor cost per unit is $1.20. (c) Interpret the value of r^2. (d) State the rule-of-thumb interpretation of the value of s_e. (e) How many degrees of freedom are there in this problem? (f) Test the independent variables for significance at the 5 percent level. What do you conclude from these tests?

TABLE B

Multiple r-square = 0.914		Standard error = 0.2404
Variable	**Coefficient**	**Standard error coefficient**
1	−0.03516	0.004178
2	2.07660	0.294900
	Constant term = 5.1988	

5. Linda Martin, an executive of Dorset Company, did a regression analysis on factors related to employees' weekly salaries. Data were obtained for 20 employees. The variables were

x_1 = number of months employed

x_2 = age of worker in years

y = worker's weekly salary in dollars

Answer the following using the computer output in Table C. (a) Write the regression equation. (b) From the equation in (a), estimate the salary of an employee who has been employed for 100 months and is 50 years old. (c) Interpret the value of r^2. (d) State the rule-of-thumb interpretation of the value of s_e. (e) How many degrees of freedom are there

TABLE C

Multiple r-square = 0.767		Standard error = 40.0352
Variable	**Coefficient**	**Standard error coefficient**
1	0.62015	0.11743
2	1.05890	0.97184
	Constant term = 247.85	

in this problem? (f) Test the independent variables for significance at the 5 percent level. What do you conclude from these tests?

6. (See Problem 5.) For the independent variable values $x_1 = 100$ and $x_2 = 50$, the computer calculated and printed the numbers in Table D. Construct the 90 percent confidence interval for the mean wage of workers who have been employed 100 months and are 50 years old.

TABLE D

Value of variable 1 = 100
Value of variable 2 = 50
Estimated Y = 362.81
Standard error for estimating mean = 14.444
Standard error for predicting Y = 42.561

7. Denning Company did a regression analysis on factors thought to affect sales of one of its products. Data were obtained for 15 sales territories. The variables were

x_1 = thousands of dollars spent by Denning on advertising

x_2 = number of stores selling Denning's product

x_3 = number of stores selling competing products

y = sales in thousands of units

Answer the following using the computer output in Table E. (a) Write the regression equation. (b) From the equation in (a), estimate sales for a territory where $4 thousand was spent on advertising if the territory has 50 stores selling Denning's product and there are 70 competitors. (c) Interpret the value of r^2. (d) State the rule-of-thumb interpretation of the value of s_e. (e) How many degrees of freedom are there in this problem? (f) Test the independent variables for significance at the 5 percent level. What do you conclude from these tests?

TABLE E

Multiple r-square = 0.997		Standard error = 4.9795
Variable	Coefficient	Standard error coefficient
1	2.1055	0.64785
2	3.5624	0.09946
3	-0.2219	0.52855
	Constant term = 178.52	

8. (See Problem 7.) For the independent variable values $x_1 = 4$, $x_2 = 50$, and $x_3 = 70$, the computer calculated and printed the numbers in

Table F. Construct the 95 percent prediction interval for sales in a territory that has the stated values of the independent variables.

TABLE F

Value of variable 1 = 4
Value of variable 2 = 50
Value of variable 3 = 70
Estimated Y = 349.529
Standard error for estimating mean = 1.8761
Standard error for predicting Y = 5.3212

9. A computer analyzed 24 (x_1, x_2, x_3, y) data points and obtained $a = -0.974$, $b_1 = 1.253$, $b_2 = 0.348$, and $b_3 = 0.445$. When supplied with the values $x_1 = 90$, $x_2 = 80$, and $x_3 = 60$, the computer found $s(\mu_Y|X_1, X_2, X_3) = 3.681$ and $s(Y|X_1, X_2, X_3) = 4.780$. Construct the 90 percent confidence interval for the mean value of the dependent variable, given the stated values for the independent variables.

10. (See Problem 9.) Construct the 90 percent interval for predicting the value of the dependent variable given the stated values of the independent variables.

13.7 CURVILINEAR REGRESSION

We have used the least-squares formulas to find the regression coefficients and the constant term of the linear equation that best fits a set of observed data. We can use the same formulas to fit an equation whose graph is a curve to a set of observed data; however, an additional step is required. Curves are fitted either because a scatter chart suggests a curvilinear tendency, or because we know from experience or theory that the variables of interest are not linearly related.

Quadratic Regression Equations

By appending an x^2 term to the linear equation $y = a + bx$, we obtain a *quadratic* equation whose form is

Standard quadratic form

$$y = a + bx + cx^2$$

Quadratic equations have graphs that are vertical parabolas. Figure 13.1 is the graph of the parabola that has $a = 60$, $b = -20$, and $c = 2$; its equation is

$$y = 60 - 20x + 2x^2$$

The parabola in Figure 13.1 is also said to be concave upward.

This parabola opens upward because the coefficient of the x^2 term, $c = 2$, is positive. It has a lowest point, called the vertex of the parabola, at (5, 10). The x coordinate of the vertex of a parabola occurs at

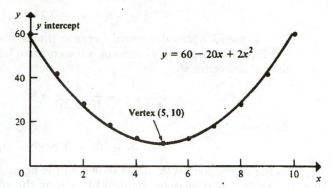

FIGURE 13.1
Section of an upward-opening vertical parabola.

$$\text{Vertex value of } x = -\frac{\text{coefficient of } x}{2(\text{coefficient of } x^2)} = -\frac{b}{2c}$$

Thus, the x coordinate of the vertex of $y = 60 - 20x + 2x^2$ is

$$x = -\frac{-20}{2(2)} = 5$$

And, when $x = 5$,

$$y = 60 - 20(5) + 2(5^2) = 10$$

so the vertex point is $(5, 10)$. The constant term 60 in $y = 60 - 20x + 2x^2$ is the y intercept; that is, as shown on the figure, $y = 60$ when $x = 0$.

Figure 13.2 is the graph of

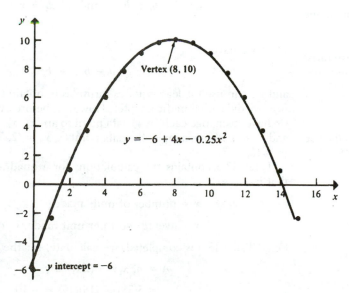

FIGURE 13.2
Section of a down-ward-opening vertical parabola.

$$y = -6 + 4x - 0.25x^2$$

This parabola opens downward because the coefficient of the x^2 term, -0.25, is negative. The y intercept is the constant term, -6. The x coordinate of the vertex is

$$x = -\frac{4}{2(-0.25)} = 8$$

At $x = 8$,

$$y = -6 + 4(8) - 0.25(8^2) = 10$$

Plotting aid:
***These parabolas are
symmetric about a
vertical line through
the vertex.***

so the vertex point is $(8, 10)$ as shown on the figure.

Vertical parabolas are graphed by plotting the vertex and several additional points found by substituting x values into the equation. Then a curve is sketched through these points.

EXERCISE What is the vertex point of the parabola $y = 11.2 - 2.4x + 0.2x^2$?
ANSWER (6, 4).

Quadratic Regression Computations Suppose we want to fit a quadratic regression equation that has x as the independent variable and y as the dependent variable. The form of the equation is

**The quadratic
equation**

$$\hat{y} = a + bx + cx^2$$

We can *transform* the quadratic into a multiple linear form by letting

The substitutions

$$b_1 = b \qquad \text{and} \qquad x_1 = x$$
$$b_2 = c \qquad \text{and} \qquad x_2 = x^2$$

**The transformed
equation (a linear
equation)**

Then we have

$$\hat{y} = a + b_1 x_1 + b_2 x_2$$

and we can use the least-squares formulas to obtain the values of a, b_1, and b_2 as we did earlier in the chapter. However, before evaluating the formulas, we have to change each (x, y) data point to an (x_1, x_2, y) point, where $x_1 = x$

**The data pairs also
must be transformed.**

and $x_2 = x^2$. For example, the data point $(x, y) = (2, 3)$ is changed to $(x_1, x_2, y) = (2, 4, 3)$.

Table 13.5 contains the calculations for a quadratic regression analysis that has

$$x = \text{number of units made}$$

$$y = \text{average cost per unit made, in dollars}$$

Once Table 13.5 is completed, we calculate, for the $n = 5$ data points,

$$A = n\Sigma x_1 y - (\Sigma x_1)(\Sigma y)$$

$$= 5(55) - (15)(19) = -10$$

TABLE 13.5
QUADRATIC REGRESSION CALCULATIONS

We start only with the
n = 5 data pairs
(x, y). The rest of the
table is calculated
from the pairs.

Number of units made (hundreds) $x_1 = x$	Average cost per unit (dollars) y	$x_2 = x^2$	$x_1 y$	$x_2 y$	$x_1 x_2$	x_1^2	x_2^2	y^2
1	6	1	6	6	1	1	1	36
2	3	4	6	12	8	4	16	9
3	2	9	6	18	27	9	81	4
4	3	16	12	48	64	16	256	9
5	5	25	25	125	125	25	625	25
$\overline{15}$	$\overline{19}$	$\overline{55}$	$\overline{55}$	$\overline{209}$	$\overline{225}$	$\overline{55}$	$\overline{979}$	$\overline{83}$

$$B = n\Sigma x_2^2 - (\Sigma x_2)^2$$

$$= 5(979) - (55)^2 = 1870$$

$$C = n\Sigma x_1 x_2 - (\Sigma x_1)(\Sigma x_2)$$

$$= 5(225) - (15)(55) = 300$$

$$D = n\Sigma x_2 y - (\Sigma x_2)(\Sigma y)$$

$$= 5(209) - (55)(19) = 0$$

$$E = n\Sigma x_1^2 - (\Sigma x_1)^2$$

$$= 5(55) - (15)^2 = 50$$

and

$$F = EB - C^2$$

$$= (50)(1870) - (300)^2 = 3500$$

Then

$$b_1 = \frac{AB - CD}{F} = \frac{(-10)(1870) - (300)(0)}{3500}$$

$$= -5.3428571$$

$$b_2 = \frac{DE - AC}{F} = \frac{0(50) - (-10)(300)}{3500}$$

$$= 0.85714286$$

and

$$a = \frac{\Sigma y - b_1 \Sigma x_1 - b_2 \Sigma x_2}{n}$$

$$= \frac{19 - (-5.3428571)(15) - (0.85714286)(55)}{5}$$

$$= 10.399999$$

The regression equation $\hat{y} = a + b_1 x_1 + b_2 x_2$ becomes

$$\hat{y} = 10.400 - 5.343x_1 + 0.857x_2$$

The linear equation must be transformed back to a quadratic.

But x_1 is x, and x_2 is x^2. So, in terms of the original variables x and y, the equation is

$$\hat{y} = 10.400 - 5.343x + 0.857x^2$$

We can now use the equation to estimate average cost per unit at a given level of output. For example, at $x = 2.5$ hundred units of output, estimated average cost per unit is

$$\hat{y} = 10.400 - 5.343(2.5) + 0.857(2.5)^2$$

$$= 2.40 \text{ dollars per unit}$$

Computer programs will handle curvilinear regression analysis as well as linear analysis.

We could go on to compute r^2 and s_e by the formulas given earlier in the chapter, but I had a computer regression program do the calculation. The output is given in Table 13.6. The regression coefficients and the constant term have the values we computed from the data in Table 13.5. Also, $r^2 = 0.989$; so 98.9 percent of the variation in y, average cost per unit, is explained by its quadratic relation to the number of units made.

TABLE 13.6
COMPUTER QUADRATIC REGRESSION OUTPUT

Multiple r-square = 0.989		Standard error = 0.2390
Variable	Coefficient	Standard error coefficient
1	−5.34286	0.39071
2	0.85714	0.06389
	Constant term = 10.4000	

EXERCISE State the rule-of-thumb interpretation of the value for s_e given in Table 13.6.

ANSWER About 68 percent of average cost per unit figures will be within ±\$0.239 of the values estimated from the regression equation.

Let's test the variable x^2 (variable x_2) for significance at the $\alpha = 0.01$ level. The hypotheses are

H_0: variable x^2 does not improve the regression equation

H_a: variable x^2 does improve the regression equation

With $n = 5$, and $p = 2$ independent variables,

$$v = n - p - 1 = 5 - 2 - 1$$

$$= 2$$

degrees of freedom. We find from Table VII that $t_{\alpha/2,v} = t_{0.005,2} = 9.92$. Hence, the decision rule is

Reject H_0 if |sample t| > 9.92

The value of the test statistic, computed from the b_2 and s_{b_2} values given in Table 13.6, is

$$\text{Sample } t = \frac{b_2}{s_{b_2}} = \frac{0.85714}{0.06389}$$

$$= 13.4$$

Since the sample t, 13.4, is greater than 9.92, we

$$\text{Reject } H_0$$

We conclude that x^2 improves the regression equation. Thus, the (quadratic) regression equation that includes $x_2 = x^2$ is an improvement over the (simple) regression equation $\hat{y} = a + bx$.

Figure 13.3 shows the five data points of the average cost example, and the graph of the parabola that we fitted to the points.

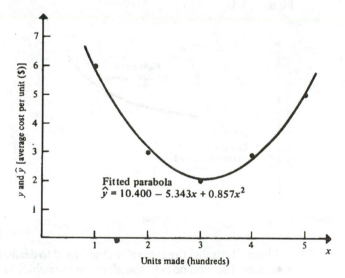

FIGURE 13.3
Quadratic fit for average cost per unit.

Other Curvilinear Regression Equations

In the economic analysis of cost, cost curves often have a shape corresponding to an equation of the form

The standard cubic form

$$y = a + bx + cx^2 + dx^3$$

This cubic equation (cubic because of the presence of the x^3 term) can be changed to a linear form by letting

$$b_1 = b \quad \text{and} \quad x_1 = x$$

$$b_2 = c \quad \text{and} \quad x_2 = x^2$$

$$b_3 = d \quad \text{and} \quad x_3 = x^3$$

We can now fit the regression equation

$$\hat{y} = a + b_1 x_1 + b_2 x_2 + b_3 x_3$$

to a set of (x, y) data points by first changing each point to an $(x_1, x_2, x_3, y) = (x, x^2, x^3, y)$ data point; then, because of the calculational burden, we would use a statistical package and have a computer determine the values of a, b_1, b_2, and b_3. Suppose the values are 60,000, 200, -0.90, and 0.0015, respectively. Then the regression equation, in terms of the transformed variables, would be

$$\hat{y} = 60{,}000 + 200x_1 - 0.90x_2 + 0.0015x_3$$

Or, in terms of the original variable x, the equation is

$$\hat{y} = 60{,}000 + 200x - 0.90x^2 + 0.0015x^3$$

The graph of this regression equation just written has the shape shown in Figure 13.4.

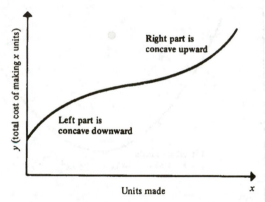

FIGURE 13.4
A cubic cost function.

I have illustrated the general method used to derive curvilinear regression equations; the method is to transform the variables in a way that leads to an equation that is a linear equation with one or more independent variables. In practice, computations with values of transformed variables are usually burdensome and should be done on a computer.

13.8 PROBLEMS

1. (a) Does the parabola $y = 10 + 6x + 0.15x^2$ open upward or downward? (b) What are the coordinates of the vertex of the parabola? (c) Find y for $x = 0$, 10, 20, 30, and 40. Then sketch a graph of the parabola.

2. (a) Does the parabola $y = 20 - 0.8x + 0.01x^2$ open upward or downward? (b) What are the coordinates of the vertex of the parabola? (c) Find y for $x = 0$, 20, 40, 60, and 80. Then sketch a graph of the parabola.

3. (a) If z is the independent variable, and m and n are regression coefficients, what transformations will change $y = a + mz + nz^2$ into the usual linear form? (b) Write the linear form.

4. (See Problem 3.) If an original data point is $(z, y) = (3, 5)$, what will be the corresponding data point for the linear form in Problem 3(b)?

5. Sam Miller, production manager for Wells Tool Co., compiled the data in Table A. Let number of hundreds of units made be the independent variable. (a) Make a scatter plot of the data. (b) Compute the regression coefficients and the constant for a quadratic regression equation. Write the equation. (c) Estimate average cost per unit when 4 hundred units are made.

TABLE A

Number of units made (hundreds)	Average cost per unit
1	8
2	5
3	3
5	2

6. Blue Dot Cab Company compiled the data in Table B. Let the number of cabs operating be the independent variable. (a) Make a scatter plot of the data. (b) Compute the regression coefficients and the constant for the quadratic regression equation. Write the equation. (c) Estimate the amount of fares collected when four cabs are operating. (d) Compute $\hat{y}$ for $x = 1, 2, \ldots, 8$. Plot the $(x, \hat{y})$ points on the graph and sketch the regression curve.

TABLE B

Number of cabs operating	Fares collected (hundreds of dollars)
1	51
2	57
3	66
5	75
6	79
7	83
8	85

7. Middle State Farm manager Neil Swenson applied different amounts of fertilizer to 10 similar plots of seeded land. Neil recorded crop yields from the plots. The variables for a quadratic regression analysis were

$$x_1 = x = \text{number of bags of fertilizer applied}$$

$$x_2 = x^2$$

$$y = \text{plot yield in hundreds of pounds}$$

Output from a computer regression program is given in Table C. (a) Write the quadratic regression equation. (b) Estimate the yield of a plot that had seven bags of fertilizer. (c) How many degrees of freedom are there in this problem? (d) Is the sample t value for x_2 significant at the $\alpha = 0.01$ level? Why? (e) What do you conclude from the answer to (d)?

TABLE C

Multiple r-square = 0.974		Standard error = 1.2926
Variable	Coefficient	Standard error coefficient
1	5.6262	0.6396
2	-0.3179	0.0541
	Constant term = 2.6273	

8. (See Problem 7.) When supplied with variable values $X_1 = 7$ and $X_2 = 49$, a computer printed out the values in Table D. (a) Construct the 90 percent prediction interval for the yield of a plot that has seven bags of fertilizer. (b) Construct the 90 percent confidence interval for the mean yield of plots that have seven bags of fertilizer.

TABLE D

Value of variable 1 = 7
Value of variable 2 = 49
Estimated Y = 26.434
Standard error for estimating mean = 0.6342
Standard error for predicting Y = 1.439

9. Write the cubic regression equation for which $a = 100$, $b_1 = 10$, $b_2 = -0.15$, and $b_3 = 0.0001$.

10. Nilo Manufacturing Company cost analyst Mary Briganti recorded cost and output data for 16 operating periods when different numbers of evening gowns were made. A cubic regression analysis was performed by a computer. The independent variable x was the number of dresses made in a period; and the dependent variable y was the cost in dollars of making x dresses. The computer output showed that $a = 28,000$, $b_1 = 200$, $b_2 = -0.9$, and $b_3 = 0.0015$. (a) Write the cubic regression equation. (b) Estimate the cost, and the cost per dress, if 150 dresses are made. (c) Estimate the cost, and the cost per dress, if 200 dresses are made.

13.9 SUMMARY

Multiple linear regression equations have the form

$$\hat{y} = a + b_1 x_1 + b_2 x_2 + b_3 x_3 + \cdots + b_p x_p$$

where p = the number of independent variables, and b_1, b_2, b_3, . . . , b_p are the regression coefficients.

The regression equation with two independent variables,

$$\hat{y} = a + b_1 x_1 + b_2 x_2$$

is fitted to n data points, each of which is an (x_1, x_2, y) number triple, as follows: First, compute Σx_1, Σx_2, and Σx_3; then compute

$$\Sigma x_1 y \qquad \Sigma x_2 y \qquad \Sigma x_1 x_2$$

$$\Sigma x_1^2 \qquad \Sigma x_2^2 \qquad \Sigma y^2$$

Next compute

$$A = n\Sigma x_1 y - (\Sigma x_1)(\Sigma y) \qquad B = n\Sigma x_2^2 - (\Sigma x_2)^2$$

$$C = n\Sigma x_1 x_2 - (\Sigma x_1)(\Sigma x_2) \qquad D = n\Sigma x_2 y - (\Sigma x_2)(\Sigma y)$$

$$E = n\Sigma x_1^2 - (\Sigma x_1)^2 \qquad F = EB - C^2$$

Then compute

$$b_1 = \frac{AB - CD}{F}$$

$$b_2 = \frac{DE - AC}{F}$$

$$a = \frac{\Sigma y - b_1 \Sigma x_1 - b_2 \Sigma x_2}{n}$$

and write the regression equation.

With two independent variables, the *formula for the standard error of estimate* is

$$s_e = \sqrt{\frac{\Sigma y^2 - a\Sigma y - b_1 \Sigma x_1 y - b_2 \Sigma x_2 y}{n - 3}}$$

The *formula for the coefficient of multiple determination* is

$$r^2 = \frac{n[a\Sigma y + b_1 \Sigma x_1 y + b_2 \Sigma x_2 y] - (\Sigma y)^2}{n\Sigma y^2 - (\Sigma y)^2}$$

The output of regression programs in statistical computer packages includes values for s_e, r^2, the regression coefficients, and the standard errors of the regression coefficients. The analyst uses the output to write the regression equation and derive statistical inferences.

The *number of degrees of freedom in multiple regression* is

$$v = n - p - 1$$

where n = number of $(x_1, x_2, x_3, . . . , x_p, y)$ data points
$\quad\quad p$ = number of independent variables

Let b_i and s_{b_i} be, respectively, the values of a regression coefficient and the standard error of that coefficient. Then

$$\text{Sample } t = \frac{b_i}{s_{b_i}}$$

is used to test the null hypothesis H_0 that the regression equation that includes the independent variable x_i is not a significant improvement over the equation that would be obtained if x_i were not included in the analysis. The decision rule at significance level α is

$$\text{Reject } H_0 \text{ if } |\text{sample } t| > t_{\alpha/2,v}$$

Some computers have programs that calculate the standard errors needed for constructing confidence or prediction intervals; these standard errors are $s(\mu_Y|X_1, \ldots, X_p)$, $s(Y|X_1, \ldots, X_p)$. The analyst supplies values for the independent variables. The computer calculates and prints out the values of $\hat{y}$ and the standard errors. Next the analyst chooses a confidence coefficient C, calculates $\alpha/2 = (1 - C)/2$, and finds $t_{\alpha/2,v}$ from Table VII. Then the analyst constructs the *interval for* μ_Y, or *for* Y, by using the respective formulas

$$\hat{y} - t_{\alpha/2,v}[s(\mu_Y|X_1, \ldots, X_p)] \le \mu_Y \le \hat{y} + t_{\alpha/2,v}[s(\mu_Y|X_1, \ldots, X_p)]$$

or $\quad \hat{y} - t_{\alpha/2,v}[s(Y|X_1, \ldots, X_p)] \le Y \le \hat{y} + t_{\alpha/2,v}[s(Y|X_1, \ldots, X_p)]$

Linear regression formulas can be used to fit curves to observed data points. A *quadratic* regression equation may be fitted to a set of (x, y) data. First, each (x, y) data point is transformed to an (x_1, x_2, y) point, where $x_1 = x$ and $x_2 = x^2$. Then the transformed data are used to determine the values of a, b_1, and b_2 in the linear regression equation

$$\hat{y} = a + b_1 x_1 + b_2 x_2$$

The last equation, expressed in terms of the original variable x, is the quadratic regression equation

$$\hat{y} = a + b_1 x + b_2 x^2$$

A *cubic* regression equation may be fitted to a set of (x, y) data. First, each (x, y) data point is changed to an (x_1, x_2, x_3, y) data point, where $x_1 = x$, $x_2 = x^2$, and $x_3 = x^3$. The transformed data are used to determine a, b_1, b_2, and b_3 in the linear regression equation

$$\hat{y} = a + b_1 x_1 + b_2 x_2 + b_3 x_3$$

The last equation, expressed in terms of the original variable x, is the cubic regression equation

$$\hat{y} = a + b_1 x + b_2 x^2 + b_3 x^3$$

13.10 REVIEW PROBLEMS

1. Bill Dorman, manager of City Credit Card Corporation, wants to estimate average monthly credit card purchases by cardholders. Bill collected the data in Table A for five cardholders. (*a*) Find the values of a, b_1, and b_2; then write the

multiple linear regression equation. (*b*) Estimate monthly credit purchases by a cardholder who earns $2.5 thousand per month and has two children. (*c*) Compute the value of s_e and state the rule-of-thumb interpretation of that value. (*d*) Compute the value of r^2 and interpret this value.

TABLE A

Monthly salary (thousands of dollars) x_1	Cardholder's number of children x_2	Monthly credit purchases (hundreds of dollars) y
2	3	5
3	2	7
3	0	4
4	1	6
6	4	18

2. Cheryl Mitchell, a securities analyst for Green Brothers and Bailey, collected data on factors thought to affect stock prices. The variables are

$$x_1 = \text{dividend paid on stock, in dollars}$$

$$x_2 = \text{the stock's P/E ratio; that is, the ratio price per share divided by earnings per share}$$

$$y = \text{the price of a share of the stock, in dollars}$$

Cheryl's data are given in Table B. (*a*) Find a, b_1, and b_2; then write the multiple linear regression equation. (*b*) Estimate the price of a share of a stock that pays a $2 dividend and has a P/E ratio of 10. (*c*) Compute the value of s_e and state the rule-of-thumb interpretation of that value. (*d*) Compute and interpret the value of r^2.

TABLE B

Dividend (dollars per share) x_1	P/E ratio x_2	Price per share y
3.2	5	74
4.0	7	72
1.3	15	60
2.3	6	41
2.4	10	58
1.4	7	15

3. Morris Bronston, an executive of Specialty Stores, Inc., studied the relationship between Specialty Stores' sales in 10 cities and factors related to sales. The variables were

$$x_1 = \text{city population in thousands}$$

$$x_2 = \text{number of competitors}$$

$$y = \text{Specialty Stores' average weekly sales in thousands of dollars}$$

Morris collected the data in Table C. (a) Find a, b_1, and b_2; then write the regression equation. (b) Estimate the sales of a Specialty Store in a city that has a population of 50 thousand if there are two competitive stores in the city. (c) Compute the value of s_e; then state the rule-of-thumb interpretation of that value. (d) Compute and interpret the value of r^2.

TABLE C

City population (thousands) x_1	Number of competitors x_2	Specialty Stores' average weekly sales (thousands of dollars) y
10	2	6
18	1	18
24	3	14
31	3	24
62	4	52
26	2	16
12	1	8
8	0	8
41	3	34
52	5	40

4. (See Problem 2.) Cheryl decided to increase the sample size to 15. A computer program provided the output given in Table D. (a) Write the regression equation. (b) From the equation in (a), estimate the price of a stock that has a dividend of $2.50 and a P/E ratio of 9. (c) Interpret the value of r^2. (d) State the rule-of-thumb interpretation of the value of s_e. (e) How many degrees of freedom are there in this problem? (f) Test the independent variables for significance at the $\alpha = 0.05$ level. What do you conclude from these tests?

TABLE D

Multiple r-square = 0.837		Standard error = 9.205
Variable	Coefficient	Standard error coefficient
1	23.471	3.053
2	3.787	0.929
	Constant term = −38.300	

5. John Salvatore, a strawberry grower, examined the relation between crop yield and factors affecting yield. The variables were

$$x_1 = \text{inches of rainfall}$$

$$x_2 = \text{pounds of fertilizer used}$$

$$y = \text{crop yield, in crates of strawberries}$$

John had 11 data points analyzed by a computer regression program and obtained the output in Table E. (a) Write the regression equation. (b) From the equation in (a), estimate crop yield when rainfall is 18 inches and 500 pounds of fertilizer are used. (c) Interpret the value of r^2. (d) State the rule-of-thumb interpretation of the value of s_e. (e) How many degrees of freedom are there in this problem? (f) Test the independent variables for significance at the 5 percent level. What do you conclude from these tests?

TABLE E

Multiple r-square = 0.854		Standard error = 73.443
Variable	**Coefficient**	**Standard error coefficient**
1	26.281	7.056
2	3.248	0.761
	Constant term = −0.00108	

6. Paula Higgins is a cost analyst for a car rental business. She wants to estimate car mileage (mpg) for a car from the car's engine size and weight. The variables are

$$x_1 = \text{car engine size in cubic inches}$$

$$x_2 = \text{car weight in pounds}$$

$$y = \text{miles per gallon}$$

Paula collected data for 18 cars, then used a computer program to obtain the output in Table F. (a) Write the regression equation. (b) From the equation in (a), estimate miles per gallon for a car with a 250 cubic inch engine if the car weighs 3000 pounds. (c) What is the value of s_e? State the rule-of-thumb interpretation of that value. (d) Interpret the value of r^2. (e) How many degrees of freedom are there in this problem? (f) Test the significance of the independent variables at the $\alpha = 0.05$ level. What do you conclude from these tests?

TABLE F

Multiple r-square = 0.931		Standard error = 1.362
Variable	**Coefficient**	**Standard error coefficient**
1	−0.05352	0.008756
2	−0.00260	0.001542
	Constant term = 42.556	

7. (See Problem 6.) A computer supplied with the values 250 for engine size and 3000 for weight provided the output in Table G. (a) Construct the 90 percent confidence interval for the mean mileage of cars with 250 cubic inch engines if the cars weigh 3000 pounds. (b) Construct the 90 percent prediction interval for the mileage of a car with a 250 cubic inch engine if the car weighs 3000 pounds.

TABLE G

Value of variable 1 = 250
Value of variable 2 = 3000
Estimated Y = 21.376
Standard error for estimating mean = 0.4589
Standard error for predicting Y = 1.4374

8. George Ryan, personnel manager for the Federal Steel Company, studied the relationship between various test scores made by 24 employees and a supervisor's rating of employee job performance. The variables are

$$x_1 = \text{employee's score on test 1}$$
$$x_2 = \text{employee's score on test 2}$$
$$x_3 = \text{employee's score on test 3}$$
$$y = \text{supervisor rating}$$

George obtained the output in Table H from a statistical package. (a) Write the regression equation. (b) From the equation in (a), estimate the supervisor's rating of an employee whose scores on tests 1, 2, and 3 are 70, 89, and 67. (c) Interpret the value of r^2. (d) State the rule-of-thumb interpretation of the value of s_e. (e) How many degrees of freedom are there in this problem? (f) Test the independent variables for significance at the 5 percent level. What do you conclude from these tests?

TABLE H

Multiple r-square = 0.945		Standard error = 3.7663
Variable	Coefficient	Standard error coefficient
1	1.2822	0.1760
2	0.3609	0.0605
3	0.3666	0.1436
	Constant term = −94.250	

9. (See Problem 8.) A computer supplied with scores of 70, 89, and 67 for tests 1, 2, and 3 calculated the values given in Table I. (a) Construct the 90 percent confidence interval for the mean rating of employees whose test scores are 70, 89, and 67. (b) Construct the 90 percent prediction interval for the rating of an employee whose scores are 70, 89, and 67.

TABLE I

Value of variable 1 = 70
Value of variable 2 = 89
Value of variable 3 = 67
Estimated Y = 52.186
Standard error for estimating mean = 2.5089
Standard error for predicting Y = 4.5245

10. (See Problem 8.) George Ryan included two more test scores for each employee. The t values for tests 1, 2, 3, 4, and 5 were, respectively, 6.338, 5.628, 2.309, 0.033, and −0.248. Interpret the t values for tests 4 and 5 at the $\alpha = 0.05$ level.

11. Fran Dahl, purchasing manager for Buster Super Markets, wants to use the wholesale price of a cut of beef to estimate the retail price of the cut. The origi-

nal variables were

$$x = \text{wholesale price per pound of the cut}$$

$$y = \text{retail price per pound of the cut}$$

Fran wants a quadratic regression equation fitted to the data of Table J. (a) Make the necessary transformation of the data; then determine and write the quadratic regression equation. (b) From the equation in (a), estimate the retail price of a cut of beef that has a wholesale price of $2.20.

TABLE J

Wholesale price per pound	Retail price per pound
$1.20	$2.00
1.60	2.40
2.00	3.00
2.40	4.40
2.60	5.20

12. Executives of Upland Steel Corp. want to know the relationship between average production cost per unit of a product and the production lot size (the number of units made). The original variables were

$$x = \text{number of units made}$$

$$y = \text{average cost per unit made}$$

Twelve data points, given in Table K, were obtained. (a) Make a scatter chart for the data. (b) Find and write the equation of the quadratic regression curve. (c) From the equation in (a), estimate the average cost per unit when 15 hundred units are made. (d) Compute $\hat{y}$ for $x = 5, 10, 15, 20$, and 25. Plot the $(x, \hat{y})$ points on the chart for (a). Then sketch the parabola passing through the points.

TABLE K

Number of units made (hundreds)	Average cost per unit (dollars)
4.5	16.00
5.5	13.50
6.5	11.50
9.0	10.00
10.0	8.00
11.5	6.50
13.5	6.50
16.5	5.50
18.0	3.50
20.5	3.50
22.5	3.00
24.5	2.50

13. A cubic regression analysis of (x, y) data values was performed by a computer. The dependent variable y is the cost of making x units of a product. The linear form of the regression equation is

$$\hat{y} = 100 + 10x_1 - 0.15x_2 + 0.001x_3$$

(a) Write the cubic regression equation. (b) Estimate the cost of making 80 units, and the cost per unit if 80 units are made. (c) Estimate the cost of making 100 units, and the cost per unit if 100 units are made.

14

CHI-SQUARE TESTS FOR INDEPENDENCE AND GOODNESS-OF-FIT

14.1 INTRODUCTION

In Chapters 12 and 13, relationships between measurements (such as gas mileage and car engine size) were expressed as equations. Frequently, however, the data of interest consist of counts (rather than measurements) in a table that has a row category (heading) and a column category; and management wants to know whether the categories are independent or dependent. For example, in a study of consumer preference for a product in various geographical regions, the consumer preference category might consist of "like," "dislike," and "no opinion"; and the geographical category might consist of East, Central, and West. Sample data gathered in the study will be summarized as counts, such as the number of consumers in the East who liked the product. In the first part of the chapter, we discuss a test of the count data to determine whether categories (such as consumer preference and geographical region) are independent or dependent.

In the second part of the chapter, you will learn how to perform tests, called *goodness-of-fit* tests, that are applied to check assumptions made about populations. The tests are important because many problems in statistical inference are solved by assuming a particular probability distribution for the population. By performing a goodness-of-fit test, you can find out whether it is reasonable to assume that a population has a particular distribution, such as a normal distribution or a binomial distribution.

Pronounce chi as you do the ki in kite.

I will start by describing the *chi-square* probability distribution. The chi-square distribution is used in a number of statistical tests, including tests for independence and goodness-of-fit.

14.2 THE CHI-SQUARE DISTRIBUTION

The mathematical expression for the chi-square distribution contains only one parameter, the number of degrees of freedom v. There is a particular chi-square distribution for each particular number of degrees of freedom. For example, the distribution of z^2 (the square of the standard normal variable) is the chi-square distribution with $v = 1$ degree of freedom. The random variable of the distributions is denoted by χ^2 (χ is the Greek letter chi). Figure 14.1 shows chi-square distributions for $v = 2$, 5, and 10 degrees of freedom. Each of the distributions is a probability distribution; so the total area under each curve is 1.

The variable χ^2 cannot be negative; so chi-square curves do not extend to the left of zero. Figure 14.1 illustrates that when v exceeds 2, chi-square curves have one mode and are skewed to the right. The skewness is less apparent when v is large. In fact, when v is very large, the chi-square distribution is almost the same as a normal distribution having a mean equal to v and a standard deviation equal to $\sqrt{2v}$; but in applications, v is not large

All χ^2 tests in this chapter are one-tail tests.

enough to permit us to use normal curve probabilities as approximations of chi-square probabilities.

The significance levels α in this chapter will be right-tail areas of chi-

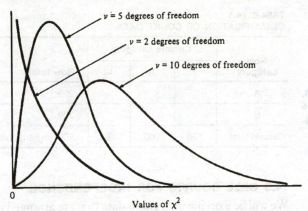

FIGURE 14.1
Chi-square distribu-
tions.

square distributions. The symbol $\chi^2_{\alpha,v}$ will mean the value of chi-square such that the distribution with v degrees of freedom has a right-tail area of α. Figure 14.2 illustrates this for

$$\chi^2_{\alpha,v} = \chi^2_{0.02,4} = 11.668$$

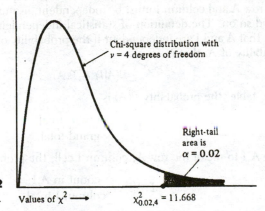

FIGURE 14.2
The meaning of $\chi^2_{\alpha,v}$.

Values of $\chi^2_{\alpha,v}$ are given in Table IV at the end of the book.

EXERCISE What is the value of $\chi^2_{0.05,3}$?
ANSWER 7.815.

It is common practice to use χ^2 to denote a random variable that has a distribution which is close to a chi-square distribution; we shall do so in this chapter. Our first application of chi-square distributions will be in performing tests of independence.

TABLE 14.1
CLASSIFICATION OF COUNT DATA

This table has 2 rows, 3 columns, and 6 cells.

Row category	Column category			Row total
	I	II	III	
A				200
B				300
Column total	120	200	180	500 = grand total

14.3 CELL COUNTS FOR INDEPENDENCE

We will be working with count data that are arranged in rows and columns of a table. There will be a row category and a column category, as illustrated in Table 14.1. The row and column rulings delineate *cells* in the table. Counts are placed in the cells. Thus, the upper left cell is the row A, column I cell.

The first step in a test for independence of the row and column categories is to determine, from given row and column totals, what the counts in each cell would be if the categories were independent. For the categories to be independent, all row and column pairs must be independent. Thus, in Table 14.1, row A and column I must be independent, as must row A and column II, and so on. The definition of statistical independence (see Section 5.12) states that A and I are independent if the probability of A *given* I equals the probability of A, that is, if

This is true if A and I are independent.

$$P(A|I) = P(A)$$

In the table, the probability $P(A)$ is

$$P(A) = \frac{\text{row A total}}{\text{grand total}}$$

Using A,I to mean the row A, column I cell, the probability of A given I is

$$P(A|I) = \frac{\text{count in A,I}}{\text{column I total}}$$

For independence, $P(A|I) = P(A)$; so

$$\frac{\text{Count in A,I}}{\text{Column I total}} = \frac{\text{row A total}}{\text{grand total}}$$

Thus, for independence, the cell count in cell A,I should be

$$\text{Count in A,I} = \frac{\text{row A total} \times \text{column I total}}{\text{grand total}}$$

$$= \frac{(200)(120)}{500}$$

$$= 48$$

In general, the *cell-count rule for independence* is

$$\text{Cell count} = \frac{(\text{cell row total}) \times (\text{cell column total})}{\text{grand total}}$$

EXERCISE Apply the cell-count rule to compute the cell count for A,II of Table 14.1.
ANSWER 80.

It is not necessary to apply the rule to every cell because some counts can be obtained by subtraction from the totals. For example, we found the first two counts in row A of Table 14.1 to be 48 and 80. The row A total is 200; so the count for row A, column III must be

$$200 - 48 - 80 = 72$$

Also, the B row counts can be obtained by subtraction after the row A counts have been determined.

The complete set of Table 14.1 cell counts for independence is given in Table 14.2. These counts are called the *expected frequencies* f_e.

TABLE 14.2
CELL COUNTS f_e FOR INDEPENDENCE

The f_e are indepen-
dence counts, not
actual sample counts.

Row category	I	II	III	Row total
A	48	80	72	200
B	72	120	108	300
Column total	120	200	180	500 = grand total

Whether some cell counts are obtained by applying the cell-count rule or by subtraction is of no importance. However, it is important to know how many counts *must* be obtained by the rule, because that number is v, the number of degrees of freedom. In general, the number of counts that must be obtained by the rule is the *number of rows minus one times the number of columns minus one*. Thus, for the two rows and three columns of Table 14.1, we must determine

Degrees of freedom
for χ^2 independence
test:

$v = (rows - 1)$
$\times (columns - 1)$

$$(2 - 1)(3 - 1) = 2$$

cell counts by the rule.

EXERCISE Suppose a table has 4 rows and 3 columns, and the row and column totals are given. In determining cell counts for independence, how many counts must be calculated by the cell-count rule?
ANSWER 6.

TABLE 14.3
CONTINGENCY TABLE OF OBSERVED AND
EXPECTED FREQUENCIES

Row category	Column category			Row total
		f_o f_e		
Column total				

14.4 THE CHI-SQUARE TEST FOR INDEPENDENCE

An r by c contingency table has r rows and c columns.

A *contingency* table consists of count data (obtained from a simple random sample) arranged in rows and columns. An *r* by *c* contingency table has *r* rows and *c* columns. The actual sample counts are called *observed frequencies*, and are denoted by f_o as illustrated in Table 14.3.

The expected and observed frequencies f_e and f_o are used to compute a sample statistic for testing the hypothesis that the row and column categories are independent. The underlying idea is that the observed frequencies should be close to the frequencies that would be expected *if* the categories are independent. Large differences will lead us to reject the hypothesis of independence. The statistic that is used for the test is called the *sample* χ^2. It is computed from the formula

H_0: row and column categories are independent

$$\text{Sample } \chi^2 = \sum \frac{(f_o - f_e)^2}{f_e}$$

Reject H_0 if sample χ^2 is large.

The formula shows that the larger the squared differences are relative to their respective expected frequencies, the larger will be the value of the sample χ^2. Therefore, large values of the sample χ^2 lead to rejecting the independence hypothesis.

The distribution of the sample χ^2 computed from a contingency table is approximated by a chi-square distribution with v degrees of freedom, where

$$v = (r - 1)(c - 1)$$

The chi-square approximation is satisfactory if the expected cell frequencies are not too small. To be specific, we shall follow the rule that each f_e value must be at least 5. If an f_e value is less than 5, we shall combine adjacent rows (or columns) in the contingency table to get f_e values of at least 5 before computing the sample χ^2; also v will be computed after combining rows or columns.

The steps followed in testing a contingency table for independence at significance level α parallel those we have followed in earlier tests; however, the hypotheses are stated in terms of independence. The hypotheses are

1. State the hypotheses.

H_0: the row and column categories are independent

H_a: the row and column categories are not independent

Significantly large values of the sample χ^2 statistic lead to the rejection of H_0; so the test is a right-tail test. The decision rule is

2. State the decision rule.

$$\text{Reject } H_0 \text{ if sample } \chi^2 > \chi^2_{\alpha,v}$$

where α = significance level of the test
$v = (r - 1)(c - 1)$

and $\chi^2_{\alpha,v}$ is found from Table IV at the end of the book.

To carry out the test, we compute the expected frequencies by the cell-count rule for independence

$$f_e = \frac{(\text{row total}) \times (\text{column total})}{\text{grand total}}$$

Then we compute

3. Compute the sample χ^2.

$$\text{Sample } \chi^2 = \sum \frac{(f_o - f_e)^2}{f_e}$$

Finally, we

4. Accept or reject H_0.

Accept or reject H_0, based on the decision rule and the sample χ^2

EXAMPLE David Gallano, a wine merchant, has collected opinions on grape wine quality from a random sample of his customers. The customers tasted wines made from grapes grown in three regions of the country; they rated wine quality on a scale of 1 (best) to 4. The sample data are given in Table 14.4. David wants to know whether quality ratings are or are not independent of the grape-growing region. Perform the test for independence at the 5 percent level.

TABLE 14.4
CUSTOMER QUALITY RATINGS OF WINE BY GRAPE-GROWING REGION

These are the sample frequencies f_o.

Quality rating	Growing region			Row total
	I	II	III	
1	15	10	6	31
2	7	13	12	32
3	11	12	8	31
4	3	8	15	26
Column total	36	43	41	120

SOLUTION The hypotheses are

1. H_0: quality rating is independent of growing region

   H_a: quality rating is not independent of growing region

Table 14.4 has $r = 4$ rows and $c = 3$ columns; it is a 4 by 3 contingency table. The number of degrees of freedom is

$$v = (r - 1)(c - 1) = (4 - 1)(3 - 1)$$
$$= 6$$

With significance level $\alpha = 0.05$, we find from Table IV that

$$\chi^2_{\alpha, v} = \chi^2_{0.05, 6} = 12.592$$

Consequently, the decision rule (illustrated in Figure 14.3) is

2. Reject H_0 if sample $\chi^2 > 12.592$

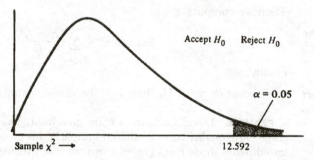

FIGURE 14.3
The decision rule for an independence test of grape region data: Reject H_0 if sample $\chi^2 > 12.592$.

Next we must compute the sample χ^2. We start by calculating the expected frequencies f_e for each cell in Table 14.4 by the cell-count rule. For example, for the cell in the first row, first column,

$$f_e = \frac{(\text{first row total}) \times (\text{first column total})}{\text{grand total}}$$

$$= \frac{(31)(36)}{120}$$

$$= 9.3$$

$v = (r - 1)(c - 1)$ **EXERCISE** See Table 14.4. (a) Compute f_e for the cell in the first row, second column. (b) How many cell frequencies must be computed by the cell-count rule?

ANSWER (a) 11.1; (b) 6.

Table 14.5 contains the observed and expected frequencies for each cell in Table 14.4. From these frequencies we compute the value of the test statistic

$$\text{Sample } \chi^2 = \sum \frac{(f_o - f_e)^2}{f_e}$$

TABLE 14.5
WINE QUALITY RATINGS: OBSERVED AND
EXPECTED FREQUENCIES
(Expected frequencies are in color)

*The expected fre-
quencies f_e (in color)
are computed from
the totals in Table
14.4.*

Quality rating	Growing region		
	I	II	III
1	15 9.3	10 11.1	6 10.6
2	7 9.6	13 11.5	12 10.9
3	11 9.3	12 11.1	8 10.6
4	3 7.8	8 9.3	15 8.9

TABLE 14.6
CALCULATION OF THE SAMPLE χ^2 VALUE

*Note that the sum of
the rightmost column
is*

$$\sum \frac{(f_o - f_e)^2}{f_e}$$

and not

$$\frac{\Sigma(f_o - f_e)^2}{\Sigma f_e}$$

Observed frequency f_o	Expected frequency f_e	$f_o - f_e$	$(f_o - f_e)^2$	$\dfrac{(f_o - f_e)^2}{f_e}$
15	9.3	5.7	32.49	3.4935
10	11.1	−1.1	1.21	0.1090
6	10.6	−4.6	21.16	1.9962
7	9.6	−2.6	6.76	0.7042
13	11.5	1.5	2.25	0.1957
12	10.9	1.1	1.21	0.1110
11	9.3	1.7	2.89	0.3108
12	11.1	0.9	0.81	0.0730
8	10.6	−2.6	6.76	0.6377
3	7.8	−4.8	23.04	2.9538
8	9.3	−1.3	1.69	0.1817
15	8.9	6.1	37.21	4.1809
				Sample χ^2 = 14.9475

as shown in Table 14.6.
We find that

3. Sample χ^2 = 14.9475

Because the value of the sample test statistic, 14.9475, exceeds the value
12.592 in the decision rule, we

4. Reject H_0

The test result means that customer quality rating of wine is not independent of the region where the wine grapes were grown. The sample provides
convincing evidence that quality rating depends on grape-growing region.

EXERCISE In the wine quality example, suppose 4 meant best and 1 meant
worst. Would this change our test result in any way? Explain.
ANSWER No. The order of the $(f_o - f_e)^2/f_e$ numbers in Table 14.6 would be
changed, but the values would be the same, and the sample χ^2 would still equal
14.9475.

14.5 TESTING THE EQUALITY OF MORE THAN TWO POPULATION PROPORTIONS

A test for the equality of two population proportions was described in Chapter 11. The hypotheses there were

$$H_0: p_1 = p_2 \quad \text{and} \quad H_a: p_1 \neq p_2$$

The chi-square test described in the last section also can be used to test for the equality of two proportions, or more than two proportions.

The test for equal proportions is performed in exactly the same way as the test for independence. In fact, the test for independence is the same as a test that, in any row, the cell proportions to column totals, p_r, are equal; and in any column, the cell proportions to row totals are equal. To illustrate this, refer to Table 14.2, where you will find that the cell proportions to column totals in the first row are

This equality of pro-
portions gives rise to
the expected fre-
quencies f_e.

$$p_r = \frac{48}{120} = \frac{80}{200} = \frac{72}{180} = 0.40$$

And the corresponding proportions in the second row are all 0.60. Similarly, the cell proportions to row totals in the first column are

$$\frac{48}{200} = \frac{72}{300} = 0.24$$

EXERCISE In Table 14.2, what are the cell proportions to row totals (a) in the second column? (b) in the third column?
ANSWER (a) 0.40; (b) 0.36.

p_r means cell
proportions to
column total.

The hypotheses of the test for equal proportions can be stated either in terms of equal row proportions or in terms of equal column proportions. We will use row proportions p_r (that is, cell proportions to column totals) in our hypotheses. The hypotheses will be

H_0: the proportions p_r in any row are equal

H_a: the p_r in at least one row are not equal

EXAMPLE Table 14.7 contains counts for a random sample of $n = 200$

TABLE 14.7
PERFORMANCE RATING OF WORKERS BY EDUCATIONAL LEVEL

Supervisor rating	Educational level			Row total
	No high school (1)	High school, but not completed (2)	Completed high school (3)	
Satisfactory	12	63	65	140
Not satisfactory	8	17	35	60
Column total	20	80	100	200

workers. It shows, for example, that 12 workers who had not gone to high school were rated as satisfactory by a supervisor. We want to test (at the $\alpha = 0.05$ level) the hypothesis that the population proportions of satisfactory workers in education levels 1, 2, and 3 are equal.

SOLUTION   The hypothesis that the population proportions are all equal, and the alternative hypothesis, are expressed as

1. Hypotheses

$$H_0: \text{the cell proportions } p_r \text{ in any row are equal}$$

$$H_a: \text{the cell proportions in at least one row are not equal}$$

Table 14.7 has $r = 2$ rows and $c = 3$ columns; so the number of degrees of freedom is

$$v = (r - 1)(c - 1) = (2 - 1)(3 - 1)$$
$$= 2$$

With $\alpha = 0.05$ and $v = 2$, we find from Table IV that

$$\chi^2_{0.05,2} = 5.991$$

Hence, the decision rule is

2. Decision rule

$$\text{Reject } H_0 \text{ if sample } \chi^2 > 5.991$$

Next we must compute the expected frequencies. For row 1, column 1 of Table 14.7, we find

$$f_e = \frac{(\text{cell row total}) \times (\text{cell column total})}{\text{grand total}}$$

$$= \frac{140(20)}{200} = 14$$

Similar computations lead to the expected frequencies shown in color in Table 14.8.

TABLE 14.8
PERFORMANCE RATING OBSERVED AND EXPECTED FREQUENCIES
(Expected frequencies are in color)

Note that we need not compute the actual proportions to do the test.

Supervisor rating	Educational level			Row total
	No high school (1)	High school but not completed (2)	Completed high school (3)	
Satisfactory	12 14	63 56	65 70	140
Not satisfactory	8 6	17 24	35 30	60
Column total	20	80	100	200

TABLE 14.9
PERFORMANCE RATING χ^2 CALCULATION

f_o	f_e	$f_o - f_e$	$(f_o - f_e)^2$	$(f_o - f_e)^2/f_e$
12	14	−2	4	0.2857
63	56	7	49	0.8750
65	70	−5	25	0.3571
8	6	2	4	0.6667
17	24	−7	49	2.0417
35	30	5	25	0.8333
				$\chi^2 = 5.0595$

Table 14.9 shows the computation of the sample χ^2 value from the observed and expected frequencies in Table 14.8. We find that

3. Sample χ^2

$$\text{Sample } \chi^2 = 5.0595$$

The sample χ^2 value does not exceed the value 5.991 in the decision rule; so we

4. Accept or reject.

$$\text{Accept } H_0$$

Accepting H_0 means that the proportion of satisfactory-rated workers is the same for all three educational levels.

14.6 PROBLEMS

1. Compute the sample χ^2 for an independence test of the random sample data in Table A. Write the null hypothesis.

TABLE A

Category I	Category II	
	C	D
A	20	40
B	61	59

2. Compute the sample χ^2 for an independence test of the random sample data in Table B. Write the null hypothesis.

TABLE B

Category I	Category II		
	C	D	E
A	9	54	57
B	11	26	43

3. In 3 by 5 contingency tables, what values of the sample χ^2 statistic will lead to rejection of the null hypothesis of independence at the 5 percent level?

4. In 2 by 4 contingency tables, what values of the sample χ^2 statistic will lead to rejection of the null hypothesis of equal proportions at the 1 percent level?

5. Jeanette Peters, a security analyst for Peters, Peters, and Paul, classified a random sample of stocks in four industries as being high, average, or low in terms of safety to buyers of the stocks. Jeanette's data are in Table C. Perform a test of the independence of safety ratings and industry classification. (Take $\alpha = 0.01$.)

TABLE C

Stock safety rating	Industry category			
	I	II	III	IV
High	25	18	29	12
Average	32	30	42	20
Low	13	32	14	33

6. Bill Cramer, an investment broker, believes that on a day when morning business activity is slack, afternoon activity also tends to be slack. Consequently, he is thinking of taking an occasional afternoon off when morning activity is slack. Bill has collected a random sample of days and tabulated morning and afternoon activity as shown in Table D. Are morning activity and afternoon activity independent? Explain. (Test at the 1 percent level.)

TABLE D

Morning activity	Afternoon activity	
	Slack	Active
Slack	13	7
Active	31	29

7. Forbes Hotel has rooms in the high, average, and low price levels. The owner advertises high-quality service in all rooms. Opinions of the service obtained from a random sample of guests are given in Table E. Are guests ratings independent of price? Test at the 1 percent level.

TABLE E

Guest service rating	Room price		
	High	Average	Low
Excellent	14	25	11
Good	20	66	14
Poor	6	19	5

8. Vota Company makes equipment for controlling the operations of machines. Vota equipment defects are of four types, A, B, C, and D. Vota operates three shifts each day, shifts 1, 2, and 3. Data for random samples of defects, by shift and type of defect, are given in Table F. Perform, at the 2 percent level, a test of the hypothesis that defect type and shift are independent.

TABLE F

Shift	Defect type			
	A	B	C	D
1	12	30	10	16
2	16	22	11	8
3	14	12	3	6

9. The credit manager of Plaza Stores obtained data for a random sample of credit customers and recorded the data in Table G. Perform, at the 5 percent level, a test of the hypothesis that time to pay is independent of residence region.

TABLE G

Days until payment of last bill	Customer residence region		
	Urban	Suburban	Rural
Under 15	31	61	28
15–30	72	87	41
Over 30	37	32	11

10. The personnel manager of Vorhees National Enterprises collected the data in Table H for a random sample of Vorhees middle managers. Perform, at the 1 percent level, a test of the hypothesis that the proportions p_r in any row are equal.

TABLE H

Top management rating of middle manager performance	Middle manager expression of satisfaction with job (5 is highest satisfaction)				
	1	2	3	4	5
Excellent	6	7	19	17	17
Average	11	10	21	16	16
Below average	15	17	6	7	5

11. The quality-control manager of Vota Company examined a random sample of parts made during the three shifts that the company operates. The manager classified the parts as good or defective as

shown in Table I. Perform, at the 5 percent level, a test of the hypothesis that equal proportions of defective parts are made by the three shifts.

TABLE I

	Shift		
	Day	Middle	Night
Number of good parts	427	273	240
Number of defective parts	23	27	10

12. The makers of Sparkle toothpaste wanted to determine if equal proportions of men, women, and children like the taste of Sparkle. They collected a random sample of opinions from toothpaste users and classified the opinions as shown in Table J. Perform, at the 5 percent level, a test of the hypothesis that equal proportions like the taste of Sparkle.

TABLE J

Opinion	Men	Women	Children
Like taste of Sparkle	20	51	32
Do not like taste of Sparkle	10	9	16

13. A company is considering four areas as possible locations for a manufacturing plant. Each area has about the same number of workers. The company needs skilled workers and wants to determine whether the proportions of skilled workers in the areas are the same. Random sample data are given in Table K. At the 5 percent level, perform a test of the hypothesis that the four areas have the same proportion of skilled workers.

TABLE K

	Area			
Number of	A	B	C	D
Skilled workers	89	99	103	82
Unskilled workers	161	151	148	168

14. Dobart Insurance Company gathered the random sample data in Table

TABLE L

	Car size		
Type of injury	Small	Medium	Large
Fatal or critical	89	35	21
Not fatal or critical	171	84	61

L. Dobart wants to determine whether the proportion of fatal or critical injury accidents is the same for different-sized cars. At the 5 percent level, perform a test of the hypothesis of equal proportions.

14.7 GOODNESS-OF-FIT TESTS

Goodness-of-fit tests use sample data as a basis for accepting or rejecting assumptions about a population's distribution. The assumptions are stated as the null hypothesis. For example, a test of

$$H_0: \text{The population is normal with } \mu = 50 \text{ and } \sigma = 5$$

A goodness-of-fit test is a hypothesis test.

is a goodness-of-fit test.

A goodness-of-fit test is performed by first computing the frequencies that would be expected if H_0 is true; then the differences between the frequencies observed in the sample f_o and the expected frequencies f_e are used to calculate

$$\text{Sample } \chi^2 = \sum \frac{(f_o - f_e)^2}{f_e}$$

Finally, the sample χ^2 is compared with the appropriate $\chi^2_{\alpha,v}$ in Table IV to decide whether H_0 should be accepted or rejected.

Goodness-of-fit tests differ from independence tests both in the methods used to compute expected frequencies and in the rule for determining the number of degrees of freedom. In a goodness-of-fit test, the method for calculating the expected frequencies depends on the population assumptions that are made; and the *number of degrees of freedom in a goodness-of-fit test* is

Degrees of freedom for a goodness-of-fit test

$$v = n_e - 1 - g$$

where n_e = number of f_e values used in computing the sample χ^2

g = number of population parameters estimated from the sample

Goodness-of-Fit: Uniform Distribution

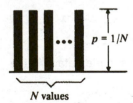

$p = 1/N$

N values

A random variable that can have one of N values has a uniform distribution if every value has the same probability $1/N$ of occurring. To test the hypothesis that a random variable has a uniform distribution we obtain a random sample of size n and record the frequency of occurrence f_o of each of the N values. Then we compute the (equal) frequencies f_e that would be expected if the variable has a uniform distribution. Since the probability of any value is $1/N$ and the sample contains n values, we expect the frequency of each value in the sample will be

$$f_e = \frac{1}{N}(n) = \frac{n}{N}$$

That is, for example, if a uniformly distributed random variable can have one of $N = 5$ values and we have a sample of $n = 400$, then the expected frequency for each value is

$$f_e = \frac{n}{N} = \frac{400}{5} = 80$$

The sample χ^2, computed as in previous sections from the f_o and f_e frequencies, is used to decide whether the uniform distribution hypothesis will be accepted or rejected.

EXAMPLE A winning number in a Massachusetts lottery is a four-digit number such as 1083 or 4416. Digits in the winning number are assumed to be drawn at random. It is assumed that the winning digit population has a uniform distribution; that is, each of the $N = 10$ integers 0, 1, 2, 3, . . . , 9 has the same probability $(1/N = ^1/_{10})$ of being selected for each place in a winning number. Lou Diamond plays the lottery regularly. She keeps a running tally of digits in past winning numbers, and plays (bets on) a four-digit number made up of digits that have occurred most frequently in the past. Lou's system is based on the supposition that some digits (the ones that have occurred most frequently in the past) have higher probabilities of occurring than others; that is, the winning digit population does not have a uniform distribution.

We will use a random sample of 400 winning digits to test, at the 5 percent level, the hypothesis that the population distribution is uniform. The hypotheses are

1. H_0: the distribution is uniform

   H_a: the distribution is not uniform

The sample data are given in the second column of Table 14.10. There are 400 observations. If H_0 is true, each of the 10 digits has a probability of

TABLE 14.10
χ^2 CALCULATION FOR LOTTERY DIGITS

Digit	Observed f_0	Expected f_e	$f_0 - f_e$	$(f_0 - f_e)^2$	$\dfrac{(f_0 - f_e)^2}{f_e}$
0	41	40	1	1	1/40
1	54	40	14	196	196/40
2	31	40	− 9	81	81/40
3	39	40	− 1	1	1/40
4	35	40	− 5	25	25/40
5	36	40	− 4	16	16/40
6	56	40	16	256	256/40
7	38	40	− 2	4	4/40
8	31	40	− 9	81	81/40
9	39	40	− 1	1	1/40
	400				$\chi^2 = $ 662/40

$1/10$ of occurring. The expected frequency for each digit f_e, given in the third column, is

$$f_e = \frac{n}{N} = \frac{400}{10}$$
$$= 40$$

Recall:
For the χ^2 approxi-
mation, each f_e must
be at least 5.

There are $n_e = 10$ computed f_e values, all of which are at least 5; and we did not estimate any population parameters in order to compute the f_e values. Consequently, the number of parameter estimates g is zero; and the number of degrees of freedom is

$$v = n_e - 1 - g = 10 - 1 - 0$$
$$= 9$$

With $\alpha = 0.05$ and $v = 9$, we find

$$\chi^2_{\alpha,v} = \chi^2_{0.05,9} = 16.919$$

from Table IV. Hence, the decision rule is

2. Reject H_0 if sample $\chi^2 > 16.919$

Table 14.10 shows the calculation leading to the sample χ^2 value $662/40$, which is 16.55. Thus,

3. Sample $\chi^2 = 16.55$

The sample χ^2 does not exceed the value 16.919 in the decision rule; so we

4. Accept H_0

Accepting H_0 means accepting the assumption that the winning digit population is uniform. Consequently, the test result does not support Lou's supposition that some digits have a higher probability of occurring than other digits.

Figure 14.4 shows the observed and expected frequencies of occurrence that led us to accept H_0. Notice that the observed sample frequencies are not exactly uniformly distributed; however, their differences from uniform frequencies are not large enough to lead us to reject the uniform distribution hypothesis at the 5 percent level.

Incidentally, the fact that the sample $\chi^2 = 16.55$ is only a little less than $\chi^2_{0.05,9} = 16.919$ might dampen our enthusiasm for accepting H_0; but the smallness of the difference does not alter the conclusion. The point of importance is this: in correctly applying statistical inference, the analyst must

You choose α; the
test will do the rest.

choose a value for α that is consistent with his or her attitude toward the consequences of rejecting a true H_0. That choice should be made before the sample statistic is computed; and that choice establishes the decision rule the analyst should be willing to apply—no matter how close the value of the sample statistic is to the value in the decision rule.

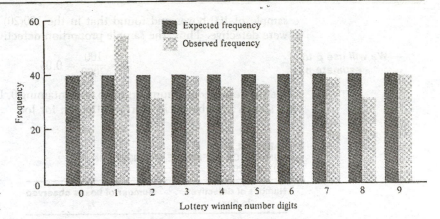

FIGURE 14.4
Expected and ob-
served lottery digit fre-
quencies.

EXERCISE Suppose the Massachusetts Lottery Commissioner set $\alpha = 0.01$, and then used the sample data of Table 14.10 to test H_0. What would the test result be? Why?

ANSWER Accept H_0 because the sample $\chi^2 = 16.55$ is less than $\chi^2_{0.01,9} = 21.666$.

Goodness-of-Fit: Binomial Distribution

A particular binomial distribution (Chapter 7) is specified by the values of two parameters, n and p, where

$$n = \text{sample size (or number of trials)}$$

$$p = \text{probability of success in a trial}$$

From tables such as IA, IB, and IC at the end of the book, we can calculate the probability of 0, 1, 2, 3, . . . successes in n trials. Each of these probabilities, when multiplied by the sample size n, is an *expected frequency* for the number of successes in n trials.

f_e of r successes =
$n \times P(r$ successes)

EXAMPLE Fizz Company makes compressed-gas cylinders used for carbonating water and inflating life vests. Cylinders are sold in boxes of 20. Occasionally, a cylinder will be defective (too low in pressure). Customers have been complaining about defectives. Many have returned all cylinders left in a box when one defective is found, stating that if one is defective the chances are that others also are defective. Joseph Popp, the quality-control manager of Fizz, states that the overall proportion of defective cylinders is at an acceptable low level, and that the number of defective cylinders in boxes of 20 has a binomial distribution. Joe also points out that if he is correct, it would be unlikely that any box would contain several defective cylinders. Joe wants to test, at the 5 percent level, the hypothesis that the number of defectives in boxes of 20 has a binomial distribution. He obtained a random sample of 100 boxes and found that in the $100(20) = 2000$ cylinders, 100 were defective. Thus, the sample proportion defective is

We will use $\bar{p}$ to estimate p.

$$\bar{p} = \frac{100}{2000} = 0.05$$

Joe also recorded the numbers of boxes containing 0, 1, 2, 3, . . . defectives as shown in Table 14.11. Perform the test for Joe.

TABLE 14.11
NUMBER OF DEFECTIVE CYLINDERS IN A
BOX OF 20

Number of defectives in box	Number of boxes observed f_o
0	39
1	34
2	20
3	4
4	1
5	2
6 or more	0
	100

SOLUTION We first need to find the expected numbers of defectives for a binomial distribution with $n = 20$ and $p = 0.05$. (Note that the value just stated for p is the sample estimate computed above. That will cost one degree of freedom when v is determined.) From Table IB with $p = 0.05$, the probability of $r = 0$ successes (defectives) is 0.3585. Therefore, the expected frequency of 0 defectives in 100 boxes is

$$f_e(0) = 0.3585(100) = 35.85$$

Now we must remember that Table IB is cumulative, so that the entry 0.7358 for $r = 1$ means $P(0) + P(1) = 0.7358$ or, in summation symbols,

$$P(0) + P(1) = \sum_0^1 P(r)$$

so that

$$P(1) = \sum_0^1 P(r) - P(0) = 0.7358 - 0.3585$$

$$= 0.3773$$

Consequently, the expected frequency for 1 defective in the 100-box sample is

$$f_e(1) = 100(0.3773) = 37.73$$

Similarly,

$$P(2) = \sum_0^2 P(r) - \sum_0^1 P(r) = 0.9245 - 0.7358$$

$$= 0.1887$$

So the expected frequency for 2 defectives is

$$f_e(2) = 100(0.1887) = 18.87$$

EXERCISE Compute the expected frequency for 3 defectives in the 100-box sample.
ANSWER 5.96.

The observed and expected frequencies for Joe's sample are shown in Table 14.12. Before computing χ^2, we will combine the bracketed fre-

TABLE 14.12
OBSERVED AND EXPECTED NUMBERS OF
DEFECTIVE CYLINDERS

	Number of boxes	
Number of defectives in box	f_o	f_e
0	39	35.85
1	34	37.73
2	20	18.87
3	4	5.96
4	1	1.33
5	2	0.23
6	0	0.03
7 or more	0	0.00
	100	100.00

These classes will be combined so that no class has $f_e < 5$.

quencies in the table so that the resultant expected frequency in each row is at least 5. The combined frequencies and the sample χ^2 calculation are shown in Table 14.13.

TABLE 14.13
CALCULATION OF χ^2 FOR
DEFECTIVE CYLINDERS

Number defective	f_o	f_e	$f_o - f_e$	$\dfrac{(f_o - f_e)^2}{f_e}$
0	39	35.85	3.15	0.2768
1	34	37.73	-3.73	0.3687
2	20	18.87	1.13	0.0677
3 or more	7	7.55	-0.55	0.0401
			$\chi^2 =$	0.7533

I did not state the decision rule at the beginning because, when goodness-of-fit tests are performed, it is often not possible to know how many degrees of freedom there will be until after the expected frequencies are computed; that's because it may be necessary to combine some frequencies before the sample χ^2 is computed. So now that we have the information needed to determine the number of degrees of freedom, let's start at the beginning. The hypotheses are

Note that n_e was reduced to 4 in Table 14.13.

1. H_0: the distribution is a binomial with $n = 20$

   H_a: the distribution is not a binomial with $n = 20$

The number of degrees of freedom is

$$v = n_e - 1 - g$$

where n_e = number of f_e values used in computing the sample χ^2
g = number of parameters estimated from the sample

In Table 14.13, we have $n_e = 4$ values of f_e. Also, we estimated the value of one parameter ($p = 0.05$) from the sample; so

$$v = 4 - 1 - 1 = 2$$

degrees of freedom. With $\alpha = 0.05$, we find

$$\chi^2_{\alpha,v} = \chi^2_{0.05,2} = 5.991$$

from Table IV. Hence, the decision rule is

2. Reject H_0 if sample $\chi^2 > 5.991$

From Table 14.13,

3. Sample $\chi^2 = 0.7533$

which does not exceed the 5.991 of the rule. Hence, we

4. Accept H_0

Thus, the sample evidence supports Joe's hypothesis that the distribution of the number of defective cylinders in boxes of 20 is a binomial distribution

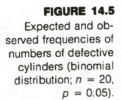

FIGURE 14.5
Expected and observed frequencies of numbers of defective cylinders (binomial distribution; $n = 20$, $p = 0.05$).

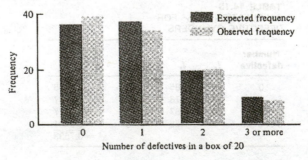

with $n = 20$. Figure 14.5 shows that the frequencies expected for a binomial with $n = 20$ and $p = 0.05$ appear to "fit" the observed frequencies quite closely.

Goodness-of-Fit: Normal Distribution

The test of a normal fit parallels the binomial fit test in the foregoing, only now the expected frequencies are determined using the normal probabilities in Table V at the end of the book.

EXAMPLE For inventory planning and control purposes, Krupp Chemical Company wants to know if its sales of a liquid chemical are normally distributed. Sales for a random sample of 200 days are given in Table 14.14. The

TABLE 14.14
SALES FOR 200 DAYS

Sales (thousands of gallons)	Number of days, f_o
Less than 34.0	0
34.0 and under 35.5	13
35.5 and under 37.0	20
37.0 and under 38.5	35
38.5 and under 40.0	43
40.0 and under 41.5	51
41.5 and under 43.0	27
43.0 and under 44.5	10
44.5 and under 46.0	1
46.0 or more	0
	$\overline{200}$

sample mean and sample standard deviation calculated from the 200 sample daily sales numbers (calculations not shown) are

$$\bar{x} = 40 \text{ thousand gallons}$$

$$s_x = 2.5 \text{ thousand gallons}$$

At the 5 percent level, perform a test of the hypothesis that sales are normally distributed. (The values to be used for the parameters μ and σ are the sample estimates. That will cost us 2 degrees of freedom when we compute the value of v.)

SOLUTION To compute the expected frequency for the "less than 34.0" class, we first find the probability for this class, and then multiply this probability by the sample size, 200. Figure 14.6 shows the hypothesized normal distribution, and the tail area that corresponds to P(less than 34 thousand).

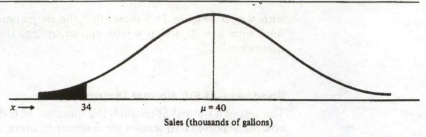

FIGURE 14.6

A normal distribution of sales.

$x \longrightarrow \qquad 34 \qquad\qquad\qquad \mu = 40$

Sales (thousands of gallons)

At $x = 34$, we compute

z values must be computed to enter Table V.

$$z = \frac{x - \mu}{\sigma} = \frac{34 - 40}{2.5}$$
$$= -2.4$$

From Table V,

$$P(0 \text{ to } -2.4) = P(0 \text{ to } 2.4) = 0.4918$$

The tail area probability we want is

$$0.5 - P(0 \text{ to } -2.4) = 0.5 - 0.4918 = 0.0082$$

Because the sample includes 200 numbers, the expected frequency for the "less than 34.0" class is

$$f_e = 0.0082(200) = 1.64$$

EXERCISE Compute the expected frequency for the "34.0 and under 35.5" class.

ANSWER 5.54.

The complete list of expected frequencies, computed as just illustrated, is given in the fourth column of Table 14.15. After combining frequencies so

TABLE 14.15

CALCULATION OF EXPECTED FREQUENCIES AND THE SAMPLE χ^2 FOR A NORMAL GOODNESS-OF-FIT TEST

Sales class	Observed f_o	Sales class probability	200 times probability, f_e	$f_o - f_e$	$\dfrac{(f_o - f_e)^2}{f_e}$
Less than 34.0	0 ⎤ 13	0.0082	1.64 ⎤ 7.18	5.82	4.7176
34.0 and under 35.5	13 ⎦	0.0277	5.54 ⎦		
35.5 and under 37.0	20	0.0792	15.84	4.16	1.0925
37.0 and under 38.5	35	0.1592	31.84	3.16	0.3136
38.5 and under 40.0	43	0.2257	45.14	−2.14	0.1015
40.0 and under 41.5	51	0.2257	45.14	5.86	0.7607
41.5 and under 43.0	27	0.1592	31.84	−4.84	0.7357
43.0 and under 44.5	10	0.0792	15.84	−5.84	2.1531
44.5 and under 46.0	1 ⎤ 1	0.0277	5.54 ⎤ 7.18	−6.18	5.3193
46.0 or more	0 ⎦	0.0082	1.64 ⎦		
				$\chi^2 =$	15.1940

that all f_e values are at least 5, the sample χ^2 is computed to be 15.1940. Now let's summarize the test.

The hypotheses are

1. H_0: the distribution is normally distributed

    H_a: the distribution is not normally distributed

The sample χ^2 was computed using $n_e = 8$ expected frequencies. Two parameters, μ and σ, were estimated from the sample. Hence, the number of degrees of freedom is

Recall: g is the number of parameter values estimated from the sample.

$$v = n_e - 1 - g$$

$$v = 8 - 1 - 2 = 5 \text{ degrees of freedom}$$

With $\alpha = 0.05$, $\chi^2_{0.05,5} = 11.070$ (Table IV); so the decision rule is

2. Reject H_0 if sample $\chi^2 > 11.070$

From Table 14.15,

3. Sample $\chi^2 = 15.1940$

The sample χ^2 exceeds the value 11.070 in the decision rule, so we

4. Reject H_0

Our conclusion is that daily sales are not normally distributed.

Figure 14.7 shows that the expected and observed frequencies appear to

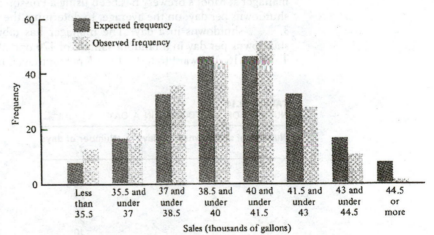

FIGURE 14.7
Expected and observed sales frequencies.

correspond quite closely. However, in each tail the difference between the frequencies is large *relative* to the expected frequency: and that makes for a large sample χ^2. To see this, check the rightmost column of Table 14.15. The first and last entries (the tails) are 4.7176 and 5.3193. Their sum, 10.0369, is about two-thirds of the total sample χ^2 value, 15.1940.

Goodness-of-Fit: Poisson Distribution

The Poisson process formula (Chapter 8) provides the probability of the number of "arrivals" in an interval of time. The formula is

When t = 1, this formula simplifies . . .

$$P(x) = \frac{e^{-\lambda t}(\lambda t)^x}{x!}$$

where x = number of arrivals in t units of time
λ = average arrival rate per unit of time
t = number of units of time

In this section we will let $t = 1$ unit of time; so $\lambda t = \lambda(1) = \lambda$. Then the formula becomes

. . . to this formula.

$$P(x) = \frac{e^{-\lambda}(\lambda)^x}{x!}$$

where x = number of arrivals in 1 unit of time
λ = average arrival rate per unit of time

The formula (or a table such as Table IIIA at the end of the book) is used to determine expected frequencies in a test of the hypothesis that a distribution is a Poisson distribution with a stated value of the parameter λ.

EXAMPLE   When a beer bottle filling machine breaks a bottle, the machine must be shut down while the broken glass is removed. The production manager at Moor's Brewery has been using a Poisson distribution with $\lambda = 3$ shutdowns per day, on the average, to determine the probabilities of 0, 1, 2, 3, . . . shutdowns in a day. The manager has tabulated the number of shutdowns per day in a random sample of 120 operating days, as shown in Table 14.16. We want to test, at the 5 percent level, the hypothesis that the

TABLE 14.16
NUMBER OF SHUTDOWNS IN A DAY

Number of shutdowns in a day x	Number of days f_o
0	3
1	20
2	29
3	22
4	23
5	10
6 or more	13

number of shutdowns in a day has a Poisson distribution with $\lambda t = \lambda = 3$.

SOLUTION   The formula for the probability of x shutdowns in a day

$$P(x) = \frac{e^{-\lambda}(\lambda)^x}{x!}$$

is

$$P(x) = \frac{e^{-3}(3)^x}{x!}$$

To compute the expected number of days when there will be $x = 0$ shut-downs, we first compute

$$P(0) = \frac{e^{-3}(3)^0}{0!}$$

$$= \frac{e^{-3}(1)}{1}$$

$$= 0.0498$$

Then we multiply $P(0)$ by the number of days in the sample, 120, to obtain

$$f_e(0) = 0.0498(120) = 5.976$$

as the expected frequency of $x = 0$ shutdowns. Poisson probabilities can be computed on a hand calculator, or they can be found in Table IIIA at the end of the book.

The probability of a or more arrivals is 1 minus the probability that the number of arrivals is 0, or 1, or 2, or . . . , or $(a - 1)$. That is,

$$P(a \text{ or more}) = 1 - \sum_{x=0}^{a-1} P(x)$$

In our example

$$P(6 \text{ or more}) = 1 - \sum_{0}^{b} P(x)$$

Thus, in the third column of Table 14.17,

TABLE 14.17
CALCULATION OF EXPECTED FREQUENCIES AND χ^2 FOR
TESTING A POISSON FIT

Number of shutdowns in a day x	Number of days f_o	$P(x)$ from Table IIIA	120 times $P(x)$ f_e	$f_o - f_e$	$\frac{(f_o - f_e)^2}{f_e}$
0	3	0.0498	5.976	−2.976	1.482
1	20	0.1494	17.928	2.072	0.239
2	29	0.2240	26.880	2.120	0.167
3	22	0.2240	26.880	−4.880	0.886
4	23	0.1680	20.160	2.840	0.400
5	10	0.1008	12.096	−2.096	0.363
6 or more	13	0.0840	10.080	2.920	0.846
					$\chi^2 = 4.383$

How to compute P
(6 or more)

$$P(6 \text{ or more}) = 1 - P(0) - P(1) - \cdots - P(5)$$
$$= 1 - (0.0498) - (0.1494) - \cdots - (0.1008)$$
$$= 0.0840$$

Therefore,

$$f_e(6 \text{ or more}) = (0.0840)(120) = 10.080$$

EXERCISE For the brewery example, use Table IIIA to compute the expected number of days when there will be 4 shutdowns.
ANSWER 20.160.

All the expected frequencies are given in the fourth column of Table 14.17.

Now, let's summarize our findings. We started with

1. H_0: the number of shutdowns per day is a Poisson distribution with $\lambda = 3$ per day

   H_a: the number of shutdowns per day is not a Poisson distribution with $\lambda = 3$ per day

In Table 14.17, we computed the sample χ^2 using $n_e = 7$ expected frequencies; the parameter λ was not estimated from the sample (it is stated in H_0). Consequently

$$v = n_e - 1 - g = 7 - 1 - 0$$
$$= 6$$

With $\alpha = 0.05$, we find $\chi^2_{0.05,6} = 12.592$ in Table IV. Hence, the decision rule is

2. Reject H_0 if sample $\chi^2 > 12.592$

Next, from Table 14.17

3. Sample $\chi^2 = 4.383$

The sample χ^2 does not exceed the 12.592 in the decision rule; so we

4. Accept H_0

Accepting H_0 means we conclude that shutdowns have a Poisson distribution with an average of $\lambda = 3$ shutdowns per day.

14.8 PROBLEMS

1. Table A contains random sample data on the number of workers absent from Muckross Company. The sample contained the same number (10) of Mondays, Tuesdays, and so on. Does it appear that number of workers absent is uniformly distributed over days of the week? (Perform a goodness-of-fit test at the 5 percent level.)

TABLE A

Day	Number of workers absent
Monday	15
Tuesday	9
Wednesday	9
Thursday	11
Friday	16

2. Fowl and Sons makes and sells large, expensive papermaking machines. Their four sales territories have been set up in a way that is supposed to provide the same sales potential in each sales territory. Sales data for a random sample of selling periods are given in Table B. Does it appear that sales are uniformly distributed over the sales territories? (Perform a goodness-of-fit test at the 5 percent level.)

TABLE B

Sales territory	I	II	III	IV
Number of machines sold	17	36	22	37

3. The possible numbers of spots showing after a die is tossed are 1, 2, 3, 4, 5, and 6. (*a*) Suppose a die is tossed 120 times. What are the expected frequencies for the spot numbers? (*b*) Toss a die 120 times and tabulate the observed frequencies of the spot numbers. (*c*) Does it appear that the spot numbers have a uniform distribution? (Perform a goodness-of-fit test at the 1 percent level.)

4. Jay Company wants to know if binomial probabilities can be used in a statistical decision analysis that involves the number of people who have seen their advertisement. They obtained 200 random samples of 10 people. The number of successes (those who saw the advertisement) in the samples of size 10 are given in Table C. At the 10 percent

TABLE C

Number of successes	Frequency
0	15
1	30
2	50
3	54
4	31
5	14
6	5
7	1
8 or more	0
	200

level, perform a test of the hypothesis that the distribution of numbers of successes is binomial with $n = 10$ and $p = 0.25$.

5. A manufacturer packages drinking glasses in boxes of 50. All glasses from a sample of 100 boxes were examined, and the number of defective glasses in each box was recorded. The sample data are given in Table D. (a) How many glasses were examined? (b) How many defective glasses were found? (c) Compute the sample proportion defective. (d) Do the sample data support the null hypothesis that the numbers of defective glasses in a box are binomially distributed? (Perform a goodness-of-fit test at the 5 percent level.)

TABLE D

Number of defectives in a box	Number of boxes
0	69
1	22
2	4
3	1
4	3
5	1

6. Sampson, Inc., a mail-order firm, sends out special item advertisements in batches of 50 at a time. Sampson's sales manager believes that the probability of receiving an order as a result of any one advertisement is 0.05. The manager wants to test the hypothesis that the distribution of numbers of orders in batches of 50 is a binomial distribution with $p = 0.05$. Data for a random sample of 120 mailings are given in Table E. Perform a goodness-of-fit test at the 5 percent level.

TABLE E

Number of orders received from a mailing of 50 advertisements	Observed frequency
0	16
1	30
2	40
3	20
4	10
5	3
6	1
7 or more	0
	120

7. Scotty McPhearson wanted to test the assumption that diameters of shafts made by an automatic machine are normally distributed. Scotty obtained a random sample of 150 shafts. Then he computed the sample

mean and the sample standard deviation. Next, using the sample mean as μ and the sample standard deviation as σ, he computed the z value for each sample shaft diameter. Finally, Scotty recorded his results in Table F. Perform a normal distribution goodness-of-fit test at the 5 percent level.

TABLE F

Shaft diameter class (z values)	Observed number of shafts
Less than −2.5	1
−2.5 and under −1.5	11
−1.5 and under −0.5	33
−0.5 and under 0.5	51
0.5 and under 1.5	47
1.5 and under 2.5	7
2.5 or more	0
	150

8. Do the random sample data in Table G support the hypothesis that the population of test scores is normally distributed with $\mu = 500$ and $\sigma = 100$. (Perform a goodness-of-fit test at the 10 percent level.)

TABLE G

Test score interval	Observed frequency
Less than 260	3
260 and under 340	5
340 and under 420	35
420 and under 500	63
500 and under 580	51
580 and under 660	28
660 and under 740	8
740 or more	7
	200

9. A seed grower sells Early Prize corn seed. A random sample of 1000 seeds was planted to determine how many hours it takes for seeds to germinate. Data for the 1000 seeds are given in Table H (at the top of page 512). The sample mean and the sample standard deviation were, respectively, 150 hours and 12 hours. Does it appear that "hours to germinate" is normally distributed? (Perform a goodness-of-fit test at the 1 percent level.)

10. (See Problem 6.) Delilah Sampson believes the receipt of orders per mailing has a Poisson distribution with an average of two orders arriving per mailing. Perform a goodness-of-fit test of Delilah's belief at the 5 percent level.

TABLE H

Hours to germinate	Number of seeds
Less than 120	10
120 and under 126	21
126 and under 132	50
132 and under 138	110
138 and under 144	160
144 and under 150	200
150 and under 156	210
156 and under 162	120
162 and under 168	60
168 and under 174	36
174 and under 180	19
180 or more	4
	1000

11. Planes landing at an airport are classified as scheduled or unscheduled. A random sample of hourly observations provided the Table I data on numbers of unscheduled plane landings. (a) Compute the sample average number of landings per hour. (b) Does number of landings per hour appear to have a Poisson distribution? (Estimate λ by calculating average landings per hour from the table. (Perform a goodness-of-fit test at the 5 percent level.)

TABLE I

Number of planes landing in 1 hour	Frequency
0	24
1	35
2	43
3	25
4	16
5	4
6	2
7	0
8	1
9 or more	0

12. Table J contains data on the number of customers entering a store in a random sample of 1-minute time intervals. Does the number of customers entering appear to have a Poisson distribution with $\lambda = 1$ arrival per minute? (Perform a goodness-of-fit test at the 5 percent level.)

13. A company mixes nuts in a large container, then fills 1-pound cans from the mixture. The mixture is supposed to contain (by count) 30 percent cashews, 20 percent Brazil nuts, and 50 percent peanuts. A sample of 300 nuts taken from the container provided the data in Table K. Does it appear that the container has the specified 30-20-50 mixture? (Perform a goodness-of-fit test at the 1 percent level.)

TABLE J			TABLE K	
Number of customers entering store	**Frequency**		**Nut type**	**Number of nuts**
0	48		Cashew	70
1	60		Brazil	50
2	37		Peanut	180
3	4			
4	0			
5	1			
6 or more	0			
	150			

14. A company makes four lines of women's dresses. Last year's total sales were 40 percent line *A*, 30 percent *B*, 20 percent *C*, and 10 percent *D*. The company will make the same percentages of lines for the coming season unless customer preference indicates a change should be made. A sample of 200 women provided the preference data in Table L. Do the data indicate that the population preference distribution is different from the distribution of last year's sales? (Perform a goodness-of-fit test at the 5 percent level.)

TABLE L	
Dress line	**Number preferring dress line**
A	70
B	67
C	48
D	15

14.9 SUMMARY

In this chapter, we analyzed discrepancies between frequencies f_o that we actually observe in a random sample and frequencies f_e that we would expect to occur if a stated null hypothesis H_0 is true. The sample test statistic used was

$$\text{Sample } \chi^2 = \sum \frac{(f_o - f_e)^2}{f_e}$$

The distribution of this test statistic is closely approximated by the mathematical chi-square distribution (with parameter v) if each f_e value is at least 5. Large values of the sample χ^2 indicate significant differences between the observed frequencies and the frequencies that would be expected if H_0 is true. Hence, the tests in this chapter are right-tail tests and the decision rule is

$$\text{Reject } H_0 \text{ if sample } \chi^2 > \chi^2_{\alpha, v}$$

where α = level of significance of the test
v = number of degrees of freedom

Values of $\chi^2_{\alpha,v}$ are given in Table IV at the end of the book.

A *contingency* table is a set of observed sample frequencies f_0 arranged in the cells of a table that has r rows and c columns. The rows constitute one category and the columns constitute another category. A contingency table is tested for independence of the row and column categories by first computing expected cell frequencies f_e using the *cell-count rule*

$$f_e = \frac{\text{(cell row total)} \times \text{(cell column total)}}{\text{grand total}}$$

The χ^2 test statistic

$$\text{Sample } \chi^2 = \sum \frac{(f_0 - f_e)^2}{f_e}$$

is computed from the pairs of f_0 and f_e frequencies. The *number of degrees of freedom in a contingency table* is

$$v = (r - 1)(c - 1)$$

where r = number of rows in the table
c = number of columns in the table

The hypotheses in a contingency table test for independence are

H_0: the row and column categories are independent

H_a: the row and column categories are not independent

In a *test for the equality of population proportions*, p_r denotes the cell proportions to column total in a *row* of a contingency table. The hypotheses are

H_0: the p_r in any row are equal

H_a: the p_r in at least one row are not equal

The rules and formulas for testing for equal proportions are the same as those given for an independence test of a contingency table.

Tests of assumptions made about a population are called *goodness-of-fit* tests. The hypotheses are

H_0: the population has a specified probability distribution

H_a: the population does not have the specified distribution

A test is made by obtaining a random sample of observed frequencies f_0. Then the probability distribution specified in H_0 is used to compute expected frequencies f_e. The sample test statistic again is

$$\text{Sample } \chi^2 = \sum \frac{(f_0 - f_e)^2}{f_e}$$

At significance level α, the decision rule is

$$\text{Reject } H_0 \text{ if sample } \chi^2 > \chi^2_{\alpha,v}$$

The number of degrees of freedom is

$$v = n_e - 1 - g$$

where n_e = number of f_e values used in computing the sample χ^2

g = number of parameter values estimated from the sample

14.10 REVIEW PROBLEMS

1. (a) What is the cell-count rule for computing expected frequencies in a contingency table test for independence? (b) From what probability rule is your answer to part (a) derived?
2. In 2 by 5 contingency tables, what values of the sample χ^2 statistic will lead to rejection of the null hypothesis of independence at the 1 percent level?
3. Using the random sample data in Table A, perform a test of the hypothesis that flavor preference is independent of age. (Test at the 5 percent level.)

TABLE A

| | Age level | | |
Candy flavor preferred	Under 18	18–40	Over 40
Sweet fruit	50	35	35
Tart fruit	19	32	30
Mint	45	38	16

4. Using the random sample data in Table B, perform a test of the hypothesis that preference for candidate Peters is independent of the sex of voters. (Test at the 5 percent level.)

TABLE B

| | Sex of voter | |
Preferred candidate	Male	Female
Peters	134	106
Others	166	94

5. See Table B. Perform a test of the hypothesis that the proportions of male and female voters preferring Peters are equal. (Test at the 5 percent level.)
6. Marsten's Department Store sells sweaters made by four suppliers. The store offers a money back guarantee on sweaters returned by customers within 15 days. Table C contains data for a random sample of sweaters sold. Perform a test of the hypothesis that the proportions returned are equal for the sweaters from the four suppliers. (Test at the 5 percent level.)

TABLE C

	Supplier			
	Weave Co.	Stitch Co.	Knit Co.	Purl Co.
Returned	14	21	19	26
Not returned	111	119	71	119

7. A random sample of cameras assembled during each of three working shifts at Casco Company provided the data in Table D. Perform a test of the hypothesis

TABLE D

Type of defect	Shift		
	First	Second	Third
Major	10	14	6
Repairable	14	18	13
Minor	36	18	21

that the type of defect is independent of the shift that assembled the cameras. (Test at the 1 percent level.)

8. A supermarket sells three brands of coffee in 1-pound cans. In a sample of selling days, sales by brand were as shown in Table E. Are sales uniformly distributed by brand? Test at $\alpha = 0.05$. State the conclusion and the evidence leading to it.

TABLE E

	Brand		
	Chico	Blanco	Allegro
Number of cans sold	175	235	190

9. The observed frequencies of number of successes in 100 random samples of size $n = 20$ are given in Table F. At the 5 percent level, perform a test of the hypothesis that the population from which the samples were drawn is binomial with $p = 0.10$.

TABLE F

Number of successes	Frequency
0	17
1	23
2	32
3	15
4	5
5	6
6	1
7	0
8	1
9 or more	0

10. Joyce Grogan, controller of Allied Fasteners, has been checking random samples of 10 invoices to find whether they have been correctly entered in company records. She found that the number of incorrectly recorded invoices in a sample was usually 0, and never was more than 6, as shown in Table G. She wants to know whether the Table G frequencies are what would be expected in binomial trials. Perform a binomial goodness-of-fit test at the 5 percent level.

TABLE G

Number of incorrectly recorded invoices in a sample of 10 invoices	Number of samples
0	39
1	21
2	9
3	6
4	3
5	1
6	1
7 or more	0
	80

11. Juan Gomez of Executive Search, Inc., wants to know whether the times taken by managerial job candidates to complete a test are normally distributed. Juan compiled the data in Table H for a random sample of 225 candidates. The mean and standard deviation, computed from the 225 sample values, were, respectively, 32 minutes and 5 minutes. Perform a normal goodness-of-fit test at the 5 percent level.

TABLE H

Minutes taken to complete test	Number of candidates
Less than 22	10
22 and under 26	15
26 and under 30	46
30 and under 34	85
34 and under 38	42
38 and under 42	19
42 or more	8
	225

12. The Steelbelt Tire Company believes that wear mileage for their tires is normally distributed with a mean of 40 thousand miles and a standard deviation of 1 thousand miles. Test sample data for 200 tires are given in Table I (at the top of page 518). Perform a goodness-of-fit test at the 5 percent level.

13. Table J (at the top of page 518) provides a summary of numbers of customers entering a store in a random sample of ninety 10-minute time periods. Perform a Poisson goodness-of-fit test at the 5 percent level.

TABLE I

Mileage class interval (thousands of miles)	Number of tires
Less than 38.2	12
38.2 and under 38.8	19
38.8 and under 39.4	29
39.4 and under 40.0	41
40.0 and under 40.6	43
40.6 and under 41.2	35
41.2 and under 41.8	18
41.8 or more	3

TABLE J

Number entering	Frequency
0	1
1	3
2	8
3	23
4	26
5	17
6	4
7	6
8	1
9	1
10 or more	0

14. D & W Road Service recorded the random sample data given in Table K on the number of calls for service received in a $\frac{1}{2}$-hour interval. D & W believes that the number of calls received per $\frac{1}{2}$-hour is a Poisson process with an average of $\lambda = 2$ calls per $\frac{1}{2}$-hour. Perform a goodness-of-fit test at the 2 percent level.

TABLE K

Number of service calls in a ½-hour period	Number of ½-hour periods
0	10
1	40
2	19
3	18
4	6
5	4
6	3
7 or more	0

15. A warehouse stock of thousands of pairs of men's socks has been damaged by water. The warehouse owner offers the entire stock for sale at a discount. The owner believes that 35 percent of the stock is undamaged, 45 percent has minor damage (but can be sold), and 20 percent is unsalable. A prospective buyer examines a random sample of 180 pairs and finds 44 pairs undamaged, 90 pairs with minor damage, and 46 pairs unsalable. At the 1 percent level, perform a goodness-of-fit test to determine whether the sample data support the warehouse owner's belief.

15

ANALYSIS OF VARIANCE

15.1 INTRODUCTION

Procedures for determining whether or not two populations have equal means were presented in Chapter 11. Often, however, management problems involve more than two populations, and decision makers want to know whether the means of these populations are, or are not, equal. For example, suppose that several methods are available for training production workers. Then management would want to know whether mean productivity (output per employee per day) is or is not the same for employees trained by different methods. In this chapter you will learn how to perform tests of the equality of several population means.

First we will apply a test called the analysis of variance (ANOVA) test. A variance, you will recall, is the square of a standard deviation; that is, if σ is a standard deviation, then σ^2 is the corresponding variance. The test is called analysis of variance because, in performing it, we decide whether to accept or reject the hypothesis of equal population means by analyzing the variations (variance) in the sample means. The ANOVA test is performed on simple random samples drawn independently, one from each of the several populations. The test assumes that the populations are normally distributed and have equal variances.

In the latter part of the chapter you will learn how to perform the Kruskal-Wallis test for the equality of population means. The Kruskal-Wallis test has the advantage of not requiring the normality assumption underlying the ANOVA test. However, ANOVA is the better test when populations can be assumed to be normal, because ANOVA can detect differences in means that might not be detected by the Kruskal-Wallis test.

15.2 THE ANOVA CONCEPT

Suppose that a typewriter manufacturer prepared three different study manuals, for use by typists learning to operate an electronic word-processing typewriter. Then each manual was studied by a simple random sample of n typists. The time to achieve proficiency (a typing rate of 80 words per minute) was recorded for each typist, and the sample mean learning times for manuals 1, 2, and 3 were $\bar{x}_1$, $\bar{x}_2$, and $\bar{x}_3$ hours. The manufacturer wants to know whether the variation in sample means is large enough to show that population mean learning times for the manuals are different.

Do different sample means indicate different population means?

Note that sample mean learning times would vary even if the typists in the samples studied from the *same* manual. That's because of the inherent variability of learning times. However, if manuals do make a difference, mean learning times for *different* manuals will vary more than mean learning times for the *same* manual.

The variance (rather than the standard deviation) is the ANOVA measure of variation. In our example, we can form the ratio

$$\frac{\text{Variance of sample means for different manuals}}{\text{Variance of sample means for the same manual}}$$

A ratio near 1 indicates "no difference"

Values of this ratio that are larger than 1 mean that, based on sample estimates, learning times for different manuals vary more than learning times for the same manual. And if the value of the ratio is significantly large (according to the test that will be described shortly), we will conclude that *population* mean learning times for the manuals are *different*. That is, we will conclude that the manuals do make a difference in learning times.

Numerator of the ratio

The numerator of the foregoing ratio, the variance of the sample means for different manuals, is simply the variance (square of the standard deviation) of the three sample means $\bar{x}_1$, $\bar{x}_2$, and $\bar{x}_3$. The denominator poses a problem, because the three samples of typists studied different manuals. However, *within* the manual 1 sample, all n typists studied the *same* manual. You learned in Chapter 9 that it is possible to compute an estimate of the standard deviation of sample means $s_{\bar{x}}$ when the standard deviation of only one sample of size n is available. In this chapter we use s (rather than s_x) to denote a sample standard deviation. The relation between $s_{\bar{x}}$ and s is

In this chapter we use s (rather than s_x) to denote a sample standard deviation . . .

$$s_{\bar{x}} = \frac{s}{\sqrt{n}}$$

Squaring both sides, we obtain the variance relation

. . . and s^2 to denote a sample variance.

$$s_{\bar{x}}^2 = \frac{s^2}{n}$$

Consequently, to obtain an estimate of the variance of sample means for typists studying the *same* manual, say manual 1, we compute the sample 1 variance s_1^2. Then we divide it by n to obtain

$$\frac{s_1^2}{n}$$

Also, we can compute s_2^2/n and s_3^2/n to estimate the variance of sample means for typists studying manual 2 and typists studying manual 3.

We now have three estimates of the variance in sample means for typists studying the same manual. In ANOVA, it is assumed that the populations from which the samples are drawn have the same variance, σ^2. Consequently s_1^2/n, s_2^2/n, and s_3^2/n are estimates of the same quantity, σ^2/n; so we may average the three estimates to obtain

Denominator of the ratio

$$\frac{\frac{s_1^2}{n} + \frac{s_2^2}{n} + \frac{s_3^2}{n}}{3} = \frac{1}{3}\left(\frac{s_1^2}{n} + \frac{s_2^2}{n} + \frac{s_3^2}{n}\right)$$

as our estimate for the variance of sample mean learning times for typists studying the same manual.

Our ratio

$$\frac{\text{Variance of sample means for different manuals}}{\text{Variance of sample means for the same manual}}$$

therefore is

One form of the ratio

Variance of sample means for different manuals

$$\frac{1}{3}\left(\frac{s_1^2}{n} + \frac{s_2^2}{n} + \frac{s_3^2}{n}\right)$$

By algebra, the last expression can be changed to

This simpler form is called the variance ratio.

$$\frac{n(\text{variance of sample means for different manuals})}{\frac{1}{3}(s_1^2 + s_2^2 + s_3^2)}$$

The general formula for the *variance ratio* is

General formula for the variance ratio

$$\text{Variance ratio} = \frac{n(\text{variance of sample means})}{\text{mean of sample variances}}$$

The variance ratio is the test statistic in the ANOVA test. I will discuss the ANOVA test after illustrating the computation of the variance ratio.

EXERCISE Five random samples, each containing n steers, were selected. The different samples of steers ate different food mixtures. Why can we not attribute a difference in the sample mean weight gains entirely to the differences in food mixtures?

ANSWER Because sample mean weight gains would vary even if all sample steers ate the same mixture.

15.3 CALCULATING VARIANCES AND THE SAMPLE F STATISTIC

In our learning-time example, suppose that three random samples of five typists were selected. Then letting

$$k = \text{number of samples}$$

and

$$n = \text{size of each sample}$$

we have $k = 3$ samples of $n = 5$ typists per sample. Samples 1, 2, and 3 studied, respectively, from manuals 1, 2, and 3. The sample learning times are shown in Table 15.1. The sample mean learning times,

TABLE 15.1
LEARNING TIMES FOR $k = 3$ SAMPLES OF $n = 5$ TYPISTS PER SAMPLE

	Manual 1	Manual 2	Manual 3
	21	17	31
	27	25	28
	29	20	22
	23	15	30
	25	23	24
Sum	125	100	135
Mean	$\bar{x}_1 = \dfrac{125}{5} = 25$	$\bar{x}_2 = \dfrac{100}{5} = 20$	$\bar{x}_3 = \dfrac{135}{5} = 27$

$$\bar{x}_1 = 25 \qquad \bar{x}_2 = 20 \qquad \bar{x}_3 = 27$$

are different, but the question, as usual, is whether the *population* mean times are different. To answer this question, we must first compute the mean of the sample variances, and the variance of the sample means.

The Mean of the Sample Variances

The standard deviatiation s of a sample of size n is computed by the formula

$$s = \sqrt{\frac{\Sigma(x - \bar{x})^2}{n - 1}}$$

The formula for the variance of a sample is

The variance of a single sample . . .

$$s^2 = \frac{\Sigma(x - \bar{x})^2}{n - 1}$$

For later reference, I mention here that the divisor in a sample variance calculation is called the *number of degrees of freedom*. Thus the variance for a *. . . has n − 1 de-* sample of size n has $n - 1$ degrees of freedom.
grees of freedom.   Table 15.2 shows the calculation of the variance s_1^2 of the learning times for the manual 1 sample.

TABLE 15.2
SAMPLE VARIANCE CALCULATION

Manual 1 learning times x		$(x - \bar{x}_1)$	$(x - \bar{x}_1)^2$
	21	21 − 25 = −4	16
	27	27 − 25 = 2	4
	29	29 − 25 = 4	16
	23	23 − 25 = −2	4
	25	25 − 25 = 0	0
Sum	125		$\Sigma(x - \bar{x}_1)^2 = 40$

$$\bar{x}_1 = \frac{125}{5} = 25 \qquad s_1^2 = \frac{\Sigma(x - \bar{x}_1)^2}{n - 1} = \frac{40}{5 - 1} = \frac{40}{4} = 10$$

EXERCISE See Table 15.2. Compute s_2^2, the variance for manual 2.
ANSWER 17.

The variance of the manual 3 sample (calculations not shown) is $s_3^2 = 15$. Hence, we have the sample variances

$$s_1^2 = 10 \qquad s_2^2 = 17 \qquad s_3^2 = 15$$

The *mean of k sample variances* $s_1^2, s_2^2, \ldots, s_k^2$ is

This is the denomina-
tor of the variance
ratio . . .
$$\text{Mean of sample variances} = \frac{s_1^2 + s_2^2 + \cdots + s_k^2}{k}$$

For our $k = 3$ sample variances,

$$\text{Mean of sample variances} = \frac{10 + 17 + 15}{3} = 14$$

For later reference, I mention here that there are $n - 1 = 4$ degrees of freedom in each of the $k = 3$ sample variance computations. Consequently, the mean of the three sample variances has $k(n - 1) = 3(4) = 12$ degrees of freedom. In general, the *mean of the sample variances has $k(n - 1)$ degrees of freedom* if all samples are of the same size n.

. . . it has $k(n - 1)$ degrees of freedom.

The Variance of the Sample Means

In Table 15.1, the sample means are

$$\bar{x}_1 = 25 \qquad \bar{x}_2 = 20 \qquad \bar{x}_3 = 27$$

The mean of the numbers in all the samples, denoted by $\bar{\bar{x}}$, is called the *grand mean*. For k samples of the same size, n, the grand mean is the mean of the sample means. That is,

$$\bar{\bar{x}} = \frac{\Sigma \bar{x}}{k}$$

In our example

$$\bar{\bar{x}} = \frac{25 + 20 + 27}{3}$$

$$= 24$$

When multiplied by n, this becomes the numerator of the variance ratio . . .

The *variance of k sample means* is

$$s_{\bar{x}}^2 = \frac{\Sigma(\bar{x} - \bar{\bar{x}})^2}{k - 1}$$

Its divisor is $k - 1$, the number of samples minus 1; so this variance has $k - 1$ degrees of freedom. In our example,

. . . it has $k - 1$ degrees of freedom.

$$s_{\bar{x}}^2 = \frac{(\bar{x}_1 - \bar{\bar{x}})^2 + (\bar{x}_2 - \bar{\bar{x}})^2 + (\bar{x}_3 - \bar{\bar{x}})^2}{3 - 1}$$

$$= \frac{(25 - 24)^2 + (20 - 24)^2 + (27 - 24)^2}{2}$$

$$= \frac{1 + 16 + 9}{2}$$

$$= 13$$

with 2 degrees of freedom.

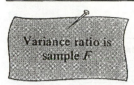

Variance ratio is sample F

The Sample F Statistic

The variance ratio constructed in Section 15.2 is called the sample F statistic. It is

$$\text{Sample } F = \frac{n(\text{variance of sample means})}{\text{mean of sample variances}}$$

As noted in the foregoing, the numerator of the sample F has $k - 1$ degrees of freedom, and the denominator has $k(n - 1)$ degrees of freedom. These separate degrees of freedom are denoted by

$$v_1 = \text{numerator degrees of freedom} = k - 1$$

$$v_2 = \text{denominator degrees of freedom} = k(n - 1)$$

For our example,

$$\text{Sample } F = \frac{n(\text{variance of sample means})}{\text{mean of sample variances}}$$

$$= \frac{5(13)}{14}$$

$$= 4.64$$

and the sample F has $v_1 = 2$ and $v_2 = 12$ degrees of freedom.

The calculations illustrated so far are summarized, step-by-step, in Table 15.3 (on page 526). We must now refer to a table of right-tail F values to determine whether the sample $F = 4.64$ is, or is not, large enough to lead us to reject, at significance level α, the hypothesis that the population means are equal. If, in our example, we reject the hypothesis of equal population means, we will conclude that mean learning times for different manuals are not equal.

15.4 THE DISTRIBUTION OF THE SAMPLE F STATISTIC

The ANOVA test is based on the assumptions that simple random samples are drawn independently from normal distributions that have the same variance. From these assumptions, mathematicians derived the probability distribution of the sample F statistic. The distribution has two parameters. They are the two degrees of freedom for the sample F, v_1 and v_2:

Degrees of freedom for sample F

$$v_1 = \text{degrees of freedom for the numerator}$$

$$v_2 = \text{degrees of freedom for the denominator}$$

When the k samples are of the same size n,

$$v_1 = \text{number of samples} - 1 = k - 1$$

$$v_2 = (\text{number of samples}) \times (\text{sample size} - 1)$$

$$= k(n - 1)$$

TABLE 15.3
CALCULATIONS OF VARIANCES AND THE SAMPLE F

	Manual 1		Manual 2		Manual 3	
	x	$(x - \bar{x}_1)^2$	x	$(x - \bar{x}_2)^2$	x	$(x - \bar{x}_3)^2$
	21	16	17	9	31	16
	27	4	25	25	28	1
	29	16	20	0	22	25
	23	4	15	25	30	9
	25	0	23	9	24	9
Sum	125	40	100	68	135	60

a. Sample means: $\bar{x}_1 = \dfrac{125}{5} = 25 \qquad \bar{x}_2 = \dfrac{100}{5} = 20 \qquad \bar{x}_3 = \dfrac{135}{5} = 27$

where $n = 5$ is the number of items per sample

b. Sample variances: $s^2 = \dfrac{\Sigma(x - \bar{x})^2}{n - 1}$

$$s_1^2 = \frac{40}{5 - 1} = 10 \qquad s_2^2 = \frac{68}{5 - 1} = 17 \qquad s_3^2 = \frac{60}{5 - 1} = 15$$

c. Mean of sample variances: $\frac{1}{3}(s_1^2 + s_2^2 + s_3^2) = \dfrac{10 + 17 + 15}{3} = \dfrac{42}{3} = 14$

where $k = 3$ is the number of samples

d. Grand mean: $\bar{\bar{x}} = \dfrac{\Sigma\bar{x}}{k} = \dfrac{25 + 20 + 27}{3} = \dfrac{72}{3} = 24$

e. Variance of sample means: $s_{\bar{x}}^2 = \dfrac{\Sigma(\bar{x} - \bar{\bar{x}})^2}{k - 1}$

$$s_{\bar{x}}^2 = \frac{(25 - 24)^2 + (20 - 24)^2 + (27 - 24)^2}{3 - 1} = \frac{1 + 16 + 9}{2} = 13$$

f. Sample $F = \dfrac{n(\text{variance of sample means})}{\text{mean of sample variances}} = \dfrac{n(\mathbf{e})}{\mathbf{c}}$

Sample $F = \dfrac{5(13)}{14} = \dfrac{65}{14} = 4.64$

Here are six good reasons for doing ANOVA on a computer!

There is a separate F distribution for each pair of degrees of freedom. The distributions have one mode and are skewed to the right as illustrated in Figure 15.1. In general, the larger v_1 and v_2 are, the smaller is the F value where the right tail almost touches the horizontal axis. In particular, when v_1 and v_2 are both at least 10, less than 1 percent of the area (probability) will be in the tail to the right of $F = 5$.

The random variable for an F distribution is the variance ratio

$$\text{Sample } F = \frac{n(\text{variance of sample means})}{\text{mean of sample variances}}$$

Variances are never negative and, of course, n cannot be negative; so the sample F is never negative. The larger the numerator of the variance ratio relative to the denominator, the larger is the sample F and the more likely it

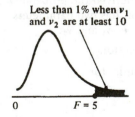

Less than 1% when v_1 and v_2 are at least 10

0      $F = 5$

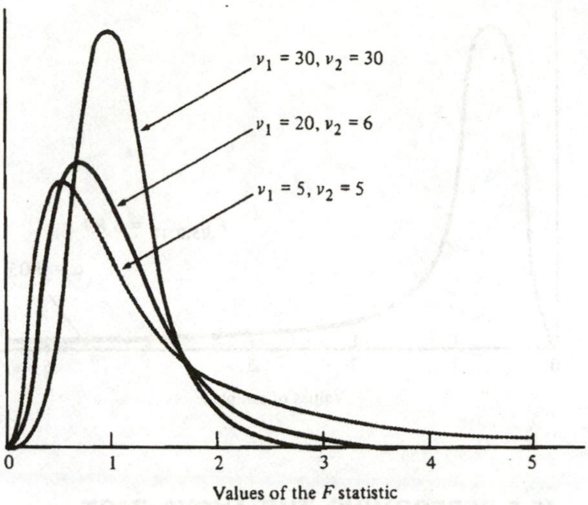

FIGURE 15.1
Distributions of the sample F statistic.

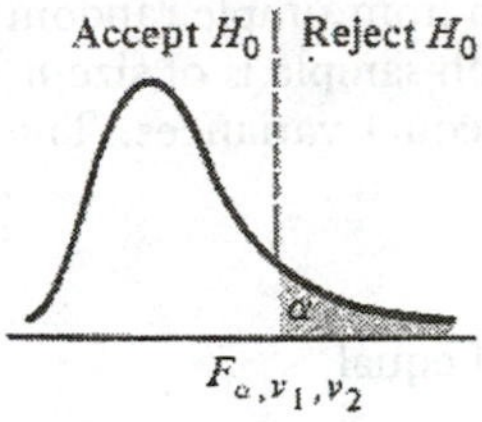

is that the samples came from populations with different means. That is, large values of the sample F indicate relatively large variations in the sample means. Consequently, the ANOVA test is a right-tail test. The decision rule, at significance level α, will be to reject the null hypothesis of equal population means if the sample F exceeds F_{α,ν_1,ν_2}. The symbol F_{α,ν_1,ν_2} means the value of F for a right-tail area of α when there are ν_1 and ν_2 degrees of freedom. Table VIII at the end of the book contains values of F_{α,ν_1,ν_2} for two commonly used significance levels, $\alpha = 0.01$ and $\alpha = 0.05$. The entries in Table 15.4 were taken from Table VIII. The entry for $\nu_1 = 2$ and $\nu_2 = 12$ is 3.89; that is, for $\alpha = 0.05$, $\nu_1 = 2$, and $\nu_2 = 12$,

$$F_{\alpha,\nu_1,\nu_2} = F_{0.05,2,12} = 3.89$$

TABLE 15.4
F VALUES FOR A RIGHT-TAIL AREA OF 0.05

Degrees of freedom for denominator	Degrees of freedom for numerator 2	3	4	5
10	4.10	3.71	3.48	3.33
11	3.98	3.59	3.36	3.20
12	3.89	3.49	3.26	3.11
13	3.81	3.41	3.18	3.03

Thus, in Figure 15.2, the area in the tail to the right of 3.89 is $\alpha = 0.05$. We will use values of F_{α,ν_1,ν_2} to formulate ANOVA test decision rules.

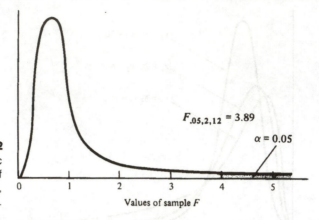

FIGURE 15.2
Value of the F statistic
for a right-tail area of
0.05 when $v_1 = 2$,
$v_2 = 12$.

$F_{.05,2,12} = 3.89$

$\alpha = 0.05$

Values of sample F

15.5 PERFORMING THE ANOVA TEST

The ANOVA test summarized in this section uses data from simple random samples drawn independently from k populations. Each sample is of size n. The populations are normally distributed and have equal variances. The hypotheses are

1. Hypotheses

H_0: the k population means are equal

H_a: the k population means are not all equal

The decision rule at significance level α is

2. Decision rule

Reject H_0 if sample $F > F_{\alpha,v_1,v_2}$

where F_{α,v_1,v_2} is found from Table VIII and

$$v_1 = k - 1 \qquad v_2 = k(n - 1)$$

Next we must compute the value of the sample F from the formula

3. Sample F

$$\text{Sample } F = \frac{n(\text{variance of sample means})}{\text{mean of sample variances}}$$

The calculation of the sample F is illustrated in Table 15.3. Finally, we

4. Accept or reject

Accept or reject H_0

If H_0 is accepted, we conclude that the population means are equal; if H_0 is rejected, we conclude that the population means are not all equal.

In the context of our learning-time example, we have

1. H_0: mean learning times for the three manuals are equal

H_a: mean learning times for the three manuals are not all equal

There are $k = 3$ samples of $n = 5$ typists; so

$$v_1 = k - 1 = 3 - 1$$
$$= 2$$

and
$$v_2 = k(n - 1) = 3(5 - 1)$$
$$= 12$$

Taking $\alpha = 0.05$ as the significance level, we find from Table VIII that $F_{0.05,2,12} = 3.89$. Hence, the decision rule is

2. Reject H_0 if sample $F > 3.89$

The sample F is calculated in Table 15.3. It is

3. Sample $F = 4.64$

The sample $F = 4.64$ exceeds the value 3.89 in the decision rule, so we

A sample F > 3.89 is
significant in our
example.

4. Reject H_0

Consequently, we conclude that mean learning times are not the same for the three manuals. Figure 15.3 shows that we rejected H_0 because the sample F falls in the rejection region of the decision rule.

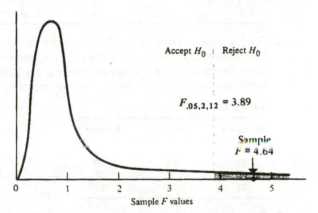

Accept H_0 : Reject H_0

$F_{.05,2,12} = 3.89$

Sample
$F = 4.64$

FIGURE 15.3
ANOVA test decision
rule for learning times.

Sample F values

Our conclusion that population mean learning times are different suggests that manual 2, which had the lowest sample mean time of $\bar{x}_2 = 20$ hours, should be selected for self-study. However, the suggestion is not a statistical inference, because the rejection of H_0 arose from the combined variations of all three samples. It cannot be assumed from the sample averages

$$\bar{x}_1 = 25 \qquad \bar{x}_2 = 20 \qquad \bar{x}_3 = 27$$

alone that μ_2 is less than both μ_1 and μ_3, or that μ_1 is less than μ_3. *Multiple comparison* procedures, discussed in advanced texts, are needed to establish such relationships.

The test we performed involved only one factor that might influence learning times—the manual used. Consequently, the test is called *one-factor* (or one-way) ANOVA. If we had wanted also to determine whether learning times vary for new and for experienced typists, a second factor (experience) would enter the analysis. Then we would need learning-time sample data for the three manuals for new typists, and learning-time sample data for the three manuals for experienced typists. The analysis of these data would be *two-factor* ANOVA. Multifactor and other advanced ANOVA procedures should be done on a computer.

15.6 PROBLEMS

1. For the data in Table A: (*a*) Compute the sample (column) means. (*b*) Compute $\bar{x}$. (*c*) Compute the mean of the sample variances. (*d*) Compute the variance of the sample means. (*e*) Compute the value of the sample *F* statistic. (*f*) What are the values of v_1 and v_2?

TABLE A

Sample 1	Sample 2	Sample 3	Sample 4
2	3	6	4
3	1	7	6
7	5	8	8

2. For the data in Table B: (*a*) Compute the sample (column) means. (*b*) Compute $\bar{x}$. (*c*) Compute the mean of the sample variances. (*d*) Compute the variance of the sample means. (*e*) Compute the value of the sample *F* statistic. (*f*) What are the values of v_1 and v_2?

TABLE B

Sample 1	Sample 2	Sample 3
20	39	14
30	28	28
32	31	32
34	22	26

3. Three methods for assembling a product are to be tested at the 0.05 level to determine whether mean times per assembly for the methods are equal. Random sample assembly times in minutes are given in Table C. Perform the ANOVA test.

TABLE C

Method 1	Method 2	Method 3
11	19	19
13	25	14
19	16	13
18	22	14
14	18	20

4. Random samples of workers from four sections of a metropolitan area were given a job aptitude examination. Scores for the workers are given in Table D. Perform an ANOVA test at the 0.01 level to determine whether mean scores for the sections are equal.

TABLE D

Section 1	Section 2	Section 3	Section 4
61	46	75	59
68	53	64	73
59	59	68	70
66	56	78	63
51	61	75	75

5. A consumer research agency tested four random samples of types of light bulbs by keeping bulbs lit until they burned out. Table E gives burning times in tens of hours (78 means 780 hours). Perform an ANOVA test at the 0.01 level to determine if mean burning times for the bulb types are equal.

TABLE E

Type 1	Type 2	Type 3	Type 4
78	65	77	76
78	73	69	83
72	75	68	77
71	71	75	83
77	67	77	82
80	69	72	85

6. A rancher selected a random sample of 18 steers of the same age. The 18 were divided, at random, into three groups of 6. The groups were fed different grain and nutrient mixtures. Weight gains, in pounds, at the end of the test period are given in Table F. Perform an ANOVA test at the $\alpha = 0.05$ level to determine if mean weight gains for the mixtures are equal.

TABLE F

Mixture 1	Mixture 2	Mixture 3
220	204	265
245	248	219
230	250	235
255	189	288
280	204	253
210	249	240

7. A new store is to be built upon one of three street corner locations in a city. To determine if the numbers of potential customers are different for the corners, passersby counts were made for a random sample of eleven $1/2$-hour periods at each corner. Sample means and sample variances are given in Table G. Perform an ANOVA test at the 0.01 level to determine if the mean number of passersby at the corners are equal.

TABLE G

Corner	Sample mean	Sample variance
1	125	288
2	141	248
3	124	304

8. A sporting goods maker is considering four different running (bottom) surfaces for racing skis. An expert made runs down a mountain with random samples of skis having these surfaces, making $n = 5$ runs with each surface. The sample means and variances are given in Table H. Perform an ANOVA test at the $\alpha = 0.01$ level to determine if mean run times for the surfaces are equal.

TABLE H

Ski surface	Mean run time (seconds)	Sample variance
1	124	8.4
2	116	10.6
3	123	9.0
4	125	12.0

9. Jill Stone, an executive career adviser, wanted to determine if the age at which chief executives of companies attain their position is different in the three types of firms in which she specializes. Jill obtained random samples of six executives for each type of firm and recorded the age data given in Table I. Perform an ANOVA test at the $\alpha = 0.05$ level to determine if mean ages to attain the position of chief executive in the three types of firms are equal.

TABLE I

Age at which position of chief executive was attained		
Firm type A	Firm type B	Firm type C
37	44	46
42	39	39
38	47	46
44	40	43
35	44	47
42	50	38

10. Sam Wilks, the vice president for marketing at Princeton Distributors, noted a variation in unit marketing costs at Princeton's distribution centers. Wilks sent one of his staff members to visit the centers, observe their operations, and try to find reasons for the cost variations. The staff member found that operations were similar at the centers, except for order-processing procedures, and that order-processing times appeared to vary from center to center. Wilks decided to have an order-processing time study carried out. Random samples of seven new orders for each of Princeton's five distribution centers were selected. Times to process the sample orders are given in Table J. Perform an ANOVA test at the $\alpha = 0.01$ level to determine if mean order-processing times at the centers are equal.

TABLE J

	Order-processing time in days			
Center 1	**Center 2**	**Center 3**	**Center 4**	**Center 5**
4.1	2.8	2.1	3.9	2.7
3.9	3.4	2.7	2.9	4.0
3.2	2.6	1.9	3.4	2.9
3.1	3.1	2.8	3.7	3.2
3.5	3.3	2.6	4.2	3.5
2.9	2.5	2.0	4.5	4.1
3.0	3.5	2.9	4.1	3.7

11. Clair Oil Company wanted to determine if the amounts of oil delivered by its trucks to customers are the same in its three sales districts. They obtained the random sample data in Table K. Perform an ANOVA test at the 0.05 level to determine if mean amounts per delivery in the sales districts are equal.

TABLE K

Gallons of oil delivered in one delivery		
District 1	**District 2**	**District 3**
81	100	295
179	158	82
142	272	155
199	248	271
124	62	212

12. In Problem 11, the sample means for districts 1, 2, and 3 are, respectively, 145, 168, and 203 gallons. The sample means appear to vary substantially, yet the hypothesis of equal population means was accepted. What feature of the numbers in Table K accounts for the fact that the sample F is small even though the sample means vary substantially?

15.7 ANOVA BY MEAN SQUARES

Method and Terminology

The procedure we have followed thus far in performing ANOVA tests is important, because it shows us what the sample F means; that is,

$$\text{Sample } F = \frac{n(\text{variance of sample means})}{\text{mean of sample variances}}$$

In this section you will learn an alternative method, called the *mean-squares* method, for computing the sample F. The calculations involved in the mean-squares method do not bring out the meaning of the sample F. However, the method is widely applied because of its calculational efficiency, and because it can be applied to problems where the sample sizes are not equal.

To begin with, we note that the quantity $\Sigma(x - \bar{x})^2$ in the numerator of the formula

$$\text{Variance} = \frac{\Sigma(x - \bar{x})^2}{n - 1}$$

is equal to $\Sigma(x^2) - (\Sigma x)^2/n$. That is,

$$\Sigma(x - \bar{x})^2 = \Sigma(x^2) - \frac{(\Sigma x)^2}{n} \qquad .$$

Note that the expression on the right involves a sum of squares, $\Sigma(x^2)$, and the square of a sum, $(\Sigma x)^2$. In general, the mean-squares method, involves these sums of squares and squares of sums.

EXERCISE   For the x values 1, 3, and 8, compute (a) $\bar{x}$; (b) $\Sigma(x - \bar{x})^2$; (c) $\Sigma(x^2) - (\Sigma x)^2/n$.
ANSWER   (a) 4; (b) 26; (c) 26.

Within-sample and between-sample variances

In the terminology of the mean-squares method, the variance of the numbers in a particular sample is called a within-sample variance; and the variance of sample means is called a between-sample variance. Variances are computed from sums of squares (SS). Between-sample and within-sample sums of squares are denoted, respectively, by SSB and SSW. A sum of squares divided by its associated number of degrees of freedom is called a mean square (MS). Between-sample and within-sample mean squares are denoted, respectively, by MSB and MSW.

Test statistic for mean squares:

MSB
MSW

It can be proved by algebra that when the samples are all of size n,

$$\text{Sample } F = \frac{\text{MSB}}{\text{MSW}} = \frac{n(\text{variance of sample means})}{\text{mean of sample variances}}$$

When the sample sizes are unequal, the MSB/MSW ratio will produce a sample F that is weighted properly to reflect the differences in sample sizes.

Suppose that we have k random samples. The sample sizes n_1, n_2, . . . , n_k may or may not be equal. Denote the total sample size by N; that is,

$$N = n_1 + n_2 + \cdots + n_k$$

The steps in calculating the sample F by the mean-squares method are as follows: Compute

Here are 10 more reasons for using a computer!

1. The sample totals (sums), T_1, T_2, . . . , T_k
2. The sum of the sample totals, $\Sigma T = T_1 + T_2 + \cdots + T_k$
3. The square of the sum of the sample totals, $(\Sigma T)^2$
4. $\displaystyle \sum \frac{T_i^2}{n_i} = \frac{T_1^2}{n_1} + \frac{T_2^2}{n_2} + \cdots + \frac{T_k^2}{n_k}$
5. The sum of the squares of all the sample numbers, $\Sigma(x^2)$
6. The between-sample sum of squares, SSB, which is

$$\text{SSB} = \sum \frac{T_i^2}{n_i} - \frac{(\Sigma T)^2}{N}$$

7. The within-sample sum of squares, SSW, which is

$$\text{SSW} = \Sigma(x^2) - \sum \frac{T_i^2}{n_i}$$

8. The between-sample mean square, MSB, which is

$$\text{MSB} = \frac{\text{SSB}}{k - 1} \qquad \text{with } v_1 = k - 1 \text{ degrees of freedom}$$

9. The within-sample mean square, MSW, which is

$$\text{MSW} = \frac{\text{SSW}}{N - k} \qquad \text{with } v_2 = N - k \text{ degrees of freedom}$$

10. The test statistic:

$$\text{Sample } F = \frac{\text{MSB}}{\text{MSW}} \qquad \text{with } v_1 \text{ and } v_2 \text{ degrees of freedom}$$

If the samples all are of size n, step 4 in the foregoing can be simplified by computing $(T_1^2 + T_2^2 + \cdots + T_k^2)/n$, which is then used in steps 6 and 7.

EXERCISE Suppose that there are $k = 5$ samples, each sample of size $n = 10$. (a) What is the value of N? (b) What is the value of v_2?
ANSWER (a) 50; (b) 45.

To illustrate that the mean-squares method and the earlier method lead to the same sample F value when sample sizes are equal, let's apply the mean-squares method to the learning-time data in Table 15.1. Table 15.5 gives the learning times, sample totals, and sample sizes.

There are $k = 3$ samples whose sizes are

TABLE 15.5
LEARNING TIMES FOR $k = 3$
SAMPLES OF TYPISTS

Manual 1	Manual 2	Manual 3
21	17	31
27	25	28
29	20	22
23	15	30
25	23	24
$T_1 = 125$	$T_2 = 100$	$T_3 = 135$
$n_1 = 5$	$n_2 = 5$	$n_3 = 5$

$$n_1 = 5 \qquad n_2 = 5 \qquad n_3 = 5$$

so that

$$N = n_1 + n_2 + \cdots + n_k = 5 + 5 + 5$$
$$= 15$$

From Table 15.5, we have

For equal sample sizes n, you may compute item 4 as

$$\frac{\Sigma T_i^2}{n}$$

1. The sample totals: $T_1 = 125$, $T_2 = 100$, $T_3 = 135$
   Now we compute
2. $\Sigma T = 125 + 100 + 135 = 360$
3. $(\Sigma T)^2 = (360)^2 = 129{,}600$
4. $\sum \dfrac{T_i^2}{n_i} = \dfrac{(125)^2}{5} + \dfrac{(100)^2}{5} + \dfrac{(135)^2}{5} = 8770$
5. $\Sigma(x^2) = (21)^2 + (27)^2 + (29)^2 + \cdots + (22)^2 + (30)^2 + (24)^2$
   $= 8938$
6. $\text{SSB} = \sum \dfrac{T_i^2}{n_i} - \dfrac{(\Sigma T)^2}{N} = 8770 - \dfrac{129{,}600}{15} = 130$
7. $\text{SSW} = \Sigma(x^2) - \sum \dfrac{T_i^2}{n_i} = 8938 - 8770 = 168$
8. $\text{MSB} = \dfrac{\text{SSB}}{k - 1} = \dfrac{130}{3 - 1} = 65 \qquad \nu_1 = k - 1 = 2$ degrees of freedom
9. $\text{MSW} = \dfrac{\text{SSW}}{N - k} = \dfrac{168}{15 - 3} = 14 \qquad \nu_2 = N - k = 12$ degrees of freedom

Dan: The six-step method in Table 15.3 looks simpler.

10. Sample $F = \dfrac{\text{MSB}}{\text{MSW}} = \dfrac{65}{14} = 4.64 \qquad \nu_1 = 2$ and $\nu_2 = 12$ degrees of freedom

The sample $F = 4.64$ is the same as the value computed in Table 15.3. Also, you can verify that MSB = 65 is 5(13) which is n times the variance of the sample means; and MSW = 14 is the mean of the sample variances.

Fran: Maybe — but that method doesn't work for unequal sample sizes.

EXERCISE Suppose we have $k = 3$ samples of size $n = 2$. The first sample is 1 and 3, the second is 2 and 4, and the third is 5 and 9. Compute the value of the sample F by mean squares.
ANSWER 3.5.

In the next example, the mean-squares method is applied to a case where the sample sizes are unequal.

EXAMPLE   One random sample of people followed diet 1. A second random sample followed diet 2, and a third random sample followed diet 3. Weight losses for the people in the samples are given in Table 15.6. Perform

TABLE 15.6
WEIGHT LOSSES IN POUNDS FOR $k = 3$
SAMPLES OF DIFFERENT SIZES

	Diet 1	Diet 2	Diet 3
	7	11	4
	8	9	6
	7	9	5
	9	8	8
	9	12	5
		11	8
			6
Total	$T_1 = 40$	$T_2 = 60$	$T_3 = 42$
Sample size	$n_1 = 5$	$n_2 = 6$	$n_3 = 7$

an ANOVA test by mean squares at the $\alpha = 0.01$ level to determine whether or not population mean weight losses are equal.

SOLUTION   The total sample size for the $k = 3$ samples is

$$N = n_1 + n_2 + n_3 = 5 + 6 + 7$$

$$= 18$$

Following the 10-step procedure, we obtain

Fran: You have to use this formula for unequal sample sizes.

1. Sample totals $T_1 = 40$, $T_2 = 60$, $T_3 = 42$
2. $\Sigma T = 142$
3. $(\Sigma T)^2 = 20{,}164$
4. $\displaystyle \Sigma \frac{T_i^2}{n_i} = \frac{T_1^2}{n_1} + \frac{T_2^2}{n_2} + \frac{T_3^2}{n_3}$

$$= \frac{(40)^2}{5} + \frac{(60)^2}{6} + \frac{(42)^2}{7} = 1172$$

5. $\Sigma(x^2) = (7)^2 + (8)^2 + (7)^2 + \cdots + (5)^2 + (8)^2 + (6)^2 = 1202$
6. $\displaystyle \text{SSB} = \Sigma \frac{T_i^2}{n_i} - \frac{(\Sigma T)^2}{N}$ where $N = 18$

$$= 1172 - \frac{20{,}164}{18} = 51.778$$

7. $\displaystyle \text{SSW} = \Sigma(x^2) - \Sigma \frac{T_i^2}{n_1}$

$$= 1202 - 1172 = 30.000$$

8. $\displaystyle \text{MSB} = \frac{\text{SSB}}{k-1}$ $v_1 = k - 1$ degrees of freedom

$$= \frac{51.778}{3 - 1}$$

$$= 25.889 \qquad v_1 = 2 \text{ degrees of freedom}$$

9. $\text{MSW} = \dfrac{\text{SSW}}{N - k} \qquad v_2 = N - k \text{ degrees of freedom}$

$$= \frac{30.000}{18 - 3}$$

$$= 2.000 \qquad v_2 = 15 \text{ degrees of freedom}$$

10. $\text{Sample } F = \dfrac{\text{MSB}}{\text{MSW}} \qquad v_1 \text{ and } v_2 \text{ degrees of freedom}$

$$= \frac{25.889}{2.000}$$

$$= 12.94 \qquad 2 \text{ and } 15 \text{ degrees of freedom}$$

The hypotheses are

1. H_0: the population mean weight losses are equal
   H_a: the population mean weight losses are not all equal

With $\alpha = 0.01$, $v_1 = 2$, and $v_2 = 15$, we find from Table VIII that

$$F_{\alpha, v_1, v_2} = F_{0.01, 2, 15} = 6.36$$

Hence, the decision rule is

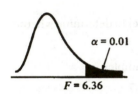

$\alpha = 0.01$

$F = 6.36$

2. Reject H_0 if sample $F > 6.36$

From our calculations

3. Sample $F = 12.94$

so we

4. Reject H_0

Consequently, we conclude that the population mean weight losses for the three diets are not equal.

In the diet example, the sample mean weight losses were

$$\bar{x}_1 = \frac{T_1}{n_1} = \frac{40}{5} = 8 \text{ pounds}$$

$$\bar{x}_2 = \frac{T_2}{n_2} = \frac{60}{6} = 10 \text{ pounds}$$

$$\bar{x}_3 = \frac{T_3}{n_3} = \frac{42}{7} = 6 \text{ pounds}$$

Comparison of the sample means suggests that diet 2 leads to the largest mean weight loss, but as discussed earlier, that suggestion is not a statistical inference.

EXERCISE Suppose we have $k = 2$ samples. The first sample is 1 and 3; the second sample is 2, 4, and 6. Compute the value of the sample F.
ANSWER 1.44.

Incidentally, the small sample test for the equality of *two* population means given in Section 11.14 has as its test statistic the sample t value. For the last exercise, the sample t (I computed it) is 1.2. Now notice that the sample $F = 1.44$ in the exercise is the *square* of the sample $t = 1.2$. In general, for $k = 2$ samples,

$$\text{Sample } F = (\text{sample } t)^2$$

Equivalence of ANOVA and the t test for two means.

This relationship between the sample statistics states that you will get the same result (i.e., accept H_0 or reject H_0) whether you apply an ANOVA test or a t test for the equality of $k = 2$ population means.

The ANOVA Table

The results of ANOVA calculations are summarized in an ANOVA table whose general format is shown by Table 15.7. The bottom row, Total, con-

TABLE 15.7
ANOVA TABLE FORMAT

The color symbols are, of course, replaced with computed values.

Source of variation	Degrees of freedom	Sum of squares	Mean square	Sample F
Between-samples	$k - 1$	SSB	MSB = SSB/$(k - 1)$	F = MSB/MSW
Within-samples	$N - k$	SSW	MSW = SSW/$(N - k)$	
Total	$N - 1$	SST		

As a check, make sure that $v_1 + v_2 = N - 1$.

tains the total sum of squares, SST, and the total number of degrees of freedom, $N - 1$. That is,

$$\text{SST} = \text{SSB} + \text{SSW}$$

and

$$(k - 1) + (N - k) = N - 1$$

The total sum of squares can be computed from the sample data. It is

$$\text{SST} = \Sigma(x^2) - \frac{(\Sigma T)^2}{N}$$

Often analysts compute SSB with the formula given earlier, and SST with the formula just stated. Then they compute SSW as

$$\text{SSW} = \text{SST} - \text{SSB}$$

Table 15.8 is the ANOVA table for the diet example. To perform the ANOVA test at the $\alpha = 0.01$ level using the information in the ANOVA table, we must understand that the 2 and 15 degrees of freedom in the table are $v_1 = 2$ and $v_2 = 15$. Then we must find F_{α, v_1, v_2} from Table VIII. It is, for $\alpha = 0.01$,

To use the numbers in the ANOVA table:
1. Choose α.
2. Look up F_{α, v_1, v_2}.
3. Compare it with the sample F.

$$F_{0.01, 2, 15} = 6.36$$

Next, we must compare the sample F with F_{α, v_1, v_2} and apply the decision

TABLE 15.8
ANOVA TABLE FOR DIET EXAMPLE

Source of variation	Degrees of freedom	Sum of squares	Mean square	Sample F
Between-samples	2	51.778	25.889	12.94
Within-samples	15	30.000	2.000	
Total	17	81.778		

rule: Reject the hypothesis of equal means if the tabulated F exceeds F_{α, v_1, v_2}. In the example, the sample $F = 12.94$ exceeds $F_{0.01,2,15} = 6.36$; so we conclude that the population means are not equal.

Computer printouts of ANOVA results have the format of Table 15.7; however, the labels may be different. Table 15.9 shows some output of the

TABLE 15.9
PARTIAL OUTPUT OF SPSS ANOVA COMPUTER PROGRAM

	Analysis of variance			
Source	D.F.	Sum of squares	Mean squares	F ratio
Between-groups	2	51.7778	25.8889	12.944
Within-groups	15	30.0000	2.0000	
Total	17	81.7778		

This contains the same information as Table 15.8.

ANOVA program that is part of SPSS (Statistical Package for the Social Sciences). The data that were supplied to the program are those of the diet example. The order of rows and columns in the SPSS output is the same as the row and column order of Table 15.8. Notice that the row labels for SPSS have the word "group" rather than "sample."

To use a computer package, all that you need to do is command the computer to perform the ANOVA program with the sample data that you supply. The computer then will make the calculations and print out the results in an ANOVA table. You, of course, will have to decide whether the sample F in the computer output is, or is not, large enough to lead to the rejection of the null hypothesis of equal means: To make that decision, you first set the significance level α; then you determine whether the sample F is, or is not, larger than the value of F_{α, v_1, v_2} that you obtain from Table VIII.

15.8 PROBLEMS

1. An investor selected random samples of stock purchases recommended by three stock brokers a year ago. The investor calculated the percent returns on each stock during the year, as given in Table A (at the top of the next page). Perform an ANOVA test by mean squares at the $\alpha = 0.05$ level to determine if mean returns for the three advisory firms are equal.

TABLE A

Percent returns		
Firm A	Firm B	Firm C
7.6	8.7	3.4
2.8	5.2	8.1
5.1	4.9	4.2
4.6	7.0	2.6

2. A tree farmer planted random samples of three each of four varieties of dwarf fir trees. The heights of the sample trees at maturity, in centimeters, are given in Table B. Perform an ANOVA test by mean squares at the $\alpha = 0.01$ level to determine if the mean heights at maturity are equal for the four varieties.

TABLE B

Variety 1	Variety 2	Variety 3	Variety 4
17	23	17	25
23	28	28	23
26	24	21	20

3. Instruments for correcting a power plant malfunction are mounted on a control panel. Three panels were designed, with the instruments arranged differently on different panels. Then three random samples of four control engineers per sample were selected. Each sample was assigned to one panel. The times, in seconds, taken by engineers to correct a simulated malfunction are given in Table C. Perform an ANOVA test by mean squares at the $\alpha = 0.05$ level to determine if the mean times to correct the malfunction are the same for the three panels.

TABLE C

Panel A	Panel B	Panel C
17	9	13
12	16	8
15	11	14
20	12	9

4. Brightglow Company, the manufacturer of a new hair shampoo, wanted to determine whether package design affected sales. Brightglow had four packages designed. Then they selected four random samples of five stores each and stocked the stores in each sample with one of the designs. Table D gives sales for the designs in number of packages during a 3-day period. Perform an ANOVA test by mean squares at the $\alpha = 0.05$ level to determine if mean sales for the designs are equal.

TABLE D

Design 1	Design 2	Design 3	Design 4
39	39	25	38
37	43	38	35
27	38	33	44
27	29	29	33
30	31	25	32

5. The admissions officer of a college rated accepted applicants' chances of success at the college as poor, good, or excellent. The college's cumulative grade index is a scale from 1 (lowest) to 12. Three random samples of students, one sample for each chance-of-success rating, were selected. Table E gives the cumulative grade indexes of the sample students. Perform an ANOVA test by mean squares at the $\alpha = 0.05$ level to determine whether mean cumulative grade indexes for the chance-of-success ratings are equal.

TABLE E

	Chance of success rating	
Poor	**Good**	**Excellent**
6.8	7.3	6.3
5.4	5.9	10.3
4.2	6.4	8.9
6.5	8.2	11.1
6.6	4.0	9.4
7.1	6.7	8.6
6.9	7.6	9.5
7.5	9.0	7.0
7.3	10.3	8.2

6. A consumer research agency wanted to determine if different brands of batteries have the same mean hours of life. They selected random samples of four different brands of batteries. Each sample contained five batteries. The sum of the squares of hours of life for all 20 batteries was 6909. The sample sums for brands 1, 2, 3, and 4, in hours, were 107, 64, 82, and 106. Perform an ANOVA test by mean squares at the $\alpha = 0.01$ level to determine if mean hours of life are the same for the battery brands.

7. Kitchen utensils made by K & F Company are sold in supermarkets. K & F wanted to determine whether sales of their utensils are affected by the store location of the utensil display. They considered four locations: left, right, central, and rear. Then they selected four random samples of six stores per sample and assigned one of the locations to each sample. At the end of the trial period, K & F recorded their utensil sales, in hundreds of dollars, for each of the 24 stores. The sum of squares of sales for all sample stores was 43,626. The sample sums of sales for the locations were 364, 124, 224, and 208. Perform an ANOVA test by mean squares at the 0.01 level to determine if mean sales of utensils are the same for the locations.

8. Perform an ANOVA test by mean squares at the $\alpha = 0.05$ level to determine if the random samples in Table F came from populations having the same mean. Note that the sample sizes are not equal.

TABLE F

Sample 1	Sample 2	Sample 3
10	14	7
11	12	9
12	12	8
	11	11
	15	8
		10
		9

9. The Four A Automobile Club tested random samples of three models of cars to determine if they obtained the same mean number of miles per gallon of gasoline. The sample data, miles per gallon for 17 cars, are given in Table G. Perform an ANOVA test by mean squares at the $\alpha = 0.05$ level to determine if mean mileages for the models are equal.

TABLE G

Model A	Model T	Model Z
20	18	24
24	17	21
19	21	19
23	22	23
	20	25
	19	22
		27

10. An educational testing company wanted to determine if the mean difficulty levels of four alternative versions of a test are the same. They selected four random samples of 10 students and had each sample take

TABLE H

Version 1	Version 2	Version 3	Version 4
97	76	62	93
55	56	85	73
84	59	56	67
63	60	77	99
57	62	63	94
52	85	86	53
70	62	94	78
56		57	92
99			97
74			

one version of the test. Some students became ill and could not complete their tests. The scores for students who did complete their tests are given in Table H. Perform an ANOVA test by mean squares at the $\alpha = 0.05$ level to determine if mean scores for the tests are equal.

11. A trucking firm makes frequent trips to a city in a nearby state. The firm has the choice of three different routes and wants to determine if mean trip times for the routes are the same. Random samples of 23 trips via route A, 21 via B, and 19 via C were obtained. The sum of the squares of trip time for all the trips was 19,340. The sums of the trip times, by route, were 368 for A, 399 for B, and 323 for C. Perform an ANOVA test by mean squares at the $\alpha = 0.01$ level to determine if mean trip times for the routes are equal.

12. Four types of solar panels were tested for heat output. Sample data are summarized in Table I. Perform an ANOVA test by mean squares at the $\alpha = 0.05$ level to determine if mean heat outputs for the panels are equal.

TABLE I

	Type A	Type B	Type C	Type D
Number of panels in sample	9	12	11	12
Sum of sample heat outputs	135	120	99	228
Sum of squares of sample heat outputs	1932	2574	2362	2580

13. Set up and fill in an ANOVA table for Problem 6.
14. Set up and fill in an ANOVA table for Problem 7.
15. Set up and fill in an ANOVA table for Problem 11.
16. Set up and fill in an ANOVA table for Problem 12.
17. Interest rates earned by random samples of the securities of four different types of firms were analyzed to determine if mean interest rates for the types of firms are equal. The sample sizes were 7, 9, 8, and 10. The sums of squares for ANOVA are given in Table J. (a) through (g) Fill in (a) through (g) in Table J. (h) Are mean interest rates for the firms equal? Test at the $\alpha = 0.01$ level.

TABLE J

Source of variation	Degrees of freedom	Sum of squares	Mean square	Sample F
Between-samples	(a)	1080	(e)	(g)
Within-samples	(b)	1740	(f)	
Total	(c)	(d)		

18. A company wanted to determine whether better discount offers affect the time it takes customers to pay their bills. The company selected five samples of nine customers per sample. Each sample of customers received a different discount offer. Records were kept of the time in days it took sample customers to pay their bills. The sums of squares for ANOVA are given in Table K. (a) through (g) Fill in (a) through (g) in Table K. (h) Are the mean days it takes for payment the same for different discount offers? Test at the $\alpha = 0.01$ level.

TABLE K

Source of variation	Degrees of freedom	Sum of squares	Mean square	Sample F
Between-samples	(a)	793.74	(e)	(g)
Within-samples	(b)	(d)	(f)	
Total	(c)	2758.46		

15.9 THE KRUSKAL-WALLIS TEST

The Hypotheses

The Kruskal-Wallis test, in its broadest form, analyzes data in k independent samples to determine whether or not k populations have identical continuous distributions. The hypotheses can be stated briefly as

$$H_0: \text{the } k \text{ populations are identical}$$

$$H_a: \text{the } k \text{ populations are not identical}$$

When this form of H_0 is rejected, we conclude that the populations differ in some respect, but we cannot say how they differ.

Now suppose we can assume, as we do in this section, that the populations have the same continuous distribution but they may have different means. Then the Kruskal-Wallis test can be used to determine whether or not the k populations have the same mean. Figure 15.4 is an illustration of

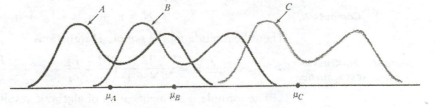

FIGURE 15.4
Three distributions that are the same except for differences in means.

three populations that have the same distribution (same curve), but they have different means as shown by μ_A, μ_B, and μ_C on the figure. Hence, under the condition that k populations have the same distribution, the hypotheses of the Kruskal-Wallis test are those of the ANOVA test; namely,

$$H_0: \text{the } k \text{ population means are equal}$$

$$H_a: \text{the } k \text{ population means are not equal}$$

The Kruskal-Wallis condition that we will use (populations all have the same distribution) is less restrictive than the ANOVA condition that all populations have a normal distribution. Hence, the Kruskal-Wallis test is more generally applicable than the ANOVA test. However, if the normality condition is satisfied, ANOVA is the better test because it can detect differences in means that are not detected by the Kruskal-Wallis test; that is, ANOVA may lead to rejection of an H_0 that is accepted by the Kruskal-Wallis test.

The Sample *H* Statistic

The Kruskal-Wallis test statistic is denoted by H. To compute the sample H, we first rank all the sample data (that is, all the numbers in the k samples) in order of size, assigning rank 1 to the smallest number. If two or more of the numbers are equal, each number is assigned the average rank for the group. For example, if the four smallest numbers are not equal, they have ranks 1, 2, 3, and 4. The next two larger numbers, if not equal, will have ranks 5 and 6; but if they are equal, they will each have the rank 5.5 (the average of 5 and 6).

EXERCISE The five smallest numbers are not equal. The next larger number occurs three times. What rank will each of these equal numbers have?
ANSWER $(6 + 7 + 8)/3 = 7$.

After ranking the data, we compute the rank sum (sum of the ranks) for each of the k samples. Now, let

$$R_1, R_2, \ldots, R_k$$

be the rank sums for the respective samples; and let

$$n_1, n_2, \ldots, n_k$$

be the respective sample sizes so that N, the total sample size, is

$$N = n_1 + n_2 + \cdots + n_k$$

Then the *formula for the sample H statistic* is

$$\text{Sample } H = \frac{12}{N(N+1)} \left(\frac{R_1^2}{n_1} + \frac{R_2^2}{n_2} + \cdots + \frac{R_k^2}{n_k} \right) - 3(N+1)$$

The formula is a simplification of algebraic results that are too cumbersome to include here. However, it is instructive to know that the algebra includes an expression for the squares of differences between observed and expected sample mean ranks. We used a similar expression in Chapter 14 where we found the squares of the differences between observed and expected frequencies. In Chapter 14 you learned that the distribution of the resulting sample statistic is close to a chi-square distribution if the expected frequencies are all at least 5. Similarly, the distribution of the sample H statistic is close to a chi-square distribution with $k - 1$ degrees of freedom if

$\chi^2_{\alpha,k-1}$ *is used in the* **Kruskal-Wallis test.** every sample size is at least 5. Consequently, we will use χ^2 (chi-square) values from Table IV at the end of the book in stating the decision rule for the Kruskal-Wallis test. The decision rule, at significance level α, will be to

$$\text{Reject } H_0 \text{ if sample } H > \chi^2_{\alpha,k-1}$$

Performing the Test

The hypotheses of the Kruskal-Wallis test are

1. H_0: the k populations have equal means
   H_a: the k population means are not all equal

The decision rule at significance level α is

2. Reject H_0 if sample $H > \chi^2_{\alpha,k-1}$

We rank all the sample numbers, compute the rank sum for each sample, and then calculate the test statistic

3. Sample $H = \dfrac{12}{N(N+1)} \left(\dfrac{R_1^2}{n_1} + \dfrac{R_2^2}{n_2} + \cdots + \dfrac{R_k^2}{n_k} \right) - 3(N+1)$

where $R_1, R_2, \ldots, R_k$ are the rank sums of samples $1, 2, \ldots, k$
$n_1, n_2, \ldots, n_k$ are the sizes of samples $1, 2, \ldots, k$
$N = n_1 + n_2 + \cdots + n_k$

Finally, we

4. Accept or reject H_0

EXAMPLE In the learning-time example earlier in the chapter the significance level α was 0.05. The ANOVA test rejected the hypothesis of equal means. Let's see what happens if we perform the Kruskal-Wallis test for this example.

SOLUTION The hypotheses are

1. H_0: mean learning times for the $k = 3$ manuals are equal

   H_a: mean learning times for the manuals are not all equal

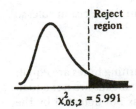

Reject region

$\chi^2_{.05,2} = 5.991$

With $\alpha = 0.05$ and $k = 3$ samples, we find from Table IV that

$$\chi^2_{\alpha,k-1} = \chi^2_{0.05,2} = 5.991$$

Hence the decision rule is

2. Reject H_0 if sample $H > 5.991$

Next we must rank the data, compute the rank sums, then compute the value of the sample H. The data are given in Table 15.10. The table also shows the ranks of the sample numbers and the rank sums.
We work now with the rank sums. They are

TABLE 15.10
LEARNING TIMES AND RANKS FOR $k = 3$ SAMPLES

Two "ties" have been
awarded average
ranks here.

Manual 1		Manual 2		Manual 3	
Learning time	Rank	Learning time	Rank	Learning time	Rank
21	4	17	2	31	15
27	11	25	9.5	28	12
29	13	20	3	22	5
23	6.5	15	1	30	14
25	9.5	23	6.5	24	8
Sum	44		22		54

$$R_1 = 44 \quad R_2 = 22 \quad R_3 = 54$$

The sample sizes are

$$n_1 = 5 \quad n_2 = 5 \quad n_3 = 5$$

so

$$N = n_1 + n_2 + n_3 = 5 + 5 + 5$$
$$= 15$$

Therefore,

$$\text{Sample } H = \frac{12}{N(N+1)} \left(\frac{R_1^2}{n_1} + \frac{R_2^2}{n_2} + \cdots + \frac{R_k^2}{n_k} \right) - 3(N+1)$$

$$= \frac{12}{15(15+1)} \left[\frac{(44)^2}{5} + \frac{(22)^2}{5} + \frac{(54)^2}{5} \right] - 3(15+1)$$

$$= 0.05(1067.2) - 3(16)$$

$$= 5.36$$

Hence,

3. Sample $H = 5.36$

The sample $H = 5.36$ does not exceed $\chi^2_{0.05,2} = 5.991$ in the decision rule; so we

4. Accept H_0

Kruskal-Wallis says
accept, but ANOVA
said reject, Why?

The Kruskal-Wallis leads us to conclude that mean learning times are equal, but the earlier ANOVA test led us to conclude that the means are not equal. Thus, the ANOVA test detected a difference that was not detected by the Kruskal-Wallis test. The reason the Kruskal-Wallis test failed to detect the difference in means is that differences in rank do not show the actual differences in the numbers that are ranked. Thus, for example, the difference between numbers ranked 1 and 2 could be substantially larger than the difference between numbers ranked 7 and 8. Consequently, we say that ANOVA, which uses the sample numbers, makes better use of the sample information than does the Kruskal-Wallis test, which uses ranks. Frequently, however, the two tests lead to the same conclusion.

EXERCISE Suppose the three lowest grades on a midterm exam taken by a class are 35, 70, 71; so the ranks of the grades are 1, 2, 3. Which set of numbers, the grades or the ranks, provide more information about student differences? Why?

ANSWER The grades, because the equally spaced ranks, 1, 2, and 3, do not show that the difference between grades ranked 1 and 2 (35 and 70) is substantial, and that there is very little difference between the grades ranked 2 and 3 (70 and 71).

Advantage of Kruskal-Wallis:
1. *It does not require normal populations.*
2. *It can be used for ranked data.*
3. *Its test statistic is easy to compute.*

Compared with the ANOVA test, the advantages of the Kruskal-Wallis test are (1) the conditions are less restrictive; (2) it can be applied to sample data that are recorded as ranks; (3) H is easier to compute than F. Item (2) refers, for example, to situations where an executive ranks the performances of managers, or where a jeweler ranks the hardness of different gemstones. If the populations from which samples are drawn and ranked have continuous distributions, the Kruskal-Wallis test can be applied in analyzing the ranked data, but the ANOVA test cannot be applied.

For the reasons just stated, statisticians consider the Kruskal-Wallis test to be an important alternative to the ANOVA test for determining whether one factor has an effect on population means, that is, for example, whether manuals (one factor) have an effect on mean learning times. However, ANOVA is by far the most extensively developed method for studying factor effects. It can be applied to analyze multifactors effects and the effects of interactions of factors.

15.10 PROBLEMS

1. A sporting goods maker is considering three different running surfaces (bottoms) for racing skis. An expert made runs down a mountain with random samples of skis having these surfaces, making five runs with each surface. Run times, in seconds, are shown in Table A. Perform the Kruskal-Wallis test at the $\alpha = 0.01$ level to determine if mean run times for the surfaces are equal.

TABLE A

Surface 1	Surface 2	Surface 3
127.8	129.7	129.2
128.5	130.4	127.3
127.6	128.3	128.7
128.8	130.1	128.0
126.1	129.0	127.2

2. Four foods were tested to determine if cholesterol content is the same for each food. Random sample data (grams of cholesterol per 1000

grams of food) are given in Table B. Perform the Kruskal-Wallis test at the $\alpha = 0.05$ level to determine if mean cholesterol contents for the foods are equal.

TABLE B

Food 1	Food 2	Food 3	Food 4
45.5	45.8	43.7	42.0
44.5	45.1	44.0	45.4
44.4	46.0	44.8	42.0
45.0	44.2	45.0	44.1
42.5	43.6	42.0	43.3
		43.0	43.1

3. A consumer research agency tested random samples of four types of light bulbs by keeping bulbs lit until they burned out. Table C gives burning lives in tens of hours (thus, 78 means 780 hours). Perform the Kruskal-Wallis test at the $\alpha = 0.05$ level to determine if mean burning lives for the bulb types are equal.

TABLE C

Type 1	Type 2	Type 3	Type 4
78	65	77	66
78	73	69	83
72	75	68	77
71	71	75	83
77	67	77	82
80	69	72	85

4. A rancher selected 18 steers of the same age at random. The 18 were divided at random into three groups of six each. The groups were fed different food mixtures. Weight gains at the end of the test period, in pounds, are shown in Table D. Perform the Kruskal-Wallis test at the $\alpha = 0.05$ level to determine if mean weight gains for the mixtures are equal.

TABLE D

Mixture 1	Mixture 2	Mixture 3
220	204	265
245	248	219
230	250	235
255	189	288
280	204	253
210	249	240

5. If gemstone A can produce a scratch on gemstone B, then A is said to be harder than B. Thus, by scratching, it is possible to rank the

hardness of different gemstones. Suppose a jewelry firm obtained random samples of simulated diamonds from each of three suppliers. Then the firm ranked the hardnesses of the diamonds. The ranks (1 is the least hard) are given in Table E. Perform the Kruskal-Wallis test at the $\alpha = 0.05$ level to determine whether the mean hardnesses of diamonds from the three suppliers are equal.

TABLE E

Supplier 1	Supplier 2	Supplier 3
9.5	2	7
6	3	14
15	1	4.5
11	4.5	8
13	12	9.5

6. Random samples of three types of batteries, $B1$, $B2$, and $B3$, were tested for hours of useful life. The sample data, hours of life for each sample battery, are given in Table F. Perform the Kruskal-Wallis test at the $\alpha = 0.05$ level to determine if the mean lives of the three types of batteries are equal.

TABLE F

Type $B1$	Type $B2$	Type $B3$
13.7	13.9	12.1
14.8	13.1	10.4
12.3	11.0	15.2
16.1	14.3	12.5
14.8	10.0	11.6
	12.0	17.0

7. Several hundred mosquitoes were trapped in each of 18 containers. The containers were divided randomly into three groups of six containers per group. Then the mosquitoes in each group of containers were sprayed with one of three chemicals, A, B, or C. The kill percentages for the chemicals are given in Table G. Perform the Kruskal-Wallis test at the $\alpha = 0.05$ level to determine if mean kill percentages for the chemicals are equal.

TABLE G

Chemical A	Chemical B	Chemical C
63	60	70
74	56	65
68	71	52
73	54	75
66	69	59
76	51	62

8. Five types of house insulation were tested for heat loss. Random samples of size $n = 10$ were used for each insulation type. The rank sums for the heat-loss measures were 200, 190, 310, 360, and 215. Perform the Kruskal-Wallis test at the $\alpha = 0.05$ level to determine if mean heat losses for the insulation types are equal.
9. See Section 15.8. Perform the Kruskal-Wallis test for Problem 4.
10. See Section 15.8. Perform the Kruskal-Wallis test for Problem 10.
11. The sizes of random samples from four populations of credit balances, $n_1, n_2, n_3,$ and n_4, are 14, 16, 15, and 13. Respective rank sums for the samples are 380, 401, 430, and 500. Perform the Kruskal-Wallis test at the $\alpha = 0.05$ level to determine if mean credit balances for the populations are equal.

15.11 SUMMARY

The two tests in this chapter use random samples drawn independently, one sample from each of k populations, to determine whether or not the means of the populations are equal. The k sample sizes are $n_1, n_2, \ldots, n_k$, and the total sample size is

$$N = n_1 + n_2 + \cdots + n_k$$

The conditions of the ANOVA test are that the populations are normally distributed and have equal variances. The test statistic is usually computed by the mean-squares method, as follows: Compute
1. The sample totals, $T_1, T_2, \ldots, T_k$
2. The sum of the totals, $\Sigma T = T_1 + T_2 + \cdots + T_k$
3. The square of the sum of the totals, $(\Sigma T)^2$
4. $\displaystyle \sum \frac{T_i^2}{n_i} = \frac{T_1^2}{n_1} + \frac{T_2^2}{n_2} + \cdots + \frac{T_k^2}{n_k}$
5. The sum of the squares of all the sample numbers, $\Sigma(x^2)$
6. The between-sample sum of squares, $\displaystyle \text{SSB} = \sum \frac{T_i^2}{n_i} - \frac{(\Sigma T)^2}{N}$
7. The within-sample sum of squares, $\displaystyle \text{SSW} = \Sigma(x^2) - \sum \frac{T_i^2}{n_i}$
8. The between-sample mean square, $\displaystyle \text{MSB} = \frac{\text{SSB}}{k - 1}$
9. The within-sample mean square, $\displaystyle \text{MSW} = \frac{\text{SSW}}{N - k}$
10. The test statistic, sample $\displaystyle F = \frac{\text{MSB}}{\text{MSW}}$, which has $v_1 = k - 1$ and $v_2 = N - k$ degrees of freedom

In step 10, v_1 and v_2 are, respectively, the numbers of degrees of freedom for the numerator and the denominator of the F statistic. The value of F_{α, v_1, v_2}, which is used in stating the decision rule, is found in Table VIII. At significance level α, the hypotheses for the ANOVA test are

$$H_0: \text{ the } k \text{ population means are equal}$$

H_a: the k population means are not equal

The decision rule is

$$\text{Reject } H_0 \text{ if sample } F > F_{\alpha, v_1, v_2}$$

When the samples are of the same size n, the ANOVA test statistic can be computed with the formula

$$\text{Sample } F = \frac{n(\text{variance of the sample means})}{\text{mean of the sample variances}}$$

The condition of the Kruskal-Wallis test is that, except for possible differences in means, the k populations have the same distribution. The steps in this test are as follows:

1. Rank all N sample numbers in order of size, assigning rank 1 to the smallest number. Assign each of a group of equal numbers the average of the ranks those numbers would have been assigned if they were not equal.

2. Find the sum of the ranks for each sample. Designate the respective rank sums by $R_1, R_2, \ldots, R_k$.

3. Compute the test statistic

$$\text{Sample } H = \frac{12}{N(N + 1)} \left(\frac{R_1^2}{n_1} + \frac{R_2^2}{n_2} + \cdots + \frac{R_k^2}{n_k} \right) - 3(N + 1)$$

When all sample sizes are at least 5, the value of $\chi^2_{\alpha, k-1}$ from Table IV is used in stating the decision rule. At significance level α, the hypotheses are:

$$H_0: \text{ the } k \text{ population means are equal}$$

$$H_a: \text{ the } k \text{ population means are not all equal}$$

The decision rule is

$$\text{Reject } H_0 \text{ if sample } H > \chi^2_{\alpha, k-1}$$

15.12 REVIEW PROBLEMS

1. Fifteen workers with similar skills were divided at random into three groups of five each. Different training methods were used for each group. Output (units per day) for the workers after training are given in Table A. Perform an ANOVA test at the $\alpha = 0.05$ level to determine if mean outputs for the training methods are equal.

TABLE A′

Method 1	Method 2	Method 3
17	33	33
21	23	45
33	21	27
31	23	39
23	35	31

2. Perform the Kruskal-Wallis test for Problem 1.
3. Random samples of six tires, one sample for each of four brands of tires, were selected. Tread wear lives in thousands of miles for the sample tires are given in
   Table B. Perform an ANOVA test at the $\alpha = 0.05$ level to determine if mean
   lives of the brands are equal.

TABLE B

Brand A	Brand B	Brand C	Brand D
38	25	37	36
32	33	29	43
38	35	28	37
31	31	35	43
37	27	37	42
40	29	32	45

4. Perform the Kruskal-Wallis test for Problem 3.
5. Golf balls were tested for hitting distance on a ball-driving machine. Four brands
   were tested using random samples of seven balls of each brand. Summary test
   data are shown in Table C. Perform an ANOVA test at the $\alpha = 0.01$ level to determine if mean distances are equal for the four brands. State the conclusion and
   the evidence leading to the conclusion.

TABLE C

Brand	Sample mean distance (yards)	Sample variance
K1	280	130
K2	292	120
K3	276	122
K4	300	128

6. A softball team has three candidates for one outfield position. The coach had
   each of the three throw a ball as far as possible. Each candidate made 11 throws.
   The total distances of the 11 throws for each candidate were, in yards, 385, 418,
   and 440. The sum of the squares of the 33 throw distances was 47,099. Perform
   an ANOVA test at the $\alpha = 0.05$ level to determine if mean throw distances for
   the candidates are equal.
7. Milk prices were sampled in four sections of a region. Summary data are given in
   Table D. The sum of the squares of all the prices in all the samples was 29.46092.
   Perform an ANOVA test at the $\alpha = 0.01$ level to determine if mean prices for
   the sections are equal.

TABLE D

Section	Number of prices in sample	Sum of sample prices (dollars)
1	7	7.14
2	9	9.27
3	6	5.94
4	7	6.86

8. Three package designs were tested by obtaining sales data for each design in random samples of stores. The sample data are given in Table E. Perform an ANOVA test at the $\alpha = 0.05$ level to determine if mean sales for the designs are equal.

TABLE E

Design 1	Design 2	Design 3
28	34	29
26	35	34
39	31	34
36	41	38
39	32	25
24		39
22		42
33		

9. Perform the Kruskal-Wallis test for Problem 8.
10. Random samples of three car models were tested for gas mileage. The mileages, in miles per gallon, for each sample car are given in Table F. Perform an ANOVA test at the $\alpha = 0.05$ level to determine if mean mileages for the models are equal.

TABLE F

Model 1	Model 2	Model 3
33	24	20
24	29	30
27	26	30
38	31	18
30	30	20
28		30
26		42
31		

11. Perform the Kruskal-Wallis test for Problem 10.
12. Random samples of workers from three sections of a metropolitan area took a job aptitude test. Test scores for workers in all three samples were ranked in order of size. Sample sizes were 9, 10, and 12 workers. Rank sums for the samples were, respectively, 180, 130, and 186. Perform the Kruskal-Wallis test at the $\alpha = 0.05$ level to determine if mean scores for the sections are equal.
13. A supermarket research agency tested three brands of processed cheese to find out how long it takes for cheese to get moldy. Random samples of eight packages each of brands A, B, and C were placed on a shelf. The first package to get moldy was of brand C: it was recorded as $1C$, meaning that the lowest rank, 1, was a brand C package. The sample data are given in Table G. Perform the Kruskal-Wallis test at the $\alpha = 0.05$ level to determine if mean times to get moldy are equal for the brands.

TABLE G

1C	5A	9A	13A	17B	21B
2B	6B	10C	14B	18B	22A
3C	7B	11B	15A	19C	23A
4C	8C	12C	16C	20A	24A

14. Construct and fill in the ANOVA table for Problem 6.
15. Construct and fill in the ANOVA table for Problem 7.
16. A real estate agency obtained a random sample of family incomes in each of seven suburbs of a large city. The sample size for suburb 3 was $n_3 = 13$; all other samples were of size 19. ANOVA sums of squares are given in Table H. (*a*) through (*g*). Fill in (*a*) through (*g*) in Table H. (*h*) Test at the $\alpha = 0.01$ level to determine if mean incomes in the suburbs are equal.

TABLE H

Source of variation	Degrees of freedom	Sum of squares	Mean square	Sample F
Between-samples	(a)	187.2649	(e)	(g)
Within-samples	(b)	(d)	(f)	
Total	(c)	1269.6891		

16

NONPARAMETRIC TESTS

16.1 INTRODUCTION

In general, nonparametric tests are tests that are relatively free of conditions which restrict their applicability. In particular, the nonparametric tests in this chapter do not require (1) that samples be drawn from normal populations or (2) that sample numbers be high-level measurements. I'll discuss measurement levels in the next section. But, as an example, weights (say, in pounds) are high-level measurements, whereas a consumer's 1, 2, 3, 4 preference rating numbers are not high-level measurements. Thus, in Chapter 15, the Kruskal-Wallis test is a nonparametric test; it does not require that samples be drawn from normal populations, and it can be performed on ranks (e.g., 1, 2, 3). The ANOVA test in Chapter 15 is a parametric test; it has the condition that samples be drawn from normal populations, and it requires high-level measurements. Nonparametric tests are important in management problems because they can be performed with numbers such as an executive's 1, 2, 3, 4 ranking of the performances of four managers, or a consumer's 1, 2, 3, 4, 5 ranking of preferences for five products.

In this chapter you will learn how to perform five nonparametric tests. Special tables, such as those in Sidney Siegel's book *Nonparametric Statistics* (McGraw-Hill, 1956), are available for small sample tests. We shall work with samples that are large enough to permit the use of familiar tables, particularly the normal Table VI, in constructing decision rules. You should understand, however, that our use of the normal table is not a restriction on a parametric test. That is, using Table VI to construct a decision rule means only that, for sufficiently large samples, the distribution of the nonparametric test statistic can be approximated by a normal distribution. This use of Table VI does not mean that samples must come from normal populations.

16.2 LEVELS OF MEASUREMENT

High-level measure:
Differences in measurements are meaningful numbers.

A high-level measure is one that produces numbers (measurements) for which differences are meaningful. Thus, weight in pounds (or any other unit) is a high-level measure because it is meaningful to say, for example, that the weight difference between 4 and 5 pounds is the same as the weight difference between 9 and 10 pounds. Other familiar high-level measures, each with an illustrative unit, include time (minutes), distance (meters), temperature (degrees Celsius), interest rates (percent), speed (miles per hour), monetary value (dollars), and fluid content (gallons).

Ordinal measure:
Only the ranking (order) of measurements is meaningful.

Numbers representing order, called *ordinal* measurements, are not high-level measurements because they do not have the "meaningful difference" property. Thus, suppose a consumer's preference ratings of four brands of a product are 1, 2, 3, and 4, with 1 meaning least preferred. Then it would be unwise, and usually wrong, to say that the preference difference between products rated 1 and 2 is the same as the preference difference between products rated 3 and 4. We can say that 2 is a higher preference than 1, but we cannot say how much higher.

A test that can be performed on ordinal measurements can also be performed on high-level measurements; that's because high-level measurements can be changed to ordinal measurements by arranging them in ascending order of size and assigning rank order 1 to the smallest measurement, rank 2 to the next larger, and so on. For example, weights of 3.4, 1.6, and 5.8 pounds can be assigned rank orders 2, 1, 3. We cannot, on the other hand, perform high-level tests on ordinal measurements—because we cannot change ordinal measurements to high-level measurements. Thus, for example, if Brown, Peters, and Jones finish 3, 1, 2 in a 1-mile race, we cannot change these numbers to minutes taken to run the race.

Nonparametric tests must be performed on ordinal measurements.

The point of the foregoing is that nonparametric tests which can be performed on ordinal measurements can be performed with high-level measurements, but parametric tests requiring high-level measurements cannot be performed on ordinal measurements. When high-level measurements are at hand, we may have the choice of performing a parametric test or a nonparametric alternative. The choice should be the parametric test *if* the conditions of the test are met; that's because the parametric test can detect a difference that the nonparametric test may not detect. If we are unable or unwilling to assume that the conditions of the parametric test are met, then the nonparametric alternative test should be performed.

16.3 THE MATCHED PAIRS SIGN TEST

Suppose each person in a random sample is asked to rate, say, two brands of shampoo; then the rating pairs are said to be *matched* because each pair was assigned by the same person.

Here, for the matched pair (A, B), the sign is + if A > B.

In the matched pairs sign test, the sign (+ or −) of the difference between a pair is determined for each matched pair in the sample. Next the number of + signs (e.g., a higher preference number for shampoo A than for shampoo B) is counted, and the sample proportion $\bar{p}$ of + signs is computed. We can think arbitrarily of a + sign as being a success (e.g., shampoo A preferred over shampoo B) and a minus sign as being a failure. And we can construct decision rules based on the normal distribution to perform tests of hypotheses about p, the unknown population proportion of successes. That is, if p_h is our hypothesized value of p, we can test the null hypothesis that $p = p_h$, or that $p \leq p_h$, or that $p \geq p_h$. For the normal approximation to be valid, the sample size n (the number of + and − signs) must be large enough so that both np_h and $n(1 - p_h)$ are at least 5.

Suppose $\bar{p}$ is the proportion of successes in a sample. Then the mean and standard deviation of the distribution of $\bar{p}$ are, respectively, from Chapter 9,

$$\mu_{\bar{p}} = p$$

$$\sigma_{\bar{p}} = \sqrt{\frac{pq}{n}}$$

where p = population proportion of successes in H_0
$q = 1 - p$
n = sample size (number of + and − signs)

For a hypothesis test of the population proportion p, we assume p is equal to the hypothesized proportion p_h, and $q = q_h = 1 - p_h$. Then in the normal approximation of the distribution of $\bar{p}$, the standard normal variable z is

Test statistic for the matched pairs sign test

$$\text{Sample } z = \frac{\bar{p} - \mu_{\bar{p}}}{\sigma_p}$$

$$= \frac{\bar{p} - p_h}{\sqrt{p_h q_h / n}}$$

This sample z is the test statistic that we shall compute for the sign test.

EXAMPLE A randomly selected sample of consumers took part in a clothes detergent "whiteness" test. Each person washed soiled white clothes—one batch in detergent A and another batch in detergent B. Washed clothes were rated on a whiteness scale of 1 to 4, with 4 being the whitest. Rating data are given in Table 16.1. The table also gives the sign of

TABLE 16.1
SAMPLE WHITENESS RATINGS FOR DETERGENTS A AND B

Ratings		Sign	Ratings		Sign	Ratings		Sign	Ratings		Sign	Ratings		Sign
A	B	A − B	A	B	A − B	A	B	A − B	A	B	A − B	A	B	A − B
2	3	−	4	1	+	4	3	+	3	2	+	4	3	+
1	2	−	1	3	−	3	3	0	3	3	0	3	2	+
3	2	+	3	3	0	2	2	0	2	4	−	4	2	+
2	2	0	3	1	+	1	3	−	3	1	+	3	2	+
4	2	+	4	2	+	4	2	+	4	2	+	1	3	−
4	3	+	3	2	+	4	1	+	4	1	+	4	1	+

the difference, $A - B$, for each pair of ratings. Perform, at the $\alpha = 0.05$ level, a test of the hypothesis that, in the population of consumers who detect a difference, more than half rate A whiter than B.

SOLUTION Rating A whiter than B makes the sign of $A - B$ positive; so we want to know if p, the proportion of + signs in the population of signs, is greater than 0.5. The hypotheses are

1. $H_0: p \leq 0.5 \qquad H_a: p > 0.5$

The test is a "greater than" one-tail test. With $\alpha = 0.05$ we find $z_{0.05} = 1.64$ in Table VI. The decision rule is

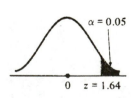

$\alpha = 0.05$

$0 \qquad z = 1.64$

2. Reject H_0 if sample $z > 1.64$

Next we need to determine the sample size n. In Table 16.1 there are 19 plus signs, 6 minus signs, and 5 zeros. We are interested only in consumers who detect a whiteness difference; so the zeros (no difference) are dis-

Here, $np_h = nq_h = 12.5$, so the normal approximation is O.K.

carded. The usable sample size is the number of plus and minus signs,

$$n = 19 + 6 = 25$$

From the null hypothesis, $p_h = 0.5$ and $q_h = 1 - p_h = 0.5$. Hence,

$$\sigma_{\bar{p}} = \sqrt{\frac{p_h q_h}{n}} = \sqrt{\frac{(0.5)(0.5)}{25}} = 0.1$$

The sample proportion of plus signs is

$$\bar{p} = \frac{19}{25} = 0.76$$

The value of the sample test statistic is

$$\text{Sample } z = \frac{\bar{p} - p_h}{\sigma_{\bar{p}}} = \frac{0.76 - 0.5}{0.1}$$

$$= 2.6$$

Hence,

3. Sample $z = 2.6$

The sample $z = 2.6$ exceeds the value 1.64 in the decision rule; so we

4. Reject H_0

Rejecting H_0 means that more than half the population rate A whiter than B. Figure 16.1 shows that H_0 was rejected because the sample z value is in the rejection region.

FIGURE 16.1
Clothes' whiteness detergent test. Rejecting H_0 means that more than half the population rates clothes washed in detergent A as whiter than clothes washed in detergent B.

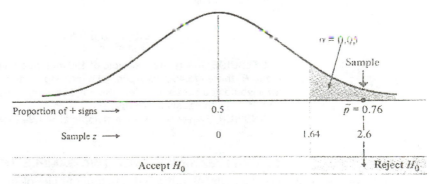

EXERCISE In the whiteness example, suppose we test at the $\alpha = 0.05$ level to determine if the proportion of minus signs is less than 0.5. (a) What are the hypotheses and the decision rule? (b) Compute the value of the sample z. (c) What do you conclude?
ANSWER (a) $H_0: p \geq 0.5$, $H_a: p < 0.5$; reject H_0 if sample $z < -1.64$. (b) Sample $z = -2.6$. (c) Reject H_0 and conclude that the proportion of minus signs is less than 0.5.

To illustrate the two-tail test, suppose that, from previous sampling, the maker of detergent A in the whiteness example believes that 58 percent find A whiter than B. The maker wants to determine at the 5 percent level of significance whether, on the basis of the current sample data that appears in Table 16.1, the current proportion differs from 58 percent. Now the hypotheses are

Two-tail hypotheses   1. $H_0: p = 0.58$ $H_a: p \neq 0.58$

$\frac{\alpha}{2} = 0.025$ With $\alpha = 0.05$, $\alpha/2 = 0.025$. From Table VI we find $z_{0.025} = 1.96$. The decision rule is

2. Reject H_0 if |sample z| > 1.96

As before, $n = 25$ and $\bar{p} = 0.76$. But p_h now is 0.58; so $q_h = 1 - p_h = 0.42$. Therefore,

$$\sigma_{\bar{p}} = \sqrt{\frac{p_h q_h}{n}} = \sqrt{\frac{(0.58)(0.42)}{25}} = 0.0987$$

The test statistic is

$$\text{Sample } z = \frac{\bar{p} - p_h}{\sigma_{\bar{p}}} = \frac{0.76 - 0.58}{0.0987} = 1.82$$

Hence,

3. Sample $z = 1.82$

The sample $z = 1.82$ does not exceed the 1.96 in the decision rule, so we

4. Accept H_0

Accepting H_0 means that the proportion that rates A whiter is 0.58; that is, the proportion does not differ from 0.58.

EXERCISE In a random sample of 100 matched pairs of ratings for products A and B, there are 45 plus signs, 45 minus signs, and 10 zeros. At the $\alpha = 0.10$ level would you accept or reject the null hypothesis that the population proportion of + signs equals 0.6? Why?
ANSWER Reject H_0 because |sample z| = 1.94 exceeds $z_{\alpha/2} = 1.64$.

16.4 THE MANN-WHITNEY TWO-SAMPLE TEST

Mann-Whitney is a test of the equality (or inequality) of two means.

For the Mann-Whitney test, random samples of sizes n_1 and n_2 are selected independently from populations 1 and 2. The conditions are that the population distributions be continuous and that, except for possible differences in their means μ_1 and μ_2, the populations have the same distribution. The test can be performed on the null hypotheses $H_0: \mu_1 = \mu_2$, or $H_0: \mu_1 \leq \mu_2$, or $H_0: \mu_1 \geq \mu_2$. The Mann-Whitney test is the nonparametric alternative to the parametric t test for means given in Chapter 11. However, unlike the t test, the Mann-Whitney test does not require that samples be drawn from normal populations.

Rank Sum Distributions

The first step in the Mann-Whitney test is to assign size rank numbers, 1, 2, 3, 4, and so on, to the $n_1 + n_2$ sample items. The conclusions drawn from a test are the same whether the ranks represent ascending order or descending order. For consistency, we will use ascending order, so that rank 1 is assigned to the smallest item (e.g., the smallest number or least preferred).

The sum of the ranks for a sample R is called its *rank sum*. Thus,

$$R_1 = \text{sum of the } n_1 \text{ sample ranks}$$

$$R_2 = \text{sum of the } n_2 \text{ sample ranks}$$

For example, Table 16.2 gives operating rates for factory A for $n_1 = 5$ days

TABLE 16.2
**RANKING OPERATING RATES FOR
TWO FACTORIES**
(Percent of capacity)

Factory A		Factory B	
Rate	Rank	Rate	Rank
71	1	85	5
82	3.5	82	3.5
77	2	94	8
92	7	97	9
88	6		
Rank sums →	$R_1 = \overline{19.5}$		$R_2 = \overline{25.5}$

and for factory B for $n_1 = 4$ days. Also shown in the table are the ranks and the rank sums. The smallest numbers, 71 and 77 for factory A, are assigned ranks 1 and 2. Where the *tie* occurs (82 appears twice), each of the tied numbers is given the average of the ranks the numbers would have had if they were not tied. After all $n_1 + n_2 = 9$ numbers have been ranked, the rank sums are computed. They are

$$R_1 = 19.5 \quad \text{and} \quad R_2 = 25.5$$

The main idea of the Mann-Whitney test is this: When R_1 (or R_2) is much larger or smaller than would be expected if the samples came from populations having the same mean, then the hypotheses of equal means will be rejected. What we have to know is the mean and standard deviation of the distributions of R_1 and R_2 if the samples came from populations with the same mean. So let's suppose that a pair of samples of sizes n_1 and n_2 are drawn from the same population. Then we compute R_1 and R_2 for the samples. Next suppose we repeat the process with another pair of samples, over and over again, to generate the sampling distributions of R_1 and R_2 for samples of sizes n_1 and n_2. These sampling distributions will have means and standard deviations. By algebra, it can be shown that μ_{R_1}, the mean of the distribution of R_1, is

*If the R_1 and R_2
samples were from
the same population,
they would have
these means . . .*

$$\mu_{R_1} = \frac{n_1(n_1 + n_2 + 1)}{2}$$

and the mean μ_{R_2} of the distribution of R_2 is

$$\mu_{R_2} = \frac{n_2(n_1 + n_2 + 1)}{2}$$

Also, both distributions have the same standard deviation σ_R; it is calculated with the formula

*. . . and this
standard deviation.*

$$\sigma_R = \sqrt{\frac{n_1 n_2 (n_1 + n_2 + 1)}{12}}$$

When both n_1 and n_2 are at least 10, the distributions of R_1 and R_2 can be approximated by normal distributions that have the means and the standard deviation stated above.

Suppose, for example, that we select independent random samples of sizes $n_1 = 15$ and $n_2 = 20$ from a population. Then the distribution of the R_1 values will have as its mean

*We use μ_R, and σ_R to
compute the sample
z for R_1.*

$$\mu_{R_1} = \frac{n_1(n_1 + n_2 + 1)}{2}$$

$$= \frac{15(15 + 20 + 1)}{2}$$

$$= 270$$

The standard deviation of the distribution will be

$$\sigma_R = \sqrt{\frac{n_1 n_2 (n_1 + n_2 + 1)}{12}}$$

$$= \sqrt{\frac{(15)(20)(15 + 20 + 1)}{12}}$$

$$= 30$$

Since both n_1 and n_2 are at least 10, the distribution of the R_1 values can be approximated by the normal distribution shown in Figure 16.2.

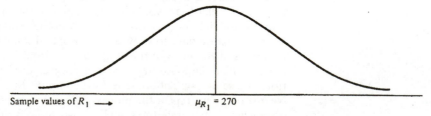

FIGURE 16.2
Distribution of rank
sum R_1 for samples of
$n_1 = 15$ and $n_2 = 20$
($\mu_{R_1} = 270$, $\sigma_R = 30$).

Sample values of $R_1 \longrightarrow$ $\mu_{R_1} = 270$

EXERCISE With $n_1 = 15$ and $n_2 = 20$, what will be the mean and standard deviation of the R_2 distribution?
ANSWER $\mu_{R_2} = 360$ and $\sigma_R = 30$.

One-Tail Test

Suppose we want to determine, at significance level α, whether the mean of population 1 is greater than the mean of population 2. The hypotheses are

1. $H_0: \mu_1 \leq \mu_2$ $H_a: \mu_1 > \mu_2$

The decision rule is

This is the usual one-tail "greater than" decision rule.

2. Reject H_0 if sample $z > z_\alpha$

We select independent random samples of sizes n_1 and n_2 from the populations (n_1 and n_2 must be at least 10). Now we rank the $n_1 + n_2$ sample items in order of size, and then compute the rank sum R_1. (We need only R_1 because μ_1 is the subject of the H_0.) Next we compute

$$\mu_{R_1} = \frac{n_1(n_1 + n_2 + 1)}{2}$$

and
$$\sigma_R = \sqrt{\frac{n_1 n_2 (n_1 + n_2 + 1)}{12}}$$

Now we compute the test statistic

3. Sample $z = \dfrac{R_1 - \mu_{R_1}}{\sigma_R}$

Finally, we

4. Accept or reject H_0

The alternative hypothesis written above is $H_a: \mu_1 > \mu_2$. We could also have written the hypothesis as $H_a: \mu_2 < \mu_1$. Then the hypotheses would be

If $\mu_1 \leq \mu_2$ (as above), then $\mu_2 \geq \mu_1$ (as here).

1. $H_0: \mu_2 \geq \mu_1$ $H_a: \mu_2 < \mu_1$

The decision rule would be

2. Reject H_0 if sample $z < -z_\alpha$

Now, because the subject of the hypotheses is μ_2, we would compute R_2, μ_{R_2}, and σ_R. Then we would compute

3. Sample $z = \dfrac{R_2 - \mu_{R_2}}{\sigma_R}$

Reversing H_0 does not change the conclusion.

The *value of the sample z obtained with* $H_0: \mu_2 \geq \mu_1$ *will be the negative of the value obtained with* $H_0: \mu_1 \leq \mu_2$. Consequently the conclusion will be the same for both sets of hypotheses. That is, a test that rejects $H_0: \mu_1 \leq \mu_2$ will also reject $H_0: \mu_2 \geq \mu_1$.

EXAMPLE Operating rates (percent of capacity) have been obtained for random samples of $n_1 = 10$ days for factory 1 and $n_2 = 12$ days for factory 2. The $n_1 + n_2 = 22$ operating rates have been ranked in order of size; the rank sums for factories 1 and 2 are 145.5 and 107.5. At the $\alpha = 0.05$ level, perform a test to determine whether the mean operating rate of factory 1 is greater than the mean rate for factory 2.

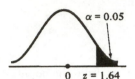

$\alpha = 0.05$

$0 \quad z = 1.64$

SOLUTION   Let μ_1 and μ_2 be the mean operating rates for factories 1 and 2. Then the hypotheses are

1. $H_0 : \mu_1 \leq \mu_2 \qquad H_a : \mu_1 > \mu_2$

With $\alpha = 0.05$, we find $z_\alpha = z_{0.05} = 1.64$ from Table VI. The decision rule is

2. Reject H_0 if sample $z > 1.64$

Now we compute, from $n_1 = 10$ and $n_2 = 12$,

$$\mu_{R_1} = \frac{n_1(n_1 + n_2 + 1)}{2}$$

$$= \frac{10(10 + 12 + 1)}{2} = 115$$

and

$$\sigma_R = \sqrt{\frac{n_1 n_2 (n_1 + n_2 + 1)}{12}}$$

$$= \sqrt{\frac{(10)(12)(10 + 12 + 1)}{12}} = 15.166$$

Next we calculate

$$\text{Sample } z = \frac{R_1 - \mu_{R_1}}{\sigma_R} = \frac{145.5 - 115}{15.166}$$

$$= 2.01$$

So

3. Sample $z = 2.01$

Finally, noting that the sample $z = 2.01$ is greater than the 1.64 in the decision rule, we

4. Reject H_0

Rejecting H_0 means that the mean operating rate for factory 1 is greater than the mean rate for factory 2.

EXERCISE   For the operating rate example, test at the $\alpha = 0.05$ level the hypotheses $H_0 : \mu_2 \geq \mu_1$; $H_a : \mu_2 < \mu_1$. (a) What is the decision rule with $\alpha = 0.05$? (b) Compute μ_{R_2} and the sample z. (c) What do you conclude from the test?
   ANSWER   (a) Reject H_0 if sample $z < -1.64$. (b) $\mu_{R_2} = 138$ and sample $z = -2.01$. (c) $\mu_2 < \mu_1$.

Comparison of the z value for the exercise, -2.01, and the z value for the example, 2.01, shows that these values are the same except for their signs.

The reversed H_0 does lead to the same conclusion.

The conclusion of the exercise, $\mu_2 < \mu_1$, and the conclusion of the example, $\mu_1 > \mu_2$, are different ways of stating the same fact.

Two-Tail Test

The hypotheses in a two-tail Mann-Whitney test are

1. $H_0: \mu_1 = \mu_2$ $H_a: \mu_1 \neq \mu_2$

At significance level α, the decision rule is

2. Reject H_0 if |sample z| > $z_{\alpha/2}$

Either R_1 or R_2 can be used in computing the sample t because, as illustrated above, |sample z| will be the same whether R_1 or R_2 is used.

EXAMPLE Mel Jaffrey, an executive of company 1, wanted to compare opinions his managers have about the company's benefit package (e.g., bonuses, health insurance) with the opinions that managers in competing company 2 have about their benefit package. Mel obtained random samples of $n_1 = 14$ and $n_2 = 11$ managers from companies 1 and 2. The managers indicated their ratings of their benefit package on a scale of 1 (very poor) to 10 (outstanding). Mel ranked the 25 sample responses in order of size. Then he computed the rank sums for the company 1 and company 2 packages and found them to be $R_1 = 205$ and $R_2 = 120$. Perform a test at the $\alpha = 0.10$ level to determine whether the mean ratings of the two benefit packages differ.

SOLUTION The hypotheses for this two-tail test for a difference are

1. $H_0: \mu_1 = \mu_2$ $H_a: \mu_1 \neq \mu_2$

With $\alpha = 0.10$, we have $\alpha/2 = 0.05$ and $z_{0.05} = 1.64$. The decision rule is

2. Reject H_0 if |sample z| > 1.64

We can use either R_1 or R_2 in the test. Let's use $R_1 = 205$. Then

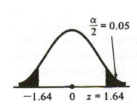

$\frac{\alpha}{2} = 0.05$

$-1.64 \quad 0 \quad z = 1.64$

$$\mu_{R_1} = \frac{n_1(n_1 + n_2 + 1)}{2}$$

$$= \frac{14(14 + 11 + 1)}{2} = 182$$

Next,

$$\sigma_R = \sqrt{\frac{n_1 n_2(n_1 + n_2 + 1)}{12}}$$

$$= \sqrt{\frac{14(11)(14 + 11 + 1)}{12}} = 18.267$$

Then

$$\text{Sample } z = \frac{R_1 - \mu_{R_1}}{\sigma_R} = \frac{205 - 182}{18.267}$$

$$= 1.26$$

So

3. Sample $z = 1.26$

The sample $z = 1.26$ does not exceed the 1.64 in the decision rule; so we

4. Accept H_0

Accepting H_0 means we conclude that $\mu_1 = \mu_2$; or, we might say, managers in the two companies have the same mean ratings of their benefit packages. Figure 16.3 shows that H_0 was accepted because the sample $z = 1.26$ lies in the acceptance region of the test.

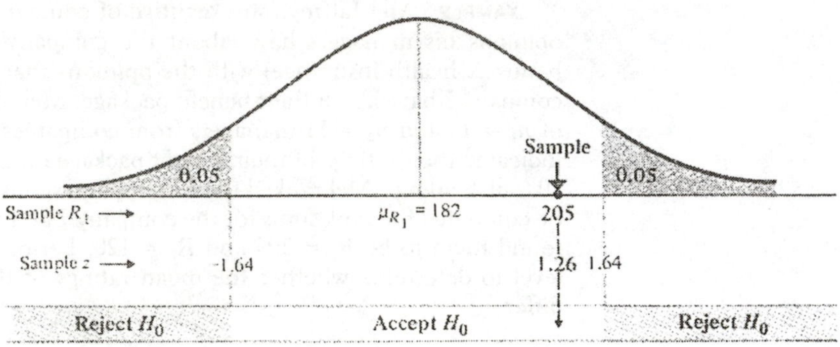

FIGURE 16.3
Mann-Whitney test of managers' ratings of two benefit packages. Accepting H_0 means that the managers in the two companies have the same mean ratings of their benefit packages.

Nonparametric tests may be performed on high-level measurements after ranking.

The Mann-Whitney test is performed on ordinal measurements. It can also be performed on high-level measurements by arranging the $n_1 + n_2$ sample numbers in ascending order of size and assigning rank 1 to the smallest, 2 to the next larger, and so on. If two or more numbers are *tied* (equal), each is assigned the average of the ranks they would have if they were not tied. Thus, for example, the seven numbers

| 3.7 | 4.9 | 5.2 | 5.2 | 8.0 | 8.0 | 8.0 |

would be given the ranks

| 1 | 2 | 3.5 | 3.5 | 6 | 6 | 6 |

16.5 PROBLEMS

1. Each of a randomly selected sample of 40 adults living below the take-off flight pattern of an airport rated aircraft noise level on a scale of 1 to 5, where 5 means exceptionally loud. Later, after experimental noise suppressors had been installed on aircraft, the same adults again rated noise levels. The before and after rating pairs are given in Table A. Perform a matched pairs sign test at the $\alpha = 0.01$ level to determine if more than half of those whose ratings changed thought the noise level was reduced after installation of the suppressors. What do you conclude from the test result? Why?

TABLE A

Before	After	Before	After	Before	After	Before	After	Before	After
3	3	4	5	3	2	2	2	1	1
4	2	2	4	1	2	2	3	3	2
3	4	2	2	4	4	4	3	2	3
2	3	4	2	5	4	5	1	3	3
5	3	3	1	3	2	5	5	4	2
2	2	2	3	1	2	4	1	5	3
4	3	4	1	4	2	2	4	5	1
5	4	5	5	3	3	3	1	4	3

2. A random sample of 36 voters in a town rated their preferences for candidates Spivey and Convey on a scale of 1 to 4, where 4 means highest preference. Sample results are given in Table B. Perform a matched pairs sign test at the $\alpha = 0.05$ level to determine whether, among voters having different preferences, more than half prefer Spivey. What do you conclude from the test result? Why?

TABLE B

Preference ratings		Preference ratings		Preference ratings		Preference ratings	
Spivey	Convey	Spivey	Convey	Spivey	Convey	Spivey	Convey
1	4	4	1	3	2	2	1
3	2	3	2	3	1	2	2
4	1	2	1	2	3	4	3
1	1	2	4	2	1	4	2
3	1	4	2	3	3	2	4
3	2	1	4	3	1	3	1
2	3	3	1	4	2	4	1
4	1	4	4	3	2	1	1
2	1	4	2	3	4	4	3

3. A random sample of 100 consumers rated brand X and brand Y furniture waxes on a scale of 1 to 5, where 5 means the highest quality of finish obtained by a wax. The samp'e data pairs had 59 plus signs (X rated higher than Y), 21 minus signs, and 20 zeros. Perform the matched pairs sign test at the $\alpha = 0.01$ level to determine if more than 60 percent of consumers rate brand X higher than Brand Y. What do you conclude from the test result? Why?

4. Each of a randomly selected sample of 35 workers was timed while assembling a television circuit following standard procedure A. The workers then practiced with procedure B. After achieving proficiency, they were timed while assembling following procedure B. The signs of the time differences, $A - B$, had 3 zeros and 22 pluses. Perform a matched pairs sign test at the $\alpha = 0.05$ level to determine whether more than half of all workers who have a time difference are faster with procedure B. What do you conclude from the test result? Why?

5. Each of a randomly selected panel of 50 consumers rated the flavors of toothpastes X and Y on a scale from 1 (dislike) to 5 (strong like). The pair differences, $X - Y$, had 15 plus signs, 27 minus signs, and 8 zeros. Perform a matched pairs sign test at the $\alpha = 0.05$ level to determine whether less than half the consumers prefer the flavor of X. What do you conclude from the test result? Why?

6. (a) Find the rank sums R_1 and R_2 for the data in Table C. (b) Compute μ_{R_1}, μ_{R_2}, and σ_R.

TABLE C

Sample 1	30.7	31.0	30.6	31.1	30.2	31.6	32.5
Sample 2	31.3	31.9	31.0	32.4	33.0	31.0	33.5

7. (a) Find the rank sums R_1 and R_2 for the data in Table D. (b) Compute μ_{R_1}, μ_{R_2}, and σ_R.

TABLE D

Sample 1	126	131	127	122	128	
Sample 2	125	123	120	127	129	133

8. Random samples of 18 brand A and 18 brand B golf balls were driven from a tee. Distances traveled by the balls were not measured. Instead, the ball nearest the driving tee (shortest distance) was ranked 1, the next further ball was ranked 2, and so on. It was found that six balls had been damaged by the driver; these balls were not ranked. Ranks and brands are given in Table E. Perform a Mann-Whitney test at the $\alpha = 0.05$ level to determine whether the mean distance for brand A balls is greater than the mean distance for brand B balls. What do you conclude from the test result? Why?

TABLE E

Rank	Brand	Rank	Brand	Rank	Brand	Rank	Brand	Rank	Brand
1	B	7	B	13	B	19	B	25	B
2	B	8	A	14	A	20	A	26	A
3	B	9	B	15	A	21	A	27	A
4	B	10	B	16	A	22	A	28	B
5	B	11	A	17	A	23	B	29	A
6	A	12	A	18	A	24	B	30	A

9. Suppose a psychologist interviewed a random sample of professional football players who frequently carry the ball on running plays. Each player was classified as, say, an introvert (type A) or an extrovert (type

B). Then average yards per carry were calculated for each player and ranked in ascending order of size. Ranks and personality types are given in Table F. Perform a Mann-Whitney test at the $\alpha = 0.05$ level to determine if mean yards per carry for type A is less than mean yards per carry for type B. What do you conclude from the test result? Why?

TABLE F

Rank	Type	Rank	Type	Rank	Type	Rank	Type	Rank	Type
1	A	6	B	11	A	16	B	21	A
2	B	7	A	12	B	17	B	22	B
3	B	8	A	13	A	18	A	23	B
4	A	9	B	14	B	19	B	24	B
5	A	10	A	15	B	20	B	25	B

10. The arrangement of switches, gauges, and other devices on an airplane control panel may affect the time it takes for a pilot to bring an emergency situation under control. Two arrangements, panel A and panel B, were tested. Two random samples of 10 pilots were selected. One sample was assigned to A and the other to B. The times (in seconds) taken by pilots to establish control over a simulated emergency are given in Table G. Perform a Mann-Whitney test at the $\alpha = 0.05$ level to determine if the mean times for the panels are equal. What do you conclude from the test result? Why?

TABLE G

Panel A	2.05	2.03	2.19	2.12	2.20	2.08	2.21	2.14	2.21	2.21
Panel B	2.06	2.04	2.17	2.01	2.10	2.06	2.06	2.07	2.13	2.16

11. A random sample of 30 new automobile engines was divided into two random groups of 15. One group was equipped with emission control device A, the other with device B. Sample data on emission contaminants are given in Table H. Perform a Mann-Whitney test at the $\alpha = 0.05$ level to determine whether mean emission for device B is less than that for device A.

TABLE H

Control device A			Control device B		
796	861	820	780	812	857
793	824	853	790	817	877
784	830	884	791	822	798
838	895	889	802	834	881
815	850	870	807	811	844

12. The parametric t test (Chapter 11) could be applied in Problems 10 and 11. What condition should be satisfied if the t test is to be performed?

13. A security analyst ranked the growth potentials of a sample of companies, assigning rank 1 to the company with the lowest potential. Some companies were in industry group A. The others were in group B. Summary data are given in Table I. Perform a Mann-Whitney test at the $\alpha = 0.05$ level to determine if mean growth potential is greater for B companies than for A companies. What do you conclude from the test result? Why?

TABLE I

	Sample size	Rank sum
Group A sample	11	140
Group B sample	18	295

14. Random samples of industrial diamonds made by two processes were examined for quality. The poorest quality was assigned rank 1. Summary data are given in Table J. Perform a Mann-Whitney test at the $\alpha = 0.05$ level to determine if the mean quality rating for process A is less than the mean for process B.

TABLE J

	Sample size	Rank sum
Process A sample	23	345
Process B sample	10	216

16.6 THE SPEARMAN RANK CORRELATION TEST

The Rank Correlation Coefficient

Suppose that we have a sample of (x, y) data pairs where the x values are ranks such as 1, 2, 3, and the y values are, except for order, the same set of ranks. For example, $n = 4$ rank pairs might be (2, 1), (3, 2), (1, 3), and (4, 4). We want to determine if the (x, y) data pairs are correlated, that is, for example, to determine whether the y ranks tend to increase as the corresponding x ranks increase. We will measure the correlation between x and y with the linear rank correlation coefficient r_s. You learned the formula for the (parametric) simple linear correlation coefficient in Chapter 12. If the formula of Chapter 12 is applied to rank pairs, it can be shown by algebra that the rank correlation coefficient is

Formula for the Spearman rank correlation coefficient

$$r_s = 1 - \frac{6\Sigma d^2}{n(n^2 - 1)}$$

where r_s = Spearman rank coefficient of linear correlation
$d = x - y$ (the difference of ranks in a pair)
n = sample size (number of pairs)

$r_s = 1$ means perfect direct correlation

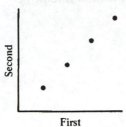

$r_s = -1$ means perfect inverse correlation

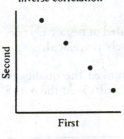

$r_s = 0$ means no correlation

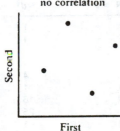

Thus, for the number pair $(2, 1)$, $d = (2 - 1) = 1$. And for the set of $n = 4$ pairs $(2, 1)$, $(3, 2)$, $(1, 3)$, and $(4, 4)$,

$$\Sigma d^2 = (2 - 1)^2 + (3 - 2)^2 + (1 - 3)^2 + (4 - 4)^2 = 6$$

Applying the formula to the $n = 4$ pairs, we find that

$$r_s = 1 - \frac{6\Sigma d^2}{n(n^2 - 1)}$$

$$= 1 - \frac{6(6)}{4(4^2 - 1)} = 0.4$$

When the ranks in every data pair are equal, r_s will equal 1, and the sample data will exhibit perfect positive (or direct) correlation. If the ranks are in perfect inverse order, as in $(1, 4)$, $(2, 3)$, $(3, 2)$, $(4, 1)$, then $r_s = -1$. We say that $r_s = -1$ means the sample data exhibit perfect negative (or inverse) correlation.

EXERCISE Compute r_s for the rank pairs $(1, 3)$, $(2, 1)$, $(3, 4)$, and $(4, 2)$.
ANSWER $r_s = 0$.

When $r_s = 0$, we say that the sample data pairs are uncorrelated. The examples and exercise illustrate the fact that r_s is a number in the interval from -1 to 1. That is,

$$-1 \le r_s \le 1$$

The Test

The sample r_s is used in a test to determine whether population ranks are correlated. The population rank correlation is denoted by ρ_s (ρ is the Greek letter rho). The null hypothesis of the test can be $H_0: \rho_s = 0$, or $H_0: \rho_s \ge 0$, or $H_0: \rho_s \le 0$. If n, the number of pairs of sample ranks, is at least 10, z values from Table VI can be used to construct decision rules. The test statistic is

$$\text{Sample } z = r_s \sqrt{n - 1}$$

The formula emerges from the fact that if $\rho_s = 0$, the distribution of r_s values in large samples is closely approximated by a normal distribution that has a mean of 0 and a standard deviation of $1/\sqrt{n - 1}$. Thus the standard normal variate

$$z = \frac{\text{sample statistic} - \text{mean}}{\text{standard deviation}}$$

$$= \frac{r_s - 0}{1/\sqrt{n - 1}}$$

$$= r_s \sqrt{n - 1}$$

I will give the steps for a one-tail "greater than" test. You can make the usual changes in steps 1 and 2 if a "less than" or a two-tail test is to be performed. For a "greater than" test, the hypotheses are

1. $H_0: \rho_s \leq 0$ $H_a: \rho_s > 0$

At significance level α, the decision rule is

2. Reject H_0 if sample $z > z_a$

Now we have to calculate r_s and compute the

Test statistic when   3. Sample $z = r_s \sqrt{n - 1}$
n ≥ 10

Finally, we

4. Accept or reject H_0

Accepting H_0 means that the ranks are either uncorrelated or negatively correlated. Rejecting H_0 means that the ranks are positively correlated.

EXAMPLE Marlene and Roger, security analysts, ranked the quality of $n = 12$ stocks as shown in the M and R columns of Table 16.3. At the $\alpha = 5$

TABLE 16.3
QUALITY RANKINGS OF 12 STOCKS

Stock code letter	Marlene's rank M	Roger's rank R	M − R = d	d²
A	5	4	1	1
B	8	6	2	4
C	3	1	2	4
D	10	8	2	4
E	7	9	−2	4
F	1	2	−1	1
G	9	5	4	16
H	2	7	−5	25
I	11	10	1	1
J	4	3	1	1
K	6	11.5	−5.5	30.25
L	12	11.5	0.5	0.25
				$\Sigma d^2 = \overline{91.50}$

percent level, perform a test to determine whether the analysts tend to agree in their ranks.

SOLUTION Translating "tend to agree" to mean that the ranks are positively correlated ($\rho_s > 0$), the hypotheses are

1. $H_0: \rho_s \leq 0$ $H_a: \rho_s > 0$

With $\alpha = 0.05$,

$$z_\alpha = z_{0.05} = 1.64$$

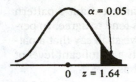

$\alpha = 0.05$

$0 \quad z = 1.64$

The decision rule is

2. Reject H_0 if sample $z > 1.64$.

Next we must compute Σd^2 as shown in Table 16.3. Then

$$r_s = 1 - \frac{6\Sigma d^2}{n(n^2 - 1)}$$

With $\Sigma d^2 = 91.50$ and $n = 12$ rank pairs, we find

$$r_s = 1 - \frac{6(91.50)}{12[(12)^2 - 1]} = 0.6801$$

Next we compute

$$\text{Sample } z = r_s \sqrt{n - 1} = 0.6801 \sqrt{12 - 1}$$
$$= 2.26$$

Hence

3. Sample $z = 2.26$

The sample $z = 2.26$ exceeds the 1.64 in the decision rule; so we

4. Reject H_0

Rejecting H_0 means that $\rho_s > 0$; or, we can say, Marlene and Roger exhibit a significant level of agreement in their rankings of the quality of stocks. Figure 16.4 shows that H_0 was rejected because the sample $z = 2.26$ lies in the rejection region of the decision rule.

FIGURE 16.4
One-tail test for positive rank correlation. Rejecting H_0 means that the stock quality ranks assigned by the two analysts are positively correlated.

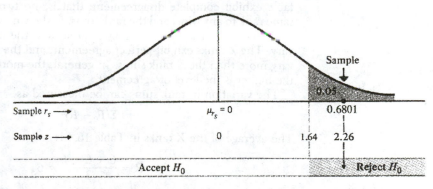

Sample

0.05

0.6801

Sample $r_s \longrightarrow$ $\mu_{r_s} = 0$

Sample $z \longrightarrow$ 0   1.64   2.26

Accept H_0 Reject H_0

16.7 THE KENDALL TEST OF CONCORDANCE

The Hypotheses

A concordance test is a test for agreement among more than two sets of rankings.

In the rank correlation test of the last section, we used two sets of rankings of n items, such as Marlene's set and Roger's set of rankings of 12 stocks. When three or more people rank n items, the Kendall test of concordance can be performed to determine whether or not the sets of ranks exhibit a pattern which indicates that the people who assigned the ranks tend to agree. In performing the concordance test at significance level α, we shall say that a pattern indicating a tendency for people to agree "exhibits a significant level of agreement." The hypotheses of the test will be stated as

Hypotheses of the Kendall test

H_0: the sets of ranks do not indicate a significant level of agreement

H_a: the sets of ranks exhibit a significant level of agreement

The Sample Statistic and the Decision Rule

Suppose three people, A, B, and C, each ranked the qualities of three wines, W1, W2, and W3. Table 16.4 shows three of the ways in which ranks could

TABLE 16.4
QUALITY RANKS FOR THREE WINES

This table shows three sets of rankings, for comparison.

Person	X ranks (no agreement)			Y ranks (some agreement)			Z ranks (perfect agreement)		
	W1	W2	W3	W1	W2	W3	W1	W2	W3
A	3	1	2	1	2	3	1	2	3
B	1	2	3	3	2	1	1	2	3
C	2	3	1	1	2	3	1	2	3
Rank sum R	$\overline{6}$	$\overline{6}$	$\overline{6}$	$\overline{5}$	$\overline{6}$	$\overline{7}$	$\overline{3}$	$\overline{6}$	$\overline{9}$

be assigned, and R, the sum of the ranks for each wine. The X ranks in the table exhibit complete disagreement: that is, no two people assigned the same rank to any wine; and the rank sums, 6, show no variation from wine to wine. The Y ranks show some agreement, and the rank sums 5, 6, and 7 vary. The Z ranks exhibit perfect agreement, and the rank sums 3, 6, and 9 vary more than the Y rank sums. In general, the more the rank sums vary, the higher is the level of agreement.

The variation in rank sums can be measured as

$$\Sigma(R - \bar{R})^2$$

The average of the X ranks in Table 16.4 is

$$\bar{R} = \frac{6 + 6 + 6}{3} = 6$$

The Y and Z ranks also have $\bar{R} = 6$. For the X ranks we have

$$\Sigma(R - \bar{R})^2 = (6 - 6)^2 + (6 - 6)^2 + (6 - 6)^2 = 0$$

For the Y ranks

$$\Sigma(R - \bar{R})^2 = (5 - 6)^2 + (6 - 6)^2 + (7 - 6)^2 = 2$$

And for the Z ranks

Larger $\Sigma(R - \bar{R})^2$ means greater agreement.

$$\Sigma(R - \bar{R})^2 = (3 - 6)^2 + (6 - 6)^2 + (9 - 6)^2 = 18$$

In general, the larger $\Sigma(R - \bar{R})^2$, the higher is the level of agreement in the ranks people assign.

Suppose that k people assign ranks to each of n different items. Statisticians have found that when n, the number of items being ranked, is at least 8, the distribution of the statistic

$$\frac{12[\Sigma(R - \bar{R})^2]}{kn(n + 1)}$$

can be approximated by the chi-square distribution with $v = n - 1$ degrees of freedom. We will call this statistic the sample χ^2 and use it as the concordance test statistic. However, to simplify calculations, the statistic can be changed by algebra to the equivalent statistic

Test statistic for concordance, $n \geq 8$

$$\text{Sample } \chi^2 = \frac{12\Sigma R^2 - 3n[k(n + 1)]^2}{kn(n + 1)}$$

where R = sum of the ranks assigned to an item
n = number of items that are ranked
k = number of people assigning ranks

Large values of $\Sigma(R - \bar{R})^2$ indicate a high level of agreement and make for a large sample χ^2. The decision rule for the concordance test at significance level α is

Decision rule for concordance test

$$\text{Reject } H_0 \text{ if sample } \chi^2 > \chi^2_{\alpha,v}$$

where $v = n - 1$

Thus, large values of the sample χ^2 lead us to reject H_0 and conclude that the ranks exhibit a significant level of agreement.

In Table 16.4, $k = 3$ people ranked $n = 3$ wines. For the Y ranks, the rank sums R are 5, 6, 7. Hence,

$$\Sigma R^2 = (5)^2 + (6)^2 + (7)^2 = 110$$

and

$$\text{Sample } \chi^2 = \frac{12\Sigma R^2 - 3n[k(n + 1)]^2}{kn(n + 1)}$$

$$= \frac{12(110) - 3(3)[3(3 + 1)]^2}{(3)(3)(3 + 1)}$$

$$= 0.667$$

EXERCISE Compute the sample χ^2 for the Z ranks in Table 16.4.
ANSWER 6.

The Test

Suppose that each of $k = 3$ people A, B, and C ranked the qualities of $n = 8$

TABLE 16.5
QUALITY RANKS FOR EIGHT WINES

Person	Wine							
	W1	W2	W3	W4	W5	W6	W7	W8
A	3	2	1	5	8	6	7	4
B	2	5	1	3	4·	7	6	8
C	4	3	2	1	7	5	8	6
Rank sum R	9	10	4	9	19	18	21	18

wines as shown in Table 16.5. We want to determine at $\alpha = 0.05$ whether or not the rankings exhibit a significant level of agreement. The hypotheses of the test are

1. H_0: the sets of ranks do not indicate a significant level of agreement

   H_a: the sets of ranks indicate a significant level of agreement

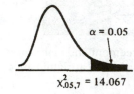

$\alpha = 0.05$

$\chi^2_{.05,7} = 14.067$

The number of items ranked is $n = 8$; so $v = n - 1 = 7$. With $\alpha = 0.05$, we find from Table IV that $\chi^2_{\alpha,v} = \chi^2_{0.05,7} = 14.067$. The decision rule is

2. Reject H_0 if sample $\chi^2 > 14.067$

We need the value of ΣR^2 to compute the sample χ^2. It is, from the rank sums R in Table 16.5,

$$\Sigma R^2 = (9)^2 + (10)^2 + (4)^2 + \cdots + (21)^2 + (18)^2 = 1728$$

Now, with $k = 3$ sets of $n = 8$ ranks we compute

$$\text{Sample } \chi^2 = \frac{12\Sigma R^2 - 3n[k(n + 1)]^2}{kn(n + 1)}$$

$$= \frac{12(1728) - 3(8)[3(8 + 1)]^2}{3(8)(8 + 1)}$$

$$= 15$$

Hence,

3. Sample $\chi^2 = 15$

The sample $\chi^2 = 15$ exceeds the value 14.067 in the decision rule; so we

4. Reject H_0

Rejecting H_0 means that the three people exhibit a significant level of agreement in their rankings of wine qualities. Figure 16.5 shows that H_0 was rejected because the sample $\chi^2 = 15$ lies in the rejection region of the decision rule.

EXERCISE College coaches voted to select the top 10 college football teams in the country. Then each of four sports editors ranked the 10 teams. The sum of

FIGURE 16.5
Kendall concordance
test of agreement
among three rankings
of wine qualities. Re-
jecting H_0 means that
the three judges of
wine qualities exhibit a
significant level of
agreement in their
rankings.

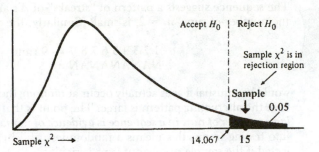

the squares of the rank sums was $\Sigma R^2 = 5094$. At the $\alpha = 0.10$ level, do the editors exhibit a significant level of agreement? Why?

ANSWER No: because the sample χ^2, 6.93, is less than $\chi^2_{0.10,9} = 14.684$.

16.8 THE RUNS TEST FOR RANDOMNESS

The Hypotheses

Statistical inference requires that samples be selected at random. The purpose of the runs test is to determine whether or not a selection *sequence* appears to be random. The test is based upon the number of runs in a sample

Definition of runs sequence. A *run* is one or more identical symbols (or occurrences) preceded
and followed by a different symbol or no symbol at all. For example, in the
sequence

$$\underbrace{XX}_{1} \ \underbrace{YYY}_{2} \ \underbrace{X}_{3} \ \underbrace{Y}_{4} \leftarrow 4 \text{ runs}$$

the pair XX at the left is a run because it is preceded by no symbol and followed by a different symbol. The YYY triple is a run because it is preceded
and followed by a different symbol. The single symbol X is a run because it is
preceded and followed by Y, and the final Y is a run because it is preceded by
X and followed by no symbol. The number of runs n_r in the sequence is 4.

EXERCISE How many runs are there in the sequence *A BB AAA B A BB A
BBB*?

ANSWER $n_r = 8$.

In tennis, a player who serves a ball so well that the opponent cannot
reach it is said to have scored an "ace." Suppose that a player has served an
ace A in four of the last nine serves. The other five serves were N, for not
ace. If the player's aces occur at random, we would not expect to observe the
sequence

$$\underbrace{AAAA}_{1}\underbrace{NNNNN}_{2} \leftarrow 2 \text{ runs}$$

Runs and randomness

The sequence suggests a pattern of "streaks" of A's and N's. Note that here the number of runs, $n_r = 2$, is small. Similarly, the alternating pattern

$$1\ 2\ 3\ 4\ 5\ 6\ 7\ 8\ 9 \leftarrow 9 \text{ runs}$$
$$NANANANAN$$

would be unusual if aces actually occur at random: the number of runs, $n_r = 9$, in the alternating pattern is large. The point is that *an unusually small or large number of runs in a sequence is evidence of nonrandomness*. Translated into testing terms, this means a randomness null hypothesis should be rejected if the sample number of runs is significantly large or small; thus, our test will be two-tailed. Our hypotheses will be

*The runs-test
hypotheses*

1. H_0: the symbol sequence is random

   H_a: the symbol sequence is not random

The Sample Statistic and the Decision Rule

For a sequence that contains two symbols, let

n_1 = number of times one symbol occurs

n_2 = number of times the other symbol occurs

$n = n_1 + n_2$

n_r = number of runs in the sequence

Suppose that in a sequence of $n = 4$ symbols there is 1 A and there are 3 B's. Then $n_1 = 1$ and $n_2 = 3$. The four possible sequences are

$$ABBB \quad BABB \quad BBAB \quad BBBA$$

The numbers of runs in the four sequences are, respectively, 2, 3, 3, 2. The mean number of runs is

$$\mu_r = \frac{2 + 3 + 3 + 2}{4} = 2.5$$

The standard deviation of the number of runs is

$$\sigma_r = \sqrt{\frac{(2 - 2.5)^2 + (3 - 2.5)^2 + (3 - 2.5)^2 + (2 - 2.5)^2}{4}}$$

$$= 0.5$$

It can be shown by algebra that μ_r and σ_r can be computed by the formulas

$$\mu_r = \frac{2n_1 n_2}{n} + 1$$

$$\sigma_r = \sqrt{\frac{2n_1 n_2 (2n_1 n_2 - n)}{n^2(n - 1)}}$$

EXERCISE Verify with the formulas that, when $n = 4$, $n_1 = 1$, and $n_2 = 3$, $\mu_r = 2.5$ and $\sigma_r = 0.5$.

When both n_1 and n_2 are at least 10, the distribution of the number of runs can be approximated by a normal distribution that has μ_r as its mean and σ_r as its standard deviation. Consequently the test statistic of the runs test for randomness is

Test statistic for runs test: n_1 and n_2 at least 10

$$\text{Sample } z = \frac{n_r - \mu_r}{\sigma_r}$$

Large positive or large negative values of the sample z mean that an observed sequence is not random because its number of runs is either too small or too large. At significance level α, the decision rule for the two-tail test is

Decision rule for runs test

$$\text{Reject } H_0 \text{ if } |\text{sample } z| > z_{\alpha/2}$$

The Test

Count n, n_1, n_2, and n_r . . .

In the runs test for randomness, we use one symbol for one occurrence and a different symbol for the other occurrence. Then we record an observed sequence of n symbols in their order of occurrence. Next we count to obtain n_1 and n_2, the respective numbers of symbols of one kind and of the other kind. Finally, we count the number n_r of runs in the sequence.

The hypotheses are

. . . then do the usual hypothesis test for a randomness hypothesis H_0.

1. H_0: the symbol sequence is random

   H_a: the symbol sequence is not random

At significance level α, the decision rule is

2. Reject H_0 if $|\text{sample } z| > z_{\alpha/2}$

Next we compute

$$\mu_r = \frac{2n_1 n_2}{n} + 1$$

and

$$\sigma_r = \sqrt{\frac{2n_1 n_2(2n_1 n_2 - n)}{n^2(n - 1)}}$$

Then we compute the value of the sample statistic

3. $\text{Sample } z = \frac{n_r - \mu_r}{\sigma_r}$

Finally, we

4. Accept or reject H_0

Accepting H_0 means that the sequence is random. Rejecting H_0 means that the sequence is not random.

EXAMPLE The following ace (A), not ace (N), sequence was observed for tennis player Riley:

$$NN\ A\ N\ AA\ N\ A\ N\ A\ N\ A\ NN\ A\ NNNNNNN\ AA\ N\ A\ NN\ AA\ NNNNNN$$

At the $\alpha = 0.05$ level, perform a runs test to determine if Riley's ace, not ace sequence is random.

SOLUTION

First, by counting, we find that

$$n_1 = \text{number of } N\text{'s} = 24$$
$$n_2 = \text{number of } A\text{'s} = 12$$
$$n = n_1 + n_2 = 36$$
$$n_r = \text{number of runs} = 19$$

The hypotheses are

1. H_0: Riley's ace, not ace sequence is random

   H_a: Riley's sequence is not random

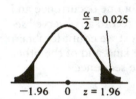

$\frac{\alpha}{2} = 0.025$

$-1.96 \quad 0 \quad z = 1.96$

With $\alpha = 0.05$, $\alpha/2$ is 0.025 and $z_{0.025} = 1.96$. The decision rule is

2. Reject H_0 if |sample z| > 1.96

Next, with $n_1 = 24$, $n_2 = 12$, and $n = 36$, we compute

$$\mu_r = \frac{2n_1 n_2}{n} + 1 = \frac{2(24)(12)}{36} + 1$$
$$= 17$$

and

$$\sigma_r = \sqrt{\frac{2n_1 n_2 (2n_1 n_2 - n)}{n^2(n - 1)}}$$

$$= \sqrt{\frac{2(24)(12)[2(24)(12) - 36]}{(36)^2(36 - 1)}}$$

$$= \sqrt{\frac{576(540)}{(1296)(35)}} = 2.62$$

The value of the test statistic is

$$\text{Sample } z = \frac{n_r - \mu_r}{\sigma_r} = \frac{19 - 17}{2.62}$$
$$= 0.76$$

Hence,

3. Sample $z = 0.76$

The sample $z = 0.76$ does not exceed the 1.96 in the decision rule; so we

4. Accept H_0

Accepting H_0 means we conclude that Riley's ace, not ace sequence is random. Figure 16.6 shows that H_0 was accepted because the sample $z = 0.76$ lies in the acceptance region of the decision rule.

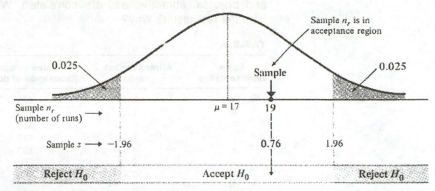

FIGURE 16.6
Runs test for randomness of tennis aces. Accepting H_0 means that the ace, not ace sequence is random.

EXERCISE A sequence of 50 parts made by an automatic machine had 10 defective (D) parts and 40 good (G) parts. There were 10 runs in the sequence of G's and D's. At the $\alpha = 0.05$ level perform a runs test to determine whether the sequence is random. What do you conclude? Why?

ANSWER The sequence is not random because |sample z| = |−3.163| = 3.163 exceeds $z_{0.025}$, which is 1.96.

16.9 PROBLEMS

1. Compute the rank correlation coefficient for each of the following sets of rank pairs.

(a) x	y	(b) x	y	(c) x	y	(d) x	y
1	5	1	4	1	4	1	1
2	4	2	3	2	3	2	3
3	3	3	5	3	2	3	2
4	2	4	1	4	1	4	4
5	1	5	2	5	5	5	5

2. Interviews with random samples of workers in 35 occupation classifications were used to construct a job satisfaction rating index for each occupation. Annual salaries for each occupation also were recorded. Satisfaction indexes and salaries were then ranked to give a pair of ranks for each occupation. The lowest satisfaction and salary numbers were ranked 1. The sum of the squares of the differences of the rank pairs was 3390. At the $\alpha = 0.01$ level, perform a test to determine if satisfaction index and salary are correlated. What do you conclude from the test result? Why?

3. The sales manager of Fordhart Insurance Company ranked the physical attractiveness of a random sample of 10 sales representatives. The

ranks (1 is lowest) are given in Table A, together with the amounts of insurance that the representatives sold. Rank the sales volumes. Then perform a test at the $\alpha = 0.05$ level to determine whether sales volume and physical attractiveness are correlated. What do you conclude from the test result? Why?

TABLE A

Sales representative	Attractiveness rank	Sales volume (thousands of dollars)
A	6	325
B	1	210
C	5	420
D	7	182
E	4	160
F	2	250
G	10	360
H	3	295
I	8	495
J	9	315

4. Jane and John, two women's fashion buyers, ranked a random sample of 14 blouse styles in order of preference. The ranks are given in Table B. At the $\alpha = 0.01$ level, perform a test to determine whether the ranks are positively correlated. What do you conclude from the test result? Why?

TABLE B

Blouse style	Jane's rank	John's rank
A	6	4
B	9	6
C	12	9.5
D	2	1
E	1	2
F	5	9.5
G	13	11
H	8	,8
I	11	12
J	4	7
K	14	14
L	7	3
M	3	5
N .	10	13

5. John P. Claus, president of Claus Band Instruments, interviewed 12 candidates for the position of general manager. John ranked the candidates from 1 to 12 (highest). Each candidate also completed a written personality inventory which was scored on a 0 to 100 scale. John's ranks and the personality inventory scores are given in Table

C. John wants to know if his ranks and the inventory scores are correlated. Rank the personality inventory scores; then perform a rank correlation test at the $\alpha = 0.05$ level. What do you conclude from the test results? Why?

TABLE C

Candidate	John's rank	Personality score
A	5	92
B	9	64
C	3.5	70
D	3.5	39
E	2	55
F	7.5	76
G	10	61
H	11	79
I	1	51
J	6	44
K	12	81
L	7.5	87

6. Selling price and dividend paid per share for a random sample of 40 stocks are given in Table D. Perform a rank correlation test at the $\alpha = 0.01$ level to determine whether price and dividend are positively correlated. What do you conclude from the test result? Why?

TABLE D

Price	Dividend	Price	Dividend	Price	Dividend	Price	Dividend
$38	$2.70	$19	$2.18	$ 5	$ 0.30	$29	$0.11
23	0.60	31	2.75	8	1.00	8	0.12
13	0.65	43	2.80	17	1.22	35	0.50
46	1.20	24	1.60	6	0.05	19	1.60
14	1.28	26	1.90	104	10.70	14	0.96
28	2.00	8	0.55	48	4.75	40	4.30
21	1.50	25	0.90	11	0.10	19	1.40
40	2.40	7	0.30	61	5.85	23	1.50
33	2.55	53	3.00	27	0.64	10	1.17
23	1.45	57	5.00	49	4.20	22	1.80

7. Each of a panel of three people ranked the qualities of a random sample of nine stereo systems. The sum of the squares of the rank sums was $\Sigma R^2 = 2500$. Perform a Kendall concordance test at the $\alpha = 0.10$ level. What do you conclude from the test result? Why?

8. Five management professors at a business college ranked the term papers submitted by a random sample of 15 students. The sum of the squares of the rank sums was $\Sigma R^2 = 27,106$. Perform a Kendall concordance test at the $\alpha = 0.01$ level. What do you conclude from the test result? Why?

9. Three executives of a company ranked the performances of a random sample of eight managers. Their ranks are given in Table E. Perform a Kendall concordance test at the $\alpha = 0.05$ level. What do you conclude from the test result? Why?

TABLE E

Executive	Manager							
	A	B	C	D	E	F	G	H
Crowley	2	8	1	3	6	7	4	5
Green	3	7	1	2	8	4	5	6
Mackay	4	8	1	6	2	5	3	7

10. Venture Capital, Inc., provides money to companies in return for part ownership of the companies. Venture is considering 10 companies that are seeking money. Each of Venture's three partners ranked the 10 companies. Rank 10 was assigned to the company a partner believed would yield the highest return on Venture's investment. The ranks are given in Table F. Perform the Kendall concordance test at the $\alpha = 0.01$ level. What do you conclude from the test result? Why?

TABLE F

Partner	Company									
	A	B	C	D	E	F	G	H	I	J
Klein	5	1	3	2	4	7	6	8	9	10
Morrisey	4	2	3	1	8	5	7	6	10	9
Pringle	3	2	4	1	5	6	9	7	8	10

11. Four security analysts ranked the growth potentials of a random sample of 10 stocks. The ranks are given in Table G. Perform the Kendall concordance test at the $\alpha = 0.05$ level. What do you conclude from the test result? Why?

TABLE G

Analyst	Stock									
	A	B	C	D	E	F	G	H	I	J
Bremer	9	4	1	6	2	3	8	10	5	7
Gorman	6	1	3	4	7	5	8	9	2	10
Phillips	8	5	4	1	2	3	9	10	6	7
Wright	9	1	2	5	3	8	6	7	4	10

12. (a) What is the expected (mean) number of runs for a random sample containing three A's and four B's? (b) How many runs does the sample AAABBBB have?

13. (a) What is the expected (mean) number of runs for a random sample that has four A's and six B's? (b) How many runs does the sample *BABABABABB* have?

14. After completing his business in Las Vegas, Jim Stone visited a gambling casino. Jim recorded the red (R), black (B) sequence of 50 winning numbers on the roulette wheel. There were 30 R's and 20 B's; and there were 29 runs in the sequence. Perform the runs test at the $\alpha = 0.05$ level to determine whether the order of the R, B sequence is random. What do you conclude from the test result? Why?

15. The planning staff of a corporation uses quarterly forecasts of the GNP (gross national product) in its projections. The forecasts are sometimes too high (H) and sometimes too low (L). The sequence of H and L forecasts for 24 consecutive quarters was

$$H, L, H, H, L, H, L, H, H, L, H, H, L, L, H, H, L, H, L, H, L, L, H, L$$

Perform the runs test at the $\alpha = 0.05$ level to determine whether the order of the H, L sequence is random. What do you conclude from the test result? Why?

16. Sharon Rodak, a stockbroker, recorded a plus sign for each day that the Dow Jones stock price average was higher than the previous day's average. She recorded a minus sign for each day that the average was below the previous day's average. No record was made on a day when the average was the same as the previous day's average. Sharon's record was

$$+, +, -, +, +, +, +, +, +, +, -, +, +, +, +, +, +, +, -, -,$$

$$-, +, -, -, -, -, +, +, +, +, +, +, +, -, -, +, +, +, +, -$$

Perform the runs test at the $\alpha = 0.05$ level to determine whether the $+$, $-$ sequence is random. What do you conclude from the test result? Why?

17. To raise money for expansion, a company sold 5000 bonds at $1000 each. The bond buyers are paid 18 percent interest ($180 per bond per year). The bonds are callable; that is, the company can buy them back after 5 years, at $1020 each. Interest rates declined markedly; so the company decided to call 50 bonds at a time (as cash became available) to avoid paying 18 percent interest. Bondholders, of course, preferred not to sell their high-interest bonds. To be fair, the company decided to call the bonds at random. The bonds are numbered serially from 1 to 5000. The first 50 called had the sequence of serial numbers listed in Table H. The median of the bond serial numbers is (5000 + 1)/2 = 2500.5. Mark each serial number that is above the median as A, and mark each number below the median as B. Perform the runs test at the $\alpha = 0.05$ level to determine whether the A, B sequence is random. What do you conclude from the test result? Why?

TABLE H

1. 4861	11. 684	21. 2290	31. 3499	41. 185
2. 1947	12. 3267	22. 4391	32. 4582	42. 400
3. 1540	13. 3984	23. 1342	33. 3128	43. 3619
4. 1404	14. 848	24. 3411	34. 3282	44. 49
5. 985	15. 3933	25. 3401	35. 2192	45. 3396
6. 479	16. 2118	26. 153	36. 1043	46. 3726
7. 2191	17. 1328	27. 4909	37. 1742	47. 869
8. 4116	18. 1951	28. 3734	38. 4170	48. 2613
9. 2377	19. 350	29. 814	39. 1095	49. 1818
10. 3322	20. 1156	30. 2471	40. 3216	50. 3201

16.10 SUMMARY

The *matched pairs sign test* is a nonparametric test of a population proportion, based on a sample of paired rankings. For each pair, the difference between its rankings is noted as either + or −. (Zero differences are discarded.) Let n be the total number of + and − signs in the sample. Compute $\bar{p}$, the sample proportion of plus signs. Let p be the unknown population proportion of plus signs, and p_h be the population proportion of plus signs stated in the null hypothesis. If np_h and $n(1 - p_h)$ are at least 5, the steps in a one-tail "greater than" test are: First, state the hypotheses

1. $H_0: p \le p_h$ $H_a: p > p_h$

At significance level α, the decision rule (using Table VI) is

2. Reject H_0 if sample $z > z_\alpha$

Next, compute

3. Sample $z = \dfrac{\bar{p} - p_h}{\sqrt{p_h(1 - p_h)/n}}$

Finally,

4. Accept or reject H_0

The hypotheses and decision rule for a one-tail "less than" test and a two-tail "equal to" test are determined similarly.

The *Mann-Whitney two-sample test* is a nonparametric test of the equality of two population means. For two independent samples of sizes n_1 and n_2 from respective populations 1 and 2, all $n_1 + n_2$ numbers are ranked in ascending order of size. Then

$$R_1 = \text{sum of sample 1 ranks}$$

$$R_2 = \text{sum of sample 2 ranks}$$

$$\mu_{R_1} = \frac{n_1(n_1 + n_2 + 1)}{2}$$

$$\mu_{R_2} = \frac{n_2(n_1 + n_2 + 1)}{2}$$

$$\sigma_R = \sqrt{\frac{n_1 n_2(n_1 + n_2 + 1)}{12}}$$

If both n_1 and n_2 are at least 10, the steps in a one-tail "greater than" test of means are: First state the hypotheses

1. $H_0: \mu_1 \leq \mu_2$ $H_a: \mu_1 > \mu_2$

At significance level α, the decision rule (using Table VI) is

2. Reject H_0 if sample $z > z_\alpha$

Next, compute

3. Sample $z = \dfrac{R_1 - \mu_{R_1}}{\sigma_R}$

Finally,

4. Accept or reject H_0

The hypotheses and decision rule for a one-tail "less than" test and a two-tail "equal to" test are determined similarly. If H_0 has μ_2 at the left, as in $\mu_2 \leq \mu_1$ or $\mu_2 \geq \mu_1$, the test statistic is

$$\text{Sample } z = \frac{R_2 - \mu_{R_2}}{\sigma_R}$$

And, in a two-tail test we may use either

$$\text{Sample } z = \frac{R_1 - \mu_{R_1}}{\sigma_R} \qquad \text{or} \qquad \text{sample } z = \frac{R_2 - \mu_{R_2}}{\sigma_R}$$

as the sample test statistic. The two formulas yield numbers that are the same except for sign.

The *Spearman rank correlation test* is a nonparametric test of the correlation between two sets of rankings. Suppose we have a pair of rankings (x, y) for each of n items. For each pair, compute

$$d = x - y$$

Next compute r_s, the Spearman rank correlation coefficient, by the formula

$$r_s = 1 - \frac{6\Sigma d^2}{n(n^2 - 1)}$$

Let ρ_s be the population rank correlation coefficient. When n is at least 10, the steps in a one-tail "greater than" test are: First, state the hypotheses

1. $H_0: \rho_s \leq 0$ $H_a: \rho_s > 0$

At significance level α, the decision rule is (using Table VI)

   2. Reject H_0 if sample $z > z_\alpha$

Next, compute

   3. Sample $z = r_s \sqrt{n - 1}$

Finally,

   4. Accept or reject H_0

Again, the other forms of the hypotheses are tested similarly.

   The *Kendall test of concordance* is a nonparametric test of the concordance (agreement) among more than two sets of rankings. Suppose there are k rankings of a set of n items. For each item, compute R^2, the square of the sum of the ranks. Then compute ΣR^2, the sum of the R^2 values. When n is at least 8, the steps in the test are: First, state the hypotheses

   1. H_0: the ranks do not exhibit a significant level of agreement

   H_a: the ranks exhibit a significant level of agreement

At significance level α, the decision rule (using Table IV) is

   2. Reject H_0 if sample $\chi^2 > \chi^2_{\alpha,v}$

where $v = n - 1$

Next, compute

   3. Sample $\chi^2 = \dfrac{12\Sigma R^2 - 3n[k(n + 1)]^2}{kn(n + 1)}$

Finally,

   4. Accept or reject H_0

   The *runs test for randomness* is a nonparametric test of the randomness of a sequence made up of two symbols, as in *AABBBAABA*. A run is one or more symbols preceded and followed by a different symbol, or none at all. Count the number of runs in the sequence and call this number n_r. Also count to obtain

$$n_1 = \text{number of letters of one kind}$$

$$n_2 = \text{number of letters of the other kind}$$

$$n = n_1 + n_2$$

Next compute

$$\mu_r = \frac{2n_1 n_2}{n} + 1$$

and

$$\sigma_r = \sqrt{\frac{2n_1 n_2(2n_1 n_2 - n)}{n^2(n - 1)}}$$

The randomness test is two-tailed. When n_1 and n_2 are at least 10, the hypotheses are

1. H_0: the symbol sequence is random

H_a: the symbol sequence is not random

At significance level α, the decision rule (using Table VI) is

2. Reject H_0 if |sample z| $> z_{\alpha/2}$

Next, compute

3. Sample $z = \dfrac{n_r - \mu_r}{\sigma_r}$

Finally,

4. Accept or reject H_0

16.11 REVIEW PROBLEMS

1. Each of a randomly selected sample of 30 airline pilots rated the clarity of reception for radio receivers P and Q. The rating scale was from 1 to 4 (clearest). Three pilots gave the same rating to three receivers. In the remaining set of $P - Q$ differences there were 18 plus signs and 9 minus signs. Perform a matched pairs test at the $\alpha = 0.05$ level to determine whether, for pilots who have different ratings, more than half rate P higher than Q. What do you conclude from the test result? Why?

2. Each of a randomly selected sample of consumers rated two package designs, X and Y, for a new shampoo. The rating scale was from 1 to 5 (most appealing). Sample data are given in Table A. Perform a matched pairs sign test at the $\alpha = 0.05$ level to determine whether the proportion of consumers rating one design more appealing than the other differs from 0.5. What do you conclude from the test result? Why?

TABLE A

Design		Design		Design		Design		Design	
X	Y	X	Y	X	Y	X	Y	X	Y
4	2	2	4	3	5	5	4	4	4
3	3	1	3	3	3	4	4	1	5
3	2	1	2	3	1	4	2	2	1
2	4	2	2	1	3	3	2	2	3
4	3	1	2	1	1	3	5	2	5
2	3	4	4	4	2	2	2	4	3
2	4	3	4	1	2	2	4	3	5
3	2	4	5	2	2	1	3	1	5
2	5	2	4	3	1	4	2	4	5
3	4	2	5	2	4	3	3	3	5

3. Answers to a set of personal questions are used to measure a person's tension level. The questions were answered by random samples of managers in two companies. The combined sample of tension measures then was ranked, with 1 being the lowest tension level. Summary data are given in Table B. Perform the Mann-Whitney test at the $\alpha = 0.05$ level to determine whether the mean ten-

sion level is lower in company 2 than in company 1. What do you conclude from the test result? Why?

TABLE B

Company	Sample size	Rank sum
1	11	226
2	20	270

4. A grower experimented with two methods, X and Y, of raising red maple trees. The heights of two random samples of trees were ranked at the end of 2 years. The shortest tree was ranked 1. The ranks and methods are given in Table C. Perform a Mann-Whitney test at the $\alpha = 0.05$ level to determine whether the mean height of trees grown by method X is greater than the mean height of trees grown by method Y. What do you conclude from the test result? Why?

TABLE C

Rank	Method	Rank	Method	Rank	Method	Rank	Method
1	X	8	Y	15	Y	22	X
2	X	9	X	16	Y	23	Y
3	X	10	X	17	X	24	Y
4	X	11	Y	18	Y	25	X
5	Y	12	Y	19	X	26	Y
6	X	13	Y	20	Y	27	Y
7	Y	14	X	21	Y		

5. The personnel director of an insurance company tried two methods, 1 and 2, for training new sales agents. Sales records in thousands of dollars, 18 months after training, are given in Table D. Perform a Mann-Whitney test at the $\alpha = 0.05$ level to determine whether mean sales for the methods are different. What do you conclude from the test result? Why?

TABLE D

Method 1	561	510	498	579	628	527	465	539	550	593	601	641	681	722
Method 2	826	472	532	544	572	584	904	705	743	632	617			

6. Two property value assessors ranked the values of a random sample of 15 properties. The property having the lowest assessed value received rank 1. The ranks are given in Table E. Perform the rank correlation test at the $\alpha = 0.01$ level to determine if the assessors' ranks are positively correlated. What do you conclude from the test result? Why?

TABLE E

	Property														
Assessor	A	B	C	D	E	F	G	H	I	J	K	L	M	N	O
Finlay	5	14	10	12	1	4	2	8	13	3	15	7	9	11	6
Moran	3	15	9	8	1	5	2	11	12	4	14	7	6	13	10

7. Amcar Company prepared 12 interior-exterior car color combinations. Then they had each person in a random sample of women and a random sample of men choose the most pleasing combination. The number of people choosing each combination is given in Table F. Rank the choices in each sample. Then, at the $\alpha = 0.05$ level, perform a rank correlation test to determine whether the choices of men and women are correlated.

TABLE F

	Color combination											
	A	**B**	**C**	**D**	**E**	**F**	**G**	**H**	**I**	**J**	**K**	**L**
Women	17	4	9	6	12	38	17	42	21	9	17	8
Men	5	9	19	23	15	29	27	16	12	2	34	6

8. Table G lists the ranks of the percent return to investors in a random sample of 20 corporations. The lowest percent return has rank 1. Also listed are the sales of the corporations in millions of dollars. Perform a rank correlation test at the $\alpha = 0.05$ level to determine whether percent return and sales are correlated.

TABLE G

Percent return (rank)	Sales (millions)	Percent return (rank)	Sales (millions)
1	$ 740	11	$2481
2	594	12	3615
3	1986	13	854
4	1505	14	6513
5	8861	15	9230
6	4270	16	5328
7	1071	17	508
8	981	18	1266
9	457	19	2126
10	652	20	595

9. For a period of 5 years, Fran Hartman, manager of Rockland Stores, ranked the sales volumes for the 12 months of each year from 1 to 12 (highest). Fran computed the rank sum R for each month; then she calculated $\Sigma R^2 = 14{,}496$. Perform a Kendall concordance test at the $\alpha = 0.01$ level. What do you conclude from the test result? Why?

TABLE H (See Problem 10)

	Blouse style									
Buyer	**A**	**B**	**C**	**D**	**E**	**F**	**G**	**H**	**I**	**J**
Lord	3	1	8	2	5	10	4	7	9	6
Jordan	6	4	3	5	10	7	1	8	9	2
Taylor	2	8	6	1	3	9	7	4	5	10

10. Each of three buyers of women's fashions rated the probable sales volume of 10 blouse styles on a scale of 1 to 10 (highest sales volume). The ranks are given in Table H. Perform a Kendall concordance test at the 5 percent level. What do you conclude from the test result? Why?

11. Sivro Company makes and sells high-quality fresh water fishing tackle. The company is developing a new graphite fly casting rod. They made nine rods, each with a different graphite composition. Then they found how far each of four expert flycasters could cast a fly with each rod. The distances for each caster then were ranked. The ranks are given in Table I. Perform a Kendall concordance test at the $\alpha = 0.01$ level. What do you conclude from the test results? Why?

TABLE I

Caster	Rod								
	A	B	C	D	E	F	G	H	I
Bean	8	9	7	5	6	1	2	3	4
Gaddis	9	7	6	3	8	1	5	2	4
Garcia	6	8	7	4	9	3	2	5	1
Orvis	9	6	8	4	7	2	1	5	3

12. If the 366 days of a leap year are numbered from 1 through 366, the median number is 183.5. Suppose that capsules containing the numbers 1 to 366 are mixed, and then drawn out one at a time in a draft lottery. The order in which the days are drawn determines the order in which eligible people are drafted into military service. Suppose the sequence drawn has 170 runs of A's and B's, where A means a number above the median and B means a number below the median. Perform a runs test for randomness at the $\alpha = 0.05$ level. What do you conclude from the test result? Why?

13. The environmental protection staff of an industrial plant collected the following sample measurements of contaminants emitted by the plant. The median measurement is 40. Mark each measurement as A (above median) or B (below median). Perform a runs test for randomness at the $\alpha = 0.05$ level. What do you conclude from the test result? Why?

53 49 47 31 29 49 13 35 41 49 19 55 51 44 37 39 59 41 31 35

29 49 35 41 27 63 37 47 21 39 27 41 35 49 46 33 39 57 47 39

14. Country Grain Company sells cereal in 8-ounce (226.8-gram) boxes. Its filling machine is set to pour 230 grams per box. Country's quality-control manager believes that one characteristic of a properly operating filling machine is that the above-setting (A) and below-setting (B) sequence of filled boxes should be random, The manager obtained the following sequence.

B, B, A, B, A, A, A, B, B, B, B, A, A, B, A,

B, B, B, A, B, A, A, B, B, A, B, B, B, B, A

Perform a runs test for randomness at the $\alpha = 0.10$ level. What do you conclude from the test result? Why?

17

INDEX NUMBERS

17.1 INTRODUCTION

The word *index* is applied in a wide variety of contexts. There are indexes computed to measure the effectiveness of school systems, a human discomfort index which measures the combined effect of temperature and humidity, utility indexes (Chapter 6), price indexes, and a host of others. In this chapter we shall compute three types of indexes of major interest to managers. These are price indexes, quantity (produced or sold) indexes, and productivity (output per labor-hour) indexes.

Index numbers are measures that express a current (changing) price, quantity, or productivity level in terms of the level at some fixed point in time called the *base period*. Almost all index numbers are in the form of percentage relatives that have 100 as the base period level. For example, suppose the per gallon prices of no-lead gasoline for January, June, and November were, respectively, $1.20, $1.26, and $1.28. Then, taking January as the base period,

$$\frac{\text{June price}}{\text{January price}} \times 100 = \frac{\$1.26}{\$1.20} \times 100 = 105$$

so the June gas price index is 105 with January as the base period. Similar computation shows the November index is 106.7 with January as 100. Note that the changing price indexes are both expressed relative to 100, which is the base period (January) index.

An index number for a single product, such as the no-lead gas price index, is called a *simple* index. An index involving more than one product is called a *composite* index. Managers use composite indexes computed within their companies as summary measures of costs and selling prices, quantities produced and sold, and productivity.

Index numbers also are "big business" in government. Currently, for example, the Bureau of Labor Statistics (BLS) spends about $8 million per year to gather data and prepare the nation's best-known composite measure of prices, the consumer price index (CPI). It is estimated that a 1 percent increase in the CPI will trigger the transfer of about $1 billion to individuals affected by legislation or contractual agreements that call for adjustments tied to the index. Many of the latter contractual agreements are those reached in labor and management negotiations. Managers also use segments of another set of BLS indexes, the producer price indexes (PPI), to trigger contractual price adjustments in long-term contracts for the purchase of materials.

In this chapter we shall first discuss how composite price, quantity, and productivity indexes are computed for a business. Then I will describe a few widely used indexes published by governmental agencies.

17.2 UNWEIGHTED PRICE INDEXES

The two most commonly used formulas for computing price indexes are the *aggregate* formula and the *average of relatives* formula. Each of these formulas may involve an unweighted or a weighted type of calculation. In this section we consider the unweighted versions of price index formulas.

The Unweighted Aggregate Price Index

Disco Company sells three brands of stereo receivers, Volunteer, Magnum, and Sanko. Table 17.1 shows unit prices for each receiver in January, Febru-

TABLE 17.1
DISCO COMPANY STEREO RECEIVER PRICES

Receiver brand name	Price per unit		
	January p_0	February p_1	March p_2
Volunteer	$150	$153	$156
Magnum	250	260	260
Sanko	525	588	609

ary, and March. Disco's manager wants a single composite measure which compares prices in February with prices in January. One composite measure is obtained by dividing the sum of February prices by the sum of January prices. This gives

$$\frac{\text{Sum of February prices}}{\text{Sum of January prices}} = \frac{\$153 + \$260 + \$588}{\$150 + \$250 + \$525} = \frac{\$1001}{\$925} = 1.082$$

The sum of a group of prices is called an *aggregate* price. The number 1.082 shows that the February aggregate price was 1.082 times, or 108.2 percent of, the aggregate January price. It is customary to express index numbers as percents but to omit the percent symbol. Thus, the price index just computed would be stated as 108.2. The index number compares February with January as the *base* period. The price index for the base period is 100. That is,

Index numbers are percent relatives, expressed without the percent symbol.

$$\frac{\text{February aggregate price index}}{\text{January aggregate price index}} = \frac{108.2}{100}$$

The base period has an index of 100.

Disco's February index of 108.2 is interpreted to mean that February prices are $108.2 - 100 = 8.2$ percent greater than January prices. The 8.2 percent is, of course, a composite number computed from prices of different receivers; so it does not mean that any one receiver necessarily rose 8.2 percent in price. The advantage of a composite measure is that it is a summary measure that managers can use to represent several (or, frequently, many) prices.

In index symbols, subscripts are used to specify time periods. Thus, in Table 17.1, the 0 in p_0 means the *zeroth* or *base* period. The 1 and 2 on p_1 and p_2 mean, respectively, the first and second periods after the base period. Similarly, p_n would mean price in the *nth* period after the base period. A current period is called the *n*th period. With these symbols, the index number just computed may be written

$$\frac{\Sigma p_1}{\Sigma p_0} \times 100 = \frac{1001}{925} \times 100 = 108.2$$

Unweighted aggregate price index

where Σp_0 means the sum of the prices in the January column, and similarly for Σp_1. In general, *the unweighted aggregate price index for period n with period 0 as base is*

$$\frac{\Sigma p_n}{\Sigma p_0} \times 100$$

The period *n* (current period) prices change period by period; but in the formula, the same base period prices p_0 are used in computing all period *n* indexes. In other words, all period *n* indexes are computed with period 0 as 100.

EXERCISE   (*a*) Compute Disco's unweighted aggregate price index for March with January as 100 (base). (*b*) Interpret the March index.
ANSWER   (*a*) 110.8. (*b*) Disco's March prices are 10.8 percent above January prices.

The Unweighted Average of Relatives Price Index

In Table 17.1, the January and February prices of a Volunteer receiver are $150 and $153. Expressing p_1 as a percent of p_0, again dropping the percent sign, we obtain the Volunteer period 1 price relative

$$\frac{p_1}{p_0} \times 100 = \frac{153}{150} \times 100 = 102$$

Table 17.2 shows the February price relatives for the three receivers. The average of the three relatives is

TABLE 17.2
PRICE RELATIVES FOR THREE STEREO RECEIVERS

Receiver brand name	January price p_0	February price p_1	Price relatives $(p_1/p_0) \times 100$
Volunteer	$150	$153	102
Magnum	250	260	104
Sanko	525	588	112

Form each price relative . . .

. . . then find their average.

$$\text{Average of price relatives} = \frac{102 + 104 + 112}{3}$$

$$= \frac{318}{3}$$

$$= 106$$

The price relatives for January compared with January are, of course, all equal to 100; so the January average of relatives is the base period value 100. The index of 106 for February is interpreted to mean that February prices are 6 percent above January prices.

In general, a price relative for period n is $(p_n / p_0) \times 100$.

The unweighted average of relatives price index for period n with period 0 as 100 is

Unweighted average of relatives price index

$$\frac{\Sigma[(p_n / p_0) \times 100]}{\text{Number of relatives}}$$

EXERCISE   From Table 17.1, compute Disco's March price index with January as 100 by the unweighted average of relatives formula.
ANSWER   108.

Recall that the unweighted aggregate price index for Disco in February was 108.2. The unweighted average of relatives index is a different number, 106. That's because the aggregate method assumes that equal amounts of change are of equal importance, while the relative method assumes that equal percent changes are of equal importance. The proper method to use, therefore, depends upon which of the two assumptions is the better one. Frequently, neither assumption is reasonable, because the importance of a price change to a manager usually depends on the number of units sold. Weighted price indexes take this into account.

17.3 WEIGHTED PRICE INDEXES

A weighted price index can be computed by the weighted aggregate formula or the weighted average of relatives formula.

The Weighted Aggregate Price Index

Price is weighted according to the quantity sold.

Suppose the manager of Disco is not satisfied with unweighted price indexes, because Volunteer sales are much higher than sales of Magnum or Sanko. The manager wants a price index that takes into account the importance of price changes as measured by the quantities sold. Table 17.3 contains quantity sold (q_0) data for the base period, January.

TABLE 17.3
DISCO QUANTITY AND PRICE DATA

Receiver brand name	Quantity sold January q_0	Price per unit		
		January p_0	February p_1	March p_2
Volunteer	30	$150	$153	$156
Magnum	15	250	260	260
Sanko	5	525	588	609

The total dollar value of receiver sales for January is found by multiplying (weighting) each January price by the number of units sold, then summing the results to obtain $\Sigma p_0 q_0$. Then suppose we compute how much the *same* quantities q_0 would have cost in February. This is $\Sigma p_1 q_0$. Because the quantities (weights) have been held constant, the change from $\Sigma p_0 q_0$ to $\Sigma p_1 q_0$ is due to price changes only. The ratio of these two sums, multiplied by 100, is called a weighted aggregate price index. Additionally, when the fixed weights are *base period weights*, the index is called a *Laspeyres* index. In Table 17.4, $\Sigma p_1 q_0 = 11{,}430$ and $\Sigma p_0 q_0 = 10{,}875$. Dividing $\Sigma p_1 q_0$ by $\Sigma p_0 q_0$, and then multiplying by 100, gives the period 1 price index 105.1.

TABLE 17.4
WEIGHTED AGGREGATE PRICE INDEX CALCULATION (LASPEYRES)

Here the weights are base period dollar sales value for each item.

Receiver type	q_0	p_0	p_1	$p_0 q_0$	$p_1 q_0$
Volunteer	30	150	153	4,500	4,590
Magnum	15	250	260	3,750	3,900
Sanko	5	525	588	2,625	2,940
				10,875	11,430

Weighted aggregate price index for period 1 with period 0 as 100 $= \dfrac{\Sigma p_1 q_0}{\Sigma p_0 q_0} \times 100 = \dfrac{11{,}430}{10{,}875} \times 100 = 105.1$

In general, the Laspeyres *weighted aggregate price index for period n with period* 0 *as* 100 *is*

$$\frac{\Sigma p_n q_0}{\Sigma p_0 q_0} \times 100$$

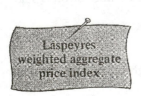

Laspeyres weighted aggregate price index

The important points to note in the formula are that prices vary (p_0 to p_n) but the weights q_0 are the same. Consequently, only price changes influence the index; so it is a price index.

EXERCISE   See Table 17.3. (a) Write the formula for the March (period 2) weighted aggregate price index with January as 100. (b) Compute the index in (a).
ANSWER   (a) $(\Sigma p_2 q_0/\Sigma p_0 q_0) \times 100$; (b) 106.9.

There are two formulas that can be used in computing weighted aggregate price indexes, the *fixed weight* and the *current period weight* formulas. Both formulas require that the same set of weights be used for period *n* and for the base period when calculating a particular period *n* index. *Fixed weights* mean that the same weights are used period after period. The Disco price index is a fixed weight index. If Disco continues to use the 30, 15, 5 sales quantity weighting pattern, its price indexes will become less meaningful if the pattern changes. When it becomes necessary, Disco will choose a new base period, update its weighting pattern, and continue to use the new fixed weights for as long as possible. If Disco uses the sales pattern of its base

The same weights must be used for periods 0 and n.

period as weights, its price indexes, as I have said, are called Laspeyres indexes. However, some fixed weight indexes have weights applying to a period other than the base period. For example, in 1981 the consumer price index had fixed weights representing the years 1972–1973, but with 1967 as 100 (base).

An index which uses *current period* weights is called a *Paasche* index. The Paasche weighted aggregate price index uses current period quantities q_n as weights. That is, the base period prices are multiplied by the q_n values and the products are summed to give $\Sigma p_0 q_n$. Next, the current period prices are multiplied by the q_n values and the products are summed to give $\Sigma p_n q_n$. Dividing $\Sigma p_n q_n$ by $\Sigma p_0 q_n$, and then multiplying by 100, gives the *Paasche weighted aggregate price index number for period n with period 0 as base*

> **Paasche weighted aggregate price index**

$$\frac{\Sigma p_n q_n}{\Sigma p_0 q_n} \times 100$$

In the formula, note that the same weights q_n are used for the current prices and for base period prices.

As an example, suppose p_{75} and q_{75} mean 1975 prices and 1975 quantities, and similarly for p_{82} and q_{82}. Then the Paasche weighted aggregate price index for 1982 with 1975 as base would be $(\Sigma p_{82} q_{82} / p_{75} q_{82}) \times 100$.

EXERCISE Write the formula for the Paasche weighted aggregate price index for 1980, with 1975 as base.
ANSWER $(\Sigma p_{80} q_{80} / \Sigma p_{75} q_{80}) \times 100$.

A current period Paasche index number measures the effect of price changes from the base period to that current period. The important advantage of the Paasche formula is that is uses up-to-date weights. However, both prices and quantity weights can change from one current period to the next. Consequently, it is not possible to say that period-to-period changes in Paasche index numbers are due to price change alone. This is a disadvantage not present in fixed weight index numbers. Another disadvantage is that it may be too costly or time-consuming to obtain the new current period weights needed each time a Paasche index is to be computed.

The Weighted Average of Relatives Price Index

In Section 17.2 we computed an unweighted average of relatives by finding the current period price relatives, adding them, and then dividing the sum by the number of relatives. As the term suggests, in a weighted average of relatives computation, each relative is multiplied by its weight, the products are added, and then the sum of the products is divided by the sum of the weights. Letting w be weights, the general formula for a *weighted average of relatives price index for period n with period 0 as base* is

> **Weighted average of relatives price index**

$$\frac{\Sigma[(p_n / p_0) \times 100w]}{\Sigma w}$$

We shall consider only fixed weights in average of relatives index calculations. These *weights, w, are dollar values or proportions of total dollar value.* Let's return to Disco Company and compute its period 1 index by the formula just written, letting the weights be base period dollar values, $w = p_0q_0$. Table 17.5 shows the calculation. The given data are in the columns headed

TABLE 17.5
THE WEIGHTED AVERAGE OF RELATIVES PRICE INDEX FOR DISCO CO.

Receiver type	q_0	p_0	p_1	Price relative $\left(\dfrac{p_1}{p_0} \times 100\right)$	Weight $w = p_0q_0$	Relative times weight $\left(\dfrac{p_1}{p_0} \times 100w\right)$
Volunteer	30	150	153	102	4,500	459,000
Magnum	15	250	260	104	3,750	390,000
Sanko	5	525	588	112	2,625	294,000
					10,875	1,143,000

$$\frac{\Sigma[(p_1/p_0) \times 100w]}{\Sigma w} = \frac{1,143,000}{10,875} = 105.1$$

q_0, p_0, and p_1. The next column contains the computed price relatives, $(p_n/p_0) \times 100$. The weight column, w, contains the computed base period dollar values, p_0q_0 (dollar value is price per unit times number of units). The results of multiplying each price relative by its dollar value weight are shown in the last column. Then, applying the formula as shown at the bottom of the table, we find the index number to be 105.1. This result is exactly the same as the index computed from the same data by the weighted aggregate method in Table 17.4. The two formulas always give the same result when applied to the same q_0, p_0, and p_n data. The weighted aggregate formula is easier to evaluate and understand than the weighted average of relatives formula. Nevertheless, the weighted average formula is encountered frequently because often the available weights are dollar values or proportions of total dollar value. The weighted average of relatives method must be used when weights are dollar values, or proportions of total dollar value. The following example illustrates the use of weights that are proportions of total dollar value. It also illustrates how a sample can be used to provide a timely index at a low cost.

You can use the simpler weighted aggregate method if you know the base period quantity weights . . .

. . . but you must use the weighted average of relatives method if you know only base period dollar values or proportions.

EXAMPLE Sue and Nick Muller own several stores. One is Quality, Inc., a New England store which sells meats, poultry, and fish. The Mullers do not work in their stores. They employ store managers. Sue has a concern about the prices Quality pays for meats, poultry, and fish. To check on prices, Sue calls Quality once a week to find what prices are being paid for beef for hamburg, broiler chickens, and haddock. She uses hamburg, chicken, and haddock prices to represent, respectively, all meats, all poultry, and all fish. Thus, she is using a sample of prices to represent all prices.

From complete data gathered in 1978, Sue knows that in that year Quality's total dollar value of purchases averaged 50 percent for meats, 30 percent for poultry, and 20 percent for fish. Sue changes the percents to the proportions 0.5, 0.3, and 0.2 and uses them as weights. Note that the weights are proportions of the total dollar value of purchases. All that Sue will use in computing the price index are the 1978 and current week's prices for hamburg, chicken, and haddock, and the 0.5, 0.3, and 0.2 weights. An illustrative calculation for the first week in January 1981 (period n) is shown in Table 17.6.

TABLE 17.6
QUALITY, INC., PRICE INDEX CALCULATION

Category	Sample item	Category weight	Price per pound 1978 p_0	Current week p_n	Price relatives $\frac{p_n}{p_0} \times 100$	Relatives times weights $\left(\frac{p_n}{p_0} \times 100w\right)$
Meat	Hamburg	0.5	$1.90	$2.15	113.16	56.58
Poultry	Chicken	0.3	0.70	0.75	107.14	32.14
Fish	Haddock	0.2	2.40	2.70	112.50	22.50
		1.0				111.22

Here the weights are proportions of base period total dollar sales value.

Applying the formula, we find

$$\frac{\Sigma[(p_1/p_0) \times 100w]}{\Sigma w} = \frac{111.22}{1.0}$$

$$= 111.22$$

Sue therefore concludes that Quality's purchase prices in the first week of January 1981 are about 11.2 percent above 1978 prices.

EXERCISE A company sells products A, B, and C. From period 0 to period 1, prices of A, B, and C rose, respectively, from $80, $25, and $50 to $88, $27, and $53. In period 0, products A, B, and C contributed, respectively, 25, 45, and 30 percent to the total dollar sales volume. (a) Which formula should be used to compute the price index for period 1 with period 0 as base? Why? (b) Compute the index in (a).

ANSWER (a) The weighted average of price relatives because the weights (changed to 0.25, 0.45, and 0.30) are proportions of the total dollar value of sales. (b) 107.9.

17.4 USING PRICE INDEXES

Composite price indexes serve the needs of a manager who needs summary measures of, say, costs and selling prices, rather than an extensive listing of individual prices. They also are used for the purposes described below.

Price Escalators

A wage *escalator* clause in a labor contract is a negotiated agreement which ties wage rates to a price index. The clause may, for example, specify a 1 per-

cent wage rate increase for each 1 percent advance in the price index. The index usually specified in a wage escalator clause is the CPI (consumer price index) published by the Bureau of Labor Statistics. The CPI is relevant for this purpose because it measures the changing cost of a fixed "market basket" of goods and services purchased by urban consumers. Similarly, a materials price escalator may be inserted in a long-term construction contract to adjust for changing materials costs. And escalators have been included in divorce agreements to provide for increases in alimony when prices rise.

Purchasing Power of $1

The current purchasing power of $1 is defined as follows:

$$\text{Current purchasing power of \$1} = \frac{100}{\text{current price index}}$$

For example, in October 1978, the CPI (with 1967 as 100) reached 200. Hence,

As the CPI goes up, purchasing power goes down.

$$\frac{\text{Purchasing power of}}{\text{October 1978 consumer dollar}} = \frac{100}{200} = 0.50 \text{ or } \$0.50$$

The idea here is simply that if prices doubled (index values went from 100 to 200), then an October 1978 dollar was worth only half as much as a base period (1967) dollar; that is, the 1978 dollar purchased only half the goods and services that could have been purchased with a base period (1967) dollar.

> **EXERCISE** In 1980, an energy price index with 1975 as base reached 250. What was the purchasing power of the energy dollar in 1980?
> **ANSWER** $0.40.

Deflating a Dollar Value

Deflated dollar value is defined as follows:

$$\text{Deflated dollar value} = (\text{dollar value}) \times (\text{purchasing power of \$1})$$

Suppose, for example, that sales of a furniture store rose from $435,000 in 1978 to $510,000 in 1981, while a furniture price index (1975 as base) for the corresponding years rose from 125 to 150. Then

Deflated sales: Current sales in terms of base period dollars.

$$\text{Deflated 1978 sales} = (\$435,000)\left(\frac{100}{125}\right) = \$348,000$$

$$\text{Deflated 1981 sales} = (\$510,000)\left(\frac{100}{150}\right) = \$340,000$$

Note that actual dollar sales had an apparently healthy increase of

$510,000 - $435,000 = $75,000$. However, deflated sales declined by $8,000 from $348,000 to $340,000. The purpose of deflating dollar values is to remove the effect of price changes. Deflated dollar values therefore measure what the dollar values would have been if prices had remained constant.

Constant *versus* current *dollars* Consequently, deflated dollar values are often called *constant dollar* values. Constant dollars are a better measure of real change than actual dollars. Thus, in the foregoing furniture store example, the decline in deflated (constant dollar) sales cannot be attributed to prices because prices have been held constant. The implication therefore is that the store is selling less furniture. The increase in actual dollar sales could lead to the incorrect conclusion that the store sold more furniture.

Real *wages* Deflated dollar wages are called *real* wages. Actual dollar wages are the number of dollars received. Real wages measure how much (of goods and services) actual wages buy from time to time.

> **EXERCISE** Suppose that average weekly wages rose from $245 to $265 while the CPI rose from 188.4 to 207.1. What happened to real wages?
> **ANSWER** Real wages declined from $130 to $128.

17.5 PROBLEMS

1. Table A gives sales and price data for Glenville Motors. With 1980 as base, compute for 1981 (a) the unweighted aggregate price index; (b) the unweighted average of relatives price index.

TABLE A
GLENVILLE MOTORS DATA

Vehicle type	1980 Number sold	1980 Price per vehicle	1981 Number sold	1981 Price per vehicle
Car	200	$ 8,000	220	$11,000
Truck	100	12,000	90	15,000
Van	50	10,000	30	12,000

2. From the data of Table A, compute the Laspeyres weighted aggregate price index for 1981 with 1980 as base.

3. The weighted average of relatives price index for 1981 with 1980 as base is to be computed from the data of Table A. (a) What are the relatives for cars, trucks, and vans? (b) What are the weights for cars, trucks, and vans? (c) Compute the index.

4. A dairy products store sells milk, butter, and cheese. In 1980 the store sold 100 thousand quarts of milk at $0.55 per quart, 20 thousand pounds of butter at $1.50 per pound, and 10 thousand pounds of cheese at $2.50 per pound. In the current year just completed prices of milk, butter, and cheese are, respectively, $0.66, $1.68, and $2.75. The current amounts sold are 112 thousand quarts of milk, 15 thousand

pounds of butter, and 12 thousand pounds of cheese. For the current year, with 1980 as base, compute (a) the unweighted aggregate price index; (b) the unweighted average of relatives price index.

5. From the data of Problem 4, compute the Laspeyres aggregate price index for the current year with 1980 as base.

6. The weighted average of relatives price index for the current year with 1980 as base is to be computed from the data of Problem 4. (a) What are the relatives for milk, butter and cheese? (b) What are the weights for milk, butter, and cheese? (c) Compute the index.

7. From the data of Table A compute the Paasche price index for 1981 with 1980 as base.

8. From the data of Problem 4, compute the Paasche price index for the current year with 1980 as base.

9. One department in a store sells stereo systems, television sets, and radios. In 1980, the percentage distribution of the department's dollar sales volume was 25 percent stereos, 55 percent TVs, and 20 percent radios. One stereo, one TV, and one radio, priced respectively in 1980 at $400, $325, and $80, have been selected to represent the product categories. In the current year, prices are: stereo, $475; TV, $375; radio, $95. A weighted price index for the current year with 1980 as base is to be computed. (a) Which calculation procedure is appropriate? Why? (b) Compute the index.

10. Quick Foods sells sandwiches, beverages, and desserts. The respective dollar sales volumes in 1980 were, in thousands, $590, $280, and $130. A price index is to be computed using hamburger to represent sandwiches, Pop to represent beverages, and a cherry tart to represent desserts. In 1980 prices were: hamburger, $0.90; Pop, $0.30; tart, $0.40. Currently, respective prices are $1.15, $0.40, and $0.50. Compute the weighted price index for the current period with 1980 as base.

11. A store computes the number

$$\left[\frac{\Sigma p_n q_n}{\Sigma p_0 q_0} (100) \right] - 100$$

for all products sold. Interpret this number.

12. What is the advantage, and what are the disadvantages, of Paasche index numbers?

13. Sales for an industry rose from $23 billion to $27 billion while the industry's price index rose from 175 to 200. Compute the percent change in (a) actual dollar sales; (b) sales in constant dollars.

14. In January 1979, the CPI (1967 as base) was 204.7. (a) Compute the January 1979 purchasing power of the consumer dollar. (b) At what CPI level would the purchasing power of the consumer dollar be 25 cents?

15. Suppose weekly dollar wages increase by 20 percent while the CPI changes from 240 to 270. What will happen to real wages? Why?

17.6 WEIGHTED QUANTITY INDEXES

In a weighted aggregate quantity index for period n, quantities may vary from period 0 to period n, but the same weights are used for the two periods. Quantity indexes are computed by the weighted aggregate formula, or by the weighted average of relatives formula. In the weighted aggregate formula, the weights are base period prices. In the weighted average of relatives formula, the weights are determined from base period dollar values.

The Weighted Aggregate Quantity Index

In price index calculations, a change from $\Sigma p_0 q_0$ to $\Sigma p_n q_0$ is due to changing prices because the quantity weights q_0 are held constant. Similarly, a change from $\Sigma p_0 q_0$ to $\Sigma p_0 q_n$ is due to changing quantities (q_0 to q_n) because the price weights p_0 are held constant. The *weighted aggregate quantity index for period n with period 0 as base* is

$$\frac{\Sigma p_0 q_n}{\Sigma p_0 q_0} \times 100$$

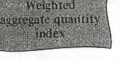

Weighted aggregate quantity index

EXAMPLE   The kitchen department of Home Appliance Company sells wall cabinets, rubbish compactors, refrigerators, sinks, and stoves. Table 17.7 shows the computation of a sales quantity index for the kitchen depart-

TABLE 17.7
SALES QUANTITY INDEX FOR THE KITCHEN DEPARTMENT USING
THE WEIGHTED AGGREGATE FORMULA

Item	Price per Item 1978 p_0	Number sold 1978 q_0	Number sold 1981 q_n	$p_0 q_0$	$p_0 q_n$
Cabinet	$120	362	410	43,440	49,200
Compactor	270	212	204	57,240	55,080
Refrigerator	809	180	160	145,620	129,440
Sink	210	540	550	113,400	115,500
Stove	270	425	360	114,750	97,200
				474,450	446,420

Quantity index for 1981 (1978 as base) $= \dfrac{\Sigma p_0 q_n}{\Sigma p_0 q_0} \times 100 = \dfrac{446,420}{474,450} \times 100 = 94.1$

The weights here are base period prices p_0.

ment. The given data are the p_0 prices and the q_0 and q_n quantities. The values of $p_0 q_0$ and $p_0 q_n$ are computed for each product. Then $\Sigma p_0 q_0$ and $\Sigma p_0 q_n$ are computed. Dividing $\Sigma p_0 q_n$ by $\Sigma p_0 q_0$, then multiplying by 100, gives the quantity index number 94.1 for period n with period 0 as 100. The decline, $100 - 94.1 = 5.9$, is interpreted to mean that the 1981 quantity of sales is 5.9 percent below the 1978 sales quantity. Or, we can say that sales in constant dollars declined 5.9 percent.

The Weighted Average of Relatives Quantity Index

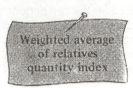

The symbol $(q_n/q_0) \times 100$ is called a quantity relative for period n with period 0 as base. The *formula for the weighted average of relatives quantity index for period n with period 0 as base* is

$$\frac{\Sigma[(q_n/q_0) \times 100w]}{\Sigma w}$$

The weights w are base period dollar values, or proportions of total value.

The weighted aggregate formula and the weighted average of relatives formula give exactly the same quantity index when applied to the same p_0, q_0, and q_n data. Consequently, if p_0, q_0, and q_n are available, the weighted aggregate formula should be used (as in Table 17.7) because it is simpler and easier to understand. However, if the weights used are dollar values, or proportions of total dollar values, the weighted average of relatives formula must be used.

$p_0q_0 = \$500$ is a dollar value.

EXAMPLE An industrial construction association publishes a construction materials index. The index measures the quantity of materials used in construction by contractors who are members of the association. The association uses the index as an indirect measure of actual construction. Three major materials, steel, cement, and lumber, are used in computing the index. In 1975, the association determined the total dollar value of materials and found that for steel, cement, and lumber, the respective proportions of the total value were 0.410, 0.070, and 0.520. Table 17.8 shows how the asso-

TABLE 17.8
CALCULATING THE CONSTRUCTION MATERIALS INDEX BY THE WEIGHTED AVERAGE OF RELATIVES FORMULA

Material	Proportion of total dollar value in 1975 w	Quantities used 1975 q_0	Quantities used 1981 q_n	Quantity relatives $\left(\frac{q_n}{q_0} \times 100\right)$	Relatives times weights $\left(\frac{q_n}{q_0} \times 100\right) w$
Steel (millions of short tons)	0.410	33.0	23.0	69.7	28.6
Cement (millions of barrels)	0.070	90.0	67.0	74.4	5.2
Lumber (billions of board feet)	0.520	42.0	38.0	90.5	47.0
	1.000				80.8

Here the weights are proportions of total dollar value . . .

Quantity index for 1981 (with 1975 as base) $= \dfrac{\Sigma[(q_n/q_0)100w]}{\Sigma w} = \dfrac{80.8}{1} = 80.8$

. . . so the weighted average of relatives method must be used.

ciation computed the 1981 construction index from the given weights (w), and the quantities q_0 and q_n. First, they computed the relative $(q_n/q_0) \times 100$ for each material. Then (last column), each relative was multiplied by its weight. The sum of the last column is the quantity index. The result, 80.8, is interpreted to mean that the quantity of materials used in 1981 was 19.2 percent below the base period (1975) level.

> **EXERCISE** Prior to publishing the index in Table 17.8, computations were checked and it was found that the cement figure for 1981, 67, was transposed; that is, it should have been 76. Compute the index using 76 for cement.
> **ANSWER** 81.5.

Value Added Weighting

In a weighted aggregate quantity-of-production index, fixed base period prices p_0 are used as weights. These prices should reflect the importance of the various items produced. That is, for example, if items A and B have $40 and $20 as respective price weights, one A should represent twice as much production as one B. Frequently, selling prices are not suitable weights. To see why, suppose you buy an old house, refinish it, and sell it at a price higher than you paid. Your selling price includes your cost price, the cost of materials you used, as well as the value added by your work. The importance of your work, your production or output, is measured only by the value your work added to the house—not by your selling price.

Value added: Amount by which the value of a product is increased by a process

In a producing industry, value added is determined by starting with total dollar value, then subtracting the cost of materials, supplies, containers, purchased energy, and other parts of total dollar value not contributed by that industry. Using value added makes an output index for a specific industry a better measure of that industry's output than an index which includes some of the output of other industries. However, our quantity index formulas still apply, only now p_0 is value added per unit in the base period. Similarly, $p_0 q_0$ and $p_0 q_n$ are, respectively, base period and current period quantities weighted by base period value added per unit.

> **EXERCISE** In 1977, the base period, Delta Company's outputs, in thousands of units, consisted of 114 valves, 84 whistles, and 170 gauges. Respective values added per unit in 1977 were $20, $12, and $40. In the current period, n, Delta's outputs, in thousands, were 120 valves, 80 whistles, and 200 gauges. Compute Delta's output index for the current period with 1977 as base.
> **ANSWER** 112.6.

17.7 PRODUCTIVITY INDEXES

Meaning of Productivity

Production versus productivity

In everyday language, the words *production* and *productivity* sometimes are used interchangeably. But in business and economics, these words have distinctly different meanings. Production means a quantity or amount of output. Productivity is a ratio of output divided by input. Thus, if 20 laborers made 320 chairs in a 40-hour week, their production was 320 chairs, but productivity was

$$\frac{320 \text{ chairs}}{(20 \text{ laborers})(40 \text{ hours})} = \frac{320 \text{ chairs}}{800 \text{ labor-hours}}$$

$$= 0.4 \text{ chair per labor-hour}$$

Productivity is output per unit of some (or all) input.

In the last computation, the input factor was labor-hours, and the resultant ratio is called *labor productivity*. Labor, of course, is only one of several input factors. Others include money invested in plant equipment, land, training of workers, and the skills and efforts of management. The ratio of output to *all* input factors is called *total factor* productivity. In this section we discuss only labor productivity; so it is necessary to call attention to the fact that changes in labor productivity (output per labor-hour) seldom disclose why the changes occurred. To identify reasons for changes, output/input ratios for various input factors have to be examined.

The Labor-Hour Equivalents Productivity Index

Suppose that 800 labor-hours were expended in the current period to make 400 chairs. Then

$$\text{Current period productivity} = \frac{400 \text{ chairs}}{800 \text{ labor-hours}}$$

$$= 0.5 \text{ chair per labor-hour}$$

Next, suppose that 1000 labor-hours would have been expended to make the same (current period) number of chairs, 400, in a base period. Then

$$\text{Base period productivity} = \frac{400 \text{ chairs}}{1000 \text{ labor-hours}}$$

$$= 0.4 \text{ chair per labor-hour}$$

Finally, we compute the simple chair productivity index for the current period as

Simple (one-item) productivity index

$$\frac{\text{Current productivity}}{\text{Base period productivity}} \times 100 = \frac{0.5}{0.4} \times 100 = 125$$

The index 125 means that the output of chairs per labor-hour increased 25 percent.

We can, and want to, compute the index number 125 in a different manner, as follows:

$$\frac{\text{Base period labor-hours to produce 400 chairs}}{\text{Current period labor-hours to produce 400 chairs}} \times 100$$

The ratio is

$$\frac{1000}{800} \times 100 = 125$$

as before. Note carefully that the base period labor-hours are in the numerator of the ratio. In earlier-computed indexes, the base period numbers were in the denominators of the ratios. The *labor-hour equivalents formula for computing a productivity index for period n* is

Labor-hour equivalent (LHE) productivity index

$$LHE = \frac{\text{Base period labor-hours required to make period } n \text{ quantities}}{\text{Period } n \text{ labor-hours expended to make period } n \text{ quantities}} \times 100$$

To use the LHE formula, it is necessary to know how many labor-hours *would have been* required in the base period to make period n quantities. The base period requirement is determined from base period *unit labor requirements*. These are the ratios labor-hours per unit for each product included in the index.

EXAMPLE In 1977, the base period, Fine Woods Company's unit labor requirements were 2 labor-hours per chair, 4 labor-hours per table, and 3 labor-hours per bookcase. In 1980, Fine Woods expended 50,000 labor-hours to produce 21,000 chairs, 3000 tables, and 2000 bookcases. Compute the 1980 productivity index.

SOLUTION To make the 1980 number of chairs, 21,000, in 1977 would have required

(21,000 chairs)(2 labor-hours per chair) = 42,000 labor-hours

Similarly, for tables and bookcases we find

(3000 tables)(4 labor-hours per table) = 12,000 labor-hours

and   (2000 bookcases)(3 labor-hours per bookcase) = 6000 labor-hours

Thus, in 1977 it would have required

42,000 + 12,000 + 6000 = 60,000 labor-hours

to make the quantities produced in 1980. Hence,

Note that the base period labor-hours are in the numerator.

$$LHE = \frac{\text{labor-hours required in 1977 to make 1980 quantities}}{\text{labor-hours required in 1980 to make 1980 quantities}} \times 100$$

$$= \frac{60,000}{50,000} \times 100$$

$$= 120$$

So 1980 productivity was 20 percent above the base period (1977) level.

EXERCISE In 1978, Delta's unit labor requirements were, in labor-hours per unit, 1.0 hour per valve, 0.5 hour per whistle, and 2.0 hours per gauge. In 1980 Delta expended 500,000 labor-hours in producing 120,000 valves, 80,000 whistles, and 200,000 gauges. Compute Delta's productivity index for 1980 with 1978 as base by the LHE formula.

ANSWER 112.

The Constant Dollars per Labor-Hour Productivity Index

Suppose the dollar value of output for an industry was $31,230 million in 1975 and $49,160 million in 1980. The price index for the products made by the industry (1970 as 100) was 143.1 in 1975 and 174.4 in 1980. We can express 1975 output in constant dollars by multiplying actual dollar output by 100/price index. Thus, in millions of 1970 dollars,

This is the deflation procedure (Section 17.4).

$$1975 \text{ constant dollar output} = \$31,230 \left(\frac{100}{143.1} \right) = \$21,824$$

Similarly,

$$1980 \text{ constant dollar output} = \$49,160 \left(\frac{100}{174.4} \right) = \$28,188$$

Changes in the actual dollar values of output are attributable to changes in both price and quantity of output. But constant dollars hold prices constant; so changes in constant dollar outputs are attributable to output quantity changes. Thus, constant dollar output is a measure of output quantity. We can obtain a productivity ratio by dividing constant dollar output by labor-hours worked. The *constant dollar per labor-hour productivity index for period n* is

Constant dollar per labor-hour (DC/L-H) productivity index

$$\text{CD/L-H} = \frac{\begin{array}{c}\text{constant dollars of output per labor-hour} \\ \text{in period } n\end{array}}{\begin{array}{c}\text{constant dollars of output per labor-hour} \\ \text{in base period}\end{array}} \times 100$$

An example of application of the CD/L-H formula is given in Table 17.9.

TABLE 17.9
CALCULATING A PRODUCTIVITY INDEX BY THE CD/L-H FORMULA

Item	Year	
	1975	1980
(a) Dollar value of output (millions)	$31,230	$49,160
(b) Price index (1970 as 100)	143.1	174.4
(c) Constant dollar output (millions): (a) [100/(b)]	$21,824	$28,188
(d) Labor-hours worked (millions)	2,040	2,285
(e) Constant dollar output per labor-hour: (c)/(d)	$10.70	$12.34
(f) CD/L-H productivity index (1975 as 100)	100	115.3*

* CD/L-H = $\dfrac{\text{constant dollars per labor-hour in 1980}}{\text{constant dollars per labor-hour in 1975}} \times 100$

$= \dfrac{\$12.34}{\$10.70} \times 100 = 115.3$

The given data are (a) dollar values of output, (b) price index numbers, and (d) labor-hours worked. Constant dollars outputs, computed in the foregoing, are shown in (c). Then, dividing (c) by (d), we obtain the constant dollar output per labor-hour figures in (e). Finally, the productivity index for 1980 with 1975 as base, 115.3, is computed as shown at the bottom of the table.

Value added, discussed earlier, is a better measure of output than total dollar value of product. Consequently, dollars of value added, if available, should be used in computing a CD/L-H productivity index. That is, the numerator and denominator of the formula should be in constant dollars of value added per labor-hour.

EXERCISE Merger, Inc., is a conglomerate owning 27 manufacturing plants that make a wide variety of products. From 1978 to 1980, Merger's total value added rose from $842 million to $1221 million, while labor-hours worked rose from 35.6 million to 38.7 million. The price index for products made by Merger (1969 as 100) rose from 169 in 1978 to 192 in 1980. Compute Merger's productivity index for 1980, with 1978 as base, by the CD/L-H formula.
ANSWER 117.

Rising productivity is a source of higher living standards and higher profits. Managers in the eighties will be directing more effort than in the past to the challenge of increasing productivity. Productivity indexes will be needed to measure the effects of various management efforts, so that successful efforts can be identified and unsuccessful efforts can be abandoned.

17.8 PROBLEMS

1. Data for Bright Lights Company, a lamp store, are given in Table A. Compute the index of quantity sold for August 1980 with the average month of 1977 as base.

TABLE A
BRIGHT LIGHTS SALES AND PRICE DATA

Lamp type	Average monthly price 1977	Number of lamps sold Average per month 1977	August 1980
Floor	$100	210	180
Table	60	150	190
Desk	40	300	420
Bed	25	120	80

2. (Production figures are in thousands.) In 1978 ABG Electronics made 70 Alphatrons, 40 Betatrons, and 100 Gammatrons whose values added per unit were, respectively, $10, $20, and $5. In 1981, ABG made 75 Alphatrons, 30 Betatrons, and 120 Gammatrons. Compute ABG's output index for 1981 with 1978 as base.

3. In Problem 2, the value added for an Alphatron is $10. However, ABG's accounting data show the cost of a completed Alphatron as $17.50. Why is $10 used in Problem 2?

4. (See Problem 2.) ABG Electronics plans to maintain the 1981 production of Alphatrons in 1982 but to increase the outputs of each of the other two products by 20 percent. If plans materialize, what will be ABG's 1982 output index, with 1978 as 100?

5. Under what circumstances must the weighted average of relatives formula be used in computing an output index?

6. Data for Sox Shop are given in Table B. Compute the sales quantity index for 1980 with 1978 as base.

TABLE B
SOX SHOP SALES DATA

Type of socks	Total dollar value of sales	Numbers of pairs of socks sold	
	1978	1978	1980
Women's	$34,500	21,200	24,380
Men's	25,500	18,500	17,575
Girls'	40,500	32,200	31,556
Boys'	49,500	43,500	52,200

7. Boxes, Inc., makes Exboxes (X), Whyboxes (Y), and Zeeboxes (Z). In 1980, total value added figures for X, Y, and Z were, in thousands of dollars, $60, $80, and $60. Outputs of X, Y, and Z, in thousands, were 60, 40, and 20 in 1980. In 1981, respective outputs were 72, 44, and 18. Compute Boxes' output index for 1981 with 1980 as base.

8. State the meanings of production and productivity in the business-economic context.

9. Name three input factors that would be included in a measure of total factor productivity.

10. The AKS Company makes Alphas, Kappas, and Sigmas. A work study in 1980 showed that unit labor requirements were 1.5 hours for an Alpha, 0.5 hour for a Kappa, and 0.8 hour for a Sigma. During the current year just completed, 189 thousand labor-hours were spent in producing 30 thousand Alphas, 78 thousand Kappas, and 120 thousand Sigmas. Compute the current index of labor productivity with 1980 as 100.

11. Shaft, Inc., makes Exshafts, Whyshafts, and Zeeshafts in three separate departments. Output and labor-hour data are given in Table C. (a) How many labor-hours would have been expended in 1980 to produce current year output? (b) Compute the labor productivity index for the current year with 1980 as 100.

12. Moulton Company compiled the data given in Table D. Compute the productivity index for 1981 with 1980 as base.

TABLE C

Product	1980		Current year	
	Units made (thousands)	Labor-hours (thousands)	Units made (thousands)	Labor-hours (thousands)
Exshaft	20	36	30	65
Whyshaft	30	105	40	136
Zeeshaft	50	100	55	95

TABLE D

	1980	1981
Dollar value of output (millions)	$9420	$11,210
Price index (1980 = 100)	100	116
Labor-hours worked (millions)	480	552

13. Reliable Auto Parts manufactures replacement parts for automobiles. The value of products made by Reliable fell from $18,345 thousand in 1979 to $15,186 thousand in 1980. The auto parts price index (1975 as 100) rose from 136 in 1979 to 154 in 1980. Reliable also reduced its labor force; so labor-hours worked fell from 1256 thousand in 1979 to 1152 thousand in 1980. Compute Reliable's productivity index for 1980 with 1979 as base.

17.9 CURRENT INDEX NUMBERS

Four widely used indexes will be described briefly in this section. The first three are price indexes.

The Consumer Price Index (CPI)

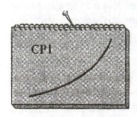

From 100 in 1967 to 261 in Jan. '81

If you should happen to see someone in a supermarket copying prices into a blue notebook, it is likely that the notebook cover will be stamped with the title *Consumer Price Index*. If so, that person is one of the BLS data collectors who gather about 1.5 million price quotations yearly. Each month, the Department of Labor's *Monthly Labor Review* includes several pages of closely packed price indexes by major category and subcategories, and indexes for some individual products and services. The CPI makes front-line news. Changes in the index may affect the income of approximately one-half the population of the United States. The index was first published in 1919 and used to adjust wages in the shipbuilding industry. Since 1919, revisions in weights, basket contents, and computation methods have been made at 10- to 15-year intervals. The revision of 1978 was the outcome of 8 years of study and cost about $50 million. More than $20 million of that cost was spent on a consumption expenditure survey in 1972–1973. Weights for the hundreds of goods and services included in the index were determined

TABLE 17.10
MAJOR CATEGORY WEIGHTS IN THE CONSUMER
PRICE INDEX

Category	Category percent weight
Food and beverages	18.8
Housing	43.9
Apparel and upkeep	5.8
Transportation	18.0
Medical care	5.0
Entertainment	4.1
Other goods and services	4.4
	100.0

A BLS dilemma:
What is the "price" of
housing?

from this survey. Major category weights are shown in Table 17.10.

The CPI often is described as measuring the changing cost of a fixed "market basket" of goods and services, which implies a weighted aggregate method of calculation. BLS calls the CPI formula a modified Laspeyres formula but states a formula that looks more like a modified weighted average of relatives. Whatever the computational details, the method involves fixed weights so that the index measures price change alone. And the concept of the changing price of a fixed market basket gives an easily understood idea of what the index seeks to measure.

BLS collects price data from a sample of 85 urban areas selected to represent all urban places in the United States. Monthly national indexes are computed as population-weighted averages of area indexes. Indexes also are available monthly for the five largest metropolitan areas and bimonthly for another 23 large metropolitan areas. Additionally, indexes are published for the four regions of the country—Northeast, North Central, South, West—and for metropolitan areas in five different size classes. It should be noted, however, that weighting patterns differ by area. Thus, a Boston worker who moves to San Diego can use the difference in CPIs to gauge the difference in consumer prices—provided the Bostonian adopts the San Diego urban consumer living style. Boston, by the way, has a lower CPI than San Diego.

The Fixed Weight Issue If the CPI is to measure price change only, the market basket must be fixed. However, the index loses relevance when consumers are not buying this fixed basket of goods and services; so, as stated earlier, the basket has been revised from time to time in the past. Recognizing that more frequent revisions will be needed in the future, BLS has obtained funds from the Congress to conduct an ongoing survey of consumer expenditures which will make more frequent revisions possible. We may expect the interval between future revisions to be perhaps 5 years, rather than 10 to 15 years as in the past. This ongoing survey will also provide data of use to government policy makers and to business decision makers who plan production and marketing efforts to satisfy changing customer demand patterns.

Our "market basket"
keeps changing in form
and quality

The Quality Issue To understand the quality issue, suppose that a 19-inch color TV is in the market basket at an original price of $300 and, several years later, "this" TV bears a price of $420, yielding a relative of $(420/300)100 = 140$. The issue is that "this" TV is not the same for both periods because of technological changes which improve quality. And the 140 relative overstates the price change that would have occurred if quality had remained constant. On the other hand, claims of deterioration in quality imply an understatement of price change.

The Bureau of Labor Statistics does make adjustments for quality changes, but many economists and others contend that these adjustments are inadequate and that the CPI has a consistent upward bias; that is, the CPI is higher than it would be if quality were held constant. The quality issue has not been resolved. About all that can be said is that studies do not provide conclusive evidence that the CPI has an upward or a downward bias. Of course, labor unions, retired persons' associations, and other groups whose incomes are, in part, tied to the CPI would almost certainly lobby actively against quality adjustments that led to lower CPI values.

CPI versus "cost of living"

The Cost of Living The CPI is not intended to be a measure of the cost of living because the market basket cost does not include all costs (e.g., income taxes and Social Security taxes are excluded) and because living costs are determined in part by the style of living rather than the price of a fixed list of goods and services. At the present time, we have no cost of living index; so the CPI is used by some as though it did measure living costs. The differences between the CPI and the cost of living could be small during stable periods but significant during times of major changes in taxation and consumption patterns—but no one has solid evidence to support these suppositions.

Finally, it should be noted that, over time, the CPI has been improved by introducing random sampling procedures in selecting particular items to be priced, sharpening of concepts, expanding coverage, and better pricing and price-checking techniques while at the same time adhering to the original market basket concept.

The Producer Price Index (PPI)

How to agree now on future prices, if prices are unstable

In 1902, the Bureau of Labor Statistics began publication of its wholesale price index (WPI), based upon price quotations for 250 commodities. In 1978, some 10,000 prices were collected monthly and used to compute about 2800 individual commodity price indexes, various stage-of-processing (i.e., crude materials, intermediate materials, finished goods) indexes, and other indexes. These indexes have been applied extensively in long-term contracts to reflect changes in the costs of materials, and can have a substantial effect upon business and public policy. The prices entering the indexes correspond more to prices charged by producers for their products than prices connoted by the word "wholesale." So, in 1978, BLS changed the name of the composite all-commodity index to the producer price index (PPI) and the name of the set of various subindexes to producer price indexes. Indexes are published in the *Monthly Labor Review* by stage-of-processing (with subgroups), by commodity groups (with subgroups), and by other groupings. Additionally, price indexes for the products of about 150 mining and manufacturing industries (e.g., iron ore, construction sand and clay, beet sugar, men's and boys' neckware, paper mills, canned fruits and vegetables) are published. Table 17.11 shows the major commodity groups.

TABLE 17.11
PRODUCER PRICE INDEXES, MAJOR COMMODITY GROUPS

Farm products
Processed foods and feeds
Manufactured animal feeds
Textile products and apparel
Hides, skins, leather, and related products
Fuels and related products and power
From A to Z (alfalfa   Chemicals and allied products
to zinc)   Rubber and plastic products
Lumber and wood products
Pulp, paper, and allied products
Metals and metal products
Machinery and equipment
Furniture and household durables
Nonmetallic mineral products
Transportation equipment
Other miscellaneous products

Major revision of the PPI coming in the 1980s

In 1978, BLS also announced the start of the first complete revision of the index. If the funds needed are made available, the revision is expected to be completed by the end of 1984. In the interim, revision results will be published as they become available. The revision will attempt to eliminate the past practice of multiple counting of the same price change. To illustrate this point, suppose the price of a crude material increases and the change is, in turn, passed on to an intermediate materials producer, then to a finished goods producer. The price change then is counted three times in a composite index that includes prices of goods at the three stages of processing. It is such triple counting that is to be eliminated.

This change is related to the concept of "value added."

Other improvements planned for the revision include an expanded sample of producers and products, and replacement of judgment selection by scientific (random) sampling. BLS also expects to obtain price quotations that better reflect actual transaction prices and avoid quotations of list prices that, because of discounts, are not operative. The computational procedure, which is a weighted price index calculation, will not be changed. Weights are based on dollar values of shipments by producers: These dollar values are obtained in the *Census of Manufacturers*. The weights will be adjusted in the future at 5-year intervals as later census data become available.

We can expect the period until 1984, and perhaps longer, to be characterized by changes in various components of the producer price indexes. Business executives will have to keep track of these changes because they will affect contractual agreements already made or to be made, and they can influence governmental regulations which apply to business. Finally, I should add, business itself is vitally concerned with price movements and, because it voluntarily supplies many of the price data, has a right to expect that the indexes will serve business needs as well as the needs of governmental policy makers.

Supplying data to government consumes millions of business labor-hours.

The Implicit Price Deflator (IPD)

The gross national product (GNP) is computed by the Bureau of Economic Analysis of the U.S. Department of Commerce. The GNP measures the total output of goods and services produced in the nation. In one set of computations, current dollar values for the component parts of GNP are summed to give the *current* dollar GNP. In another set of computations, individual component dollar values are first deflated, and then the deflated components are summed to give the *constant* dollar GNP.

The ratio of current dollar GNP divided by constant dollar GNP, when multiplied by 100, *implies* a price index. The source of the implication is the deflating formula discussed earlier; that is,

$$\text{Constant dollars} = (\text{current dollars}) \times \frac{100}{\text{price index}}$$

After rearrangement, the last says

$$\text{Price index} = \frac{\text{current dollars}}{\text{constant dollars}} \times 100$$

When GNP dollars are used in the last expression, the index is called the *implicit price deflator*, IPD. Thus,

$$\text{IPD} = \frac{\text{current dollar GNP}}{\text{constant dollar GNP}} \times 100$$

The IPD measures the level of all prices.

GNP measures the total value of just about all goods and services produced in the nation, including the services of government. Consequently, the IPD is a measure of the general level of all prices. Managers, forecasters, economic analysts, and others use the IPD rather than the consumer price index as a measure of overall price changes.

The Federal Reserve Board Index of Industrial Production

This is a quantity index.

The Federal Reserve Board industrial production index measures the output of the important industrial sector of the economy. It is a quantity index computed by a weighted average of relatives formula which uses percentages of total value added in the base period as weights. Production indexes are computed for hundreds of individual industrial groups. Weighted combinations of individual group indexes are used to obtain broader major industry indexes. These are durable manufacturing, nondurable manufacturing, mining, and utilities. The composite index, in turn, is a weighted combination of all individual indexes.

Managers who plan and direct the activities of large businesses need to know what has happened, and what is likely to happen, in the industrial sector of the economy. The industrial production index and its subcategory indexes help fill the need to know what has happened: Forecasts of probable coming changes, purchased by managers from economic forecasting firms, help in planning ahead.

Stock Price Indexes

Considering the almost immediate availability of price quotations for stocks listed on the New York Stock Exchange (NYSE), and computer capabilities, it would appear to be easy to compute an index of stock prices. However, there are day-by-day occurrences that lead to complications. For example, a company may replace 1 share of old stock with 2 shares of new stock, a so-called "2 for 1" split; or, a company may issue "rights" to purchase stock at a later time. These and other occurrences have arbitrary effects on prices; so index numbers must be adjusted frequently to take account of such effects. Adjustments have to be made also for other occurrences, such as new listings, delistings, mergers, and stock dividends.

The "S & P 500" measures the per-share price of stocks.

Its base period level is 10, not 100.

The *Standard and Poor's 500* stock price index measures average price per share of stock. It is described as a base-weighted aggregate index. The base period (1941–1943) level of the index is 10, not 100. The base level 10 was chosen to make the index value approximate the average price per share for all stocks listed on the NYSE. If you hear on a newscast that the price of an average share of stock advanced 12 cents, the reference is to the S & P 500. The composite 500-stock index and indexes for its components are published daily. The components are 400 industrial stocks, 20 transportation stocks, 40 utility stocks, and 40 financial stocks.

The NYSE index measures the total value of stocks.

The monthly *NYSE composite index* measures the total *value* of all stocks listed on the exchange. The index base period is December 31, 1965. The base period level of the index was set at 50.00. Note carefully that this index is neither a price nor a quantity index. Rather, it is a *value* index which changes when prices or quantities (numbers of shares) change, or both prices and quantities change. Daily NYSE indexes for common, industrial, transportation, utility, and finance stocks are now available. You can find them in many newspapers.

Fran: What's the stock market doing today?
Dan: The Dow was up 12 points at noon.

The *Dow Jones industrial average* (DJIA) is not an index number in the sense that we have used the term. That is, the Dow has no base period or base period level. But the Dow should be included here because it has a long history and is widely quoted. The Dow started as a simple arithmetic average of the prices of 30 high-quality ("blue chip") stocks. In the beginning, then, the numerator of the Dow average was the sum of 30 prices and the denominator (divisor) was the number of stocks, 30. The last time I looked (in the *Wall Street Journal*) the divisor was around 1.5. What happened? Stock splits for one thing. For example, suppose that a stock selling for $50 a share "splits" 2 for 1. Now there are twice as many shares with a price of $25 per share. The DJIA will use the new $25 price in the numerator, but adjust the denominator (decrease it) so that at the time of the split, the average using $25 and the new divisor equals the average using $50 and the old divisor.

The composition of the Dow changes occasionally. For example, a substitution will be made when an included stock becomes inactive, or when its price becomes too low to have a significant effect upon the average. A substitution can have a marked effect on the average. As an illustration, IBM was brought into the average in June 1979. Subsequently, stock prices declined. IBM dropped from $73.50 to $50 per share and accounted for about 20 percent of the decline in the 30-stock DJIA.

17.10 PROBLEMS

1. Why would it be virtually impossible to use the Paasche formula in computing the consumer price index?
2. Suppose improved pollution-control devices are to be installed on next year's automobiles, causing a price increase. Do you think the price increase should be reflected in the CPI? Why?
3. How does BLS plan to keep the CPI weighting pattern more current than has been the case in the past?
4. State a specific reason why the CPI should not be considered a "cost of living" index.
5. Does the CPI (1967 as 100) have base period weights? Explain.
6. The CPI is called a "market basket" index. What's in the "basket"? (Name four categories of items.)
7. The Bureau of Labor Statistics takes surveys from time to time to obtain data for revising the CPI weighting pattern. Why are the results of such surveys of interest to managers?
8. Why, and in what way, would revisions which raise the CPI affect wage rates paid by businesses?
9. Why did the Bureau of Labor Statistics change the name of its wholesale price index to producer price index?
10. How do managers use producer price indexes in long-term contracts?
11. Why does the industrial production index use value added weights?
12. Labor-hours worked, rather than actual production, are used in the industrial production index as substitute measures of the output in the shipping industry. Why not count and use ships built (or their tonnage) rather than substitute labor-hours in computing monthly indexes? (*Hint:* Think about a shipyard that has been closed down, then gets an order to build five large oil tankers.)
13. What does the S & P 500 stock price index measure?

14. What does the NYSE composite index measure?

15. Dividing the dollar value of stocks owned by an investor today by the dollar value of stocks owned a year ago, then multiplying by 100, will give an index number. What type of index number is this (price, quantity, or what)?

16. Why is the divisor in the Dow Jones average of 30 stock prices not equal to 30?

17. For certain purposes, the Securities and Exchange Commission (SEC) requires that a corporation revalue its machinery and equipment at replacement cost. This is difficult in many cases because current machinery and equipment, for which prices can be obtained, differs in many ways from that purchased years ago. Suggest how the SEC requirement might be met.

17.11 SUMMARY

Index numbers are percentages relative to a base period which has the level 100. The percent symbol is omitted when writing index numbers. An index number for one item (e.g., the price or quantity of one product) is called a *simple* index. An index which combines data for more than one item is called a *composite* index. Price and quantity index number formulas use the following symbols:

p_0 for prices in the zeroth (base) period

p_n for prices in the nth (current) period

q_0 for quantities in the zeroth (base) period

q_n for quantities in the nth (current) period

w for dollar value weights

Note: The weights w may be dollar values or proportions of total dollar value.

Period n index numbers with period 0 as base (100) are computed from the following formulas:

$$\text{Unweighted aggregate price index} = \frac{\Sigma p_n}{\Sigma p_0} \times 100$$

$$\text{Unweighted average of relatives price index} = \frac{\Sigma[(p_n/p_0) \times 100]}{\text{number of relatives}}$$

$$\text{Weighted aggregate price index} = \frac{\Sigma p_n q_0}{\Sigma p_0 q_0} \times 100$$

$$\text{Weighted average of relatives price index} = \frac{\Sigma[(p_n/p_0) \times 100w]}{\Sigma w}$$

$$\text{Weighted aggregate quantity index} = \frac{\Sigma p_0 q_n}{\Sigma p_0 q_0} \times 100$$

$$\text{Weighted average of relatives quantity index} = \frac{\Sigma[(q_n/q_0) \times 100w]}{\Sigma w}$$

Value added in production is found by starting with the total dollar value of a producer's output, then subtracting the cost of items (e.g., raw materials purchased by the producer) supplied by other producers. When computing output quantity indexes, value added per unit should be used, where possible, in place of selling price per unit; weights w should be dollars of value added or proportions of total dollars of value added.

Weighted index numbers may have *fixed* or *current period* (changing) weights. In both cases, the same weights must be used for the base period and for period n when a current period index number is computed. An index that has fixed weights applying to the index base period is called a *Laspeyres* index. An index that has current period weights is called a *Paasche* index.

In general, at a given time:

$$\text{Purchasing power of } \$1 = \frac{100}{\text{price index}}$$

Also, in general:

Deflated dollar value = (dollar value) × (purchasing power of $1)

Deflated dollar values are called *constant* dollars. Deflated wages are called *real* wages.

Productivity is a ratio computed by dividing output by input. Output per labor-hour is called labor productivity. The labor-hour equivalent, LHE, formula for computing labor productivity is

$$\text{LHE} = \frac{\text{base period labor-hours required to make period } n \text{ quantities}}{\text{period } n \text{ labor-hours expended in making period } n \text{ quantities}} \times 100$$

The constant dollar per labor-hour, CD/L-H, formula for computing labor productivity is

$$\text{CD/L-H} = \frac{\text{constant dollars of output per labor-hour in period } n}{\text{constant dollars of output per labor-hour in base period}} \times 100$$

Three widely used United States price indexes are (1) the consumer price index, which measures changes in the price of a fixed "market basket" of goods and services purchased by urban consumers; (2) the producer price index, which measures changes in prices received by producers; (3) the implicit price deflator, which measures changes in the prices of all goods and services included in the gross national product.

The Federal Reserve index of industrial production is a quantity index that measures changes in the output of the industrial sector of the economy.

The Standard and Poor's 500 composite stock price index measures the average per share price of stocks listed on the New York Stock Exchange. The composite New York Stock Exchange index measures the total value of all shares listed on the exchange. The Dow Jones industrial average is an indicator of movements in industrial stock prices rather than a price index number with a fixed base period.

17.12 REVIEW PROBLEMS

1. A store sells milk, butter, and eggs. In 1980, sales were 112 thousand quarts of milk at $0.55 per quart, 15 thousand pounds of butter at $1.50 per pound, and 8 thousand dozen eggs at $1.00 per dozen. In the current year just completed, the store sold 120 thousand quarts of milk at $0.66 per quart, 20 thousand pounds of butter at $1.68 per pound, and 15 thousand dozen eggs at $0.90 per dozen. For the current year, with 1980 as 100, compute (a) the unweighted aggregate price index; (b) the unweighted average of relatives price index.

2. (See Problem 1.) Change milk prices to prices per gallon (4 times the per quart price) and compute (a) and (b) of Problem 1. What is shown by comparing the answers to Problems 1 and 2?

3. From the data of Problem 1, compute the Laspeyres weighted aggregate price index for the current year with 1980 as 100.

4. From the data of Problem 1, compute the Paasche price index for the current year with 1980 as 100.

5. One department in a store sells cameras, projectors, and film. In 1980, the percentage distribution of dollar sales volume was 50 percent cameras, 30 percent projectors, and 20 percent film. In 1980, one camera at $125, one projector at $150, and one type of film at $2.50 were selected to represent the product categories. In the current year, prices for the selected items are: camera, $140; projector, $156; film, $2.75. A weighted price index for the current year with 1980 as 100 is to be computed. (a) Which index formula is appropriate? Why? (b) Compute the index.

6. One department in a store sells stereo systems, television sets, and radios. In 1980 dollar sales in thousands were: stereo, $625; TV, $137.5; radio, $50. In 1980, one stereo at $350, one TV at $320, and one radio at $80 were selected to represent the product categories. In the current year, prices are: stereo, $399; TV, $384; radio, $88. Compute the weighted price index for the current year with 1980 as 100.

7. A price index with 1975 as 100 rose to 140 in 1980 and 155 in the current year. What will the index numbers for the three years be if the base year is changed to 1980?

8. Currently, over 60 percent of the workers in major bargaining units have escalator clauses in their wage contracts. What is meant by the term "escalator clause"?

9. When the CPI, with 1967 as 100, reaches 250, what will be the purchasing power of a consumer dollar?

10. A furniture price index, with 1978 as 100, reached 125 in 1980 and 135 in the current year. Furniture store sales in an urban area were $300 million in 1980 and $378 million in the current year. (a) Compute sales in constant 1978 dollars for 1980 and for the current year. (b) Compute the percent change in dollar volume of sales. (c) Compute the percent change in constant dollar sales.

11. Compute real wages if dollar wages average $275 per week and the purchasing power of a dollar is 95 cents.

12. (a) Compute real wages if the CPI (1967 as 100) is 225 and wages are $360 per week. (b) Interpret the answer to (a).

13. The BCD Company makes Bees, Cees, and Dees. The respective outputs, in thousands, for these products were 20, 5, and 6 in 1980 and 15, 8, and 4 in the current year. In 1980, values added per unit were: Bees, $10; Cees, $30; Dees, $25. Compute the weighted aggregate output index for the current year with 1980 as 100.

14. In 1980, the output of the GKY Company, in thousands of units, consisted of 100 Gees, 160 Kays, and 200 Whys. The respective outputs in the current year are, in thousands, 110, 168, and 240. Total values added in 1980, by product, were, in thousands of dollars: Gees, $120; Kays, $480; and Whys, $400. Compute the output index for the current year with 1980 as 100.

15. A furniture producer charges customers $20 for a chair and $60 for a table. Should the producer view a table as representing three times as much output as a chair? Explain.

16. (a) Write the weighted average of relatives price index formula. (b) If we have data for p_0, q_0, and p_n, what would be the proper weights w in (a)? (c) Substitute the proper weights (b) into the formula (a), simplify, and write the simplified result. (d) The simplified result in (c) is a price index formula. What is the name of this formula? (e) What statement made in the text about the formulas (a) and (d) is proved by (b) and (c)?

17. A subscript means a year. For example, p_{75} means 1975 prices. The following are price index formulas for 1981 with 1975 as base. Which of the formulas is (1) a Laspeyres index? (2) a Paasche Index?

(a) $100 \times \dfrac{\Sigma p_{81} q_{78}}{\Sigma p_{75} q_{78}}$; (b) $100 \times \dfrac{\Sigma p_{81} q_{75}}{\Sigma p_{75} q_{75}}$; (c) $100 \times \dfrac{\Sigma p_{81} q_{81}}{\Sigma p_{75} q_{81}}$.

18. Which of the following formulas is (1) a price index? (2) a quantity index?

(a) $100 \times \dfrac{\Sigma p_n q_0}{\Sigma p_0 q_0}$; (b) $100 \times \dfrac{\Sigma p_0 q_n}{\Sigma p_0 q_0}$; (c) $100 \times \dfrac{\Sigma p_n q_n}{\Sigma p_0 q_0}$.

19. Write a formula for a fixed weight price index that is not a Laspeyres index.

20. In 1980, DSK Company found that unit labor requirements were 1.2 hours for a Delta, 0.8 hour for a Sigma, and 0.4 hour for a Kappa. During the current year, 96 thousand labor-hours were worked and outputs, in thousands of units, were: Delta, 20: Sigma, 70; Kappa, 100. Compute the labor productivity index for the current year with 1980 as 100.

21. In the following, all numbers are in thousands and, for example, (40, 72) means 40 thousand units made in 72 thousand labor-hours. Operational results of TVZ Company in 1980 were: Tees, (40, 72); Vees (60, 210); Zees (100, 200). In the current year results were: Tees (60, 136); Vees (80, 272); Zees (110, 198). (a) How many hours would have been spent in 1980 to produce current year outputs? (b) Compute the labor productivity index for the current year with 1980 as 100.

22. Women's Fashions, Inc., makes dresses selling in four price categories; low (L), average (A), high (H), and very expensive (E). In the base period, labor-hours spent in making one dress were, for L, A, H, and E, respectively, 1, 2, 4, and 6. In the current period, Women's Fashions expended 82,500 labor-hours making 9000 L's, 12,000 A's, 6000 H's and 3000 E's. Compute the current period productivity index.

23. The dollar value of output of Carson Manufacturing Company rose from $22.428 million in 1980 to $27.416 million in the current year. Over the same period, the

Carson products price index rose from 164 to 181, and labor-hours worked declined from 1.231 to 1.082 million labor-hours. Compute Carson's productivity index for the current year with 1980 as 100.

24. In 1975 Steel Industries, Inc., worked 2.37 million labor-hours and made products valued at $72.96 million. In 1981, 2.62 million labor-hours were expended in making products valued at $102.14 million. The steel product price index rose from 113 in 1975 to 134 in 1981. Compute Steel Industries' productivity index for 1981 with 1975 as 100.

25. In one year, a standard new car model priced by BLS (for inclusion in the CPI) was available with tinted glass as an option at additional cost. The next year's new standard model comes equipped with tinted glass, and the manufacturer raises the price of the car. BLS, when pricing the new car, reduces the manufacturer's price by the amount attributable to tinted glass. Why does BLS make such an adjustment?

26. In January, a buyer of glass containers signed a contract to buy a fixed number of containers per month for 12 months. The January cost was established at $25,000, and the purchase contract specified a cost escalator based upon percentage changes in the producer price index for glass containers, which was 280 in January. What will the buyer pay in September if the index has risen to 294?

27. Suppose that the implicit price deflator is 180, with 1967 as 100. How was the number 180 computed?

28. The New York Stock Exchange index is not a price index. What type of index is it?

18

TIME-SERIES ANALYSIS

18.1 INTRODUCTION

Frequently, the data needed by managers for making decisions consist of numbers recorded by time period. These data include sales by year, units of output by week, selling expenses by month, and so on. A series of values of a variable recorded for succeeding time periods is called a *time series*. Time series are analyzed to obtain measures that can be used for making current decisions, for forecasting, and for planning future operations. There are many methods for analyzing time series. In this chapter you will learn the methods that are based upon the classical time-series model.

18.2 TIME-SERIES COMPONENTS

Trends

Cycles

Seasons

Irregularities

In the classical concept, or *model*, a time series has four components. They are long-term trend (T), cycles (C), seasonal (S) variation, and irregular (I) fluctuations. A particular series may contain all or only some of these components. The classical model assumes that (1) observed time-series values are a combination of the T, C, S, and I components; and (2) the combination is multiplicative. That is, the form of the model is the product

$$T \times C \times S \times I$$

In this section I will illustrate the four time-series components. In later sections you will learn how to measure the components and use the measures for forecasting and planning.

Long-Term Trend +

Table 18.1 gives data on sales of electric toasters, in hundreds, by an appli-

TABLE 18.1
TOASTER SALES IN HUNDREDS,
BY QUARTER, 1973–1981

| Year | Toaster sales (hundreds) | | | |
	Quarter 1	Quarter 2	Quarter 3	Quarter 4
1973	187	243	209	291
1974	198	263	270	297
1975	274	363	294	336
1976	232	273	241	289
1977	206	295	239	317
1978	237	366	300	429
1979	282	424	383	478
1980	375	429	393	560
1981	373	423	387	433

ance manufacturer for the period 1973–1981. Sales are by quarter (3-month period). I will use 1973:1 to refer to the first quarter of 1973. Similarly, 1978:4 means the fourth quarter of 1978, and so on.

EXERCISE What were toaster sales in 1980:2?
ANSWER 429 hundred.

The data of Table 18.1 are plotted as points in Figure 18.1. Thus, for

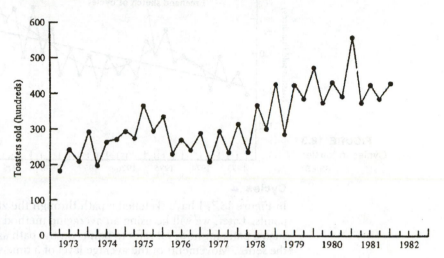

1973:1, the height of the point is 187. The plotted points are connected by
line segments, but only the plotted points have meaning; the line segments
serve to guide the eye in tracing point-to-point movements.

*The long-term trend
is a line or a curve
showing a general
tendency.*

A line or curve describing a time-series movement that persists for many
years is called a *long-term trend*. I stretched a piece of thread across the central region of the entire set of data points to obtain the straight-line, or
linear, long-term trend shown in Figure 18.2. Later we will discuss methods
for calculating the equations of both linear and curvilinear trends.

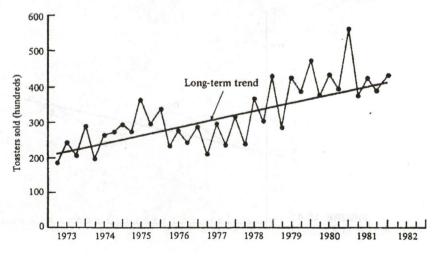

FIGURE 18.2
Long-term trend in
toaster sales.

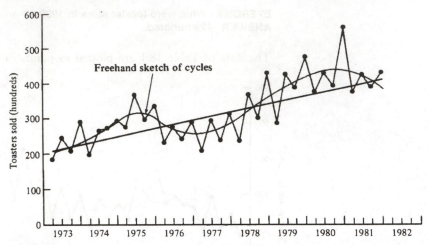

Cycles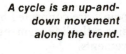

In Figure 18.3, I have sketched a path through the zigzag of quarterly data points. Later, we will be using an averaging method to calculate values for such a path; for now, I'll refer to points on the path as the "average" level of the series. Movements of the average level of a time series above and below the long-term trend are called cyclical movements, or *cycles*. In my sketch, the cyclical movement reached a *peak* in mid-1975, and then contracted to a low point called a *trough* at the end of 1976. The ensuing cyclical expansion (increase) peaked at the end of 1980. In general, a cycle has the following phases: an initial peak, a contraction, a trough, an expansion, and a terminal peak. (Alternatively, the order of the phases can be listed as initial trough, expansion, peak, contraction, and terminal trough.) The phases of a cycle are shown in Figure 18.4. The time it takes for a full cycle, say, from peak to peak, is called the *duration* of a cycle.

A cycle is an up-and-down movement along the trend.

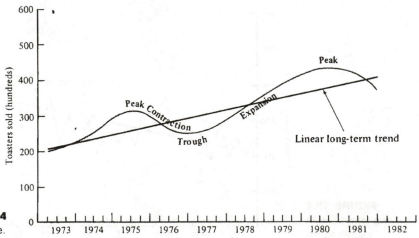

FIGURE 18.4
Phases of a cycle.

Seasonal patterns·show peaks and troughs similar to those in Figure 18.4, but the duration is always 1 year or less. To avoid confusing cycles with seasonal patterns, we shall call a cyclelike pattern a cycle only when its duration is longer than 1 year.

The percent difference between the peak points and the trend line is called the cycle's peak *amplitude*. The percent difference between the trough point and the trend line is called the cycle's trough *amplitude*. Thus, a peak amplitude of 20 percent means that the peak was 20 percent above the trend line. And a trough amplitude of 15 percent means that the trough was 15 percent below the trend line. Cycles recur continually in business and economic time series, but the durations and amplitudes may vary considerably from cycle to cycle. Consequently, you should not think of cycles as having one pattern that repeats over and over, as time goes on; each cycle can exhibit its own amplitude and duration.

Seasonal Variation

Figure 18.5 shows toaster sales by quarter for five of the years of data in Table 18.1. For each year, the first quarter is a low point; then there is a rise to the second quarter, a decline to the third quarter, and a rise to the fourth

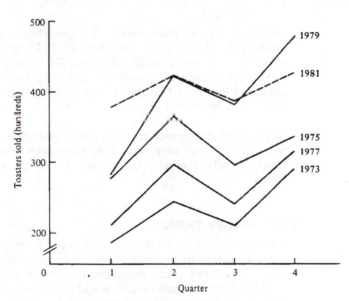

FIGURE 18.5
The seasonal pattern
of toaster sales.

quarter. To avoid complicating the figure, I did not include four of the years, but the omitted years show the same up-down-up pattern; it is a seasonal pattern. In general, a *seasonal pattern* is a within-a-year pattern whose shape repeats year after year. Many time series exhibit seasonal patterns that arise

*Seasonal variation is
a short-term repeated
pattern.*

because of the change in seasons and events such as school openings and closings or holidays. Managers need measures of seasonal variation, which we will compute later in the chapter, for short-term (1 year or less) forecasting and planning.

Irregularities are random (unpredictable) variations in a time series.

Irregularities

Irregularities are random variations in a time series. Figure 18.6 shows the irregularities in the toaster sales time series (I introduced them when I made

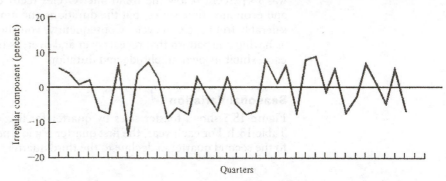

FIGURE 18.6
Irregular fluctuations in toaster sales.

up the time-series illustration). The first plotted point is at 5 percent, meaning that the irregular component of 1973:1 sales (187) is 5 percent. But we shall not measure irregularities in a time series because their size and their direction cannot be predicted; thus, measures of past irregularities are not useful for forecasting and planning. Sometimes a reason for an irregularity (say, a larger than usual or smaller than usual seasonal change) can be found *after* the irregularity occurs. For example, an unexpected strike may have caused an unexpected decline in a production time series, or an income tax cut may have caused an unexpected rise in a retail-sales time series. Usually, however, the reasons for irregularities cannot be determined.

18.3 LINEAR TRENDS

If we want to see the long-term trend in a time series, and not be misled by cyclical expansions or contractions, the period of time examined should cover at least one cycle, and preferably two or more cycles. As a rule of thumb, 15 or more years of data should be used when measuring a trend; but here, in explaining and applying trend measurement methods, we shall often work with shorter time periods to reduce the calculational burden. Also, because annual trend projections are used in long-term forecasting and planning, trend measurements will be made from annual data rather than quarterly or monthly data.

Coded years simplify trend calculations.

Coded Time Variable

To simplify computations, we should use coded year numbers instead of actual year numbers (such as 1980) in trend measurement. Actual year numbers will be denoted by t, and coded year numbers will be denoted by x. Table 18.2 shows the coded year numbers x for a period with an odd number

TABLE 18.2
CODED YEAR NUMBERS

| | Odd number of years | | Even number of years | |
	Year t	Coded year x	Year t	Coded year x
	1976	−2	1975	−2.5
The	1977	−1	1976	−1.5
middle →	1978	0	1977	−0.5 *x = 0 lies between*
year is	1979	1	1978 →0 0.5 ← *the two middle years*
coded	1980	2	1979	1.5
$x = 0$			1980	2.5

of years and a period with an even number of years. At the middle of the time period, $x = 0$. In general, for a sequence of years, the middle point $\bar{t}$ is the average of the first and last years. That is,

$\bar{t}$ is the "average year number" in the period.

$$\bar{t} = \frac{\text{first year} + \text{last year}}{2}$$

Thus, at the left of the table,

$$\bar{t} = \frac{1976 + 1980}{2} = 1978$$

The code for year t is

$$x = t - \bar{t}$$

so for 1978, $x = 1978 - 1978 = 0$. The coded year is zero at $\bar{t}$. At 1977,

$$x = t - \bar{t} = 1977 - 1978$$
$$= -1$$

Actually, the only computation we need is that for $\bar{t}$. Then, after entering $x = 0$ at the middle of an odd number of years, we assign -1, -2, and so on for years before the middle year, and 1, 2, and so on for years after the middle year, as shown in the table.

The even-number-of-years period 1975–1980 at the right of Table 18.2 has

$$\bar{t} = \frac{1980 + 1975}{2}$$
$$= 1977.5$$

as the middle point. So $x = 0$ halfway between 1977 and 1978. For $t = 1977$,

$$x = t - \bar{t} = 1977 - 1977.5$$
$$= -0.5$$

Again, as shown in the table, for years before the middle, x is -0.5, -1.5, -2.5, and so on; and for years after the middle, x is 0.5, 1.5, 2.5, and so on.

> **EXERCISE** (a) For the period 1970–1980, what is the coded year x for 1972?
> (b) For the period 1968–1981, what is the coded year x for 1979?
> **ANSWER** (a) -3; (b) 4.5.

Caution:
y_t refers to points on the trend line.

Linear Trend Equations

Let y_t be the trend value, the vertical height of a point on a trend line at coded year x. Then the coded form of the equation of a straight-line trend is

We use x to simplify computation of the trend line . . .

$$y_t = a + bx$$

But $x = t - \bar{t}$; so the equation for y_t in terms of actual years t is

. . . then replace x by $t - \bar{t}$.

$$y_t = a + b(t - \bar{t})$$

For a specific line, a and b are specific numbers. The number a is the height of the trend line at the middle time period $\bar{t}$; and b is the *constant vertical change* (rise or decline of the line) *per year* as time goes forward. For example, suppose that we have the following coded trend equation for the period 1965–1982, for which $\bar{t} = 1973.5$:

a is the y_t value for year $\bar{t}$.

$$y_t = 2046 - 12x$$

Because $x = t - \bar{t}$, and $\bar{t} = 1973.5$, we can write

$$y_t = 2046 - 12(t - 1973.5)$$

In the equation, $a = 2046$ is the trend value at the midperiod, 1973.5; and $b = -12$ means that the line declines by 12 each year as time goes forward. We compute trend values y_t for year t by substituting t into the equation. Thus, for $t = 1965$, the trend value is

b is the slope of the trend line.

$$y_t = 2046 - 12(1965 - 1973.5)$$
$$= 2046 - 12(-8.5)$$
$$= 2046 + 102$$
$$= 2148$$

We now have the number pair $(t, y_t) = (1965, 2148)$.

> **EXERCISE** From the foregoing equation, what is the (t, y_t) number pair for 1982?
> **ANSWER** (1982, 1944).

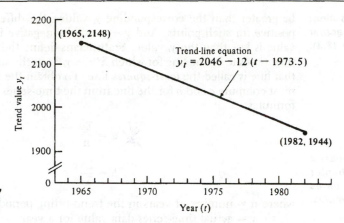

FIGURE 18.7
Trend line.

TABLE 18.3
TOASTER SALES, IN
HUNDREDS, 1973–1981

Year t	Toaster sales (hundreds) y
1973	930
1974	1028
1975	1267
1976	1035
1977	1057
1978	1332
1979	1567
1980	1757
1981	1616

To graph a linear trend equation, we plot any two (t, y_t) pairs as points and then draw a line through the points. Figure 18.7 shows the trend line through the points just computed, (1965, 2148) and (1982, 1944).

EXERCISE The coded trend equation for the period 1960–1980 is $y_t = 500 + 10x$. Compute (t, y_t) points for 1960 and 1980.
ANSWER (1960, 400); (1980, 600).

Computing Trend-Line Equations

Table 18.3 gives annual toaster sales y of an appliance manufacturer for the period 1973–1981. Figure 18.8 is the graph of the data. We want to find the equation of a line that follows a middle course between the data points. The height of that line for each year is a y_t value. Some of the actual y values will

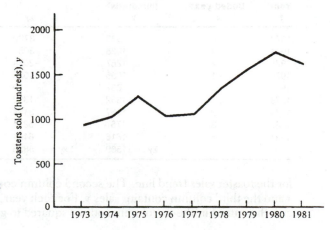

FIGURE 18.8
Toaster sales by year,
1973–1981.

Caution:
*y values are actual
values (Table 18.3).*

be greater than the corresponding y_t values; the differences $y - y_t$ will be positive for such points. And $y - y_t$ will be negative for years where the y value is less than the y_t value. Statisticians define the best-fitting line for a time series to be the line for which $\Sigma(y - y_t)^2$ has the smallest possible value; that line is called the *least-squares* line. To obtain the least-squares line, we must compute a and b for the line from the time-series data by the following formulas:

$$a = \frac{\Sigma y}{n}$$

*Use of coded years x
simplifies the Chapter
12 least-squares
formulas.*

$$b = \frac{\Sigma xy}{\Sigma x^2}$$

where n = number of years in the trend-fitting period
y = actual time-series data value for a year
x = coded year, $t - \bar{t}$
$\bar{t}$ = middle of time period

After values for a and b are computed, the trend equation in coded years can be written by substituting a and b into

$$y_t = a + bx$$

Or, in actual years t, the equation is

$$y_t = a + b(t - \bar{t})$$

If we had not used coded years, we would have had to compute Σty and Σt^2, and use more complicated formulas for a and b.

Table 18.4 shows the computations needed to obtain the values of a and b

TABLE 18.4
TOASTER SALES-TREND COMPUTATIONS

Year t	Coded year x	Toaster sales (hundreds) y	xy	x^2
1973	−4	930	−3720	16
1974	−3	1028	−3084	9
1975	−2	1267	−2534	4
1976	−1	1035	−1035	1
1977	0	1057	0	0
1978	1	1332	1332	1
1979	2	1567	3134	4
1980	3	1757	5271	9
1981	4	1616	6464	16
		$\Sigma y = 11589$	$\Sigma xy = 5828$	$\Sigma x^2 = 60$

for the toaster sales trend line. The second column contains the coded years x and the third column contains sales y. For each year, x is multiplied by y to give the entries in the xy column; and x is squared to give the entry in the x^2

column. The sums of the last three columns are used to compute a and b. Thus, for the $n = 9$ years,

$$a = \frac{\Sigma y}{n} = \frac{11,589}{9}$$

$$= 1287.667$$

and

$$b = \frac{\Sigma xy}{\Sigma x^2} = \frac{5828}{60}$$

$$= 97.133$$

Rounding gives $a = 1287.7$ and $b = 97.1$. Therefore, the coded equation $y_t = a + bx$ is

$$y_t = 1287.7 + 97.1x$$

But, $\bar{t}$, the middle year, is 1977; so the equation in terms of actual year numbers is

The trend equation in actual year numbers

$$y_t = 1287.7 + 97.1(t - 1977)$$

Substituting $t = 1973$ and $t = 1981$ into the last equation gives the data points (1973, 899) and (1981, 1676). These points were used to plot the trend line shown in Figure 18.9.

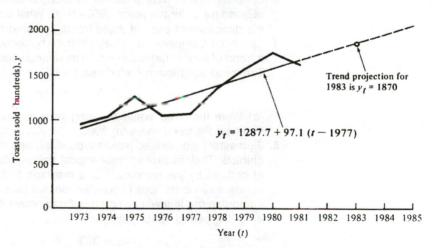

FIGURE 18.9
Computed trend line
for toaster sales.

The dashed section of the line of Figure 18.9 projects the trend to 1985. On that line, the computed projection for, say, $t = 1983$, is

$$y_t = 1287.7 + 97.1(t - 1977)$$

$$= 1287.7 + 97.1(1983 - 1977)$$

$$= 1870 \text{ hundred toasters}$$

Projections are forecasts of future trend levels, but they do not take into account cyclical movements that may lead to actual annual sales levels which are above or below the forecasts. In planning, managers often work out (by accounting methods) what implications the forecasted trend levels have for such items as profit and production facility requirements. Then they do *sensitivity* analyses; that is, they work out the implications of actual levels that might be, say, 10 percent above and 10 percent below trend forecasts. Such analyses may reveal that the accomplishment of planning objectives is relatively insensitive to variations from trend forecasts. Or, the analyses may identify a problem that could arise: then a contingency plan is made to handle the problem if it does arise.

EXERCISE Production data in thousands of units for 1977–1981 were 12, 17, 14, 19, and 16. Compute the linear trend equation for production.
ANSWER $y_t = 15.6 + 1(t - 1979)$.

18.4 PROBLEMS

1. Name the four components that may be present in a time series.
2. Name two factors that help explain why many business and economic time series exhibit upward rather than downward trends.
3. Suppose charts were made of passenger-miles of airline travel and railroad travel for the years 1950–1980. What do you believe would be the directions of each of these trends, upward or downward?
4. Spruance Company makes automobile batteries. Spruance computed a trend of annual battery sales, in thousands, for the years 1960–1980. The trend equation in coded years x is

$$y_t = 94 + 10.8x$$

(a) Write the trend equation using year numbers t rather than x. (b) Forecast the trend value for 1985.
5. Jigmaster Incorporated makes taps, dies, and other tools used by machinists. They multiplied their annual dollar volumes of sales (millions of dollars) by the reciprocal of a machine tool price index to obtain annual sales in millions of constant dollars (see Chapter 17). Then they computed the following trend line for constant dollars, in coded years x, for the period 1966–1981:

$$y_t = 320 - 6.4x$$

(a) Write the trend equation using year numbers t rather than x. (b) Forecast the trend value for 1985.

(*Note:* Trend computations should be made from data for long periods of time, say, 15 years or more. Shorter time periods are used in most of the following problems in order to reduce the number of calculations required.)

6. Sanford Company sales in millions of constant dollars are given in

Table A. (a) Compute a and b for the least-squares trend line. Then write the trend equation in the form $y_t = a + b(t - \bar{t})$. (b) Make a time-series chart of the data. Then draw the trend line on the chart. (c) Forecast Sanford Company's sales in millions of constant dollars for 1983.

TABLE A

Year	1977	1978	1979	1980	1981
Sales	10	15	13	16	21

7. Mercator Electronics, Inc., makes special ignition systems for large eight-cylinder cars. Sales, in thousands of systems per year, are given in Table B. (a) Compute a and b for the least-squares trend line. Then write the trend equation in the form $y_t = a + b(t - \bar{t})$. (b) Make a time-series chart of the data. Then draw the trend line on the chart.

TABLE B

Year	1976	1977	1978	1979	1980	1981
Sales	50	40	40	30	16	20

8. Table C gives annual productivity data for Gelso Company, in units made per labor-hour worked. (a) Compute a and b for the least-squares trend line. Then write the equation in the form $y_t = a + b(t - \bar{t})$. (b) Forecast Gelso's trend level of productivity for 1983.

TABLE C

Year	1975	1976	1977	1978	1979	1980	1981
Units per labor-hour	8	10	13	13	16	19	18

9. Table D gives the number of hundreds of new production employees hired each year by Pitman Company. (a) Compute a and b for the least-squares trend line. (b) Forecast the trend level for 1985.

TABLE D

Year	1974	1975	1976	1977	1978	1979	1980	1981
Hundreds of employees	4.8	4.7	4.4	4.1	4.3	4.1	3.8	4.0

10. Table E gives output data for Allied Fertilizer, Inc., in thousands of tons. (a) Find a and b for the least-squares trend line. Then write the equation of the trend line. (b) Forecast Allied's trend level for 1985.

TABLE E

Year	Output	Year	Output	Year	Output	Year	Output	Year	Output
1956	534	1961	655	1966	737	1971	926	1976	1075
1957	576	1962	669	1967	755	1972	981	1977	1108
1958	598	1963	681	1968	800	1973	1007	1978	1171
1959	622	1964	680	1969	831	1974	1057	1979	1233
1960	614	1965	720	1970	874	1975	1079	1980	1211

11. The trend of Javits Company sales, in thousands of units, is

$$y_t = 324 + 28.6(t - 1975)$$

Company president Frank Hammer wants to know what sales in 1982 will be if sales for that year are 10 percent below the forecasted trend level. Compute the number that Frank wants.

12. Haymarket Seafoods computed a linear trend of lobster sales in thousands of pounds for the period 1968–1981. They found $a = 126$ and $b = -3.2$. Haymarket wants to know what sales would be in 1985 if sales are 8 percent below the trend forecast. Compute the number that Haymarket wants.

18.5 QUADRATIC TREND EQUATIONS

Suppose the trend of a time-series graph appears to be a curve rather than a straight line. Then we may use the equation of a curve to measure the trend. Curves called parabolas often are used for this purpose. Figure 18.10 shows

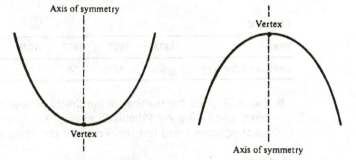

FIGURE 18.10
Parabolas.

two parabolas. Each has a vertical axis of symmetry that goes through its vertex (lowest or highest point). Frequently, trend curves are only sections of parabolas such as those shown in Figure 18.11. Straight-line trends either rise or fall by a *constant* amount per year. However, sections of parabolas rise by *decreasing* or *increasing* amounts per year; or they fall by decreasing or increasing amounts per year.

The equation of a parabola is called a *quadratic* equation. In coded years x, the quadratic trend equation is

*Coded quadratic
trend*

$$y_t = a + bx + cx^2$$

Rising by decreasing amounts per year

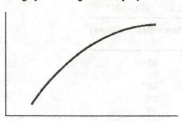

Rising by increasing amounts per year

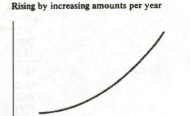

Falling by decreasing amounts per year

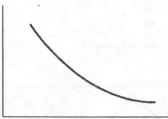

Falling by increasing amounts per year

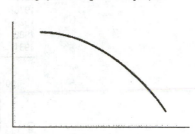

FIGURE 18.11
Sections of parabolas.

Or, in actual years t,

Uncoded quadratic trend

$$y_t = a + b(t - \bar{t}) + c(t - \bar{t})^2$$

where, as earlier, $\bar{t}$ is the middle of the trend-fitting time period and $x = t - \bar{t}$. To obtain a quadratic trend equation, we must compute a, b, and c from the given time-series data. The formulas for a, b, and c in coded years are derived from the least-squares quadratic regression formulas in Chapter 13. They are

a, b, and c are the same for both coded and uncoded quadratic trends.

$$a = \frac{(\Sigma y)(\Sigma x^4) - (\Sigma x^2 y)(\Sigma x^2)}{n(\Sigma x^4) - (\Sigma x^2)^2}$$

$$b = \frac{\Sigma xy}{\Sigma x^2}$$

$$c = \frac{n(\Sigma x^2 y) - (\Sigma x^2)(\Sigma y)}{n(\Sigma x^4) - (\Sigma x^2)^2}$$

where n = number of years in the trend-fitting period
y = time-series data value for a year
x = coded year

After computing a, b, and c from the data, we obtain the parabolic trend equation by substituting these values into $y_t = a + bx + cx^2$. And we can change coded years to actual years to give

$$y_t = a + b(t - \bar{t}) + c(t - \bar{t})^2$$

EXAMPLE Table 18.5 gives the freight ton-miles (in millions) carried by a railroad for the period 1971–1981. (One ton-mile is one ton of freight carried 1 mile.) The data are plotted in Figure 18.12. The central course between

TABLE 18.5
FREIGHT TON-MILES, 1971–1981

Year t	Freight ton-miles (millions) y
1971	93
1972	91
1973	96
1974	89
1975	90
1976	82
1977	88
1978	86
1979	87
1980	94
1981	92

FIGURE 18.12
Freight ton-miles,
1971–1981.

the data points appears to decline, and then rise. We shall compute a quadratic trend equation for the data, and then plot the equation to see whether or not it does follow the central course of the data.

Table 18.6 shows the calculation of the numbers required in the formulas for a, b, and c. We find that

$$\Sigma y = 988 \quad \Sigma xy = -28 \quad \Sigma x^2 = 110 \quad \Sigma x^2 y = 10,110 \quad \Sigma x^4 = 1958$$

Hence, with $n = 11$ years

The complexity of these calculations would increase threefold if coded years were not used.

$$a = \frac{(\Sigma y)(\Sigma x^4) - (\Sigma x^2 y)(\Sigma x^2)}{n(\Sigma x^4) - (\Sigma x^2)^2}$$

$$= \frac{(988)(1958) - (10,110)(110)}{11(1958) - (110)^2} = \frac{822,404}{9438}$$

$$= 87.14$$

Next,

$$b = \frac{\Sigma xy}{\Sigma x^2} = \frac{-28}{110}$$

$$= -0.2545$$

TABLE 18.6
QUADRATIC TREND COMPUTATIONS

Year t	Coded year x	Ton-miles (millions) y	xy	x²	x²y	x⁴
1971	−5	93	−465	25	2325	625
1972	−4	91	−364	16	1456	256
1973	−3	96	−288	9	864	81
1974	−2	89	−178	4	356	16
1975	−1	90	−90	1	90	1
1976	0	82	0	0	0	0
1977	1	88	88	1	88	1
1978	2	86	172	4	344	16
1979	3	87	261	9	783	81
1980	4	94	376	16	1504	256
1981	5	92	460	25	2300	625
		988	−28	110	10110	1958

As usual, coded years simplify computation.

and

$$c = \frac{n(\Sigma x^2 y) - (\Sigma x^2)(\Sigma y)}{n(\Sigma x^4) - (\Sigma x^2)^2}$$

$$= \frac{11(10,110) - (110)(988)}{11(1958) - (110)^2} = \frac{2530}{9438}$$

$$= 0.2681$$

Hence, in coded years, the equation $y_t = a + bx + cx^2$ is

$$y_t = 87.14 - 0.2545x + 0.2681x^2$$

Or, with $\bar{t} = 1976$, so that $x = t - 1976$, we have

$$y_t = 87.14 - 0.2545(t - 1976) + 0.2681(t - 1976)^2$$

We need several points to plot the graph of a quadratic trend. For $t = 1971$, we obtain from the trend equation

$$y_t = 87.14 - 0.2545(1971 - 1976) + 0.2681(1971 - 1976)^2$$

$$= 87.14 - 0.2545(-5) + 0.2681(-5)^2$$

$$= 87.14 + 1.2725 + 6.7025$$

$$= 95.1 \text{ million ton-miles}$$

so one point is $(t, y_t) = (1971, 95.1)$.

EXERCISE Compute the ton-mile trend value for 1972.
ANSWER 92.4 million ton-miles.

I used 11 points to plot the quadratic. The quadratic trend curve, sketched through plotted (t, y_t) points computed from the equation, is shown in Figure 18.13. Projections of the curve are forecasts of trend levels that can be used in planning future operations.

EXERCISE Compute the quadratic trend equation for the (t, y_t) data points (1979, 3), (1980, 15), (1981, 10).

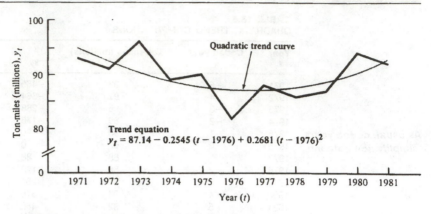

FIGURE 18.13
Quadratic trend of
freight ton-miles.

ANSWER $y_t = 15 + 3.5(t - 1980) - 8.5(t - 1980)^2$.

18.6 COMPARING TREND FITS

$\Sigma(y - y_t)^2$ *measures*
how well the trend
fits the data.

Statisticians use the sum of the squares of the $y - y_t$ differences, $\Sigma(y - y_t)^2$, to measure how well different trends fit a time series. The least-squares line is always the best-fitting *straight-line* trend because, of all possible *lines*, it has the smallest value for $\Sigma(y - y_t)^2$. Similarly, the least-squares quadratic equation always provides the best-fitting *parabola*. But, for a given time series, a linear and a parabolic trend will not lead to the same $\Sigma(y - y_t)^2$.

Smaller $\Sigma(y - y_t)^2$
means better fit.

Then the better-fitting trend is the one that has the smaller $\Sigma(y - y_t)^2$. For example, I computed y_t values for each year from the quadratic trend equation for the data in Table 18.6. Then I computed $(y - y_t)^2$ for each year and added the results to obtain $\Sigma(y - y_t)^2 = 90.3$. Next, I found the equation of the straight-line trend for the same data and computed $\Sigma(y - y_t)^2 = 152.1$ for the linear trend. The quadratic trend has the smaller sum of squares, 90.3 versus 152.1; so the quadratic trend is the better-fitting trend.

The computation of $\Sigma(y - y_t)^2$ for two or more trend equations by hand is time-consuming. The calculations should be made by using a computer program. I will not ask you to compute $\Sigma(y - y_t)^2$, but you should understand the principle: for two or more possible trend equations, the best-fitting equation is the one that has the smallest $\Sigma(y - y_t)^2$.

18.7 EXPONENTIAL TRENDS

Hand Calculators

In this section you will need a hand calculator with keys for finding powers, logarithms, and antilogarithms of numbers. The power key will be labeled something like x^y or y^x. Learn how to use the power key on your calculator. Then verify that, rounded,

$$(1.1037)^{15} = 4.39304$$

and with the fractional power $^1/_8$,

$$(217)^{1/8} = 1.95910$$

A calculator may have two keys for finding logarithms. A key containing the label *log*, as in log x, is for finding *common* (base 10) logarithms. The other, containing the label *ln*, as in ln x, is for finding *natural* (base = 2.71828) logarithms. We will use natural (ln x) logarithms because some calculators do not have a common logarithm key. However, computations can be made with either natural or common logarithms. On your calculator, verify that, rounded,

Pronounce **ln** *as you do Lynn.*

$$\ln 21.2 = 3.05400$$

and

$$\ln 0.747 = -0.29169$$

Calculators usually do not have a key with the label antilog or antiln for finding the antilogarithm of a number x. If your calculator has an e^x key, then the anti natural logarithm of x is

The antilogarithm of x is the number whose logarithm is x.

$$\text{antiln } x = e^x$$

If your calculator has an INV (for inverse) key, or a second function key, the steps in finding antiln x are

1. Enter number x.
2. Press INV (or second function) key.
3. Press ln x key.

Verify that, rounded,

Antiln x is sometimes written as **ln** ⁻¹ *x.*

$$\text{antiln } (2.617) = 13.69458$$

$$\text{antiln } (-1.6472) = 0.19259$$

Semilog Graphs

Exponential equations are used to measure trends that have a constant *percent rate* of change per year. Before computing an exponential trend equation, you should find out whether the trend of the data appears to rise (or fall) by a constant percent rate per year. To find out, plot the time series on graph paper called *semilog* paper. If the trend of the series appears to be linear (i.e., a straight line), on semilog paper, then the trend is exponential. Figure 18.14 shows the appearance of semilog paper that you can buy at a college bookstore. The horizontal divisions are evenly spaced; such an evenly spaced scale is called an *arithmetic* scale. The vertical scale divisions are based on logarithms; so that scale is called a *log* scale. The reference numbers on the vertical scale (1, 2, 3, and so on) can all be multiplied by the *same positive* number to obtain a scale for plotting a given set of data. Thus, for example, suppose the time-series values y run from 140 to 577. In that case, we would multiply the reference numbers by 100 and replace them with 100, 200, 300, 400, 500, 600, and so on. Then, after marking the (arithmetic) horizontal time scale for years t, we would plot the (t, y) data to obtain a semilog time-series chart.

If you can't find semilog paper, copy Figure 18.14.

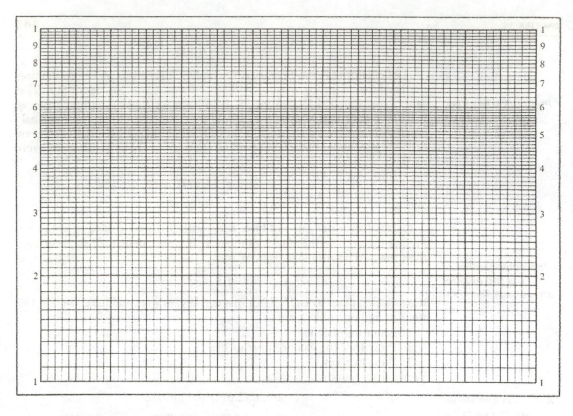

FIGURE 18.14
Semilog graph paper.

TABLE 18.7
FACTORY OUTPUT, 1971–1981

Year	Units of output (thousands)
1971	210
1972	250
1973	260
1974	240
1975	300
1976	310
1977	330
1978	380
1979	470
1980	530
1981	560

Table 18.7 gives data on a factory's output for the years 1971–1981.

Figure 18.15 is an ordinary (arithmetic) chart of the data. The trend appears to curve upward. To determine whether the trend has a constant percent rate of increase, I made the semilog chart shown in Figure 18.16. Now the trend appears to be linear. A straight line on a semilog time-series chart has an exponential equation.

Semilog paper "removes" the exponential part.

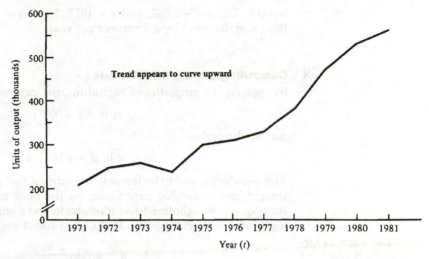

FIGURE 18.15
Arithmetic chart of output time series.

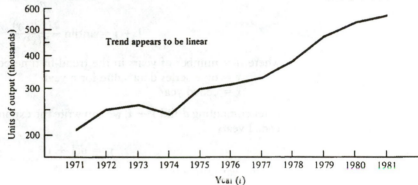

FIGURE 18.16
Semilog chart of output time series.

Exponential Trend Equations

The form of an exponential trend equation is

$$y_t = d(1 + i)^{t-\bar{t}} \qquad \text{or} \qquad y_t = d(1 + i)^x$$

The numbers d and $(1 + i)$ are computed from a given time series. As before, t means year and $\bar{t}$ is the middle of the trend-fit time period; and $x = t - \bar{t}$. The number i is the *constant* annual rate of change; and $100i$ percent is the annual percent rate of change. The equation is called exponential because the variable t is in the exponent. For example, the equation

100i percent is the constant annual percent change.

$$y_t = 175(1 + 0.094)^{t-1975}$$

d is the trend value for year $\bar{t}$.

has $d = 175$, $i = 0.094$, and $\bar{t} = 1975$. This trend increases by $100i$ percent = 9.4 percent per year. Similarly,

$$y_t = 527(1 - 0.062)^{t-1973}$$

has $d = 527$, $i = -0.062$, and $\bar{t} = 1973$. Here, $i = -0.062$ is negative; so this trend decreases by 6.2 percent per year.

 ### Computing Exponential Trends (—)

By applying the properties of logarithms, the exponential equation

$$y_t = d(1 + i)^x$$

can be changed to

$$\ln y_t = \ln d + x \ln (1 + i)$$

This equation is said to be linear in logarithms; that's why the equation is a straight line on semilog paper; and, for the same reason, we can use the least-squares straight-line trend formulas to find d and $1 + i$ *if* we work with logarithms. The least-squares formulas in coded years x are

Least-squares for-
mulas for d and 1 + i

$$d = \text{antiln} \, \frac{\sum \ln y}{n}$$

$$1 + i = \text{antiln} \, \frac{\sum(x \ln y)}{\sum(x^2)}$$

where n = number of years in the trend-fit time period
y = time-series data value for a year
x = coded year

After computing d and $1 + i$, we can write the exponential trend equation in coded years as

$$y_t = d(1 + i)^x$$

Or, in year numbers t,

$$y_t = d(1 + i)^{t - \bar{t}}$$

Table 18.8 shows the calculations needed to determine an exponential trend equation for the units of output in Table 18.7. With $\bar{t} = 1976$, $x = 0$ in 1976; this and the remaining coded x values are in the second column. The natural logarithms $\ln y$ of the output data values y found on a calculator are in the fourth column. For each year, the x and $\ln y$ values are multiplied to give the $x \ln y$ values in the fifth column; and the last column contains the square of each x value. The column sums we need are

$$\sum \ln y = 63.84305$$

$$\sum(x \ln y) = 10.70035$$

$$\sum(x^2) = 110$$

Next, for the $n = 11$ years, we compute

$$d = \text{antiln} \, \frac{\sum \ln y}{n} = \text{antiln} \, \frac{63.84305}{11}$$

TABLE 18.8
EXPONENTIAL TREND CALCULATIONS

Year t	Coded year x	Units of output (thousands) y	ln y	x ln y	x^2
1971	−5	210	5.34711	−26.73555	25
1972	−4	250	5.52146	−22.08584	16
1973	−3	260	5.56068	−16.68204	9
1974	−2	240	5.48064	−10.96128	4
1975	−1	300	5.70378	−5.70378	1
1976	0	310	5.73657	0	0
1977	1	330	5.79909	5.79909	1
1978	2	380	5.94017	11.88034	4
1979	3	470	6.15273	18.45819	9
1980	4	530	6.27288	25.09152	16
1981	5	560	6.32794	31.63970	25
			63.84305	10.70035	110

$\bar{t} = 1976$

$$= \text{antiln } 5.80391$$

$$= 331.6$$

and
$$1 + i = \text{antiln } \frac{\Sigma(x \ln y)}{\Sigma x^2} = \text{antiln } \frac{10.70035}{110}$$

$$= \text{antiln } 0.097276$$

$$= 1.1022$$

Then the exponential trend equation is, with $\bar{t} = 1976$,

$$y_t = 331.6(1.1022)^{t-1976}$$

The base of the exponent is $1 + i = 1.1022$, so $i = 0.1022$; that is, the annual percent rate of increase is 10.22 percent.

Computing trend values y_t

We compute values of y_t either to make a graph of the trend, or to forecast trend levels, by substituting t values into the equation. Thus, for $t = 1971$,

$$y_t = 331.6(1.1022)^{t-1976}$$

$$= 331.6(1.1022)^{1971-1976}$$

$$= 331.6(1.1022)^{-5}$$

$$= 331.6(0.61475)$$

$$= 203.85$$

or, rounded, 204 thousand units.

EXERCISE Compute the output trend value for 1980.
ANSWER 489 thousand units.

Arithmetic graph of the exponential trend

The output trend, drawn through (t, y_t) points computed for 1971–1981,

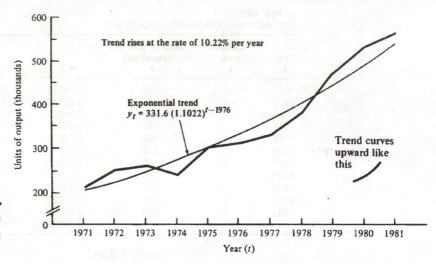

FIGURE 18.17
Exponential trend of
output time series
(arithmetic chart).

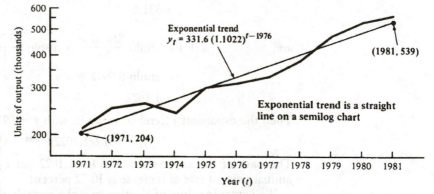

FIGURE 18.18
Exponential trend of
output time series
(semilog chart).

The semilog graph is
easier to draw and
use.

is shown on an arithmetic chart in Figure 18.17. It is a curve rising by
increasing amounts (but the same percent, 10.22 percent) each year. Figure
18.18 shows the trend on a semilog graph. Here the trend is a straight line; so
only two points are needed to draw it. When the graph (rather than the
equation) is used to forecast trend, the forecasts can be made more easily
from the semilog graph than from the arithmetic graph.

EXERCISE (a) Compute the exponential trend equation for the three data
points (1979, 33), (1980, 23), (1981, 18). (b) What is the annual percent rate of
change?
ANSWER (a) $y_t = 23.9(0.739)^{t-1980}$. (b) $(1 + i)$ is 0.739. Hence, $i = 0.739 -$
$1 = -0.261$; that is, the trend declines by 26.1 percent per year.

18.8 PROBLEMS

1. Jackson Company computed a quadratic trend for their basic wage
rate (dollars per hour) for the period 1970–1980. They found $a = 4$,

$b = 0.2$, and $c \doteq 0.01$. (a) Write the equation for the trend value y_t at time t years. (b) Forecast the trend value of the wage rate for 1985.

2. Greer Company computed a quadratic trend for their sales of tractors for the period 1968–1981. They found $a = 3920$, $b = -7$, and $c = -0.8$. (a) Write the equation for the trend value y_t at time t years. (b) Forecast the trend value of sales for 1990.

3. Table A gives Fowler Company's output of room air conditioners, in thousands, for 1977–1981. (a) Compute a, b, and c for the quadratic trend equation. Then write the equation for the trend value y_t at time t years. (b) Forecast the trend value of output for 1986. (c) Compute the trend values for 1977–1981. Then make a graph showing the quadratic trend curve.

TABLE A

Year	1977	1978	1979	1980	1981
Output	12.0	16.0	19.4	21.4	22.8

4. Table B shows the cost in dollars of an electronic filter made by Transitron Company. (a) Compute a, b, and c for the quadratic trend equation. Then write the equation for the trend value y_t at time t years. (b) Forecast the trend value of price for 1984. (c) Compute the trend values for 1975–1980. Then make a graph showing the points in Table B and *the quadratic trend curve.*

TABLE B

Year	1975	1976	1977	1978	1979	1980
Price (dollars)	56	47	45	43	48	37

5. Table C gives the tuition charge in dollars per credit hour at a large university. (a) Compute a, b, and c for the quadratic trend equation. Then write the equation for the trend value y_t at time t years. (b) Forecast the trend value of charge per credit hour in 1984.

TABLE C

Year	1973	1974	1975	1976	1977	1978	1979	1980	1981
Tuition charge	74	76	78	84	92	108	126	140	150

6. Dawson Manufacturing computed the exponential trend of an index of prices paid for the raw materials they buy. The price index has 1975 as 100. For the years 1965–1981, they found that $d = 75$ and that the annual percent rate of increase is 12 percent. (a) Write the exponential equation for the trend value y_t at time t years. (b) Forecast the trend value of the price index for 1985.

7. Wildcat Oil Company computed the exponential trend of the number of thousands of barrels of oil pumped from an oil field for the period

1970–1981. They found $d = 14,000$, and the annual percent rate of change was -14 percent (a decline of 14 percent per year). (a) Write the exponential equation for the trend value y_t at time t years. (b) Forecast the trend value of output for 1988.

8. Computer Equipment, Inc., constructed a measure of the price of computer systems with the same data-processing capabilities for the period 1976–1980. Their measures, in millions of dollars, are given in Table D. (a) Compute d and $1 + i$. Then write the least-squares exponential equation for computing the trend value y_t at time t years. (b) What is the annual percent rate of change of the trend values? (c) Forecast the trend value of the price measure for 1983.

TABLE D

Year	1976	1977	1978	1979	1980
Price measure	4.6	3.1	2.2	1.7	1.2

9. Table E gives the cost in millions of dollars of fuel consumed by Tri-State Electric Company for the period 1976–1981. (a) Compute d and $1 + i$. Then write the least-squares exponential trend equation for computing the trend value y_t at time t years. (b) What is the annual percent rate of change of the trend values? (c) Forecast the trend value of fuel cost for 1986.

TABLE E

Year	1976	1977	1978	1979	1980	1981
Fuel cost	47	58	68	77	92	119

10. In 1970, a telephone company built a facility planned to handle calls made by subscribers during the next 10 to 15 years. In 1980 it was decided that in order to have adequate lead time, construction of an additional facility would start 2 years before the number of subscribers reaches 1.5 million. The equation of the exponential trend of millions of subscribers was found to be

$$y_t = 0.52(1.085)^{t-1973}$$

(a) Compute the trend values for 1981 and 1982. (b) Continue the computations as in (a) until the trend value first exceeds 1.5 million. (c) In what year should additional facility construction start?

11. Suppose the graph of a time series appears to have a trend that increases by an increasing amount per year. Both a rising exponential trend and one type of rising quadratic trend increase by increasing amounts each year. Suppose that an exponential trend equation and a quadratic trend equation are computed for the series. What statistical measure would be computed to determine how well each trend fits the data? In terms of the statistical measures, which trend would be called the better-fitting trend?

12. Corrogon Company's net profits, in millions of dollars, are given in Table F. (a) Make a semilog chart of the data. (b) Does it appear that the series has an exponential trend? Why? (c) Find d and $1 + i$. Then write the exponential trend equation for y_t at time t years. (d) Compute the y_t values for 1976–1980. (e) Make an arithmetic chart showing the data of Table F and the trend curve.

TABLE F

Year	1976	1977	1978	1979	1980
Net profit	21.6	25.5	30.1	35.5	41.9

13. Sales of Farragut, Inc., in thousands of units, are given in Table G. (a) Make an arithmetic chart of the data. (b) Make a semilog chart of the data. (c) Would you use a linear, a quadratic, or an exponential trend equation for these data? Why?

TABLE G

Year	1975	1976	1977	1978	1979	1980	1981
Sales	25	40	56	63	70	81	83

18.9 MOVING AVERAGES

Averages called *m*-period *moving averages* for the data values in a time series are calculated as follows: (1) compute and record the average of the earliest remaining set of *m* values; (2) then discard the first value; (3) repeat (1) and (2) until the latest data value has been used.

Table 18.9 gives a time series of output values for 1976–1981. To com-

TABLE 18.9
OUTPUT TIME SERIES, 1976–1981

Year	1976	1977	1978	1979	1980	1981
Output (thousands of units)	17	22	18	26	16	27

pute, say, $m = 3$-year moving averages, we first compute the average of the earliest set of three output values, which is

Start with the earliest m data values.

$$\frac{17 + 22 + 18}{3} = 19$$

and then discard the first value, 17. Next we compute the average of the earliest remaining set of $m = 3$ values, which is

To "move":
*For each average,
discard the earliest
used and add the
earliest unused.*

$$\frac{22 + 18 + 26}{3} = 22$$

We repeat the process until the last output value has been used. The averages are called "moving" averages because we move one period later as each successive average is computed.

EXERCISE The first two 3-year moving averages just computed for the output data of Table 18.9 are 19 and 22. Compute the next two 3-year moving averages.
ANSWER 20 and 23.

*Dan: How would I
center a moving
average if m is even?*

*Fran: Compute 2-
period moving
averages of your
m-period moving
averages.*

A moving average is tabulated at the average (center) of the time period for which it is computed. Then it is called a *centered* moving average. Table 18.10 gives the centered 3-year moving averages for the output data of Table 18.9. Moving averages vary less than the data values from which they are computed. Thus, for example, the moving averages in the table vary from 19 to 23, but the output values vary from 16 to 27. Hence, we say that moving averages tend to *smooth* a time series. Notice in the table that the sequence of centered moving averages is "out of date" in the sense that there is no average centered on 1981, the latest year for which the output value is available.

TABLE 18.10
CENTERED MOVING AVERAGES

Year	1976	1977	1978	1979	1980	1981
Output (thousands of units)	17	22	18	26	16	27
Centered 3-year moving average	—	19	22	20	23	—

EXERCISE If 7-year moving averages of values of a 1950–1981 time series are computed, at what year will the last moving average be centered?
ANSWER 1978.

Figure 18.19 shows the output series of Table 18.10 and the smoothing tendency of its 3-year centered moving averages. Sometimes 3-year or 5-year or 7-year moving averages are used to expose the combined trend and cycle movement in a time series; but, as discussed in what follows, four-quarter or 12-month moving averages are a more useful measure (for forecasting purposes) of the combined trend and cycle movement in a series.

18.10 MEASURES OF TREND AND CYCLE

In our classical time-series model, observed data values occur because of the interactive effects of four components. The components are long-term trend (*T*), cyclical (*C*) effects, seasonal (*S*) variation, and irregular (*I*) fluctua-

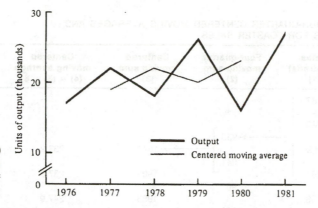

FIGURE 18.19
Three-year centered
moving average of
output data.

tions. If we can remove the seasonal (S) and irregular (I) effects, we will be
left with the combined effects of trend and cycle. Now suppose that we have
data recorded by month for a period of years, and we compute 12-month
centered moving averages of the data. Each average will be computed from
a 12-month total (but, of course, the 12 months are not always January
through December). Twelve-month *totals* do not exhibit a seasonal
(month-by-month) pattern; so computing 12-month centered moving
averages removes seasonal variation from monthly data. And moving
averages of 12 months of data smooth out irregularities. Hence, we can use
12-month centered moving averages to remove seasonal variations and irregularities.

12-month moving
averages smooth out
(remove) S and I,
leaving T and C.

When the seasonal variations and irregularities are removed, only trend
and cycle remain. Thus, 12-month centered moving averages are measures
of the combined effect of trend and cycle for monthly data. Similarly,
four-quarter centered moving averages are combined trend and cycle measures for quarterly data.

EXERCISE A company divides each year into thirteen four-week periods.
How would you measure the combined trend and cycle levels in the company's
period-by-period sales data?
ANSWER By computing 13-period centered moving averages.

Table 18.11 shows the computations of four-quarter centered moving
averages of the toaster sales data of Table 18.1. (For the moment, disregard
the entries in the last column of the table.) The column numbered (2) contains the four-quarter moving sums centered at the middle of each four-
quarter period; the middle falls halfway between two quarters. Thus, the
sum of the first four sales numbers is

$$187 + 243 + 209 + 291 = 930$$

When m is even,
moving sums center
between periods.

and that sum is entered between 1973:2 and 1973:3. Moving ahead one
quarter, the next sum is

$$243 + 209 + 291 + 198 = 941$$

TABLE 18.11
COMPUTATION OF FOUR-QUARTER CENTERED MOVING AVERAGES AND
SEASONAL RELATIVES FOR TOASTER SALES

Year	Q	Sales (hundreds) (1)	Four-quarter moving sum (2)	Centered moving sum (3)	Centered moving average (4) = (3) ÷ 8	Seasonal relative (5) = [(1) ÷ (4)] × 100
1973	1	187				
	2	243				
			930			
	3	209		1871	233.9	89.4
			941			
	4	291		1902	237.8	122.4
			961			
1974	1	198		1983	247.9	79.9
			1022			
	2	263		2050	256.2	102.7
			1028			
	3	270		2132	266.5	101.3
			1104			
	4	297		2308	288.5	102.9
			1204			
1975	1	274		2432	304.0	90.1
			1228			
	2	363		2495	311.9	116.4
			1267			
	3	294		2492	311.5	94.4
			1225			
	4	336		2360	295.0	113.9
			1135			
1976	1	232		2217	277.1	83.7
			1082			
	2	273		2117	264.6	103.2
			1035			
	3	241		2044	255.5	94.3
			1009			
	4	289		2040	255.0	113.3
			1031			
1977	1	206		2060	257.5	80.0
			1029			
	2	295		2086	260.8	113.1
			1057			
	3	239		2145	268.1	89.1
			1088			
	4	317		2247	280.9	112.9
			1159			
1978	1	237		2379	297.4	79.7
			1220			
	2	366		2552	319.0	114.7
			1332			
	3	300		2709	338.6	88.6
			1377			
	4	429		2812	351.5	122.0
			1435			

TABLE 18.11
(Continued)

Year	Q	Sales (hundreds) (1)	Four-quarter moving sum (2)	Centered moving sum (3)	Centered moving average (4) = (3) ÷ 8	Seasonal relative (5) = [(1) ÷ (4)] × 100
1979	1	282		2953	369.1	76.4
			1518			
	2	424		3085	385.6	110.0
			1567			
	3	383		3227	403.4	94.9
			1660			
	4	478		3325	415.6	115.0
			1665			
1980	1	375		3340	417.5	89.8
			1675			
	2	429		3432	429.0	100.0
			1757			
	3	393		3512	439.0	89.5
			1755			
	4	560		3504	438.0	127.9
			1749			
1981	1	373		3492	436.5	85.5
			1743			
	2	423		3359	419.9	100.7
			1616			
	3	387				
	4	433				

This calculation [column (0)] centers the moving sums on, rather than between, quarters.

and this sum is entered between 1973:3 and 1973:4.

Next we want to center the sums on, rather than between, quarters. To do this, a moving sum of pairs of column (2) entries is computed and entered on the quarters as shown in column (3). The column (3) sums are for 8 quarters; so these sums, divided by 8, are the centered quarterly moving averages. The centered moving averages are entered in column (4) of the table. They measure the quarterly combined trend and cycle level of the data values.

Figure 18.20 shows the graph of quarterly toaster sales data and the centered moving averages computed in Table 18.11. The expansions and contractions of the moving averages show the cycles in the data. But the moving averages also have an upward trend; so the moving averages contain both trend and cycles.

EXERCISE Suppose coffeemaker sales for quarters 1, 2, 3, and 4 of 1972 were, in hundreds, 170, 200, 180, and 230. Sales data for quarters 1, 2, and 3 of 1973 were 187, 243, and 209 hundred. (a) Following the steps in Table 18.11, compute as many quarterly centered moving averages as you can with the 7 quarters of data. (b) In what quarters will the averages in (a) be centered?
ANSWER (a) 197.1, 204.6, 213.6; (b) 1972:3, 1972:4, 1973:1.

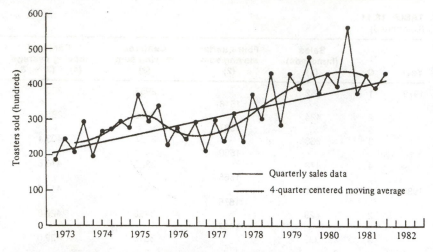

FIGURE 18.20
Trend and cycle
(moving average) for
toaster sales.

18.11 RATIO-TO-MOVING AVERAGE MEASURES OF SEASONAL VARIATION

T × C × S × I repre-
sents the actual data
value for a period.

In our classical model, time-series components are assumed to be multiplicative; that is, actual values that we observe are the product $T \times C \times S \times I$ (trend times cycle times seasonal times irregular). If we remove S and I by computing centered moving averages as we did in the last section, $T \times C$ remains. Now suppose we divide observed $T \times C \times S \times I$ values by the corresponding $T \times C$ values. Then

T × C is the moving
average for that
period.

$$\frac{T \times C \times S \times I}{T \times C} = S \times I$$

Dividing leaves S × I.

The outcome is $S \times I$, the product of seasonal and irregular components. That is, division of a period's sales (or output, or whatever) value by the moving average (or $T \times C$) for that period gives a measure of combined seasonal and irregular effects ($S \times I$) for that period. The $S \times I$ measure, multiplied by 100, is called a *seasonal relative*. Thus,

This is S × I × 100.

$$\text{Seasonal relative} = \frac{\text{actual data value for a period}}{\text{moving average centered on that period}} \times 100$$

Seasonal relatives computed for toaster sales are given in column (5) of Table 18.11. The first entry is

$$\text{Seasonal relative, 1973:3} = \frac{\text{1973:3 toaster sales}}{\text{1973:3 centered moving average}} \times 100$$

$$= \frac{209}{233.9} \times 100$$

$$= 89.4$$

Similar computations provided the remaining entries in column (5). The en-

TABLE 18.12
SEASONAL RELATIVES FOR TOASTER SALES

Year	Quarter			
	1	2	3	4
1973			89.4	122.4
1974	79.9	102.7	101.3*	102.9*
1975	90.1*	116.4*	94.4	113.9
1976	83.7	103.2	94.3	113.3
1977	80.0	113.1	89.1	112.9
1978	79.7	114.7	88.6*	122.0
1979	76.4*	110.0	94.9	115.0
1980	89.8	100.0*	89.5	127.9*
1981	85.5	100.7		
Sums	498.6	644.4	551.6	699.5
Average	83.1	107.4	91.9	116.6 → sum = 399.0
Seasonal index	83.3	107.7	92.1	116.9 → sum = 400

This averaging process removes the effect of I, leaving only S.

* Discard these relatives before computing sums.

tire set of seasonal relatives, arranged by quarter, is given in Table 18.12.

The eight relatives for a given period in Table 18.12 are $S \times I$ measures that vary because of the influence of irregularities I. Consequently, we average the relatives for a period to remove irregularities and obtain the seasonal component S. Because an unusually large or small relative can distort the average (i.e., the arithmetic mean), it is common practice (which we will follow) to discard the smallest and largest relatives in each column before the average is computed. The discarded relatives are marked * in the table. The sum of the remaining six relatives in each column is given at the bottom of the column. Each sum divided by 6 yields the average on the next line; the sum of the four averages, shown at the right, is 399.0.

The classical model assumes that seasonal effects for a year should average out; that is, the average of seasonal measures should be 100. Consequently, the four quarterly measures must have a sum of 400 (not 399.0). Multiplying the sum 399.0 by 400/399.0 gives 400. We therefore multiply each average in the table by 400/399.0 to give the seasonal indexes shown on the bottom line in the table. These indexes have 400 as their sum. Thus, *seasonal indexes* for the periods of a year are averages of seasonal relatives adjusted so that their average is 100 per period. This method of computing the seasonal indexes is called the *ratio-to-moving average* method, because seasonal relatives are computed by dividing actual data values by their corresponding moving averages (then multiplying by 100).

For monthly data, we would compute 12 seasonal indexes; for semiannual data, 2 indexes, etc.

EXERCISE Assume the following: (1) Seasonal relatives for January are 91.5, 94.5, 97.8, 103, 96.2, and 84.0; (2) the averages of seasonal relatives for the 12 months of a year, computed after discarding the largest and smallest relatives for a month, have a sum of 1206. (a) Discard the largest and smallest January relative, and compute the average of the remaining relatives. (b) Compute the January seasonal index.
ANSWER (a) 95; (b) 94.5.

18.12 ADJUSTING FOR SEASONAL VARIATION

Multiplying an observed time-series data value for a period by

$$\frac{100}{\text{that period's seasonal index}}$$

is called *adjusting for seasonal variation*. Thus,

Formula for seasonal adjustment

$$\text{Period's seasonally adjusted data value} = \frac{\text{period's actual data value}}{\text{period's seasonal index}} \times 100$$

In terms of the $T \times C \times S \times I$ model, dividing by the seasonal measure S gives

$$\frac{T \times C \times S \times I}{S} = T \times C \times I$$

Thus, seasonally adjusted data contain the effects of trend, cycle, and irregularities. We will say that *seasonal adjustment of data values gives estimates of $T \times C$ that have an error component due to irregularities*.

In Table 18.11, toaster sales for 1981:3 are 387 hundred. There is no centered moving average in column (4) for 1981:3. However, the third quarter seasonal index (see Table 18.12) is 92.1. Hence,

$$\text{Seasonally adjusted sales, 1981:3} = \frac{\text{1981:3 sales}}{\text{quarter 3 seasonal index}} \times 100$$

$$= \frac{387}{92.1} \times 100$$

$$= 420.2$$

or, rounded, 420 hundred toasters.

EXERCISE Toaster sales for 1981:4 are 433 hundred, and the fourth-quarter seasonal index is 116.9. Compute seasonally adjusted sales for 1981:4.
ANSWER 370 hundred.

Seasonal adjustment helps us estimate missing moving averages.

Seasonal adjustment is important because trend and cycle measures are used in forecasting; and our $T \times C$ measure (the centered moving average) is out of date. That is, for example, we do not have values of the centered moving average for the last two quarters of quarterly data or for the last 6 months of monthly data. Seasonal adjustment of the last two quarters (or last 6 months) provides estimates of the centered moving average (estimates of $T \times C$). Figure 18.21 shows the moving averages computed in Table 18.11, and the estimated moving averages for the toaster sales data. The estimated values are the seasonally adjusted values 420 and 370 hundred computed in the foregoing example and exercise. The larger than usual decline in the seasonally adjusted values from 1981:3 to 1981:4 may be an irregularity. It may also be a signal to a manager that the trend and cycle level are in a contraction phase.

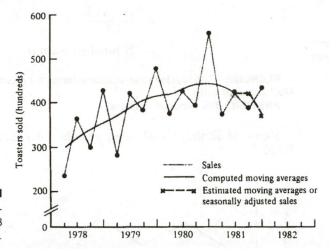

FIGURE 18.21

Toaster sales: seasonally adjusted in 1981:3 and 1981:4.

18.13 SHORT-TERM FORECASTING AND PLANNING

Forecasting

We will call forecasting for a period of 1 year or less short-term forecasting. In short-term forecasting, we will use projections of the centered moving averages as $T \times C$ forecasts. The moving-average ($T \times C$) forecast for a period will then be multiplied by the seasonal index for that period, and divided by 100 to obtain a $T \times C \times S$ forecast. Thus,

$$\text{Period forecast} = \frac{(\text{projected period moving average}) \times (\text{seasonal index})}{100}$$

We cannot forecast irregularities that may occur; so our forecasts make no provisions for irregularities.

In the toaster example, suppose that for ordering and inventory control purposes, forecasts are made at the beginning of each quarter for that quarter's and the next quarter's sales. For example, at the beginning of 1982:1 (after 1981:4 sales data are available) forecasts are to be made for 1982:1 and 1982:2. Then we will need projections of the moving average for 1982:1 and 1982:2. Different projections are obtained when different assumptions are made about the direction and amount of change in the moving average. Here, we shall make the assumption that the level of the moving average for both 1982:1 and 1982:2 will equal the average of the last two (estimated) values of the moving average, 420 and 370. This average is

First forecast the moving averages . . .

$$\frac{420 + 370}{2} = 395.0$$

Then the sales forecast for 1982:1 is

. . . then apply the seasonal factor . . .

$$\frac{(1982{:}1 \text{ moving average forecast}) \times (\text{quarter 1 seasonal index})}{100}$$

$$= \frac{395.0(83.3)}{100}$$

*. . . to obtain fore-
casts.*

$$= 329 \text{ hundred toasters}$$

EXERCISE   The toaster sales seasonal index for quarter 2 is 107.7. Forecast
1982:2 toaster sales.
ANSWER   425 hundred toasters.

Figure 18.22 shows 1981 sales, and the sales forecasts for 1982:1 and
1982:2.

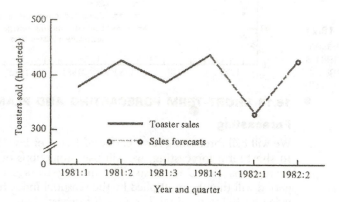

FIGURE 18.22
Forecasting toaster
sales.

Planning

A manager who decides, or is told by a superior, that next year's sales must
reach a certain level takes that level as a planned objective rather than a
forecast. Then the manager has to convert the planned annual level into
quarterly or monthly sales levels that need to be attained if the annual level
is to be reached. Suppose, for example, that our toaster company manager
decides that 1982 sales should be 1800. (Keep in mind that sales are in
hundreds of toasters.) Sales in 1981 were 1616. Consequently, the 1982 objective of 1800 is

$$1800 - 1616 = 184$$

above 1981 sales, or about 11 percent above 1981 sales.

The objective of 1800 is the planned-for sum of quarters 1, 2, 3, and 4
sales for 1982. To reach the objective, the moving four-quarter total for
Start with the   1982, entered halfway between quarters 2 and 3 should be 1800, as shown in
objective increase.   the first column of Table 18.13. The increase of 184 is

*Allocate the increase
among the quarterly*

$$\frac{184}{4} = 46 \text{ per quarter}$$

totals.   or 23 per half quarter. So we add a half quarter to 1800 to give 1800 + 23 =

TABLE 18.13
PLANNING OBJECTIVE CALCULATIONS

Year	Q	Annual sales objective (1)	Moving 4-quarter objective (2)	Quarterly moving average objective (3) = (2)/4	Seasonal index (4)	Sales objective (unadjusted) $(5) = \frac{(3) \times (4)}{100}$	Sales objective (adjusted) $(6) = (5) \times \frac{1800}{1804}$
1982	1		1731	432.75	83.3	360	359
	2	1800	1777	444.25	107.7	478	477
	3		1823	455.75	92.1	420	419
	4		1869	467.25	116.9	546	545
						1804	1800

1823 for the quarter 3 entry in column (2). Then add a full quarter to give 1823 + 46 = 1869 for quarter 4. Now subtract a full quarter from 1823 to give 1777 for quarter 2; and subtract a full quarter from 1777 to give 1731 for quarter 1.

Find the objective moving averages.

Next, divide each column (2) entry by 4 to get the quarterly moving average objectives in column (3). The seasonal factor is introduced by multiplying a column (3) entry by the seasonal index in column (4), then dividing by 100; the result is the unadjusted sales objective in column (5). The sum of the four quarterly objectives should be the annual objective, 1800; but the column (5) sum is 1804. Consequently, each column (5) entry is adjusted by multiplying it by $^{1800}/_{1804}$ to give the final adjusted sales objectives in column (6). After planned objectives have been approved by top management, they become the starting point for the detailed accounting analyses needed to determine personnel and raw materials requirements, lay out production schedules, prepare financial budgets, and so on. Thus, business planning starts by setting objectives, and time-series analysis is used in setting these objectives.

Apply the seasonal factor.

And adjust to 100 percent of the objective.

EXERCISE In Table 18.13, start with an annual planned objective of 1712 for 1982. Then compute adjusted quarterly sales objectives for 1982.
ANSWER 348, 457, 396, and 510.

The methods described in the foregoing are illustrative rather than comprehensive. They show you one approach to the important business problem of forecasting and planning for an uncertain future. And they provide you with the background you will need to devise alternative methods. Nowadays, computer programs often are used to refine, extend, or replace the classical model that underlies the analyses I have shown.

18.14 PROBLEMS

1. Table A gives the numbers of deep freezers sold by Brian Appliances, Inc. (*a*) Compute four-quarter moving averages centered on the quarters. (*b*) On what quarters do the respective averages in (*a*) center?

TABLE A

Year	Quarter			
	1	2	3	4
1980	40	46	36	52
1981	40	54	50	72

2. Table B gives the numbers of houses built by Ross-DiMatteo Construction Company. (a) Compute four-quarter moving averages centered on the quarters. (b) On what quarters do the respective averages in (a) center?

TABLE B

Year	Quarter			
	1	2	3	4
1980	62	82	48	72
1981	65	85	55	82

3. Table C gives the numbers of new cars sold by Jacar dealers in a three-state area. (a) Compute 12-month moving averages centered on the months. (b) On what months do the respective averages in (a) center?

TABLE C

Year	Jan.	Feb.	Mar.	Apr.	May	June	July	Aug.	Sept.	Oct.	Nov.	Dec.
1980	736	775	964	863	972	909	808	686	754	858	778	574
1981	551	568	654	703	767	698	691	668	591	628	506	430

4. Table D gives the numbers of deep freezers sold by Brian Appliances, Inc. Compute the seasonal index for each quarter by the ratio-to-moving average method.

TABLE D

Year	Quarter			
	1	2	3	4
1977	·28	30	22	24
1978	20	30	28	44
1979	34	46	44	62
1980	40	46	36	52
1981	40	54	50	72

5. Table E gives the numbers of houses built by Ross-DiMatteo Construction Company. Compute the seasonal index for each quarter by the ratio-to-moving average method.

TABLE E

Year	Quarter			
	1	2	3	4
1977	60	72	42	65
1978	58	70	45	65
1979	62	80	52	75
1980	62	82	48	72
1981	65	85	55	82

6. Table F gives the numbers of new cars sold by Jacar dealers in a three-state area. Compute the seasonal index for each month by the ratio-to-moving average method.

TABLE F

Year	Jan.	Feb.	Mar.	Apr.	May	June	July	Aug.	Sept.	Oct.	Nov.	Dec.
1977	612	655	742	770	792	821	734	590	655	799	792	644
1978	586	637	756	737	748	798	668	566	756	934	848	649
1979	610	698	772	774	888	877	769	656	741	932	891	719
1980	736	775	964	863	972	909	808	686	754	858	778	574
1981	551	568	654	703	767	698	691	668	591	628	506	430

7. Why would it be advisable to adjust monthly sales data to obtain average sales per selling day before calculating seasonal indexes?

8. Actual sales for August and September were, respectively, 895 and 984 units. The seasonal indexes for August and September are, respectively, 92 and 110. (a) Compute seasonally adjusted sales. (b) Compute the percent change in actual sales. (c) Compute the percent change in seasonally adjusted sales from August to September.

9. Actual sales for June and July were, respectively, 1680 and 1520 units. Respective seasonal indexes for June and July are 105 and 95. (a) Compute the percent change in actual sales. (b) Compute the percent change in seasonally adjusted sales from June to July.

10. Kondor Stores sales in thousands of dollars, and the latest available four-quarter moving averages, are given in Table G. The seasonal indexes (1 to 4) are 81.6, 97.7, 99.3, and 121.4. (a) Compute seasonally adjusted sales for 1981:3 and 1981:4. Enter the adjusted sales in the moving average row of Table G. (b) Compute the average of the two adjusted sales values in (a). Use the average just computed as the projected moving average for both 1982:1 and 1982:2. Then forecast sales for 1982:1 and 1982:2.

TABLE G

Year	1980	1981			
Quarter	4	1	2	3	4
Sales	3226	2185	2623	2552	3382
Moving average	2565	2612	2666		

11. (a) Do Problem 10(a) first. Then compute $b = \Sigma xy / \Sigma x^2$ for the least-squares line fitted to the five numbers in the moving average row. ($x = 0$ at 1981:2.) (b) To obtain projected moving averages, start with the last given moving average, 2666, in Table G. Then add the value of b, just computed, successively, to obtain projected moving averages for quarters 1, 2, 3, and 4 of 1982. (c) Forecast sales for quarters 1, 2, 3, and 4 of 1982.

12. Atlas Company sells decorative illuminated globes of the world. Their seasonal indexes, their sales in thousands, and the latest computed moving average, are given in Table H. (a) Compute seasonally adjusted sales for the last 6 months of 1981. Enter the adjusted sales in the moving average row of Table H. (b) Compute the average of the seven entries in the moving average row. Use the average just computed as the projected moving average for January, February, and March of 1982. Then forecast sales for January, February, and March of 1982.

TABLE H

	June	July	Aug.	Sept.	Oct.	Nov.	Dec.	Jan.	Feb.	Mar.
Seasonal index	98	97	102	98	102	116	150	80	73	92
1981 sales	820	805	842	804	849	937	1208			
Moving average	830									

13. (a) Do Problem 12(a) first. Then compute $b = \Sigma xy / \Sigma x^2$ for the least-squares line fitted to the seven numbers in the moving average row. ($x = 0$ at September.) (b) To obtain projected moving averages, start with the last given moving average, 830, in Table H. Then add the value of b, just computed, successively, to obtain moving average projections for the first 3 months of 1982. (c) Forecast sales for the first 3 months of 1982.

14. Sales of computers in 1981 by Lindquist Analog, Inc., and seasonal indexes, are given in Table I. Lindquist's chief executive officer has set a sales objective of 3200 analog computers for 1982. (a) Compute total sales for 1981. Where will this total center? (b) Where will the 1982 objective sales center? (c) Using the results of (a) and (b), compute projected moving average values for the four quarters of 1982. (d) Compute quarterly sales objectives for 1982.

TABLE I

Quarter	1	2	3	4
Seasonal index	97	122	99	82
Sales, 1981	657	850	678	535

15. Sales of women's pocketbooks in 1981 by Fine Leather Products, Inc., and seasonal indexes, are given in Table J. Management has set a sales objective of 9100 pocketbooks for 1982. (a) Compute total sales for 1981. Where will this total center? (b) Where will the 1982 objective sales center? (c) Using the results of (a) and (b), compute projected moving average values for the quarters of 1982. (d) Compute quarterly sales objectives for 1982.

TABLE J

Quarter	1	2	3	4
Seasonal index	90	110	85	115
Sales, 1981	1960	2390	1824	2510

16. It is common practice to compare sales for the current month with sales for the same month a year ago. With reference to the $T \times C \times S \times I$ model, what could account for a change shown by the comparison?

18.15 SUMMARY

The classical time-series model, $T \times C \times S \times I$, contains four components: long-term trend (T), cycle (C), seasonal (S) variation, and irregular (I) fluctuations.

Long-term (say, 15 or more years) *trend* is measured by equations of straight lines or curves. Trend equations are "fitted" to n observed (t, y) time-series number pairs, where

n = number of years in the trend-fit time interval

t = year number (as in 1981)

y = data value (sales, output, or whatever) for the year number

The variables in a trend equation are

$\bar{t}$ = middle of the trend-fit time interval = $\dfrac{\text{first year} + \text{last year}}{2}$

x = coded year = $t - \bar{t}$

y_t = trend value for year t, calculated from the trend equation

The *straight-line trend equation* is

$$y_t = a + b(t - \bar{t}) \qquad \text{or} \qquad y_t = a + bx$$

where a and b are computed from the (x, y) pairs as follows:

$$a = \frac{\Sigma y}{n}$$

$$b = \frac{\Sigma xy}{\Sigma x^2}$$

The *quadratic* trend equation is

$$y_t = a + b(t - \bar{t}) + c(t - \bar{t})^2 \qquad \text{or} \qquad y_t = a + bx + cx^2$$

where a, b, and c are computed from the (x, y) pairs as follows:

$$a = \frac{(\Sigma y)(\Sigma x^4) - (\Sigma x^2 y)(\Sigma x^2)}{n(\Sigma x^4) - (\Sigma x^2)^2}$$

$$b = \frac{\Sigma xy}{\Sigma x^2}$$

$$c = \frac{n(\Sigma x^2 y) - (\Sigma x^2)(\Sigma y)}{n(\Sigma x^4) - (\Sigma x^2)^2}$$

The *exponential trend* equation is

$$y_t = d(1 + i)^{t - \bar{t}} \qquad \text{or} \qquad y_t = d(1 + i)^x$$

where d and $(1 + i)$ are computed from the $(x, \ln y)$ pairs as follows:

$$d = \text{antiln} \frac{\Sigma \ln y}{n}$$

$$1 + i = \text{antiln} \frac{\Sigma(x \ln y)}{\Sigma x^2}$$

Values on an exponential trend curve change by a constant percent rate of $100i$ percent per year.

Combined trend and cycle measures are centered m-period moving averages where m periods equals 1 year; for example, $m = 4$ quarters or $m = 12$ months. m-period moving averages are calculated as follows: (1) compute and record the average of the earliest remaining m time-series data values; (2) discard the first value; (3) repeat (1) and (2) until the latest data value has been used. Each m-period average is entered at the middle of its time period. When m is even, the moving averages will center between two periods; then two-period moving averages of the first computed averages are calculated and centered on the periods.

The steps in computing ratio-to-moving average *seasonal indexes* are

1. Compute the seasonal relative for every period by the formula

$$\text{Seasonal relative} = \frac{\text{actual } y \text{ value}}{\text{centered moving average}} \times 100$$

2. (*a*) Discard the largest and smallest seasonal relative for a given period.

Compute the unadjusted seasonal index for that period by averaging the remaining relatives. (*b*) Repeat (*a*) for each period.

3. Multiply the unadjusted seasonal indexes computed in step 2 by the number that will make the average of all the indexes equal 100.

An observed data value for a period is *adjusted for seasonal variation* as follows:

$$\text{Seasonally adjusted value} = \frac{\text{actual data value } y \text{ for a period}}{\text{that period's seasonal index}} \times 100$$

Seasonally adjusted values are estimates of trend and cycle that include errors caused by irregularities.

Short-term (1 year or less) *forecasts* are made by projecting the centered moving average to obtain forecasts of moving average values. Then the forecast for a period is found by computing

$$\frac{(\text{Period's moving average forecast}) \times (\text{period's seasonal index})}{100}$$

The steps in computing period-by-period *planning objectives* for planning periods are:

1. Compute the difference between last year's total and the objective.
2. Allocate the difference to obtain one-year moving totals for the periods of the planning year.
3. From step 2 compute projected moving averages.
4. Apply the seasonal factor to obtain the objective for each planning period by computing

$$\frac{(\text{Period's moving average objective}) \times (\text{period's seasonal index})}{100}$$

18.16 REVIEW PROBLEMS

1. Table A gives the number of computer systems sold by High Speed Computers, Inc. (*a*) Compute *a* and *b* for the linear trend equation. Then write the trend equation. (*b*) Make a times-series chart of the data. Then draw the trend line on the chart. (*c*) Forecast the trend value y_t of High Speed's sales for 1984.

TABLE A

Year	1971	1972	1973	1974	1975	1976	1977	1978	1979	1980	1981
Sales	468	491	576	622	655	681	720	755	831	926	1008

2. The outputs of large-size car tires by Richstone Rubber Company, in thousands, are given in Table B. (*a*) Compute *a* and *b* for the linear trend equation. Then write the trend equation. (*b*) Make a time-series chart of the data. Then draw the trend line on the chart. (*c*) Forecast the trend value y_t of Richstone's sales for 1985.

TABLE B

Year	1972	1973	1974	1975	1976	1977	1978	1979	1980	1981
Output	91	100	96	90	91	92	86	86	83	72

3. A trend line for the period 1960–1980 has a y_t value of 487 in 1970, and the trend rises by 12.8 per year. Write the trend equation.
4. Table C shows sales (in hundreds) of power-plant control equipment units made by Wolfboro Instruments, Inc. (*a*) Compute *a*, *b*, and *c* for the quadratic trend equation. Then write the trend equation. (*b*) Forecast the trend value y_t of Wolfboro's sales for 1986.

TABLE C

Year	1973	1974	1975	1976	1977	1978	1979	1980	1981
Sales	18	20	35	39	40	39	40	44	43

5. (See Problem 4.) Compute trend values y_t for the years 1973–1981 from the quadratic trend equation. Then, on the same chart, plot the time series of Table C and the graph of the trend equation.
6. Table D gives the interest rates paid on money borrowed by Volta Company. (*a*) Compute *a*, *b*, and *c* for the quadratic trend equation. Then write the trend equation. (*b*) Forecast the trend value y_t of the interest rate for 1983.

TABLE D

Year	1972	1973	1974	1975	1976	1977	1978	1979	1980	1981
Interest rate, percent	6	8	7	7	8	10	12	13	18	17

7. (See Problem 6.) Compute trend values y_t for the years 1972–1981 from the quadratic trend equation. Then, on the same chart, plot the time series of Table D and the graph of the trend equation.
8. (*a*) What is the percent rate of change per year for the following trend equation?

$$y_t = 260(1.187)^{t-1974}$$

(*b*) Compute trend values y_t for the years 1967 to 1981. Then make an arithmetic chart of the (t, y_t) series. (*c*) What will be the form of the graph of the equation if the (t, y_t) points are plotted on semilog graph paper?
9. (*a*) What is the percent rate of change per year for the following trend equation?

$$y_t = 1294(0.885)^{t-1975}$$

(*b*) Compute y_t values for the years 1970–1980. Then make an arithmetic chart of the (t, y_t) series. (*c*) What will be the form of the graph of the equation if the (t, y_t) points are plotted on semilog paper?
10. Table E gives the number of water-driven electric generators sold by Fossil Power Equipment Corporation. (*a*) Compute *d* and $1 + i$ for the exponential trend equation. Then write the trend equation. (*b*) What is the annual percent rate of change of the trend values? (*c*) Forecast the sales trend value y_t for 1983.

TABLE E

Year	1973	1974	1975	1976	1977	1978	1979	1980	1981
Sales	525	625	650	600	750	775	825	950	1175

11. Table F gives the number of members of the New York Stock Exchange for 10 succeeding years. (a) Compute d and $1 + i$ for the exponential trend equation. Then write the trend equation. (b) What is the annual percent rate of change of the trend values?

TABLE F

Year	1968	1969	1970	1971	1972	1973	1974	1975	1976	1977
Number of members	646	622	572	577	558	523	508	494	481	473

12. From the data in Table F, compute a, b, and c for the quadratic trend equation. Then write the trend equation.
13. What criterion would be used to determine whether the exponential trend equation of Problem 11 or the quadratic trend equation of Problem 12 is the better-fitting trend for the data of Table F?
14. Table G gives the number of stereo systems sold by Quality Stereo Company. Compute seasonal indexes for quarters 1, 2, 3, and 4 by the ratio-to-moving average method.

TABLE G

	Quarter			
	1	2	3	4
1976	134	110	74	120
1977	130	106	80	120
1978	150	114	94	140
1979	154	114	86	134
1980	160	120	100	154

15. Table H gives the number of new trucks sold by National Truck, Inc., in a five-state area. Compute seasonal indexes for each month of the year by the ratio-to-moving average method.

TABLE H

Year	Jan.	Feb.	Mar.	Apr.	May	June	July	Aug.	Sept.	Oct.	Nov.	Dec.
1976	411	454	541	569	591	620	533	389	454	598	591	443
1977	385	436	555	536	547	597	467	365	555	733	647	448
1978	409	497	571	573	687	676	568	455	540	731	690	518
1979	535	574	763	662	771	708	607	485	553	657	577	373
1980	350	367	453	502	566	497	490	467	390	427	305	229

16. Sales for May and June were, respectively, 1264 and 1152 units. Seasonal indexes are 109 for May and 89 for June. (a) Compute seasonally adjusted sales. (b) Com-

pute the percent change in unadjusted sales. (c) Compute the percent change in seasonally adjusted sales.

17. Table I gives sales data and the latest computed centered moving averages for Fordson Company. Seasonal indexes for quarters 1, 2, 3, and 4 are 115, 94, 105, and 86. (a) Compute seasonally adjusted sales for 1981:3 and 1981:4. Enter the adjusted sales in the moving average row of Table I. (b) Compute the average of the two adjusted values computed in (a). Use the average just computed as the projected moving average for both 1982:1 and 1982:2. Then forecast sales for 1982:1 and 1982:2.

TABLE I

Year and quarter	1980:4	1981:1	1981:2	1981:3	1981:4
Sales	681	948	789	897	760
Moving average	800	816	839		

18. (a) Do Problem 17(a) first. Then compute $b = \Sigma xy/\Sigma x^2$ for the least-squares line fitted to the five numbers in the moving average row. ($x = 0$ at 1981:2.) (b) To obtain projected moving averages, start with the latest given moving average, 839, in Table I. Then add the value of b, just computed, successively, to obtain projected moving averages for quarters 1, 2, 3, and 4 of 1982. (c) Forecast sales for quarters 1, 2, 3, and 4 of 1984.

19. See Table I, and suppose that management has set 3650 as the sales objective for 1982. (a) Compute total sales for 1981. Where will this total center? (b) Where will the 1982 objective total center? (c) Using the information from (a) and (b), project the moving average values for the four quarters of 1982. (d) Compute quarterly sales objectives for 1982.

20. Table J gives seasonal indexes, and monthly sales for 1981, for Green Brothers, Inc. Management has set a sales objective of 75,000 for 1982. (a) Compute total sales for 1981. Where will this total center? (b) Where will the 1982 objective total center? (c) Using the information from (a) and (b) compute projected moving averages for the months of 1982. (d) Compute sales objectives for the months of 1982.

TABLE J

Month	Jan.	Feb.	Mar.	Apr.	May	June	July	Aug.	Sept.	Oct.	Nov.	Dec.
Index	108	102	112	110	92	96	94	88	104	106	90	98
Sales, 1981	5522	5316	5956	5968	5086	5421	5416	5167	6229	6478	5610	6231

ANSWERS TO ODD-NUMBERED PROBLEMS

CHAPTER 1

Section 1.5

1. Statistics are numbers, but statistics s a field of study.
3. A probability is a number that measures relative frequency of occurrence of some event over tl e long run, or expresses a degree of belief that an event will occur.
5. Population means all elements of some specified type.
7. A statistical inference is a conclusion about a population that is based on a random sample drawn from the population.

CHAPTER 2

Section 2.4

1. (a) 4; (b) 3; (c) 3; (d) 3
3. (a) 12 hundred; (b) 1.5 thousand; (c) 12.5 thousand; (d) 34.6 thousand
5. (a) 8.6; (b) 2.95; (c) 112; (d) 693 thousand; (e) 23 hundred; (f) 0.0062; (g) 6.2; (h) 0.0256; (i) 2.1; (j) 40; (k) 0.196; (l) 25 thousand; (m) 5.95; (n) 15.5; (o) 94 07; (p) 298; (q) 0.078; (r) 5.6; (s) 22.249; (t) 0.376; (u) 158.6; (v) 0.0; (w) 15.7; (x) 9.3; (y) 0.0160; (z) 0.331

Section 2.7

1. Sales were 142 radios per 100 television sets.
3. Sales were $9.38 per cubic foot of shelf space.
5. $14.17
7. $18.52
9. (a) 47.5 percent; (b) 8.75 percent; (c) 0.25 percent; (d) 164.14 percent
11. December sales were 12.5 percent of annual sales.
13. Sales this month are 92.5 percent as great as, or 7.5 percent less than, sales of the same month a year ago.
15. The super model cost 129.4 percent as much as, or 29.4 percent more than, the standard model.
17. Increase of 3.57 percent
19. (a) -0.6 percentage points; (b) -4.20 percent
21. (a) 100, 105.4, 113.5, 120.3; (b) 97.4, 102.6, 110.5, 117.1
23. See Table A.1

TABLE A.1

Item	This year	Last year
Cash	4.94%	5.82%
Marketable securities	3.25	2.78
Accounts receivable	35.23	34.36
Inventory	27.35	29.56
Plant and equipment	29.23	27.49

25. 0.0175 percent

Section 2.11

1. (a) The effect of varying totals; (b) Taxes paid by manufacturing companies in Illinois are greater than taxes paid by manufacturing companies in Idaho.
3. Exray may have more shares of stock outstanding. Compare dividends per share.
5. There may be more cardholders this year than last year. Compare percentages defaulting for the two years.
7. Compare Carol's operating data with averages for similar (small, suburban) fashion shops.
9. Test the other-than-best workers. Compare the percent who make better-than-average grades with the stated 70 percent.
11. The dollar ratio can change because of inflation.
13. See Table A.2.

TABLE A.2
HOURLY CLERICAL WAGE RATES, PLANTS A AND B, BY JOB CLASSIFICATION AND SEX

Job classification	Plant A		Plant B	
	Male	Female	Male	Female
I				
II				
III				
IV				

15. (a) See Table A.3.

TABLE A.3

	Delinquency rate per 100 borrowers
Owners	1.64
Renters	3.39

Delinquency and own-or-rent appear to be associated, with renters having the higher delinquency rate, 3.39.

(b) See Table A.4.

TABLE A.4

Time on job	Delinquency rate per 100 borrowers
Less than 2 years	2.60
2 years or more	1.95

Delinquency and time-on-job appear to be associated, with borrowers who have less than 2 years on the job having the higher delinquency rate, 2.60.

(c) See Table A.5.

TABLE A.5

Time on job	Delinquency rate per 100 borrowers	
	Owners	Renters
Less than 2 years	2.14	3.67
2 years or more	1.39	3.25

The associations in (a) and (b) appear still to hold. Delinquency rates (3.67 and 3.25) are higher for renters than for owners in both time-on-job categories; and rates (2.14 and 3.67) are higher for less-than-2-years-on-job in both the owner and renter categories.

17. A cross-classified table is a table which classifies entries down the side and across the top.

CHAPTER 3

Section 3.7

1. (a) See Table A.6.

TABLE A.6

Miles per gallon	Number of cars
13.5 and under 14.5	2
14.5 and under 15.5	6
15.5 and under 16.5	23
16.5 and under 17.5	36
17.5 and under 18.5	25
18.5 and under 19.5	7
19.5 and under 20.5	1

(b) See Figure A.1.

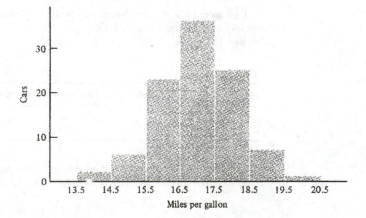

FIGURE A.1
Histogram of Table A.6.

(*c*) A normal distribution

3. (*a*) See Table A.7.

TABLE A.7

Weekly earnings	Number of workers
$130–$139	2
140– 149	3
150– 159	5
160– 169	6
170– 179	6
180– 189	8
190– 199	10
200– 209	8
210– 219	2

(*b*) See Figure A.2.

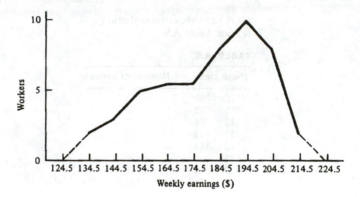

FIGURE A.2
Frequency polygon for
Table A.7.

(*c*) A left-skewed distribution

5. (*a*) See Table A.8.

TABLE A.8

Percent return class	Percent of corporations
(50)*–(31)	0.7
(30)–(11)	4.1
(10)– 9	13.3
10– 29	26.7
30– 49	23.9
50– 69	15.4
70– 89	8.5
90–109	4.3
110–129	1.7
130–149	0.9
150–169	0.4

* Numbers in parentheses are negative.

(b) See Figure A.3.

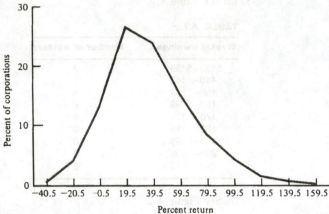

FIGURE A.3
Percentage frequency
polygon for Table A.8.

(c) A right-skewed distribution
7. (a) See Table A.9.

TABLE A.9

Wage class	Number of areas
$110– $124	1
125– 139	10
140– 154	7
155– 169	15
170– 184	17
185– 199	28
200– 214	16
215– 229	11
230– 244	1
245– 259	4

(b) See Figure A.4.

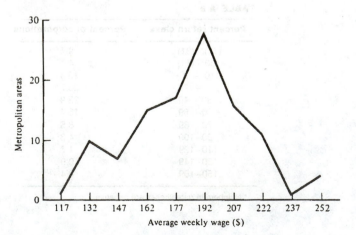

FIGURE A.4
Frequency polygon for
Table A.9.

(c) A left-skewed distribution

9. (a) $25; (b) See Figure A.5.

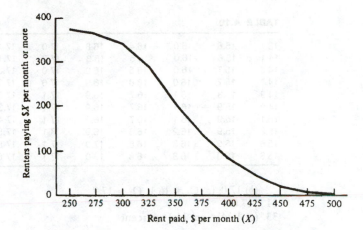

FIGURE A.5
"Or more" chart for
rent paid.

11. A right-skewed distribution because account balances vary over a wide dollar interval, but most of the balances fall in a small section of the lower part of this interval

CHAPTER 4

Section 4.8

1. (a) $\sum_{i=1}^{5} x_i$; (b) $\sum_{i=1}^{P} y_i$

3. (a) 40; (b) 450; (c) 1600; (d) 10; (e) 0; (f) 50

5. (a) 38; (b) 48

7. (a) μ = 3.5 days for both suppliers. (b) Supplier A can be depended on because A's delivery times do not vary as much as B's do.

9. (a) $38,250; (b) the total value property of μ

11. 83

13. Marginal cost because marginal cost must be larger than average cost if average cost per unit is to increase

15. No. The mean, which is the balance point, is to the left of 50.

17. $2.52

19. (a) $5.20; (b) $5.17; (c) Yes. The average hourly rate declined because the increase in the proportion of low-rate A workers more than canceled the effect of the 10 percent wage rate increase.

21. (a) $47 and $49.69; (b) 5.72 percent increase; (c) The 5 percent increase is less than (b) because the largest percent increase (10 percent) was for A, which has the largest weight (0.5).

23. $229

25. $17

27. (a) $24,940; (b) Because the median, $275 (the 50 percent point), is less than $290; (c) Near $275 because the distribution apparently is skewed; and for a

skewed distribution, the median is a more likely figure because it is closer to the mode than is the arithmetic average
29. (a) See Table A.10.

TABLE A.10

13.7	15.6	16.0	16.4	16.8	17.0	17.1	17.6	17.9	18.4
14.1	15.6	16.0	16.5	16.8	17.0	17.1	17.6	17.9	18.4
14.6	15.7	16.0	16.5	16.9	17.0	17.3	17.7	17.9	18.6
14.7	15.7	16.0	16.6	16.9	17.0	17.3	17.7	17.9	18.6
14.9	15.8	16.1	16.7	16.9	17.1	17.3	17.7	18.1	18.6
14.9	15.9	16.1	16.7	16.9	17.1	17.3	17.7	18.1	18.8
15.1	15.9	16.1	16.7	16.9	17.1	17.4	17.7	18.1	18.8
15.2	15.9	16.2	16.8	16.9	17.1	17.5	17.7	18.2	19.1
15.5	15.9	16.3	16.8	17.0	17.1	17.5	17.8	18.2	19.2
15.6	16.0	16.3	16.8	17.0	17.1	17.6	17.8	18.2	20.2

(b) 17.0; (c) $Q_1 = 16.1$, $Q_3 = 17.7$
31. $17.00
33. (a) 1.1414; (b) 14.14 percent

Section 4.13

1. (a) Zero; (b) The variance is the square of the standard deviation.
3. 0.11 and 6.01 percentage points
5. 17.2 years
7. $21.64
9. $2.23
11. For 68 percent of the weeks, sales were 400–600 boxes. For 95 percent of the weeks, sales were 300–700 boxes. For 99.7 percent of the weeks, sales were 200–800 boxes.
13. Knowing that $\sigma = 0.5$, we find that the decline of $5.2 - 4 = 1.2$ accidents per 1000 worker-hours is $1.2/0.5 = 2.4$ standard deviations; so the decline is unusual. That unusual decline strengthens the implication that the safety devices have helped to reduce the accident rate.
15. (a) At least 75 percent lie in the interval. (b) Yes, because *at least* 75 percent could be more than 95 percent.
17. $107 to $1493
19. No. Increasing by 10 percent will multiply σ by 1.1; so the new salaries have a wider variation than the old salaries.
21. (a) Large, 0.44 percent; small, 0.88 percent; (b) Relatively more variable in filling small boxes

CHAPTER 5

Section 5.9

1. An objective probability of an event is a computed relative frequency of occurrence of that event. A subjective probability is a person's degree-of-belief that an event will occur.
3. (a) 0.8; (b) 0.4375; (c) 0.55; (d) 0.636

5. (a) 0.320; (b) 0.800; (c) 0.340; (d) 0; (e) 0.040; (f) 0.040; (g) 0; (h) 0.700; (i) 0.292; (j) 0.375; (k) 0.800; (l) 0.540; (m) 0.800; (n) 1; (o) 0.840

Section 5.16

1. (a) $P(A \text{ or } B) = P(A) + P(B) - P(AB)$; (b) $P(A \text{ or } B) = P(A) + P(B)$; (c) $P(B|A) = P(BA)/P(A)$; (d) $P(AB) = P(A)P(B|A)$; (e) $P(AB) = P(A)P(B)$
3. (a) Let A mean A rises and let B mean B rises. Then $P(A \text{ or } B) = P(A) + P(B) - P(AB) = 0.7 + 0.4 - 0.3 = 0.8$. (b) See Table A.11.

TABLE A.11

	B	B'	Total
A	0.3	0.4	0.7
A'	0.1	0.2	0.3
Total	0.4	0.6	1.0

(c) $P(AB) + P(AB') + P(A'B) = 0.8$. (d) $P(A \text{ or } B) = 0.8$; $1 - P(A'B') = 1 - 0.2 = 0.8$. The event A or B is the complement of the event A'B'.
5. 0.995 because $P(\text{at least 1 detects smoke}) = 1 - P$ (none of the four detects smoke)
7. $P(G|H) = P(GH)/P(H) = 0.80$
9. (a) 0.24; (b) $P(DF) = P(D)P(F|D)$
11. (a) $P(SSS)$; (b) 0.8574; (c) independently; (d) 0.9999; (e) $P(\text{at least 1 success}) = 1 - P(0 \text{ successes}) = 1 - P(\text{all fail}) = 1 - (0.5)(0.5)(0.5) = 0.9999$
13. $P(A \text{ or } B) = P(A) + P(B) - P(AB)$. For independent events $P(AB) = P(A)P(B)$, so $P(A \text{ or } B) = P(A) + P(B) - P(AB) = 0.3 + 0.4 - (0.3)(0.4) = 0.58$.
15. $P(B|A) = P(AB)/P(A)$. Substituting the given numbers, we have $0.5 = 0.2/P(A)$, from which $P(A) = 0.2/0.5 = 0.40$.
17. Zero, because $P(AB) = 0$ for mutually exclusive events. Hence, $P(B|A) = P(AB)/P(A) = 0/P(A) = 0$.
19. $P(S|C')$ could be 0.5 or some other probability. Knowing that $P(S|C) = 0.7$ does not fix the value of $P(S|C')$.
21. F
23. T
25. F
27. T
29. T
31. T
33. F
35. T
37. T
39. F

Section 5.20

1. $^2/_3$
3. 0.496

5. $^4/_7$

7. (a) 0.8; (b) 0.675; (c) 60 percent; (d) 200; (e) 135

9. 0.706

11. (a) About 15; (b) about 16

13. 0.57

15. 0.556

17. 0.86

19. 0.286

CHAPTER 6

Section 6.3

1. (a) 4.6, (b) 230

3. 0.037

5. (a) $1560; (b) $2340

7. $2000

Section 6.10

1. (a) Make the product; (b) $32 thousand

3. (a) Make 4 units; (b) $15,200

5. (a) See Table A.12.

TABLE A.12

Number demanded	Number bought					
	0	1	2	3	4	5
0	0	−50	−100	−150	−200	−250
1	0	60	10	− 40	− 90	−140
2	0	60	120	70	20	− 30
3	0	60	120	180	130	80
4	0	60	120	180	240	190
5	0	60	120	180	240	300

(b) Buy 3 boxes; (c) $134.90

7. See Figure A.6.

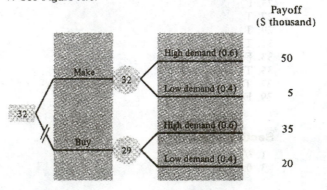

Payoff
($ thousand)

High demand (0.6)   50

Make   32

Low demand (0.4)   5

32

High demand (0.6)   35

Buy   29

Low demand (0.4)   20

FIGURE A.6
Tree diagram for
make-or-buy decision.

9. See Figure A.7. Do not order a tentative shutdown. EMV = $10,000

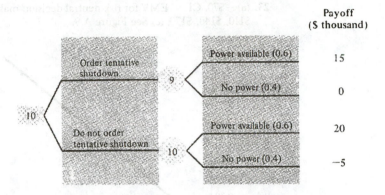

Payoff
($ thousand)

Order tentative shutdown

Power available (0.6) — 15

No power (0.4) — 0

Do not order tentative shutdown

Power available (0.6) — 20

No power (0.4) — −5

FIGURE A.7
Tree diagram for shutdown decision.

11. See Figure A.8.

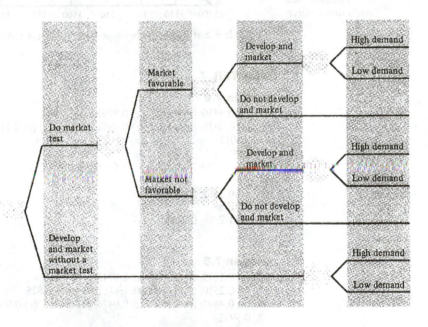

Market favorable

Develop and market

High demand

Low demand

Do not develop and market

Do market test

Develop and market

High demand

Low demand

Market not favorable

Do not develop and market

Develop and market without a market test

High demand

Low demand

FIGURE A.8
Tree diagram for marketing decision problem.

13. (a) $90,000 or − $50,000; (b) a loss of $10,000; (c) Secure the option, buy if developments are favorable; otherwise, do not exercise the option. EMV is $49,160.
15. (a) Hire the plane. Then if a location 3 is found, move to 3; otherwise, move to 2. (b) The decisions in (a) have the highest EMV. It is $14.8 thousand.
17. (a), (b), (c) I would take the 50-50 chance in each case because I do not consider $1000 (or $100 or $1) to be important sums of money. Consequently, the certainty values would have to be higher than $1, $100, and $1000 before I would prefer them to the 50-50 chance situation.

19. (a) An 80-20 chance at $10 million and − $5 million; (b) risk-neutral
21. Action A_3
23. (a) − $70. CE = EMV for risk-neutral decision makers. (b) − $40, $20, $50, $80, $110, $140, $170; (c) See Figure A.9.

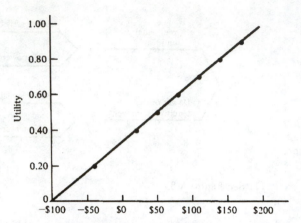

FIGURE A.9
Cleo's utility curve.

(d) It is a straight line because Cleo is always risk-neutral.

CHAPTER 7

Section 7.6

1. (a) 0.3456; (b) 0.6561; (c) 0.0595; (d) 0.2734
3. (a) 0.3828; (b) 0.6172; (c) 0.5852; (d) 0.5813; (e) 0.1124
5. 0.1013
7. 0.09
9. (a) 0.0769; (b) 0.2199; (c) 0.5405; (d) 0.1036; (e) 2.5
11. $a = 2$
13. (a) 0.1122; (b) 0.4439
15. 0.01985
17. (a) 1.2; (b) 0.9165

Section 7.8

1. (a) 0.1353; (b) 0.7408; (c) 0.0743
3. (a) 0.2510; (b) 0.0002500; (c) 0.1678; (d) 0.8825
5. (a) 0.4493; (b) 0.3595; (c) 0.0474; (d) 0.1910; (e) 0.9909
7. 0.3935
9. 0.0079
11. (a) 0.2681; (b) 0.0616
13. 0.1813
15. (a) 0.2678; (b) 0.1205
17. (a) 0.3012; (b) 0.6988; (c) 0.2105
19. 0.0821

Section 7.10

1. The probabilities of 0, 1, and 2 defectives are, respectively, $^7/_{15}$, $^7/_{15}$, and $^1/_{15}$.
3. (a) Getting a secretary who can use a word processing typewriter; (b) The probabilities of 0, 1, 2, and 3 successes are, respectively, 0.045, 0.318, 0.477, and 0.159. (Note: Because of rounding, the probabilities have a sum of 0.999 rather than 1.) (c) 0.636
5. (a) 0.388; (b) 0.422

CHAPTER 8

Section 8.6

1. (a) There is a normal distribution for each pair of μ, σ numbers, and the number of μ, σ pairs is unlimited. (b) Changing every value of the random variable x to its corresponding z value which is $(x - \mu)/\sigma$; (c) $z = (x - \mu)/\sigma$
3. (a) $(z|P = 0.3944) = 1.25$; (b) $(z|P = 0.4610) = 1.76$; (c) $(z|P = 0.4933) = 2.48$
5. (a) $a = 52$. See Figure A.10a. (b) $a = 67$; interval is $1000 - 67$ to $1000 + 67$, or 933 to 1067. See Figure A.10b. (c) $a = 795$. See Figure A.10c. (d) $a = 1164$. See Figure A.10d.

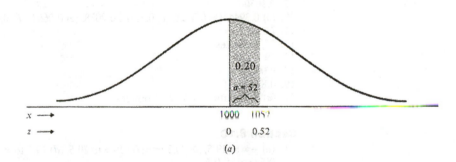

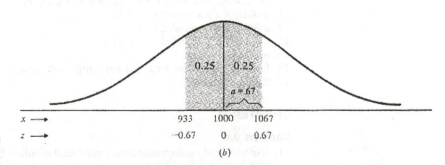

FIGURE A.10
(a) $a = 52$; (b) $a = 67$.

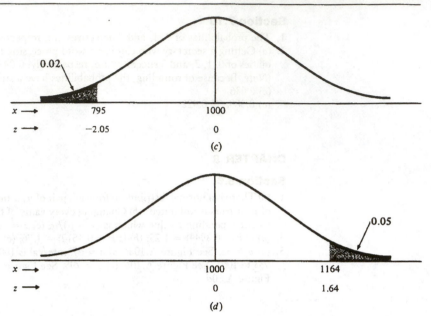

FIGURE A.10
(c) $a = 795$; (d) $a = 1164$.

7. 0.1056
9. (a) 0.3944; (b) 0.3721; (c) 0.5; (d) 0.2038; (e) 0.0668; (f) 0.0013; (g) 0.6915
11. 24 months
13. 27,100 miles
15. 20
17. 0.097 mm
19. 0.874
21. (a) 7.34 ounces; (b) 12.51 ounces

Section 8.10

1. (a) $-\infty$ to 19.5; (b) 20.5 to ∞; (c) 19.5 to 20.5; (d) 19.5 to ∞; (e) 14.5 to 25.5; (f) $\mu - 0.5$ to $\mu + 0.5$
3. (a) 0.1294; (b) 0.1293, if z is rounded to -0.33; (c) 0.000
5. (a) 0.3816; (b) 0.3707, if z is rounded to -0.33; (c) -0.011
7. 0.0681, if z is rounded to -1.49
9. 0.0401, if z is rounded to 1.75
11. 0.7324, if z is rounded to -0.62
13. (a) $1/3$; (b) $2/3$
15. (a) 0.02, so that the area of the rectangle will equal 1; (b) 25
17. 0.2231 ·

CHAPTER 9

Section 9.4

1. Use a table of random numbers. Take 4-digit numbers that are 3400 or less (with no repetitions) until 340 numbers are obtained. Then check the invoices having

those 340 numbers. The foregoing sample is a simple random sample. A systematic sample also could be selected.

3. (a) Systematic sampling is being used. (b) The problem is that in a 16-hour run, the sample bottles are all filled and capped at the same station; so the filling stations are not being sampled.

5. No, because the voters called were not selected randomly. And, moreover, voters not at home when volunteers call have a zero chance of being included in the sample.

7. The auditors are using a sample of account holders to check the bank's records of deposit balances.

9. Stratify by plant so that each plant is adequately represented in the sample. The stratified sample can provide a better estimate than a simple random sample if the proportions of faulty cylinders made at the plants are different.

11. Cluster sampling is used mainly because it is economical.

Section 9.13

1. (a) 15 (b)

$\bar{x}$:	3	5	6	7	8	9	10
$P(\bar{x})$:	0.067	0.133	0.267	0.133	0.067	0.267	0.067

3. Because $\sigma_{\bar{x}} = \sigma_x/\sqrt{n}$, the larger n is, the smaller will be $\sigma_{\bar{x}}$; that is, averages of samples of $n = 100$ will vary less than averages of samples of $n = 30$.

5. 0.0668

7. 0.0456

9. (a) 1000 for Massachusetts and 200 for Rhode Island; (b) No, because $\sigma_{\bar{x}}$ will be larger for Rhode Island owing to its smaller sample size.

11. (a) Because it does not include the finite population multiplier that is needed to make the formula mathematically correct; (b) Discarding the finite population factor has a negligible effect on the value of $\sigma_{\bar{x}}$ when, as often is the case, the sample contains only a small fraction (say less than 5 percent) of the population.

13. (a) $p = 0.40$; (b) $\sigma_p = 0.00980$, (c) Compute the sample proportion $\bar{p}$ for every sample; then compute the standard deviation of the values of $\bar{p}$.

15. 0.9772

CHAPTER 10

Section 10.3

1. (a) $\bar{x}$ is a sample mean; μ is a population mean. (b) s_x is a sample estimate of a population standard deviation; σ_x is a population standard deviation. (c) $\sigma_{\bar{x}}$ is called the standard error of the mean; it is the standard deviation of the means of all samples of a given size that can be drawn from a population. $s_{\bar{x}}$ is a sample estimate of the standard error of the mean. (d) $\bar{p}$ is a sample proportion of successes; p is a population proportion of successes. (e) $\sigma_{\bar{p}}$ is the standard error of the proportion; it is the standard deviation of the proportions of successes in all samples of a given size that can be drawn from a population. s_p is a sample estimate of the standard error of the proportion.

3. Yes, by computing $s_{\bar{x}} = s_x/\sqrt{n}$, where

$$s_x = \sqrt{\Sigma(x - \bar{x})^2/(n - 1)}$$

and n is the sample size.

5. 0.428

7. An interval estimate

Section 10.5

1. (a) 2.33; (b) The tail area of a normal distribution is 0.01 when $z = 2.33$.

3. 3.41 hours $\leq \mu \leq$ 3.99 hours

5. (a) $t_{0.01,5}$ is the value of t for which the tail area of the t distribution with 5 degrees of freedom is 0.01. (b) $\bar{x} - 1.83s_{\bar{x}} \leq \mu \leq \bar{x} + 1.83s_{\bar{x}}$

7. 478.8 ml $\leq \mu \leq$ 481.2 ml

9. 17.9 min $\leq \mu \leq$ 42.1 min

11. (a) \$1.598 $\leq \mu \leq$ \$1.602; (b) \$1.595 $\leq \mu \leq$ \$1.605; (c) The (a) interval is more precise (narrower) because it has the smaller confidence coefficient.

13. (a) Multiply μ by 2000; (b) 90,700 units $\leq$ total purchases $\leq$ 109,300 units

15. 1.9996 inches $\leq \mu \leq$ 2.0036 inches

17. (a) The sample size n; (b) Increase the sample size.

19. 53.0 $\leq \mu \leq$ 67.0

Section 10.8

1. 0.16 $\leq p \leq$ 0.24

3. 0.354 $\leq p \leq$ 0.446

5. 0.708 $\leq p \leq$ 0.792

7. 2401

9. 269

11. (a) 426.01; round to 427; (b) 106.5; round to 107

13. 96.04; round to 97

15. You can still construct a confidence interval, but it will be less precise (wider) than you wanted because you underestimated the standard deviation when you determined the sample size.

CHAPTER 11

Section 11.9

1. (a) Rejecting a true null hypothesis; (b) accepting a false null hypothesis

3. Low requirements in order to hold the chance of rejecting a good applicant at the small value α

5. (a) $H_0: p' \geq 0.25$; $H_a: p < 0.25$. Reject H_0 if sample $z < -1.28$. The sample z is -1.96. Reject H_0. (b) Institute the policy.

7. (a) $H_0: p \geq 0.40$; $H_a: p < 0.40$. Reject H_0 if sample $z < -1.88$. The sample z is -2.01. Reject H_0. (b) Cancel Guess Who.

9. (a) $H_0: p \leq 0.075$; $H_a: p > 0.075$. Reject H_0 if sample $z > 2.05$. The sample z is 1.70. Accept H_0. (b) Do not grant unemployment aid.

11. $H_0: p = 0.42$; $H_a: p \neq 0.42$. Reject H_0 if |sample z| > 2.58. The sample z is 1.22. Accept H_0. Conclude that p has not changed.
13. (a) $H_0: p = 0.9$; $H_a: p \neq 0.9$. Reject H_0 if |sample z| > 2.58. The sample z is 2.74. Reject H_0. (b) The implication is that the proportion of high-quality hot dogs exceeds 0.90.

Section 11.12

1. (a) Use z when the population is normal and σ_x is known; or when $n > 30$. (b) Use t when the population is normal, σ_x is unknown, and $n \leq 30$.
3. (a) $H_0: \mu \leq 5000$; $H_a: \mu > 5000$. Reject H_0 if sample $z > 2.58$. The sample z is 3.20. Reject H_0. (b) Links from Big Deal are up to specifications. Buy them.
5. (a) $H_0: \mu \leq 490$; $H_a: \mu > 490$. Reject H_0 if sample $z > 1.64$. The sample z is 1.39. Accept H_0. (b) Tutored students do not have a mean grade that exceeds 490.
7. Reject H_0 if sample $z > 2.33$.
9. $H_0: \mu \leq 4.5$; $H_a: \mu > 4.5$. Reject H_0 if sample $t > 2.13$. Sample t is 1.41. Accept H_0. The mean yield is less than or equal to 4.5 barrels per ton of shale.
11. (a) $H_0: \mu = 50$; $H_a: \mu \neq 50$. Reject H_0 if |sample z| > 1.96. The sample z is 2.26. Reject H_0. (b) Mean output exceeds 50 units per worker per day.
13. (a) $H_0: \mu = 100$; $H_a; \mu \neq 100$. Reject H_0 if |sample t| > 2.14. The sample t is 1.94. Accept H_0. (b) Install the odometers.
15. When $\mu > 30$ and H_0 is accepted
17. When $\mu < 500$ and H_0 is accepted
19. Lives may be lost if the snap links break in use. So I would want $\mu > 5000$. That is, I would take $H_0: \mu \leq 5000$; $H_a: \mu > 5000$ and then use the links only when H_0 is rejected.

Section 11.16

1. Let p_m and p_w be, respectively, proportions of men and women favoring the candidate. (a) $H_0: p_m - p_w = 0$; $H_a: p_m - p_w \neq 0$. Reject H_0 if |sample z| > 1.96. The sample z is -3.16. Reject H_0. (b) The proportion of men favoring the candidate is less then the proportion of women favoring the candidate.
3. (a) $H_0: p_1 - p_2 = 0$; $H_a: p_1 - p_2 \neq 0$. Reject H_0 if |sample z| > 1.64. The sample z is 2.48. Reject H_0. (b) Shift 1 makes a larger proportion of defectives than shift 2.
5. (a) $H_0: \mu_2 - \mu_1 \leq 0$; $H_a: \mu_2 - \mu_1 > 0$. Reject H_0 if sample $z > 1.64$. The sample z is 2.83. Reject H_0. (b) Amcar should buy brand 2 to get a higher mean tire mileage.
7. (a) $H_0: \mu_1 - \mu_2 = 0$; $H_a: \mu_1 - \mu_2 \neq 0$. Reject H_0 if |sample z| > 1.64. The sample z is 2.16. Reject H_0. (b) Variety 1 has the higher mean yield.
9. (a) $H_0: \mu_1 - \mu_2 = 0$; $H_a: \mu_1 - \mu_2 \neq 0$. Reject H_0 if |sample t| > 1.76. The sample t is 2.94. Reject H_0. (b) Assign alarms to station 2.
11. $H_0: \mu_1 - \mu_2 = 0$; $H_a: \mu_1 - \mu_2 \neq 0$. Reject H_0 if |sample t| > 2.23. The sample t is 6.85. Reject H_0.
13. $H_0: D \geq 0$; $H_a: D < 0$. Reject H_0 if sample $t < -1.76$. The sample t is -5.68. Reject H_0. The mean typing rate is lower on model 2.

CHAPTER 12

Section 12.5

1. (a) See Figure A.11a. (b) See Figure A.11b. (c) See Figure A.11c.

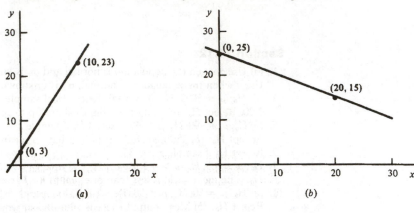

(a)

(b)

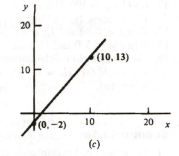

(c)

FIGURE A.11

(a) Graph of $y = 3 + 2x$; (b) graph of $y = 5 - 0.5x$; (c) graph of $y = -2 + 1.5x$.

3. (a) $y = 10,000 - 1000x$; (b) \$4500

5. (a) See Figure A.12. (b) Sales do not appear to be related to number of employees.

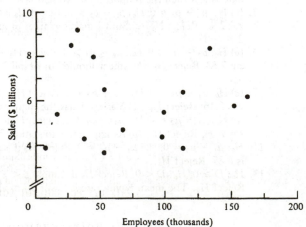

FIGURE A.12

Scatter plot of number of employees and sales.

7. (*a*) See Figure A.13. (*b*) A curved (curvilinear) relationship

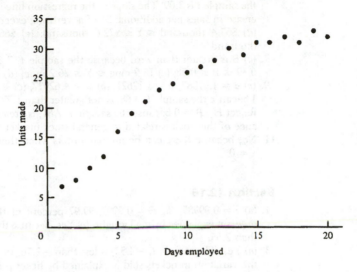

FIGURE A.13
Scatter plot of days
employed and number
of units made.

9. (*a*) $a = 4$; $b = -0.5$; $\hat{y} = 4 - 0.5x$; (*b*) See Figure A.14. (*c*) $(\bar{x}, \bar{y}) = (2, 3)$ satisfies $\hat{y} = 4 - 0.5x$; that is, $3 = 4 - 0.5(2)$.

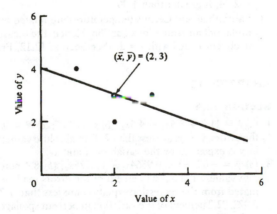

FIGURE A.14
Regression line
$\hat{y} = 4 - 0.5x$.

11. (*a*) $\hat{y} = 60.9 - 2.66x$; (*b*) 21
13. (*a*) $\hat{y} = 17.9 + 3.11x$; (*b*) 39.7 boxes

Section 12.12

1. (*a*) $s_e = 5.0218$; (*b*) $s_b = 0.09096$; (*c*) Reject H_0: $B = 0$ because the decision rule is to reject H_0 if |sample t| > 5.84; and the sample t is 9.36.
3. (*a*) $\hat{y} = 32 + 1.8x$; (*b*) $s_e = 0$; (*c*) All the points are on the regression line; that's because Fahrenheit temperatures can always be computed exactly from Celsius temperatures.

5. (a) Reject H_0: $B \leq 2$. The decision rule is to reject H_0 if the sample $t > 1.81$; and the sample t is 3.09. The slope of the regression line is greater than 2. (b) The increase in sales per additional \$1 of advertising exceeds \$2. (c) $2.22 \leq B \leq 3.38$; (d) \$63.4 thousand $\leq Y \leq$ \$72.6 thousand; (e) \$66.4 thousand $\leq \mu_Y \leq$ \$69.6 thousand

7. (a) B is greater than zero because the sample t, 7.59, is greater than 2.58. (b) $0.39 \leq B \leq 0.88$; (c) 16.9 mpg $\leq Y \leq$ 26.2 mpg; (d) 20.4 mpg $\leq \mu_Y \leq$ 22.6

9. (a) $a = 1.97087$, $b = 1.12621$; (b) $s_e = 4.62927$; (c) $s_b = 0.14424$; (d) Accept $B \leq 1$ because the sample t, 0.88, is not greater than 1.77. B is not greater than 1. (e) Reject H_0: $B = 0$ because the sample t, 7.81, is greater than 2.16. The performance of the stock is related to general stock market performance.

11. No, because there can be no mail orders when there is no mail; that is, when $x = 0$.

Section 12.16

1. (a) $r = 0.99985$; (b) $r^2 = 0.9997$; 99.97 percent of the variation in number of orders is explained by mail weight. (c) Yes, because the sample t, 245.2, is greater than 2.55.

3. (a) Yes. The sample t, -4.53, is less than -2.76. (b) $r^2 = 0.672$; 67.2 percent of the variation in tickets sold is explained by ticket price.

5. Age and days absent are not correlated. The sample t, 1.86, is less than 2.31.

7. $s_e = 0$ when $r = \pm 1$ because all points lie on the regression line.

9. (With $n = 2000$, use z in place of t.) Yes, r is different from 0 because the sample z, 2.24, is greater than 1.96.

11. Fahrenheit and Celsius temperatures are related by an exact mathematical formula, not an estimating equation. Hence, the measures should be perfectly positively correlated with $r = 1$. (See Section 12.12, Problem 3.)

CHAPTER 13

Section 13.4

1. (a) $\hat{y} = 11.3 + 5.5x_1 - 4.5x_2$; (b) $s_e = 3.07$; (c) $r^2 = 0.915$; (d) About 68 percent of the errors, $\hat{y} - y$, are less than 3.07 in absolute value; 91.5 percent of the variation in y is explained by the variables x_1 and x_2.

3. (a) $\hat{y} = -0.7033 + 0.9564x_1 + 0.3725x_2$; (b) 8.4 percent; (c) $s_e = 1.2$. The absolute values of about 68 percent of the errors made when percent spoilage is estimated from the regression equation are less than 1.2 percentage points. (d) $r^2 = 0.922$; 92.2 percent of the variation in percent spoilage is explained by temperature and miles transported.

5. (a) $\hat{y} = 41.70 - 8.58x_1 - 0.31x_2$; (b) 16.7 mpg; (c) $s_e = 1.38$ mpg. The absolute values of about 68 percent of the errors made when mpg is estimated from the regression equation are less than 1.38 mpg. (d) $r^2 = 0.961$; 96.1 percent of the variation in mpg is explained by engine size and weight.

7. (a) $\hat{y} = 0.3541 + 0.5630x_1 - 0.03585x_2$; (b) \$1.85 hundred thousand; (c) $s_e = 0.13$ hundred thousand dollars, or \$13,000. The absolute values of about 68 percent of the errors made when sales are estimated from the regression equation are less than \$13,000. (d) $r^2 = 0.962$; 96.2 percent of the variation in sales is explained by population and income.

9. (a) $\hat{y} = 6.7625 + 40.9759x_1 + 0.1729x_2$; (b) \$49.5 thousand; (c) $s_e = $ \$6.2 thousand, or \$6200. The absolute values of about 68 percent of the errors made when lot price is estimated from the regression equation are less than \$6200. (d) $r^2 = 0.958$; 95.8 percent of the variation in lot prices is explained by shore frontage and lot size.

Section 13.6

1. $\hat{y} = 10 + 2.5x_1 - 1.4x_2 + 0.2x_3$
3. (a) $\hat{y} = 562.44 - 5.446x_1 - 20.010x_2$; (b) 239 gallons; (c) 96.6 percent of the variation in fuel consumption is explained by temperature and thickness of insulation. (d) About 68 percent of the errors made when fuel consumption is estimated from temperature and thickness of insulation are less than 25.970 gallons. (e) 12; (f) Both temperature and thickness of insulation improve the estimating equation.
5. (a) $\hat{y} = 247.85 + 0.62015x_1 + 1.05890x_2$; (b) \$363; (c) 76.7 percent of the variation in weekly wages is explained by time-on-the-job and age. (d) About 68 percent of the errors made when weekly wage is estimated from the regression equation are less than \$40.0352. (e) 17; (f) Including number of months improves the estimating equation that contains age; but including age does not improve the estimating equation that contains number of months.
7. (a) $\hat{y} = 178.52 + 2.1055x_1 + 3.5624x_2 - 0.2219x_3$; (b) 350 thousand units; (c) 99.7 percent of the variation in sales is explained by advertising, number of stores, and number of competitors. (d) About 68 percent of the errors made when sales are estimated from the regression equation are less than 4.9795 thousand units. (e) 11; (f) Both advertising and number of stores improve the estimating equation that contains the other variables; but number of competitors does not improve the equation that contains advertising and number of stores.
9. $160 \le \mu_Y \le 173$

Section 13.8

1. (a) Downward, (b) (20, 70); (c) See Figure A.15.

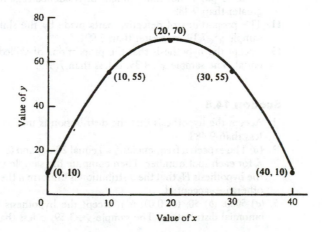

FIGURE A.15
The parabola $y = 10 + 6x - 0.15x^2$.

3. (a) Let $b_1 = m$, $x_1 = z$, $b_2 = n$, $x_2 = z^2$. (b) $y = a + b_1 x_1 + b_2 x_2$
5. (a) See Figure A.16. (b) $\hat{y} = 12 - 4.5x + 0.5x^2$; (c) \$2.00

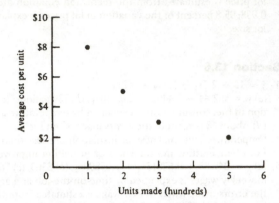

FIGURE A.16

Scatter plot of units made and average unit cost.

7. (a) $\hat{y} = 2.6273 + 5.6262x - 0.3179x^2$; (b) 26.4 hundred pounds; (c) $v = 7$; (d) Yes, because the sample t, -5.9, in absolute value, is greater than 3.50. (e) The quadratic regression equation is an improvement over the linear regression equation.
9. $\hat{y} = 100 + 10x - 0.15x^2 + 0.0001x^3$

CHAPTER 14

Section 14.6

1. $\chi^2 = 4.95$. H_0: category I and category II are independent.
3. Sample $\chi^2 > 15.507$
5. Safety rating and industry category are not independent. The sample χ^2, 25.80, is greater than 16.812.
7. Yes. The sample χ^2, 3.75, is less than 13.277.
9. Time to pay is not independent of residence region. The sample χ^2, 9.54, is greater than 9.488.
11. The proportions of defective parts made by the shifts are not all equal. The sample χ^2, 7.19, is greater than 5.991.
13. Accept the hypothesis that the proportions of skilled workers in the areas are equal. The sample χ^2, 4.35, is less than 7.815.

Section 14.8

1. Accept the hypothesis that the distribution is uniform. The sample χ^2, 3.67, is less than 9.488.
3. (a) The expected frequencies f_e all equal 20. (b) and (c). Tabulate the frequencies f_o for each spot number. Then compute the sample χ^2, $[\Sigma(f_o - 20)^2]/20$. Reject the hypothesis H_0 that the distribution is uniform if the sample χ^2 exceeds 15.086; otherwise, accept H_0.
5. (a) 5000; (b) 50; (c) 0.01; (d) Accept the hypothesis that the distribution is a binomial distribution. The sample χ^2, 3.59, is less than 3.841.

7. Accept the hypothesis that the distribution is a normal distribution. The sample χ^2, 5.502, is less than 5.991.
9. Reject the hypothesis that the distribution is the normal distribution with μ = 150 and σ = 12. The sample χ^2, 30.32, is greater than 21.666.
11. (a) 2; (b) Accept the hypothesis that the distribution is a Poisson distribution with $\lambda t = \lambda = 2$ landings per hour. The sample χ^2, 2.30, is less than 9.488.
13. Reject the hypothesis of a 30-20-50 percent mixture. The sample χ^2, 12.11, is greater than 9.210.

CHAPTER 15

Section 15.6

1. (a) 4, 3, 7, 6; (b) 5; (c) 4; (d) $^{10}/_3$; (e) 2.5; (f) 3 and 8
3. Accept the hypothesis that the mean learning times for the three methods are equal. The sample F, 3.04, is less than 3.89.
5. The mean burning times for the four bulb types are not all equal. The sample F, 9.43, is greater than 4.94.
7. Accept the hypothesis that the mean number of passersby at the three corners are equal. The sample F, 3.575, is less than 5.39.
9. Accept the hypothesis that the three mean ages are equal. The sample F, 2.14, is less than 3.68.
11. Accept the hypothesis that mean delivery amounts for the three regions are equal. The sample F, 0.711, is less than 3.89.

Section 15.8

1. Accept the hypothesis that the mean percent returns for the three firms are equal. The sample F, 0.886, is less than 4.26.
3. Accept the hypothesis that the mean times for the three panels are equal. The sample F, 2.93, is less than 4.26.
5. The mean cumulative grade indexes for the three ratings are not all equal. The sample F, 5.65, is greater than 3.40.
7. Mean sales for the four locations are not all equal. The sample F, 9.69, is greater than 4.94.
9. Accept the hypothesis that mean mileages for the three car models are equal. The sample F, 3.625, is less than 3.74.
11. The mean trip times for the three routes are not all equal. The sample F, 7.99, is greater than 4.98.
13. See Table A.13.

TABLE A.13 .

Source of variation	Degrees of freedom	Sum of squares	Mean square	Sample F
Between-samples	3	256.95	85.65	6.588
Within-samples	16	208.00	13.00	
Total	19	464.95		

15. See Table A.14:

TABLE A.14

Source of variation	Degrees of freedom	Sum of squares	Mean square	Sample F
Between-samples	2	101.270	50.635	7.995
Within-samples	60	380.000	6.333	
Total	62	481.270		

17. (a) through (g). See Table A.15. (h) The mean interest rates for the firms are not all equal. The sample F, 6.207, is greater than 4.51.

TABLE A.15

Source of variation	Degrees of freedom	Sum of squares	Mean square	Sample F
Between-samples	3	1080	360	6.207
Within-samples	30	1740	58	
Total	33	2820		

Section 15.10

1. Accept the hypothesis that mean run times are equal. The sample H, 6.08, is less than 9.210.
3. The mean burning lives are not all equal. The sample H, 8.71, is greater than 7.815.
5. Accept the hypothesis that the mean hardnesses are equal. The sample H, 5.255, is less than 5.991.
7. Accept the hypothesis that the mean kill percentages are equal. The sample H, 4.36, is less than 5.991.
9. Accept the hypothesis that mean sales for the designs are equal. The sample H, 4.33, is less than 7.815.
11. Accept the hypothesis that the mean credit balances are equal. The sample H, 5.08, is less than 7.815.

CHAPTER 16

Section 16.5

1. Accept the hypothesis that half, or less than half, of the population thought the noise level was reduced. The sample z, 1.83, is less than 2.33.
3. More than 60 percent prefer X over Y. The sample z, 2.51, is greater than 2.33.
5. Less than half prefer the flavor of X. The sample z, -1.85, is less than -1.64.
7. (a) $R_1 = 31.5$, $R_2 = 34.5$; (b) $\mu_{R_1} = 30$; $\mu_{R_2} = 36$; (c) $\sigma_R = 5.477$
9. The mean for type A is less than the mean for type B. The sample z, -1.78, is less than -1.64.
11. Accept the hypothesis that the mean emission of B is equal to, or greater than, that of A. The sample z, -1.56, is greater than -1.64.
13. The mean growth potential for B companies is equal to, or less than, the mean for A companies. The sample z, 1.12, is less than 1.64.

Section 16.9

1. (a) -1; (b) -0.6; (c) 0; (d) 0.9
3. Accept the hypothesis that physical attractiveness and sales volume are not correlated. The absolute value of the sample z, 1.54, is less than 1.96.
5. Accept the hypothesis that the ranks and inventory scores are not correlated. The absolute value of the sample z, 1.62, is less than 1.96.
7. The sets of ranks exhibit a significant level of agreement. The sample x^2, 21.11, is greater than 13.362.
9. The sets of ranks exhibit a significant level of agreement. The sample x^2, 14.56, is greater than 14.067.
11. The sets of ranks exhibit a significant level of agreement. The sample x^2, 25.09, is greater than 16.919.
13. (a) 5.8; (b) 9
15. The sequence of H's and L's is not random. The absolute value of the sample z, 2.14, is greater than 1.96.
17. The sequence of A's and B's is random. The absolute value of the sample z, 0.97, is less than 1.96.

CHAPTER 17

Section 17.5

1. (a) 126.7; (b) 127.5
3. (a) 137.5, 125, 120; (b) 1,600,000; 1,200,000; 500,000; (c) 130.3
5. 115.5
7. 131.5
9. (a) Use the weighted average of relatives method because the weights are proportions of total dollar value. (b) 116.9
11. The number is the percent change in the total dollar volume of sales from period zero to period n.
13. (a) 17.4 percent; (b) 2.7 percent
15. Real wages will rise because dollar wages increased by a greater percent (20 percent) than the percent increase (12.5 percent) in the CPI.

Section 17.8

1. 107.1
3. Dollars of value added are better than dollars of cost as a measure of amount of production or output.
5. The weighted average of relatives calculation must be used if the weights available are dollar values, or proportions of total dollar value.
7. 107
9. Labor, land, invested capital, management efforts and skills
11. (a) 304; (b) 102.7
13. 79.7

Section 17.10

1. The cost of conducting a month-by-month survey of consumer expenditures (to use for weighting) would be prohibitive.

3. By conducting more frequent consumer expenditure surveys to update weights for the index
5. No. The weights apply to the time of the last consumer expenditure survey which currently (March 1981) is the period 1972–1973.
7. The surveys reveal trends in consumer expenditure patterns that managers use in planning production schedules and marketing strategy.
9. The prices in the index are mostly prices charged by suppliers (producers); so the term "wholesale" price index does not describe what the index measures.
11. Value added is a better measure of production than is the total dollar value of production.
13. The S & P 500 measures the average price per share for stocks traded on the NYSE.
15. It is an index of dollar value; it is neither a price nor a quantity index.
17. Let P_0 and P_n be the values of the machinery and equipment producer price index at, respectively, the time an item was bought and at the current time; and let C be the original cost of an item. Then determine the replacement cost of the item by computing $C(P_n/P_0)$.

CHAPTER 18

Section 18.4

1. Long-term trend, cycles, seasonal variation, and irregular fluctuations
3. I believe (and research verifies) that airline travel has an upward trend and railroad travel has a downward trend.
5. (a) $y_t = 360 - 6.4(t - 1973.5)$; (b) $286.4 million
7. (a) $y_t = 32.67 - 6.63(t - 1978.5)$; (b) see Figure A.17.

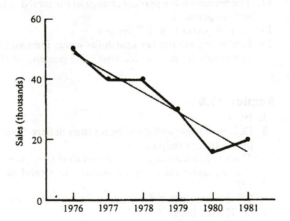

FIGURE A.17
Mercator Electronics
sales trend.

9. (a) $y_t = 4.3 - 0.13(t - 1977.5)$; (b) 3.3 hundred
11. 471.8 thousand units

Section 18.8

1. (a) $y_t = 4 + 0.2(t - 1975) + 0.01(t - 1975)^2$; (b) \$7 per hour
3. (a) $y_t = 19.263 + 2.700(t - 1979) - 0.4714(t - 1979)^2$; (b) 15.1 thousand; (c) See Figure A.18.

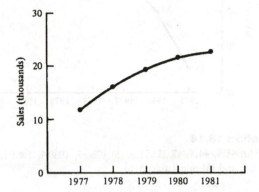

FIGURE A.18
Fowler Company quadratic trend.

5. (a) $y_t = 95.550 + 10.267(t - 1977) + 1.134(t - 1977)^2$; (b) \$223 per credit-hour
7. (a) $y_t = 14{,}000(0.86)^{t-1975.5}$; (b) 2125 thousand barrels
9. (a) $y_t = 73.391(1.192)^{t-1978.5}$; (b) 19.2 percent; (c) \$274 million
11. Compute $\Sigma(y - y_t)^2$ for each trend. The better fit is the trend which has the smaller $\Sigma(y - y_t)^2$.
13. (a) See Figure A.19. (b) See Figure A.20. (c) Use a quadratic trend. Both Figures A.19 and A.20 appear to show a curved trend; so neither a straight-line trend nor an exponential trend will fit the data as well as will a quadratic trend.

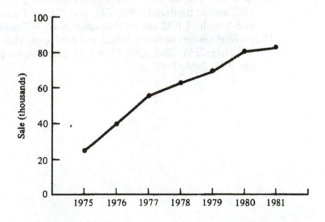

FIGURE A.19
Farragut Company sales on an arithmetic chart.

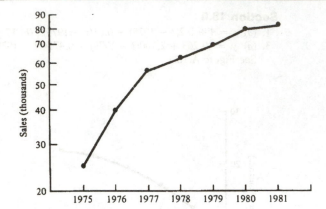

FIGURE A.20
Farragut Company
sales on a semilog
chart.

Section 18.14

1. (a) 43.5, 44.5, 47.25, 51.5; (b) 1980:3, 1980:4, 1981:1, 1981:2
3. (a) and (b) See Table A.16.

TABLE A.16

	Jan.	Feb.	Mar.	Apr.	May	June	July	Aug.	Sept.	Oct.	Nov.	Dec.
1980							798.7	782.4	760.8	741.2	726.0	708.7
1981	695.0	689.4	681.9	665.5	644.6	627.2						

5. The respective indexes for quarters 1, 2, 3, and 4 are 96.2, 121.1, 73.8, and 108.9.
7. The number of selling days for a given month may vary from year to year. Use of average sales per day removes the effect of the varying number of days.
9. (a) A decrease of 9.5 percent; (b) no change
11. (a) $b = 40$; (b) 2786, 2826, 2866, and 2906; (c) In thousands, the forecasts for quarters 1, 2, 3, and 4 of 1982 are $2273, $2761, $2846, and $3528.
13. (a) $b = -4$; (b) Moving average projections for January, February, and March of 1982 are, in thousands, 802, 798, and 794. (c) Forecasts for January, February, and March of 1982 are, in thousands, 642, 583, and 730.
15. (a) 8684 centers between 1981:2 and 1981:3; (b) 9100 centers between 1982:2 and 1982:3; (c) 2236, 2262, 2288, 2314; (d) Objectives for quarters 1, 2, 3, and 4 of 1982 are 2011, 2486, 1944, 2659.

TABLES

TABLE IA
BINOMIAL CUMULATIVE PROBABILITIES, $n = 10$: $\sum_{0}^{r} P(r)$

					p				
r	0.01	0.05	0.10	0.25	0.50	0.75	0.90	0.95	0.99
0	0.9044	0.5987	0.3487	0.0563	0.0010				
1	0.9957	0.9139	0.7361	0.2440	0.0107	0.0000			
2	0.9999	0.9885	0.9298	0.5256	0.0547	0.0004			
3	1.0000	0.9990	0.9872	0.7759	0.1719	0.0035	0.0000		
4		0.9999	0.9984	0.9219	0.3770	0.0197	0.0001	0.0000	
5		1.0000	0.9999	0.9803	0.6230	0.0781	0.0016	0.0001	
6			1.0000	0.9965	0.8281	0.2241	0.0128	0.0010	0.0000
7				0.9996	0.9453	0.4744	0.0702	0.0115	0.0001
8				1.0000	0.9893	0.7560	0.2639	0.0861	0.0043
9					0.9990	0.9437	0.6513	0.4013	0.0956
10					1.0000	1.0000	1.0000	1.0000	1.0000

TABLE IB
BINOMIAL CUMULATIVE PROBABILITIES, $n = 20$: $\sum_{0}^{r} P(r)$

					p				
r	0.01	0.05	0.10	0.25	0.50	0.75	0.90	0.95	0.99
0	0.8179	0.3585	0.1216	0.0032	0.0000				
1	0.9831	0.7358	0.3917	0.0243	0.0000				
2	0.9990	0.9245	0.6769	0.0913	0.0002				
3	1.0000	0.9841	0.8670	0.2252	0.0013				
4		0.9974	0.9568	0.4148	0.0059				
5		0.9997	0.9887	0.6172	0.0207				
6		1.0000	0.9976	0.7858	0.0577	0.0000			
7			0.9996	0.8982	0.1316	0.0002			
8			0.9999	0.9591	0.2517	0.0009			
9			1.0000	0.9861	0.4119	0.0039			
10				0.9961	0.5881	0.0139	0.0000		
11				0.9991	0.7483	0.0409	0.0001		
12				0.9998	0.8684	0.1018	0.0004		
13				1.0000	0.9423	0.2142	0.0024	0.0000	
14					0.9793	0.3828	0.0113	0.0003	
15					0.9941	0.5852	0.0432	0.0026	
16					0.9987	0.7748	0.1330	0.0159	0.0000
17					0.9998	0.9087	0.3231	0.0755	0.0010
18					1.0000	0.9757	0.6083	0.2642	0.0169
19						0.9968	0.8784	0.6415	0.1821
20						1.0000	1.0000	1.0000	1.0000

TABLE IC
BINOMIAL CUMULATIVE PROBABILITIES, $n = 50$: $\sum_{0}^{r} P(r)$

r	0.01	0.05	0.10	0.25	0.50	0.75	0.90	0.95	0.99
					p				
0	0.6050	0.0769	0.0052	0.0000					
1	0.9106	0.2794	0.0338	0.0000					
2	0.9862	0.5405	0.1117	0.0001					
3	0.9984	0.7604	0.2503	0.0005					
4	0.9999	0.8964	0.4312	0.0021					
5	1.0000	0.9622	0.6161	0.0070					
6		0.9882	0.7702	0.0194					
7		0.9968	0.8779	0.0453					
8		0.9992	0.9421	0.0916					
9		0.9998	0.9755	0.1637					
10		1.0000	0.9906	0.2622					
11			0.9968	0.3816	0.0000				
12			0.9990	0.5110	0.0002				
13			0.9997	0.6370	0.0005				
14			0.9999	0.7481	0.0013				
15			1.0000	0.8369	0.0033				
16				0.9017	0.0077				
17				0.9449	0.0164				
18				0.9713	0.0325				
19				0.9861	0.0595				
20				0.9937	0.1013				
21				0.9974	0.1611				
22				0.9990	0.2399				
23				0.9996	0.3359				
24				0.9999	0.4409	0.0000			
25				1.0000	0.5561	0.0001			
26					0.6641	0.0004			
27					0.7601	0.0010			
28					0.8389	0.0026			
29					0.8987	0.0063			
30					0.9405	0.0139			
31					0.9675	0.0287			
32					0.9836	0.0551			
33					0.9923	0.0983			
34					0.9967	0.1631	0.0000		
35					0.9987	0.2519	0.0001		
36					0.9995	0.3630	0.0003		
37					0.9998	0.4890	0.0010		
38					1.0000	0.6184	0.0032		
39						0.7378	0.0094	0.0000	

TABLE IC
(Continued)

r					p				
	0.01	0.05	0.10	0.25	0.50	0.75	0.90	0.95	0.99
40						0.8363	0.0245	0.0002	
41						0.9084	0.0579	0.0008	
42						0.9547	0.1221	0.0032	
43						0.9806	0.2298	0.0118	
44						0.9930	0.3839	0.0378	0.0000
45						0.9979	0.5688	0.1036	0.0001
46						0.9995	0.7497	0.2396	0.0016
47						0.9999	0.8883	0.4595	0.0138
48						1.0000	0.9662	0.7206	0.0894
49							0.9948	0.9231	0.3950
50							1.0000	1.0000	1.0000

TABLE II
VALUES OF e^{-x}

x	0.0	0.1	0.2	0.3	0.4	0.5	0.6	0.7	0.8	0.9
0	1.0000	0.9048	0.8187	0.7408	0.6703	0.6065	0.5488	0.4966	0.4493	0.4066
1	0.3679	0.3329	0.3012	0.2725	0.2466	0.2231	0.2019	0.1827	0.1653	0.1496
2	0.1353	0.1225	0.1108	0.1003	0.0907	0.0821	0.0743	0.0672	0.0608	0.0550
3	0.0498	0.0450	0.0408	0.0369	0.0334	0.0302	0.0273	0.0247	0.0224	0.0202
4	0.0183	0.0166	0.0150	0.0136	0.0123	0.0111	0.0101	0.0091	0.0082	0.0074
5	0.0067	0.0061	0.0055	0.0050	0.0045	0.0041	0.0037	0.0033	0.0030	0.0027
6	0.0025	0.0022	0.0020	0.0018	0.0017	0.0015	0.0014	0.0012	0.0011	0.0010

TABLE IIIA

POISSON DISTRIBUTION: PROBABILITY OF EXACTLY *r* OCCURRENCES OR *x* ARRIVALS*

	μ or λt								
r or *x*	**0.2**	**0.4**	**0.6**	**0.8**	**1**	**2**	**3**	**4**	**5**
0	0.8187	0.6703	0.5488	0.4493	0.3679	0.1353	0.0498	0.0183	0.0067
1	0.1637	0.2681	0.3293	0.3595	0.3679	0.2707	0.1494	0.0733	0.0337
2	0.0164	0.0536	0.0988	0.1438	0.1839	0.2707	0.2240	0.1465	0.0842
3	0.0011	0.0072	0.0198	0.0383	0.0613	0.1804	0.2240	0.1954	0.1404
4	0.0001	0.0007	0.0030	0.0077	0.0153	0.0902	0.1680	0.1954	0.1755
5		0.0001	0.0004	0.0012	0.0031	0.0361	0.1008	0.1563	0.1755
6				0.0002	0.0005	0.0120	0.0504	0.1042	0.1462
7					0.0001	0.0034	0.0216	0.0595	0.1044
8						0.0009	0.0081	0.0298	0.0653
9						0.0002	0.0027	0.0132	0.0363
10							0.0008	0.0053	0.0181
11							0.0002	0.0019	0.0082
12							0.0001	0.0006	0.0034
13								0.0002	0.0013
14								0.0001	0.0005
15									0.0002

* Columns may not sum to 1 because of rounding.

TABLE IIIB
POISSON CUMULATIVE PROBABILITIES: $\sum_0^r P(r)$ or $\sum_0^x P(x)$

r or x	μ or λt								
	0.1	0.2	0.3	0.4	0.5	0.6	0.7	0.8	0.9
0	0.9048	0.8187	0.7408	0.6703	0.6065	0.5488	0.4966	0.4493	0.4066
1	0.9953	0.9825	0.9631	0.9384	0.9098	0.8781	0.8442	0.8088	0.7725
2	0.9998	0.9989	0.9964	0.9921	0.9856	0.9769	0.9659	0.9526	0.9371
3	1.0000	0.9999	0.9997	0.9992	0.9982	0.9966	0.9942	0.9909	0.9865
4		1.0000	1.0000	0.9999	0.9998	0.9996	0.9992	0.9986	0.9977
5				1.0000	1.0000	1.0000	0.9999	0.9998	0.9997
6							1.0000	1.0000	1.0000
7									
8									
9									
10									
11									
12									
13									
14									
15									
16									

				μ or λ				
1.0	1.2	1.4	1.6	1.8	2	3	4	5
0.3679	0.3012	0.2466	0.2019	0.1653	0.1353	0.0498	0.0183	0.0067
0.7358	0.6626	0.5918	0.5249	0.4628	0.4060	0.1991	0.0916	0.0404
0.9197	0.8795	0.8335	0.7834	0.7306	0.6767	0.4232	0.2381	0.1247
0.9810	0.9662	0.9463	0.9212	0.8913	0.8571	0.6472	0.4335	0.2650
0.9963	0.9923	0.9857	0.9763	0.9636	0.9473	0.8153	0.6288	0.4405
0.9994	0.9985	0.9968	0.9940	0.9896	0.9834	0.9161	0.7851	0.6160
0.9999	0.9997	0.9994	0.9987	0.9974	0.9955	0.9665	0.8893	0.7622
1.0000	1.0000	0.9999	0.9997	0.9994	0.9989	0.9881	0.9489	0.8666
		1.0000	1.0000	0.9999	0.9998	0.9962	0.9786	0.9319
				1.0000	1.0000	0.9989	0.9919	0.9682
						0.9997	0.9972	0.9863
						0.9999	0.9991	0.9945
						1.0000	0.9997	0.9980
							0.9999	0.9993
							1.0000	0.9998
								0.9999
								1.0000

TABLE IV

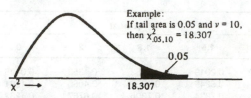

Example:
If tail area is 0.05 and $\nu = 10$,
then $\chi^2_{.05,10} = 18.307$

0.05

$\chi^2 \longrightarrow$ 18.307

VALUES OF χ^2 FOR SPECIFIED RIGHT-TAIL AREAS

Degrees of freedom ν	Right-tail area				
	0.20	0.10	0.05	0.02	0.01
1	1.642	2.706	3.841	5.412	6.635
2	3.219	4.605	5.991	7.824	9.210
3	4.642	6.251	7.815	9.837	11.345
4	5.989	7.779	9.488	11.668	13.277
5	7.289	9.236	11.070	13.388	15.086
6	8.558	10.645	12.592	15.033	16.812
7	9.803	12.017	14.067	16.622	18.475
8	11.030	13.362	15.507	18.168	20.090
9	12.242	14.684	16.919	19.679	21.666
10	13.442	15.987	18.307	21.161	23.209
11	14.631	17.275	19.675	22.618	24.725
12	15.812	18.549	21.026	24.054	26.217
13	16.985	19.812	22.362	25.472	27.688
14	18.151	21.064	23.685	26.873	29.141
15	19.311	22.307	24.996	28.259	30.578
16	20.465	23.542	26.296	29.633	32.000
17	21.615	24.769	27.587	30.995	33.409
18	22.760	25.989	28.869	32.346	34.805
19	23.900	27.204	30.144	33.687	36.191
20	25.038	28.412	31.410	35.020	37.566
21	26.171	29.615	32.671	36.343	38.932
22	27.301	30.813	33.924	37.659	40.289
23	28.429	32.007	35.172	38.968	41.638
24	29.553	33.196	36.415	40.270	42.980
25	30.675	34.382	37.652	41.566	44.314
26	31.795	35.563	38.885	42.856	45.642
27	32.912	36.741	40.113	44.140	46.963
28	34.027	37.916	41.337	45.419	48.278
29	35.139	39.087	42.557	46.693	49.588
30	36.250	40.256	43.773	47.962	50.892

Source: Taken from Table IV of Fisher & Yates, Statistical Tables for Biological, Agricultural and Medical Research, published by Longman Group, Ltd., London (1974), 6th edition. (Previously published by Oliver & Boyd, Ltd., Edinburgh.) By permission of the authors and publishers.

TABLE V

Example:
If $z = 1.96$, then
$P(0$ to $z) = 0.4750$

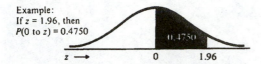

0.4750

$z \longrightarrow$ 0 1.96

AREAS UNDER THE NORMAL CURVE

z	0.00	0.01	0.02	0.03	0.04	0.05	0.06	0.07	0.08	0.09
0.0	0.0000	0.0040	0.0080	0.0120	0.0160	0.0199	0.0239	0.0279	0.0319	0.0359
0.1	0.0398	0.0438	0.0478	0.0517	0.0557	0.0596	0.0636	0.0675	0.0714	0.0753
0.2	0.0793	0.0832	0.0871	0.0910	0.0948	0.0987	0.1026	0.1064	0.1103	0.1141
0.3	0.1179	0.1217	0.1255	0.1293	0.1331	0.1368	0.1406	0.1443	0.1480	0.1517
0.4	0.1554	0.1591	0.1628	0.1664	0.1700	0.1736	0.1772	0.1808	0.1844	0.1879
0.5	0.1915	0.1950	0.1985	0.2019	0.2054	0.2088	0.2123	0.2157	0.2190	0.2224
0.6	0.2257	0.2291	0.2324	0.2357	0.2389	0.2422	0.2454	0.2486	0.2517	0.2549
0.7	0.2580	0.2611	0.2642	0.2673	0.2704	0.2734	0.2764	0.2794	0.2823	0.2852
0.8	0.2881	0.2910	0.2939	0.2967	0.2995	0.3023	0.3051	0.3078	0.3106	0.3133
0.9	0.3159	0.3186	0.3212	0.3238	0.3264	0.3289	0.3315	0.3340	0.3365	0.3389
1 0	0.3413	0.3438	0.3461	0.3485	0.3508	0.3531	0.3554	0.3577	0.3599	0.3621
1.1	0.3643	0.3665	0.3686	0.3708	0.3729	0.3749	0.3770	0.3790	0.3810	0.3830
1.2	0.3849	0.3869	0.3888	0.3907	0.3925	0.3944	0.3962	0.3980	0.3997	0.4015
1.3	0.4032	0.4049	0.4066	0.4082	0.4099	0.4115	0.4131	0.4147	0.4162	0.4177
1.4	0.4192	0.4207	0.4222	0.4236	0.4251	0.4265	0.4279	0.4292	0.4306	0.4319
1.5	0.4332	0.4345	0.4357	0.4370	0.4382	0.4394	0.4406	0.4418	0.4429	0.4441
1.6	0.4452	0.4463	0.4474	0.4484	0.4495	0.4505	0.4515	0.4525	0.4535	0.4545
1.7	0.4554	0.4564	0.4573	0.4582	0.4591	0.4599	0.4608	0.4616	0.4625	0.4633
1.8	0.4641	0.4649	0.4656	0.4664	0.4671	0.4678	0.4686	0.4693	0.4699	0.4706
1.9	0.4713	0.4719	0.4726	0.4732	0.4738	0.4744	0.4750	0.4756	0.4761	0.4767
2.0	0.4772	0.4778	0.4783	0.4788	0.4793	0.4798	0.4803	0.4808	0.4812	0.4817
2 1	0.4821	0.4826	0.4830	0.4834	0.4838	0.4842	0.4846	0.4850	0.4854	0.4857
2.2	0.4861	0.4864	0.4868	0.4871	0.4875	0.4878	0.4881	0.4884	0.4887	0.4890
2.3	0.4893	0.4896	0.4898	0.4901	0.4904	0.4906	0.4909	0.4911	0.4913	0.4916
2.4	0.4918	0.4920	0.4922	0.4925	0.4927	0.4929	0.4931	0.4932	0.4934	0.4936
2.5	0.4938	0.4940	0.4941	0.4943	0.4945	0.4946	0.4948	0.4949	0.4951	0.4952
2.6	0.4953	0.4955	0.4956	0.4957	0.4959	0.4960	0.4961	0.4962	0.4963	0.4964
2.7	0.4965	0.4966	0.4967	0.4968	0.4969	0.4970	0.4971	0.4972	0.4973	0.4974
2.8	0.4974	0.4975	0.4976	0.4977	0.4977	0.4978	0.4979	0.4979	0.4980	0.4981
2.9	0.4981	0.4982	0.4982	0.4983	0.4984	0.4984	0.4985	0.4985	0.4986	0.4986
3.0	0.4987	0.4987	0.4987	0.4988	0.4988	0.4989	0.4989	0.4989	0.4990	0.4990

TABLE VI

Example:
If tail area = 0.05,
then z = 1.64

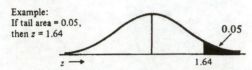

0.05

z ⟶   1.64

z FOR ONE-TAIL AREAS UNDER THE NORMAL CURVE
(Locate tail area in margins; take z from body of table)

Area	0.000	0.001	0.002	0.003	0.004	0.005	0.006	0.007	0.008	0.009
0.00		3.09	2.88	2.75	2.65	2.58	2.51	2.46	2.41	2.37
0.01	2.33	2.29	2.26	2.23	2.20	2.17	2.14	2.12	2.10	2.07
0.02	2.05	2.03	2.01	2.00	1.98	1.96	1.94	1.93	1.91	1.90
0.03	1.88	1.87	1.85	1.84	1.83	1.81	1.80	1.79	1.77	1.76
0.04	1.75	1.74	1.73	1.72	1.71	1.70	1.68	1.67	1.66	1.65
0.05	1.64	1.64	1.63	1.62	1.61	1.60	1.59	1.58	1.57	1.56
0.06	1.55	1.55	1.54	1.53	1.52	1.51	1.51	1.50	1.49	1.48
0.07	1.48	1.47	1.46	1.45	1.45	1.44	1.43	1.43	1.42	1.41
0.08	1.41	1.40	1.39	1.39	1.38	1.37	1.37	1.36	1.35	1.35
0.09	1.34	1.33	1.33	1.32	1.32	1.31	1.30	1.30	1.29	1.29
0.10	1.28	1.28	1.27	1.26	1.26	1.25	1.25	1.24	1.24	1.23

TABLE VII

Example:
If tail area is 0.05 and
$\nu = 10$, then $t_{.05,10} = 1.81$

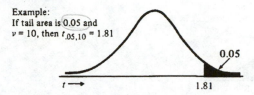

0.05

$t \longrightarrow$ 1.81

THE STUDENT t DISTRIBUTION
(Entries are t values for selected tail areas)

Degrees of freedom ν	Tail area					
	0.25	0.10	0.05	0.025	0.01	0.005
1	1.00	3.08	6.31	12.71	31.82	63.66
2	0.82	1.89	2.92	4.30	6.96	9.92
3	0.76	1.64	2.35	3.18	4.54	5.84
4	0.74	1.53	2.13	2.78	3.75	4.60
5	0.73	1.48	2.02	2.57	3.36	4.03
6	0.72	1.44	1.94	2.45	3.14	3.71
7	0.71	1.41	1.89	2.36	3.00	3.50
8	0.71	1.40	1.86	2.31	2.90	3.36
9	0.70	1.38	1.83	2.26	2.82	3.25
10	0.70	1.37	1.81	2.23	2.76	3.17
11	0.70	1.36	1.80	2.20	2.72	3.11
12	0.70	1.36	1.78	2.18	2.68	3.05
13	0.69	1.35	1.77	2.16	2.65	3.01
14	0.69	1.35	1.76	2.14	2.62	2.98
15	0.69	1.34	1.75	2.13	2.60	2.95
16	0.69	1.34	1.75	2.12	2.58	2.92
17	0.69	1.33	1.74	2.11	2.57	2.90
18	0.69	1.00	1.73	2.10	2.55	2.88
19	0.69	1.33	1.73	2.09	2.54	2.86
20	0.69	1.33	1.72	2.09	2.53	2.85
21	0.69	1.32	1.72	2.08	2.52	2.83
22	0.69	1.32	1.72	2.07	2.51	2.82
23	0.69	1.32	1.71	2.07	2.50	2.81
24	0.68	1.32	1.71	2.06	2.49	2.80
25	0.68	1.32	1.71	2.06	2.49	2.79
26	0.68	1.31	1.71	2.06	2.48	2.78
27	0.68	1.31	1.70	2.05	2.47	2.77
28	0.68	1.31	1.70	2.05	2.47	2.76
29	0.68	1.31	1.70	2.05	2.46	2.76
30	0.68	1.31	1.70	2.04	2.46	2.75
40	0.68	1.30	1.68	2.02	2.42	2.70
60	0.68	1.30	1.67	2.00	2.39	2.66
∞	0.67	1.28	1.64	1.96	2.33	2.58

TABLE VIII

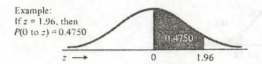

Example:
If $z = 1.96$, then
$P(0 \text{ to } z) = 0.4750$

0.4750

$z \longrightarrow$ 0   1.96

F VALUES FOR RIGHT-TAIL AREA OF 0.01

	Degrees of freedom for numerator									
	1	2	3	4	5	6	7	8	9	10
1	4052	5000	5403	5625	5764	5859	5928	5982	6022	6056
2	98.5	99.0	99.2	99.2	99.3	99.3	99.4	99.4	99.4	99.4
3	34.1	30.8	29.5	28.7	28.2	27.9	27.7	27.5	27.3	27.2
4	21.2	18.0	16.7	16.0	15.5	15.2	15.0	14.8	14.7	14.5
5	16.3	13.3	12.1	11.4	11.0	10.7	10.5	10.3	10.2	10.1
6	13.7	10.9	9.78	9.15	8.75	8.47	8.26	8.10	7.98	7.87
7	12.2	9.55	8.45	7.85	7.46	7.19	6.99	6.84	6.72	6.62
8	11.3	8.65	7.59	7.01	6.63	6.37	6.18	6.03	5.91	5.81
9	10.6	8.02	6.99	6.42	6.06	5.80	5.61	5.47	5.35	5.26
10	10.0	7.56	6.55	5.99	5.64	5.39	5.20	5.06	4.94	4.85
11	9.65	7.21	6.22	5.67	5.32	5.07	4.89	4.74	4.63	4.54
12	9.33	6.93	5.95	5.41	5.06	4.82	4.64	4.50	4.39	4.30
13	9.07	6.70	5.74	5.21	4.86	4.62	4.44	4.30	4.19	4.10
14	8.86	6.51	5.56	5.04	4.70	4.46	4.28	4.14	4.03	3.94
15	8.68	6.36	5.42	4.89	4.56	4.32	4.14	4.00	3.89	3.80
16	8.53	6.23	5.29	4.77	4.44	4.20	4.03	3.89	3.78	3.69
17	8.40	6.11	5.19	4.67	4.34	4.10	3.93	3.79	3.68	3.59
18	8.29	6.01	5.09	4.58	4.25	4.01	3.84	3.71	3.60	3.51
19	8.19	5.93	5.01	4.50	4.17	3.94	3.77	3.63	3.52	3.43
20	8.10	5.85	4.94	4.43	4.10	3.87	3.70	3.56	3.46	3.37
21	8.02	5.78	4.87	4.37	4.04	3.81	3.64	3.51	3.40	3.31
22	7.95	5.72	4.82	4.31	3.99	3.76	3.59	3.45	3.35	3.26
23	7.88	5.66	4.76	4.26	3.94	3.71	3.54	3.41	3.30	3.21
24	7.82	5.61	4.72	4.22	3.90	3.67	3.50	3.36	3.26	3.17
25	7.77	5.57	4.68	4.18	3.86	3.63	3.46	3.32	3.22	3.13
30	7.56	5.39	4.51	4.02	3.70	3.47	3.30	3.17	3.07	2.98
40	7.31	5.18	4.31	3.83	3.51	3.29	3.12	2.99	2.89	2.80
60	7.08	4.98	4.13	3.65	3.34	3.12	2.95	2.82	2.72	2.63
120	6.85	4.79	3.95	3.48	3.17	2.96	2.79	2.66	2.56	2.47
∞	6.63	4.61	3.78	3.32	3.02	2.80	2.64	2.51	2.41	2.32

(Degrees of freedom for denominator — left axis labels)

Source: Extracted from M. Merrington and C. M. Thompson, "Tables of Percentage Points of the Inverted Beta (*F*) Distribution," *Biometrika*, vol. 33 (1943). Reprinted by permission of the *Biometrika* trustees.

TABLE VIII
(Continued)
F VALUES FOR RIGHT-TAIL AREA OF 0.05

		Degrees of freedom for numerator								
	1	**2**	**3**	**4**	**5**	**6**	**7**	**8**	**9**	**10**
1	161	200	216	225	230	234	237	239	241	242
2	18.5	19.0	19.2	19.2	19.3	19.3	19.4	19.4	19.4	19.4
3	10.1	9.55	9.28	9.12	9.01	8.94	8.89	8.85	8.81	8.79
4	7.71	6.94	6.59	6.39	6.26	6.16	6.09	6.04	6.00	5.96
5	6.61	5.79	5.41	5.19	5.05	4.95	4.88	4.82	4.77	4.74
6	5.99	5.14	4.76	4.53	4.39	4.28	4.21	4.15	4.10	4.06
7	5.59	4.74	4.35	4.12	3.97	3.87	3.79	3.73	3.68	3.64
8	5.32	4.46	4.07	3.84	3.69	3.58	3.50	3.44	3.39	3.35
9	5.12	4.26	3.86	3.63	3.48	3.37	3.29	3.23	3.18	3.14
10	4.96	4.10	3.71	3.48	3.33	3.22	3.14	3.07	3.02	2.98
11	4.84	3.98	3.59	3.36	3.20	3.09	3.01	2.95	2.90	2.85
12	4.75	3.89	3.49	3.26	3.11	3.00	2.91	2.85	2.80	2.75
13	4.67	3.81	3.41	3.18	3.03	2.92	2.83	2.77	2.71	2.67
14	4.60	3.74	3.34	3.11	2.96	2.85	2.76	2.70	2.65	2.60
15	4.54	3.68	3.29	3.06	2.90	2.79	2.71	2.64	2.59	2.54
16	4.49	3.63	3.24	3.01	2.85	2.74	2.66	2.59	2.54	2.49
17	4.45	3.59	3.20	2.96	2.81	2.70	2.61	2.55	2.49	2.45
18	4.41	3.55	3.16	2.93	2.77	2.66	2.58	2.51	2.46	2.41
19	4.38	3.52	3.13	2.90	2.74	2.63	2.54	2.48	2.42	2.38
20	4.35	3.49	3.10	2.87	2.71	2.60	2.51	2.45	2.39	2.35
21	4.32	3.47	3.07	2.84	2.68	2.57	2.49	2.42	2.37	2.32
22	4.30	3.44	3.05	2.82	2.66	2.55	2.46	2.40	2.34	2.30
23	4.28	3.42	3.03	2.80	2.64	2.53	2.44	2.37	2.32	2.27
24	4.26	3.40	3.01	2.78	2.62	2.51	2.42	2.36	2.30	2.25
25	4.24	3.39	2.99	2.76	2.60	2.49	2.40	2.34	2.28	2.24
30	4.17	3.32	2.92	2.69	2.53	2.42	2.33	2.27	2.21	2.16
40	4.08	3.23	2.84	2.61	2.45	2.34	2.25	2.18	2.12	2.08
60	4.00	3.15	2.76	2.53	2.37	2.25	2.17	2.10	2.04	1.99
120	3.92	3.07	2.68	2.45	2.29	2.18	2.09	2.02	1.96	1.91
∞	3.84	3.00	2.60	2.37	2.21	2.10	2.01	1.94	1.88	1.83

Degrees of freedom for denominator

TABLE IX
SQUARE ROOT OF N AND 10N FOR N = 100 TO 199*

N	√N	√10N	N	√N	√10N	N	√N	√10N	N	√N	√10N
100	10.00	31.62	125	11.18	35.36	150	12.25	38.73	175	13.23	41.83
101	10.05	31.78	126	11.22	35.50	151	12.29	38.86	176	13.27	41.95
102	10.10	31.94	127	11.27	35.64	152	12.33	38.99	177	13.30	42.07
103	10.15	32.09	128	11.31	35.78	153	12.37	39.12	178	13.34	42.19
104	10.20	32.25	129	11.36	35.92	154	12.41	39.24	179	13.38	42.31
105	10.25	32.40	130	11.40	36.06	155	12.45	39.37	180	13.42	42.43
106	10.30	32.56	131	11.45	36.19	156	12.49	39.50	181	13.45	42.54
107	10.34	32.71	132	11.49	36.33	157	12.53	39.62	182	13.49	42.66
108	10.39	32.86	133	11.53	36.47	158	12.57	39.75	183	13.53	42.78
109	10.44	33.02	134	11.58	36.61	159	12.61	39.87	184	13.56	42.90
110	10.49	33.17	135	11.62	36.74	160	12.65	40.00	185	13.60	43.01
111	10.54	33.32	136	11.66	36.88	161	12.69	40.12	186	13.64	43.13
112	10.58	33.47	137	11.70	37.01	162	12.73	40.25	187	13.67	43.24
113	10.63	33.62	138	11.75	37.15	163	12.77	40.37	188	13.71	43.36
114	10.68	33.76	139	11.79	37.28	164	12.81	40.50	189	13.75	43.47
115	10.72	33.91	140	11.83	37.42	165	12.85	40.62	190	13.78	43.59
116	10.77	34.06	141	11.87	37.55	166	12.88	40.74	191	13.82	43.70
117	10.82	34.21	142	11.92	37.68	167	12.92	40.87	192	13.86	43.82
118	10.86	34.35	143	11.96	37.82	168	12.96	40.99	193	13.89	43.93
119	10.91	34.50	144	12.00	37.95	169	13.00	41.11	194	13.93	44.05
120	10.95	34.64	145	12.04	38.08	170	13.04	41.23	195	13.96	44.16
121	11.00	34.79	146	12.08	38.21	171	13.08	41.35	196	14.00	44.27
122	11.05	34.93	147	12.12	38.34	172	13.11	41.47	197	14.04	44.38
123	11.09	35.07	148	12.17	38.47	173	13.15	41.59	198	14.07	44.50
124	11.14	35.21	149	12.21	38.60	174	13.19	41.71	199	14.11	44.61

* To find square roots using Table IX:

1. Let x be the number whose square root is to be found. Place a ∧ to the right of the first significant digit in x. (See Chapter 2 for a discussion of significant digits and rounding.)
2. Count the number of decimal positions *from the* ∧ *to* the decimal point in x. This is the *count*. Counts to the right are positive (+); counts to the left are negative (−).
3. Divide the count by 2, rounding to the next *smaller* whole number; this gives the *half-count*. (Note, e.g., that −³/₂ rounded is −2.)
4. Use the √N column for even counts; use the √10N column for odd counts. Write the entry, leaving out the tabulated decimal point; mark the ∧ position in the entry. Then place the decimal point the half-count number of positions from the ∧.
5. Follow the rules for significant digits and rounding (Chapter 2) to determine the number of significant digits in √x.
6. Examples follow.

Original number x	x to 3 significant digits with ∧ inserted	Count	Half-count	√N	√10N	√x
192	1∧92	2	1	1∧386		13.86
0.00192	0.001∧92	−3	−2		4∧382	0.04382
4639	4∧640	3	1		6∧812	68.12
7.544	7.54∧	0	0	2∧746		2.746

TABLE IX
(Continued)
SQUARE ROOT OF N AND 10N FOR N = 200 TO 299

N	$\sqrt{N}$	$\sqrt{10N}$	N	$\sqrt{N}$	$\sqrt{10N}$	N	$\sqrt{N}$	$\sqrt{10N}$	N	$\sqrt{N}$	$\sqrt{10N}$
200	14.14	44.72	225	15.00	47.43	250	15.81	50.00	275	16.58	52.44
201	14.18	44.83	226	15.03	47.54	251	15.84	50.10	276	16.61	52.54
202	14.21	44.94	227	15.07	47.64	252	15.87	50.20	277	16.64	52.63
203	14.25	45.06	228	15.10	47.75	253	15.91	50.30	278	16.67	52.73
204	14.28	45.17	229	15.13	47.85	254	15.94	50.40	279	16.70	52.82
205	14.32	45.28	230	15.17	47.96	255	15.97	50.50	280	16.73	52.92
206	14.35	45.39	231	15.20	48.06	256	16.00	50.60	281	16.76	53.01
207	14.39	45.50	232	15.23	48.17	257	16.03	50.70	282	16.79	53.10
208	14.42	45.61	233	15.26	48.27	258	16.06	50.79	283	16.82	53.20
209	14.46	45.72	234	15.30	48.37	259	16.09	50.89	284	16.85	53.29
210	14.49	45.83	235	15.33	48.48	260	16.12	50.99	285	16.88	53.39
211	14.53	45.93	236	15.36	48.58	261	16.16	51.09	286	16.91	53.48
212	14.56	46.04	237	15.39	48.68	262	16.19	51.19	287	16.94	53.57
213	14.59	46.15	238	15.43	48.79	263	16.22	51.28	288	16.97	53.67
214	14.63	46.26	239	15.46	48.89	264	16.25	51.38	289	17.00	53.76
215	14.66	46.37	240	15.49	48.99	265	16.28	51.48	290	17.03	53.85
216	14.70	46.48	241	15.52	49.09	266	16.31	51.58	291	17.06	53.94
217	14.73	46.58	242	15.56	49.19	267	16.34	51.67	292	17.09	54.04
218	14.76	46.69	243	15.59	49.30	268	16.37	51.77	293	17.12	54.13
219	14.80	46.80	244	15.62	49.40	269	16.40	51.87	294	17.15	54.22
220	14.83	46.90	245	15.65	49.50	270	16.43	51.96	295	17.18	54.31
221	14.87	47.01	246	15.68	49.60	271	16.46	52.06	296	17.20	54.41
222	14.90	47.12	247	15.72	49.70	272	16.49	52.15	297	17.23	54.50
223	14.93	47.22	248	15.75	49.80	273	16.52	52.25	298	17.26	54.59
224	14.97	47.33	249	15.78	49.90	274	16.55	52.35	299	17.29	54.68

TABLE IX
(Continued)
SQUARE ROOT OF *N* AND 10*N* FOR *N* = 300 TO 399

N	$\sqrt{N}$	$\sqrt{10N}$	N	$\sqrt{N}$	$\sqrt{10N}$	N	$\sqrt{N}$	$\sqrt{10N}$	N	$\sqrt{N}$	$\sqrt{10N}$
300	17.32	54.77	325	18.03	57.01	350	18.71	59.16	375	19.36	61.24
301	17.35	54.86	326	18.06	57.10	351	18.73	59.25	376	19.39	61.32
302	17.38	54.95	327	18.08	57.18	352	18.76	59.33	377	19.42	61.40
303	17.41	55.05	328	18.11	57.27	353	18.79	59.41	378	19.44	61.48
304	17.44	55.14	329	18.14	57.36	354	18.81	59.50	379	19.47	61.56
305	17.46	55.23	330	18.17	57.45	355	18.84	59.58	380	19.49	61.64
306	17.49	55.32	331	18.19	57.53	356	18.87	59.67	381	19.52	61.73
307	17.52	55.41	332	18.22	57.62	357	18.89	59.75	382	19.54	61.81
308	17.55	55.50	333	18.25	57.71	358	18.92	59.83	383	19.57	61.89
309	17.58	55.59	334	18.28	57.79	359	18.95	59.92	384	19.60	61.97
310	17.61	55.68	335	18.30	57.88	360	18.97	60.00	385	19.62	62.05
311	17.64	55.77	336	18.33	57.97	361	19.00	60.08	386	19.65	62.13
312	17.66	55.86	337	18.36	58.05	362	19.03	60.17	387	19.67	62.21
313	17.69	55.95	338	18.38	58.14	363	19.05	60.25	388	19.70	62.29
314	17.72	56.04	339	18.41	58.22	364	19.08	60.33	389	19.72	62.37
315	17.75	56.12	340	18.44	58.31	365	19.10	60.42	390	19.75	62.45
316	17.78	56.21	341	18.47	58.40	366	19.13	60.50	391	19.77	62.53
317	17.80	56.30	342	18.49	58.48	367	19.16	60.58	392	19.80	62.61
318	17.83	56.39	343	18.52	58.57	368	19.18	60.66	393	19.82	62.69
319	17.86	56.48	344	18.55	58.65	369	19.21	60.75	394	19.85	62.77
320	17.89	56.57	345	18.57	58.74	370	19.24	60.83	395	19.87	62.85
321	17.92	56.66	346	18.60	58.82	371	19.26	60.91	396	19.90	62.93
322	17.94	56.75	347	18.63	58.91	372	19.29	60.99	397	19.92	63.01
323	17.97	56.83	348	18.65	58.99	373	19.31	61.07	398	19.95	63.09
324	18.00	56.92	349	18.68	59.08	374	19.34	61.16	399	19.97	63.17

TABLE IX
(Continued)
SQUARE ROOT OF N AND 10N FOR N = 400 TO 499

N	$\sqrt{N}$	$\sqrt{10N}$	N	$\sqrt{N}$	$\sqrt{10N}$	N	$\sqrt{N}$	$\sqrt{10N}$	N	$\sqrt{N}$	$\sqrt{10N}$
400	20.00	63.25	425	20.62	65.19	450	21.21	67.08	475	21.79	68.92
401	20.02	63.32	426	20.64	65.27	451	21.24	67.16	476	21.82	68.99
402	20.05	63.40	427	20.66	65.35	452	21.26	67.23	477	21.84	69.07
403	20.07	63.48	428	20.69	65.42	453	21.28	67.31	478	21.86	69.14
404	20.10	63.56	429	20.71	65.50	454	21.31	67.38	479	21.89	69.21
405	20.12	63.64	430	20.74	65.57	455	21.33	67.45	480	21.91	69.28
406	20.15	63.72	431	20.76	65.65	456	21.35	67.53	481	21.93	69.35
407	20.17	63.80	432	20.78	65.73	457	21.38	67.60	482	21.95	69.43
408	20.20	63.87	433	20.81	65.80	458	21.40	67.68	483	21.98	69.50
409	20.22	63.95	434	20.83	65.88	459	21.42	67.75	484	22.00	69.57
410	20.25	64.03	435	20.86	65.95	460	21.45	67.82	485	22.02	69.64
411	20.27	64.11	436	20.88	66.03	461	21.47	67.90	486	22.05	69.71
412	20.30	64.19	437	20.90	66.11	462	21.49	67.97	487	22.07	69.79
413	20.32	64.27	438	20.93	66.18	463	21.52	68.04	488	22.09	69.86
414	20.35	64.34	439	20.95	66.26	464	21.54	68.12	489	22.11	69.93
415	20.37	64.42	440	20.98	66.33	465	21.56	68.19	490	22.14	70.00
416	20.40	64.50	441	21.00	66.41	466	21.59	68.26	491	22.16	70.07
417	20.42	64.58	442	21.02	66.48	467	21.61	68.34	492	22.18	70.14
418	20.45	64.65	443	21.05	66.56	468	21.63	68.41	493	22.20	70.21
419	20.47	64.73	444	21.07	66.63	469	21.66	68.48	494	22.23	70.29
420	20.49	64.81	445	21.10	66.71	470	21.68	68.56	495	22.25	70.36
421	20.52	64.88	446	21.12	66.78	471	21.70	68.63	496	22.27	70.43
422	20.54	64.96	447	21.14	66.86	472	21.73	68.70	497	22.29	70.50
423	20.57	65.04	448	21.17	66.93	473	21.75	68.77	498	22.32	70.57
424	20.59	65.12	449	21.19	67.01	474	21.77	68.85	499	22.34	70.64

TABLE IX
(Continued)
SQUARE ROOT OF *N* AND 10*N* FOR *N* = 500 TO 599

N	√N	√10N	N	√N	√10N	N	√N	√10N	N	√N	√10N
500	22.36	70.71	525	22.91	72.46	550	23.45	74.16	575	23.98	75.83
501	22.38	70.78	526	22.93	72.53	551	23.47	74.23	576	24.00	75.89
502	22.41	70.85	527	22.96	72.59	552	23.49	74.30	577	24.02	75.96
503	22.43	70.92	528	22.98	72.66	553	23.52	74.36	578	24.04	76.03
504	22.45	70.99	529	23.00	72.73	554	23.54	74.43	579	24.06	76.09
505	22.47	71.06	530	23.02	72.80	555	23.56	74.50	580	24.08	76.16
506	22.49	71.13	531	23.04	72.87	556	23.58	74.57	581	24.10	76.22
507	22.52	71.20	532	23.07	72.94	557	23.60	74.63	582	24.12	76.29
508	22.54	71.27	533	23.09	73.01	558	23.62	74.70	583	24.15	76.35
509	22.56	71.34	534	23.11	73.08	559	23.64	74.77	584	24.17	76.42
510	22.58	71.41	535	23.13	73.14	560	23.66	74.83	585	24.19	76.49
511	22.61	71.48	536	23.15	73.21	561	23.69	74.90	586	24.21	76.55
512	22.63	71.55	537	23.17	73.28	562	23.71	74.97	587	24.23	76.62
513	22.65	71.62	538	23.19	73.35	563	23.73	75.03	588	24.25	76.68
514	22.67	71.69	539	23.22	73.42	564	23.75	75.10	589	24.27	76.75
515	22.69	71.76	540	23.24	73.48	565	23.77	75.17	590	24.29	76.81
516	22.72	71.83	541	23.26	73.55	566	23.79	75.23	591	24.31	76.88
517	22.74	71.90	542	23.28	73.62	567	23.81	75.30	592	24.33	76.94
518	22.76	71.97	543	23.30	73.69	568	23.83	75.37	593	24.35	77.01
519	22.78	72.04	544	23.32	73.76	569	23.85	75.43	594	24.37	77.07
520	22.80	72.11	545	23.35	73.82	570	23.87	75.50	595	24.39	77.14
521	22.83	72.18	546	23.37	73.89	571	23.90	75.56	596	24.41	77.20
522	22.85	72.25	547	23.39	73.96	572	23.92	75.63	597	24.43	77.27
523	22.87	72.32	548	23.41	74.03	573	23.94	75.70	598	24.45	77.33
524	22.89	72.39	549	23.43	74.09	574	23.96	75.76	599	24.47	77.40

TABLE IX
(Continued)
SQUARE ROOT OF N AND 10N FOR N = 600 TO 699

N	$\sqrt{N}$	$\sqrt{10N}$	N	$\sqrt{N}$	$\sqrt{10N}$	N	$\sqrt{N}$	$\sqrt{10N}$	N	$\sqrt{N}$	$\sqrt{10N}$
600	24.49	77.46	625	25.00	79.06	650	25.50	80.62	675	25.98	82.16
601	24.52	77.52	626	25.02	79.12	651	25.51	80.68	676	26.00	82.22
602	24.54	77.59	627	25.04	79.18	652	25.53	80.75	677	26.02	82.28
603	24.56	77.65	628	25.06	79.25	653	25.55	80.81	678	26.04	82.34
604	24.58	77.72	629	25.08	79.31	654	25.57	80.87	679	26.06	82.40
605	24.60	77.78	630	25.10	79.37	655	25.59	80.93	680	26.08	82.46
606	24.62	77.85	631	25.12	79.44	656	25.61	80.99	681	26.10	82.52
607	24.64	77.91	632	25.14	79.50	657	25.63	81.06	682	26.12	82.58
608	24.66	77.97	633	25.16	79.56	658	25.65	81.12	683	26.13	82.64
609	24.68	78.04	634	25.18	79.62	659	25.67	81.18	684	26.15	82.70
610	24.70	78.10	635	25.20	79.69	660	25.69	81.24	685	26.17	82.76
611	24.72	78.17	636	25.22	79.75	661	25.71	81.30	686	26.19	82.83
612	24.74	78.23	637	25.24	79.81	662	25.73	81.36	687	26.21	82.89
613	24.76	78.29	638	25.26	79.87	663	25.75	81.42	688	26.23	82.95
614	24.78	78.36	639	25.28	79.94	664	25.77	81.49	689	26.25	83.01
615	24.80	78.42	640	25.30	80.00	665	25.79	81.55	690	26.27	83.07
616	24.82	78.49	641	25.32	80.06	666	25.81	81.61	691	26.29	83.13
617	24.84	78.55	642	25.34	80.12	667	25.83	81.67	692	26.31	83.19
618	24.86	78.61	643	25.36	80.19	668	25.85	81.73	693	26.32	83.25
619	24.88	78.68	644	25.38	80.25	669	25.87	81.79	694	26.34	83.31
620	24.90	78.74	645	25.40	80.31	670	25.88	81.85	695	26.36	83.37
621	24.92	78.80	646	25.42	80.37	671	25.90	81.91	696	26.38	83.43
622	24.94	78.87	647	25.44	80.44	672	25.92	81.98	697	26.40	83.49
623	24.96	78.93	648	25.46	80.50	673	25.94	82.04	698	26.42	83.55
624	24.98	78.99	649	25.48	80.56	674	25.96	82.10	699	26.44	83.61

TABLE IX
(Continued)
SQUARE ROOT OF *N* AND 10*N* FOR *N* = 700 TO 799

N	$\sqrt{N}$	$\sqrt{10N}$	N	$\sqrt{N}$	$\sqrt{10N}$	N	$\sqrt{N}$	$\sqrt{10N}$	N	$\sqrt{N}$	$\sqrt{10N}$
700	26.46	83.67	725	26.93	85.15	750	27.39	86.60	775	27.84	88.03
701	26.48	83.73	726	26.94	85.21	751	27.40	86.66	776	27.86	88.09
702	26.50	83.79	727	26.96	85.26	752	27.42	86.72	777	27.87	88.15
703	26.51	83.85	728	26.98	85.32	753	27.44	86.78	778	27.89	88.20
704	26.53	83.90	729	27.00	85.38	754	27.46	86.83	779	27.91	88.26
705	26.55	83.96	730	27.02	85.44	755	27.48	86.89	780	27.93	88.32
706	26.57	84.02	731	27.04	85.50	756	27.50	86.95	781	27.95	88.37
707	26.59	84.08	732	27.06	85.56	757	27.51	87.01	782	27.96	88.43
708	26.61	84.14	733	27.07	85.62	758	27.53	87.06	783	27.98	88.49
709	26.63	84.20	734	27.09	85.67	759	27.55	87.12	784	28.00	88.54
710	26.65	84.26	735	27.11	85.73	760	27.57	87.18	785	28.02	88.60
711	26.66	84.32	736	27.13	85.79	761	27.59	87.24	786	28.04	88.66
712	26.68	84.38	737	27.15	85.85	762	27.60	87.29	787	28.05	88.71
713	26.70	84.44	738	27.17	85.91	763	27.62	87.35	788	28.07	88.77
714	26.72	84.50	739	27.18	85.97	764	27.64	87.41	789	28.09	88.83
715	26.74	84.56	740	27.20	86.02	765	27.66	87.46	790	28.11	88.88
716	26.76	84.62	741	27.22	86.08	766	27.68	87.52	791	28.12	88.94
717	26.78	84.68	742	27.24	86.14	767	27.69	87.58	792	28.14	88.99
718	26.80	84.73	743	27.26	86.20	768	27.71	87.64	793	28.16	89.05
719	26.81	84.79	744	27.28	86.26	769	27.73	87.69	794	28.18	89.11
720	26.83	84.85	745	27.29	86.31	770	27.75	87.75	795	28.20	89.16
721	26.85	84.91	746	27.31	86.37	771	27.77	87.81	796	28.21	89.22
722	26.87	84.97	747	27.33	86.43	772	27.78	87.86	797	28.23	89.27
723	26.89	85.03	748	27.35	86.49	773	27.80	87.92	798	28.25	89.33
724	26.91	85.09	749	27.37	86.54	774	27.82	87.98	799	28.27	89.39

TABLE IX
(Continued)
SQUARE ROOT OF N AND $10N$ FOR N = 800 TO 899

N	$\sqrt{N}$	$\sqrt{10N}$	N	$\sqrt{N}$	$\sqrt{10N}$	N	$\sqrt{N}$	$\sqrt{10N}$	N	$\sqrt{N}$	$\sqrt{10N}$
800	28.28	89.44	825	28.72	90.83	850	29.15	92.20	875	29.58	93.54
801	28.30	89.50	826	28.74	90.88	851	29.17	92.25	876	29.60	93.59
802	28.32	89.55	827	28.76	90.94	852	29.19	92.30	877	29.61	93.65
803	28.34	89.61	828	28.77	90.99	853	29.21	92.36	878	29.63	93.70
804	28.35	89.67	829	28.79	91.05	854	29.22	92.41	879	29.65	93.76
805	28.37	89.72	830	28.81	91.10	855	29.24	92.47	880	29.66	93.81
806	28.39	89.78	831	28.83	91.16	856	29.26	92.52	881	29.68	93.86
807	28.41	89.83	832	28.84	91.21	857	29.27	92.57	882	29.70	93.91
808	28.43	89.89	833	28.86	91.27	858	29.29	92.63	883	29.72	93.97
809	28.44	89.94	834	28.88	91.32	859	29.31	92.68	884	29.73	94.02
810	28.46	90.00	835	28.90	91.38	860	29.33	92.74	885	29.75	94.07
811	28.48	90.06	836	28.91	91.43	861	29.34	92.79	886	29.77	94.13
812	28.50	90.11	837	28.93	91.49	862	29.36	92.84	887	29.78	94.18
813	28.51	90.17	838	28.95	91.54	863	29.38	92.90	888	29.80	94.23
814	28.53	90.22	839	28.97	91.60	864	29.39	92.95	889	29.82	94.29
815	28.55	90.28	840	28.98	91.65	865	29.41	93.01	890	29.83	94.34
816	28.57	90.33	841	29.00	91.71	866	29.43	93.06	891	29.85	94.39
817	28.58	90.39	842	29.02	91.76	867	29.44	93.11	892	29.87	94.45
818	28.60	90.44	843	29.03	91.82	868	29.46	93.17	893	29.88	94.50
819	28.62	90.50	844	29.05	91.87	869	29.48	93.22	894	29.90	94.55
820	28.64	90.55	845	29.07	91.92	870	29.50	93.27	895	29.92	94.60
821	28.65	90.61	846	29.09	91.98	871	29.51	93.33	896	29.93	94.66
822	28.67	90.66	847	29.10	92.03	872	29.53	93.38	897	29.95	94.71
823	28.69	90.72	848	29.12	92.09	873	29.55	93.43	898	29.97	94.76
824	28.71	90.77	849	29.14	92.14	874	29.56	93.49	899	29.98	94.82

TABLE IX
(Continued)
SQUARE ROOT OF N AND 10N FOR N = 900 TO 999

N	$\sqrt{N}$	$\sqrt{10N}$	N	$\sqrt{N}$	$\sqrt{10N}$	N	$\sqrt{N}$	$\sqrt{10N}$	N	$\sqrt{N}$	$\sqrt{10N}$
900	30.00	94.87	925	30.41	96.18	950	30.82	97.47	975	31.22	98.74
901	30.02	94.92	926	30.43	96.23	951	30.84	97.52	976	31.24	98.79
902	30.03	94.97	927	30.45	96.28	952	30.85	97.57	977	31.26	98.84
903	30.05	95.03	928	30.46	96.33	953	30.87	97.62	978	31.27	98.89
904	30.07	95.08	929	30.48	96.38	954	30.89	97.67	979	31.29	98.94
905	30.08	95.13	930	30.50	96.44	955	30.90	97.72	980	31.30	98.99
906	30.10	95.18	931	30.51	96.49	956	30.92	97.78	981	31.32	99.05
907	30.12	95.24	932	30.53	96.54	957	30.94	97.83	982	31.34	99.10
908	30.13	95.29	933	30.55	96.59	958	30.95	97.88	983	31.35	99.15
909	30.15	95.34	934	30.56	96.64	959	30.97	97.93	984	31.37	99.20
910	30.17	95.39	935	30.58	96.70	960	30.98	97.98	985	31.38	99.25
911	30.18	95.45	936	30.59	96.75	961	31.00	98.03	986	31.40	99.30
912	30.20	95.50	937	30.61	96.80	962	31.02	98.08	987	31.42	99.35
913	30.22	95.55	938	30.63	96.85	963	31.03	98.13	988	31.43	99.40
914	30.23	95.60	939	30.64	96.90	964	31.05	98.18	989	31.45	99.45
915	30.25	95.66	940	30.66	96.95	965	31.06	98.23	990	31.46	99.50
916	30.27	95.71	941	30.68	97.01	966	31.08	98.29	991	31.48	99.55
917	30.28	95.76	942	30.69	97.06	967	31.10	98.34	992	31.50	99.60
918	30.30	95.81	943	30.71	97.11	968	31.11	98.39	993	31.51	99.65
919	30.32	95.86	944	30.72	97.16	969	31.13	98.44	994	31.53	99.70
920	30.33	95.92	945	30.74	97.21	970	31.14	98.49	995	31.54	99.75
921	30.35	95.97	946	30.76	97.26	971	31.16	98.54	996	31.56	99.80
922	30.36	96.02	947	30.77	97.31	972	31.18	98.59	997	31.58	99.85
923	30.38	96.07	948	30.79	97.37	973	31.19	98.64	998	31.59	99.90
924	30.40	96.12	949	30.81	97.42	974	31.21	98.69	999	31.61	99.95

INDEX

INDEX